D1083533

WITHDRAWN FROM
MACALESTER COLLEGE
LIBRARY

WITHDRAWN FROM
MACALESTER COLLEGE
LIBRARY

Participation in Social and Political Activities

*A Comprehensive Analysis
of Political Involvement,
Expressive Leisure Time,
and Helping Behavior*

David Horton Smith

Jacqueline Macaulay

and Associates

Participation in Social and Political Activities

Jossey-Bass Publishers

San Francisco • Washington • London • 1980

PARTICIPATION IN SOCIAL AND POLITICAL ACTIVITIES
A Comprehensive Analysis of Political Involvement,
Expressive Leisure Time, and Helping Behavior
by David Horton Smith, Jacqueline Macaulay, and Associates

Copyright © 1980 by: Jossey-Bass Inc., Publishers
433 California Street
San Francisco, California 94104
&
Jossey-Bass Limited
28 Banner Street
London EC1Y 8QE

Copyright under International, Pan American, and
Universal Copyright Conventions. All rights
reserved. No part of this book may be reproduced
in any form—except for brief quotation (not to
exceed 1,000 words) in a review or professional
work—without permission in writing from the publishers.

Library of Congress Cataloging in Publication Data

Smith, David Horton.
   Participation in social and political
activities.

   Bibliography: p. 545
   Includes indexes.
   1. Social participation—Addresses, essays,
lectures. 2. Leisure—Addresses, essays, lectures.
3. Political participation—Addresses, essays,
lectures. 4. Voluntarism—Addresses, essays,
lectures. I. Macaulay, Jacqueline, joint author.
II. Title.
HM131.S564   302   80-16362
ISBN 0-87589-463-1

Manufactured in the United States of America

JACKET DESIGN BY WILLI BAUM

FIRST EDITION

Code 8023

The Jossey-Bass
Social and Behavioral Science Series

*To Talcott Parsons
and George Homans*

Preface

This book presents and makes a case for two interrelated theoretical models that will permit more precise explanation and prediction of human discretionary behavior or voluntary action by using an integrative approach to understanding the patterns of daily human activities over the life span. These models are part of a new worldview paradigm for the social and behavioral sciences, although this paradigm still needs further development and testing. The names of the two models suggest their nature, but a distinctive new term helps to refer to my broader theoretical approach as a whole—*synanthrometrics.*

As the root words of this neologism suggest, *synanthrometrics is a scientific approach that emphasizes comprehensive, interdisciplinary synthesis and precise, complex measurement and analysis of human behavior in time and space.* The present interdisciplinary sequential specificity time allocation life span (ISSTAL) and general activity (GA) models described in this book argue for synanthrometrics because the evidence of the many review chapters in this volume, in turn, make a substantial case for the validity of these two models. Synanthrometrics is not a "grand" theory or "abstract" theory lacking strong roots in empirical research. Although it is certainly abstract and comprehensive within its domain, the theory stems from on-going social and behavioral research and theory on individual discretionary behavior, as a glance at the references at the end of this volume and a careful reading of the chapters will verify.

The synanthrometric approach is readily testable (see Chapter Twenty) and serves as a guide to promising future lines of research. Synanthrometrics, thus, is not a doctrine, a faith, a dogma, or a dream, though it does involve a vision and a challenge. It aspires to a unified science of human behavior, only partially described and validated in this volume. It challenges the existing social structure, the customary practices, and the culture of the human sciences (psychology, sociology, political science, anthropology, economics, and so forth), a challenge outlined here.

The substantive focus of this volume is on informal social participation, a kind of voluntary action (Smith, 1975). The development of synanthrometrics has grown out of my work on voluntary action and on modernization. Informal social participation is the principal category of behavior that people engage in during their leisure or discretionary time. Though I myself and others have often given more attention to discretionary participation in formal contexts such as "voluntary associations," churches, political parties, and unions, discretionary participation in quasi-formal or informal settings is far more frequent in an average day (Robinson, Converse, and Szalai, 1972). Indeed, when one subtracts obligatory behavior such as sleeping, working, and activities related to sheer subsistence or existence as a socialized human being (such as grooming or eating), informal social participation occupies the vast majority of our remaining time.

For various reasons, among them a powerful prejudice (against the importance of discretionary time activities and for the importance of work related activities) in our society and in our social and behavioral sciences, individual discretionary behavior in informal settings or informal social participation has failed to receive the theoretical attention it deserves. The importance of discretionary time activities to the average individual is clearly demonstrated in major studies of individual well-being, satisfaction, or happiness, such as that of Campbell, Converse, and Rodgers (1976). They show that informal social participation, as a major component of free-time activities, is crucial to individual satisfaction and well-being at the practical level of everyday life.

Most adults work, but most people do *not* attend concerts, stop to help strangers with a flat tire, or campaign for a political candidate. If one can understand the great variability of individual discretionary behavior by means of an empirically grounded, comprehensive, and interdisciplinary theoretical model, then such a model has a high probability for being useful. With modification and amplification, it may be applicable to the entire range of individual human behavior. In short, a thorough understanding of discretionary behavior will lead us toward a unified theory of human behavior, a general theory of action.

This book is the result of an "experiment" aimed at moving toward the goal of better understanding of individual discretionary behavior, regardless of the disciplinary boundaries that had to be crossed. Jacqueline Macaulay and I sought to test the hypothesis that whatever the form taken by informal social participation, a broad review of the literature extant on one form would usually show a pattern of results and correlates similar to the pattern for other forms. We hoped that this would lead to a synthesis of specific, detailed research results from different fields and disciplines and to the emergence of a new model or perspective. The main challenge of working on this book has been to bring and hold together the disparate research literatures on informal social participation while deriving this new synanthrometric paradigm and its components from the vast amount of discipline-bound research of customary social and behavioral science. Social and behavioral scientists are ordinarily limited in both the methods and the kinds of independent variables they use when studying individual human behavior. But in this volume we have collectively established some important communalities across the various types of social participation and shown that participation in different discretionary activities is significantly and positively correlated.

This volume brings together scholars in psychology, sociology, and political science who review literature in these fields. I have integrated the results and elaborated a theoretical framework for synthesis of this otherwise apparently disparate data on informal social participation. This volume differs from most books containing literature reviews because it represents a quest for new and overarching perspectives on basically familiar bodies of slowly changing research. It differs in challenging directly the adequacy of customary "discipline-bound" theoretical and methodological approaches to the study of informal social participation, and in devoting substantial space to a theoretical framework for synthesis. We have asked what social and behavioral science research on informal social participation adds up to and how more of the variance in such participation might be explained both directly and indirectly (through mediated relationships).

In this volume we have limited the literature reviews to three major social science disciplines, although many more have relevant data and concepts for the study of informal social participation. The contents should interest economists concerned with nonmarket activity, household economics, and consumer behavior. Further, the time budget research paradigm that draws on the methodology of economic research will interest them. Similarly, social anthropologists will find the litera- ture reveiws or theory and concepts presented here related to their work. These theoretical models have cross-cultural relevance, as well as a culture and personality adaptation component that connects with their field.

Jacqueline Macaulay and I expected that the intrinsic similarity of the phenomena studied, combined with a common focus on several major classes of predictor variables, would generate a clearly discernible and cohesive interdisciplinary perspective on social and political partic- ipation. However, we did not get all that we sought. Some of the review chapters reflect concerns of their authors that are somewhat tangential to the original conception of the book, although still interesting. Practi- cal concerns also affected when each author ended his or her literature review period. Given the constraints of time, energy, and space available in this volume, we believe these chapters form a cohesive whole and provide evidence for a new paradigm for future study of informal social participation and discretionary behavior generally—synanthrometrics.

The core of this book is literature review chapters that cover a wide range of available data and theoretical work. Parts Two through Four contain chapters on political participation (both conventional and unconventional), altruistic and helping behavior, and expressive leisure activities (mass media use, outdoor sports and recreation, and participa- tion in sects and cults). Each major area of informal social participation has at least one chapter considering the special aspects of socialization or "humanization" for that kind of participation.

Besides ignoring formal voluntary group participation here (see Smith, 1975), some important types of *informal* social participation are not covered by this volume in separate chapters, although analytically they belong here. These areas include such research topics as par- ticipation in indoor expressive leisure and recreation, informal in- terpersonal relations, adult education, tourism, and relaxation. With the exception of informal interpersonal relations, the empirical litera- ture is rather small for these topics. To some extent they have been incorporated into the empirical groundwork for the synanthrometric paradigm derived here by examining some representative research or research reviews in Chapters Eighteen and Nineteen, along with the empirical evidence from the other review chapters. Still other activities, somewhat discretionary in nature, are more basically obligatory in our view and hence need not be dealt with here. These activities include house- work and home maintenance, child care, attention to personal needs and grooming, nonrecreational community resource use, and activities that maintain or enhance one's work skills.

Parts One and Five represent my attempt to synthesize the various areas of knowledge about informal social participation as presented in the central part of the book. Part One describes the need for and problems in arriving at a general synanthrometric paradigm for research on human discretionary activity, both formal and informal. Chapter One is in part a critique of the social and behavioral science academic system as found today, and in part a discussion of the reasons that interdisciplinary integrative synthesis is little sought or used at present. The first chapter also introduces the GA and ISSTAL models. Chapter Two describes in detail the main types of state variables (as opposed to process variables) that make up the ISSTAL model. Later, in Part Five, I return to systematically elaborate and examine evidence for the ISSTAL and GA models from the review chapters in this book and elsewhere.

The contents of this volume have important relationships to the larger context of methodology in the human sciences. The review chapters of Parts Two, Three, and Four reveal a wide range of methodologies currently in use, sometimes complementary, sometimes almost contradictory. But the synanthrometric approach I urge finds nearly all current methodological approaches lacking and inadequate to the task of understanding even some small aspect of human behavior. The discipline-bound nature of virtually all human science research, in terms of both variables and methodology, prohibits adequate understanding in nearly every instance. Inevitably these customary approaches to such research fail to take account of important variables and research methods. An unknown but potentially quite significant and substantial number of their findings are likely to be spurious or superficial and the interpretations placed upon these findings only partly accurate or even dead wrong.

Chestnut Hill, Massachusetts   DAVID HORTON SMITH
June 1980

Acknowledgments

When I first conceived the plan for this volume, I sought and received the official sponsorship of the Association of Voluntary Action Scholars (AVAS) for this endeavor. I have received a variety of help—both intellectual and material—from leaders and members of the association, particularly Eugene D. White, Jr., a former executive officer of AVAS. Boston College has also been very helpful. I am especially grateful to Donald White, dean of the Graduate School of Arts and Sciences, for making available special typing funds at crucial times, and to Lorraine Bone, administrative assistant of the Department of Sociology, for her exceptional care and conscientiousness in helping with the production of the manuscript. She put her considerable talents to work in numerous ways, not only in deciphering the hieroglyphics that pass for my handwriting but also in serving as a liaison between myself and others involved in the writing, editing, and critiquing of the contents of this volume. Not least of her contributions was organizing, supervising and participating in the massive and tedious job of typing and proofing the references section. Alice Close and Shirley Urban were also most helpful in typing various parts of this volume.

A year or so after I had begun to plan and solicit papers for this volume, I invited Jacqueline Macaulay, a social psychologist, to become actively involved as the author of a chapter and as a co-editor. She agreed and assisted in elaborating the design of the volume as well as in soliciting most of the chapters in Part Four. She edited nearly all of the review chapters (except my own) and Part One in an earlier version. I thank her for helping the chapter authors express their own ideas more clearly and felicitously. I regret that she was not able to write a chapter on the determinants of altruism and helping behavior as planned, but I fully understand and sympathize with her reasons. I also thank her for aid with many of the tedious mechanical tasks involved in completing the manuscript, including collating and proofing of the references prior to copy editing by the publisher. I would also like to express my appreciation to the various chapter authors who were all conscientious in meeting their deadlines and regret any inconveniences caused by my own slowness. Their contributions, although prepared for the volume by special invitiation, do not necessarily represent a consensus of opinion.

A number of friends and scholars at various universities have been kind enough to comment on draft versions of one or more of the chapters that I have written. I wish I could have done justice to all of their comments and criticisms but to do so as comprehensively as deserved will take much additional writing and research. Nonetheless, I have freely incorporated many of the ideas and suggested references from each of the following persons in one degree or another. Most have been very encouraging and all have valuable ideas and volunteered their scarce time to help me improve my work; I hold them blameless for its remaining faults. I add special thanks to those who gave the most time and thought to the task: Marc Fried, Boston College; Stanley Heshka, McMaster University; Alex Inkeles, Stanford University; David Knoke, University of Indiana; J. Miller MacPherson, University of South Carolina; James N. Morgan, University of Michigan; Jone Pearce, University of California at Irvine; Richard D. Reddy, College at Fredonia, State University of New York; David L. Rogers, Colorado State University; Milton Rokeach, Washington State University; Hans B. C. Spiegel, Hunter College, City University of New York; Nancy Theberge, University of Waterloo; Randall J. Thomson, North Carolina State University; and Louis A. Zurcher, University of Texas at Austin.

I have drawn insights from numerous other researchers and theorists. Although I have cited references throughout Parts One and Five to indicate these persons, some special debts cannot be indicated so simply. These debts are both personal and intellectual but essential to what I have undertaken and what I have accomplished here. First, I thank my undergraduate mentor, then at the University of Southern California, Edward McDonagh, who encouraged me to attend graduate school at Harvard rather than elsewhere. The intellectual climate of the Department of Social Relations at Harvard in the early and middle 1960s turned out to be just what I needed. Though a fragile joint enterprise now much changed, it then nourished in numerous ways my already keen interest in interdisciplinary synthesis of the social and behavioral sciences. Certain teachers there had a particularly powerful and lasting impact on my thinking in ways that are difficult to describe. Thus, without holding them in any way responsible for my errors or follies, I thank Alex Inkeles, Daniel Levinson, Talcott Parsons, George Homans, Gordon Allport, J.W.M. Whiting, S. M. Lipset, David McClelland, Thomas Pettigrew, Neal Gross, and Stanton Wheeler, all of whom in various ways contributed significantly to my present thinking.

For those who know their work, it is clear how much I draw on the personality and social structure/culture conceptualizations of Inkeles and Levinson, as well as on my long association with Inkeles (see Inkeles and Smith, 1974, for example). But the empirically grounded theory of accommodation between character and the sociocultural system that I first learned and tested for myself as a result of these associations has always been an approach that I have tried to see in the larger context of a unified theory of human behavior. In the latter aspiration, I have been most influenced by Parsons and Homans. These two teachers and theorists, almost diametrically opposite in their styles and approaches, one working from the top down and the other from the bottom up, one excruciatingly complex and difficult to read in his formulations and the other shockingly direct and easy to read, have somehow created in me a kind of dynamic tension.

Leaving the first for last, I must acknowledge the emotional inspiration I received from two of my earliest teachers in college (at the California Institute of Technology). They first made me realize and feel the sheer joy of theoretical inquiry about complex natural phenomena— Linus Pauling and Richard Feynman. I continue to draw strength from them, even though I search other realms than theirs for different patterns and models. Without the direct personal experience of such dedicated and fearless intellectual giants, I might not have had the courage to tread the difficult path I now turn to in Parts One and Five of this volume. But it is a path only begun, and its end is out of sight.

I cannot adequately express my profound gratitude to my wife, Barbara. But I thank her here for the acceptance, help, and essential emotional and intellectual companionship she has given so freely during these past several years.

DAVID HORTON SMITH

Contents

Contents

The Authors

DAVID HORTON SMITH is professor of sociology at Boston College. He earned his B.S. degree in sociology, psychology, and philosophy from the University of Southern California (1960) and his M.A. and Ph.D. degrees in sociology from Harvard University (1962, 1965).

In 1971, Smith found the Association of Voluntary Action Scholars (North America) and its principal publication, the *Journal of Voluntary Action Research*. He has assisted in stimulating similar associations elsewhere in the world. His interest in modernization and economic development, particularly as it affects individuals, is exemplified in his book *Becoming Modern* (1974, with Alex Inkeles). He has also contributed to the *Annual Review of Sociology* (1975) and written or edited numerous articles and several books on the subject of voluntary action and voluntary groups. His long-term projects include continuing the development of the International Voluntary Action and Voluntary Associations Research Organization, which he initiated and currently serves as secretary general, and of his synanthrometric theory of human behavior.

JACQUELINE MACAULAY is a social psychologist and freelance editorial consultant who does research, writing, and editing in the social sciences. She earned her A.B. degree in English from Stanford University (1955) and her M.S. and Ph.D. degrees in psychology from the University of Wisconsin (1960, 1965).

Macaulay has previously taught and done research at the State University of New York in Buffalo and the University of Wisconsin in Madison. Her research interests include law and psychology, employment discrimination, and the psychology of women. Among her publications are *Altruism and Helping Behavior* (edited with Leonard Berkowitz, 1970) and two contributions to *Rocking the Boat: Academic Women and the Academic Process* (forthcoming). She shared (with A. Frodi and P. R. Thome) the 1978 Distinguished Publication Award from the Association for Women in Psychology for an article examining the levels of aggression exhibited by women and men.

KAREN SMITH DAWSON has a joint appointment in the Department of Political Science and the Center for the Study of Public Affairs at Washington University in St. Louis.

RUSSELL R. DYNES is executive officer of the American Sociological Association in Washington, D.C.

CLYDE W. FAULKNER is professor of sociology and associate dean of arts and sciences at Georgia State University in Atlanta.

HELENE K. FEINBERG is visiting lecturer in psychology at the Community College of Philadelphia.

M. LAL GOEL is professor of political science at the University of West Florida in Pensacola.

ALAN E. GROSS is professor and head of the Department of Psychology at the University of Maryland in College Park.

ROBERT W. HUNT is associate professor of political science at Illinois State University in Normal.

LEO W. JEFFRES is assistant professor of communication at Cleveland State University.

JOHN R. KELLY is associate professor of leisure studies at the University of Illinois in Urbana.

THEODORE D. KEMPER is associate professor of sociology at St. John's University in Jamaica, New York.

KURT H. PARKUM is associate professor and head of the Division of Administrative and Social Sciences at Queens College in Charlotte, North Carolina.

VIRGINIA COHN PARKUM is public sector course consultant at the School of Organization and Management at Yale University in New Haven, Connecticut.

IRVING M. PILIAVIN is professor of social work at the University of Wisconsin in Madison.

BARBARA PITTARD-PAYNE is professor of sociology and director of the Gerontology Center at Georgia State University in Atlanta.

E. L. QUARANTELLI is professor of sociology and director of the Disaster Research Center at Ohio State University in Columbus.

RICHARD D. REDDY is associate professor and head of the Department of Sociology and Anthropology at the College at Fredonia, State University of New York.

JOHN P. ROBINSON is professor of communication and director of the Communication Research Center at Cleveland State University.

ERVIN STAUB is professor of psychology at the University of Massachusetts in Amherst.

BARBARA S. WALLSTON is associate professor of psychology and human development at Vanderbilt University in Nashville, Tennessee.

Participation in Social and Political Activities

*A Comprehensive Analysis
of Political Involvement,
Expressive Leisure Time,
and Helping Behavior*

PART I

Informal Social Participation

David Horton Smith

In this volume we seek to identify consistent underlying patterns in the ways people spend their discretionary time (the time available for activities not essential to making a living or sustaining life in a society). The focus is on individual social behavior, not on the behavior of aggregates or social groups. We are not trying to understand why nations, communities, organizations, or other social systems behave as they do. Nor are we concerned with the social behavior of nonhuman animals. When the term "social behavior" is used here, it refers to the forms of human behavior significantly shaped by culture, custom, and norms and by the presence (actual or imagined) of others. Of course, it is difficult to say any form of human behavior is not social in some sense—for example, the need for sleep is physiologically based, but where and when we sleep are shaped by custom and culture. I am not considering physiologically compelled behaviors because they are at most quasi-social. I am instead directing attention to behavior in which society or its representatives or symbols plays a central role.

There are many possible reasons one might be interested in finding consistent underlying patterns in the ways people spend their discretionary time. One source of my interest was a need to integrate a wide variety of social and behavioral science data on phenomena that obviously had many elements in common but that were seldom seen as related in the literature. These data are part of the great social behavior information explosion of the past few decades. There is as much published each year in some specialized fields of study as was published three decades ago in an entire discipline—sociology, political science, or psychology (Crane, 1972, figs. 1–16). It has become a herculean task just to integrate the ever-increasing data into a synthesis that covers a subfield within a discipline, and we no longer expect to find more than a few attempts at syntheses that span adjacent disciplines, let alone several at once. Thus, we can dip into topics that would be closely related in any comprehensive social or behavioral science theoretical scheme and find reams of research without any reference to their communality. Even theoretical efforts to synthesize data within subfields seldom include more than a few references across disciplinary or subfield lines. Specialists in one subfield are often unaware of closely parallel work or relevant theoretical advances in related subfields or disciplines. The data explosion and synthesis lack are compounded by the arbitrarily compartmentalized disciplinary structure of the social and behavioral sciences. Campbell (1969) has produced an original and provocative model of this situation, viewing scholarly fields as overlapping scales, positioned like the scales of a fish. Conventional disciplines are areas consensually defined over time as particular subsets of scales (or overlapping circles). Some scales are in the center of these sets and for various historical, political, and perceptual reasons come to be seen as its core. Other scales fall between disciplines or are at the periphery of one or another discipline.

Scholars who work in what appear to be the core areas of a discipline are viewed as doing important "mainstream" work, the work others in their discipline feel they must keep up with. They find more journals in which to publish than workers at the margins of a discipline, and the journals they publish in tend to be the most prestigious in their discipline. These mainstream scholars also usually have the advantage of readily being able to find colleagues to discuss their ideas with, which gives them an edge over those who work in relative isolation because of their nonmainstream focuses of study. Further, mainstream scholars are more likely to derive intrinsic satisfactions from their work in most cases because it is more socially legitimated than work at the margins and intersections of disciplines. Most important, the mainstream scholars are more likely to survive and advance in the academic world—to achieve tenure, rank, and power within their department and field, while those who deviate by venturing into interdisciplinary areas are more likely to find themselves in trouble, other things equal. Not only is it difficult to be a competent scholar in more than a few areas simultaneously, given the volume of published work, but ventures into collaborative work with those from other disciplines tend to be difficult to bring off successfully (Sherif and Sherif, 1969). Alliances created to meet specific research goals often turn out to be very fragile. Even if outright warfare does not ensue, such alliances may die from the effects of disciplinary snobbery, competing interests, differences in methodological approaches and theoretical perspectives, problems of geographical location, and lack of material support.

In spite of this harsh reality, some scholars in the social and behavioral sciences, including myself, believe integrative syntheses are not only possible but vitally needed for the maintenance of theoretical vitality and for real advancement of scientific knowledge. I am interested in finding consistent underlying patterns of individual discretionary time activity because I am convinced that as a sociologist I share a common substantive interest with scholars in many other fields, that we would all profit by sharing our discipline-limited syntheses, and that it is essential for the development of a broader theory of social behavior to generate an interdisciplinary synthesis of our pooled knowledge about both formal and informal social participation. The digression into the description of the fragmented world of social and behavioral science was a necessary introduction to some of the difficulties we face in accomplishing this goal. For nearly two decades, I have been intrigued by the task of devising a broad, general, and empirically grounded explanation of individual social behavior that covers the full range of everyday activities both formally organized and informal as contrasted to general and highly abstract theories that have little linkage to either empirical research or everyday behavior. (And I achieved academic advancement and tenure in spite of that consuming interest, though not because of it.)

It has seemed curious to me, during these decades, that so little relative attention has been paid in any discipline to the patterning of the activities of daily life, and particularly to lifetime patterns of role entry, performance, and exit. After the early work on time budgets by Sorokin and Berger (1939) and Lundberg, Komarovsky, and McInerny (1934), this topic was neglected for a long time. Some modest work has been done in the last decade or so, but mostly in Eastern Europe (see bibliography in Szalai and others, 1972, pp. 841–868). There tends to be an ethnocentric ignorance in North American social science of work not originally published in English and little of this work has been integrated into recent English-language social science.

These two gaps in social science research and theory are related. Both reflect a dominant concern with fragmented areas of social life and *our scientific understanding of discretionary social behavior (T. Kuhn, 1964). With alternative paradigms, it is possible that more real growth in our knowledge, rather than spurious, inflationary growth, will result.*

As mentioned briefly in the Preface, discretionary time activity, particularly informal social participation, is obviously an important aspect of human behavior and life because it fills our waking hours to an extent rivalled only by income-generating activity or its equivalent. However, discretionary activity is seldom subjected to broad interdisciplinary theoretical or empirical scrutiny; and it is seldom given the importance in theory that it has in our daily lives. Formally organized discretionary activity (for example, participation in associations or churches as a member) has received far more attention even though it accounts for far less of our discretionary time (see Smith, 1975, for instance). Further, discretionary time activity, particularly informal social participation, is or can be the source of major satisfactions and dissatisfactions we experience over our lifetimes (see Andrews and Withey, 1976; Bradburn, 1969; Bradburn and Caplovitz, 1965; Campbell, Converse, and Rodgers, 1976; Phillips, 1967a, 1967b; E. Scott, 1971; Wilson, 1967). Also, virtually by definition this area of human behavior involves the most individual discretion or voluntary action (Smith, 1975). Leisure time activity (which may be taken here as synonymous with discretionary time activity) is the most variable and least predictable behavior (Bull, 1971, 1972). The majority of adults in modern society must "work" for a living, and both custom and economic market forces severely limit the nature of that work. But our options when it comes to nonwork activity are infinitely more varied. (I put work in quotation marks at this point because discretionary time activity also may involve work; for instance, worklike activity can be undertaken for something other than subsistence or direct income generation.) Thus, if one can explain this highly variable form of social behavior, one may well find the conceptual tools developed will make it easier to explain the less variable, more obligatory forms of social participation and behavior. Facilitating a more comprehensive explanation of individual human behavior beyond the realms of informal and formal discretionary social participation is an important secondary purpose of this volume.

This introduction and Chapters One and Two begin to provide a conceptual framework and methodological perspective for understanding individual discretionary time activity. The first chapter is particularly concerned with the most appropriate paradigms of inquiry in this field. It suggests two related but distinct aspects of discretionary social participation viewed as a set of dependent variables being studied here. The first aspect involves identification of relevant analytical variables of social participation in discretionary time—a subproblem of the larger problem of the relevant general analytical variables for understanding how individuals use their time in everyday life over their life spans. The second aspect involves discussion of a general activity model which postulates an important underlying pattern of consistent positive covariation that can and does occur in the interrelationships among various kinds of discretionary social participation because of underlying character, body, and context accommodation processes. Chapter Two describes the range of state-variables that must be taken into account in order to understand and explain individual discretionary time activity. The various major categories of independent or predictor state-variables described constitute the general framework for most of the substantive literature review chapters in the next three parts.

CHAPTER 1

Methods of Inquiry and Theoretical Perspectives

David Horton Smith

An important beginning point for the study of informal social participation and, more broadly, of discretionary time activity, is to consider how such activity can be most fruitfully categorized in analytical terms. Most of the existing typologies for the analysis of discretionary time use by individuals are designed to cover nondiscretionary time use as well and to cover both formal and informal contexts of such participation. One such typology developed for use in coding time budget data is presented in Table 1. The significance of such schemes (see also the more extended scheme in Chapin, 1974) extends far beyond their use as coding tools for dealing with the raw data of time budgets of human behavior because the categories in a coding scheme ideally relate both to empirical data and to major theoretical categories. Also, analyses using them provide some tests of the theoretical assumptions on which categorization is based. For example, Chapin's (1974, p. 98) data on nonobligatory activities show a substantial proportion of his metropolitan sample

Table 1. Complete Two-Digit Activity Code

Working Time and Time Connected to It (00–09)

00 Normal professional work (outside home)
01 Normal professional work at home or brought home
02 Overtime if it can be specifically isolated from 00
03 Displacement during work if it can be specifically isolated from 00 (travel for job)
04 Any waiting or interruption during working time if it can be isolated from work (for example, due to supply shortage or breakdown of machines)
05 Undeclared or auxiliary work (moonlighting or second job)
06 Meal at the work place
07 Time spent at the work place before starting or after ending work
08 Regular breaks and prescribed nonworking periods during work time
09 Travel to (and from) work place, including waiting for means of transport

Domestic Work (10–19)[a]

10 Preparation and cooking of food
11 Washing up and putting away the dishes
12 Indoor cleaning (sweeping, washing, bed making)
13 Outdoor cleaning (sidewalk, disposal of garbage)
14 Laundry, ironing
15 Repair or upkeep of clothes, shoes, underwear
16 Other repairs and home operations
17 Gardening, animal care
18 Heat and water supplies upkeep
19 Others (for example, dealing with bills and various other papers and usual care to household members)

Care to Children (20–29)

20 Care to babies
21 Care to older children
22 Supervision of schoolwork (exercises and lessons)
23 Reading of tales or other nonschoolbooks to children, conversations with children
24 Indoor games and manual instruction
25 Outdoor games and walks
26 Medical care (visiting the childrens' doctor or dentist or other activities related to the health of children)
27-28 Others (including babysitting)
29 Travel to accompany children, including waiting for means of transport

Purchasing of Goods and Services (30–39)

30 Purchasing of everyday consumer goods and products
31 Purchasing of durable consumer goods
32 Personal care outside home (for example, hairdresser)
33 Medical care outside home

Table 1 (continued)

34 Administrative services, offices
35 Repair and other services (for example, laundry, electricity, mechanics)
36 Waiting, queueing for the purchase of goods and services
37–38 Others (other services)
39 Traveling connected to the above-mentioned activities, including waiting for means of transport

Private Needs: Meals and Sleep (private and nondescribed activities) (40–49)

40 Personal hygiene, dressing (getting up, going to bed, and such)
41 Personal medical care at home
42 Care given to adults, if not included in household work
43 Meals and snacks at home
44 Meals outside home or the canteen[b]
45 Night sleep (essential)
46 Daytime sleep (incidental)
47 Nap or rest
48 Private activities, nondescribed, others
49 Traveling connected to the above-mentioned activities, including waiting for means of transport

Adult Education and Professional Training (50–59)

50 Full-time attendance to classes (undergraduate or postgraduate student), studies being the principal activity
51 Reduced programs of professional or special training courses (including after-work classes organized by the plant or enterprise in question)
52 Attendance to lectures (occasionally)
53 Programs of political or union training course
54 Homework prepared for different courses and lectures (including related research work and self-instruction)
55 Reading of scientific reviews or books for personal instruction
56–58 Others (other study)
59 Traveling connected to the above-mentioned activities, including waiting for means of transport

Civic and Collective Participation Activities (60–69)

60 Participation as member of a party, a union, or such
61 Voluntary activity as an elected official of a social or political organization
62 Participation in meetings other than those covered by 60 and 61
63 Nonpaid collective civic activity (volunteers)
64 Participation in religious organizations
65 Religious practice and attending religious ceremonies
66 Participation in various factory councils (committees, commissions)
67 Participation in other associations (family, parent, military, and so on)
68 Others (other associations)
69 Traveling connected to the above-mentioned activities, including waiting for means of transport

Table 1 (continued)

Spectacles, Entertainment, Social Life (70-79)

70 Attending a sports event
71 Circus, music hall, dancing, show, nightclub (including a meal in the entertainment locale)
72 Movies
73 Theater, concert, opera
74 Museum, exhibition
75 Receiving visit of friends or visiting friends
76 Party or reception with meal offered to or offered by friends
77 Cafe, bar, tearoom
78 Attending receptions (other than those mentioned above)
79 Traveling connected to the above-mentioned activities, including waiting for means of transport

Sports and Active Leisure (80-89)

80 Practice a sport and physical exercise
81 Excursion, hunting, fishing
82 Walks
83 Technical hobbies, collections
84 Ladies' work (confection, needlework, dressmaking, knitting, and so on)
85 Artistic creations (sculpture, painting, poetry, literature, and so on)
86 Playing a musical instrument, singing
87 Society games
88 Others (other pastimes)
89 Traveling connected to the above-mentioned activities, including waiting for means of transport

Passive Leisure (90-99)

90 Listening to the radio
91 Watching television
92 Listening to records
93 Reading books
94 Reading reviews, periodicals, pamphlets, and so forth
95 Reading newspaper
96 Conversations, including telephone conversation
97 Writing private correspondence
98 Relaxing, reflecting, thinking, planning, doing nothing, no visible activity
99 Traveling connected to the above-mentioned activities, including waiting for means of transport

Source: Szalai and others, 1972, pp. 562–564.

[a]Such activities (especially gardening and animal care) are to be recorded as domestic work only if not part of professional work or gainful employment.
[b]A number of special types of meals outside the home and the canteen have special codes, different from 44 (see especially codes 71, 76–78).

engaged in each major type of discretionary activity coded, indicating these are not unimportant activities in the daily lives of those in the sample. From 7 to 33 percent of the population took part in church or other organizational activities in the course of a single week. From 29 to 67 percent of the adults sampled participated in family activities, socializing, and various recreational diversions ranging from the most active to the most passive in nature. Similarly, data collected by Szalai and others (1972, p. 581) from a forty-four-city U.S. sample show 78 percent participating in non-work-related travel; 20 percent in educational, religious, or organizational activities; and 79 percent in sports, cultural, or social (interpersonal) activity. Eighty-seven percent were entertained by mass media. (See Tables 1 and 2 for the typologies used here.) Data from a national sample of older adolescents and adults drawn in 1957 (De Grazia, 1962, p. 462) yielded the following participation ranking for various leisure activities engaged in during the prior week:

- Watching television: 57 percent
- Visiting with friends or relatives: 38 percent
- Working in yard and garden: 33 percent
- Reading magazines: 27 percent
- Special hobbies (woodworking, knitting, and so forth): 19 percent
- Reading books: 18 percent
- Pleasure driving: 17 percent
- Listening to records: 14 percent
- Going to meetings and other organizational activities: 11 percent

Other activities not on this list (going out to dinner, sports, playing games, and watching sports events or movies) occupied the time of only a small percentage of this sample. This list would probably look quite different if the data had been gathered in 1977 or today instead of 1957 because television is now in nearly every home and has drastically changed many of our time use patterns (Robinson and Converse, 1972). Nonetheless, the data contrast a popularity ranking based on participation frequency with one based on amount of time allocated to each activity (ignoring here the problem of overlapping activities and coding only the primary activity for any time period).

Table 2 ranks fifteen activities according to amount of time spent on each by a 1965 national U.S. urban sample. Some activities we might expect to be very important to respondents—religious, organizational, and educational activities—take up rather small average amounts of time. Active sports and outdoor recreation and attendance at sports and other events such as popular and classical music concerts, plays, and museum shows show similarly low average time expenditures. Even

Table 2. Rank Order of Activities for National Urban Sample of Adults in Terms of Total Average Minutes per Day

 1 Sleep (470 minutes)
 2 Paid work and related travel (266 minutes)
 3 Housework and household care (189 minutes)
 4 Mass media usage (134 minutes)
 5 Eating (81 minutes)
 6 Social leisure and conversation (81 minutes)
 7 Personal care (69 minutes)
 8 Nonwork travel (50 minutes)
 9 Child care (32 minutes)
10 Resting and miscellaneous leisure (29 minutes)
11 Study (12 minutes)
12 Religious activities (10 minutes)
13 Active sports and outdoor activities (8 minutes)
14 Entertainment and cultural events (6 minutes)
15 Voluntary organization participation (6 minutes)

Note: The rank ordering presented here is based on the author's computations, with collapsing of categories, from Robinson, Converse, and Szalai, 1972, table 1, p. 114. The average minutes per day has been weighted to ensure equality of days of the week and eligible respondents per household. Eligible respondents were persons in the United States of either sex between the ages of eighteen and sixty-four (not sixty-five plus) who were not in some institution or in a household wholly engaged in agriculture.

child care shows a much lower average time than its probable importance to people. Those discretionary activities that do take up relatively large amounts of time are mass media use (television viewing in particular—about 90 minutes per day, as noted in Chapter Twelve) and casual social activities (conversation and visiting, for example), which one would not expect to be given a high rating. We find the same discrepancy when we look at several obligatory activities—sleep, housework and household care, personal care, and nonwork travel. These take relatively large amounts of time but most people would probably not list them as important direct contributors to their satisfaction with life in either the long or short term. Many would also fail to list work-related travel (25 minutes per day average) and paid work (241 minutes per day average) as very satisfying.

The array of topics presented in this volume reflects these facts. Pages are allotted not on the basis of amount of time we believe various activities consume in the life of the average American but on the basis of our assumption that each of our categories reflects a type of activity the average American might rate as reasonably important—at least in general, if not in his or her own life. Thus, although nearly half the

American population's discretionary time may be spent consuming mass media, mass media usage does not take up half this book. But political participation (formal and informal), which takes up an average 0.2 minutes per day for urban U.S. adults (Szalai and others, 1972, p. 577), is a topic to which we devote several chapters. Altruistic or helping behavior occurs too infrequently to be included in Szalai's coding scheme, though it does occur in Chapin's (1974, p. 225) most detailed scheme. We do not believe this justifies ignoring the topic. Our assignment of topic importance is made on the basis of our general socialization in Western culture and our specific shaping by education in the social sciences. Although I have made a brief for the importance of studying the mundane, frequent, but seldom studied behaviors that fill our everyday lives, I am also assuming some of those activities are more important than others and amount of time allocated is not the only measure of importance. Time allocation is one measure of topic importance; we cannot slight the largely passive, time-filling, and often time-wasting activity of television (and other mass media use) because it occupies tremendous stretches of time. But another equally valid criterion of importance is that an activity is held to be important by the performer or leaves its mark on the world (altruism and political activity, for example).

ISSTAL Model: Dependent Variables

I am proposing as a general research paradigm a conceptual scheme or loose theoretical model called the ISSTAL model (interdisciplinary sequential specificity time allocation-life span model) of individual social participation. A special variant of this scheme is the general activity model, a scheme that I have referred to earlier as the General Activity Syndrome (Smith, 1969). The principal independent or explanatory variables of the ISSTAL model are described and discussed in Chapters Two and Eighteen. The latter chapter presents my general notions of causal linkages within the ISSTAL model and the larger theoretical linkages between it and other important concepts in the social and behavioral sciences. This section focuses on the time allocation-life span perspective as an aspect of the larger model. The time allocation-life span perspective refers to a consideration of social participation in terms of the fine grain of everyday behavior through the individual's life span. This perspective contrasts with the widespread tendency in the social and behavioral sciences to focus mainly on behavior or participation taken out of its daily and life span context, ignoring certain types of behavior completely and usually failing to relate adequately the behavior studied to its temporal context for the individual.

The point seems simple; but in practice, there are many methodological complexities that militate against taking this approach to the study of social participation and discretionary activity. Two main methodological approaches are important here, one a short-range and one a long-range approach.

Time Budget Studies. One major methodological approach to the study of individual social behavior is the short-term study of time budgets (see Warwick and Bishop, 1972). A time budget is the observed or recorded daily or weekly time allocation by an individual to various activities for every period of the day. Time periods used for reporting and recording are usually quarter- or half-hour segments. A comprehensive time budget study obtains data on what people do, approximately how long they do it, where, with whom, and with what resources. Such a study covers the full twenty-four-hour day and, ideally, a seven-day week and considers seasonal variations in time use through appropriate sampling techniques (sampling can also be used to deal with day-of-the-week variations). Good examples of this kind of study are the multinational study by Szalai and others (1972), the study of a U.S. national urban sample by Robinson (1977)—one of the data sets from Szalai and others, a major metropolitan area by Chapin (1974), the series of works of Barker and his colleagues on psychological ecology (Barker, 1963, 1968; Barker and Schoggen, 1973; Barker and Wright, 1955), and a national U.S. panel study by Juster (forthcoming).

A detailed coding scheme is, of course, necessary if one is to draw conclusions about time use patterns from time budget data. Some kind of abstract beginning and ending rules must be imposed on the ongoing behavior stream in order to have analyzable units. One such scheme, as developed by Szalai and others (1972), was presented in this chapter. Chapin (1974) has also developed a detailed coding scheme, the original extended version having 236 categories. As can be noted from Tables 1 and 2, one striking aspect of the time budget approach to human behavior is the wide range of activities that must be coded, symbolizing the range of naturally occurring variation existing but usually not well studied, especially as regards patterns of interrelationships of these behaviors in everyday life. For example, assume we examine the data for one individual for one day, using the Szalai and others (1972) 96-category scheme presented earlier. If we code only one activity at a time, we usually code the apparently primary activity, although time budget research has shown that people often perform two or more activities simultaneously (radio listening being a good example of an activity frequently combined with something else). If we assume each activity can recur twice a day and individuals perform an average of twenty different activities per day, using this coding scheme (as indicated by the research results of Szalai and others, 1972, pp. 400–407), we have some-thing like 10^{48} (10 to the 48th power, or one with forty-eight zeros) possible permutations of daily activity sequences. If we use instead Chapin's 236-category scheme, quarter-hour observation data (ninety-six per day), or extend the temporal unit of analysis from a day to a week or a month, the number of possible sequences rises to figures beyond my patience to calculate. Not all sequences are possible or probable, but taking just a small fraction of the possibilities leaves us with a set of mammoth size—larger than the number of atoms in the universe in all likelihood.

Obviously, then, the task of research on individual time alloca-tion is as much a task of analysis—of drawing generalizations from massive data sets—as it is a task of observation. Szalai and others (1972) have, fortunately, been able to abstract some fairly regular daily, weekly, monthly, and seasonal cycles from their data, as have other researchers; so the task is not impossible. Most time budget research so far, however, has been mainly descriptive, and we understand relatively little as yet about common patterns of time use and their determinants. One way to simplify the analytical task is to reduce the number of categories (as done in Table 2 relative to Table 1); but even these simplifications may be too complex for easy analysis, especially in the absence of a specific and clear theoretical focus. At the extreme, excessive collapsing of time budget coding categories oversimplifies the very real and meaningful complexi-ties of human life that are precisely what the time budget approach otherwise helps us to recover and attend to in social and behavioral science research. Hence, such reduction of analytical categories should be done judiciously and preferably with particular theoretical purposes in mind.

For example, Parker (1971, pp. 25–27), following DeGrazia (1962) and others, has suggested a set of basic categories for the "components of life space" or range of human activities. According to Parker, these components represent all human activities or ways of spending time. I suggest this reduction of time budget categories is useful as a means of elucidating the major differences among work or work-related activities, socially compelled activities, and discretionary activities. The five cate-gories are as follows:

1. *"Work, working time, sold time, and subsistence time."* Activities in this category include all those likely to lead to remuneration and those done around the home or elsewhere that enable the individual and those dependent on him or her to subsist.
2. *"Work-related time, work obligations."* Apart from actual working time, most people have to spend . . . time traveling to and from . . .

work and in preparing or 'grooming' themselves for work." Included here are such things as work-related reading, learning, and meetings (a union meeting, for example). The key element in this category is that these activities are not directly remunerated but are necessary in order to maintain or enhance remuneration from activities in the first category.

3. *"Existence time, meeting physiological needs."* This category covers the minimum time we all must spend sleeping, eating, washing, eliminating, and so forth. Only the minimum necessary time is included here (for a given society) and *not* any extra time taken in such things as eating for pleasure or grooming in preparation for a party.

4. *"Nonwork obligations, semileisure."* Parker (1971, p. 26) quotes Dumazedier (1967) in defining semileisure as "activities which, from the point of view of the individual, arise in the first place from leisure; but which represent in differing degrees the character of obligations." Such obligations may be to other people, pets, homes, gardens, deities, and so on. The differentiation between a nonwork obligation and a leisure activity depends on the individual's attitudes toward the activity.

5. *"Leisure, free time, spare time, uncommitted time, discretionary time, choosing time."* All these phrases describe some aspect of what we mean by leisure or discretionary time in this volume. The essence of discretionary activities is the existence of choice. They take place during time we can use as we choose. Parker's fourth and fifth categories parallel the definition of "voluntary action" my associates and I presented in 1972. We emphasized the differentiation of voluntary action as activity not biologically or socially determined by needs or compulsions, not economically determined by the imperatives of subsistence, and not compelled by political, physical, or legal force. Voluntary action is activity freely entered into either for short-term enjoyment or to realize some long-term goal not rooted in biological, political, or economic necessity, or both (Smith, Reddy, and Baldwin, 1972 a, p. 163). Generally, then, we will use the terms "discretionary," "voluntary," and "leisure" interchangeably.

The fifth category (and some aspects of the fourth category) is the central concern of this volume. We are interested in relatively unorganized or only informally organized discretionary activities. The other major category of voluntary action is that of participation in "formal" or explicitly organized activity, undertaken under the aegis of some formal organization (overlapping partially with Parker's fourth category). Formal voluntary action has been the subject of several other works (Smith, 1975; Smith, Reddy, and Baldwin, 1972b; Tomeh, 1973).

Informal voluntary participation has never before been subject to such comprehensive scrutiny.

Although "participation" usually implies relatively active behavior and even exclusion of passive behavior, its usage here includes every kind of activity. Uses of time that one might in everyday speech call inaction (sitting and thinking), nonmovement (immobile absorption in, say, a television show), passive receptivity (listening to music), and similar concepts are here considered informal voluntary action or participation in an informal discretionary or leisure activity. However, the activation level or intensity of such participation varies from high to low—a measure of physical activity in the sense of body or body part movement and energy expenditure—as well as in terms of frequency and duration (Szalai and others, 1972). To give some examples of activation quantifications, one could participate at an intense activity level in a handball game or at a relaxed activity level in watching television. One can do these things often, several times a day or week, and one can do these things for a long time on each occasion. These are high but not intense activation levels.

Longitudinal Studies. The other appropriate major approach is that of the long-term study of individuals across their life spans or at least across a major stage of their lives, with several data collection points. The dependent variables in the long-term approach, in contrast to the coded time samples of activity found with the short-term approach, are likely to be derived from data on role performance, role entries and exits, major or minor life events, and so forth (see Tuma, Hannan, and Groeneveld, 1979). Because of the greater variety of activities engaged in across the life span as compared to the already great variety found within a single day, it is necessary to use simpler categorizations than in short-term studies.

Occasionally, cross-sectional or short-time span longitudinal data can substitute for more extensive longitudinal study. Instead of following individuals for long periods of time, overlapping age-cohort methodologies attempt to draw inferences about differences across the life span through comparisons of individuals at different overlapping stages. This takes the most sophisticated sampling, statistical tools, and logical analyses in order to ensure one's results represent longitudinal processes and not artifacts of the short-term comparisons. Such analyses are not always possible with the data available. Because social systems are characterized not by stability but by change and development, there are phenomena that cannot be analyzed in short-term longitudinal, let alone cross-sectional, frameworks.

Besides the previously mentioned reasons for the dearth of longitudinal studies of human behavior in any field, such research is rare because it requires a commitment of many years. If the researcher cannot obtain long-term funding, he or she must engage in a never-ending search for grants. Furthermore, there is more risk of failure in longitudinal studies. One must plan ahead and anticipate essential data and problems for which there is no post hoc remedy. One must draw a sample that will be (or can be made) available for long periods and maintain contact with the sample even when data is not being collected. The analysis required is highly sophisticated; and ideal analyses may prove to be beyond the researcher's or computer's capability, especially because of sample attrition over time or inadequate numbers of data-collection points. In spite of all these problems, longitudinal research is well worth doing; it is hoped this book underscores the great advantage of longitudinal research over static research. The development of dynamic theory that can explain and predict large blocks of human behavior (and the overdue fall from dominance of static theory in the social and behavioral sciences) depends on the existence of high-quality longitudinal work. As yet we have only a slim base on which to build.

Existing longitudinal studies have usually been limited to single segments of human life, such as specific age ranges (for example, for studies of children and youth, see Jessor and Jessor, 1977; Kagan and Moss, 1962; Stone and Onque, 1959; for studies of the aged, see Cumming and Henry, 1961; Palmore, 1970; for a study of young families, see Geismar, 1973; for a study of students' college years, see Newcomb, 1943). Several other studies where fuller life span data have been collected are samples of special populations and/or have had limited purposes, which in turn limits the usefulness of the data for our understanding social behavior generally. Examples of such studies are the Terman study of the intellectually gifted (Terman and Oden, 1947, 1959; Terman, Burks, and Jensen, 1930; Terman and others, 1925), Vaillant's (1977) study of Harvard men, Newcomb and others' (1967) twenty-five-year follow-up on Bennington College women, and Maas and Kuypers's (1974) study of the parents of children receiving child guidance at the University of California at Berkeley. In spite of these limitations, the existing longitudinal studies do have something to offer the study of social participation over the life span. As Banton (1965), Biddle and Thomas (1966), Nadel (1957), Sarbin and Allen (1968), and others have suggested, the study of roles is an important key to understanding the structure of human behavior. Some longitudinal studies have much to tell us about role performance and about life events that signify role exits and entries; thus, they shed light on patterns of social participation and changes in those patterns.

Other information about patterns in social participation can be gleaned from the study of language, as suggested by Nadel (1957, p. 20).

A catalog of all social position and role names used in the society's main language, especially those role names used frequently in everyday life, will yield an inventory of the roles available to the people in that society. Changes in role language mirror changes in social structure and role. With close analysis, one can find language data as well as life span longitudinal study data indicating role overlaps, conflicts, sequences, and so forth.

These two approaches to the study of social behavior—daily time budgets and life span longitudinal study—are the most important that social scientists can undertake, providing part of the broad paradigm for research on individual social behavior that the social and behavioral sciences have sorely lacked so far. Only when we have a broad understanding of the total pattern of human individual activity—across all types of activities, individuals, activity sites, and the life span—will we be able to understand fully the significance of research into specific types of activities and people in specific social groups and sites at particular times of life. Without knowledge of the total pattern provided by the time allocation and life span research perspectives, particular pieces of research on individual social behavior lose their proper interpretive context, and the pieces of this vast puzzle cannot be assembled as readily. Analogously, I do not propose to supplant existing theories or models of social participation, but rather I hope to develop a larger context into which narrow theories will fit (or may be altered to fit) and which will yield a broader understanding of social behavior in general. The IS-STAL model is part of that larger theoretical context or paradigm. As a research paradigm or perspective, this model asserts, in part, the forgoing propositions about the necessary approaches to studying individual social behavior. It states unequivocally that real (versus spurious or apparent) progress in the study of human individual social behavior is most likely to result from testing purported contributions to knowledge (including the ISSTAL model itself) against a new or little-used standard—the ability to explain and predict meaningfully the patterns of daily and life span social activities and social roles of individuals in their natural contexts. The ISSTAL model also asserts that real intellectual progress in the study of human individual behavior is most likely when a broad and interdisciplinary range of relevant independent variables is used instead of the usual narrow range of variables and variable classes.

The next chapter outlines the broad range of relevant independent or explanatory variables the ISSTAL model suggests will aid in understanding human individual behavior. There is a very definite interdisciplinary sequential specificity aspect of the model involved in the independent variables and in the manner they will likely be associated with the dependent social participation variables. Together, the various aspects of the ISSTAL model constitute a paradigm that involves new ways to study social behavior. At present, elements of this paradigm are widespread, but their use in combination is extremely rare. The ISSTAL model has at least the following characteristics: (1) focus on the full range of individuals' everyday and life span social behavior; (2) use of the full range of relevant contextual, social-psychological, and situational variables to explain individual behavior, without regard to the established and customary disciplinary boundaries; and (3) consideration of complex, mediated interactive, and feedback effects in causal systems for the explanation of individual behavior. One variant of this ISSTAL model is the general activity model.

General Activity Model

The general activity model, like the ISSTAL model, involves specification of both independent and dependent variables and of their interrelationships. The G A model may be characterized initially and superficially in terms of its most obvious face, namely, the interrelationships among various kinds of discretionary social participation. The various kinds of individual social participation in discretionary time are usually sorted into political, social, religious, recreational, cultural, altruistic, and other similar categories—that is, into types with names that match the purposes of various activities. These are often further subdivided into formal and informal categories, according to whether the participation takes place in an organized social context. Participation levels tend to be positively and significantly correlated across categories for all valued discretionary activities. That is, a person who participates in one kind of socioculturally valued activity will tend to participate at roughly the same level in other kinds (inter-type covariation). Even within broad types of social participation, there tends to be a positive covariation of major subtypes of social participation, for example, among recreational activities (intra-type covariation). This covariation tends to exist both at a given time and through time. Of course, the finite character of energy, time, and other individual resources, as well as opportunity limitations, place upper limits on an individual's total social participation. The great variety of relevant determinants, the number and complexity of various forms of participation, and the upper limits on individual participation keep this correlation level rather low. Nonetheless, the positive covariation involved (as will be seen later) is a consistent and thus highly significant finding, both statistically and theoretically.

The roots of this GA model primary pattern lie in the general accommodation between individual character and culture and social structure (see Fromm, 1947, 1955; Gerth and Mills, 1953; Kardiner, 1939, 1945; Linton, 1945). This accommodation tends to shape all forms of social behavior—discretionary and obligatory, informal and formal. If this assumption is correct, then some evidence for this accommodation should be found in all the relevant reviews in this book. Any type of society—whatever its environment, culture, social structure, and degree and nature of role differentiation—must recruit and socialize individuals into its positively valued roles. In order to assure the continued satisfactory performance by incumbents of valued social roles or positions, a society must arrange or evolve appropriate reward systems. If a role incumbent no longer possesses the proper characteristics or fails to behave appropriately for a role, there will be mechanisms to induce the person to exit from that role.

Various societies tend to produce different mixes of characters and to fill their most important roles with people having certain types of character. Studies of national character document the first half of this assertion (for example, Inkeles and Levinson, 1969; Lynn, 1971; Mead, 1956; Triandis, Malpass, and Davidson, 1973). For the second half, one could cite the vast body of ethnographic studies that document the nature of differences among societies, though such studies tell little about the characters of different roles' incumbents. However, within the subgroup of modern industrial societies, where one might expect to find character similarities among certain role incumbents, such similarities seem to exist, at least among adult men (Inkeles and Smith, 1974).

Next I would argue there will be a strain toward consistency in any society such that those most suited by their characters for one kind of valued role will also be reasonably well suited for other valued roles, though not necessarily *all* valued roles. For one thing, it is more efficient for a society to produce socialized individuals with broad rather than narrow role performance capabilities. There will be more human resource flexibility in the system if there is greater interchangeability among highly active or high-quality role participants. Furthermore, there is a tendency toward cognitive consistency such that those labeled as "good" and worthy of filling one kind of socially valued role in a society will be viewed as more appropriate for other kinds of roles as well, especially in modern and postindustrial society (for reasons to be noted a bit later). Thus, we see generals becoming president, politicians becoming professors, and bankers becoming cabinet members at the highest levels in our society, with analogous transitions at middle or even lower prestige and power levels.

Looking at this strain toward consistency from another perspective, we would not only expect to find that those who fill various highly valued social positions and roles within a single society are more like than unlike each other but would also expect to find (both simultaneously and sequentially) an uneven distribution of societal roles among those available to fill them. That is, a person who performs a role accorded high social value will occupy relatively many socially valued positions, both simultaneously and sequentially, in comparison with those who perform less highly socially valued roles. We would also expect to find the social prestige value of any role performed to correlate positively with the value of perceived individual characteristics or character of its incumbents. That is, those with high-status roles will be viewed as having characters of all-around social value; those in low-status roles will be viewed as possessing fewer or no highly valued personal characteristics. Not only is there status consistency, as others have shown, in regard to the roles (for example, occupation prestige level, education, income class, or race-ethnicity) most basic to social stratification in a society, but the social prestige value of individual character and the occupancy of socially valued roles are positively correlated and may be a positively accelerated function. Hence, as we move from low to high value sets of individual characteristics (from less to more valued characters), the total number of high-prestige value positions occupied in a given society will increase accordingly—possibly geometrically rather than arithmetically. At the top, we will find the highly regarded individual occupying (simultaneously and sequentially) a wide array of high-status positions, while those of an average or lower than average socially valued character will occupy few or no high-status positions at all and fewer nondeviant positions or roles in general. Indeed those with the least valued (most disvalued) characters will tend to be criminals and incumbents of other deviant, disvalued roles.

All of the foregoing can be viewed as helping to explain the general activity syndrome if one notes that the kinds of roles (and corresponding role performances) involved in that discussion include discretionary behavior roles. The same people whose characters are most suited in a given society for optimal performance of the highest prestige work and other obligatory roles will also have characters most suited for optimal performance of the highest prestige (most socioculturally valued) discretionary behavior roles. Similarly, people at middle and lower prestige levels of both work and discretionary roles are likely to have correspondingly fewer of the socioculturally preferred aspects of character in the given society. Mobility is usually possible in either direction, up or down, in modern societies, but at any given time there tends to be a fairly close correspondence between the degree to which an individual approximates society's preferences and the degree of prestige of all roles played by the person—work roles, other obligatory roles (kin, racial, gender roles, and so on), and discretionary time roles. When mobility occurs, it can arise either from an individual's increasing (or decreasing) fit with society's preferred character type, from an individual's entry into a higher (or lower) prestige role of importance than is socioculturally appropriate given his or her character, or both. Individual mobility can be best explained by changes in individual character as it relates to the socioculturally preferred character types. Changes in the role opportunity structure also play a part, mainly in recognizing character changes and validating them. And either initial source of mobility can be successful or unsuccessful according to whether the person is able to achieve some reasonable consistency, in time, between character type and role prestige level.

Another element of this theoretical explanation of the existence of a pattern corresponding to a general activity model in modern and postindustrial societies is that in such societies characterized by a high degree of social-structural role differentiation, the nature of the socialization process tends to be such that individuals are encouraged not only to learn certain basic ascribed and achieved roles but also to seek out and become satisfactory performers of a *variety* of achieved roles. Insofar as social mobility (both vertical and horizontal) is encouraged by the cultural values and social structure, people in a modern or postindustrial society are urged generally to seek out the more valued social roles in the society. This "encouragement" in the socialization process involves both the inculcation of appropriate aspirations and expectations regarding simultaneous and sequential role incumbencies as well as the molding of the individual's character into the most socially approved form feasible. Both processes make either mobility to or maintenance of highly valued achieved social positions and roles as likely as possible, given initial individual limitations. The individuals in any modern society will thus show a mix of "inherited" and "earned" valued characteristics, with changes in this mix for any given individual over the life span, usually. Changes in individual prestige level will occur as a result of net changes in valued characteristics.

This is all a kind of "metasocialization" in that it is not directed so much toward achievement of particular roles in a given society as toward encouraging the individual to seek out, become socialized into, and perform well over the life span in various highly valued, achieved social roles. The equivalent concept in the psychological theory of learning is "learning how to learn"; I have applied this concept to the learning of valued social roles rather than to the learning of problem solution techniques. Modern societies are thus more flexible in allowing either valued character or valued social roles to precede the other. In premodern societies, valued social roles of an ascribed (inherited) sort are much more likely to precede valued character, limiting social mobility.

When one speaks of playing or performing multiple roles, one usually is referring to being an incumbent of several different roles more or less simultaneously (that is, during the same day, week, or month). For example, one might be at once a professor, father, husband, church member, voter, hospital volunteer, friend, neighbor, and museum goer. The general activity syndrome refers to a positive covariation of such simultaneous roles, particularly of highly valued roles in society, as well as a positive covariation of highly valued role incumbencies and performances for the individual over the life span or sequentially. People with several highly valued roles are likely to hold other roles of high value; people with several disvalued or low value roles are likely to hold others of low value. The same is true for people with roles of moderate value, at a given time and over the life span. The sequential covariation is not so strong that social mobility is precluded. Nonetheless, it represents an important type of patterning of human lives in modern societies. I have already discussed why such patterning is, for the most part, overlooked and have taken social science research on individuals to task for its failure to give adequate attention to life span patterns of role entry, performance, and exit. The attention that is given to status consistency by sociologists falls far short of the more general and life span consistency patterns I note.

This point leads to the other element that helps both to describe and explain the existence of the pattern corresponding to the general activity model, namely, linkage among roles in modern and postindustrial societies. Social positions and roles in modern societies have a much greater tendency to be linked to each other than in peasant or preliterate societies. I am not using the term "linkage" to refer to the fact that incumbents of a given role are likely to have normatively provided role partners (for instance, fathers have children as role partners, employers have employees, club leaders have club members, and so on). The term here refers to the probability that an incumbent of a given role will also be or become an incumbent of some other specified role or roles. This concept of "role linkage" refers either to a *role overlap probability* or a *role transition probability*. When I speak of the probability of an individual being simultaneously an incumbent of two specific roles, this may be termed the "simultaneous role linkage" for the two given roles. This linkage can be measured by the degree of observed overlap, as best it can be estimated, between the incumbents of any two roles in a given society or social system. If all members of the first role are also incumbents of the second, the overlap is perfect, the probability of a member of the second role being a member of the first role is 1.00, and the role linkage from role one to role two is as strong as it can be. One example of a 1.00 simultaneous role linkage is that between the voluntary group leader role and the voluntary group member role (within the same specific voluntary group, such as the Sierra Club). On the other hand, the simultaneous role linkage of the role of Republican Club leader and Communist Party member (overtly) or even Democratic Party member is likely to be 0.00. For most roles in modern society, however, the simultaneous role overlap probability is a number between zero and one, not at these extremes. Note that the notion of role linkage, whether simultaneous or sequential, involves direction or ordering of the two roles involved. All fathers are men, but not all men are fathers.

The concept of *sequential* role linkage refers to the probability that an incumbent of a given role at time 1 will become an incumbent of a second role at time 2. (This concept is similar to but broader than Merton's concept of status sequence. See Merton, 1957, p. 381.) When the interval is very short, sequential role linkage almost reduces to simultaneous role linkage. However, in general, the interval involved will be measured in years. If the maximum time interval for an individual is considered, sequential role linkage becomes *lifetime* role linkage, referring to the probability that an incumbent of a given role at time 1 will ever subsequently in his or her lifetime become an incumbent of some second role. Once again, for certain ascribed roles based on physical characteristics, the sequential and lifetime role linkages are zero, as with male and female gender roles. For most roles, especially achieved roles, in modern society, the sequential and lifetime role linkages are neither zero nor one but somewhere between these extremes. Role transition probabilities can change over time, of course, and are directional, as with the role overlap probabilities.

I can now state more precisely my initial point that both the simultaneous and sequential role linkages are greater on the average in modern or postindustrial society than in peasant or preliterate societies. This variable can be termed "role permeability." Thus, modern society is distinguished from traditional society not solely by greater role multiplicity, a greater number and variety of roles (Parsons, 1966), but also by greater probabilities of linkages among them. In premodern society, there is a greater tendency for occupational or social class/caste/estate role to determine most other roles and to be relatively unchangeable, in comparison with modern societies or the modern sectors of premodern societies. The general activity model is most relevant and valid in modern societies for several reasons, including the general shift in the ratio of ascribed to achieved roles (with a greater proportion of the latter and hence more opportunities for the mutual accommodation of character and roles), the greatly increased social structural interdependency of achieved roles, and the nature of the "modern person" required to be an effective, functioning member of modern society. As demonstrated by Inkeles and Smith (1974), the "modern man" is distinguished from others by usually having more aspiration, a feeling of efficacy, an interest in new experiences, and a willingness to meet new people, among other characteristics. I have no systematic and quantitative comparative evidence of this suggested differential in role permeability, although it would be welcome. Moreover, the generalization I have made probably will hold better for nonkin roles than for kin roles. However, ethnographic, historical, and sociological studies of traditional and modern societies generally and impressionistically confirm my basic point.

Whether or not there is a greater level of role linkage, especially achieved role linkage, in modern than in traditional society, the general activity model is partly explained by the higher average role linkage among high-prestige as well as less powerful roles in modern society. In part, these higher role linkage levels derive from factors already mentioned, including the socialization process that encourages role seeking, role learning, and role mobility; the resulting modal or national character that is appropriate to complex modern social structure, with its high degree of role differentiation and interrole mobility; and the interdependence of roles in modern society that leads incumbents of a given role to learn a good deal about not only the expectations and activities of their role partners (incumbents of other roles with whom the given individual role incumbent interacts) but also about the nature of related, similar, or indirectly linked roles.

Then, too, there is the important factor of normative role linkage, both simultaneous and sequential. Normative role linkage refers to role linkage that results from social norms that prescribe a connection between two given roles. This normative prescription can vary in intensity from an absolute requirement (very rare) to a mildly preferred situation (total lack of role linkage preference in the sociocultural system indicating a lack of normative linkage at all, though there may still be a probabilistic role linkage for other reasons). Such normative role linkages are essential parts of the social structure of a society. Indeed, Banton (1965, p. 167) has gone so far as to argue that a society's structure can be viewed essentially as a set of rules (norms) regarding role linkages.

An example of a normative role linkage would be the fairly strong linkage between high social class role and the roles of consumer of live classical opera or ballet performances, with the former role normatively prescribing some involvement in the latter roles (contrary to the social class norms of lower or working class roles). Normative role linkages are likely to be stronger and more frequent at higher status levels (especially upper-middle-class or lower-upper-class levels, with some decline at the highest levels where people are relatively impervious to many norms that affect lesser mortals in their society) than at lower status levels. This results from the greater accommodation of higher status people, on the average, to societal needs and norms and from the greater deviance of lower status people from such norms; "higher" and "lower" here refer to halves of the social prestige status continuum. Naturally, high-status people receive appropriately greater rewards and fewer punishments from society than do low-status people as a result of being so accommodating. The net result is that there are greater probabilities of role linkage at high-status levels in modern society than at low levels, which contributes to the validity of a general activity model.

Another factor contributing to the greater average role linkage for high-status persons in modern society is interpersonal role entry and role performance pressure. There is greater structural role linkage at high- than at low-status levels in part as a cumulative result of the facts that (1) high-status persons tend to have friends and acquaintances in more different kinds of roles than low-status persons, (2) such friends and acquaintances in these various roles tend to exert systematic interpersonal pressure to induce their peers (other high-status persons and sometimes upwardly mobile middle-status persons) to take note of and get involved in their roles and/or with their role partners, and (3) such friends and acquaintances tend to serve as role models, thus providing indirect interpersonal pressure on their peers and would-be peers to take note of and get involved in such roles or similar and related ones. Such "significant other" and "peer modeling" effects are far more important at higher status levels in modern society than at lower levels, because of meta-socialization for role-seeking being greater at such levels. The result is again greater role linkage of all types and hence more structural pressure for a general activity model to be valid. Thus, the social structure of modern society is patterned such that one kind of social participation opportunity tends to lead to others, particularly for those who are of high status and have the appropriate set of personal characteristics—social, psychological, and physical.

The general activity model may seem analogous to the sociological concept of status consistency or status crystallization (Lenski, 1954). However, there are a number of important differences between them, the former being much more general in scope. Unlike the status consistency concept, the general activity model is concerned not only with social positions in major hierarchies relevant to the general social status (prestige) level of an individual in society, but also with the whole range of other kinds of social positions in a society, even ones that have very little to do with one's basic social prestige level. For instance, not only occupational prestige, educational level, income, and race or ethnicity are involved, but also such other social positions and roles as voter, association member, mass media consumer, sports participant, donor to philanthropy, helper of strangers with problems, married person, friend, female, and so forth. Thus, the general activity model is much broader in the scope and variety of roles with which it is concerned than is the status consistency concept. The general activity model also differs from status consistency in focusing on the performance aspects of social positions or roles as well as the sheer social identity or labeling aspect. That is, instead of being mainly concerned with the idea that levels in various hierarchies of social characteristics tend to be similar and move toward consistency, the general activity model is more concerned with communalities in individuals' daily and lifetime activity patterns. Furthermore, the general activity model, unlike the status consistency concept, is integrally related to a certain kind of socioculturally preferred character of individuals in a given society; and this preferred character is related to the society's social structure and culture in a variety of ways.

In sum, the roots of the general activity model are hypothesized to lie in the interaction of modern sociocultural systems with individual character. The general activity model reflects a dynamic accommodation, both for the individual and the larger society, between societal needs (in the functionalist sense) and individual needs. This accommodation is brought about through the processes of socialization, interpersonal influence, social selection or recruitment, and social conformity. Varying degrees of social change, deviance, and conflict over time in the whole system make this process of accommodation a continuing one.

Evidence for the General Activity Model

There are two analytical levels at which we might expect to find evidence in this volume for the existence of a general activity model. First, we may seek evidence for the hypothesized positive covariation of social positions, roles, and participation both within and across major types of valued social activity. Because most social science studies of individuals are cross-sectional rather than longitudinal, evidence is more likely to be found for simultaneous role linkage than for sequential role linkage. This sort of evidence will be observable to a minor degree in the review chapters that follow when a given type of social participation being studied is related to other forms of social participation. However, the most direct evidence is to be found in studies explicitly designed for analysis of multiple forms of discretionary social participation. A brief review of this evidence is found in Chapter Nineteen.

Second, one may seek evidence of the existence of the general activity model in the patterning of correlates or determinants of the various forms of informal social participation to be reviewed in subsequent chapters. I use the term "determinants" with some uneasiness because the general activity model, if valid, will require some significant rethinking of our ideas on direction of causality and causal systems in the study of individual social participation. Indeed, the GA model highlights the relativity of the independent versus the dependent variable distinction in the study of individual social participation, particularly when we analyze the relationship of demographic variables (age, education, income, race, social class, and so forth) to the apparently more psychological variables (attitudes, beliefs, perceptions of the situation, and so forth), and the relationship of both to actual social behavior. What are customarily viewed as wholly ascribed and exogenous variables by most human scientists actually have important and often crucial learned and normative psychological components (sex or gender roles, age roles, racial roles). Hence they can and at times should be viewed as endogenous or even dependent variables.

In the review chapters in this volume, the major social class variables, such as occupational prestige, educational level, and income, and the additional arrays of ethnicity, race, age, gender, marital status, employment status, and others will be treated mainly as independent variables. However, many of the factors can be treated as either independent or dependent variables. For example, a volunteer position may result from occupancy of a particular paid position or may be the cause of it. One may become a volunteer ombudsperson because one is director of a large corporation; or one might be invited to join a corporate board of directors, as an attempt at cooptation, because one has been active in a consumer group with goals relevant to the corporation's business.

Thus, when one observes a statistically significant correlation between such role incumbency variables in cross-sectional analyses, the general activity model perspective directs one to investigate the possibility that the correlation stems from the concurrent effect upon these variables of another variable. If this is true, the latter variable will usually be more basic to understanding the observed behavior and the causation involved. For instance, the observed correlation between socioeconomic status and a particular kind of informal or formal social participation may in fact stem largely from the underlying importance of particular character types in the society being studied. Such character types, in turn, are comprised of various cognitive, conative, affective, and physical characteristics and prior experiences that facilitate higher levels of social participation in that society and that are learned or induced by socioeconomic status roles in part.

Another substantial part of the observed correlation may derive from the combination of certain contextual and situational variables that determine the roles, formal or informal, present in the society. A matrix, expressing the directional probabilities of linkage between all relevant pairs of roles, represents the general *role opportunity structure* for an individual having any given role (or no roles at all, if we care to add such an improbable possibility) in that society. The remaining direct effect of socioeconomic status level on the particular form of social participation may be quite small and certainly reduced from the effect apparent when the implications of the general activity model are not taken into account. Thus, instead of a simple causal system in which normative expectations associated with higher socioeconomic status lead to higher levels of social participation (which, indeed, I believe they do), an accurate causal system is likely to be more complex, replete with non-recursive features and feedback effects as well as additional variable categories and interactions.

In the review chapters that follow, then, we expect to find an emerging pattern of individual characteristics that will collectively define for modern industrial and postindustrial society (particularly U.S. society) the kind of character most likely to be associated with higher social participation in informal discretionary activities. This character will show some significant consistency across types of informal social participation, if the general activity model is broadly correct. Further, the kind of character that emerges consistently in the study of informal discretionary social participation should be consistent with the character pattern that has emerged from other reviews of the correlates of formal voluntary association participation (Smith, 1975; Smith, Reddy, and Baldwin, 1972b) and with whatever scant data there are on the character correlates of a general discretionary activity index.

The emergent pattern of relationships observed in the following review chapters should also confirm two separate facets of the general activity model, if it is indeed valid. One facet is the positive relationship between informal social participation measures and socially valued or "dominant" (see Lemon, Palisi, and Jacobson, 1972) social position and role characteristics such as formal education. A second facet is the positive relationship between informal social participation measures and certain psychological aspects of the active-effective character in modern society such as the trait extroversion. If the general activity model is not valid, neither of the two facets of the GA model should be observed in the succeeding chapters with significant consistency across types of social participation. Insofar as significant correlates of informal social participation are found, whether social or psychological in nature, these correlates will in that case be highly inconsistent in both direction and strength across types of participation. Whatever consistency is found between social and psychological characteristics themselves should be interpretable as isolated instances of accommodation of personality (broadly construed) and particular social roles.

If valid, the general activity model will both synthesize a great many otherwise disparate findings regarding the determinants of individual social participation and explain many inconsistencies in such research. I have already indicated the kind of synthesis the theoretical paradigm will make possible, but I have not mentioned how important inconsistencies may also be explained. The inconsistencies I have in mind here are troublesome variations in the relationship of social roles such as age, gender, marital status, and religion to the forms of social participation we are terming discretionary activity. All too often there appears in the social science literature a jumbled and inconsistent pattern of relationships between certain social role characteristics (often called social background or demographic variables) and dependent social participation variables. My perspective, drawing on the work of Lemon, Palisi, and Jacobson (1972), would attempt to explain such inconsistencies partly in terms of methodological differences and partly in terms of variations in the sociocultural preference value or dominance of the inconsistent social role characteristics in particular societies at different times, in different societies at the same time, or in different social subsystems of a society at the same or different times. In any given society and social subsystem at a particular time, some social roles and individual characteristics will tend to be more highly valued than others and hence more strongly associated with general social participation. For specific types of social participation, there will be additional variations in the value placed on particular characteristics. The most important stable qualifications are likely to be ascribed (such as gender, age, race, or handicapped status), though some very stable achieved characteristics are also likely to be important (for instance, level of formal education or language spoken fluently), as are those positions that involve substantial control over others or over resources and benefits (see Nadel, 1957). For many other achieved roles (such as occupation) or characteristics (such as attitudes) the social value placed upon them may be highly variable in terms of time, geography, social system, and type of social participation. The general activity model may help explain such variations. That is, the active character in a given social system at a particular time, mediating the effects of the usual social background and demographic variables, should also be an important factor in explaining the apparent inconsistencies of relationships. Further, such inconsistencies should be explicable in part by variations in the normative expectations (over time, space, and social systems) for the roles and social positions involved and by variations in the general and specific (local) role opportunity structures involved (interpreted in terms of role linkage matrices, whether simultaneous, sequential, or lifetime).

Having sketched roughly the outlines of the general activity model and the dependent variables of discretionary social participation that are the focus of explanation of the larger ISSTAL model, I turn in the next chapter to a detailed description of the predictor *state*-variables and variable classes of the model. A brief listing of the relevant *process*-variables of the ISSTAL model is given in Chapter Eighteen; such variables are of secondary importance here because so few of the studies available focus on dynamics of discretionary behavior. Indeed, much of the inconsistency seen in cross-sectional, synchronic studies of discretionary behavior may simply be the result of viewing complex dynamics from different static perspectives methodologically.

CHAPTER 2

Determinants of Individuals' Discretionary Use of Time

David Horton Smith

In an attempt to categorize and identify all the factors that might shape individual social behavior, I have devised a five-class scheme over the years (Smith, 1966; Smith and Fisher, 1971; Smith and Reddy, 1972a). This sequential specificity model draws on a variety of earlier works, most particularly on books by Allport (1954) and by Campbell and others (1960) as well as on a seminar by Alex Inkeles and Daniel Levinson in which I participated (Department of Social Relations, Harvard University, 1961). I have recently revised and elaborated the sequential specificity model, adding a sixth class of factors, retained information. Figure 1 provides an overview of the ISSTAL model sequence of major variable types. The major classes of predictor state-variables in the present version of the sequential specificity model, thus, are as follows:

1. External contextual factors
2. Social background and social role factors
3. Personality and intellectual capacity factors
4. Attitudinal dispositions: values, attitudes, expectations, and intentions

5. Retained information: images, beliefs, knowledge, and plans
6. Situational factors: immediate awareness and definition of the situation.

Together with the time allocation-lifespan perspective on what people do in their lives, the sequential specificity model forms part of the broader ISSTAL model being presented and, in part, tested in this volume as a general explanatory model for individual discretionary behavior. In the planning of this volume, the contributors were presented with the earlier five-category version of the sequential specificity scheme in order to foster conceptual communality among the planned review chapters. For various reasons, including a respect for genuine differences in intellectual interests and perspectives, we were not able to achieve the hoped for communality of approach in all of the chapters, although many of the chapters come very close to the proposed design. Even though the plan to work with a common conceptual framework in each review chapter (other than the socialization chapters) was not entirely realized (or perhaps even realizable in such an unfunded collaborative project), this scheme was nonetheless influential at many points. The reader can use it in seeking conceptual likenesses among the chapters just as I subsequently use it in Part Five to assess communalities in the findings of research from the various fields and disciplines on different types of discretionary informal social participation.

Note, however, that the use of a common conceptual scheme for organizing the research findings on a given type of informal social participation in no way guarantees confirmation of the ISSTAL model or general activity model. Rather, such use merely facilitates testing of the utility and validity of these models. The relationship between empirical results and the ISSTAL model or general activity model is the crucial point. The review chapters of Parts Two, Three, and Four lend substantial confirmation to both schemes. But a great deal of additional research is needed to test other aspects of these models on which there is presently little or no research extant. The conclusion of this volume suggests a number of these future research tests.

External Contextual Factors

The first class of factors includes the whole range of determinants of present social behavior that stem from past events external to and largely independent of a given person. This includes characteristics of cultures and subcultures, of social structures, of the physical and biological environment, and of the human population (as physiological beings) in which the individual is embedded or acting. These characteristics may be of recent origin or may have direct roots in the distant past.

External contextual factors can be divided into four types: biophysical environmental, human population, cultural, and social structural.

All the nonhuman aspects of the world in which social systems exist—biological and physical—comprise the biophysical environmental factors. These include climate, topography, soil types, natural resources or lack of resources, pollution, vegetation, wild and domestic animal populations, and all human-made objects and forces that impinge upon our lives, from buildings to roads to electricity to radio waves. Marking the start of life from conception, the intrauterine environment is also included for the child before birth (see Joffe, 1969). There has been little work on the effects of this class of factors on social behavior (but see Craik, 1973; Huntington, 1945; Michelson, 1971).

The second subset includes the various biological and physical characteristics of human populations. A single population may be defined as all those living in a given nation, society, culture, or territory. Human population variables include average stature, general level of physical health, modal skin pigmentation and physiognomy, spatial distribution, and population density. Again, there is relatively little research on the effects of such factors, with the recent exception of population or crowd density effects on individual social behavior (see Carson, 1969; Marx and Wood, 1975; Milgram and Toch, 1969).

The subset of cultural factors includes all the socially created and transmitted general values, ideas, beliefs, and symbolizing systems that differentiate societies, ethnic groups, linguistic groups, or even different age-cohorts. This definition of "culture" focuses on abstract or general but pervasive and powerful ideas, values, and technology that are relatively stable across time and within individuals. Norms, customary attitudes, and other cognitive, conative, and affective aspects of more specific role behavior will be referred to as characteristics of the social structure rather than of the culture. It is these very basic patterns of values and ideas that are an integral part of early childhood socialization and are taught by the chief socializers in childhood that I am defining as "cultural."

In contrast to cultural factors, social-structural factors generally vary markedly as we move from one role or one group to another within a society or subculture. This subset includes those normative expectations for patterned behaviors that are associated with specialized role performance, specific social settings or institutional contexts, and particular groups or organizations. They may be learned at any stage of life (rather than only or mainly during the basic childhood socialization period). In general, specification of these factors will be more detailed and precise in its referents than specification of cultural factors; but the main distinguishing feature of a social-structural factor is that it does not characterize all or nearly all members of a society or ethnic group.

Social structure can be called the fine grain of customs and culture, the coarse grain. Social structure is an abstraction from the details of social life; culture is an abstraction from broad social patterns. Social-structural factors involve norms for specific roles and behaviors; and cultural factors involve broad values, ideas, and world views. Both social structure and culture have clear effects on individual personality and behavior (see Triandis, Malpass, and Davidson, 1973).

The study of these various social and historical contextual factors properly involves sampling not only individuals but sites and situations that differ significantly in terms of the contextual factors of interest. For example, one might study the effects on individual social behavior of average income levels across census tracts, the percentage of women employed in different organizations, or the suicide rates of different ethnic groups. In actuality, researchers most often use individual's self-reports, which are assumed to reflect contextual influences, because this is the cheapest way to answer many research questions. Thus, we do not have a large body of research concerning the directly and accurately measured impact of contextual factors on individual behavior—research in which it has been possible to separate and thus control for the effect of personal individual characteristics as contrasted with the contextual effects. When we have only self-reports of important present and prior contextual variables, these measures inevitably combine personal attitudes and beliefs with objective contextual factors in a manner that makes impossible the independent accurate assessment of the latter.

The proper study of contextual variables also involves measurement of changes in an individual's social and historical context. Such changes may be of two distinct types. In one case, the individual remains in the same place but there are important changes in the nature of the context (for example, a disease epidemic, an economic depression, cultural or social change, or an earthquake or weather disaster). In the second case, the individual changes location of residence or work and is thus exposed to a different social and historical context. In the latter case, the nature and causes of the migration or travel involved and length of time in the new context become important variables. Such information falls in the life history and experience subcategory of the social background category.

Finally, contextual variables must be clearly distinguished from contextual social roles. Place of residence (suburban rather than inner-city or urban, for example) may affect social behavior not only because the physical or social nature of different kinds of living areas have different effects, but also because of contextual social role variations. People in the suburbs may be socialized into different normative expectations, images, or feelings than people in innercities and rural areas. The same kind of contextual role variations may be found with regard to particular cities (for example, New Yorkers versus Bostonians), regions of the country (for example, southerners versus westerners), countries, neighborhoods, even blocks or buildings. The only way to determine whether contextual social roles are operating is to analyze role characteristics (over time) of individuals from various contexts and to investigate directly context-linked expectations, images, and feelings as they are relevant to some particular kind of social behavior of interest. Unless this is done, it will be impossible to say for sure whether any apparent contextual effects are really the result of physical and social aspects of the contexts or also the result of the normative expectations usually learned by the inhabitants. If contextual social roles are present, this kind of variable falls into the category of social background variables and its subcategory of achieved social roles.

Social Background and Social Role Factors

The second major category of determinants of discretionary social behavior includes all the familiar demographic categories of age, sex, race, ethnicity, marital status, religion, occupation, employment status, income, education, health, physical abilities or handicaps, organizational and political affiliations, position in kin and friendship networks, neighborhood relations, and whatever other role, status, and social experience differentiations researchers find necessary to make. These factors can all be used to characterize individuals in terms of past, present, and potential social positions, roles and relationships, personal experiential and activity history, and physical states, past and present. Some of these kinds of roles and activities can be viewed also as parts of dependent discretionary behavior variables, depending on one's causal and analytic perspective. Five subcategories can be distinguished.

Physical and Physiological Characteristics. There are a number of characteristics with social implications of a type that might require the services of a physician or physical anthropologist to determine. These factors include individuals' height, weight, sex, age, physiology, physiognomy, body morphology, skin, hair and eye colors, physical coordination, perceptual-motor skills, general health, handicaps, and disfigurements. They may have only a minor direct effect on individual behavioral potential, but they become social factors because (or when) society has assigned a social meaning to them. With the exception of sex and age, these factors are usually ignored in behavioral research unless its focus happens to be directly relevant to one of them. For example, one consistently finds general health variables only in studies of medical services utilization and one consistently finds data on race only in studies of discrimination and similar topics. When included in studies where they are not directly relevant to the main focus (as relevance is conventionally defined in social science theory), such variables are often rather inadequately measured—by means of self-reports, which are often inaccurate, or through indicators that may correspond poorly to the variable of interest (for example, adult skin color and designation of race at birth or physical health and visits to a physician). The incipient growth of "physiological sociology" (Barchas, 1976a) is a positive sign that future research in the area may far outstrip the past.

Ascribed Social Positions and Roles. Some of the roles an individual occupies (or is assumed to occupy) are dictated by physiology as interpreted by society. For example, physical age or visible incapacitating handicaps define an individual as elderly or handicapped. Such roles tend to bring with them certain restrictions and privileges not accorded to those whose physical characteristics do not qualify them for the role. For example, doors are held open for the elderly and handicapped but the doors to social participation tend to be closed to them (through retirement rules, discriminatory practices, or socioculturally derived architectural barriers). As students of our own culture, we may be well aware that many ascribed role characteristics are in the eye of the beholder rather than actually true of a specific individual. However, social and behavioral scientists often ignore this truism in their research, using physical characteristics as proxies (surrogate variables) for positions or roles occupied by individuals, even when they have no solid information on the probability of being correct. An example of this can be found in the literature on marriage and the family. "Adult female in a family" is still often assumed to be a proxy for one whose chief role is unpaid domestic, in spite of the fact that about half the American adult women now have jobs outside the home.

In many cases, we find researchers assuming one-to-one correspondence without being aware of their own analytical confusion. The best case in point is the question of the physiological variable of sex, usually assumed to be a dichotomy, with the continuous social variable of gender. Gould and Kern-Daniels (1977, pp. 183–184) define sex as "the biological dichotomy between female and male, chromosomally determined and, for the most part, unalterable. Gender is that which is recognized as masculine or feminine by society." Gender is thus a continuous variable, not a dichotomy. "Sex role" then properly refers to positions in sexual intercourse and reproductive behavior; "gender role" refers more broadly to sex-typed social behavior, including a series of normative expectations, self-imagery, and beliefs. (See Tresemer, 1975, for more on this point and for a discussion of the concomitant misconceptions and misuses of "masculine" and "feminine.") This error or confusion is particularly flagrant in view of the recent changes in gender roles in modern society (especially U.S. society; see Seward and Williamson, 1970). The result of this habit of using physical characteristics as proxies for ascribed social positions or roles is that the significance of the physical variable is likely to remain obscure and its apparent "effect" inconsistent across studies. This is true not only for gender but also for race, age, and disability characteristics. In fact, until very recently, a neglected field of social-psychological study was that of the effects on the individual and on society of ascription of social meaning to physical characteristics. Much of what currently falls under the headings of the sociology or psychology of minorities and women (or "women's studies" and "minority studies") involves the initiation of this study.

Unless and until one has established for a given population that there is a perfect or near-perfect association between a given physical characteristic (or complex of physical characteristics) of human individuals and certain social position and role expectations, images, and feelings, one should not use the physical characteristic as a proxy for the latter. This can only obscure the social meaning of the physical characteristic. Instead, one should directly measure the variations in position and role expectations, images and feelings and use them as independent variables to help explain the social behavior of interest (see Sechrest, 1976). The determinants of the relationship between a particular physical characteristic, such as skin color, and a particular social position or role expectation, image, or feeling are themselves worthy of study. Such study would involve human societies or social systems and role changes within them rather than individual behavior, however.

Voluntary or Achieved Social Positions and Roles. Another kind of social position or role is more purely social than those previously discussed. It is usually entered voluntarily or at least can be left voluntarily. This type is based on elements in an individual's social identity stemming from position in religious, political, geographical, occupational, educational, organization, friendship, and kinship systems. (In the case of a position such as "son of," there is a biological element, unless the relationship is adoptive; but the important aspect of this is social, not biological. And though it is initially ascribed, one can voluntarily exit from a kinship role.) Such voluntary roles, like the ascribed roles, are usually treated as dichotomous or nominal variables and are measured by simple self-report. Such measures are treated as coherent and accurate, often without justification or good results. For example, the Democrat-Independent-Republican scale does not index three distinct groups but rather a continuum of attitudes, perceptions, expectations, and behavior, say, from radical to conservative and perhaps several other continua as well that may be logically or statistically independent. (One might be a fiscal conservative and a civil libertarian, for example.) One cannot predict either attitudes or votes from the three traditional political labels with any great accuracy. In some cases, there is a strong correlation between traditional social labels and attitudes or behaviors, but this is a matter for demonstration rather than something that can be safely assumed. Again, researchers are generally rather sloppy when it comes to justifying their use or interpretation of achieved social position and role data, and the reliability and validity of their results suffer accordingly.

Thus, for achieved social positions as well as ascribed ones, social identity labels or role names are again used as proxies for a series of expectations, images, and feelings that vary greatly among individuals who are incumbents of the same position or role. Again, the only adequate way to approach the matter is to measure the social position or role expectations, images, and feelings of each individual and to use these to help understand the individual social behavior being studied. Failure to do this has resulted in a great deal of unreliability and invalidity in research on human individual social behavior. The result is that the amount of explained variance in such behavior using socio-demographic variables is rather low or modest at best (seldom above 30 percent). Moreover, because the studies do not contain adequate information on the variations in role expectations involved, it is virtually impossible to resolve discrepancies among studies and to synthesize their results into a coherent whole.

Generally, my reading of the literature on individual social behavior suggests that when a social position or role category (such as female, Jewish, or upper class) is consistently found to be strongly related to a particular behavior or type of social participation, we will find among the role incumbents involved (women, Jews, or the rich) an unusually high degree of consensus on some beliefs, feelings, attitudes, or expectations relevant to that behavior. When we come across a set of studies that sometimes shows a strong relationship and sometimes does not, we are probably dealing with lack of such a consensus within the set of role incumbents and their role partners and thus lack of any strong or consistent relationship between the social position and behavior. In short, degree of role consensus is a major determinant of the strength of relationships found between social role measures and behavior.

Experience and Activity History. Another set of social background determinants of discretionary behavior involves the individual's personal experience and activity history. For example, one might glean from life histories information on whether a person has ever been raped, had a mystical experience, visited a psychiatrist, voted in a local election, migrated across the country by car, or gone skiing in the winter.

Obviously, some such experiences are likely to be very influential in shaping present behavior. Most of these background factors are rather easy to identify—they occurred or they did not. Determination of timing and frequency is much more difficult because there is almost always a problem of error due to poor memory when using self-report (and, of course, longitudinal data collection of such material is very rare). In some studies, where the life history variable of interest is likely to have become an official statistic (for example, epidemiological studies of general health or mental health such as those by Roff and Ricks, 1970; Roff, Robins, and Pollack, 1972), these kinds of background data may be relatively easily gathered. In other cases, particularly when individual memories of specific events are not likely to be vivid or reliable, it may be necessary to use the expensive longitudinal observation or time budget methodologies to get the accuracy needed.

Resources, Possessions, and Access to Resources. One's stock of resources is a strong determinant of discretionary behavior. For participation in some activities, one may need a high level of wealth or income or perhaps, more specifically, ownership of (or other right of access to) a car, pet, boat, home, telephone, or television set. These variables are usually fairly easy to measure; but as with other categories of this type, the variable commonly measured is often only a crude indicator of the variable of interest. The most common example here is use of individual or family income as a proxy variable for possession of specific goods necessary to undertake some behavior. It is far preferable to investigate the latter directly. Thus, if one is interested in leisure travel behavior, income may be a partial determinant; but after a given income level is reached, further variation may not be strongly related to such travel behavior. Instead, access to a car or public transportation is likely to be more crucial, as well as freedom from domestic or employment responsibilities, length of vacation periods, possession of major consumer goods (as alternative expenditures) and attitude or life history variables. Some of these variables of resource access or possession are often misused or too crudely used as measures of social status or life-style. Income, for example, has not proven to be a very good predictor of various kinds of social behavior; and its predictive power has become substantially weaker over the past few decades of increasing affluence in the United States and other industrial or postindustrial societies. Direct measures of social class role or life-style role expectations should be used if one wants increased accuracy and explanatory power.

A subset of the category of possessions and resources includes those resources and services available in or provided by both the sociopolitical and physical environment. Geographic location or place of residence often serves as a crude proxy for measurement of these resources, though more direct measurement is preferable. One cannot go skiing without snow, and skiing will not be a casual discretionary activity for those who live in Florida. If one lives in a rural area, plentiful public transportation is not likely to be a resource that facilitates discretionary behavior. If one lives in a central city area, one has many more cultural and social service resources (museums and perhaps even public transportation to them, for example) than those who live in the suburbs. For many of these variables, direct measurement of the context itself is most appropriate and reliable and generally superior to self-report. In other cases, both self-report and direct examination of the context might be essential. For example, pollution might constitute a negative resource for some people in that they cannot play tennis when pollution interferes with their breathing. But people will differ in their self-reports of how much pollution levels affect their activity. And finally, there is a geographical determinant of discretionary behavior that arises from the arrangement of the physical setting in interaction with social factors. For example, the social system resources that arise or do not arise in a Los Angeles-type urban sprawl are likely to be substantially different from those that arise in hilly, compact, foggy San Francisco. Studies of the effect of this kind of determinant have rarely been done.

Taken together, the set of factors referred to in this category help to define for each person a unique resource opportunity structure. By resource opportunity structure is meant the set of probabilities that any and all kinds of activities may be performed, given knowledge only of an individual's external possessions, resources, and access to resources. Obviously, the individual's contextual characteristics play a major role in determining his or her resource opportunity structure, in addition to personal possessions and access factors not directly linked to the particular larger social and historical context of individual action. Note that the concept of resource opportunity structure is different from the previous concept of role opportunity structure. The former is individually linked or person-specific; the latter is a broader contextual characteristic affecting many people. Thus, an individual's resource opportunity structure is a personal "modifier" of the more general role opportunity structure an individual faces in a given society or social system.

Personality and Intellectual Capacity Factors

There is a variety of individual psychological characteristics (which may or may not have some physiological elements) believed to affect social behavior consistently in many situations over time. Personality traits and intellectual (versus physical) capacities are prime examples. The relative importance of personality trait versus situational influences on behavior and the enduringness of such traits—in fact, their very reality as significant hypothetical constructs—have been hotly contested among psychologists in the last few years. I take the traditional view that personality traits are meaningful and useful abstractions and that some relatively invariant characteristics of individual behavior can be observed over time and across situations that can usefully be referred to as deriving from personality traits. It would be difficult to cover the existing literature if I took the opposite view because many high-quality studies show firm relationships between measured personality traits and social participation of various kinds. The psychologists' debate may end in a major reconceptualization of the construct of personality, but it seems unlikely that the trait notion can be dropped altogether as an explanatory construct for human behavior. In contrast, there is little argument about the meaningfulness and utility of concepts of intellectual capacities, although there is much debate about the origins of such capacities and their number and nature.

Each individual has some uniqueness. Psychologists' attempts to codify and categorize psychological traits and intellectual capacities have allowed them to group people according to specific combinations or patterns, but the great variety of these traits and capacities makes any categorization a rough one. There is within any major psychological trait or capacity category a great deal of variation that reflects individuals' natural uniqueness. For example, Guilford (1967) distinguished a hundred and twenty intellectual capacity factors. Suppose we take a sample of individuals and categorize them as high or low on only ten of these. The possible number of individual capacity patterns is in the area of a trillion, even with our crude two-level measure. If we dealt with the full hundred and twenty capacity factors that Guilford listed plus, say, thirty personality traits and again categorized people merely as high or low on each, there would be about 10^{45} (ten to the forty-fifth power, or 1,000,000,000,000,000,000,000,000,000,000,000,000,000,000,000) possible patterns individuals could manifest. In short, in addition to the tremendous variation in patterns of human activity over the life span mentioned earlier, we have to deal with tremendous variation in patterns of human personality traits and capacities. Adding variations in numerous attitudinal dispositions, images, and beliefs makes the problem still greater and the possible number of patterns still more mind-boggling. Any scientific attempt to use psychological variables in the study of social behavior is of necessity reductionist and will never be able to deal fully with all the human variation we observe and manifest on a daily basis. The best the social and behavioral sciences can do is explain some of the variance in patterns of individual social behavior using some of the important psychological variable patterns (but we can do this and thus can find some regularities in the great and sometimes bewildering profusion of unique individual actions and characters). It is heartening that the human psyche, which must be the major proximate cause of most individual behavior, shows a variability theoretically adequate to explain the astronomically large variability in human activity patterns noted earlier.

I have found it useful to view personality traits as relatively enduring (over time and situations) dispositions of individuals to think, feel, want, and act in certain ways and not in others, depending on the circumstances. Like a substance subject to magnetism, humans react to certain "force fields" in predictable ways. Unlike most substances subject to magnetism, the human reactions are subject not only to external force fields but also to the internal influence of changing cognitions, physical states, emotions, intentions, and so on that mediate between the external social and physical force fields and the observed individual reaction. Thus, we speak of human behavior as being under "conscious control" or as subject to capacity limitations or "will power" and use a variety of other terms that point to internal forces interacting with external forces to produce observed individual action or inaction. For an example of such a trait, consider "introversion-extroversion," a personality construct used to describe people's habitual attraction and repulsion tendencies toward other individuals. Although the trait may be thought of as one that has developed over time and continues to develop or change, it is relatively stable compared to such internal behavior-modifying forces as hunger and pain. It is a construct that can be applied to a wide variety of reactions to other individuals in a wide variety of situations and thus allows the scientific observer to detect consistent, repeated patterns in the flow of human behavior.

Although specific traits are defined in relation to particular observable behavior, my definition of personality traits includes associated thoughts, feelings, intentions, wants, habits, and other internal motivators or behavior shapers. In this chapter, I have been using the terms "behavior" and "activity" to refer to observable behavior, without attempting to specify any unobservable processes or "covert behavior," which has relevance for the topic at hand. When we come to the construct "personality trait," however, we are implicitly dealing with covert as well as overt behavior. That is, to name a "trait" as a causative factor in observable behavior is to refer to internal behavior sequences involving cognition, emotion, and conation (the latter term referring to will, wanting, intention). If I am an introvert, for example, not only will I be observed to react to the presence of others in a certain way (by remaining silent, by leaving, by avoiding contact or interaction, and so on); but I will tend also to react with feelings of shyness or discomfort, with expectations for an unsatisfying interpersonal experience, or with the formation of intentions to leave the situation as soon as possible.

It is useful to distinguish the *capacity* to behave a certain way or to perform at a certain level from personality traits. I define capacities as "probabilities of response and behavior of a certain kind, given the disposition to respond" (Reddy and Smith, 1972, p. 278). Capacities thus cannot be observed in the absence of willingness to respond with a particular class of behaviors. Once the person is willing, the overt response provides the scientific observer with a measure of the individual's capacity to respond with a type or level of behavior belonging to a certain class—for example, responding quickly and correctly or slowly and incorrectly to a request for an antonym of a particular word. Limitations on current individual capacities may result from contextual factors (being immersed in water), from temporary individual physical characteristics (having a brain concussion), or from the nature of the individual's intellect per se (lack of knowledge of how best to make a desired reaction or perform an activity). The latter category of factors is relevant to the definition of capacity as one kind of individual character disposition. The other limiting or incapacitating factors will be entered into my general explanatory model either as contextual or as individual physical and physiological factors.

Like personality traits, *intellectual capacities* tend to be relatively transsituational and enduring. They are not, however, the same as personality traits and could be treated as a separate category of variables in my general model. I treat them together with personality traits because of the similarities of these two types of dispositions. Intellectual capacity has received much attention by students of human character and individual behavior because of its presumed relevance for a wide variety of behavior. This kind of capacity is properly measured by the level of intellectual performance an individual achieves in the absence of external contextual or temporary internal physiological limitations on behavior. The most common tests involve performance on a written form filled out in a well-lit room by a healthy, awake, seeing, hearing, nonparalyzed, non-brain-damaged individual. Guilford's (1967) theory of the structure of the intellect, the most comprehensive view extant, involves a hundred and twenty intellectual capacities based on combinations of the performance of five kinds of operations (cognition, memory, convergent production, divergent production, and evaluation) on four types of information content (figural-spatial, symbolic-numerical, semantic-verbal, and behavioral-social) with six resulting information "product" types (units, classes, relations, systems, transformations, and implications). What is usually called information, knowledge, and beliefs are treated as operations by Guilford and subsumed under the categories of cognition or memory in his scheme. The operations of convergent thinking and evaluation include what is usually called reasoning and problem solving; divergent thinking covers what is often called creative thinking. Although subject to criticism, Guilford's model seems to have substantial support (Guilford and Hoepfner, 1971), particularly in terms of its emphasis on a faceted organizational system (Horn, 1976). The scheme allows for both verbal and social intelligence (the latter referring to understanding how people behave). Although spatial and numerical abilities are specifically recognized in this scheme, perceptual-motor skills are not. The latter I would place into the earlier described category of physiological factors rather than the intellectual capacities category.

Only a small number of intellectual capacity variables have been examined in research on social behavior, and this has been done only rarely. The literature that does exist deals mainly with educational and employment settings, and what studies there are of other categories of social behavior (such as discretionary participation) that include intellectual capacity variables have used only the crudest measures of verbal intelligence. This situation undoubtedly represents the legacy of the extreme specialization present in the social and behavioral sciences. Those interested in the study of intellectual capacities tend to believe a few social background variables and perhaps a few personality or attitude variables are all they need to attend to, and then just for control purposes. Those on the other side of the disciplinary fence have similar limitations. These two groups rarely have the chance or find reason to communicate with each other, either face to face or through journal publication. In other words, a narrowness of focus in terms of dependent variables studied tends to be accompanied by narrowness in terms of independent variables studied, a situation fostered by the current social structure of science. The ISSTAL model remedies both problems.

Guilford's comprehensive structure of the intellect model is not paralleled by as comprehensive a structure for understanding personality traits and dynamics. There are many competing theories that have generated organizing schemes, but no one theory has yet gained an edge over the others in terms of predictive power or persuasive cogency. In general, existing schemes tend to be limited by the theoretical focus that generated them. Many researchers stick to one trait as their principal interest and overgeneralize from results reflecting the operation of that trait (see discussions of personality theories by Hall and Lindzey, 1970; Maddi, 1968; Mischel, 1971; Phares and Lamiell, 1977). In Maddi's view, there are three principal models of the core of personality: a conflict model espoused by theorists such as Freud, Sullivan, and Rank; a fulfillment model espoused by theorists such as Rogers, Maslow, Adler, White, and Allport; and a consistency model espoused by theorists such as Kelly, McClelland, and Fiske and Maddi. Mischel (1971) classified personality theories into type and trait theories (Murray, Guilford, and Cattell), psychodynamic theories (Freud, Jung, and Fromm), psychodynamic behavior theory (Dollard and Miller), social behavior theory (Skinner, Rotter, Bandura and Walters), and phenomenological theory (Rogers, Festinger, and Kelly). In addition to these grand theories, there are many minitheories dealing with a single trait or type of behavior (see, for example Phares and Lamiell, 1977, and chapters on personality in the *Annual Review of Psychology* series). At still another level, Anderson (1968) distinguished 555 personality trait words distilled from Allport and Odbert (1936), who reported about 18,000 in English.

With no comprehensive and integrative personality theory yet available (although several would lay this claim) and with evidence that all major theories have some predictive power, I have found an eclectic stance to be most appropriate when trying to understand how personality traits affect discretionary social behavior. For convenience, a colleague and I grouped traits (other than capacities) into clusters that organized our understanding of the relationship between traits and participation in formal voluntary associations (Reddy and Smith, 1972, p. 179). I have since changed and elaborated these clusters, which seem useful also for understanding the relationship between personality traits and informal social participation. The number of clusters could easily be extended by separating some into subclusters; the elements within each cluster bear varying degrees of similarity to other elements of the cluster. Nonetheless, the list serves a useful heuristic purpose. The clusters are as follows:

1. Extraversion, sociability, likeability, gregariousness, friendliness, affiliation and belongingness needs, love (giving and receiving) needs, trust in people, cooperativeness, solidarity, conformity, and social confidence versus introversion, distrust of people, interpersonal cynicism, shyness, unfriendliness, surliness, rejection of others, nonconformity, anomie, alienation, and interpersonal hostility

2. Ego strength, adjustment, defense of selfhood, identity, satisfaction, happiness, optimism, self-confidence, positive self-image, and high self-esteem versus anxiety, insecurity, inferiority feelings, excessive guilt, fear of humiliation, excessive harm avoidance, negative self-image, low self-esteem, unhappiness, depression, hopelessness, pessimism, psychopathology, neuroticism, and psychoticism

3. Emotional stability, emotional control, mood stability, and impassiveness versus emotionality, emotional expressiveness, moodiness, mood and affect variability, and temperamental nature

4. Intimacy, empathy, emotional openness, self-disclosure, nurturance, succorance, intuitiveness, and need for relational closeness versus emotional coldness, lack of empathy, emotional closedness, nondisclosure of self, interpersonal exclusion, denial of nurturance and succorance needs, and lack of interpersonal intuition

5. Assertiveness, aggressiveness, need for control or dominance over others, need for power, superordination, independence, high reactance, and personal autonomy need versus unassertiveness, submissiveness, unaggressiveness, subordination, low needs for power or control over others, dependency, low reactance, interpersonal acquiescence, need for abasement, and need for protection

6. Efficacy, mastery, competence, internal locus of control, initiative, responsibility, conscientiousness, task interest and commitment versus fatalism, powerlessness, apathy, irresponsibility, lack of task commitment, and external locus of control

7. High needs for prominence, achievement, prestige, recognition, acceptance, attention, status, reputation, and appreciation from others; need for exhibition; reasonable risk-taking; and high level of aspiration versus indifference to or avoidance of prestige, attention, and such from others; need to show deference and admiration of others; and fear of failure

8. Morality, altruism, benevolence, and superego strength versus selfishness, amorality, weak superego, lack of concern for welfare of others, malevolence, and misanthropy

9. Flexibility, adaptability, readiness to change, spontaneity, need for complexity, tolerance of ambiguity, need for novelty and new experience, sense of humor, and transsituational inconsistency versus rigidity, dogmatism, authoritarianism, intolerance of ambiguity, need for consistency, need for simplicity, dislike of novelty or new experiences, sameness, compulsivity, need for order, seriousness, and transsituational consistency

10. High energy levels, high activity rate, activation, and arousal versus low energy level, low activity rate, passivity, inertia, conservation of effort, and lethargy

11. Deliberateness, impulse control, perseverance, and deferral of gratification versus impulsiveness, impetuousness, quickness of response, and nondeferral of gratification (immediate gratification preference)

12. High need for stimulation, sensory impressions, excitement, sensation, danger, sexual experience, play, fantasy, and beauty versus avoidance of sensory stimulation, excitement, play, and so forth and low need for or indifference to aesthetic stimuli

13. Pragmatism, tough-mindedness, realism, reality-orientation versus impracticality, tender-mindedness, idealism, lack of reality-orientation

14. Curiosity; need for understanding, analysis, and synthesis; and inquisitiveness versus lack of curiosity, inquisitiveness, or need for understanding
15. Need for self-actualization, personal growth, and personal creativity versus satisfaction with current stage of character development and growth of self (Goble, 1970; Maslow, 1954, 1962)
16. Effective ego defense mechanisms (Eriksen and Pierce, 1968; A. Freud, 1932), projection, repression, reaction formation, sublimation, rationalization, denial, regression, and so forth
17. Effective ego expression styles (Carlson, 1975, pp. 406–408); vocal styles (Rice and Gaylin, 1973); expressive movements and nonverbal communication styles (Buck, Miller, and Caul, 1974); cognitive styles such as field dependence, perceptual differentiation, stimulus control, and tendency to plan for the future (for instance, Morrison and Centers, 1969); test taking styles (Edwards and Abbott, 1973)

The final categorization includes the personality traits mentioned most often in the psychological literature. Although all the trait names that can be found are not included, I believe most can be fitted into these categories as the need arises. At any rate, the division into clusters gives the reader an idea of the variety and types of traits relevant to the understanding of individual social behavior. In recent years, many psychologists have suggested abandoning the notion of transsituational traits in favor of a more situational view of personality. It now seems clear, however, that both traits and situational variables are useful and important (see Bowers, 1973; Ekehammar, 1974; Phares and Lamiell, 1977, pp. 121–123; Sechrest, 1976, p. 9).

Attitudinal Dispositions: Values, Attitudes, Expectations, and Intentions

The fourth category might be broadly termed "attitudinal dispositions." They are theoretically similar to the previously described category of personality traits in being internal psychological characteristics of individuals and in representing dispositions of individuals to think, feel, want, and act in certain ways. They are a type of internal motivator or behavior shaper. They also may be inferred from observable behavior but implicitly involve covert behavior. Like personality traits, they are learned and involve some cognitive integration (Greenwald, 1968).

However, where personality traits are by definition relatively enduring across time and situations, this set of attitudinal dispositions is by definition less enduring or more situationally linked. Where there is a discrepancy between the enduring and the transsituational quality of a disposition, the transsituational quality should be taken as paramount. The continua of motivational dispositions, ranging from personality traits to highly specific intentions, is clearer for degree of situational specificity than for temporal stability in the individual. Indeed, many general values and broad attitudes can be as enduring as personality traits, as can some more specific attitudes, expectations, and intentions. This would lead some to argue that values, for instance, may be taken as synonymous with personality traits because of the highly transsituational and temporally enduring nature of the former. One might readily do this without much loss in terms of the present scheme, although I am inclined to preserve the term "values" to refer to the most transsituational attitudinal dispositions that fall just short of being personality traits. This seems to fit better with usual social and behavioral science terminology and to be a meaningful distinction. For example, Rokeach's (1973) ultimate value of equality seems to me to be best viewed as a very general attitudinal disposition, not a personality trait.

I will not try to specify precisely how transsituational a behavior disposition must be to qualify as a trait rather than as an attitudinal disposition (particularly a value). The classification is somewhat arbitrary because continua of transsituationality and duration are involved, but nonetheless it is useful. We can, for example, easily distinguish between an enduring transsituational trait like extroversion, which is likely to manifest itself in all interpersonal situations and to characterize individuals across their entire lifetimes, and something like my attitude toward grasshoppers as a food, which manifests itself in a more limited set of situations and might be changed by a single, intense encounter. Although the latter change might be possible for some personality traits, this is unlikely to be the case generally.

Values, attitudes, expectations, and intentions are not usually grouped together in a single category. I have done so on the basis of their being motivational dispositions with generally less enduringness and greater situational relativity than personality traits. Much research remains to be done on the relative enduringness of various kinds of motivational dispositions, from personality traits to intentions, although the relative transsituational relevance or specificity of these dispositions is clear by definition. Furthermore, the order in which they are listed is meaningful; one can view this set of determinants as ranging from those most likely to apply across many situations (values) to those likely to be most situation bound (intentions). At the most transsituational and enduring end of this category of dispositions (for instance, broad values like "liberalism"), the distinction between these and personality traits can become arbitrary. However, in addition to the heuristic value of this distinction, the separation of these more limited attitudinal dispositions from the class of personality traits is reflected in observed modes of measurement in existing studies. Values, attitudes, expectations, and intentions have generally more specific referents than do personality traits. One can measure very simply the content, say, of an attitude; but one must devise a relatively complex test in order to cover the more general personality trait adequately. For the latter, one ideally samples reactions to many situations or test items of widely varying content; for an attitude, a few well-designed questions focused on a particular situation might suffice.

The degree of transsituational relevance versus situation bound-edness is the essential, defining aspect of the various motivational dispositions from personality traits to intentions in my scheme. The enduringness of a disposition tends to be closely correlated with its transsituationality but is not essential to my definitions of these various types of dispositions when there is an inconsistency of situation boundedness and enduringness of a particular disposition. In the literature, one occasionally finds what I have termed values referred to as "general attitudes." "Attitudes," in turn, may refer to dispositions relevant for many or few situations or objects. If the scope of their situational relevance is narrower, the dispositions in the present category are termed expectations, and the most specific expectations are termed intentions. There is no clearly defined break between these subcategories; they form a continuum. It is of heuristic value, however, to demarcate sections of this continuum. The following is an example of how this continuum might be used: My need for achievement is a personality trait; my general liking for productive intellectual endeavors is a value; my liking for my own job is an attitude; my wanting to finish this book is an expectation; and my immediate plan and determination to finish this particular chapter today is an intention. All these are behavior dispositions involving both overt and covert behavior—thoughts, feelings, desires, and activities—but varying markedly in situation bound-edness (and enduringness). The generally greater enduringness of the more transsituational dispositions is to be expected because the latter are more generalized response dispositions, presumably based on more numerous experiences and occupying a larger and more salient portion of the individual's conscious self-image than more specific and situation-bound dispositions.

My general categorization scheme for motivational dispositions is a departure from common conceptualizations. Among those conceptualizations similar to mine, Rokeach (1968) makes a sharp distinction between attitudes and values and Fishbein and Ajzen (1972) clearly distinguish between attitudes and behavioral intentions. I accept these distinctions, generally, but view them in the larger context of the continuum I have described, a perspective with various theoretical virtues. Values and attitudes are usually defined in ways that emphasize affective or evaluative components (liking or disliking). Yet there are cognitive and conative components—one can scarcely have an attitude without having a cognition of what that "something" is and of whether one's feelings are positive or negative (or mixed, as the case may be). Furthermore, the concept of attitude implies the likelihood of some specific behavior—at the least, moving toward or away from the "something" involved. Although these implications are often not brought out in the usual definition, they cannot be dismissed. Thus, I define attitudes and values explicitly as not just a matter of affect but as a complex matter of thoughts, feelings, desires, and relevant actions—in short, as motivational dispositions. Motivational dispositions are *not* used here as synonymous with personality traits; they refer to the full range of behavior dispositions from highly transsituational traits to situationally specific intentions.

Although there have been many value categorizations developed over the years (see Robinson and Shaver, 1973, chap. 8), some very brief (such as Allport and Vernon, 1931) and some very lengthy (such as Judge, 1976), the lists of eighteen terminal (ultimate or intrinsic) values and eighteen instrumental (intermediate or means) values developed by Rokeach (1973, p. 28) seems to be a very useful scheme. Rokeach lists as terminal values the following: a comfortable life, an exciting life, a sense of accomplishment, a world at peace, a world of beauty, equality, family security, freedom, happiness, inner harmony, mature love, national security, pleasure, salvation, self-respect, social recognition, true friendship, and wisdom. As instrumental values, he lists the following, each corresponding in order to one of the forgoing terminal values: ambitious, broadminded, capable, cheerful, clean, courageous, forgiving, helpful, honest, imaginative, independent, intellectual, logical, loving, obedient, polite, responsible, and self-controlled.

As Rokeach (1973, p. 17) notes, researchers over the past half century have paid much more attention to measuring attitudes than to measuring values. Therefore, the numbers of specific and general attitudes of interest in empirical research and theory are far too extensive to encompass with any brief scheme. The most we can do here is note there are several excellent compendiums of the more frequently used attitude scales and indexes (see Bonjean, Hill, and McLemore, 1967; Chun, Cobb, and French, 1975; Miller, 1977; Shaw and Wright, 1967). Some such compendiums focus on broad attitude areas, such as Robinson, Rusk, and Head's (1969) on political attitudes; Robinson, Athanasiou, and Head's (1969) on occupational attitudes; Robinson and Shaver's (1973) on social-psychological attitudes; and Straus' (1969) on family attitudes. The most frequently studied and important attitudes from the standpoint of psychology can be seen in the chapters on attitudes in the *Annual Review of Psychology* over the years. For sociology and political science, it is necessary to peruse the major journals in each field to see what types of attitude measures are most commonly being used (although several of the compendiums previously referred to include the most important attitude measures from these fields). Whatever type or aspect of social behavior one is studying, there is a variety of relevant attitudes to be included if one wants to understand the phenomena thoroughly.

Sociologists usually define expectations in relation to social roles. Psychologists usually define them in relation to beliefs about the likelihood of future events. Psychologists define intention as a conscious will to act. These definitions emphasize conation (wanting, willing, and being committed to action) but include affect (feelings about what is expected or intended) and cognitions (knowledge of what the behavior will lead to, of the properties of things, of the likelihood of events, and so forth). Thus, both expectations and intentions clearly have elements of thinking, feeling, wanting, and action, as do values and attitudes. On the basis of this communality, I place values, attitudes, expectations, and intentions on a single continuum of motivational character dispositions and personality traits at the extreme end of this continuum (see Greenwald, 1968, p. 386, for a related suggestion).

The elaboration of my dispositions relevant to the production of this chapter is of analytic value and should increase understanding of this particular social behavior. It is also a kind of thorough analysis of motivational character disposition seldom seen in the literature. Studies of political behavior (especially voting) and consumer behavior are two exceptions (see, for example, Britt, 1966; Campbell and others, 1960; Jacoby, 1976; Kassarjian and Robertson, 1968; Milbrath and Goel, 1977; Verba and Nie, 1972). In these areas, one can find a number of highly productive studies that pay attention to the differentiation of traits, values, attitudes, expectations, and intentions. It is striking that both of these research areas are concerned, more than any others perhaps, with the prediction for practical purposes of natural human social behavior. One reason for the lack of specificity seen in other areas is the expectation that one will find strong positive relationships between various similar independent or explanatory variables when they represent different aspects of the same complex. This expectation may often be valid, but I think the conclusion that analytic differentiation then is unnecessary is a mistake because it results in disregard of important determinants of social behavior. That is, if one focuses on a specific intention without attention to values that apply to broader situations, one limits one's understanding of the factors that "cause" that behavior. More generally, the principal virtues of my approach to motivational character dispositions are that it both increases predictive and explanatory power and provides an interpretive context that permits theoretical integration of otherwise disparate research.

The neglect of analytical schemes such as the one I have proposed stems partly from the general neglect of time allocation and life span research paradigms in favor of narrower perspectives on social behavior dependent variables to be studied. To put this another way, social behavior researchers have seldom been concerned with the relationship between what people normally do with their time and the particular behavior the researchers are interested in, a lack of concern that leads to serious limitations on the value of their research. There is also, generally, a lack of concern for naturally occurring social behavior because of the emphasis on theory or hypothesis testing rather than on understanding social behavior. As I suggested earlier, these limitations can be seen partly in the overdependence on social background variables as proxies for more specific social position or role expectation information. It can be seen, too, in dismissal of the relatively "narrow" expectation and intention variables as too obvious or trivial to study. This prevalent but mistaken view is often rationalized by the argument that such dispositions are tautologously or circularly related to the dependent variable of interest and that nearly perfect correlations are to be expected here routinely. As far as I am aware, there is relatively little research on the relationship between intentions or expectations and natural social behavior; and what research there is makes it clear that the relationships are far from perfect (Deutscher, 1966; Ehrlich, 1969; Wicker, 1969). Schuman and Johnson (1976), in a review of studies on relationships between attitudes and behavior, found that one can show strong relationships in some cases but only moderate or weak relationships in most instances, confirming my general point about the nontrivial and non-tautologous nature of research that includes attitude, expectation, and intention variables. They further point out that as attitudes increase in specificity (with regard to what behavior or situation), the relationship between attitudes and observed behavior becomes stronger. This can be translated into the conclusion that the ordering of constructs (values, attitudes, expectations, and intentions) in my scheme probably also represents an order of increasing predictive relevance and explanatory power for any given type of social behavior, in addition to representing an order of increasing situation boundedness and specificity for the behavior involved.

We can view the full set of personality traits not only as components of individual "personality" but also as components of motivation.

Values, attitudes, expectations, and intentions form other parts of motivation. I have defined all these as parts of a single continuum of motivational character dispositions (of varying degrees of transsituational relevance) to think, feel, want, and act in certain ways, a definition in which the concept of motivation is implicit (see Staats, 1968, p. 37). To be more specific, I define human motivation generally as a dynamic mix of this continuum of motivational dispositions to behave (overtly or covertly) in certain ways in certain situations (capacities not included). In a specific situation, the individual's *current motivation* can be thought of as the net or combined resultant of all such motivational dispositions relevant to that situation. I use the term "current motivation" approximately as does Fishbein (1967) when he uses the term "behavioral intention"—both refer to what an individual is motivated to do at a given time and in a given situation. Intellectual capacity dispositions are contingent on the individual's motivation to act in a certain way. Hence, although motivational dispositions are contingent on the situation, in that they are manifest only when relevant situations are encountered, intellectual capacity dispositions are contingent on both relevant motivation and relevant situations. An individual's current motivation in a specific situation is the result of internal psychodynamic integrative action involving, variously, rational analysis and decision making, conscious and unconscious emotional weighting, pressures toward cognitive consistency, the unconscious operation of ego defense mechanisms, and the like. I would term this internal integrative behavior the process of "psychodynamic synthesis." It tends to be what most interests personality theorists, who usually refer to it as involving "internal dynamics" or use similar process-oriented terms.

The notion of current motivation as a net resultant is relevant to the time allocation-life span dependent variable paradigm I have been proposing for the study of individual social behavior. It is one of the most important elements in the scheme of "sequential specificity" determinants that make up my model. Current motivation, along with current capacities, largely determines the activities of any individual at any point. In the time lag between the presentation of stimuli to behave and overt behavior, relevant motivational dispositions are activated and the unobservable psychodynamic synthesis occurs. The size of the lag (or the duration of "reaction time") is itself in part a function of the particular individual's capacity for fast- or slow-paced psychodynamic synthesis in particular situations. From this viewpoint, then, nearly all other determinants of overt individual social behavior ultimately tend to operate through their effect on current motivation and current capacities.

Retained Information: Images, Beliefs, Knowledge, and Plans

The fifth major class of determinants of individual social behavior in my model includes images, beliefs, knowledge, and plans. Together these make up "retained information." Following Rokeach (1968) and Fishbein and Ajzen (1975)—and contrary to an earlier version of the scheme (Smith and Reddy, 1972a)—I have separated retained information from the category of attitudes. The distinction appears to be theoretically useful to introduce at this point, although this retained information category was not included in the pattern that authors of review chapters for this volume were asked to follow.

Information is defined as consisting of discriminable stimuli. The basic unit of information is the "bit." The original operational definition of a bit in information theory was a discrimination that a stimulus light (or switch) was on or off. In this definition, items of information are assumed to involve perceptions of single but more complex configurations of stimuli than an on-or-off light—shapes, letters, words, numbers, and so on. Information is perceived, sometimes immediately and sometimes from memory, as a result of learning. Immediate awareness of information falls into the subsequent category of situational variables; the present retained information category refers to the individual's continuing, enduring, and usually growing stock of information in the brain. Information may be symbolic or nonsymbolic. Nonsymbolic information consists of images, that is, of material not coded into a conventional symbolic structure (language, number system, and signs). Images can be sensory impressions from the past (a remembered sunset) or from immediately present stimuli (the look on a spouse's face). This use of the term "image" is related to but narrower than that of Boulding (1956). Symbolic information items, when complex in combination, can be termed beliefs or knowledge. Beliefs are information encoded into conventional symbols, such as pictograms, language, or mathematical notation. The usual meaning of belief implies recognition that several items of information are involved, with the focus of the belief on their relationship. For example, one believes there is more light in daytime than nighttime. In this broader usage, a single item of information is also included in the category of beliefs if it is known by someone. For example, the spoken word "light" is not a meaningless sound to a speaker of English but represents a complex concept (or set of concepts). We believe light to be something we know or understand. "Knowledge" is a term reserved for those beliefs the individual thinks have a high probability of being true, of corresponding to reality. What an individual believes to be knowledge is not necessarily true in terms of current scientific knowledge, of course. The truth of beliefs that are treated as knowledge is, in this scheme, determined by the individual, not by scientific consensus of rigorous reality tests. Plans are another special kind of belief, involving items of information intended, at least potentially, to serve as guides for overt action.

Images, beliefs, knowledge, and plans play a major role in the covert behavior process of cognitive synthesis that leads to an individual's definition of the situation. These forms of information also are integrally involved to some degree in individuals' current capacities (which always depend to some degree on retained information) and in the psychodynamic synthesis that leads to an individual's current motivation at any point. Barring amnesia or brain damage and assuming normal forgetting, an individual remembers much information about prior contexts, physical and emotional states, social role expectations and enactments, external and internal resources, activities, events, and so forth. In addition to immediate awareness of present stimuli, the individual is affected by retained items of information from the past, whether called up by present stimuli, the will to remember, or random thought processes. The information an individual retains has been discriminated, sensed, perceived, or thought about by the individual. But things once known and now forgotten can also be important in understanding individual behavior, as Freud convincingly pointed out. Their effect is on the ongoing covert psychodynamic processes and cognitive synthesis without being part of immediate awareness. Only with a life span approach can we adequately incorporate into our model an individual's past experiences, which, in the form of retained information, act as determinants of social behavior. In the ahistorical approach to individual social behavior, one is limited to what is present in immediate awareness. The time allocation-life span perspective encourages measurement of important information in terms of when it is initially learned or processed by an individual, how much is remembered for how long, and what is retained versus forgotten—all in relation to individual social behavior through time.

The kind of symbolic information entered into an individual's plans (see Miller, Galanter, and Pribram, 1960), estimates of future probabilities for certain events and their effects on individuals or context, and the symbolic information involved in beliefs about social norms are particularly important as determinants of social behavior. The cognitive processing of such information involves not only memory capacity but also other intellectual capacities (particularly the operations of evaluation and divergent production) operating on the complex of retained information and current stimuli in the individual's immediate awareness. The outcomes of these operations are often termed "expectancies." Note that neither expectancies nor any other kind of retained information accessible to the individual's consciousness is necessarily related to conation or motivation. Psychodynamic synthesis leading to current motivation does involve the processing of information and may be in part based on expectancies. However, the mere presence of retained information of any kind does not imply that such information will be used in psychodynamic synthesis or affect motivation. Retained information, including remembered information that is instantaneously present in the individual's cognition, is a kind of mental library or computer memory bank from which different items of information may be accessed at different times in different situations for different purposes.

As with other major categories of psychological variables I have included in my ISSTAL model, so too with information there are numerous possible categorizations, the most extensive being the Library of Congress indexing system (although it refers primarily to symbolic information). For present purposes, a good example of a classification scheme for symbolic information is Rokeach's list of categories of "the belief system": cognitions about self, the terminal value system (as cognized), the instrumental value system (as cognized), the attitude system, (particular) attitudes, cognitions about one's behavior and about significant others' attitudes, cognitions about significant others' values or needs, cognitions about significant others' behavior, and cognitions about behavior of nonsocial objects (Rokeach, 1973, p. 220). This scheme bears further refinement in terms of differentiating reference groups and reference others (see Schmitt, 1972); differentiating perceptions of expected outcomes of behavior (expectancies) from subjective expected utilities (particularly multiattribute utilities of such outcomes; see Jacoby, 1976; Slovic, Fischhoff, and Lichtenstein, 1977); differentiating personal beliefs about social norms for a given situation from beliefs about others' beliefs about social norms for a situation (see Ajzen and Fishbein, 1969; Fishbein and Ajzen, 1975); differentiating a variety of aspects of self-cognitions (see Allport, 1955; Super and others, 1963; Wylie, 1974); differentiating cognitions of the nonsocial environment in terms of customary behavior and sites and their attributes (see Barker and Schoggen, 1973); and differentiating images, symbolic cognitions (beliefs), plans, and knowledge, as noted earlier. This set of additional differentiations is only a rough beginning in what is obviously a very complex area. Note, too, that some, but not necessarily all, information may also have affective elements.

Situational Variables: Immediate
Awareness and Definition of the Situation

The sixth set of determinants of social behavior involves individuals' immediate awareness and their definition of situations as they occur. By definition of the situation I mean the end result of the cognitive process by which an individual takes in sensations and perceptions or remembers stored information, puts it all together, and makes wholistic sense of what is currently happening. Inputs, of course, arrive continuously and from a variety of sources. Experiencing these inputs comprises what I mean by immediate awareness. There are fairly specific stimuli from one's body (pain due to exposure to too much sun, heat sensations after drinking hot soup, or an itch on one's foot) as well as nonlocational, emotional inputs (anger or joy). There are stimuli from the environment that are usually relatively specific in terms of what the individual takes in—sounds of people talking, sights of others moving or doing, the odor of leaking gas, or the pressure of a hand on one's shoulder. There are also stimuli from "the mind"—thoughts, memories, gestaltlike cognitions, or definable emotions and obscure feelings.

Immediate awareness variables include not only inputs from the external environment but also inputs from the individual's "internal environment." Thus, we need not only measures of immediately observable situations, events, motion, action, objects, and so forth; we need to be able to measure the individual's internal stimuli if we are to understand the full range of situational determinants of individual social behavior. Sometimes we can use physiological measures that are relatively objective—at least insofar as our measurement involves something like reading numbers off a dial. But self-report is also inevitably needed, using this methodological term broadly to cover all kinds of measures of the content of a person's conscious "mind" or psyche based on individual reporting or overt activity. Only with self-report can we know much of what is happening in the individual's consciousness, and we usually even need self-report to understand the meaning (to the individual) of physiological measures. Of course, we often must resort to other than self-report, using observable behavior as a proxy; but the ideal measures involve some element of self-report.

I have separated out this class of situational variables in order to emphasize that human social behavior involves unique individual consciousness of feeling, wanting, knowing, acting, controlling, and changing one's own behavior. In this category, we have the most proximal cognitive and affective determinants of human voluntary behavior—and even of some involuntary behavior (that stemming from the activity of the autonomic nervous system). In order to understand social behavior, we need to know something of how past experience affects present behavior; but in order to understand this, we must view past experience as it is filtered through present states. Both past and present states are factors in the internal cognitive synthesis behavior that occurs during the time lag between reception of situational stimuli and observable behavior. In short, this class of situational variables directs the researcher to consider how immediate stimuli of all kinds affect individual behavior in addition to considering more enduring aspects of individual character.

There has been relatively little attention to most situational variables as determinants of social behavior in natural situations. Much laboratory work by psychologists involves elaborate control of some situational variables while others that are equally important go unnoticed. There has been a debate on issues related to this problem going on for some time in psychology, with arguments revolving around how serious the "artificiality" of laboratory research is (see, for instance, Kruglanski, 1975; Rosenthal and Rosnow, 1969; Silverman, 1976). The basis of the artificiality problem is, essentially, neglect of factors of immediate awareness and definition of the situation in the laboratory that make it very different from "real world" situations to which the researcher wishes to generalize. Existing research on the impact of situational variables, both from external and internal stimuli, suggests they are of substantial importance, although longer term dispositions are also important (see Endler and Magnusson, 1975; Mehrabian and Russell, 1974; Plutchik, 1980a; Sarason, Smith, and Diener, 1975).

Again, I believe the lack of adequate research on the effects upon natural social behavior of immediate individual awareness and definition of the situation stems substantially from a failure to view social behavior in a time allocation-life span perspective. When the focus is on an individual's particular action, process, decision, or experience, extracted from his or her larger life context, consideration of awareness and seemingly unrelated elements in the situation seems tangential to the purpose of the research. Instead of employing the full range of possible determinants for social behavior, the researcher concentrates on the traditional social background, motivational, capacity, or contextual variables customarily used in prior research in the particular area involved. But when a time allocation-life span paradigm is employed, it is not possible to ignore individual awareness and the immediate definition of the situation. At every point in an individual's life span, there exists both a current definition of the present situation and an ongoing cognitive synthesis through which the present situation is being continually redefined. This awareness constitutes a crucial factor and is one of the most proximal determinants of much behavior. I am not denying that unconscious processes and character dispositions play a role, but their manifestation is usually through their influence on the gestalt of which the individual is aware. Emotions, beliefs, and other information or stimuli, past and present, are dealt with in the ongoing synthesis that defines the present situation for a given individual. This definition of the situation continuously affects the individual's psychodynamic synthesis and resulting current motivation, which in turn determine social behavior within the limits set by current capacities, current context, and current resources.

An important part of social behavior research should be not only to determine individual reactions to situational stimuli but also to classify customary sites or settings of behavior and to deal with both reactions and sites in a coherent and theoretically meaningful way. Mehrabian and Russell (1974), for instance, propose a framework for environmental psychology that emphasizes three primary dimensions of emotional response to environmental stimuli: pleasure, arousal (activation), and dominance and their opposites. They view the inputs that determine individual responses as both characteristic emotions associated with personality (or internal environmental stimuli, in terms of my earlier discussion) and external environmental stimuli. Within the latter category, the most important variables are the sense modality variables (such as color, temperature, and sound) and information rate, which characterizes the spatial and temporal relationships among the stimuli from the individual's environment. Individual emotional responses to a situation are viewed, in turn, as determining individual approach-avoidance behavior with regard to the particular situation, whether it involves social or nonsocial behavior. Their research supports this scheme.

Plutchik (1980a) takes an even more refined and persuasive approach to the understanding and classification of human emotions as states of immediate awareness. Though generally related to and caused by some internal or external stimulus event, which is processed by the individual's sensory, perceptual, and cognitive capacities, feelings or emotions can be categorized into eight primary categories: anger, anticipation, joy, acceptance, fear, surprise, sadness, and disgust (Plutchik, 1980b, p. 75). Each of these is viewed as analogous to a primary color that can be mixed with other adjacent colors to give secondary emotional state colorings (for instance, anger and disgust combine to form contempt in this scheme). Plutchik (1980b, p. 74) argues that all of the primary emotions vary in possible intensity (for instance, sadness ranges from mild pensiveness to extreme grief), as well as in difference or psychological distance from each other (for instance, joy and sadness are distant emotions from each other, while joy and acceptance are adjacent or similar emotions). Being simultaneously complex, reasonable, comprehensive, logically coherent, and empirically grounded, Plutchik's theory of emotions and its classifications seem to me to be the best available general approach, and I accept these as integral parts of the larger ISSTAL model.

Note, however, that although most emotions and feelings are best dealt with as aspects of the category of immediate awareness in the ISSTAL model, there are also affective or emotional aspects of other elements and variables in the model. For example, there are emotional components to social role and other social background variables as well as emotional effects on the manifestation of intellectual and physical capacities. All motivations have some emotional elements or colorings (see DeCharms, 1968), as do most external contexts. One of the principal clusters of personality traits distinguished by the ISSTAL model is emotional stability, a kind of enduring tendency of the individual to be less susceptible to emotions (especially frequent wide emotional variations) than emotionally volatile persons. Further, emotions are remembered, so that one's retained information includes images, beliefs, and knowledge about emotional states experienced by oneself and others. No major class of ISSTAL model variables escapes the pervasive influence of human emotions. However, their principal direct placement in the model and the primary source of their effects on human behavior are in an immediate awareness and definition of the situation, the two main types of situational variables. The immediate awareness of the individual, almost always colored by some emotions, influences one's definition of the situation, giving it in turn an emotional coloration of some sort. Thus, the emotions affect both the perceptual-cognitive synthesis that creates a definition of the situation for the individual as well as the psychodynamic synthesis that creates a net or resultant motivation.

Barker and his colleagues take a very different approach to situational variables. They term it "ecological psychology" (for instance, see Barker and Schoggen, 1973). In a sense following up on and making measureable Murray's (1938) concept of "press," their concern is with describing and classifying in detail the spatial and temporal settings in which human behavior takes place naturally in the community. Using mainly naturalistic observation and existing records, they have focused most of their work on two small towns, one in the American Midwest and one in England, with special emphasis on children. Barker and Schoggen (1973) present a catalogue of two hundred genotypic behavior settings (that is, broad types of behavior settings such as animal feed mills, barbershops, bus stops, funeral services at churches, classes and meetings of various kinds, and so forth) for their Midwest town and two hundred thirty-one genotypic settings for their English town. Within some genotypic behavior settings, they also distinguish various sub-types. For instance, under the genotype of libraries, there are various specific libraries; and under business meetings, there are many organizations listed as subtypes. For other genotypes, there is only a single setting involved (such as the Midwest county jail and sheriff's residence). This level of detail, though tedious and time consuming to collect, is precisely what is needed in order to understand how individuals behave in natural situations, particularly social situations. Having described the settings in which behavior tends to take place, Barker and Schoggen turn to questions of what kind of and how much behavior occur in each setting. They measure "behavior output" in terms of person-hours of behavior in settings. The total person-hours of behavior generated by all the inhabitants of a town (whether residents or visitors) is termed the gross behavior product of the town. A particular behavior setting entered by an individual is called an inhabitant-setting intersection. The performance of a particular activity by a person in a particular behavior setting is termed a claim-operation when that activity is a responsible, important, and difficult action that is part of the process of operating and maintaining the behavior setting (that is, implementing the programs of a behavior setting and maintaining their milieu).

With these data and definitions, Barker and Schoggen describe their towns in terms of time spent in different behavior settings (total times entered and total duration for a given period, such as day, year, or even hour), amount of habitat (behavior setting) variety, most popular behavior settings, and such. Particularly interesting is their investigation of eleven action pattern qualities of the towns' habitats, which correspond roughly to both major institutions of human society and to a collapsed time budget coding scheme as follows: aesthetics, business, education, government, nutrition, personal appearance, physical health, professional involvement, recreation, religion, and social contact (Barker and Schoggen, 1973, p. 81). Their data permit generalizations regarding both the time spent in settings having these different qualities and the number and type of settings in which behavior with each of these different qualities takes place. Having data from 1954–1955 and 1963–1964 on both towns, they are also able to make some simple cross-national and longitudinal comparisons on all these matters and to determine how a particular individual's behavior differs from the norm for his or her town at a given time. Age, gender, race, and social class information permit analysis of their data in these terms as well. In sum, the ecological psychology approach of Barker and his colleagues (see also Barker, 1963, 1968; Barker and Wright, 1955) is in many ways a breakthrough in the study of situational variables in natural settings of human behavior. Something like his approach is necessary perhaps in combination with an approach like that of Mehrabian and Russell (1974) and Goffman's (1974; also Gonos, 1977) "frame analysis," if we are to do justice to the impact of the situation on social behavior. Thus, it is sad that so few researchers have followed up on Barker's work (see Craik, 1973; Moos, 1974).

This entire class of situational variables can be seen as attempts to make measurable in more rigorous terms the impressionistic conceptual and research work of the symbolic interactionist school of sociology and social psychology (see Blumer, 1969; Coutu, 1949; McHugh, 1968). As summarized succinctly by Coser (1976, p. 156), the major tenets of symbolic interactionism are as follows:

> Human beings act toward social objects mainly in terms of the meaning they attribute to these objects rather than to their intrinsic character. Such meanings are constructed and reconstructed in the process of social interaction. Shaped as they are by the actual or anticipated response of others, human actions cannot be accounted for by background characteristics, prepotent impulses, structural requirements, or external stimuli. Social reality, far from being stable, is the result of ongoing negotiations between mutually involved sets of actors. These actors are always engaged in fluid interpretative, evaluational, and definitional process so that only strictly inductive procedures can help elucidate their behavior. Any sociological theory that proceeds deductively or attempts to build nomothetic propositions is bound to founder on the rock of the inevitable particularities and the ever-changing character of human conduct. Hence symbolic interactionism is at bottom an antitheoretical sociological theory that refuses in principle to transcend the peculiar characteristics of social processes in the here and now. It rejects conceptual generalization and abstraction and allows concepts to perform at best a sensitizing function.

In the ISSTAL model, I accept the importance of individual definitions of the situation and the ever-changing nature of such definitions, which are based on cognitive syntheses that differ through time, site, and from person to person. However, I reject the antitheoretical and antipositivistic (antiscientific, antideterministic) assumptions of symbolic interactionism (see Gonos, 1977). It is clear from the kinds of work cited earlier that one can go beyond impressionistic understanding of others as a researcher concerned with human social behavior. Human social behavior is indeed partly and very importantly a function of unique individuals' definitions of unique situations, but immediate awareness and the cognitive processes that synthesize internal and external stimuli can be studied rigorously and systematically, as Mehrabian and Russell (1974) and Barker and Schoggen (1973) have convincingly shown. Moreover, many other researchers have shown personality and attitudinal dispositions, as well as social background characteristics and roles rooted in the larger social structure, to be important elements in human social behavior. Rigorous and systematic study of all these elements leads to useful nomothetic generalizations. For these reasons, my ISSTAL model includes the full range of such variables. I accept the insightful substantive principle of symbolic interactionism while rejecting its methodological limitations and its tendency to overgeneralize and overemphasize the importance of a single class of variables to the exclusion of consideration of other classes. It is paradoxical that the methodological limitations of symbolic interactionism have prevented its adherents from demonstrating empirically in a rigorous fashion the core of substantive truth that this perspective has to offer.

The Self. One loose end in theoretical terms is the concept of the self. It may reasonably be asked how the forgoing analytical scheme takes account of the self and if it does so adequately. I see the self mainly in terms of a set of self-cognitions that fall into the broader category of retained information, but information of strong emotional associations and intensity, generally. However, there are other aspects as well. I find Allport's (1955) treatment particularly useful for its breadth. He suggests the self is basically an organizing principle for the individual. As such, the self helps the individual to distinguish between matters of importance to the person and mere matters of fact, "between what [one] feels to be vital and central in becoming and what belongs to the periphery of [one's] being" (Allport, 1955, p. 39). He further defines "the proprium" (derived from the word "propriate," meaning in this sense central to one's sense of existence) as including "all aspects of personality that make for inward unity" (p. 40). Then he indicates several important analytical aspects of the proprium or self, so defined. First there is the bodily sense of "me," which is basically a stream of sensations from the individual's body about that body (as contrasted with sensations from outside the body and about things other than one's body). In my analytical scheme, this aspect of the self falls into the category of situational variables. Another facet of the proprium for Allport is the "ego-extension," which refers to those objects, animals, or persons an individual considers to be "mine." It includes all the physical things and intangibles (for instance, one's name) that are important to the individual but external to the body. In terms of my scheme, an individual's ego extension falls into the "possessions" subcategory of the broader category of social background variables. Other facets Allport distinguishes, such as ego-enhancement tendencies, propriate striving (central motivational dispositions), and the self as rational agent (synthesizer of motivational dispositions in relation to external reality), fall into my analytical scheme's broad categories of personality dispositions and attitudinal dispositions. Finally, the sense of continuing self-identity (memories of oneself and one's experiences through time) and the self-image (actual and ideal) both fall into the category of retained information in my analytical scheme. And the self as knower (the sense of "I") for an individual conscious of cognizing things, including oneself, at any time when the individual is not unconscious is a way of labeling and describing the psychological process of experiencing, one of several process variables mentioned in Chapter Eighteen.

My scheme has all the aspects of self or the proprium that Allport distinguishes. However, his point that to understand individual behavior one must pay very careful attention to the role of each of these aspects of the self is well taken. Put another way, those aspects of an individual's total character that are part of the self, broadly defined (including all aspects Allport notes), are particularly important determinants of behavior in many though not all situations and for many though not all activities. It is further interesting to note that the aspect of the self Allport terms the "rational agent" corresponds more or less to what in my scheme might be referred to as the individual engaging in the psychodynamic synthesis that results in current motivation. Similarly, what he terms "the knower" corresponds more or less to what in my scheme might be referred to as the individual engaging in the cognitive synthesis that results in current definition of the situation. Although I would prefer "conscious agent" to "rational agent," so as to allow for "irrational" conation and motivation, I will use Allport's terminology here. I find it useful to have these terms available to use for aspects of the self, just as the whole set of facets of the self he distinguishes is useful. Together, these terms and facets draw proper attention to the self as a critical organizing principle for individual character, as well as providing a human quality to what otherwise might seem, at this point, to be a rather mechanical analytical scheme. Thus, the self stands in a position analogous to the emotions in my analytical scheme: It pervades several of the major categories (perhaps all, including at times as part of ego extension, the social and historical context) and is important to keep in mind when considering any one of them.

The importance of the self as an organizing principle of human individual character and behavior has long been recognized in psychological theory (see Lecky, 1945; Symonds 1951) dating back to Freud, William James, and earlier thinkers. Much research on aspects of the self, its nature, development, and effects on behavior, has been performed in the last few decades, though relatively little progress seems to have been made in understanding individual behavior as a result (see Gergen, 1971; Wylie, 1968, 1974). Nonetheless, there has been some progress both theoretically and empirically. Empirical research has now demonstrated that in certain circumstances there are very real effects on behavior of such constructs as self-esteem or self-acceptance, body image, ego enhancement or ego defense motivation, and both ideal and actual self-image. On the theoretical side, several new aspects or facets of the self have been delineated in the past two decades, including the constructs of self-disclosure and self-actualization. The work of Super and others (1963) is particularly interesting in specifying a variety of so-called "metadimensions" of self-concepts and self-concept systems. These metadimensions include not only the well-known self-esteem construct but also clarity, abstraction, refinement (elaboration), certainty, stability, and realism. For the self-concept system as a whole, there are also such important metadimensions as structure, scope, harmony (consistency), flexibility, idiosyncrasy, and regnancy (prepotency, or amount of emotional and ego investment of particular aspects of the total self-concept system). Little research has followed up on these constructs; and there are many flaws in research on the self in general, as Wylie (1968, 1974) has shown. She suggests one possible reason for the inadequacy of such research is its failure to take into account other relevant variables, such as prior experience, current stimuli, and objective individual characteristics. (In my terms, this amounts to having too narrow a model for behavior.) Wylie (1968) also suggests, however, that failure to take account of the unconscious is another possible reason for there being relatively little real progress in the empirical study of the self as a factor in behavior. This leads to another important topic, the unconscious.

The Unconscious. There are important unconscious processes of cognition, conation, and affection that affect individual human behavior. To ignore such processes would hinder our understanding of individual social behavior. In my analytical scheme, I have not set aside a special category for the unconscious; instead, I view each of the major categories of variables comprising human character as having both conscious and unconscious components. This is particularly true of personality dispositions, attitudinal dispositions, retained information, and situational variables, where unconscious variables can be important behavior determinants. Both the psychodynamic synthesis and cognitive synthesis processes I have postulated as part of my analytical model have important unconscious components and determinants, varying with the individual, time, situation, and activity involved. Finally, I assume those unconscious elements most closely related to the self are most likely to affect individual behavior; hence, it makes sense to speak of the unconscious self as the most important aspect of the unconscious in general. The degree of importance the unconscious has in determining individual behavior is itself an important differentiating characteristic among people. If the general Freudian hypothesis is correct, the personality trait of adjustment or ego strength reflects the importance of the unconscious in determining one's behavior, with there being less unconscious determination of behavior where adjustment is greater. Hence, this particular aspect of the unconscious—its relative importance in determining individual social behavior—is included in my analytical scheme under personality dispositions. Similarly, ego defense mechanisms (which may be conscious but are frequently unconscious) are also included in my scheme under personality dispositions as a major cluster of traits.

Character and Personality. I define individual or human character as the total set of an individual's internal psychological characteristics. External characteristics, such as social and contextual variables, possessions and access to resources, and situational variables arising from outside the body, are not part of human character as I define it nor is the human body itself. However, human character does include short-term and ephemeral states or characteristics, in my broad definition, as well as longer term, relatively stable states and characteristics. In so defining human character, I am departing from conventional usage of the term "character." I prefer to reserve the term "personality" for the much narrower construct of highly transsituational motivational dispositions. Some kind of broad term is needed to refer to the totality of human internal psychological characteristics. I prefer to use the term "character" for this entity rather than devising a neologism. In taking this approach, I am following Gerth and Mills (1953, p. 22), who define "character structure" as "the relatively stabilized integration of the organism's psychic structure linked with the social roles of the person." However, their definition emphasizes the individual's more enduring psychosocial characteristics; mine includes the more ephemeral as well.

Socialization. Human behavior is essentially learned behavior, and physiologically based instincts play a rather small role in determining human social behavior. The important human instincts, physiologically based needs like hunger or physical pain avoidance, are expressed by socialized adult humans in ways that reflect powerful learning. My analytical scheme provides for socialization and learning in the subcategory of individual prior experiences and activities (which comes under the broader heading of social background and role characteristics). The most important individual prior experiences and activities tend to be socialization experiences and prior social role performances, because humans are preeminently social animals living in a society based on learned roles rather than on physiologically determined roles (as is true of such social animals as ants or bees). Not all important prior experiences and activities involve socialization, of course; there can be important idiosyncratic individual experiences and activities that play a major role in shaping subsequent individual behavior. Because socialization is so important a determinant of individual social behavior, however, we have given special attention to this kind of determinant of informal social participation in Parts Two, Three, and Four. A chapter on the socialization relevant to each type of social participation precedes the chapters on other, more immediate determinants of participation. For the political and helping behavior parts, there is only one chapter on socialization; but for the part on expressive-leisure participation, there are separate socialization chapters for mass media, sports, and religious participation. We did not give the authors of these chapters any guidelines, so any similarity among them is partly fortuitous and partly a result of similarities in the types of research performed on socialization irrespective of the behavior involved. In Chapter Eighteen, I shall assess the degree of similarity present, if any, among these chapters and the implications of this for the general ISSTAL model.

Conclusion

Most social and behavioral science research on individuals has shown a narrow focus in terms of both the dependent and independent variables traditionally studied. The time allocation-life span research perspective broadens this focus by including a wide array of dependent variables. In addition, the total explanatory model has an interdisciplinary sequential specificity perspective that broadens the range of independent variables that can (and must) be taken into account. In one respect, the interdisciplinary sequential specificity portion of the paradigm is little more than an accounting scheme designed to make sure all relevant major classes and subcategories of variables that are likely to have an influence on social behavior are taken into account. The term "sequential specificity" was chosen because the scheme presented (see Figure 1) progresses generally from the most general to the most specific variables in terms of breadth of relevance to individual behavior, in terms of long range temporal sequence of effects on behavior, and in terms of degree of short range spatio-temporal relevance to the behavior in situation/role. The proper order of the basic explanatory variable categories is as follows:

1. External contextual factors
2. Social background and social role variables

3. Personality traits and intellectual capacities
4. Attitudinal dispositions: values, attitudes, expectations, and intentions
5. Retained information: images, beliefs, knowledge, and plans
6. Situational variables: immediate awareness and definition of the association

This set of categories is more than just an accounting scheme; it also involves a theoretical statement, elaborated further in Chapter Eighteen, that permits one to explain or predict more variance in individual social behavior than any other, less comprehensive models of important state-variables. I have two kinds of evidence for this assertion. First, research on participation in formal voluntary associations (Smith, 1966, and similar research by others—for example, Reddy, 1974; Rogers, 1971; Smith, 1975) has shown that the inclusion of several broad classes of variables (social background, personality, and attitudes) in the set of explanatory constructs significantly increases the amount of variance explained over that explained in preceding studies on the same general topic and over that explained in the studies using fewer classes of variables. Second, the review chapters in this book show the necessity of considering several broad classes of variables in order to fulfill our charge to the contributors that they produce a comprehensive review of their area. Although few of them have been able to find single studies that are comprehensive enough to meet the requirements of the full ISSTAL paradigm, they have found it possible to draw some conceptually broad conclusions through synthesis of the results of narrow studies. In Chapter Eighteen, I have similarly attempted synthesis of the whole book in terms of the ISSTAL model.

As I argued earlier, I believe the limitations of most prior social and behavioral research on individuals stem from the confinement of most researchers within disciplinary walls—from their use of discipline-bound research paradigms. It is not entirely voluntary confinement; if scholars are to be allowed to go ahead with their work, they need a base of operations, and that base is provided by what is known as a "tenure track" position. The security of having a fully tenured position comes only to those who impress others *within* their discipline, in part by showing familiarity with the way their colleagues do things and with the way things have conventionally been done in their particular discipline. Innovation is supposedly honored, but one must also respect conventional wisdom of the discipline. In terms of research, this means studying the "right" variables; and the rightness of variables differs from discipline to discipline. For example, psychologists explain human social behavior mainly with personality trait, intellectual capacity, attitude, and situational variables; sociologists use mainly social background and a few contextual or attitudinal variables. Political scientists, social anthropologists, and economists, among other social scientists in established disciplines, each have their own "boxes" and preferred variables.

Researchers are not rewarded for efforts to explain as much variance in individual social behavior as they can. The rewards of recognition and advancement come from explaining a *significant* portion of the variance using the "right" variables and methods for one's discipline—that is, finding some variable, defined as important within one's discipline, to be reliably related to an acceptable form of behavior being studied using acceptable methods for that discipline. If the variable is only a minor determinant and explains very little variance, this is no problem—and perhaps it is not even noticed as long as the variable is statistically significant. The variable may even explain a major portion of the variance; but if it is not important within the discipline, it may not garner the rewards that gain a scholar tenure. For example, sociologists strongly favor social and demographic variables and often deliberately ignore individual psychological variability as mere "random error." In contrast, psychologists feel free to concentrate their research on white, middle-class, male college youth because they consider social and demographic variables of relative unimportance in the psychological understanding of behavior dynamics.

Thus, in my view, all current and prior research on individual social behavior tends generally to be limited by various discipline-bound paradigms of research, explanation, and prediction. This severely limits scientific progress. The paradigm presented here, with its time allocation-life span model of dependent variable focus and its interdisciplinary sequential specificity model of explanatory variables, offers a way out of this dilemma. It is much needed as a tool for productive research and much needed in the effort to reform the present restrictive character of social and behavioral science inquiry into human individual social behavior. The substantive literature reviews in this volume tend to confirm the forgoing argument. Use of several broad classes of explanatory variables, as in the interdisciplinary sequential specificity model, with multivariate analyses attempting to explain as much of the variance as is possible in some form of informal social participation, is extremely rare. Thus, it is usually difficult, if not impossible, to point to more than a few studies in any social participation research area that explain a substantial portion of the variance. This is even truer because the discipline-bound paradigms tend to ignore, rather systematically, multivariate statistics that permit proportional reduction in error variance (PRE) interpretations. By ignoring

PRE statistical analyses, the inadequacy of discipline-bound research paradigms is in turn more readily ignored. Hence, it is conventional in social and behavioral science research on individual social behavior not to use PRE statistics, and the conventionality of discipline-bound paradigms helps explain this otherwise somewhat curious fact. By contrast, proper use of my proposed ISSTAL paradigm requires use of PRE statistical analyses. I shall return to this matter and other aspects of the ISSTAL model in Chapter Eighteen.

PART II

Political Activities

M. Lal Goel
David Horton Smith

Political action or participation is defined in this volume as comprising all those activities that, one way or another, are intended to affect the workings of and outcomes in the political system. Our using the phrase "social action" reflects our desire to recognize that much of what political scientists call "political participation" is known as "social action" to others. Political participation covers a very broad territory. The conceptualization of political participation political scientists use has recently increased in complexity and breadth. It may, perhaps, be understood now that political participation includes not only such traditional behaviors as voting and joining parties, but also such nontraditional behaviors as social protest and social activism. We find a conceptual communality among all these behaviors and believe the results of the study of one kind of political participation are likely to have relevance for understanding other kinds of political and social participation.

As an introduction to the following chapters, we will describe how social scientists presently conceptualize political participation. This will serve not only to anchor the terminology in the subsequent

Note: Goel wishes to thank Kay Trine, Jane Marques, and Alisia Robinson for secretarial assistance on this project.

chapters but also to provide some idea of how well the existing literature reported here actually covers all the activities that might fall under the heading of political and social action.

Our first division is into "conventional" and "unconventional" participation. The major activities subsumed under each category are shown in Table 1. Conventional activities are those regarded as "normal" and legitimate for a citizen to do. What is regarded as normal and legitimate may vary from culture to culture or over time; the list presented in Table 1 covers conventional and unconventional political participation as seen in the United States in midtwentieth century.

Table 1. Forms of Political Participation

Conventional	Unconventional
Voting	Demonstrating
Discussing politics	Marching and sitting in
Campaigning	Engaging in civil disobedience
Attending meetings and rallies	Holding political strikes
Forming a group	Rioting
Contacting government officials	Engaging in guerrilla activity
Belonging to a political party	Engaging in revolutions and rebellions

Another common dimension applied to political participation is the active-inactive dimension. Milbrath's (1965) review showed this to be the most commonly used dimension. He divided the United States public into three broad categories: (1) apathetics, who participate only passively (about 33 percent of the adult population); (2) spectators, who are minimally involved (about 60 percent of the adult population); and (3) gladiators, who are true political activists (about 5 percent to 7 percent of the adult population). In line with the views of Lane (1959) and Berelson, Lazarsfeld, and McPhee (1954), Milbrath argued that political participation is cumulative in that participants in the most active and difficult (effortful) forms of political participation are highly likely also to participate in the less active forms. This view of participation as being essentially cumulative and unidimensional is prevalent in much of the literature (see, for example, Alford and Scoble, 1968; Almond and Verba, 1963; DiPalma, 1970; Erbe, 1964; Inkeles, 1969; Matthews and Prothro, 1966; Nie, Powell, and Prewitt, 1969; Olsen, 1973).

This prevailing view has recently been challenged in two studies. One is a cross-national comparative study with data from seven countries (Verba and Nie, 1972; Verba, Nie, and Kim, 1971; Verba and

*others, 1973). The other study was conducted in Buffalo, New York,
between 1966 and 1969. (Results are reported in Milbrath and Goel,
1977.) Both these path-breaking studies viewed political participation as
multidimensional. Through cluster and factor analysis, both sought to
uncover distinct "modes" or "styles" of political participation. Political
acts were then distinguished not only in terms of their frequency or
difficulty but also in terms of the kind of relationship between citizen
and government each act represented. In this view, there are not only
gladiators and nongladiators, but a variety of gladiators and nongladiators with different goals and different styles and techniques of action.
Verba and his colleagues studied Austria, India, Japan, the Netherlands,
Nigeria, the United States, and Yugoslavia. Thus, where their results
coincide with the Buffalo results, we can view them as having cross-
cultural reliability. Verba and his colleagues and Milbrath and Goel
discuss six modes or styles: voting, campaign and party work, communal activity, parochial participation, protest, and communication.*

*Both studies found voting to be a distinct mode of participation.
In the Buffalo study, voting was included in a "patriotism" cluster
along with love of country, showing patriotism by flying the flag,
paying all taxes, respecting the police, and supporting the country even
in wars not approved of. This suggests a view of voting as an act of
affirming loyalty to the system rather than as making demands on it. It
has been understood for some time that those casting their votes rarely
believe individual votes make an important difference to political outcomes. Voting does not require as much information and motivation as
do most other political activities. Many people who are not politically
involved vote and many who are highly involved may not bother to vote.
However, these facts have not prevented political scientists from using
voting behavior as an operational definition for general political participation. Some research has measured political "mobilization" through
voting (see, for example, Deutsch, 1961; Lerner, 1958; Lipset, 1960;
McCrone and Cnudde, 1967.) The findings from these cluster analyses of
the various forms of political participation should caution researchers
against assuming this kind of significance for voting.*

*Both the Buffalo and cross-national studies found campaign and
party work to belong to a separate mode of political participation.
Included in this cluster were such activities as persuading others to vote a
certain way, attending political rallies, giving money to a party or
candidate, working to get people registered to vote, joining and supporting a political club or party, and being a candidate for public office.
These activities can be seen as a distinct cluster in all seven nations Verba
and his colleagues studied.*

Citizens who work with formal and informal groups for the purpose of redressing community grievances constitute a distinct type. Communal activity is defined as that form of participation that aims to solve broad social problems in the community. The following activities were loaded on this factor in the Verba study: working through local groups, forming local groups, being an active member in community social action organizations, and contacting local or national leaders on social issues. Verba and Nie (1972) report that in the United States, 20 percent of adults can be classified as communal activists.

Parochial participation is defined as voting or becoming politically active because one is personally concerned about a specific issue that directly affects one, such as property taxes, road improvements, or social security. Parochial participants are seldom generally involved in other political matters. Verba and Nie (1972) report that only a small fraction (4 percent) of the United States citizenry fall into this distinct category.

The category of protester emerged only in the Buffalo study. Questions that might have disclosed these types were not asked in the cross-national study. The protest cluster in the United States involves activities such as joining in demonstrations, marches, and riots; refusing to obey unjust laws; and generally protesting both vigorously and publicly about immoral government action.

Black citizens scored higher than white citizens on items measuring this cluster in the Buffalo study (reported in Milbrath and Goel, 1977). The morality of refusing to obey unjust laws was found to have sizable acceptance among both blacks and whites, with 23 percent and 14 percent of the black and white samples, respectively, reporting that they had so acted "fairly often." Although society at large may regard protest as illegitimate and outside the normal workings of the political system, most protesters view their activity as legitimate and as one among many weapons citizens may use in efforts to correct governmental wrongs. Among blacks, there was a positive correlation between protesting and expressing patriotic sentiments. In the sample as a whole, there was a positive correlation between conventional and unconventional political participation: Those who chose protesting to articulate their demands were also more active in conventional activities.

The last factor, communication, includes keeping informed about politics, sending support messages to political leaders when they are doing well, sending protest messages to leaders when they are doing badly, engaging in political discussion, and writing letters to newspapers. The communication mode of political activity requires a high level of sophistication, interest, and information about politics. Educated and verbal people may engage in this activity.

Implications

The six modes or styles of participation are not discrete, mutually exclusive behaviors. Verba, Nie, and Kim (1971) computed the intercorrelations of thirteen different political acts encompassing four different modes of political participation previously distinguished (the first four types or modes). There was a significant positive correlation among all the different acts, indicating a general covariance among conventional political acts. The correlation coefficients between different political acts ranged from a low of .10 to a high of .71; the average value for all the coefficients was .25. Thus, the various kinds of conventional political acts are intercorrelated to a statistically significant degree, though the magnitudes of the correlations and their common variance are small. Nevertheless, the first principal components factor extracted in a factor analysis procedure accounted for about 31 percent of the total variance in the items, which indicates again a moderate and significant general political participation factor.

When one examines correlations in these data between different acts within the same mode of participation (for example, communal participation), the average correlation coefficient is .45. By contrast, the average correlation for items in any given mode with items outside that mode is less than .20. The Buffalo data (Milbrath and Goel, 1977) indicate the same kind of clustering. Although the correlations between activities within the same mode are much higher than between activities in different participation modes, there is a small but significant positive correlation among all kinds of political participation, even including protest.

Therefore, even though citizens tend to concentrate their political participation by mode, the performance of any kind of a political act means the performance of other political acts of the same or different kinds is more likely. In this sense, the data are compatible with the hypothesis of a general political activity dimension or syndrome, in which people can be ranged from inactive to highly active in political participation in general. Voting behavior is the kind of political participation least closely related to the other modes and to the general political participation syndrome or dimension. But even voting is a significant part of the clustering of political acts of all kinds.

In summary, political participation is simultaneously unidimensional and multidimensional, depending on how one wants to emphasize one or another aspect of the data. *On the one hand, there is clear evidence of a general activism dimension in the realm of political participation, both conventional and unconventional (at least at the level of symbolic protest and direct action, though the inclusion of violent protest acts is less clear). On the other hand, there is strong evidence that certain modes of political participation form fairly coherent clusters in and of themselves. Either of these circumstances could have been true without the other also being true, but such is not the case. There is both a significant if weak general clustering of political activities and a significant and moderate specific clustering of political activities into several distinct and different modes.*

Explaining Political Participation

Given the forgoing conclusions regarding the nature and modes of informal political participation, the chapters in this section have as their ultimate task the explanation of both the unity and the diversity of political participation. It is not by chance, moreover, that the section on political participation is the first substantive section of the book. We have chosen to present this material first because in some sense the most work has been done on the unity and diversity of political participation, as compared with the other types of informal or quasi-formal participation dealt with in this volume. To say this is far from saying that the necessary analyses have been done to answer all the questions of our general analytical scheme with the desirable degree of sophistication and certainty.

Part Two begins with a chapter on socialization of children into political roles. The aim here is to shed some light on why people learn to act in certain politically relevant ways and how socialization affects politically relevant personality and attitudinal dispositions of individuals. By examining the socialization processes, we will begin to see how both unity and diversity come to characterize political participation.

Chapters Four and Five take a more contemporary or cross-sectional look at the determinants (correlates, predictors) of political participation. We have divided the literature review effort along the lines suggested earlier in this introduction: conventional versus unconventional political participation. The latter is only one of the six modes of political participation distinguished here, but it is sufficiently distinct in its legitimacy and relation to the larger political system to deserve special and separate treatment. Perhaps because of its general "illegitimacy" in the broadest sense, unconventional political participation is far more poorly studied an area of political participation than is conventional participation. The riots and protests of the 1960s and early 1970s in the United States led to an upsurge of research interest in this kind of activity; but, in comparison with research on more conventional political participation, the surface has only been scratched.

There is another analytical reason why we have presented a separate chapter on unconventional political participation. We are broadly concerned with looking at the issue of unity within diversity. And we are concerned with stimulating more thinking among all kinds of behavioral and social scientists regarding the implications of such a unity within diversity, if it be present. It follows that, in the realm of political participation, the severest test of our hypothesis of unity within diversity will be to examine that mode of political participation that seems qualitatively most different from the other modes. If even that mode of political participation fits the unity within diversity pattern, it will confirm the value of the broader model. We expect data to show that unconventional political participation (at least at the gross level of self-reported and potential political activity) is a part of the general unity (or syndrome) of political activism. At the same time, we must and do expect to find some differences in the determinants of conventional versus unconventional political participation. If the latter differences did not appear, we would be hard pressed to explain why so few people generally engage in unconventional political participation and why those particular people do so. We must seek to explain the diversity as well as the unity, the unidimensionality as well as the multidimensionality of political participation.

Chapter Six reviews the literature on still another kind of political participation, namely, participation in community planning and decision making. This kind of involvement, common in the early years of the American republic and still present in most smaller towns in America, experienced a resurgence of major proportions in the 1960s. Although involving only a tiny portion of the population, this resurgence grew out of the thrust in the cities for community control and localized decision making. Such basically conventional participation is often ignored in most studies by political scientists of the general range of political behaviors. Instead, it is mainly studied by researchers from the fields of city planning, community development, and social work. Nonetheless, its increasing importance, at least in the United States, is undeniable, with implications for the political system and quality of life far in excess of its numerical frequency of occurrence. For this reason, we have included a special literature review chapter on such participation in Part Two of this volume.

Yet the web of the crude theoretical scheme we are attempting to present, illustrate, and develop in this book requires we place the greatest emphasis on still broader levels of unity within diversity. We encour-

age readers to form their own opinions regarding this matter. Though there will doubtless be arguments about the validity of our line of reasoning, we believe it is nonetheless worthwhile to stimulate each reader to experience the degrees of unity and diversity that seem to be present across apparently different types of informal (or quasi-formal) social participation.

CHAPTER 3

Political Socialization and Behavior

Karen Smith Dawson

Persons mature politically as they mature biologically and socially. Political learning begins early in life. Apprentice citizens are shaped by political socialization long before they reach adulthood and before they are able to participate with full legal status as citizens. This chapter examines the personal and social origins of political orientations and behavior.

Individuals are not born citizens of a particular nation-state. They are developed into citizens over time. The declaration "I am an American" or "I am a Frenchman" has great consequence for both the nation and the individual. Interest and involvement in political life is not evenly distributed throughout any society. Some individuals are very active political participants. They vote, campaign, attend political meetings, contact public officials, and express their political interest in numerous conventional ways. Others demonstrate dissatisfaction with public policy and political leaders through less conventional means,

Note: Much of the material in this chapter is drawn from Dawson, Prewitt, and Dawson (1977).

such as marches, sit-ins, civil disobedience, and riots. Still other people choose to be little involved in political life.

The distribution of these various types of political participants differs from one political system to another. Some regimes encourage widespread participation; others limit active involvement to only a few (Almond and Verba, 1963). The political life of any nation reflects both individual similarities (the common culture) and individual differences in political attachments, attitudes toward politics, and evaluations of leaders and policies. Within any system, there are divisions among those who share the common national identity. These divisions are related to demographic characteristics and to individual memberships in various groups (Almond and Verba, 1963; Bardwick and Douvan, 1972; Battle and Rotter, 1963; Easton and Dennis, 1969; Greenberg, 1970; Greenstein, 1965; Hess and Torney, 1967; Jaros, Hirsch and Fleron, 1968; Laurence, 1970; Lefcourt and Lading, 1965; Lyons, 1970). Members of different subgroups often have different expectations as to what political leaders should and should not do (Jaros, Hirsch, and Fleron, 1968) and tend to hold somewhat different values for political life.

Participation differences are related also to personal experiences and needs. Some people learn to respect and trust their political leaders and institutions; others view politics with indifference, distrust, or a sense of alienation. Some people identify actively with different political viewpoints and express their personal commitment and involvement by saying "I am a conservative," "I am a feminist," "I belong to the Democratic party," and so on. Others remain uncommitted and uninvolved and refuse to identify themselves in any way, except "I am not interested in politics."

Why do some people develop a sense of involvement in politics while others do not? When and how do individuals develop political attitudes toward and responsiveness to political stimuli? What factors tend to encourage or discourage active political stimuli? These are some of the issues political socialization research has focused on. Since Hyman's (1959) pioneering work, which presented an inventory of research findings bearing on the sources of political outlooks, the assumption has been that political behavior can be investigated as a form of *learned* behavior. The idea that political learning has its origins in early life and that what happens during childhood is important for shaping the political outlooks of later life has its roots in Hyman's book. This emphasis is evident in Hyman's (1959, pp. 25–26) attempt to identify patterns of political behavior:

> Regularities in the political behavior of adult individuals
> and stable differences between groups of adults have become a

commonplace in social research. Such patterns of behavior may well be interpreted in terms of contemporaneous features present in the adult lives of particular individuals or groups. But, certainly it is true that the *continuity* of such patterns over time and place suggests that the individual has been modified in the course of his development in such a way that he is likely to exhibit certain persistent behavior apart from transient stimulation in his contemporary environment. One is naturally directed to the area of *learning;* more specifically to the *socialization* of the individual, his learning of social patterns corresponding to his societal position as mediated through various agencies of society. One searches therefore for psychological studies which will establish the beginning of political behavior in preadult life, the process by which it emerges, and the subsequent changes in the course of further experiences.

In 1960, a year after the publication of Hyman's book, two field studies of the development of political orientation among American children were published (Greenstein, 1960; Hess and Easton, 1960). Using samples of American grammar school children, the studies focused on orientations toward political authority and emphasized the role of the presidency as a central concept in the political maturation of young Americans. These two studies provided the foundation for much subsequent research and discussion on political learning among the young (Easton and Dennis, 1969; Greenstein, 1965; Hess and Torney, 1967). Although most research has been done in the United States, there is some work (and a growing interest) in microcomparisons across nations (see Adelson, 1971; Torney, Oppenheim, and Farnen, 1975). The concept of political socialization has been utilized also by scholars interested in the properties and processes of political systems (Almond and Coleman, 1960; Easton, 1956–57, 1965). Studies of political socialization can be a useful tool for understanding internation similarities and differences as well as intranation variance and common culture.

One is not born with an awareness of the political world, and it does not develop very fully for a number of years after birth. The "political self" (Mead, 1934) is made during a gradual and incremental process. The concept of a political self comes from Mead (1934, p. 135): "The self is something which has a development; it is not initially there at birth, but arises in the process of social experience and activity, that is, develops in the given individual as a result of his relations to that process as a whole and to other individuals within the process." There is no turning point at which a child or youth can be declared to have acquired a political self not subject to alteration. Political socialization is an ongoing, perhaps a never-ending, process.

This does not mean, of course, that all periods in a person's life are equally important for the development of the political self. Although political learning is continuous, some periods in the life cycle are more important than others. Childhood has received most attention and will be the major focus of this review, but continuing socialization during adulthood is an important determinant of political participation and needs to be examined with greater care than it has so far.

Models of Political Socialization

Political socialization is one form of the more general phenomenon of socialization. Political scholars have reformulated the concept of socialization to fit their particular subject matter and theoretical interests. The study of political socialization has been particularly strongly influenced by cultural anthropologists' views of the socialization process (LeVine, 1960; Pye, 1962) and by Freudian assumptions about personality development (Davis and Dollard, 1940; Kardiner, 1939; Whiting and Child, 1953).

However, political scientists have tended to ignore the Freudian emphasis on socialization as a process of repression of certain individual behavior impulses. Rather than asking the question, "How does political socialization control the natural antipolitical predispositions of children?," researchers into political socialization have tended to ask, "How are children introduced to citizenship roles? When and how do they develop attachments to their nation? To other political groups? How do they come to have particular attitudes toward political authorities and policy issues?" Political socialization is seen as opening up the world of politics and political participation to the individual rather than acting as a restraint. Although some behavior might be considered negative and in need of suppression for the stability and well-being of the political community, the emphasis in political socialization literature is on the more positive aspect of what is added to the individual through the process. There is also a built-in conservative bias toward studying system maintenance, to understand the persistence of political systems and the transmittance of political values from one generation to another (Easton, 1965; Easton and Dennis, 1969). The study of the development of nonconventional political behavior, which may have stronger effects on political life than conventional political activity, has received less attention.

Another perspective that has influenced the study of political socialization is that of developmental psychology. This influence is prominent in studies of the development of political outlooks over the childhood years (Adelson, 1971; Adelson and O'Neill, 1966; Greenstein,

1965; Hess and Torney, 1967; Sears, 1975). Two of these studies trace the development of children's political outlooks from the beginning of elementary school through the end of high school (Dennis, 1973; Sears, 1975). All these studies focus on the relationship between developing political concepts and development of cognitive capacities. They pay particular interest to a child's developing ability to generalize from immediate to less immediate relationships, as from family to school and to the political world.

The work of Piaget (1965), Maccoby (1968), and Kohlberg (1969) has been particularly influential here. Piaget and Kohlberg argue that a child's intellectual growth follows a series of stages, and students of political socialization have argued that the development of children's political outlooks follow a parallel course. At six or seven years, children have vague, personalized, and nondiscriminating perceptions of the political universe. As their cognitive capacity matures and they interact with their environment, they begin to understand more complex and abstract relationships and roles in the political world.

Generally, then, students of political socialization have viewed the childhood years as critical for the development of individual personality, social attitudes, and cultural values. In addition to the psychoanalytically oriented anthropologists and cognitive development theorists mentioned, political socialization researchers have also been influenced by social learning theorists, who similarly treat childhood learning as a crucial determinant of adult behavior (Bandura and Walters, 1963; Miller and Dollard, 1941). Easton and Dennis (1969, pp. 106–107) illustrate this dominant viewpoint: "Those children who begin to develop positive feelings toward the political authorities will tend to grow into adults who will be less easily disenchanted with the system than those children who early acquire negative, hostile sentiments. . . . [B]asic childhood sentiments are less easily dislodged and modified than those acquired later in life." Early positive and supportive orientations toward the existing political system in childhood are assumed to be important determinants of general social support for the political system among adults. The importance of childhood socialization has been further characterized by Weissberg (1974) as severely limiting the effective political choices open to adults. Weissberg views childhood learning as determining not only general support of the existing system but also assuring adult adherence to normative political values.

The question of to what extent early childhood training persists and structures later political action has not been settled (see Searing, Schwartz, and Lind, 1973). The conventional wisdom is expressed in such ideas as "the child is father to the man." But early acquired political outlooks are not always found to be closely associated with adult political choices (Searing, Schwartz, and Lind, 1973). Almond and Verba (1963, p. 324) argue that contemporaneous events and experience have more influence on adult political choices than childhood political learning and conclude, "Early socialization experiences significantly affect an individual's basic personality predispositions and may therefore affect his political behavior, but numerous other factors intervene between these earliest experiences and later political behavior that greatly inhibit the impact of the former on the latter. Such basic dimensions of political behavior as the degree of activity or involvement in politics or the individual's partisan affiliation seem to be best explained in terms of later experiences."

One can distinguish three basic models among existing explanations of the process of political socialization (Weissberg, 1974): the primacy model, the intermediate period model, and the recency model, all shown in Figure 1.

In the primacy model, early years are very important, with not much significant political learning taking place during the adult years. Choices in later life are structured by early-formed basic preferences for and attachments to political symbols.

In the intermediate period model, late childhood (about age nine to thirteen) is designated as the period when the most substantial political learning takes place. The child who says, "I am a Democrat" or "I am a Republican" begins to understand the substance of those labels at about this age. Greenstein (1965, p. 245) writes, "It is not until the fifth grade that the model child can name at least one party leader, and not until eighth grade that the children typically name leaders in both parties." According to Easton and Hess (1962), political learning peaks sometimes between the age of eleven and thirteen, when children learn to distinguish between political roles and the individuals who fill them. For young children, the incumbent president and the presidency are one and the same. By late childhood, distinctions are made between incumbents, candidates, and the presidency as a role. Research done in the early 1970s showed younger children (second through fourth grade) giving only positive responses to questions about the presidency, with the tendency to idealize presidential authority decreasing as the child became older (Arterton, 1974; Greenstein, 1975; Hershey and Hill, 1975). Post-Watergate surveys show an effect on children of negative political events, with a growth of political cynicism. The effect, however, was found to be age related, with sixth and eighth graders more affected than second and fourth graders (Hershey and Hill, 1975). Greenstein (1975) found in mid 1973 that the negative judgments of seventh graders concerned the performance of the incumbent president and not the presidential role. He concluded (p. 1390), "Children appear able—in a

Figure 1. Three Models for the Relevance of Early Political Learning
for Adult Political Attitudes and Behavior

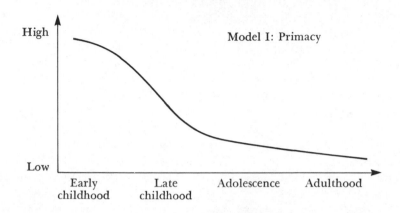

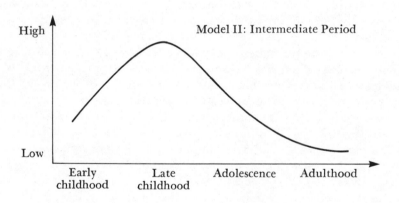

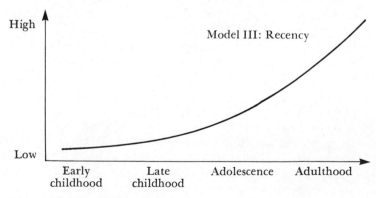

Source: Weissberg, 1974, p. 26.

wholly un-self-conscious way—to distinguish between roles and the individuals who fill them."

In the recency model, the closer a particular political experience is to a relevant decision or activity, the greater its impact is assumed to be. This model calls into question the persistence and structuring power of early learning for later political action. In this perspective, only when persons are old enough to vote, pay taxes, have children in school, rely on a union's health benefits, and such are they going to hold firm opinions on relevant issues and be likely to act on them. Political learning here is seen as tied to relatively transient political entities—day-to-day events, particular candidates and issues, and so forth. Adult orientations change as circumstances change.

Implicit within these models are three types of political orientation that vary in breadth, ranging from broad and usually unchanging to narrow and more easily changed. Figure 2 shows a hypothesized relationship between age and these three types of orientation (Weissberg, 1974). Figure 2 combines the three basic models for political socialization into a single model that adds the dimension of breadth of political orientation. Here we assume the most basic, effective, and enduring orientations are developed early in life, as a child takes on other important identities. Knowledge and the behavioral components of the political self develop as the individual's cognitive capacity develops. The most specific political choices, those available only to adults, are determined generally by the individual's immediate social and political situation.

**Figure 2. The Scope of Political Orientations Acquired
at Different States of Life**

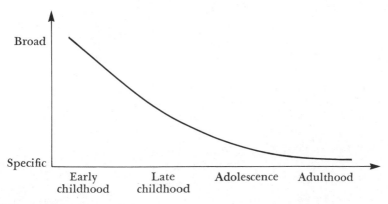

Source: Weissberg, 1974, p. 30.

These characterize adult political life. Thus, findings on the relative importance of various socialization periods will depend on the type of political attitude or action studied. Socialization processes may differ somewhat for different classes and races, and for men and women.

Dawson, Prewitt, and Dawson (1977, chap. 3) have used the model in Figure 2 to explain the gap between the evidence for the importance of early childhood learning and evidence that adult behavior is more strongly determined by contemporaneous influences. When children announce they are "an American," "a Communist," or "a Democrat," they are announcing their basic political identity, at that point. But the child's self-identification also includes ties to racial, religious, ethnic, or other groups. The core elements of identity and basic political sentiments seem to be acquired during early childhood and maintained over the years (Sears, 1975), but it is important to note that apparently nonpolitical attachments and outlooks may have consequences for political behavior (for example, the Catholic church and the issue of abortion).

Political maturity encompasses relatively specific information and evaluation of political roles, institutions, parties, and processes and of the rights and duties of citizenship. The incorporation of all this into one's political outlooks takes intellectual capacity and experience beyond that of a young child (Adelson, 1971). Thus, only in late childhood and early adulthood does one think at abstract levels of political cognition (Kohlberg, 1969). Early socialization cannot completely prepare the individual for all upcoming decisions to be made and events to be evaluated. In this sense, then, childhood socialization does not complete the development of a political self because it cannot adequately prepare one for all the complexities of adult political participation (see Rose, 1960).

The question of just how important early, in comparison with contemporaneous, political learning is for determining adult political behavior is still not resolved. There is little research that looks at the persistence of specific political outlooks over the life span. Political scientists recognize the importance of longitudinal analysis (see Bailey, 1977), but it has been prohibitively expensive so far. Thus, the question of the relative importance of various stages cannot yet be completely answered.

The Development of Political Attitudes and Beliefs

Another question concerns how political learning takes place and the roles of various social agents in political socialization. The family, schools, peer groups, and media all transmit messages concerning political facts, values, and attitudes. The individual, in turn, is not a mere sponge but a cognitive being who sorts out all these stimuli and evaluates, rejects, or accepts them. Individual personality attributes, levels of political interest, predispositions to act, and other factors also enter into the political development process. One's experiences in political activities shape one's feelings about the fairness and responsiveness of the political process and one's feelings of personal efficacy regarding politics. In short, the process of political socialization is an interaction between the individual and the environment.

Political learning takes place through direct and indirect processes. Direct political learning is simple enough. One learns from lessons designed to have obvious political import. Indirect political learning involves a two-step process in which general, nonpolitical cognitions affect political cognitions. The theory of indirect political learning borrows from psychocultural theory, which explains culture as the result of the socialization of certain personality types (Almond and Verba, 1963). The roots of culture lie in the very young child's family experiences. Child-rearing practices are assumed to be the best explanations of both adult personality and general cultural patterns (Whiting and Child, 1953). Psychocultural theory regards explicit political orientations as projections from the basic personality traits acquired early in life. The important personality attributes, when it comes to understanding the acquisition of political attitudes later in life, include self-esteem, ego strength, authoritarianism, need for power, and feelings of competence.

Dawson, Prewitt, and Dawson (1977) suggest this emphasis on the child-rearing antecedents of political socialization is too narrow, with its interpretation of all postchildhood socialization as simply "projection" from basic personality traits developed in early childhood. This approach cannot account for some major discontinuities between childhood and adult political outlooks. It also discounts the process of maturation, of continuous development that allows individuals to take on a progression of roles as they age. Direct political learning appears to be much more significant than personality traits as a determinant of the acquisition of political information, political party identification, and attitudes toward specific issues. This kind of learning takes place in schools and other contexts as well as in the family, which is the main source of early indirect political learning.

I now delineate more specifically the modes of political learning. These modes are not mutually exclusive. Several may be involved in any specific learning situation. Nor is direct political learning necessarily intentional and indirect learning unintentional. They consist, rather, of a number of empirically observed processes. (See Dawson, Prewitt, and

Dawson, 1977, for a more detailed description of these.) Indirect modes are those that do *not* appear to be deliberately political; direct modes involve learning of clearly political content.

Indirect Modes of Political Learning

Interpersonal Transference. A number of scholars have explained the development of positive orientations toward political authority universally seen among children as a process of interpersonal transference (Easton and Hess, 1962; Greenstein, 1960; Hess and Torney, 1967). According to Easton and Hess (p. 242), "The authority figures with which they [children] have earliest and most intimate contact are of course their parents, and it is this image of authority that they subsequently seem to transfer to political figures that cross their vision. The child not only learns to respect and admire political authorities, but with regard to many characteristics sees them as parents writ large."

Apprenticeship Learning. Another source of mainly positive orientations toward the political system is a kind of apprenticeship that takes place in nonpolitical contexts, such as youth organizations and schools (Ziblatt, 1965). The apprenticeship continues through late childhood, adolescence, and early adulthood. Apprenticeship processes can also be seen in work place (Lipset, Trow, and Coleman, 1956) and volunteer action settings, where the learning undoubtedly includes some negative as well as positive orientations. In this mode of political learning, the individual is assumed to acquire skills, habits, and behaviors that can be transferred to political activities (see Almond and Verba, 1963). Recently, we have seen groups previously excluded from apprenticeship opportunities demanding broader access to training. On many college campuses, students have demanded more opportunity to participate in institutional decision-making processes—demands that grew out of political learning that took place in the civil rights and antiwar movements. Women and minority groups have also pressured for the right to participate in nonpolitical decision making as they have become politically more sophisticated. In new nations, we see the same phenomenon. As the population becomes knowledgeable about political processes, they demand more involvement not only in political life but also in schools, labor unions, and such. Thus, the transfer of learning takes place in both directions, from nonpolitical to political and in reverse.

Generalization. A third mode of indirect political learning involves the human tendency to generalize what is learned in one sphere to other spheres. This mode is assumed to underlie observed tendencies for various groups to hold relatively homogeneous political views. Greenberg (1970), for example, comments that the fact that inner-city black children have low political trust and little sense of political efficacy may reflect some generalizations from social attitudes.

Direct Modes of Political Learning

Imitation. Children both consciously and unconsciously copy those who are important to them. Imitation of role models may be the most common way people learn many things (Miller and Dollard, 1941). Greenstein (1965) and Easton and Hess (1962), for example, point out that it is unlikely parents or teachers explicitly teach children to say, "I am a Democrat," or the like; yet by age seven or eight, children can express definite political party identification. Presumably, they copy their parents' party labels.

Imitation works in reverse as well. In adolescent years, children may imitate their parents' political orientations or rebelliously choose antithetical orientations.

Anticipatory Socialization. Children not only imitate observed role behavior in appropriate settings when given the opportunity to fill a particular role but can also be seen practicing anticipated roles or adopting attitudes appropriate to roles they expect to fill (see Merton, 1949). The child imitates parenting by taking care of a baby doll; the premedical student takes on attitudes and opinions believed to be associated with being a doctor; the future political leader conducts full-fledged political campaigns for minor school offices. The cues that guide this anticipatory imitation come from role models, as with direct imitation, and from other elements of the environment—the baby doll parents provide to the child, the classroom performances of medical school professors who give the student cues about attitudes appropriate to anticipated role behavior, the structure of school life that promotes the imitation of partisan electoral behavior, and so on.

Political Education. In addition, most children are given some direct political education. Instruction may be carried out by parents, relatives, teachers, peers, voluntary groups such as the League of Women Voters, and work-related groups such as unions, political parties, and governmental agencies. This kind of education is deliberate. On one hand, it may be imposed on the individual, in contrast to other forms of learning in which the individual appears to choose to be educated. On the other hand, because the goal of direct political education is usually quite clear, the individual may feel he or she has some choice in the kind of education received. The student can choose not to learn certain responses; the worker can choose not to go to a union political meeting; and so forth.

Political Experience. Political education also takes place through experiential learning—learning by doing. Political education typically is not provided for young children; but by adolescence, the individual has a chance to participate in political campaigns, voluntary social action groups, and such. These political experiences tend to foster reassessment of previous learning and of current political choices. Political experience may be seen as completing or correcting earlier political learning. Obviously, this kind of learning is most important for those who are political activists or at least very attentive to political processes.

Social Role and Status Socialization: Implications for Political Behavior

Although it is essential to understand how political orientations are acquired, this alone does not explain why specific political behaviors are manifested. We assume that there is a linkage between predispositions (attitudes, orientations, and such) and behavior, but not that there is an automatic cause-and-effect relationship. The study of political learning does not answer such questions as "Who votes? What sort of people contact government officials? Why do some people and not others join protest marches?" The next step in the study of socialization for political behavior is to look at what factors besides individual predispositions may determine observed political behavior. I shall consider social class identification, educational level, occupation and income, race, gender, ethnic and religious group, and voluntary group affiliations.

Social Class. During early childhood, positive attitudes toward political authorities and symbols are universal (Sears, 1975). As children grow older, differences among groups begin to appear. Social class differences begin to emerge in third or fourth grade. Lower-class children tend to maintain naive, benevolent attitudes toward political authorities longer than middle-class children in the United States and in other countries. The pattern of depersonalizing and deidealizing political authority does not appear among lower-class children until late childhood or early adolescence (Easton and Dennis, 1969; Greenstein, 1965; Hess and Torney, 1967; Sears, 1975; Weissberg, 1974). At each age level, lower-class children tend to show somewhat lower levels of political maturity than middle-class children.

This lag is more a matter of awareness and actual participation than of normative support for political activism. Greenstein (1965) and Jennings (1971) found no socioeconomic differences in children's willingness to participate in adult politics. But Greenstein (1965) and Hess and Torney (1967) found that high-status children were significantly more likely than low-status children to engage in political discussions with their parents and friends. Middle-class homes seem to foster earlier development of the cognitive and planning skills and feelings of self-confidence and efficacy that are important for effective political action. Also, acquisition of political information is easier in middle-class homes, where it is more likely to be available and where parental interest in politics may be greater. The importance of home environment and parental influence has been found to be particularly strong when parents agree with one another in political matters, when they are consistent in their views, when they make their viewpoints and values known to their children, and when their political opinions are important to them (Jennings and Niemi, 1974; Tedin, 1974). Tedin (1974, pp. 1579–1592) set forth these hypotheses concerning effective parental transmission of specific issue positions to children:

1. The more accurate the adolescent's perception of the parent's attitudes, the more influence the parent will have on the adolescent's attitude.
2. The greater the issue and partisan salience to the parent, the more influence the parent will have on the adolescent's attitude.

Another important factor in parental influence is that of the quality of parent-child relationships (Jennings and Niemi, 1974). Middle-class parents tend to have more interest in pursuing political topics with their children and spend more time doing so. Thus, they encourage interest and attitudes that foster their children's political participation. Middle-class children have this advantage very early in life, and it increases as they grow older. At each maturation stage, the middle-class child receives greater reinforcement for political learning (Hess and Torney, 1967). Furthermore, several other factors related to the development of political awareness are correlated with class. I shall treat these other factors separately because they can be shown to have some independent influence, but it should be noted that the political socialization of children with high social status is influenced by a number of class-related factors in addition to the general process of socialization into middle-class norms.

Education. Level of political participation is most strongly related to level of educational attainment. Being educated enables one to be fully involved in social communication networks and thus to gain political information on many aspects of a wide variety of topics. The well educated tend to have more successful and generally positive political experiences than the less well educated. These experiences reinforce the well-educated person's sense of political competence and efficacy, which in turn makes him or her more likely to participate further and thus increases political sophistication and expertise, making continued participation more likely. In short, the initial middle-class socialization advantage continues to grow as a result of actual experiences.

Key (1961, pp. 323–331), in summarizing U.S. research findings on the relation between education and political orientations, concluded that better-educated citizens (1) have a greater sense of duty to participate in national life than less well educated citizens; (2) have greater confidence in their power to influence the political process, to make governmental officials listen to them and their views, and to gain access to political power; (3) are generally more interested in public affairs; and (4) are more politically active (are more likely to vote, to contribute money, and to engage in demanding types of political participation such as campaigning and working for a party).

Almond and Verba (1963, pp. 380–387) came to the same kinds of conclusions on the basis of their five-nation study. Better-educated persons in their samples were more aware of political stimuli, had greater political information, expressed more political opinions, felt more able to influence governmental decisions, and were more actively involved in political organizations than less well educated persons. The well educated also expressed more confidence in the social environment, tending to believe that other people are likely to be trustworthy and helpful.

Prewitt attempted to account for the relationship between educational level and level of political participation in terms of variation in political socialization across classes. His major points are:

1. Better-educated persons are more involved in society's communication networks. Their reading habits, travel experiences, friendship patterns, and leisure activities increase the amount of politically pertinent information available to them. Education also gives people the skills that help them act on the information they acquire.
2. Citizens with high educational status are accustomed to collective decision making. The well educated are active participants in the organizational life of society. Through their social involvement, the well educated acquire habits and skills that are easily transferred to political affairs.
3. The educated citizen acquires attitudes that are generalized to the political sphere. An illustration of this is the feeling of political competence. The well educated tend to believe that rational manipulation of social institutions can produce desired goals. This sense of mastery and control over the social environment is generalized to political matters and expressed as feelings of political efficacy.

4. The well educated, because of their high social and economic status, usually feel they have a greater stake in maintaining the status quo. Thus, the well educated tend to presume that political events will directly affect their personal well-being. In part, then, the active political role the well educated take stems from a desire to protect their investment in society (Dawson, Prewitt, and Dawson, 1977, pp. 167–168).

Occupation and Income. Political socialization in adulthood is affected by occupational standing and income. Although many of the basic aspects of the political self are established in childhood, there are other aspects that come with acquiring an occupational identity and that are related to the power that income level represents. In part, the effects of occupation are similar to those of education. Many of the skills and abilities developed in occupational roles can be generalized to the political world. In addition, work settings may be important for structuring secondary group relationships that have political effects. Friendship patterns, political and social attitudes, and values are developed, changed, and sustained within group contexts (see Cartwright and Zander, 1960; Festinger, Schachter, and Back, 1950; Verba, 1961). Union participation may strengthen democratic values as well as give members the opportunity to acquire political skills (Lipset, Trow, and Coleman, 1956).

Race. Race-related differences can be seen in political learning throughout the life cycle. Questions have been raised about the possibility that minorities are socialized to be political losers, that society teaches them the attributes of second-class citizenship rather than first-class citizenship. Black children have been found to share with lower-class white children the tendency to conceptualize government in personal rather than in institutional terms. However, black children tend to persist in holding indiscriminately benevolent attitudes toward the nation, the flag, and important authority figures longer than white children.

The existence of indiscriminately positive attitudes may reflect a need for young children to see authority in a positive light as well as the impact of parental and school socialization. Whatever the reason, when the benevolent attitudes of black children begin the shift to more realistic views, they follow a somewhat different course than the changing attitudes of white children. By the time children are in high school, their attitudes tend to reflect their social position—middle class, Chicano, black, and so on. Jennings (as reported in Weissberg, 1974), for example, indicates that 40.3 percent of white high school seniors in 1965 viewed political activism as good citizenship and only 19.5 percent of black seniors did. Greenberg (1970) reports that black youths feel much more positive toward police than do white youths. Similar patterns of diverging attitudes can be found among Chicano versus Anglo youth (Garcia, 1973). Weissberg (1974), in summarizing the relevant literature, concluded that blacks tend to be socialized into political apathy. Black youths have a much weaker sense of political efficacy than white youths. Blacks tend toward fatalism, toward seeing things as happening *to* them rather than seeing *themselves* as affecting events. They are less likely than whites to feel they are in control of their lives (Battle and Rotter, 1963).

The gap between whites and blacks widens over time. In part, this is a matter of the realities of our society. Whites can see that the political system is susceptible to their influences; blacks can see that for them often it is not (Abramson, 1972). The differences are not a consequence only of class and income or economic privileges versus deprivation; they stem from realistic perceptions of hostility toward minorities on the part of political authorities as well as white society generally.

Gender. Gender role differences appear early in childhood and continue through adolescence. Early differences are very like adult differences. Up to the present, women have tended to be socialized away from political activity and into political passivity. General socialization into gender roles steers girls away from assertiveness and leadership and toward deference to authority and general dependency (Bardwick and Douvan, 1972; Sherman, 1971; Tuma and Livson, 1960).

Girls keep their immature picture of authority figures (presidents, police, and such) longer than boys (Hess and Torney, 1967). Girls also have an idealized, personalized image of political authority longer than boys. Participation in campaign-type political activities increases markedly for both girls and boys from the third to eighth grades, but the increase is greater for boys at each grade level. By fourth grade, boys have been found to be better informed about political matters than girls, in spite of girls' generally superior school performance at this age (Greenstein, 1965). Weissberg (1974) reports that among high school seniors, men feel they have more capacity to manipulate the political environment than do women. Torney, Oppenheim, and Farnen (1975) report that female students score lower than male students in tests of knowledge of law, government, international problems, and support for individual rights. Although there are no gender differences in the amount of political discussion with friends and family, girls are less likely to take sides in these discussions (Hess and Torney, 1967).

Iglitzen (1974) speculates that young women are not interested in learning about government and politics because these areas are presented to them as aggressive, exploitative, and manipulative and generally appear to be nonfeminine. Secondary school students learn only about males in politics (because the politicians in history and social studies books are almost exclusively males) at a time when young women's chief interest is in learning about behavior appropriate to females. Torney, Oppenheim, and Farnen (1975), in a cross-cultural study of fourteen-year-olds, found that only 17 percent of U.S. students agreed women should run for political office and take part in government much the same as men do. In contrast, from 38 percent to 58 percent of students from West Germany, Ireland, Italy, and New Zealand accepted equal participation. More students from the United States than from the other countries agreed women should stay out of politics.

Weissberg (1974, p. 118) summarizes what is known about gender role differences in political socialization, in comparison with class and racial differences, as follows:

> Though most of the differences in male/female political competence are not very large, their very existence is significant, since they indicate the possibility of socializing young citizens away from knowledgeable participation despite the lack of real differences of ability. One could argue that in the case of lower-class and black children comparative political incompetence is an inevitable corollary of their general socioeconomic position that also results in low academic motivation, poor grades, poorer verbal facility, and so on. Thus, if lower-class and black children were only made educational equals, equality in political socialization would soon follow. When we examine the education of American females, however, we see that comparable academic and intellectual ability does not necessarily lead to political equality. Obviously, it is one thing to possess the potential for sophisticated political activism and quite another to be motivated to employ these abilities.

As noted, one of the demands activist women make today is the chance to redress this politically deficient socialization through apprenticeship and work opportunities. As the woman's role has become more varied, these changes in participation have been reflected also in political involvement (see Andersen, 1975; Tedin, Brady, and Vedlitz, 1977). Although educational and political institutions are slowly yielding to some of these pressures, there are still strong external (and internal) barriers to active, assertive social and political participation by women in our society (Hahn, 1976; Unger, 1978).

Ethnic and Religious Group Identification. Other types of self-identity besides race and gender affect the course of political socialization. Although there is little research in these areas, it is clear that ethnic group membership and religious identification are important factors. They serve as reference points for both children and adults, and they serve to structure relationships between individuals of different groups. Being Polish, Jewish, or Catholic tends to influence a family's choice of residential area, organizational memberships for both adults and children, dating patterns, and a whole range of behaviors. Thus, there are indirect effects on political attitudes from social contextual factors that reflect self-identification.

Political attitudes and opinions can also be directly influenced by religious and ethnic forces, and the relative salience of various issues reflects focal concerns of particular groups. For a Catholic, the most salient political issue in the 1970s may be abortion; Jewish voters may tend to take particular interest in foreign policy issues as they relate to the Middle East. The significance of these group identifications varies among those who are identified as belonging to various groups. An individual's use of a particular group as a political reference point depends on the strength of identification with the group and the perceived relevance of modal group attitudes for the issue at hand.

Voluntary Group Associations. Groups that are joined with relative freedom of choice—secondary groups and voluntary associations—tend to have some of the same effects as groups to which one belongs mainly through circumstances of birth. Of course, the individual tends to join voluntary groups that are in harmony with her or his existing political opinions, but group participation can have some influence on further development. Voluntary associations are influential to the extent that they serve as a reference point for an individual and to the extent that the group is perceived as having relevant positions on current issues. In addition, secondary groups serve as communication networks, providing social interaction and information exchange opportunities. Primary groups (the family, mainly) are the chief political socializers during a child's early years; but as the individual matures, close peer and work groups may become very influential, particularly as the individual begins to separate from her or his family of origin (Torney and Buergenthal, 1977). Some evidence suggests that during adolescence peer associations begin to replace family and school as the most significant reference points (Coleman, 1961). Peer relationships grow in variety and complexity at this age and continue to do so as the individual enters the work force, marries, becomes a resident of a specific neighborhood, joins voluntary associations as an adult member, and so on. All these social affiliations, which multiply as the individual becomes an adult, encourage various kinds of political growth and involvement. As Goel notes in Chapter Four, the effects of general social participation on political participation are cumulative. Almond and Verba (1963, p. 309), summarizing their findings for the relationship between secondary group membership and political interest, conclude, "[Citizens] who are members of a nonpolitical organization are more likely to feel subjectively competent than are those who belong to no organization. This, then, appears to confirm the fact that latent political functions are performed by voluntary associations, whether those organizations are political or not. Those who are members of some organizations, even if they report that it has no political role, have more political competence than those who have no such membership." Existing research does not allow us to resolve the question of whether this observed relationship is a matter of socialization or selection. It is probably both. It may be that political opportunity opens up to those who have the opportunity and inclination to become active participants in society generally. At the same time, research on socialization generally suggests that the more social group affiliations one has, the stronger one's tendency to participate in political activity.

Social Roles and Statuses versus Experience

The effect of particular political experiences and events can modify and even nullify the effects of socialization into social roles and group membership influences. Many women and minorities are politically active. It is a difference in modal tendency that has been observed, not all-or-nothing differences between women and men, social classes, or racial groups. Many lower-class children are upwardly mobile; and if they have positive experiences with the social and political order, their political orientations may become much like those socialized in the middle class—for example, they will show greater rather than lesser political trust as adults.

Note that the class differences reverse with age. Lower-class children retain their positive feelings about political authority longer than middle-class children, but adulthood brings more cynicism and distrustful attitudes to lower-class orientations than to middle-class orientations. To some extent, we assume this reflects class-related experiences with reality. The specific political experiences an individual has while growing up are very important. Thus, although the modal developmental tendencies for lower and middle classes are different, at the same time there is room for individual differences within classes.

Experiences in adulthood are obviously of some importance in shaping both these modal tendencies and individual differences within groups, but research findings in the area of adult socialization are sparse (Brim, 1967). The assumption that the most dramatic development of basic political perspectives took place early in life dominated research for many years. In childhood, the important processes involve significant acquisition of political knowledge and the development of complex conceptualizations of the political world. These processes do not have a counterpart in adulthood. Adult political learning is characterized by the forming of opinions on specific issues, candidates, and events. In adulthood, the main processes are usually cumulative and elaborative rather than breaking new ground.

There are two other aspects of adult socialization that are important, though little researched. First, most adults tend to experience at least once in their lifetimes, and perhaps more often, sharp social discontinuities. This may involve life-style, associates, or ways of thinking about the political world. The Great Depression of the 1930s, the end of slavery, the civil rights revolution, the Vietnam War, and the great changes in sexual morality all represent such discontinuities for many people.

Second, growth continues in adult life, but along paths we know little of as yet (for example, see Sheehy, 1974; Levinson, 1978). Gould (1975, p. 74) writes, "Adults aren't fully forged by adolescence. Growth continues, from the confidence and optimism of the twenties through the doubts of the early thirties, the urgencies of the early forties, and the mellowing and self-acceptance of the fifties." As yet, the process of normal aging has not attracted the attention of political researchers. One reason is that the necessary research must be longitudinal and will be costly and difficult. At this point, then, we can only ask, and not answer, one of the most important questions in political socialization: To what extent does early learning persist and structure later political learning and behavior?

Antecedents of Conventional versus Unconventional
Political Behavior

In subsequent chapters of this volume, modes of political participation will be divided into conventional and unconventional and discussed separately. At this point, I raise the question of differences and similarities in the socialization antecedents of these two types of political participation. Do those who participate in conventional activities (voting, discussing politics, campaigning, attending meetings, contacting government officials, or joining a party) have different socialization experiences than those who join unconventional activities (demonstrations, civil disobedience, political strikes, riots, or guerrilla action)? The distinction here is between what is considered "normal" and legitimate versus what is illegitimate and out of bounds in legal or social terms. On the basis of existing research, we can answer this question with "yes," "no," and "do not know."

One difficulty in answering this question stems from conceptual confusion. Does the distinction between conventional and unconventional concern legal or social approval of the action, the target of the action, or the motivation of the actor? Verba and Nie (1972) have argued a multidimensional concept of political participation; the specificity of unconventional behavior also needs to be spelled out.

Approval. We know the actions listed under the unconventional label are not generally approved of in the United States. Verba and Brody (1970) found that at the height of anti–Vietnam War activity only about 0.5 percent of the population was participating in the protests, but Key (1961) points out that only a small minority of the population are either conventional or unconventional activists. There is evidence that there has been more public acceptance of protest as a form of political behavior in recent years, but about half the citizenry still disapproves of unconventional political activities such as sit-ins, mass meetings, and demonstrations (Finifter and Miller, 1975). American political activism is strongly biased in the direction of electoral participation as the major form (Verba and Nie, 1972; Weissberg, 1974). Weissberg (1974, p. 93) concluded, "of all the possible ways of participating in political decisions, Americans by virtue of their socialization gravitate to only a handful of possibilities."

Motivation. Turning to the question of motivation for unconventional behavior, we do not find any simple answer. College students' political activity in the 1960s and early 1970s included participation in the civil rights movement, the peace movement, an unofficial "war" on poverty, and attempts to democratize educational institutions. Some students were motivated by hostility to authority and established institutions, some were motivated by specific policy change goals, and others may have simply gone along with a collective of friends and peers. For many of these students, protests served as an apprenticeship for political careers. However, when some of the most unconventional political behaviors are considered—the violent kind, such as riots and street warfare—it seems probable that many participants were motivated by political distrust, anger, and feelings of economic deprivation or alienation (Aberbach, 1969; Jackson, 1973).

The socialization influences for these various protest movements are not the same for all participants. The Catholic church and religious family values clearly are the roots of the antiabortion protest, and such things as the women's movement and unwanted pregnancies seem to be major determinants of proabortion activism. Political involvement seems to have radicalized student protesters (Altbach, 1966). Whatever political views the student comes to a demonstration with, he or she is likely to leave with an intensified or more extreme view. Students participating in protest actions often become part of a highly emotional, supportive group that deepens their commitment to political causes. For example, the youth movement in the late 1960s and early 1970s that emphasized the "generation gap" tended to lead many students to question their feelings of political trust. Governmental responses to the peace movement intensified students' concern, and opposition to the Vietnam War became a rallying point for many who had begun to question the general trustworthiness of the political system (Lubell, 1972). The extent to which these students were permanently affected by this activity and their experiences is yet to be determined by longitudinal study. Newcomb's (1943) study of radicalization of students suggests the antiwar movement may have a long-term impact on the participants' political orientation.

The participants in these various movements do not see each other as all belonging to the same political group. Women marching for abortion on demand do not necessarily see themselves as having much in common with student radicals; women marching in an antiabortion protest may see themselves at the opposite end of the political spectrum from those who marched for civil rights in the 1960s. Liberals who boycotted nonunion lettuce and grapes in support of California farm workers probably do not see themselves as generally alienated from the dominant political regime but simply opposed to the power of large agricultural corporations that keep farm wages unacceptably low. These relatively peaceful protesters may not, in fact, see their political activity as "nonconventional."

A related question is that of unconventionality of targets. Some unconventional participation is seen by observers and perhaps by many participants as an effort to "bring down the system." The purpose is revolutionary, not reformist. The change sought is complete policy change and not incremental policy improvement. This kind of unconventional political activity is clearly different—and likely to have different antecedents—from protest marches employed as a means of changing a school busing policy or rent strikes used to bring economic power to bear on irresponsible landlords.

In summary, then, because studies of political socialization have been mainly concerned with preparation for conventional participation, the major answer to the question of differential socialization for unconventional participation is "do not know."

Conclusion

Studies on political participation have tended to stress conventional political activities. Studies focusing on unconventional participation have tended to lack the specification needed to question whether the motivations, behaviors, and targets of unconventional political activity follow from a different pattern of political socialization or are more like variations on a theme. This conceptual confusion is not confined to research on unconventional participation. The extent to which early political learning structures and determines later political behavior is often assumed without supporting data in political socialization literature. Political socialization research deals with self-reported opinions and attitudes rather than with political behavior itself. The methodology of survey research involves asking people (including children) what they think, including sometimes what they remember doing; but actual behavior is not observed (Salisbury, 1975). Behavioral measures are needed to bridge this gap in our knowledge of what people say and what they actually do.

We need a fuller and more accurate sense of what is involved in political participation generally. Verba and Nie's (1972) delineation of conventional participation activities in a multidimensional context was a beginning. But we need subtler and deeper probing of political motivation and research into a wider range of political behavior—for example, of such activities as politically meaningful conversations between neighbors over the back fence, letters to the editors of local newspapers, and participation in radio call-in shows. Research also is needed to differentiate political learning that prepares people for verbal assessment of their attitudes (such as that found in opinion surveys) and learning that prepares people for effective political action of a type not usually assessed by such methods as survey instruments. (For example, participants in successful neighborhood advocacy groups may not "test out" politically sophisticated.)

Adult political socialization is another fertile field for exploration. Adult political activity should be observed in a variety of institutional settings—work places, courts, administrative agencies, and the street—that may reveal a range of politically relevant behaviors and experiences. We have not yet studied the full variety.

Another focus for future work in this area is the application of political socialization research findings to the development of consciousness-raising political materials, materials that will illustrate the importance of the family and the school as agents of political socialization and that will make parents and teachers more aware of their potential roles in the process. In addition, the integration of relevant political socialization findings (such as age-related cognitive-developmental learning theory findings concerning age and social group contexts) into a sequential primary and secondary social studies curriculum would enrich the political education of the country's future citizens.

CHAPTER 4

Conventional Political Participation

M. Lal Goel

This chapter summarizes the literature on conventional informal political participation. I shall refer to "unconventional" political participation for comparison purposes, but this topic is dealt with more thoroughly in the next chapter. I shall report how each of the categories of independent variables correlates with political participation. If I found that a given independent variable correlates differently with different modes of participation, I have noted this. The reader should remember, however, that political participation is usually treated as an undifferentiated phenomenon. For this reason, I have had to treat political participation as unitary activity in most places.

I have reviewed and abstracted a sizable portion of the literature, most of it dating after 1964. For a review of the literature before 1964, I

Note: I wish to thank the following for reviewing an earlier draft of this paper and making helpful suggestions: Lester Milbrath, State University of New York–Buffalo; James Hottois, University of San Diego; Yas Kuroda, University of Hawaii; Jim Munro and Arthur Doerr, University of West Florida; and Don Freeman, Texas Tech University. Secretarial help was received from Kay Trine, Karen Born, Debbie Hall, and Priscilla Meyers, University of West Florida.

depended on the summary provided by Milbrath (1965); and for later material, I depended on Milbrath and Goel (1977), which updates the previous work. The inventory of findings presented here is not exhaustive. It consists of generalizations that are empirically based. Writings devoted to theorizing about political problems or philosophical issues are omitted. Most of the literature summarized here appeared in English language books and journals. Thus, the generality of most findings is limited mainly to the United States and, to a lesser extent, other industrialized societies, although findings from other parts of the world have been included when they were available in English.

I have used the following classes of independent variables to explain political participation: social and historical contextual, demographic, personality and attitudinal.

Social and Historical Contextual Factors

Historical factors are listed here mainly for conceptual completeness; space limitations do not allow me to describe all the literature in this area. A discussion of the variety of social and historical contextual variables and their relationship to participation in organized voluntary action is available in Smith and Reddy (1972a). A full discussion of specifically political variables, such as the party system, constitutional provisions, eligibility requirements, and voting systems, is provided by Milbrath (1965) and Milbrath and Goel (1977, chap. 5).

A few examples of studies of social contextual variables will have to suffice. For instance, Needler (1968) found that the more developed Latin American countries had higher electoral political participation rates. Almond and Verba's (1963) five-nation study and a secondary analysis of the same data by Nie, Powell, and Prewitt (1969) also shows higher informal political participation in more developed nations. The United States and England led Germany, Mexico, and Italy in participation rates. This ranking corresponded (in the early 1960s) with an economic development ranking of the five nations.

Another study, focusing on cities as the level of analysis, found that cities with less well educated populations tended to have higher voting turnout than cities with better-educated populations, contrary to what might be expected (Alford and Lee, 1968). Using county-level aggregate data in the American South, Matthews and Prothro (1966) found that the presence of higher socioeconomic status blacks in the county was associated with higher political participation levels.

Among the historical factors receiving most attention in recent years is that of modernization level. The basic thesis is that, everything else equal, people in modernized societies participate politically at a higher level than do people in traditional and preindustrial societies. For a discussion of this thesis, see Inkeles (1969); Kim, Nie, and Verba (1974); Lerner (1958); and Nie, Powell, and Prewitt (1969).

Demographic Variables

Demographic, and particularly socioeconomic, variables are among the most often researched determinants of political participation. Nearly all studies of political behavior include a discussion of socioeconomic variables as a matter of routine. Social background characteristics provide important indicators of who the person is, what social positions he or she occupies, what type of socialization experiences he or she is likely to have gone through, what resulting political expectations and attitudes he or she is likely to have, and what kind of political activity he or she is likely to engage in. Socioeconomic variables stand for other variables and provide clues about personality traits and attitudes. Among the social background factors often studied are the following: place of residence, education, income, occupation, socioeconomic status, gender roles, age, and organizational involvement.

Place of Residence. Place of residence is an important variable related to political participation. Although there are many studies of the urban-rural dichotomy, there is no consensus on how and to what extent community size affects individual political action.

At least two trends can be seen in the literature. One model holds that urban living is conducive to higher involvement because urban residents are closer to the center of society than are rural dwellers and hence have more opportunity for interaction and communication. Thus, greater stimulation is supposed to result from an urban environment (Milbrath, 1965). Scholars in the field of modernization and development generally support this model. The movement of people from farms to the city is said to trigger a chain reaction that leads to increased literacy, exposure to mass communication, and higher political participation. (See, for example, Deutsch, 1961; Lerner, 1958; Russett and others, 1964).

In support of a second and contradictory model, a variety of studies have found little positive correlation between urban living and political activity, especially voting. The evidence comes from a variety of cultures (Burnham, 1965; Cameron, Hendericks, and Hofferbert, 1972; Goel, 1971; Inkeles, 1969; Kim, 1971; Kyogoku and Ike, 1959; Marquette, 1971; Matthews and Prothro, 1966; Nie, Powell, and Prewitt, 1969; Richardson, 1973; Robinson and Standing, 1960; Tarrow, 1971; Verba and Nie, 1972; Watanuki, 1972). These studies report data from fourteen countries.

The lack of relationship between urbanism and political activity is seen most clearly when the effects of other variables such as organizational involvement and social status are neutralized. Inkeles' (1969, p. 1140) finding is representative: "Our most striking finding is precisely that urbanism, despite its zero-order correlation, fails to meet the test of being an independent school of citizenship. Neither urban origin, nor the number of years of urban experience after age fifteen, produces significant increases in active citizenship when other variables are controlled. This is confirmed by many special matches." In the Verba and Nie (1972) study of the United States, after corrections were made for the socioeconomic differences, citizens in the suburbs—communities that are least well bounded and have the least identity as communities—emerged as underparticipants. However, isolated villages and towns and the core cities exhibited greater political activity.

The reason most often cited for these disparate findings is that in rural areas in most countries one is a member of a small, integrated community, whereas in the metropolitan area, one is part of a supposedly atomized, mass society. Except in the older and relatively homogeneous core areas, politics in the city and suburbs is believed to become impersonal and distant. However, note that although most rural dwellers live together in villages in Europe and Asia, in the United States, farmers tend to live on their farms, isolated from other farmers. In Japan and India, some evidence also suggests that urban living leads to greater political cynicism, negative views about politicians, and lower feelings about voting being a duty. In contrast, rural residents tend to be more dutiful and less hostile toward politicians (Eldersveld, Jagannadham, and Barnabas, 1968; Goel, 1975; Richardson, 1973).

What do we make of the contradictory findings presented in this section? Differences in measures of the dependent variable presumably contribute to the conflicting evidence. Voting may correlate differently with community size than do other, more demanding political acts. Also, differences in culture may account for part of the discrepancy. Nevertheless, most of the recent research solidly rejects the notion that urbanism is conducive to political activism. If there is a close relation between urbanism and political activity, it is the effect of other variables, such as level of education or of mass media, which have higher incidence in urban areas. However, there may be more political participation in lower-status urban areas than political scientists observe, given their usual conceptual and measurement approaches (Perlman, 1975).

Education. Among the socioeconomic variables investigated in political science literature, education is the most thoroughly researched factor. In many studies, education is not treated as a separate variable but is merged with other variables, in particular with income and occupation, to form the social status or socioeconomic status variable. A widely documented research finding is that people with greater education tend to engage in more conventional political participation than those with less education. The relationship between education and participation holds for most forms of political activity, with the possible exception of voting.

Milbrath (1965) lists twenty-three sources as supportive of the proposition linking education and political activity (Agger and Goldrich, 1958; Agger and Ostrom, 1956; Agger, Goldrich, and Swanson, 1964; Allardt and Pesonen, 1960; Almond and Verba, 1963; Benny, Gray, and Pear, 1956; Berelson, Lazarsfeld, and McPhee, 1954; Buchanan, 1956; Campbell, 1962; Campbell, Gurin, and Miller, 1954; Converse and Dupeux, 1961; Dahl, 1961; Gronseth, 1955; Jensen, 1960; Key, 1961; Kornhauser, Mayer, and Sheppard, 1956; Kuroda, 1965; Lane, 1959; Lipset, 1960; McPhee and Glaser, 1962; Miller, 1952; Sussman, 1959; Woodward and Roper, 1950). Later supporting studies are Alford and Scoble, 1968; Barber, 1969; Bowman and Boynton, 1974; DiPalma, 1970; Erbe, 1964; Goel, 1975; Inkeles, 1969; Kelley, Ayers, and Bowen, 1967; Marquette, 1971; Matthews and Prothro, 1966; Milbrath, 1972; Nie, Powell, and Prewitt, 1969; Olsen, 1973; Rosenau, 1974; Sallach, Babchuk, and Booth, 1972; Tessler, 1972; Verba and Nie, 1972; Verba, Nie, and Kim, 1971. The positive relationship between education and political participation holds not only in the United States and Western European nations, but also in the developing nations where research has been conducted; see Inkeles' research on Argentina, Chile, India, Israel, Nigeria, and Bangladesh (formerly East Pakistan); Verba, Nie, and Kim's work on Austria, India, Japan, Nigeria, and the United States; Goel's work on India; Marquette's work on the Philippines; and Tessler's work on Tunisia—all cited previously.

Why does education have such a strong impact on political behavior in such a diversity of cultures? The most important reason is that differences in educational attainment are associated with differences in other social and psychological attributes. Better-educated persons are more likely to have higher incomes, to be exposed to more mass media, to occupy higher-status positions, to be more informed about government and politics, to perceive higher stakes in politics, and to feel more efficacious. Almond and Verba (1963, pp. 381–382) comment,

> In each nation the educated classes are more likely to be cognitively aware of politics (to be aware of the impact of government, to have information about government, to follow politics in the various media), to have political opinions on a wide range of subjects, and to engage in political discussions. The

more highly educated are also more likely to consider themselves competent to influence the government and free to engage in political discussions. This set of orientations, widely distributed among those with high education and much less widely distributed among those with low education, constitutes what one might consider the minimum requirements for political participation. More complex attitudes and behavior depend upon such basic orientations as awareness of the political system, information about it, and some exposure to its operations. It is just this basic set of orientations that those of limited education tend not to have.

There is, however, one important qualification to this generalization: The effect of education is not uniform across all forms of participation. It correlates most strongly and clearly with campaign activity, participation in community affairs, and communication activities (such as talking about politics with friends). It correlates insignificantly, and sometimes negatively, with voter turnout. In India, education showed a small negative correlation with voting (Goel, 1970). In the cross-national study by Verba, Nie, and Kim (1971, pp. 75–79), only in the United States was education found to relate significantly to voting; in India, the correlation was -.04, in Austria, -.09, in Japan, .03, in Nigeria, -.03, and in the United States, .21. (In Japan, education had little impact on other modes of participation as well.) A negative correlation between education and voting has been found in urban Malaya (Rabushka, 1970) and in Japanese local elections (Richardson, 1966). In a study of Toledo, Ohio, primary elections failed to show a meaningful association of education to voting when occupational level and income were held constant (Hamilton, 1971).

Using the statistical technique of multiple-classification analysis on 1964, 1966, and 1968 election data collected by the University of Michigan Survey Research Center, Bennett and Klecka (1970) found the educational variable to be the strongest predictor of political efficacy, political interest, and political influence attempts, even when effects of occupation and income were taken into account. But with the latter controls, education retained little relationship to voter turnout.

Why do the more educated not vote in higher proportion in some cultures? One possible explanation is feelings of pessimism. In some countries, higher education levels do not correspond with patriotism and political satisfaction. In India and Nigeria, Inkeles (1969) found that the more informed, knowledgeable, and rational citizens were also more hostile and anomic and less patriotic. Similar findings are reported for India by Goel (1975) and Eldersveld, Jagannadham, and Barnabas (1968) and for Japan by Richardson (1973). Another relevant finding is that the socialization process by which the more educated assume political roles may not work for members of an ethnic minority. In a Nebraska survey of Mexican Americans, Welch, Comer, and Steinman (1973) found little positive correlation between educational attainment and the several dimensions of political participation. They felt this was "because the education process and other socialization agents do not prepare [minority] group members for political roles" (p. 813). A general lack of minority political power is also undoubtedly responsible for many of these findings.

Income. It is almost universally true that more prosperous persons are more likely than the less prosperous to participate in conventional politics. This relationship is supported by studies in several countries. Milbrath (1965) cites data from fourteen studies in support of the thesis (Agger and Ostrom, 1956; Campbell, Gurin, and Miller, 1954; Campbell and others, 1960; Campbell and Kahn, 1952; Connelly and Field, 1944; Dahl, 1961; Gronseth, 1955; Korchin, 1946; Lane, 1959; Lipset, 1960; Miller, 1952; Riesman and Glazer, 1950; Tingsten, 1937; Valen, 1961). Several more recent studies further corroborate the income-participation thesis (Alford and Scoble, 1968; Bennett and Klecka, 1970; DiPalma, 1970; Erbe, 1964; Hamilton, 1971; Inkeles, 1969; Matthews and Prothro, 1966; Nie, Powell, and Prewitt, 1969; Olsen, 1973; Rosenau, 1974; Verba and Nie, 1972).

In the South, blacks' incomes have greater impact on their political participation than other socioeconomic factors (Matthews and Prothro, 1966). DiPalma (1970) found that income and other socioeconomic factors have greater relevancy for political participation in the United States and Italy than in Germany and the United Kingdom.

Income relates differently to different participation measures. Its greatest impact is on activities that presumably require high self-esteem (convincing others to vote a particular way) or that require financial well-being (donating money to parties). In the Verba and Nie study (1972), income was more strongly related to communal and partisan activities than to voting or parochial participation. In India, income level showed no positive correlation with voting, but it did correlate positively with higher-level activities (Goel, 1975). In Japan, Kuroda (1967) found no significant correlation between income and political participation.

There are several explanations for the strong income-participation relationship. One is that income differences are related to other socioeconomic and attitudinal differences. The more affluent are likely to have had greater education, to interact with others in social and political groups, and to be exposed to mass media. The last factor is especially important in poor countries, where only the economically well-off can afford to buy newspapers and radios (Deutsch, 1962; Inkeles and Smith, 1974; Lerner, 1958). Active citizenship appears to be a luxury afforded only by those who have fulfilled more basic necessities. Political activism is also, of course, usually more profitable to those with economic power than to the poor. In general, the relations between income and political participation weaken considerably when the simultaneous effects of education and occupational prestige status are taken into account, though there is still some significant effect remaining. Among southern blacks, however, income has a stronger impact than does education, occupational status, or any other socioeconomic status variable (Matthews and Prothro, 1966).

Occupation. Occupational characteristics are highly intertwined with education and income. The relationship between occupational prestige and political participation reflects in part the effect of education and income on political involvement. But occupational characteristics also introduce independent effects in that some occupations either encourage or discourage political involvement because of their prestige level or for other, venal reasons.

Lane (1959, p. 331) suggests the following job characteristics facilitate political participation: (1) development of social and intellectual skills on the job that might carry over to politics, (2) opportunity to interact with other individuals who are politically knowledgeable and active, (3) higher than average stakes in government policies, and (4) civic or social roles certain occupations impose on their occupants. Milbrath (1965) emphasizes in addition the opportunity to get blocks of free time for politics and to interact with others interested in politics and the invulnerability of one's job to retaliatory action if one becomes active in politics.

One of the most thoroughly documented findings is that persons of higher occupational prestige status are more involved in politics than persons of lower status (Alford and Scoble, 1968; Barber, 1969; Bennett and Klecka, 1970; Berelson, Lazarsfeld, and McPhee, 1954; Dahl, 1961; Erbe, 1964; Hamilton, 1971; Lane, 1959; Lipset, 1960; Matthews and Prothro, 1966; Milbrath, 1965; Olsen, 1973). In the United States, Barber (1969, p. 12) found the following hierarchy in voting turnout in 1964 elections by occupation: professional and managerial (80 percent), other white collar (79 percent), farmers (79 percent), skilled and semiskilled (69 percent), and unskilled (64 percent).

In status-polarized societies, manual workers may achieve participation rates equal to or better than those who occupy more prestigious positions. Rokkan and Campbell (1960) suggest an interesting hypothesis to explain this: Status differences are less strongly associated with political participation in class-distinct party systems (Norway) than in heterogeneous party systems (United States). They found that active citizens were more likely to be drawn from the lower strata in Norway than in the United States. The heterogeneous character of American parties may depress participation rates among lower-status persons. A similar inference can be drawn from Butler and Stokes' (1971) British data. The gradual weakening of the Labour party's distinctive identification with working-class interests has led to a decline in the electoral turnout in traditional working-class neighborhoods.

Socioeconomic Status. In some studies, researchers have combined several measures of social prestige and economic status into a single index when relating demographic variables to political participation. Most commonly, scores on education, income, and occupational prestige status are combined to produce a single measure of socioeconomic status. Many studies have found a strong positive relationship between this kind of measure and political participation (Agger, Goldrich, and Swanson, 1964; Alford and Scoble, 1968; Campbell and others, 1960; Dahl, 1961; DiPalma, 1970; Erbe, 1964; Milbrath, 1965, 1971; Nie, Powell, and Prewitt, 1969; Olsen, 1972; Sallach, Babchuk, and Booth, 1972; Tessler, 1972; Tingsten, 1937; Verba and Nie, 1972; Watanuki, 1972).

The impact of status on turnout is higher in low-stimulus than in high-stimulus elections. Low-stimulus elections are characterized by weak partisanship (party identification), weak competitiveness, and fewer political stimuli in the environment (for example, less mass media attention to the election). In a study of Toledo, the association between turnout and social status was much higher in city elections (usually low stimulus) than in presidential elections (usually high stimulus) (Hamilton, 1971).

Verba and Nie (1972, pp. 133–134) found that the effect of socioeconomic characteristics on political participation in the United States is mediated through civic attitudes. Socioeconomic status increases political participation by increasing civic orientations, defined as feelings of efficacy, information about politics, and a sense of responsibility to contribute to the community. The original correlation between socioeconomic status and an overall index of political participation was .37. It was reduced to .16 when they removed the influence of civic orientations on participation. A similar finding was reported by Nie, Powell, and Prewitt (1969) for the United States, United Kingdom, Germany, Italy, and Mexico.

Gender Roles. Up to now politics has been almost everywhere a male-dominated activity. One of the most thoroughly substantiated research findings is that women all over the world participate less in politics than men do. Milbrath (1965) cites twenty-one studies with data drawn from nine countries that support this proposition (Agger, Goldrich, and Swanson, 1964; Allardt, 1956; Allardt and Pesonen, 1960; Almond and Verba, 1963; Benny, Gray, and Pear, 1956; Berelson, Lazarsfeld, and McPhee, 1954; Birch, 1950; Buchanan, 1956; Campbell and Cooper, 1956; Connelly and Field, 1944; Dogan and Narbonne, 1955; Gronseth, 1955; Grundy, 1950; Korchin, 1946; Lane, 1959; Lazarsfeld, Berelson, and Gaudet, 1944; McPhee and Glaser, 1962; Pesonen, 1960, 1961; Rokkan, 1962; Tingsten, 1937, with data from five countries). Additional later studies supporting this proposition include Barber (1969), DiPalma (1970), Duverger (1955), Goel (1975), Kuroda (1967), Lipset (1960), Matthews and Prothro (1966), Milbrath (1971), Nie, Verba, and Kim (1974), Olsen (1973), Verba and Nie (1972), and Watanuki (1972). The only exception to this rule has been found to exist in Argentina, where women voted slightly more often than men (Lewis, 1971).

In the United States, although the gap is becoming gradually narrower, the female voting rate is still about 10 percent lower than the male. The gap is widest among low-status people and narrowest among upper-status people; among college-educated women, political participation rates are little different from those among men. At upper educational levels, Campbell and others (1960) showed that women are more likely to express views supportive of good citizenship, with little gender difference at other levels. So women's lower participation is not a result of lack of dutiful sentiments. Campbell's data indicate, rather, that it is feelings of political efficacy that separate women from men and that may account for participation differences. As with other socioeconomic variables, the crucial factor in gender differences may be power—real and perceived.

Level of modernization is related to women's political participation. In Almond and Verba's (1963) five-nation study, the United States led other countries in overall rate of participation (except voting). But when the male-female dichotomy is introduced, it turns out that men have about the same participation level in the United States, the United Kingdom, and Germany. It is U.S. women's higher participation rate that sets this country apart from the modern European countries; participation rates of both men and women are lower in less modern countries (Mexico, Italy).

DiPalma's (1970) secondary analysis of Almond and Verba's data confirms this pattern. Gender role differences in political participation were sharper in Italy, England and Germany, even when variation due to education, occupation, and group membership was controlled, than in the United States. In another cross-national study, the male-female gap is the lowest in the United States and the greatest in India, with

Japan, Austria, and Nigeria in the middle (Nie, Verba, and Kim, 1974). This held for voting as well as other forms of participation. In the southern United States, gender differences in all forms of participation and at all levels of education are more distinct among blacks than among whites (Matthews and Prothro, 1966).

In India, the male-female differential in voting was eleven percentage points in 1967, down from seventeen percentage points in 1957. This eleven-point differential was not uniformly distributed in different regions of the country. The more modernized states recorded higher female voter participation. The correlation between size and male-female voting gap was -.652 for literacy, -.493 for income, and -.639 for urbanization (Goel, 1975, p. 93). On the basis of these findings, it can be expected that as the number of women working outside the home increases and as women's liberation movements spread, there will be greater political participation among women—continuing a trend of the past hundred years in the more developed countries.

Age. Many studies the world over have found that participation increases steadily with age until it reaches the peak in the middle years and then gradually drops with old age. Milbrath (1965) cites seventeen studies for this conclusion, based on a variety of samples in different cultures. Additional supportive studies include Campbell and others (1960), Goel (1975), Lane (1959), Lipset (1960), Matthews and Prothro (1966), Nie, Verba, and Kim (1974), Rosenau (1974), Tingsten (1937), Verba and Nie (1972).

In most cases, this generalization applies to voter turnout, but recent evidence suggests the curvilinear age-participation relationship applies with equal force to other forms of political participation. However, strong evidence in the United States indicates that when education and sex are taken into account, the decline in the voting rate of the elderly largely disappears (Glenn and Grimes, 1968; Riley and Foner, 1968). The less educated and women are overrepresented among older age-cohorts in the United States. Age makes the greatest difference among the least educated; the best educated are likely to vote at all ages.

For activities other than voting, the curvilinear pattern has been reported by Nie, Verba, and Kim (1974) in the five nations they studied—Austria, India, Japan, Nigeria, and the United States. In each nation (with minor variations), political participation of various kinds (all modes mentioned earlier, except protest) rises in the early years, reaches a peak in the middle years, and declines in old age. The heterogeneity of cultures studied gives us confidence about the validity of the findings. When the authors controlled for educational variation among different age-cohorts, the age difference disappeared. Thus, the lower activity rate among the elderly reflects their lower average educational attainment and not a withdrawal from politics. The young emerge as genuine underparticipants. If it were not for their above-average educational level, they would have still lower participation rates. Younger citizens who have had longer residence in the community are often active, which suggests that identification with the community is an important intervening variable. Being married (Olsen, 1972) and owning a home (Alford and Scoble, 1968) also lead to increased political participation.

There is little evidence connecting the number and age of children to political participation, but what exists suggests couples with young children participate less than couples with no children or with older children (Milbrath, 1965).

The usual age-participation relation may not hold for blacks in the United States. One study in the South found that blacks under thirty-five were more active than those over thirty-five (Agger, Goldrich, and Swanson, 1964). In another study in the South, two things were found to distinguish black political participation: The peak of black political activity occurs at a much earlier age than for southern whites or for Americans in general, and the drop in activity in the fifties and sixties is very steep (Matthews and Prothro, 1966). Probably some generational experiences peculiar to American blacks are at work here. Most of the older blacks in the South grew up in a period of open and often official political repression. We may expect black rates to fit the national patterns more closely after the present older generation of blacks has passed from the scene.

Why should middle-aged or older people participate more than the young? Lane (1959, p. 218) suggests several reasons:

> In maturity certain things occur in the normal lifetime which tend to increase motivation and the pressure to take part in the political life of the community. A person acquires property, hence one of the most important forces politicizing the local citizen comes to bear upon him—the question of the assessment and tax on his house. Then too, the family includes children who need playgrounds and schools and therefore the mother finds new stakes in politics. Because of the children . . . the parents become conscious of themselves as civic models. . . . They are geographically less mobile. . . . Dreams of solving status and income problems through rapid personal mobility may suffer erosion, and a more solid alignment with class and ethnic groups emerges. Vocational interests become more salient. The increased economic security associated with middle age provides freedom of attention and psychic energy for political matters often not available at an earlier stage in life.

I would add to this only that political activity may also be the result of cumulative experiences—older people have had more opportunities to acquire the habits and skills of political participation.

Organizational Involvement. Few factors compare with organizational involvement in importance as predictors of individual political participation. Many studies show that organizationally involved citizens participate in politics at rates far greater than uninvolved citizens. Erbe (1964) cites fourteen studies and Milbrath (1965) cites twenty in support of this conclusion. In addition, see Alford and Scoble, 1968; Almond and Verba, 1963; Erbe, 1964; Inkeles, 1969; G. Johnson, 1971; Lane, 1959; Lipset, 1960; Matthews and Prothro, 1966; Milbrath, 1965; Nie, Powell, and Prewitt, 1969; Olsen, 1972, 1973; Rokkan and Campbell, 1960; Rosenau, 1974; Sallach, Babchuk, and Booth, 1972; Verba and Nie, 1972; Verba, Ahmed, and Bhatt, 1971; Verba, Nie, and Kim, 1971. The close relationship between organizational and political activity occurs not only because many of the same characteristics and attitudes lead to both organizational and political participation, but also probably because organized voluntary groups are important mobilizers of political activities. In addition, organizational participation increases political participation because it broadens one's sphere of interests, concerns, interpersonal contacts, and leadership skills.

Several studies have supported this view of organizational involvement as independently related to political participation rather than a spurious reflection of socioeconomic status and other variables that correlate significantly with both organizational and political participation (Alford and Scoble, 1968; Erbe, 1964; Nie, Powell, and Prewitt, 1969; Olsen, 1972, 1974; Verba and Nie, 1972). Furthermore, it appears that organizations can mobilize their membership without first changing attitudes. Organizational members who choose to participate in politics are not necessarily more informed, nor do they feel more efficacious or more dutiful than the general citizenry (Nie, Powell, and Prewitt, 1969; Verba and Nie, 1972). Finally, the effects of organizational participation on political participation are cumulative. The greater the number of one's organizational affiliations, the greater the likelihood of one's participation in political activity.

Organizational mobilization is especially important for relatively deprived people such as blacks in the United States and the untouchables in India (Verba, Ahmed, and Bhatt, 1971). The evidence suggests group membership boosts the participation rate of lower socioeconomic status individuals to a greater extent than similar membership does for higher socioeconomic status individuals. Thus, organizations become the channels that help narrow the participation gap between the lower and the upper strata of society.

This section has dealt with demographic factors as determinants of participation in conventional political activities. In order to explain many of the findings, it has been necessary to assume that attitudes and personality traits are intermediary variables between a particular social attribute and political behavior. The next two sections discuss several personality and attitudinal characteristics as predictors of conventional political participation.

Personality Determinants

It is not easy to establish clear and reliable connections between personality and political behavior. The difficulty may stem in part from differing conceptions of personality. In the past, most psychologists have defined personality very broadly to include not only enduring personality traits but beliefs, attitudes, and values as well. Most political scientists have had narrower conceptions of personality as involving stable and enduring traits and needs but not attitudes (Greenstein, 1969; Knutson, 1973). I use Reddy and Smith's (1972, pp. 277–278) distinction between personality and attitudes: "Personality can be understood and analyzed in terms of traits or dimensions, that is, in terms of relatively enduring, transsituational dispositions which are relevant and salient in a large variety of situations. Seen in this fashion, *personality traits form a continuum with attitudes. The latter, though perhaps quite relevant and salient in their own realm, are more bound to a specific situation and are potentially less enduring.*" The concept of personality traits has been and continues to be useful in political science research. However, social psychologists are currently engaged in heated debate over the validity of the trait construct. (See, for example, Alston, 1975; Buss, 1977.)

After reviewing the literature on the nature and variety of personality traits, I identified the following clusters of traits as relevant for the study of political activity: (1) extraversion, sociability, friendliness; (2) ego strength, competence, self-confidence; (3) authoritarianism, dogmatism; (4) psychic needs (Maslow's need hierarchy); (5) anomie, alienation; (6) assertiveness, aggressiveness, dominance; (7) achievement motivation, creativity; (8) flexibility, adaptability; (9) empathy, relational closeness; (10) morality, superego strength; (11) high energy level; and (12) planning, future orientation. Most of these clusters are based on a list developed by Reddy and Smith (1972). These categories are neither exhaustive nor mutually exclusive.

The study of personality in relation to political behavior has not been a fertile undertaking, at least not in comparison with the study of demographic and attitudinal determinants of political behavior. Available research is limited mainly to the first four categories in my list. Greenstein (1969) and Knutson (1973) suggest a greater focus on personality-related political behavior research, but perhaps it is too soon for these treatises to have had any impact on research. In this section, I discuss existing research on the first four clusters in the list; studies of the latter eight clusters do not exist.

Extraversion, Sociability, Friendliness. Some studies have linked ease in social interactions with political participation. Sociable personalities are more likely to enter politics and to take leading roles once they enter it. Support for this finding comes from Kuroda (1967), Milbrath (1960), and Milbrath and Klein (1962). In the area of social participation, which is related to political participation, Gough (1952) found a positive correlation between extraversion and participation in extracurricular (voluntary) activities among high school students. Martin and Siegel (1953) found that "gregariousness" was positively associated with group participation among a sample of male undergraduate students. In his study of Chilean voluntary organizations, Smith (1966) found that various measures of extraversion were positively related with active participation among organization members. In their cross-cultural study, Almond and Verba (1963) related national differences in political participation to levels of social activity. Nations high on social interaction (the United States and the United Kingdom) were also high on participation in politics by their citizenry, as compared with nations scoring low on sociability (Italy, for example). In a study of opinion leaders, gregariousness was related to performance in leadership roles (Katz and Lazarsfeld, 1955). In a study of a small community in Japan, Kuroda (1967) found that politically active respondents were highly sociable.

The relationship between extraversion and political participation is not a mere artifact of socioeconomic variance. In a few studies where statistical controls for social status effects were introduced, sociability and political participation were still significantly related.

Ego Strength, Competence, Self-Confidence. Self-confidence is closely associated with a sense of civic competence or feelings of political efficacy. Persons who are generally self-confident are also likely to exhibit feelings of effectiveness vis-a-vis political situations. Many of the findings discussed under civic competence attitudes also therefore hold true in this context. In general, the conclusion of many studies is that persons with a sense of confidence are more likely to assume political activist roles (Campbell and others, 1960; Gore and Rotter, 1963; Lane, 1959; Milbrath, 1965, 1972; Rosen and Salling, 1971). As might be expected, persons whose parents had high status (in education and income level) are more likely to develop ego strength. Verba and Nie (1972) and Nie, Powell, and Prewitt (1969) suggest socioeconomic status affects political participation largely through shaping such personality traits as ego strength and sociability. This is truer for activities like campaigning and making political contacts, where supportive attitudes and personality traits are necessary, than for activities like voting or attending a mass meeting.

Authoritarianism, Dogmatism. Since the publication of *The Authoritarian Personality* (Adorno and others, 1950), there have been many studies on authoritarianism. Christie and Cook (1958) list two hundred and sixty bibliographic references through 1956. For later reviews, see Greenstein (1969), Knapp (1976), Knutson (1972), and Sanford (1973). The central disposition that characterizes an authoritarian personality is believed to be a submission-aggression syndrome—submission to those above and aggression toward those below. An incisive description of this trait in German folklore is caught by the symbolism of the "bicyclist's personality"—"Above they bow, below they kick" (Greenstein, 1969).

In spite of the large volume of research on authoritarianism, there is very little that strongly supports either a positive or a negative correlation between this personality trait and political participation. The Michigan Survey Research Center's 1956 election study included a shortened version of the F-scale (the original measure of authoritarianism). This scale was not significantly related to the "campaign activity index." Controls for education and for response set did not alter the results. Similar findings are reported by Harned (1961) and Hennessy (1959). A secondary analysis of a 1952 postelection study was done by Lane (1955), who found that, with education controlled, there was no difference between authoritarians and nonauthoritarians in voting and only minor differences in other political activities. The authoritarians were slightly less likely to campaign or to feel politically efficacious.

In contrast to studies reporting a lack of relationship between authoritarianism and political participation is the negative relationship between authoritarianism and political activism reported by Milbrath and Klein (1962) in their study of Washington lobbyists. Kornhauser (1959) also found support for an inverse relationship. Knutson (1972) suggests the relationship between authoritarianism and political participation will vary by the type of authoritarian being studied. Authoritarians with physical and material needs are likely to be nonparticipants; those motivated by unmet affection and esteem needs will take on activist roles. In summary, data on the relationship between authoritarianism and political activity are ambiguous and inconsistent.

A psychological trait closely related to authoritarianism is that of dogmatism or "closed mindedness" (Rokeach, 1960). There is a close association between dogmatism and psychic deprivation (Knutson, 1972), and so the relationship of this attribute to political participation should be of theoretical interest. However, very little work has been done in this area. In one study, dogmatism and political participation were found to be inversely related; but the correlation coefficient was only -.15 (Knutson, 1972). In contrast, DiRenzo (1967) found that a sample of Italian legislators scored relatively high on dogmatism, suggesting a positive correlation between this trait and political activity. However, the comparison group was not a random sample of the population or matched controls. As with authoritarianism, then, we cannot draw any firm conclusions from existing data on dogmatism and political activity.

Psychic Needs. Maslow (1954) has developed a hierarchy of five need areas: physical, safety, affection, self-esteem, and self-actualization. The first four needs may be termed deficiency needs; the fifth is a need for psychic fulfillment. These are hierarchically organized in terms of their potency—the lower needs override higher needs. Knutson (1972) has explored the relationship of this hypothesized need hierarchy to political participation. Evidence from a nonrandom sample of 495 adults in the state of Oregon supported the conclusion that lower-level unfulfilled needs are inversely related to political activism. Persons with unmet physical and security needs tend to be authoritarian, dogmatic, intolerant of ambiguity, and marred by anxiety; and all these traits were negatively related to level of political participation, lending further validity to Knutson's formulation.

When we move up the need hierarchy to the level of affection and esteem needs, contradictory predictions can be made regarding these needs and political participation. Lasswell (1930) argues that political leaders enter politics in order to compensate for their unmet esteem needs. George and George's (1956, pp. 114–115) study of Woodrow Wilson supports this thesis: "His interest in power, in political leadership, was based, we submit, on the need to compensate for damaged self-esteem."

Lane (1959), Milbrath, (1965), and Knutson (1972) take a contradictory position. Lane argues that individuals suffering from psychic conflicts spend so much energy on resolving these conflicts they have little energy left to assume activist roles in the political arena. Milbrath (1965, p. 82) reviewed several studies (Browning and Jacob, 1964; Jensen, 1960; McConaughy, 1950; Milbrath and Klein, 1962) and concluded, "The available empirical evidence on this point (for the United States only) suggests that *persons with high power motivation are not likely to enter politics.*" Knutson (1972) correlated psychic fulfillment with political participation and found that the slightly positive association (.14) was reduced to zero value when socioeconomic status (SES) controls were introduced. Thus, available empirical studies suggest that the existence of unmet psychic needs is not related to political participation; however, more research is needed to come to any firm conclusion.

The role of personality in political behavior is probably a great deal more pervasive than the brief research summary presented here suggests. However, the exact dimensions of the relation between personality variables and political activity have yet to be uncovered or convincingly described.

Attitudinal Determinants

People have predispositions and orientations toward political objects and situations. Orientations have cognitive, affective, and evaluative components. The cognitive component includes information about the political system and its various parts; the affective component involves positive or negative feelings; the evaluative component involves judgments about political matters or objects. There is a large political science literature that treats the impact of attitudinal factors on political participation. I will abstract briefly and describe a number of propositions gleaned from this literature.

Psychological Involvement. Psychological involvement (sometimes called political involvement) refers to the degree to which citizens are interested in and concerned about politics and public affairs. We can think of psychological involvement as a continuum. At one pole are those completely submerged into the political conflicts surrounding them. At the other extreme are those totally preoccupied with their private lives, who have little or no interest in public issues. During election times, the level of psychological involvement for many citizens increases dramatically—though only temporarily.

Psychological involvement is a central variable affecting exposure to political stimuli as well as participation in political activities. At least a dozen studies in several countries have shown that persons who are more concerned about political matters are more likely to be activists (Berelson, Lazarsfeld, and McPhee, 1954; Campbell, Gurin, and Miller, 1954; Campbell and others, 1960; Goel, 1975; Inkeles, 1969; Janowitz and Marvick, 1953; Kuroda, 1967; Lazarsfeld, Berelson, and Gaudet, 1944; Matthews and Prothro, 1966; Milbrath, 1972; Miller, 1952; Nie, Powell, and Prewitt, 1969; Pesonen, 1960, 1961; Verba and Nie, 1972.) In general, psychological involvement in political matters relates more strongly to campaign and community activities and less strongly to voting and parochial participation (that is, participation in political activities for personal or family reasons; Verba, Nie, and Kim, 1971). Voting is less dependent on personal factors. Many individuals vote because of partisan commitments or group pressures; and in comparison with other activities, little initiative or psychological involvement is necessary in order to vote. Psychological involvement also tends not to be related to parochial participation, which relates more to narrow and private problems of the individual or a family and has little to do with broader public issues. In the Buffalo study (Milbrath, 1971), psychological involvement related somewhat differently to political participation by race. Whites were more dependent on personal motivation for becoming active in politics; in the black community, group associations were more important.

Sense of Civic Obligation. A sense of obligation to participate in politics is another important political attitude relating to participation. The duty to participate ranks very high in the United States; in several different surveys, 80 to 90 percent of the sample indicate adherence to this norm (Campbell, Gurin, and Miller, 1954; Campbell and others, 1960; Dennis, 1970; Milbrath, 1968). In a study of Stockport, England, 82 percent said they regarded voting as a duty (Rose and Mossawir, 1967). The sense that voting is a duty may also be taking hold in nations where democratic institutions are relatively new; in Japan, between 40 and 50 percent of respondents in different samples report adherence to such an attitude (Richardson, 1974).

Feeling a duty to participate seems to carry over to political actions; several studies show that persons feeling a duty to participate are more likely to do so (Alford and Scoble, 1968; Campbell, Gurin, and Miller, 1954; Campbell and others, 1960; Dennis, 1970; Kuroda, 1965; Marvick and Nixon, 1961; Mayntz, 1961; Milbrath, 1968).

The citizen-duty attitude relates strongly to social position variables; upper socioeconomic status persons, especially those with higher education, are more likely to develop a sense of citizen duty (Almond and Verba, 1963; Campbell, Gurin, and Miller, 1954; Campbell and others, 1960; Dennis, 1970; Eulau, 1962). In the United States, race seems to play very little, if any, role in the development of this attitude (Dennis, 1970; Milbrath, 1968). However, Campbell, Gurin, and Miller (1954) found that persons growing up in the American South were less likely to develop it. In the United States, there is also very little age or gender difference in expression of a sense of political duty (Almond and Verba, 1963; Dennis, 1970; Campbell, Gurin, and Miller, 1954). The psychological mechanisms by which conscience and feelings of duty are instilled into personality structure are complex and incompletely understood. Generally, it can be said that in stable democratic societies, most citizens seem to learn early that it is their obligation to be at least minimally active in the political arena; and this sense of political obligation is positively associated with political participation.

Political Efficacy. The feeling of political efficacy is perhaps the most thoroughly researched attitude variable in political science. Measures of this feeling, originally identified by the Survey Research Center at the University of Michigan, have been employed as a predictor of a wide variety of behaviors and orientations, including both conventional and unconventional political participation. Political efficacy is the feeling that one is capable of influencing the decision-making process. When people believe they can exert influence on government officials or on public issues, they are said to be subjectively efficacious or competent. The concept of political efficacy is related to such concepts as "civic competence," "citizen efficacy," and, inversely, "political incapability," "political futility," and "political powerlessness." These terms will be used interchangeably here.

Two different ways of measuring the concept have been popular in the research literature, one developed by the Michigan team (Campbell and others, 1960) and the other by Almond and Verba (1963) for their five-nation survey. The Michigan scale taps the generalized feeling that institutions are responsive to citizen pressure. The Almond and Verba scale taps the feeling that respondents themselves have the personal capacity to wield influence. In a secondary analysis of the five-nation data, Muller (1970) found at least two dimensions to the concept of political competence. Similarly, Converse (1972a) discusses two forms of political efficacy: trust in system responsiveness and personal feelings of political competence.

The relationship between feelings of efficacy and conventional political participation is broadly documented. People in a variety of cultures who feel they can do something to influence government and politics participate at a higher level than do those who do not feel that way (Agger, Goldstein, and Pearl, 1961; Almond and Verba, 1963; Baker, 1973; Barnes, 1966; Campbell and others, 1960; Cataldo and Kellstedt, 1968; Dahl, 1961; Dean, 1960; Dennis, 1970; DiPalma, 1970; Erbe, 1964; Finifter, 1970; Goel, 1975; Hamilton, 1971; Lane, 1959; Matthews and Prothro, 1966; Milbrath, 1971; Muller, 1970; Olsen, 1969; Sallach, Babchuk, and Booth, 1972; Tessler, 1972; Thompson and Horton, 1960; Verba and Nie, 1972; Welch, Comer and Steinman, 1973). In most studies, the positive correlation persists after variation due to socioeconomic variables has been taken into account. Thus, the sense of political efficacy emerges as a powerful independent attitudinal determinant of political activism.

If feelings of efficacy increase political participation, might opportunities for participation not increase one's sense of competence? This point has been argued by several authors (Almond and Verba, 1963; Barnes, 1966; Muller, 1970) and seems highly plausible. Favorable interactions with authorities are likely to enhance one's sense of political competence; unfavorable interactions can lead to feelings of futility. Whether causality can be inferred, it is clear that political participation and subjective competence are positively related.

Political Alienation, Cynicism, Distrust. The history of the concept of alienation is a long one, with roots going back to Marx, Durkheim, and Weber. Alienation and anomie have been the subject matter of extensive study by political sociologists in the last two decades. Easton and Dennis (1967) list about thirty articles and books dealing with political efficacy and its correlates; this list can be considerably lengthened now. The earlier studies focused on the fate of the individual in the wake of industrialization and materialism; the later ones by political scientists have been concerned with the fate and survivability of regimes. In addition to alienation, much of this literature uses terms such as "political efficacy," "civic competence," "legitimacy," "diffuse support," and "system allegiance."

It is not easy to define alienation because it is a politically fashionable concept that often implies a variety of negative attitudes toward modern society in general and capitalist political systems in particular. Several writers have attempted to decompose the concept into its component parts. For instance, Seeman (1959) outlines five components of alienation: powerlessness, meaninglessness, normlessness, isolation, and self-estrangement. Finifter (1970) presents a fourfold scheme for political alienation: political powerlessness, political meaninglessness, political normlessness, and political isolation. Similar approaches are found in the works of Allardt (1970), Dean (1960), Gamson (1968), Nandy (1974), Neal and Rettig (1967), Olsen (1969), and Struening and Richardson (1965). A few of these studies are distinctive in that they demonstrate separate modes of alienation empirically through factor and cluster analysis (Finifter, 1970; Neal and Rettig, 1967; Struening and Richardson, 1965).

Borrowing from these commentators for the purposes of this review, I define alienation as having three dimensions. First, there is *political powerlessness.* This may be defined as feelings that one cannot affect or influence what goes on in politics. This is the obverse of political efficacy, discussed previously, and thus will not be discussed further except to note that powerlessness is a frequently used measure of alienation (Dean, 1960; Finifter, 1970; Nandy, 1974; Neal and Rettig, 1967; Olsen, 1969; Seeman, 1959, 1972).

Second, there is *political normlessness,* or anomie, usually defined as a lack of or conflict among perceived norms. Political normlessness involves questioning or rejecting the operating rules of the political system. It is a feeling that the rules governing the society are either fraudulent or broken often by powerful groups and individuals for selfish gain. The politically normless individual in a democratic political system does not perceive the utility of elections or of partisan conflict and may believe elections and parties do more harm than good. In a Communist system, rejection of the role of the party as the central and controlling institution suggests normlessness. Transitional or the emerging polities, where old values have broken down but new ones have not yet taken a firm hold, are likely to contain many more anomic citizens than the more established, stable polities (Dean, 1960, 1961; DiPalma, 1970; Finifter, 1970; Keniston, 1965; Nandy, 1974; Struening and Richardson, 1965). No satisfactory measurement approach for this concept exists. A short anomie scale developed by Srole has been used in several studies (Meier and Bell, 1959; Srole, 1951, 1956), but this scale emphasizes general personal life situations rather than attitudes toward political objects or situations.

The third dimension of alienation consists of feelings of *political distrust and cynicism*—distrust in the government and political leadership of the country. Trusting citizens believe that government activity tends to improve conditions, that politics is not all dirty, and that public officials in general work for the citizens' general welfare. In contrast, politically untrusting citizens tend to feel that politicians often manipulate the people, that the country's leadership is corrupt and self-serving, and that special interests wield too much power. Almond and Verba (1963) discuss "output affect," which is measured by political trust items, and distinguish it from "input affect," which is political efficacy. The level of political trust is more likely than the other two political alienation dimensions identified here to vary over time. Political trust is high in economically good times and low in bad times. A prolonged period of distrust can, of course, lead to questioning and even rejecting constitutional norms (that is, can lead to political normlessness, as previously used). The "political cynicism" scale developed by Agger, Goldstein, and Pearl (1961) is one way of measuring of this attitude; another is a battery of five items used in the Michigan studies (Miller, 1974).

There is some difficulty with this kind of multidimensional definition of alienation. If it is defined as rejection of the political system or separation from it, then it is possible that some people may feel powerless and yet remain loyal because openness in the political system is not particularly important to them. To see this distinction, one only needs to think of "subjects" under dictatorial regimes, generally powerless but not always alienated. (Both Ellen Flerlage and Guenther Kress made this distinction in personal communications.) It is also possible that one can distrust a given leadership without rejecting the whole system. For a view that powerlessness, normlessness, and cynicism ought to be regarded as sources of alienation rather than its definition, see Citrin and others (1975) and Schwartz (1973).

Whatever the best definition, when one considers the relationship between various feelings of alienation and political participation, one finds over and over again that negative feelings about the political system, no matter how measured, are inversely related to conventional political participation. Evidence comes from a variety of samples (Agger, Goldstein, and Pearl, 1961; Almond and Verba, 1963; Dean, 1960; Erbe, 1964; Finifter, 1970; Kobayashi, 1974; Miller, 1974; Muller, 1970; Nandy, 1974; Olsen, 1969; Schwartz, 1973; Seeman, 1972; Templeton, 1966; Thompson and Horton, 1960). Some other evidence indicates alienation is related positively to unconventional political participation. (See Chapter Five.)

Party Identification. For over two decades, the concept of party identification has been a fundamental explanatory variable for the level as well as the direction of U.S. electoral participation. As defined by scholars at the University of Michigan Survey Research Center, party identification is a measure of psychological attachment or commitment to a given party. The importance of party identification lies in its stability over long periods of time. Party identification represents a long-term force in contrast to candidate and issue preferences, which are short-term forces (Campbell and others, 1960, 1966). The concept of party identification has been extended to the study of electoral behavior in several European and Asian countries (Butler and Stokes, 1971; Campbell and Valen, 1961; Converse, 1969; Converse and Dupeux, 1962; Kothari, 1970).

The cross-national utility and relevance of this concept may be questionable because party identification is unstable and its psychological content is meager and poorly developed in many non-American cultures (Eldersveld and Kubota, 1973; Shively, 1972). However, a number of studies in several nations have shown that persons who strongly identify with or intensely prefer *some* party are more likely to participate actively in the political process (Butler and Stokes, 1971; Campbell and Valen, 1961; Campbell, Gurin, and Miller, 1954; Campbell and others, 1960; Goel, 1975; Marvick and Nixon, 1961; Matthews and Prothro, 1966; Milbrath, 1972; Nie and Verba, 1975; Pesonen, 1960, 1968; Valen and Katz, 1964; Verba, Ahmed, and Bhatt, 1971; Verba and Nie, 1972).

The impact of partisan attachments on political participation is independent of the impact of socioeconomic variables. At all levels of education or income, those who are strong partisans (party identified) are more active than the weak partisans or independents (Verba and Nie, 1972). The impact of party affiliation on participation varies with the mode of political activity. It correlates most strongly with voting and electoral activities, but only minimally with communal activity and parochial participation modes as defined earlier (Milbrath, 1972; Verba and Nie, 1972; Verba, Ahmed, and Bhatt, 1971). This pattern is to be expected, for both voting and electoral work are partisan activities and would therefore clearly benefit from partisan orientations. In contrast, bother communal and parochial participation tend to be nonpartisan in nature.

Unlike the positive correlation between socioeconomic status and certain other psychological factors (feelings of efficacy and duty, political interests, and such), party identification and status may be somewhat negatively correlated. In the Verba and Nie (1972) U.S. study, 43 percent among the lower-status citizens identified strongly with a political party versus 34 percent in the middle stratum and 31 percent in the upper stratum. Because party identification and political participation are positively associated and a somewhat greater proportion of the lower-status citizens have strong party identification, do the lower-status segments in the United States receive a boost in participation as a result of greater partisan orientations, as Rokkan and Campbell (1960) have suggested for the Norwegian citizenry? The answer is probably no. In contrast to Norwegian parties, U.S. parties are broad based, drawing support from across status levels. As a result, they do not contribute to narrowing the participation gap between upper- and lower-status citizens. Nie and Verba's (1975) research shows that the impact of party varies by nation. In those nations where parties are aligned with particular social and ethnic groups (such as Austria, Japan, and the Netherlands), parties narrow the socioeconomic gap in political participation. By contrast, broad-based parties (such as in the United States and India) do not perform this function.

In addition to party preference, candidate and issue preferences are also related to the level of political participation. Several studies have shown that individuals who have intense preferences for either candidates or issues are more likely to be active in politics (Campbell, Gurin, and Miller, 1954; Campbell and others, 1960; Marvick and Nixon, 1961). If a person's issue preferences pull in different directions (one issue toward one party and another issue toward another party), the likelihood of his or her participation in politics is lessened as a result of these "cross pressures" (Campbell, Gurin, and Miller, 1954; Campbell and others, 1960). Conversely, congruence in the direction of one's political preferences increases the likelihood of participation (Lane, 1959, Lipset, 1960).

Group Consciousness. Another attitudinal variable similar to party identification is group consciousness, a sense of belonging to a group (or a social category, especially an ethnic group) and awareness of the salience of one's group. Group consciousness can involve a belief system leading to greater political activity. The most vivid example of this phenomenon is to be found in the American black population. Few whites manifest a comparable group feeling as "whites." Evidence indicates that persons who exhibit consciousness of (usually ethnic) group identification participate at a higher level (Verba and Nie, 1972; Verba, Nie, and Kim, 1971). Although blacks with high socioeconomic status tend to be most conscious of a black identity, the relationship between ethnic group feelings and political participation itself is independent of the influence of socioeconomic factors.

In a study of U.S. southern blacks, a related concept—"racial pride and confidence"—was found to correlate strongly with political participation. "Feelings of racial inadequacy do not seem appreciably to reduce Negro voting rates, but they do diminish the frequency with which Negroes participate beyond the voting stage. A sense of racial inferiority is largely incompatible with high levels of political activism" (Matthews and Prothro, 1966, p. 298). Parallel data pertaining to a deprived ethnic group in India, the untouchables, sustain these generalizations (Verba, Ahmed, and Bhatt, 1971).

Conclusion

I have reviewed the extensive literature relating numerous variables to participation in conventional political activities. As the review indicates, the greatest amount of research continues to be on demographic variables as predictors of political participation, with relatively less emphasis being placed on attitudinal and personality determinants. The establishment of links between personality traits and political activity is the weakest and the least researched area, although some promising work has been published in recent years. Since Milbrath's publication of *Political Participation* in 1965, the most promising development has been improved conceptualization of the dependent variable, political participation, which is now understood to be multidimensional rather than unidimensional. It is important to note, though, that the findings synthesized in Milbrath's 1965 review continue to appear remarkably stable, as shown, for example, by the conclusions of the more recent Milbrath and Goel (1977) review.

CHAPTER 5

Unconventional
Political Participation

Robert W. Hunt
M. Lal Goel

There have been striking amounts of politicized anger in contemporary societies. In the sixties alone, efforts to change regimes, policies, or elites by public protest and violent agitation occurred in well over 90 percent of the nations of the world (Gurr, 1970). In the developing nations of Asia, Africa, and Latin America during the same time period, violence often created a politics of confrontation—strikes, riots, terrorist kidnappings, political assassinations, and bloody civil wars. Even the United States, with its extraordinary resource base and historic record of political accommodation, has seen a dramatic rise in politically motivated violence; riots and bombings have taken place throughout the country and have produced human and material destructiveness on a scale scarcely predictable a few years ago. Despite some decline from the

Note: The authors wish to acknowledge aid from the following in commenting on an earlier draft: James Hottois, Lester Milbrath, James Munro, and Emma Brossard. Typing assistance, for which the authors express much appreciation, was provided by Kay Trine, Karen Born, and Betty Harmon.

violence of the late 1960s and early 1970s, we are forced to wonder whether "normal" politics should not now clearly encompass the politics of protest and militant resistance.

This chapter discusses individual participation in unconventional political activities, primarily acts of political violence. We review the literature on the subject and present the major theoretical propositions advanced to explain such behavior. Expanding on Gurr (1970) and Nieburg (1969), we define the dependent variable as follows: Unconventional political behavior refers to acts of disruption, destruction, and injury within a political community against the political regime, its actors, or its policies. This definition includes an exceedingly wide range of behaviors, from assassinations, to military coups, to less-focused forms of militant activities by segments of the public at large. It encompasses a range of activities from protest, which is aimed at policy change without challenging the basic authority of policymakers, to partial and finally total resistance, central features of revolutionary politics (Bell, 1973).

Studies of unconventional or resistance behavior have proceeded apace with the growing public concern over the destructive and harmful quality of such activity. However, despite the exciting and often fruitful nature of current research, there is considerable tentativeness and ambiguity in it. There are competing and often overlapping paradigms but no verified comprehensive theories. More limited explanations are plentiful, but the causal factors discussed are usually not linked systematically; and the terms are not defined precisely enough to allow for significant comparative and cumulative research. Moreover, some explanatory factors are relatively well researched while other areas have been ignored (Eckstein, 1972).

As a consequence, a review of the current literature on political violence must involve primarily listing specific, limited, often overlapping, and sometimes even contradictory hypotheses. To structure such a review, we shall utilize as a general framework the sequential specificity model described by Smith and Reddy (1972a) in their discussion of the determinants of individual participation in organizations. According to them, the sequential specificity model is a set of focal points arranged in terms of proximity to the behavioral acts in question that link together in a reasonable causal and time sequence the kinds of factors pointed to in existing literature as significant independent variables. As Smith and Reddy (1972a, p. 322) noted,

> Basic to the present model is the attempt to explain individual behavior by means of a variety of levels of explanatory variables that range from *very general levels* of explanation to

very specific levels. Each level makes its own contribution to the understanding, explanation, and prediction of the phenomenon in question, and each level tends to have some influence on the next level in the sequence. Each level has its own proper focus, orientation, general mode of influence, and special areas of impact. Taken together the several levels serve to provide a reasonable comprehensive basis for the understanding, explanation, and prediction of the behavior or action in question.

Historical Context

Many writers take the movement of societies from one stage of socioeconomic development to another to be the historical backdrop against which violence becomes more probable. Participation in political violence is clearly and demonstrably more likely when old social and cultural patterns are in the process of breaking down and when new ones have not yet fully taken root. This observation is based on the extensive research conducted by Sorokin (1957) into the history of a number of nations. Olson (1963) and Huntington (1968) have argued that rapid economic change, whether up or down, also produces instability and turmoil. This proposition, of course, runs contrary to the commonly held view in the United States that economic growth produces stability. Olson has argued that rapid economic growth disrupts social groupings and thus increases the number of dislocated individuals; increases urbanization, which again undermines social ties and produces alienation; increases the number of people with "new riches," which widens the gap between the rich and the poor; and increases literacy and exposure to communications, which in turn enhance aspirations that cannot be satisfied.

In historical terms, the most fundamental source of socioeconomic change has been the advance of the industrial revolution. Dramatic changes in manufacturing and commercial processes are key precipitants of profoundly new forms of social differentiation and inequality. The instability and violence proneness of the so-called "transitional" societies can be understood as a consequence of the penetration of the industrial revolution. One of the primary early effects of this revolution is the creation of a broadly based system of markets— interdependent and monetized. Consequent to this is the transformation of material resources into commodities and of social relationships from emotional and personal into relatively impersonal. The development of national administrative and legal systems that accompanies new economic institutions has similar effects and further reduces the autonomy of local communities and their capacity to provide essential services.

The introduction of secular education and of new work organizations with achieved rather than ascribed roles helps speed disintegration of the traditional culture and development of personal expectations incompatible with conventional norms (Eisenstadt, 1966; Gamer, 1976; Hagopian, 1974; Kornhauser, 1959; Wolf and Hansen, 1972). As Greene (1974, p. 132) comments, "One of the fundamental preconditions for revolutions, then, is not so much the poverty of peasants (or workers), but economic change that threatens the relative security and traditional status of men and women living according to norms and habits that are rapidly becoming anachronistic."

These are the factors probably associated with the greater levels of protest and violence in transitional societies. But there are, of course, national differences in the scope and intensity of these activities; and a significant concern in the development literature is with what impedes or enhances the potential for protest and resistance behavior during transition periods. Among the more common conclusions are that the prospects for political instability and violence increase under the following conditions:

1. When rapid change occurs prior to the formation of a common identity and/or the emergence of indigenous leadership with substantial governing experience (Nordlinger, 1968; Schmitt, 1974)
2. When the spread of commerce and industry and the rate of development is highly uneven, thereby creating tension between the more traditional and the more modern sectors or geographic areas of the population (Gamer, 1976; Greene, 1974; Moore; 1966, Organski, 1969)
3. When vastly different cultural groupings exist side by side, accentuating problems of integration in the political system (Enloe, 1973; Geertz, 1967; Pye, 1966; von der Mehden, 1973)
4. When population pressures are especially severe, increasing land rents and creating inflationary pressures, and where outward migration is precluded (Moore, 1966; Wakeman, 1977; Wolf, 1969)
5. When commercialization and industrial development are very rapid, thereby creating problems for political adaptation (Feierabend and Feierabend, 1972; Lipset, 1960)
6. When "developmental crises," including population pressures, delegitimization of traditional authority, and growth of participant demands, occur simultaneously instead of one at a time (Binder and others, 1971; Greene, 1974; Pye, 1966)
7. When political institutions do not develop at the same rate as popular aspirations and demands (Huntington, 1968; Lerner, 1958)

Proximate Social and Political Context

Recent sociological approaches to the study of political upheaval have attempted to link it to social and economic inequality. Elaborating on or modifying Karl Marx's reductionist analysis, efforts have been directed at delineating the forms of social differentiation. A general proposition receiving extensive support is that societies are more prone to political disruption and violence when there is considerable economic inequality and when value stocks, especially economic ones, are relatively fixed, thus limiting opportunities for upward mobility (Gurr, 1970; Huntington, 1968; Russett, 1972). There is statistical validity to this proposition: Russett (1972) correlated inequality in land ownership with deaths from political violence in forty-seven nations and found a positive correlation between the two (r = .46). This relationship was even stronger in poor, predominantly agricultural societies where limitation to a small plot of land (the chief source of income) is tantamount to being condemned to perpetual poverty. Similarly, Tanter and Midlarsky (1967) found that between 1955 and 1970 revolutions occurred most often in societies with a high degree of land inequality. When economic inequality corresponds with regional, religious, ethnic, or racial divisions in the society, the probability of potential confrontation between classes or social strata becomes particularly high and dangerous (von der Mehden, 1973). U.S. racial violence is but one example of this. However, many studies of American urban riots suggest the relationships here are by no means automatic; nonwhite unemployment rates and the ratio of white to nonwhite income have not been reliable predictors of these riots. (See Marx and Wood, 1975, for a review of these studies.)

A second indicator of the prospects for political agitation and resistance movements is the viability of institutions that stand at the interface between the different elite strata on the one hand and between the elite and the masses on the other. There is substantial evidence, for example, that the prospects for these activities are particularly great in societies with few formal voluntary organizations or with narrowly sectarian organizations (Clinard and Abbott, 1973; Dahrendorf, 1959; Greene, 1974; Kornhauser, 1959). There is ample evidence as well that when voluntary organizations representing the industrial work force and the rural poor exist and are able to function as effective political power brokers, protest and resistance from these sectors of society is less likely. Labor violence, for instance, seems to have decreased universally with the development and recognition of unions (Taft and Ross, 1969). The development of intermediary organizations between the masses and the elite presumably softens social tensions and makes citizens less available for mobilization in radical, extremist activities (Kornhauser, 1959).

Huntington (1968) has argued that the level of institutionalization in a society—the development of political parties especially—is inversely related to the potential for political instability. Alternatively, other studies (Freeman, 1973; Oberschall, 1973) have suggested that membership in secondary groups can facilitate recruitment to radical and reformist political movements. This is most clearly the case, however, in well-differentiated societies with strong networks of secondary associations and relates, in any event, more to recruitment rates to limited (that is, normative) protest movements (Marx and Wood, 1975).

Next there are several political factors many authors consider conducive to unconventional political behavior. With regard to one of them, regime legitimacy, a well-supported proposition is that political protest and resistance varies inversely with the extent of regime legitimacy (Aberbach and Walker, 1970; Almond and Verba, 1963; Gamson, 1968; Gurr, 1970; Yinger, 1973). A regime is said to be legitimate when the vast majority of citizens regard it as proper and morally worthy of support. If compliance with regime rules is based primarily on coercion, the regime is not regarded as legitimate.

A second attribute of a regime that affects the potential for political agitation and violence is its flexibility and ability to adjust to changing conditions. Historically, the rise of the merchant class and later the working class, with their economic and participatory demands, has posed a considerable test of the adaptive capability of governments. The historically stable political conditions in England, as contrasted with the instability in France, is often explained in terms of the greater adaptive capacity of the British government. Working-class politics in France has always been more extreme than in England; unionization in France was not legalized until 1884 and collective bargaining not until 1936, about fifty years later than in England (Birnie, 1961; Huntington, 1968). Although such flexibility and inflexibility on the part of regime elites is difficult to predict or explain, it appears related to circumstances such as the rate at which new groups seek to enter the political arena, the relative availability of economic resources during times of political challenge, and the degree to which new demands impinge upon the most valued elite prerogatives (Lipset, 1963; Moore, 1966).

Resistance behavior is also associated with governmental coercion, but in a fairly complex way. Generally, the relationship is curvilinear, with relatively permissive and highly coercive nations experiencing less turbulence than countries relying on medium levels of coercion (Feierabend and Feierabend, 1972; Gurr, 1970). Public resistance and violence is, however, more likely when governments resort to indiscriminate repression of dissident behavior and when their response is incommensurate with the apparent threat; even highly repressive regimes may generate resistance in these cases (Downton, 1973; Gurr, 1970). In general, repressive regimes must display consistency in the application of coercion to maximize its inhibitive effect. Consistency depends on such factors as a consensus among governing elites on the use of physical coercion, on the loyalty of military and police forces, and on the availability to dissidents of sanctuaries in remote, nonurban areas or in sympathetic neighboring states (Gurr, 1970; Wolf, 1969).

In the catalogue of social and political factors that lead to collective violence, the effectiveness of protest organizations should also be included. Well-organized protest groups can crystallize and channel discontent (Downton, 1973; Gamson, 1975; Oberschall, 1973). Critical factors determining organizational effectiveness in this case include the following:

1. The existence of sensitive and creative leaders capable of articulating ideologies that focus, interpret, and politicize the strains people feel (Downton, 1973; Lipset and Raab, 1970; Wood, 1974)
2. The availability of resources (including money, land, and leadership roles) for rewarding supporters and attracting potential recruits; the "reward" of serving utopian goals may appeal to only a small percentage of all individuals (Greene, 1974)
3. The development of capacity for protecting members and sympathizers from the coercive power of the regime (Downton, 1973; Wolf, 1969)
4. The creation of affiliative norms and solidarity symbols through, for example, initiation rituals, formal renunciation of previous social ties, and public confession. On occasion, this process is aided by the early stigmatization of dissidents and their organizations by the ruling elites, thus cutting off paths of retreat to nondissident social roles (Downton, 1973; Greene, 1974). Such stigmatization also helps protest organizations avoid what might be called the "effectiveness trap." As these bodies become better able to provide immediate and varied rewards, cohesion and militancy are likely to decline; and they can become more a means for the institutionalization of protest than its exacerbation (Dasgupta, 1973; Gurr, 1970)

Individual-Level Variables

Social Background Factors. Individuals at the forefront of protest movements, as leaders or simply early converts to dramatic action, tend to share similar backgrounds. They commonly have had experiences that make them acutely aware of both the opportunities offered by their society and the obstacles to taking advantage of them. They also tend to have a variety of resources that have increased both their awareness of opportunities and their capacity for action. That is, activists, and activist leaders in particular, tend to come from relatively high-status families and to receive an above-average amount of formal education; some researchers suggest that frustration of expectations learned in the course of attaining this education spawns rebellious dispositions (Caplan, 1970; Flacks, 1970; Gurr, 1970; Keniston, 1968). It is just such a balance of opportunity and frustration in the individual's earliest experiences that Willner (1968) points to in her study of revolutionary charismatic leaders. She found, for example, that these leaders tend to come from heterogeneous family settings where there were significant differences among close relatives on one or more key social dimensions such as religion, ethnicity, education, or social class. Willner suggests these differences were a source of tension that was translated into higher than average expectations for the child. Radical leaders often come from geographically mobile families and so are more likely to have been exposed to varied environments. Many of these individuals come from regions that have historically produced the nation's rebels. These are regions bounded by seacoasts and the frontiers of other countries where foreign penetration was likely to generate the first nationalist responses (Flacks, 1970; Leiden and Schmitt, 1968: Willner, 1968; Wolf, 1971). Political unconventionality is also a factor; activists tend to come from families wherein political concerns were intense and often heretical (Keniston, 1968; Willner, 1968; Wood, 1974). This was one factor distinguishing American student activists from nonactivists all through the sixties and later—even as other social differences began to disappear with the growth in number of protesters (Marx and Wood, 1975).

    This type of background is generally typical both of leaders of the Left (equalizers) and the Right (preservationists). However, more preservationists than equalizers are from the lower-middle sectors of society. They are more often from groups facing a relative decline in competence and status in an increasingly secular and organizationally complex society. They are liable to have experienced more punitive relations with their parents and to have somewhat fewer of the negotiable resources (education, social status, and the like) required for success than their adversaries on the Left. As a result, the giant financial, labor, and industrial organizations of modern society are primary sources of provocation in their lives (Greene, 1974; Lipset, 1960; Lipset and Raab, 1970; Rohter, 1970).

    Presumably, the educational opportunities and experiences that tend to distinguish activists from nonactivists are those that make individuals less likely to internalize prevailing social norms, more sensitive to group differences and status distinctions, and more able to communicate effectively across social boundaries. Higher education generally encourages a critical awareness and tentativeness regarding conventional norms, particularly education in the social sciences, which is likely to involve critical analyses of social institutions (Keniston, 1968; Inkeles and Smith, 1974). Thus, it is not surprising to find that university students are prominent in the higher echelons of resistance organizations. The probability of such involvement is greater during times of economic stagnation, when students feel they will find relatively few outlets for their newly acquired skills (Ellul, 1970; Greene, 1974; Prizzia and Sinsawasdi, 1975).

Rebel leaders have been found to have above-average status in many studies of political resistance and political violence. Militant peasants and workers differ from most revolutionary leaders in level of education and social attainment, but they are still not typical of their own social and economic strata. Wolf (1969, 1971) found that although peasants were generally unlikely recruits for resistance activities, exceptions were "middle peasants," who were either small landowners themselves or were located in peripheral areas outside landlord control. These individuals are often the most conservative bearers of the peasant tradition; but when they find themselves under great pressure, their minimal tactical freedom becomes a facilitator of agitation. Ironically enough, therefore, it is these bastions of the rural order who are most likely to move to destroy it when forced into a precarious balancing act by the economic changes brought on by commercialism (Powell, 1969). Moreover, the probability of militant resistance activity is increased when they find the need to send their sons to the cities to seek supplementary income for the family; this transforms these peasants into channels for political ideas (Greene, 1974; Inkeles and Smith, 1974; Wolf, 1971). Urban contacts, along with leadership provided by students and professionals from the cities, then become additional catalysts for discontent and a basis for an organizational expression of this discontent (Hewitt, 1969; Landsberger, 1969).

The same factors seem to encourage militant protest and resistance in the urban work force. Workers who act forcefully and violently against political elites also tend to be "middles"—neither skilled craftspersons for whom special competence provides good and predictable income nor hardcore umemployed. Moreover, although the unemployed in general are overrepresented in radical protest movements, the most dedicated, steadfast, and ideologically motivated practitioners of violence are likely to be those skilled enough to have found jobs yet most often laid off. It is the threat or actual fact of unemployment among those who believe that steady employment is their right that is most likely to produce a commitment to militant, even violent, protest (Caplan, 1970; Greene, 1974; Zeitlin, 1967).

The record reviewed thus far suggests the background experiences most likely to produce militant resistance behavior are twofold: those that pose contradictions between what individuals see as possible for some and what is possible for them and those that provide individuals with resources for action to rectify discrepancies. By implication, then, the extremely deprived should be unlikely to act violently against the state. A frequent finding is that poor, religious peasants who are bound by semifeudal obligations and the lumpenproletariat in the cities who are impoverished and live on subsistence wages or less are the least likely candidates for revolutionary organizations and political violence. Their dire poverty precludes attraction to the usually distant and often intangible benefits of militant political activity (Davies, 1963; Huntington, 1968; Milbrath, 1965; Nelson, 1970; Wolf, 1969). On occasion, when they do become involved in political protest, their activities are more likely to be formless and short-lived, with little coherent follow-up and with participants motivated more by the potential for immediate gain than by complex reform goals (Gurr, 1970; Huntington, 1968; Ransford, 1968). But even more likely, it is argued, is formless, ill-directed, and nonpolitical protest activity, as in family feuds, petty crime, drunkenness, and religious revivalism. This is violence displaced upon safe targets rather than the sociopolitical institutions likely to be more fundamental sources of the individual's frustrations (Comer, 1969). However, a number of sociological commentators have pointed out that the same behavior tends to remain hidden in the middle and upper classes, and accurate statistics might nearly erase such apparent class differences (Hampden-Turner, 1974).

Psychobiological Factors. A recent body of research on the roots of nonconventional political behavior has focused on innate human aggressiveness. Though these theories are very fashionable, there is serious question about their theoretical utility and validity. Ethologists Konrad Lorenz (1967) and Robert Ardrey (1966) have popularized the view that aggression is part and parcel of the human biological makeup, natural, and instinctive. For Lorenz, the inherent aggressiveness of humankind is a product of the natural selection process; aggressive traits were viable in the environment in which humans developed and so have flourished as humankind evolved. For Ardrey, it is our innate passion for space or territory that creates tendencies for aggression and violence. Freud's work on the "death instinct" is comparable to that of Lorenz and Ardrey. Human aggressiveness, Freud believed, rests on an instinctual wish for destructiveness. This "death wish" is in constant tension with "eros," the life-seeking wish. Part of us wants to build and preserve, but part of us wants to erase life. With our instinctual aggressiveness, we are easily mobilized for violent action, mass movements, and war (Einstein and Freud, 1932).

These approaches have been widely criticized as being too general, as providing little information on the *varying* propensity for individuals or groups to engage in violent acts. The evidence advanced in behalf of these theories has also been questioned. Freud's data, for instance, are seen as too clinical and extremely limited. One critic suggests Freud's whole approach is more "evangelical than scientific" (Davies, 1973a). Criticisms of Ardrey and Lorenz also point to the general nature of their theories and to their tendencies to generalize too easily from animal to human behavior in the face of contradictory evidence—of which they seem unaware (Alland, 1972; Berkowitz, 1968). Consequently, students of political violence have not taken the work of Ardrey, Lorenz, or Freud very seriously.

Another reductionist approach to the study of aggression, but one with more scientific validity, involves work on the human body's central control systems—the nerves and the endocrine glands. Research indicates that individuals may become agitated and violent when these systems are activated in specific ways, either because of malfunction or as a result of external stimuli. This research could have major implications for the study of political violence. However, the majority of studies are with nonhumans, and at present these efforts have little to contribute to an understanding of why certain humans rebel in certain locales at certain times. (See Davies, 1973a, for a review of this research.)

Personality Factors. There are many psychological studies of social and political violence using a personality trait approach. These differ in degree of comprehensiveness. They involve a variety of theoretical concepts, variously measured in scales correlated with various measures of political protest and resistance. Among the personality theorists of political aggression, the concept of authoritarian personality has gained the most recognition (Adorno and others, 1950; Greenstein, 1969; Knutson, 1972; Sanford, 1973). With such related concepts as intolerance of ambiguity, compensatory power needs, conventionalism, and closed mindedness, authoritarianism and other related concepts can be validly measured by the instrument most commonly used, the F-scale (Christie and Jahoda, 1954). The F-scale is now assumed to measure right-wing authoritarianism to the exclusion of the left-wing variety. The scale is also known to be deficient because of response-set biases. However, there is some evidence that authoritarian personality traits as measured by this and other scales are related to antisocial behavior. In several studies, the authoritarian person, in comparison with the nonauthoritarian person, has been shown to be more rigid, suspicious, and less trusting; to prefer autocratic leadership; to be more accepting of authoritarian commands; and to be punitive toward low-status groups (Sanford, 1973).

The authoritarian personality is presumed to be largely the product of rigid and punitive parental behavior that develops in the child ambivalent and hostile feelings toward authority figures. Such feelings supposedly are displaced in later years toward outgroups, and there is a large body of research and theory attempting to relate specific socialization patterns to later aggressive inclinations. Findings generally indicate that the more painful and stressful one's early childhood experiences, the more likely one is to manifest adult neurosis, anxiety, suicidal tendencies, homicide, feuding, and aggression toward outsiders and low-status social groups (Bandura and Walters, 1959; most of this research reviewed in Gurr, 1970). However, some research on radical antiwar politics in the United States suggests authoritarian aggression may also be displaced through political activism against established authority (Feuer, 1969; Liebert, 1971). Moreover, building on Lasswell's (1930) argument that radical leaders of all political persuasions may be displacing frustration onto things political, Wolfenstein (1967, p. 307) interprets "the revolutionary personality" (Lenin, Trotsky, and Gandhi) as one "who escapes from the burdens of Oedipal guilt with ambivalence by carrying his conflict with authority into the political realm."

Another approach linking personality traits to collective violence is based on a theory of psychological needs common to all humans (Davies, 1973a; Knutson, 1972). Borrowing directly from Maslow (1954), researchers identify four or sometimes five need areas: physical, safety, social-affectional, self-esteem, and self-actualization. The basic needs take precedence over higher needs. If any one or a combination of several need areas remain unfulfilled, a person may be activiated to revolt in order to gratify them. As Davies (1973a, p. 251) says, "The poor man is most likely to be activated by physical deprivation—which if it is *very* severe will deactivate him politically. The person of high status and skill is more likely to be activated to revolt by deprivation of his self-actualization need to pursue an occupation suitable to his talents and training."

Deprivation of these higher needs, and especially of concerns for justice and human expressiveness, has commonly been described as a significant cause of civil rights and antiwar activism during the sixties and early seventies (Haan, Smith, and Block, 1968; Hampden-Turner, 1971, Keniston, 1968, 1969). Other research has suggested a general common association of frustration of higher needs and political activism (Davies, 1973b; Kerpelman, 1972; Knutson, 1974) and presented these needs as the root source of a "silent revolution" against material-ism in Western societies (Inglehart, 1977).

Three problems are common to most personality studies in this area. First, although these theories may be serviceable in illuminating the psychological dynamics that dispose a given revolutionary leader to radical activity, they are inadequate as general explanations of broad-based social movements or for variation in the magnitude of strife across different cultures. Second, only a limited range of personality traits has been examined in the context of political resistance and violence. Third, existing studies tend to overemphasize the negative, dysfunctional, and antisocial aspects of radical activists' personalities. Revolutionaries are most commonly characterized in these studies as social misfits who are psychically deprived, with such a characterization often based on per-sonality measurement data rarely involving positive traits. Though the recent research on Western radicalism as an expression of self-actualization needs provides a corrective to trends in earlier research, there is need for further attention to the role of ideological conviction and goals of constructive change and research into the positive aspects of revolutionary activists' personalities (Greene, 1974; Marx and Wood, 1975).

Attitudinal Factors. The major assumption of the psychobiolog-ical theories discussed earlier is that aggression is mainly instinctual. Another major theory of aggression is that it occurs primarily as a response to frustration. In their classic work, *Frustration and Aggres-sion,* Dollard and others (1939, p.1) state the basic propositions that "the occurrence of aggressive behavior always presupposes the existence of frustration" and "the existence of frustration always leads to some form of aggression." A frustration is defined as an interference with goal-directed behavior. Inhibitions learned through the socialization process can modify dispositions to respond aggressively against the frustrating agent. Aggression can also be displaced toward the self or toward less-threatening nonself objects. Berkowitz (1969) and others have called for modification in the original theory on the basis of later research.

Drawing on the frustration-aggression theory, a good portion of the literature on political resistance and violence has emphasized rela-tive deprivation as a basic cause of extremist behavior, such deprivation being perceived as inherently frustrating. For our purposes, relative deprivation may be viewed as a broad kind of attitude because it is clearly situationally rooted and largely perceptual. Leading theorists using this model are Davies (1972, 1973a); Feierabend, Feierabend, and Nesvold (1972); and Gurr (1970, 1972a, 1972b). Gurr (1970, p. 13) defines relative deprivation as "a perceived discrepancy between men's value expecta-tions and their value capabilities." Feierabend, Feierabend, and Nesvold

(1972) use a similar concept of systemic frustration, defined as the gap between social wants and social satisfactions.

The theories advanced by these theorists both encompass and extend beyond the concept of relative deprivation in an attempt to be holistic—to explain all political violence from individual agitation to civil wars. To this end, they have investigated a broad range of social and psychological conditions involving the following:

1. Social and cultural factors likely to increase the gap between personal expectations and social reality
2. Conditions under which a sense of relative deprivation is likely to be directed at political objects (including the salience of unfulfilled needs, the legitimacy accorded to political institutions, and the belief in the efficacy of political violence)
3. Social and psychological factors that facilitate or impede the expression of deprivation-generated discontent (including the size of coercive forces commanded by the regime as well as by dissidents, and their perceived effectiveness, the presence or absence of institutions promoting negotiations more then protest, and the perceived extent of success of past political violence)

Their efforts have stimulated a great deal of research, and theirs is perhaps the best known of contemporary approaches in the area of political resistance and violence. Moreover, they have been innovative in their use of quantitative data and analysis. Gurr (1970, 1972a, 1972b) and Feierabend and Feierabend (1972) utilize more multiple-level and multivariate analysis than is common in theoretical work on this topic and have been able to explain substantial variation in protest and violence levels. However, the work has also begun to generate criticism from a number of directions. For one thing, efforts to replicate the various studies cited by Gurr (1970) have not consistently borne out the findings or the theoretical model he and other deprivation theorists advance. Some studies are supportive (Pettigrew, 1971; Wedge, 1972) and others are not. For instance, in a study of two hundred and seventy black residents in a riot area in Detroit, Hahn (1970) failed to find any relationship between radicalism or violence proneness and level of deprivation. (See Marx and Wood, 1975, for other examples.)

One possible reason for these diverse findings, and another source of the criticism, is the great diversity of means used to measure deprivation and other concepts and the common use of aggregate indicators to suggest subjective states. Thus, unemployment rates become indicators of discontent, as do urban crowding, colonial domination, or the structure of land tenure. Individual attitudinal variables such as aspiration and expectation levels are inferred from educational rates, mobility patterns, or the spread of mass media. For instance, the well-known theory of Davies (1972) proposes that a sudden and rapid decline in the perceived degree to which aspirations are being met subsequent to a period of rising expectations is especially likely to precipitate dissent and lead to revolts. Yet Davies used no survey or other attitudinal data to test the theory; he relied on aggregate data from selected case histories of violent political events for this purpose. Eventually, in order to test such propositions, individual data must be used to avoid the problems of inference from aggregate to psychological levels.

Other critics have argued that resistance and violence in the political arena can better be explained by class, status, or power factors and that deprivation analysis is thus diversionary (Marx and Wood, 1975). More specifically, critics have suggested the preeminence of individual and group power struggles over feelings of deprivation in causing political conflict (Tilly, 1969) and even of career professionals and "agents provocateurs" as catalysts of certain social movements when little or no deprivation can be found to exist (McCarthy and Zald, 1973; Marx, 1974). These criticisms suggest minimally that efforts to explain so much with relative deprivation theory are rather misdirected.

Another major problem for the relative deprivation hypothesis is in some ways more fundamental. It is that empirical support for the underlying frustration-aggression hypothesis as it was first proposed by Dollard and his colleagues has been seriously eroded over the years by the work of other theorists (see Berkowitz, 1969). Whatever theory eventually proves to offer the best understanding of human aggression, it is clear that the simple frustration-aggression hypothesis has little predictive or explanatory power and needs much refinement to be scientifically useful.

Among other attitudinal dispositions having an impact on violence proneness, the cluster of attitudes usually referred to as political alienation (nonallegiance, disaffection, estrangement, political powerlessness, and anomie) has received the greatest attention in the literature. The anomic and alienated are all supposedly found disproportionately among the ranks of protesters and radical activists. Much of the literature has focused on defining the meaning of alienation and spelling out its dimensions (Finifter, 1970; Keniston, 1965; Seeman, 1959; Yinger, 1973). Many writers focus on two aspects of alienation: political normlessness (rejection of the basic institutions and governing principles of the polity, rejection of the "rules of the game") and political distrust (unhappiness with and disapproval of the governing leadership and/or the policies they pursue). Some writers include a third variant of alienation: political powerlessness. Political powerlessness is the feeling on the part of individuals that they do not count in politics and that their actions make little difference to political outcomes.

In the wake of student and minority group disturbances in the United States in the mid sixties, a number of works have been published that allow a significant test of the presumed linkage between alienation and civil strife. For instance, Milbrath, Cataldo, Johnson, and Kellstedt conducted a study in Buffalo from 1966 to 1968 of conventional and unconventional political behavior (Milbrath, 1971). Not surprisingly, protesting was found to be a largely black phenomenon in Buffalo. Participants were of slightly higher socioeconomic status, felt somewhat more confident about their capabilities, but were more distrustful of political authorities than nonparticipants. Ransford (1968) interviewed 312 black men in the Los Angeles area in 1967 and found that feelings of political inefficacy, social isolation, and racial dissatisfaction (the feeling one is being treated unfairly because of one's race) were all positively related to an attitude of willingness to participate in violence to get black rights. In another survey, 503 adults in Waterloo, Iowa, were interviewed with respect to their willingness and readiness to resort to extremist tactics to register their disapproval of government policies. Two factors explained a large portion of the variance in the dependent variables. These were trust in political authorities and belief in the effectiveness of past violence. The largest single correlation coefficient (.46) was found for the relationship of distrust in political leaders to potential for political violence (Muller, 1972).

The proposition that political distrust leads to radical action also received support in the 1967 Detroit study by Aberbach and Walker (1970). Positive answers to the question "Can you imagine a situation in which you could riot?" were more frequently given by cynical than by noncynical people. The authors concluded, "distrust clearly stimulates a willingness to engage in violence or favorably predisposes people toward voting for the extremist candidates" (p. 1213). Further support is found in the Sears and McConahay (1973) study of self-identified activists in the 1965 Watts riots. Respondents who admitted to high participation tended to be native-born Californians rather than immigrants from the rural South and were somewhat better educated, more politically sophisticated, and more optimistic of the future and of their own personal capabilities. Furthermore, a number of studies show that feelings of lack of legitimacy in the regime and a belief in the efficacy of militant resistance or even violent methods are both conducive to collective violence (Gurr, 1970).

Characterizations of the rioter as more confident of ultimate success than nonrioters is compatible with earlier discussion of social background factors where reference was made to the relative violence proneness of "middle" peasants and workers. Such findings, however, should not be allowed to obscure the equally common image of the rioter as depressed, isolated, and alienated (Ransford, 1968; D. Schwartz, 1973; Yinger, 1973). This latter hypothesis draws on a theoretical heritage at least as old as Marx and some empirical support can be found. However, most behavioral research on the psychology of political activism suggests the alienated tend to be inactive and even apathetic with regard to the political process (Almond and Verba, 1963; Lane, 1959; Milbrath, 1965; Thompson and Horton, 1960).

If alienation is both an instigation to political violence and a cause of apathy and withdrawal, additional evidence is needed to determine when one or the other will occur. One might speculate that when political distrust is combined with feelings of personal efficacy, it is likely to lead to action against the regime. But when distrust is combined with feelings of powerlessness, the consequence is likely to be withdrawal from politics. This argument, which finds some support in research on student activism and inactivism in the sixties (Marx and Wood, 1975), is more fully developed in Milbrath and Goel (1977) and in several other research reports (Crawford and Naditch, 1970; Forward and Williams, 1970; D. Schwartz, 1973; Yinger, 1973).

It bears repeating that, although there is a voluminous literature in the area of political attitudes, there is no real consistency in concepts, theoretical approaches, or measurement devices. Contradictory findings might disappear once agreement emerges on the definition and measurement of certain key concepts. Finally, the most important trait analyses, by their very avoidance of holistic models, only partly help us interpret the dependent variable; to be fully serviceable, these approaches need to be connected under more complex models or theories of personality.

Situational Factors

So far, we have been discussing preconditions of resistance and violence—that is, deep social divisions and psychological states that dispose people toward unconventional political behavior. This section deals with precipitants of civil strife—specific, situational developments that trigger the occurrence of protest and violent behavior. Our focus here is on the immediate situation in which individuals find themselves either prior to or during the commission of violence. Situations occur within a historical context and may or may not trigger political militancy; much depends on whether the participants are already primed to act in such a manner. This would suggest that for resistance or violence to occur, both the situation (growing out of the historical context) and attitudes and traits that predispose individuals toward militant, unconventional political action must be present.

Many situational factors are fortuitous and accidental; and this reduces their theoretical value as predictors of resistance behavior unless they can be systematically identified, classified, and measured. This may explain why situational factors in the occurrence of protest movements and political violence are relatively underresearched, just as they are relatively little researched in studies of voluntary action in general (Smith and Reddy, 1972b). It is not easy to develop a list of common situational precipitants because they are potentially infinite in number. However, one can outline some common categories.

Dramatic events often associated with unconventional political behavior included such things as defeat in war, natural disasters, and sudden economic crises (Greene, 1974; Hagopian, 1974). Such events are more likely to have a violent impact in situations where public expectations have recently been raised so that failure is starkly contrasted with anticipated benefits. For instance, sudden economic downturns are apparently more likely to provide antielite violence if they follow a period of improvement in living standards. Similarly, military misadventures are more likely to produce angry public reaction if they follow a period in which the need for an assertive foreign policy has been forcefully presented. Military misadventures have historically put a particular strain on colonial governments because they tend to undermine the image of potency cultivated by colonial elites (Greene, 1974; McAlister and Mus, 1970). Sudden governmental efforts either to institute reforms or to impose regressive solutions to political dilemmas are also associated with political violence. The first of these actions is more often noted in the literature, drawing as it does on de Tocqueville's (1955) famous explanation of the French Revolution. A situation that often leads to greater public violence is one in which the government uses excessive and indiscriminate force in cracking down on dissidents. The amount of coercion the public will accept as legitimate varies from culture to culture. Supposedly, under democratic forms of government, authorities can seriously erode their legitimacy if they resort to indiscriminate use of violence. The rise of student demonstrations on many U.S. college campuses in the wake of the Jackson State and Kent State incidents (in which several students were shot to death) can be interpreted as a reaction to what students perceived as undue and excessive use of force. Finally, when events such as these cause a loss of cohesion among political elites, public resistance and violence is even more likely (Eckstein, 1972; Greene, 1974).

Another precipitant of sorts can be seen in the contagion of violence from one group or region or country to another (Greene, 1974;

Gurr, 1970). Thus, a successful military coup in one country enhances chances for similar occurrences in nearby or other countries; student protests in one university give rise to student protests in others; peasant uprising in one country may lead to peasant uprising in others; and anticolonial movements may stimulate more anticolonial movements. The success of the American Revolution is often cited as a precipitant of the French Revolution (Greene, 1974). Contemporary terrorism is seen as sparked by dramatic terrorist acts elsewhere (Milbank, 1976). Moreover, Berkowitz and Macaulay (1971) have shown that a political assassination (the shooting of President Kennedy) apparently increases nonpolitical criminal violence. A reverse contagion from dramatic interpersonal violence to political violence may also occur. The strong possibility that media violence sparks disruptive and even violent behavior is one increasingly troubling students of the mass media (Lefkowitz, 1977; Liebert, Neale, and Davidson, 1973). The effects are apparently produced both via imitation and through the reduction of individual inhibitions to unconventional behavior and violence. An important contrary proposition (Feshback, 1955; Feshback and Singer, 1971) is that media violence may sometimes have a cathartic effect; but this view has been sharply challenged in recent years, and more recent evidence suggests an opposite conclusion (for example, see Liebert, Sobol, and Davidson, 1972). Moreover, evidence is accumulating (Berkowitz, 1970; Milgram, 1965) that any environmental cue for aggression increases the probability of such aggression occurring, whether the cue is direct, such as explicit instructions from a prestigious source, or subtle, such as the presence of a toy gun in a child's playroom.

Modern technology itself is a situational factor of obvious importance beyond what has been suggested here. Milbank (1976) argues that new weaponry and systems of transportation and communications are important precipitants of recent terrorist activities throughout the world. Particularly with the increasing flow of resources from radical states, revolutionary groups have been better able to break the monopoly of force normally attributed to governments and to mobilize modern technology for purposes of widespread violence (McCarthy and Zald, 1973; Milbank, 1976).

Sometimes violence springs less from deficient socioeconomic or political conditions that from the dynamics that underlie a crowd. To be sure, the impetus to the gathering of a crowd is likely to be a consequence of some long-felt deprivation; but once the crowd is formed, a so-called "milling process" (Blumer, 1939) can serve to create group solidarities and other conditions where actions that are not anticipated or initially desired by either the rank and file or the leadership are taken. For one thing, the rapid diffusion of rumor is especially likely in such a context and unsubstantiated reports can become a significant catalyst for action (Greene, 1974). It is, however, possible to overemphasize the spontaneous and irrational components of crowd behavior; rational goal seeking may occur and be facilitated by the presence of large numbers of people with common interests (Heirich, 1973; Oberschall, 1973; Rude, 1964).

Conclusion

A sequential specificity model has provided the framework for categorizing a number of hypotheses about individual participation in political violence in this chapter. The hypotheses were presented in stages, starting with the major historical, cultural, and social factors and then the psychological and situational factors most commonly found by researchers to relate to unconventional behavior by individuals in the political arena. The assumption has been that variables discussed within each of the analytical levels influence all others at that level and those at subsequent levels. Our primary integrative assumption has been that of additivity—the more causal factors present, the greater the probability of political violence. Some indication of interaction effects—of more and less volatile combinations of causal factors—is implicit in the discussion, but we have made no real attempt to link all the independent variables under any complex model. We feel this still would be premature despite the creative and productive theorizing done in the area in the past several years. It is, however, the direction in which theory and research should proceed in the future.

CHAPTER 6

Citizen Participation in Community Planning and Decision Making

Kurt H. Parkum
Virginia Cohn Parkum

New, revived, or revised methods of citizen participation in the community were the topic of much rhetoric and theorization in the 1960s. Numerous programs at all levels of government implemented many theoretical suggestions (Mogulof, 1970). Although some of the Great Society agencies no longer exist and the rhetoric has to a large extent subsided, citizen activism is by no means a dead issue in the 1970s. Local participation requirements have been written into many pieces of new American and foreign legislation (Bailey, 1975; Diamant, 1976; Fagence, 1973; Spiegel, 1973; van Meter, 1975; Yin and others, 1973), and citizen groups are active in almost every area of concern (see Foster, 1980).

This chapter deals with noninstitutionalized voluntary participation in shaping the community. Voluntarism is said to be primarily characterized by the seeking of psychic benefits and by its discretionary nature (Smith, 1975). Informal voluntary group action is defined negatively as being (1) without an explicit leadership structure that gives the leader the right under certain circumstances to make binding decisions for the group as a whole, (2) without a natural proper name, and (3) without clear group boundaries (Smith, Reddy, and Baldwin, 1972a).

Formality is a matter of degree. This chapter concerns voluntary action that is comparatively informal but more formal than "helping behavior," which is dealt with elsewhere in this volume. Citizen representation on community planning boards is included because most of these boards are relatively new and noninstitutionalized. The role of citizen representatives has been comparatively unclear and, consequently, quite informal with regard to both leadership structure and group boundaries.

The widespread advocacy of "community participation" does not reflect general agreement regarding the objectives of such participation, the forms it should take, or the means for its implementation (Arnstein, 1969; Bailey, 1975; Cahn and Cahn, 1971; Sparer, Dines, and Smith, 1970; Spiegel, 1968, 1969, 1974a; Steggert, 1975; Yin and others, 1973). For example, the community action program's vaguely stated provision for "maximum feasible participation," which was the legislative or spiritual base for the establishment of many of the boards discussed here, resulted in confusion and "maximum feasible misunderstanding" (Moynihan, 1969). Not all politicians, bureaucrats, or social scientists believe citizen participation units can or should be created. For a review of the literature on participatory democracy, see Thompson (1970). The introductory chapters in most of the books and dissertations cited in this chapter also contain concise reviews. The "loss of community" work in sociology (for example, Etzioni, 1968; Kornhauser, 1959: Stein, 1960) is also relevant but not always included in theoretical discussions.

When considering generalizations about such participation, one must bear in mind several points about the nature of existing research and theory and of the activities and issues involved. Discussions of the practical side of citizen participation are to be found in the journals or house organs of the various professions and organizations that have worked with community activists or projects, in monographs evaluating specific projects, and in journalistic reports describing citizen action in particular programs (for example, see Couto, 1975; Ebbin and Kasper, 1974; Sloan, 1974). Many such writings are rather impressionistic descriptions instead of methodologically rigorous analyses.

Reports of the comparatively few studies of citizen participation that draw upon national samples or data from a number of geographic areas usually consider the informal or quasi-formal community-shaping activity, if they do consider it, as part of a participation measure designed for use in the particular study. A number of bibliographies are available: See Meyers and Sorwart (1974), Mitchell (1972), Parkum (1974), and Ruzek (1978) for aspects of health care; Draper (1973) for environmental issues; Davies (1974) for education; Booker (1975) and Mazziotti (1974) for other areas of planning; and May (1971), Pierce (1972), and Yin and others (1973) for general bibliographies.

Community involvement often leads from informal to formal participation. The decision to be active frequently leads to a perceived need for formal organizational affiliation in order to be able to command the economic and personnel resources necessary to make one's voice heard in community decision making. As Max Weber observed, bureaucracy is *"the* means of carrying 'community action' over into rationally ordered 'societal action'" (Gerth and Mills, 1958, p. 228). A single participant may also play several changing and overlapping roles in volunteer community action (Naylor, 1976). For example, Headstart parents, basically consumers to start with, become service volunteers when they serve in educational or cultural programs, administrative volunteers when they serve on parent advisory councils, and consumer advocates when they go before a budget committee or city council for funds. Many go on to become grid employees of the same service agency they first encountered as volunteers or community members of the agency board.

Federal legislation does not always recognize a "volunteer" as a "citizen participant." This is sometimes a problem for the agency because a specified proportion of federally defined citizen participants is often required in a program if it is to receive federal matching funds. For example, persons receiving financial reimbursement for their expenses as volunteers might not be considered volunteers even though they were not actually paid for work done. "Volunteer" might also be task defined, with citizen members of advisory or planning boards being counted as volunteers but with unpaid persons involved in delivering services or in administration, and thus having no formal impact on policy making, being considered as auxiliary staff. This may be seen by activists as appropriate labeling because direct access to decision-making channels is a leading demand of many advocates of participatory democracy and citizen action.

Also, many traditional writings on voluntarism (even current publications) fail to recommend as areas for volunteer work service on the type of planning boards and activities considered in this chapter, although in the 1970s, such participation is fairly widespread. (See, for example, Hardy and Cull, 1973; Loeser, 1974). Perhaps activism with the potential for changing local power structures and reshaping the community is not yet seen as legitimate or respectable.

Another point to bear in mind is that informal community participation may be considered both political and nonpolitical, depending on the definition of "political." Empirical definitions, measures, and studies of political participation are only gradually catching up with Easton's (1965) conceptualization of political activity as dealing with the authoritative allocation of values in society, which could be seen as including local community planning and shaping activities. However, studies of informal or quasi-formal community participation are seldom included in overviews of political participation.

Taking into account all the problems with the possibilities for citizen participation, one major generalization stands out: Rates for community participation of the type we are interested in here are rather low (Friedmann, 1974; Lamb, 1975; Rich, 1976; Weissman, 1970). The remainder of this chapter describes what is known about community participation and what, if any, common characteristics can be found among those actively involved in shaping their community.

Demographic Variables

Class and Status. Numerous studies have noted a relationship between social class or status and community participation. Cunningham (1972) reported that members of health center boards were often from the influential elite rather than from the poor people eligible for program services. Wilensky (1975) characterized the United States as a welfare state in which channels for participation are dominated by the upper middle class. According to the American Public Health Association (1970, p. 180), the required consumer representation (minimum 51 percent of the membership) on the comprehensive health planning councils has come mainly from the middle and upper classes. This observation was confirmed in Pennsylvania (Parkum and Parkum, 1973) and Michigan (Bishop and Beck, 1973).

In a study of community action groups (most being formal by definition) in ten cities, Steggert (1975) found socioeconomic status (SES) to be a significant variable, with upper-class respondents more likely than others to participate in such groups and to be interested in city problems. In a study of informal but quasi-political complaint behavior in Canada and Britain, Friedmann (1974) found that lower SES respondents were more likely to say they would do nothing or not know what to do than were higher SES respondents, both when faced with a hypothetical case of maladministration and when asked about actual past complaint behavior.

Cole's (1974) data from numerous programs in several urban areas involving citizen participants showed the SES of program participants was higher than that of the neighborhood as a whole. This discrepancy increased as the program's ranking on a participation index increased. The index took into account the number of ways citizens were involved in decision making in a program and how the citizens were selected. Similarly, in a study of one community council, Weissman (1970) noted that although the neighborhood in question was predominantly working class, the middle class participated more in all committees except one dealing with sports. Weissman hypothesized that participation in the latter committee was within the self-perceived skills of potential working-class participants. He concluded, "the more often a council can offer rewards congruent with those dictated by an individual's status as a member of a social class, the more members of that class will join the council" (p. 94).

The type of action involved is also an important factor. For example, Lamb (1975) found that in poor neighborhoods, civil rights group members were generally from the middle class. In comparison, militant ethnic group members had the greatest diversity in SES, with the highest educational level of all active groups studied but the lowest average income and an income range approximating that of the community poor.

Income. People with moderate to high incomes are more likely to be active in community-oriented activities than are low-income residents. Although people may be reluctant to say so during an interview, participation may to a great extent depend on available personal resources, with attitudinal variables being more important for differentiating between participants and nonparticipants within income levels than between income levels. Participation rates are lowest among families receiving public assistance, especially among families on more than one type of assistance (Bloomberg and Rosenstock, 1968). In this study, participation included complaining about local problems, requesting aid from a city legislator, attending public meetings, belonging to neighborhood improvement committees, and voting in local elections. The very low participation rates found for those on welfare may reflect the nature of obtaining such aid and possibly some physical or social disability that leads both to the need for welfare and lack of community participation.

Studying crime prevention activities such as neighborhood watches and walks, mobile patrols, and block clubs, Washnis (1975) found it is more difficult to organize and maintain such groups or protection in low-income than middle-income areas. High-income areas were often hard to organize because residents were usually successful in demanding and getting better police protection. Volunteer municipal officials were found to have incomes higher than the community average (Pfeiffer, 1976). A study of the environmental movement in two of ten U.S. federal regions indicated that participants were mainly from the middle and upper levels (Zinger, Dalsemer, and Magargle, 1973). Two studies of comprehensive health planning showed that although the health provider participants had higher incomes than the health consumer participants, both groups' incomes were relatively high in comparison with general community levels (Bishop and Beck, 1973; Parkum and Parkum, 1973). Yates (1973) found a similar pattern in a variety of planning boards.

Occupation. The relationship of occupational variables to membership and participation in voluntary associations has been well established. This relationship is also found in studies of specific types of informal and quasi-formal community activity. Robbins (1975) found that library boards were overwhelmingly dominated numerically by relatively high status members (housewives, professionals, and managers) traditionally found on such boards, despite varying outreach efforts. Almost 75 percent of comprehensive health planning committee and board members interviewed in Pennsylvania were managers, administrators, professionals, or officials (about 63 percent of the health consumer members and 85 percent of the provider members). These figures are far greater than the corresponding proportions in the population (Parkum and Parkum, 1973). Similar professional dominance was found in the comprehensive health planning study by Bishop and Beck (1973).

Education. People who have attained relatively high levels of formal education seem more inclined both to participate in community organizations and planning-related activities and to become formal members of the organizing groups. In the Friedmann (1974) study of complaints in Canada and Britain, education appeared as one of the two major explanatory factors. Zinger, Dalsemer, and Magargle, (1973) reported that over two-thirds of the respondents in a study of the environmental movement in two of ten federal regions had college degrees, with 23 percent of these having graduate degrees. Educational level was highest in metropolitan areas. These figures are far above the corresponding population proportions at high educational levels. Pfeiffer (1976) found that volunteer municipal officials have more formal education than the community average. Several studies of health planning committees and boards yielded similar results, with both health consumer and provider participants having relatively high educational levels (Bishop and Beck, 1973; Parkum and Parkum, 1973).

Age. In general, those people in a broadly defined middle age category (thirty-five to sixty-five) were most likely to be engaged in community problem-solving activity. (See Steggert, 1975, regarding activities and interests in city; Zinger, Dalsemer, and Magargle, 1973, regarding environmental activities; Robbins, 1975, regarding library boards; Pfeiffer, 1976, regarding volunteer city officials; and Parkum and Parkum, 1973, regarding citizen participation in health planning.)

Gender. No consistent relationship between gender and participation in quasi-formal or informal community activity can be found in the many relevant studies. Rather, each problem area or specific activity showed its own pattern. Volunteer municipal officials were generally men (Pfeiffer, 1976). In the environmental movement, men were more likely to be active than women, except in metropolitan areas. Also, men were involved more than women in economic growth and development matters, preservation, forestry use planning, outdoor recreation, and with leadership and policy-making responsibilities; women were occupied with clerical work, education, recycling, boycotting, and letter writing (Zinger, Dalsemer, and Magargle, 1973).

The majority of citizens attempting to influence school policies by being members of policy or advisory groups and boards involved in educational decision making were women (Stanwick, 1975). They also comprised over 90 percent of the membership of urban recreation councils in poverty areas (Godbey and Kraus, 1973). Washnis (1975) found that anticrime crusade participants were usually white, middle-aged, middle- and upper-income women. There was no significant difference in the proportion of men to women within the health consumer and provider divisions in comprehensive health planning, although overall about 59 percent of the respondents were men and 41 percent were women (Parkum and Parkum, 1973).

Race. Several recent studies of participation have found that although blacks in general participate less actively than whites in community voluntary associations, this relationship is reversed when proper controls are made for SES (Olsen, 1970; Orbell and Uno, 1972). Steggert (1975) reported that for the ten cities surveyed, race usually made no difference except that within the upper class, blacks were much more likely than whites to be active in community improvement. Also, at all class levels, blacks consistently showed greater interest than whites in city problems and politics. However, many of the activities included in the survey would be classified as formal voluntary organizations rather than as the community participation of interest in this chapter. Gockel, Bradburn, and Sudman (1972) noted that in integrated communities, blacks' participation in community organizations exceeded that of whites with similar amounts of education; and black participation was higher in segregated than in integrated neighborhoods. Kramer (1969) described a number of poverty advisory bodies in California as having a large percentage of black members even though the target areas also contained a high proportion of low-income whites. Lamb (1975) concluded that poor black communities now have highly politicized sets of community groups, with a full 73 percent of their group memberships being in organizations devoted to civic purposes. The figure for the United States generally is reported as being closer to 15 percent.

Other types of community activity show white numerical dominance. Robbins (1975) found this to be the case with library boards, as did Zinger, Dalsemer, and Magargle (1973) for the environmental movement. About 20 percent of the Pennsylvania comprehensive health planning consumers were black (versus 9 percent black population), as were 6 percent of the providers. Most of the black representatives were in urban areas, with 42 percent black consumers in the five-county Philadelphia area, where roughly 20 percent of the population is black (Parkum and Parkum, 1973).

Organizational Involvement. The generalization could be made that many people are not active in any group concerned with community problems. Steggert (1975) found only an average of 14 percent involved in such groups in central cities. However, of those residents who are active, involvement is seldom limited to just one type of organization or problem area. Many become virtually full-time volunteers, involved in numerous activities at once. In more formal community participation, this multiple membership may be due partially to the fact that members are often appointed or elected on the basis of their reputation as leaders. Ready (1972) sees an advantage of overlapping memberships in local planning groups, civil rights groups, labor unions, and such. The overlap may result in an economy of time, effort, and money.

Onibokun and Curry (1976) found that 75 percent of those active in a metropolitan transit citizen participation program belonged to some type of community organization and 90 percent had at various times taken an active interest in local or regional issues. Those involved in a citizens revenue-sharing committee had active backgrounds in various aspects of local community affairs, especially health and social service agencies, political campaigns, and civic functions (Browne and Rehfuss, 1975). In the Pennsylvania health planning study, almost 80 percent of the respondents had high organizational activity ratings on a composite index of meeting attendance, financial contributions, number of committee memberships, and number of offices held (Chapin Social Participation Scale). When only organizational memberships were considered, the scores again were quite high, with over half the respondents belonging to six or more organizations (Parkum and Parkum, 1973). These figures show that those active on community participation boards and committees are also usually involved in other formal or informal voluntary action.

Residence. Several variables having to do with various aspects of residence were noted in the different studies. Greater length of local residence was associated with higher levels of community activity (Onibokun and Curry, 1976; Steggert, 1975) and with more interest in neighborhood problems (Steggert, 1975). Local orientation influenced the decision whether or not to vote in neighborhood council elections, with people having a tendency to vote for persons living in the same area. The more candidates from an area, the higher was the number of people voting in the elections, although the participation in the elections was very low (Peterson, 1970). Also, Godbey and Kraus (1973) found that those involved in urban recreation planning activities tended to live near each other.

Attitudinal Variables

Attitudes or Beliefs. Some studies have included direct questions as to why respondents did or did not participate in community-oriented activities. Stepwise multiple-regression analysis of data from the Pennsylvania health planning study revealed that amount of volunteer time was related to a number of significant cognitive variables: perceived need for organizational changes in health services in council area, understanding of community health planning issues, belief that community health officials care about what respondent and friends think, perceived likelihood of success in changing a harmful or unjust community health regulation, and perceived improvement in community due to council activity. These variables explained involvement (as indicated by amount of volunteer time) better than the demographic variables of sex, race, age, education, and income (Parkum, 1973). Nineteen percent of the involvement was accounted for by the five cognitive variables, but only 5 percent was explained by the demographic variables. Corresponding relationships were found when a measure of involvement adapted from Chapin's Social Participation Scale was used as the dependent variable. Predictive demographic variables were the same in the reanalysis, but different belief variables were found to be significant. These were feelings of opportunity to make views known in community meetings; feelings of having a say in committee decisions; and belief that a health care delivery system controlled solely by providers will have to be adopted, that community health officials care about what respondent and friends think, and that a health care delivery system controlled solely by consumers will have to be adopted. The variance explained in the reanalysis was only 15 percent, 13 percent by the cognitive variables and 2 percent by the demographic variables.

Reasons given for becoming active often concern personal gain or betterment and community improvement. In studies of programs financed by the federal Office of Economic Opportunity, Kramer (1969) found that members of such groups initially tended to be upwardly striving ethnic minorities, primarily black or Spanish-speaking, who had recently been poor or had lived near poor areas. Incentives for involvement included the prospect of new jobs, low-rent housing, payment for participation, access to services, and political power for themselves, for an organization to which they belonged, or for their ethnic group. They tended to seek more tangible than abstract rewards.

In contrast, health planning board and committee participants first decided to become active because they were in the habit of being involved in the community, they wanted to increase their own knowledge, they felt they had the skills necessary to make a contribution, or they wanted to improve health and welfare conditions (Parkum and Parkum, 1973). Women active in local policy matters, in either formal or ad hoc, informally organized groups in a Michigan city, listed self-oriented incentives, such as the need to keep busy, as reasons for their initial involvement. Self-actualization goals, such as personal growth and education, were given as reasons for subsequent or continued involvement (Flynn and Webb, 1975). Cole (1974) found general interest in community improvement to characterize members of boards and programs dealing with urban problems. Weissman (1970) found that members of an urban neighborhood council often reported obtaining emotional rewards and service rewards. However, he believed many also received, but did not report, "negotiable" rewards, such as the advancement of one's organization or career. For example, professions such as social work or religious ministry value community service work.

Efficacy, Competence, and Trust. Positive relations have often been found between feelings of political efficacy, competence and trust, and political participation. (See Chapters Four and Five.) Similar relationships have been found in some of the community participation studies considered here, though the attitudinal items are not measured in a standardized manner.

Friedmann (1974) notes that the sense of political efficacy is one of the two major explanatory factors for citizen complaint behavior. Bloomberg and Rosenstock (1968) found a high correlation between a sense of personal competence and citizen action. In answer to questions similar to political efficacy items but referring to the health care subsystem, active participants on community health planning boards and committees (both health consumers and providers) said they felt such participation was worthwhile. Providers felt this to a greater extent than consumers (Parkum, 1976, 1978). Providers and consumers both generally believed they would try to change a harmful health regulation, but the consumer members felt it less likely that they would actually succeed.

Positive relationships were found between feeling a high degree of efficacy on one's comprehensive health planning committee and participating actively in committee work.

Personality Variables

There is a general shortage of research regarding personality and personal capacity determinants of individual participation in organized voluntary action. This shortage is also felt in the community planning area. Available studies that include personality dimensions most frequently concern participants' reports on fellow members or reports of personal experiences rather than standard measures of personality variables (for example, Ecklein and Lauffer, 1972; Kaplan, 1976). Accumulated summaries of such information could perhaps be useful in establishing profiles of community activists or for hypothesizing personality differences among various categories of citizen participants. More structured research is also needed, of course. Until proven otherwise, there is no reason to assume that personality traits differ between those who take part in informal or quasi-formal community-shaping efforts and those who are active in more formal endeavors, especially because the former are quite likely to be members of formal organizations as well.

Historical and Social-Contextual Variables

A number of factors that are not personal attributes of the participants are associated with people becoming involved in efforts to shape their community. For the purposes of this review, they are divided into cultural, social-structural, and organizational variables.

Cultural Variables. Participation in volunteer social service and self-betterment organizations is a well-established American tradition. However, in the 1960s, the volunteer self-help ethic was revised to include popular participation in community planning and decision making. The idea itself was not new; but at the time, it received enthusiastic support from numerous community leaders, particularly after the successes of direct citizen intervention during the civil rights struggles. A general spirit of activism filled the air, as described by Jackson and Johnson (1974) for the urban poor. Lamb (1975) noted the importance of the values of critical reformism rather than of cynical discontent regarding local institutions for the presence of constructive citizen participation.

Participation was also in vogue for other areas. Consumerism became, and still remains, a national issue (Gartner and Riessman, 1974;

Hapgood and Hall, 1977; Nadel 1975). It has had extensive media coverage, as exemplified in a November 29, 1975, ABC TV presentation, "The Consumer Offensive—Who Speaks for the People?" Employee participation in shaping both the immediate work environment and long-range corporate decision making, popularly labeled organizational democracy, has received much attention. However, worker management, or codetermination, councils seem to be more popular in Europe and Latin America than in the United States, with AFL-CIO president George Meany having deemed them "a farce, and irrelevant for carrying out the workers' interests." (For codetermination, see Adizes and Borgese, 1975; Diamant, 1976; Dickson, 1975; Garson and Smith, 1976; for American quality of working life studies, see Macy, 1977; Macy and Nurick, 1977.)

Social-Structural Variables. Whether the opportunity for individual action precedes or results from demands for such opportunity is not clear, even for particular programs. Cooper (1972) stresses the long American heritage of asserting one's control over one's own life as the basis for the 1960s wave of demands for citizen participation. In contrast, Miller and Rein (1969) trace the impetus for these demands to preceding experimental programs, such as the Ford Foundation's youth projects. Whatever their origin, opportunity structures must be present in the community in question for people to have even the chance to participate in community planning and decision making.

Some researchers have tried to discover what factors are associated with the existence of citizen boards. After studying Office of Economic Opportunity, Model Cities, and Urban Renewal projects having such boards, Cole (1974) concluded that the acceptance of federal grants was a major factor in a city's having such citizen participation structures. However, Yin and Yates (1975), surveying a large number of works on decentralized urban decision making, found that federal funds made no difference in the frequency with which citizen boards arise. They explained the difference in the results of the two studies by noting that their study focused on decentralization of urban services (public safety, health, education, economic development, and multiservice programs), whereas Cole focused primarily on federal programs. Yin and Yates felt the availability of federal funds may be an important factor in building citizen participation in new programs, but the presence of such funds does not influence the outcomes of decentralization of existing service bureaucracies.

Population size may also be an important variable. Cole (1974) concluded that the majority of all citizen participation activities, especially those with more intense levels of citizen involvement, exist in the larger cities. However, Yin and Yates (using a different data base) found no consistent relationship between level or type of participation and population size, though smaller communities (under ten thousand) were found to have the greatest client control of community services.

Looking at another community characteristic, both Cole (1974) and Yin and Yates (1975) found areas that experienced urban violence were more likely to initiate citizen participation in community programs or on service-specific boards. Yin and Yates note also that the existence of preimplementation conflict has no relationship to the improvement of quality in community services.

Organizational Variables. The paper environment of legislation and regulation that touches many areas of participation must not be neglected when generalizing about community activism. The formal rules, charters, and such of many programs specify that certain categories of people may or may not receive the tangible benefits of the programs or be active in their structures. Thus, certain categories of citizens may be stimulated to participate while others remain inactive or use their extra time and energy in other activities and organizations.

Other membership selection procedures are also important factors in determining the composition of participants in the informal and quasi-formal activities discussed in this chapter. Specific interest groups may be asked to appoint members to community participation boards. People charged with selecting the board members may select people whose views are compatible with their own (Steggert, 1975). Citizen members of personal selection committees do likewise (Yates, 1973). Organizations interested in a board's central concerns also can be expected to be alert to the opportunity to exert influence by proposing candidates for elections or appointments and by sending their members to open meetings at which board members are elected (Parkum and Parkum, 1973; Weissman, 1970).

The actual effect on a person of being asked to participate has not been studied in great detail. Board members who belong to relevant interest groups do seem to attend meetings more consistently than do the representatives of the community in general on the same board. Consumer members of comprehensive health planning boards in Pennsylvania attended meetings less often than did the health provider representatives, and over a year's time this difference increased (Parkum and Parkum, 1973). Providers also increasingly dominated the meetings, both in length of time they spoke per meeting and in number of different members able to command attention during any ten-minute segment of the meetings observed.

Some citizens' participation may be limited due to the prestige surrounding particular activities and those traditionally engaged in them. There may be a perceived "credentials barrier" to citizen participation in policy making, as noted by Robbins (1975, p. 126) in reference to the "self-conscious professionalism of the library field." The potential difficulties posed by the implications of the nature of the doctor-patient relationship for health planning interactions among health consumers and providers are of a similar nature (Freidson, 1970; Parkum, 1976, 1978; Parsons, 1964, 1975). Prestige factors may also be instrumental in a person's decision to serve on a particular board.

State of organizational development and type of organization have also been considered in relation to quasi-formal citizen involvement. Some studies suggest that different types of citizens tend to be members of community participation boards at different stages of the board's development. Militants were found to dominate in number or in actual participation during meetings when the board was new and hopes were high for immediate benefits (to the community or self), but moderates tended to take over when the militants become frustrated with lack of progress and quit (Ehrenreich and Ehrenreich, 1971; Yates, 1973).

Conclusion

In general, people toward the lower end of the socioeconomic status spectrum participate less actively in the informal or quasi-informal aspects of community shaping and planning than do those at higher SES levels. The variables of race and gender show differing relationships to participation, often depending on type and location of the activity in question. Of those people who are active in community planning, many tend to be involved in a number of ways in informal and formal contexts. Participation in an organized group effort is more likely to be successful than random individual attempts to effect community change. Attitudinal variables are important correlates of the various types of participation in community shaping and planning. Many of the broad relationships found here are similar to those found for political participation generally. A cultural environment in which constructive activism is stressed and receives publicity is important both for encouraging people to participate in community shaping and planning and for creating or opening up the actual structures for such participation.

That the activities covered in this chapter vary so widely in degree of organizational structure, in geographic area studied, in problem focus, and in formal and informal membership requirements probably accounts for much of the variance in the effect of the different factors. Also, different researchers use different operational definitions of relevant variables, notably political efficacy and even participation itself.

Comparatively little research has been done on personality variables, and there is a need to explain more of the variance between participants and nonparticipants. More than one kind or class of variable must be included in analyses of participation. This has seldom been done in the case of noninstitutionalized voluntary organizations.

The average rate of community planning participation revealed in the studies cited in this chapter is low. The conclusions drawn from empirical studies range from a relatively sanguine view of the future of local citizen involvement to pessimism both for its chances of success and of its value to the communities and to larger social and governmental units. Bloomberg and Rosenstock (1968) feel that, given the stimuli in the form of funds and "facilitators" to organize and mobilize people, attitudes and patterns of nonparticipation can and will change enough so that local people, especially those in need, will even be "overrepresented" on bodies that control the allocation of goods and services. But Alford and Friedland (1975, p. 464) question whether there can be any real impact of citizen community-shaping participation at a level of government where "the political and economic power of those interests that control resources critical to the solution of such problems is not located." In the literature of a more philosophical or advocacy bent, citizen participation is seen as either a way out of the malaise said to be affecting modern, postwelfare societies or as the sand in the gears of a relatively smoothly functioning system of legitimation via electoral representation and interest group conflict. (See Benello and Roussopoulos, 1971; Carter, 1973; Crozier, Huntington, and Watanuki, 1975; Dahl, 1970; Hapgood, 1977; Lind, 1975; Pateman, 1970; and the concluding sections of many of the works cited in this chapter.) Most likely, given the trend in legislation and worker-management relations, citizen participation will remain both an issue and a solution.

Part III

Expressive
Leisure Activities

David Horton Smith

This entire volume is basically concerned with understanding the determinants of human individual leisure or discretionary behavior, broadly defined. In Part Two, we considered one societally important kind of discretionary participation that tends generally to have an instrumental focus or purpose—political participation and activity of various kinds. In this part, we turn to a few selected types of discretionary participation that have a much more expressive and consummatory focus or purpose. Rather than being kinds of participation that are means to some end, these behaviors provide mainly intrinsic satisfaction and tend to be pursued mainly for their own sake—hence, the label expressive-consummatory leisure participation.

Expressive-consummatory leisure participation such as recreational and sports participation, mass media exposure, interpersonal friendship relations, and to a lesser extent religious participation tends to comprise the majority of the discretionary time budget of individuals in most industrialized countries (see Szalai and others, 1972, p. 114). Thus, although we are not considering certain types of expressive-leisure behavior (for example, interpersonal friendship relations, rest-

ing behavior, cultural and entertainment event participation, and leisure travel or tourism), the sampling of types of expressive-leisure participation in Part Three is broadly representative of the larger category of individuals' expressive-consummatory leisure participation.

The choice of topics for these six chapters has been determined partly by their importance in human individual allocation of discretionary time and partly by the extent and quality of the literature available dealing with the topic as well as by the availability of a scholar to perform and write the necessary review. Another constraint has been our attempt to hold as closely as possible in this book to a focus on informal social participation rather than formal social participation of a discretionary nature. This has led to our including a chapter on religious participation in the newer, quasi-formal, or loosely organized sects or cults rather than omitting religious participation entirely (because there is relatively little literature strictly on the private devotional aspects of religious behavior) or dealing with participation in the more established, formally organized religious bodies. Most of the sects and cults examined, indeed most sects and cults by definition, tend to be somewhat or very deviant forms of discretionary activity relative to the norms and values of the larger (for instance, American) society of which they are a part. Hence, participation in such activity is likely to be rather different from other, more socially acceptable and valued types of informal social participation. Similarly, some forms of mass media use are socially valued little or not at all in current American society— television and radio exposure being perhaps the best general examples. Here, too, we may expect some important differences from the pattern of correlates and determinants that characterizes the more socioculturally valued forms of media use. Certain outdoor sports and recreational activities may show similar patterns of deviance because they are disvalued by the sociocultural system generally.

There is much less research on the socialization of individuals for participation in the present expressive-consummatory leisure activities than for participation in the more instrumental political or helping discretionary activities of Parts Two and Four of this volume. Partly as a result of this, the review chapters on socialization for participation in Part Three are briefer than for Parts Two and Four and the degree of analytical development here is more rudimentary. Nonetheless, we include socialization review chapters here in order to suggest the main lines of research being pursued. In the case of the religious socialization chapter, the focus is broader than the substantive review chapter it precedes—including socialization for conventional religious participation.

CHAPTER 7

Leisure and Sport Socialization

John R. Kelly

Socialization is generally considered to involve attitudes, tastes, skills, modes of behavior, role expectations, values, and norms for relationships. It is usually defined to include both processes of internalization of norms and values and processes that shape behavior. All of this is relevant for socialization in the areas of leisure activity and sports. Existing research in these areas, however, does not cover all of this. Instead, most attention so far has been given to the question of which reference groups, significant others, and institutions most influence participation. There are no landmark studies in these areas that allow us fully and authoritatively to describe leisure and sport socialization. Thus, this chapter concentrates on describing a number of studies that cumulatively suggest paths for further research.

The basic definition used here is that socialization is "the learning and internalizing of appropriate patterns, values, and feelings" (Elkin, 1960, p. 4). Introducing, teaching, supporting, exemplifying, financing, jointly participating, encouraging, rewarding, and even enforcing commitments enter into leisure and sport socialization. Both the agents and the processes of socialization are viewed as significant.

170

Three Theoretical Approaches

The three principal approaches to leisure and sport socialization may be distinguished by the inclusion or exclusion of certain social variables and the conceptual differentiation of the socialization stages.

The least-inclusive approach proposes that in childhood, dispositions are learned that determine later modes and meanings of leisure and sport participation. This approach tends to emphasize parents and older siblings as role models who set patterns for both childhood and later adult activities and attitudes. An extended version of this approach includes reference groups in the school and community as socializing influences. One variant views leisure socialization as a general function of the cultural and social context in which the child grows up. Values, skills, and experiences are related to ethnicity, community type, family social position, and opportunity. In more activity-specific variants of this approach, researchers have attempted to explain the initiation and continuation of individuals' activity preferences such as hunting, competitive team sports, and resource-based outdoor recreation. Here, family, school, and peer influences are all considered potentially significant. Socialization is assumed to involve both learning to value the activity and acquiring the necessary skills for participation.

The second major theoretical approach focuses on the learning of adult social roles. This approach is more comprehensive and more fully grounded in the social context. Leisure and sport socialization are viewed as part of the general learning and taking of appropriate roles that occur from childhood into adulthood. The social institutions of the family, school, community, and economy are seen as primary learning contexts. Leisure and sport activities are viewed also as one of many milieus in which value orientations, self-concepts, and role behavior are learned. Play is generally viewed in this approach as a crucial factor in socialization. Theorists in this approach acknowledge major debts to the work of Mead (1934), who stressed the role and rules of games in childhood socialization, and Erikson (1963), who described children's play as preparation for adult roles.

The third major theoretical approach involves the full life span. This view considers the childhood determination model too simple. It views leisure and sport participation, skills, interests, and values as an ongoing process of change and development not only in childhood but throughout adult life. Work, family, and leisure careers are not viewed as separate streams of activity but as interacting throughout the life span. Both what people do and what activities mean to them change as associations, locales, role expectations, resources, and abilities change. Researchers working in this paradigm then give attention to both roles and identities, to both continuity and change throughout individual life careers.

Pervasive Issues

There are several frequently addressed issues in theory and research in sport and leisure socialization that remain as yet unresolved. Eight issues appear to be of central concern to scholars in this area. The first deals with the most significant relationships during the childhood phase of leisure and sport socialization. To what extent do peers counter and complement parental influence, beginning when children first enter play groups? Does the presence, birth order, and gender of siblings make a difference in the outcome of sport and leisure socialization? What are the relative contributions of peers in informal settings, peers in the school setting, and adults in the school setting? Do coaches and teachers tend to replace parents as significant others? Finally, has researchers' concentration on the importance of other persons in socialization masked the importance of opportunity structures? For example, a highly competitive sports program may provide opportunity for only a very few students who early demonstrate skill and talent and preclude access to facilities and learning opportunities for most students.

The second issue concerns the critical element in sport and leisure socialization. Should attention be directed to opportunity for entry into specific activities such as classical music, basketball, and fishing or focus on skill acquisition and development of tastes and general interests? It can be argued that learning to enjoy sports in general and learning hand-eye coordination may carry over into adult life but learning to enjoy a particular sport and the specific skills necessary to participate in it may not. Interests developed over a range of areas (music, exercise, color and form in art, outdoor activities, and so forth) may be expressed through participation in different activities at different times of life, depending on opportunity and resources. In general, actual research in leisure and sport socialization has tended to be confined to the study of participation in specific activities, and only in theory have scholars explored the implications of more general socialization experiences.

The relationship between social status and leisure socialization, the third issue, has been an issue ever since Thorstein Veblen noted the value of leisure activity as status display. Social groups of differing status differ in life-styles involving costly leisure activities. We seldom find the rich hustling pool on Saturday or the poor on the golf greens. However, we do not have comprehensive research findings about the relative importance of status-connected role expectations, leisure-relevant opportunities and resources, and general life chances as determinants of leisure activity patterns.

An issue that has recently become prominent is that of sex and gender differences. The women's movement, the application of civil rights legislation to sex determination, and a general raised awareness of social limitations on women's participation in sports have all contributed to a growing body of research on the importance of both biological and socialization factors in sport participation.

A part of the "conventional wisdom" concerning sport participation is that the school is a major socializer. This fifth issue has not, however, been very carefully investigated. Reading, cultural appreciation, and sport participation alike are introduced in the curriculum because they are assumed to lead to skills that are useful in adult life. This assumption's validity is seldom demonstrated empirically.

Leisure and sport participation have frequently been assigned to the area of life known somewhat vaguely as "life-style." Factors assumed to be important here include ethnicity, culture, community, region, and generational subculture. Leisure participation, as an aspect of life that is least institutionalized and thus open to influence by these kinds of factors, obviously is often a central focus in studies of life-styles. In spite of this, there is very little research on leisure and sport participation that includes these variables of ethnicity, culture, and style.

Probably the most important issue in the area of leisure and sport participation is one of continuity and change in behavior. What factors promote continuity and change in activity, values, and associations? What are the effects of such major life events and transitions as marriage, job change, health traumas, childbirth, and retirement? As resources and opportunities change, activities change; but do satisfactions change or remain essentially the same?

The eighth issue, of increasing interest as the proportion of those over age fifty-five in our population increases, is that of the meaning of leisure activity in the later years and in retirement. There is evidence that the increase in time for leisure that comes with retirement is not always accompanied by increases in participation in leisure activities or by increased satisfaction with how leisure time is spent. We still need, however, much more data on the relationship of prior socialization to this matter of leisure activities and satisfactions in retirement years.

Research Findings

Leisure. Research into childhood determination of leisure behavior has been concentrated on outdoor recreation (camping, hunting, fishing, and such). W. Burch (1969), Hendee (1969), and Yoesting and Burkhead (1973) report that childhood experiences of outdoor activity with parents are related to the style of later outdoor recreations. In two studies of a full range of adults' leisure activities by Kelly (1974, 1977), 50 percent to 60 percent were found to have begun these adult activities in their childhood. Thus, there is some evidence that childhood experience and socialization are partial determinants of adult leisure behavior. Further, values and orientations learned in childhood may be influential in adult years even though the individual is participating in different activities than those engaged in during childhood.

The second theoretical approach assumes childhood play and games are forms of anticipatory socialization for adult roles—for sex or work roles, according to Erikson (1963), for political roles, according to Keniston (1971), and for community roles, according to Seeley, Sim, and Loosley (1963). Role expectations vary across social classes and thus socialization does, too (Kohn, 1968). In a small community, the organized activities open to youth vary by class (Hollingshead, 1949). This includes variations in type of activity, locale, and social networks as well as variations in opportunity to participate in a given activity. Seeley, Sim, and Loosely (1963) approached the study of in-school, after-school, and vacation leisure behavior among children and youth in a suburban community as a search for an implicit socialization program. They found the children they studied were being prepared, as expected, for the levels of affluence and status their parents occupied and for the symbolic leisure roles their parents valued. Thus, leisure is not only limited by class-related opportunity structures but is positively shaped by these structures. However, it must be noted here again that we know little of the influence of status factors relative to other factors or the hypothesized consequences of childhood play and leisure activities for nonleisure roles.

The third theoretical orientation, the life-career approach, demands longitudinal research that would trace continuity and change through individual leisure careers. Such research has not yet been done. However, some of Kelly's data from the previously mentioned studies are relevant here. First, in two communities studied, half the activities were found not to be carryovers from childhood. In a third community, with a younger population, about one-third of the activities were not carryovers. In all three communities, major changes in leisure behavior were found to occur after passage into marriage and parenthood. Parents' new leisure patterns involved more interpersonal relationships and fewer activities engaged in for their own sake, for satisfactions intrinsic to the experience rather than response to family role expectations.

A recent series of case studies in England also supplies some data on the interrelationship of employment, family, and leisure activities as seen in a life-cycle perspective (Rapoport and Rapoport, 1975). At different life stages, there are different roles to be performed; and these were found to be related to leisure activities engaged in and to the reasons given for engaging in them. Leisure socialization, in view of these data, appears to be a lifelong process, as hypothesized in the life-career model.

Sports. The literature on socialization specifically into sport participation is somewhat more extensive than that on leisure in general. Emphasis has been on introduction to specific sports and on acquisition of specific skills and attitudes, with a variety of methods used to sort out the relative influence of family, school, peers, and coaches (see Kenyon, 1970; Kenyon and McPherson, 1974a).

Snyder and Spreitzer (1976) applied a model of childhood determination to the sport participation of young men, using path analysis to trace major determinants. They found that parental interest in a particular sport (particularly on the part of the father) encouraged participation. The sport participant also evaluates her or his ability and whether or not participation will be rewarding. Additional data reported by Spreitzer and Snyder (1976) show not only the importance of childhood experience as a determinant of adult behavior but also that sport socialization is more than a simple cause and effect matter. Sport, like leisure, may exhibit a processual, life-career pattern.

A major theme in the study of sport socialization has been that of socialization into roles. The pervasiveness of the "dumb jock" stereotype and the significance of sport participation in the high school status system (Coleman, 1961) triggered interest in the social-psychological consequences of athletic participation. Studies by Schendel (1965) and Schafer and Rehberg (1970) have confirmed the hypothesized relevance of sport participation to high school social status. But as Snyder and Spreitzer (1974b, 1976) point out, little research has yet been done on the relationship of athletic participation to self-image development, the achievement of life satisfactions, and emotional health.

Other studies indicate athletes tend to be more conservative, conventional, and conformist than nonathletes (Phillips and Schafer, 1970; J. Scott, 1971). Hoch (1972) and others have pointed out, rather critically, that athletics tends to be an instrument of socialization into conservatism. Sport participation has been described both favorably and unfavorably as an element in student life that tends on one hand to encourage competitive, achievement-oriented behavior and gratification deferment and on the other hand to encourage mindless conformity to social norms. More recently, issues of gender and racial differences and discrimination have been added to the agenda for future research because existing research is almost entirely concerned with white males (Edwards, 1973; Snyder and Kivlin, 1975). It is clear there is differential gender role socialization (Maloney and Petrie, 1972; Webb, 1969) and racial role socialization (Castine and Roberts, 1974) for sport participation in the United States.

The validity of the life-career approach to sport socialization has been supported by research focusing on family influences. Kenyon (1970), for example, proposed a model of age-related involvement in sports, with changes in preferred activities following changes in major social roles that occur over the life span. Snyder and Spreitzer's (1976) finding that sport participation by married persons is related to the level of encouragement of one's spouse suggests this kind of model may be fruitful. Kelly (1977) found that both opportunity and social contacts were important for adults who regularly engage in a sport like tennis. But again, it must be noted that the longitudinal research necessary to explore the life-career model of leisure behavior has not yet been done.

Research Needs

The preceding description of existing research has included a full agenda of research needs in leisure and sport socialization research. The issues outlined have barely begun to be addressed. To summarize, issues needing refined research approaches include the relative significance of peers, family, and school in childhood; the carryover of both specific and general attitudes, skills, and interests from childhood to adulthood; and the relationship of leisure and sport socialization to the full set of adult behaviors (nonleisure as well as leisure). In addition, there is a pressing need for more study of sex differences, socialization into gender roles in leisure activities, life-style and cultural differences, the later effects of limited opportunities in childhood, and changes due to aging and retirement. Leisure is believed to be an increasingly important aspect of everyday life. Most theorists now view play activity as integral to the development of childhood and youth. The need for more comprehensive research on socialization processes, limitations, and consequences is great.

CHAPTER 8

Participation in Outdoor Recreation and Sports

David Horton Smith

The study of leisure behavior has grown rapidly in the past decade or so, both in North America and elsewhere. One of the most central concerns of this emerging interdisciplinary field has been individual participation in outdoor recreation and sports (ORS), with only lesser attention to participation in indoor table games, hobbies, and other leisure activities. Partly because there is a richer literature to draw on and partly because it seems more distinctive from the other forms of expressive leisure participation reviewed in Part Three, ORS participation is the focus of this chapter. ORS includes those games that require physical prowess (sports) and those kinds of relatively unorganized play that

Note: This chapter is a condensed version of a larger monograph entitled *Participation in Amateur Sports and Outdoor Recreation* in which many issues as well as particular studies are dealt with in more depth. That monograph also contains an extensive discussion of definitional issues and methodological problems prevalent in the literature, both of which topics had to be omitted almost entirely from this chapter for reasons of space. The author is grateful for useful comments and references provided by Nancy Theberge, of the University of Waterloo, and wishes to thank Lorraine Bone, Alice Close, and Shirley Urban of Boston College for typing help.

require physical exertion to at least some degree and take place outdoors (see Loy, 1968, chap. 1). So defined, ORS is not merely leisure or free time and not merely "doing nothing" or watching some amusement or entertainment; it is a physical outlet for playfulness, creativity, and self-expression (see Nash, 1962). Examples of sports are baseball, hand-ball, basketball, wrestling, tennis, and swimming. They are activities done in some sort of quasi-structured or competitive but still essentially informal setting. Examples of outdoor recreational activities, which involve even less formal structuring and a lack of competition (or else they become sports), are camping, fishing, hunting, walking for pleas-ure, jogging, boating, gardening, and sailing. My concern here is with amateur ORS rather than with paid, professional participation in such activities.

This chapter briefly reviews the literature on the determinants of ORS by individuals, using the broad categories of determinants indi-cated as part of the ISSTAL model in Part One. Because the literature to be reviewed is substantial, space limitations prevent me from discussing any of the important methodological, definitional, or broad theoretical issues in the study of ORS.

Social and Historical Contextual Factors

Of the four main types of social and historical contextual factors distinguished by the ISSTAL model, the category of *human population factors* has been virtually unstudied. DeGrazia (1962, pp. 171–173) has spoken generally of the differences in leisure time use that might be caused by such human population factors as average diet, use of alco-holic or other drinks and drugs, general health, age-gender-race compo-sition, and population density. However, I am unaware of any empirical studies of the effects of such factors at the aggregate level upon individ-ual ORS, with the sole exception of population density. The latter variable has been of some interest to geographers and specialists in recreational travel and recreational facility use (see Rooney, 1974). The models used in this very specialized field of study, however, almost invariably focus on an aggregate dependent variable of ORS as well as an aggregate independent variable of population density, among others (see, for instance, Cesario, 1975; O'Rourke, 1974; Wolfe, 1972). Popula-tion density is used principally in these kinds of studies to account for greater use of outdoor recreation facilities (and hence greater ORS) nearer areas of high population density, although per-capita participa-tion rates, which would be of interest here, are seldom studied.

For the second contextual factor, *biophysical environmental var-iables*, the situation is a bit better but still generally poor in terms of the quality and quantity of relevant research on ORS. Roberts, Arth, and Bus (1959), for instance, studied games of physical skill, strategy, and chance using data on preliterate tribal societies from the Human Relations Area Files (a set of carefully coded ethnographic materials developed initially at Yale University). Selecting about a hundred tribes from all over the world and with wide cultural variability, they sought detailed information on the games played in each society. Of the fifty tribes where the topic was well covered, all but five had at least some kind of games. Most relevant, the number of games of physical skill (sports) reported in a society was significantly higher when the society was located more than twenty degrees north or south of the equator. This suggests that mean temperature, humidity, or aspects of diet related to latitude has something to do with ORS participation—clearly an effect of biophysical environment. Of the very few other studies of possible effects of climate upon ORS participation, Michelson (1971) found that a sample of married middle-class women in Toronto showed a marked tendency to participate more in ORS in summer than in winter. A study by Converse (1972b), based on the time budget data from nearly thirty thousand people in twelve nations (Szalai and others, 1972), found clear evidence of a "north-south dimension" in the use of time. Careful examination of particular types of activities accounting for this north-south dimension made it clear that a climatic factor was responsible, with people in warmer climates spending more time sleeping, resting, and engaging in outdoor activities, including ORS. In the colder countries, more time was spent on mass media consumption, religion, organizations, shopping, and personal care. These data support the conclusion from the Michelson data regarding climatic effects of a seasonal sort; but Roberts, Arth, and Bus (1959) suggest that getting too close to the equator can have the reverse effect. Of the twelve countries Converse studied, only Peru was at all close to the equator.

Two other kinds of climatic effects on ORS participation have also been observed. In a detailed analysis of data from a national urban sample of the United States (actually part of the larger Szalai and others, 1972, study data), Robinson (1977) found evidence that outdoor leisure activities are generally less frequent in poor weather. In summarizing some results from a massive national survey of the U.S. population at different seasons of the year, Ciccheti (1972) confirms that summer is generally the season when participation rates in ORS are greatest, whether measured in terms of percentage participating or number of days on which individuals have engaged in the activity. However, he also reports marked tendencies for season-specific ORS in some cases, as might be expected: swimming being a summer activity; hunting, a fall and winter activity; and ice-skating, sledding, and snow skiing being mainly confined to winter. In sum, the studies suggest future research will probably reveal a consistently significant effect of weather on ORS, with moderate weather and a temperate climate or seasons most closely associated with higher participation in ORS generally.

Another kind of biophysical environmental factor that has been studied is urban versus rural residence, although the usual means of measuring this variable is by self-report and it has seldom been analyzed as a strict contextual variable (rather than an admixture of both contextual effects and possibly role expectations relating to urban versus rural residence). Hendee (1969) reviews a variety of studies of this factor, with most results showing some significant differences in urban versus rural ORS participation. However, the majority of these studies did not control for other individual social background factors. When the latter kinds of controls were used with the national sample survey data gathered by the U.S. Outdoor Recreation Resource Review Commission (ORRRC), few or no urban-rural differences were found. The apparent overrepresentation of urbanites in ORS of most kinds seems to be a consequence of urban-rural differences in other factors, such as income, education, and occupational prestige rather than location and biophysical environment. Other studies make it clear that, in addition, apparent urban-rural differences are partly a result of differential access to ORS facilities (see Ciccheti, 1972; Hauser, 1962, p. 51). And aside from apparent urban-rural differences, studies have shown that ORS is greater where individuals have greater average access to the relevant facilities for such activities (see Ciccheti, 1972; Kleemeier, 1961; Leigh, 1971; Meldrum, 1971; Spiegel, 1974b; Treble and Neil, 1972).

Turning to *cultural variables*, the third type of contextual factors that may affect ORS participation, we find more relevant research than for the prior two types of contextual factors, though systematic comparative studies are rare and impressionistic or historical material is usual. There are, for instance, a number of high-quality historical studies of the rise of sports and recreations of various types in the United States and elsewhere, indicating changes in cultural norms about the expenditure of leisure time and types of ORS (Betts, 1954, 1974; Diem, 1960; Eisen, 1975; Gruneau, 1976; Henderson, 1953; McIntosh and others, 1957; Manchester, 1968; Menke, 1969; Metcalfe, 1978; Steiner, 1970; Weaver, 1968). There are also many histories of particular types of ORS rather than changing patterns of ORS more generally (for instance, Andreano, 1965; Bartlett, 1951; Davis, 1911; Dunning and Sheard, 1979; Goodspeed, 1939; Hervey, 1944; Miermans, 1955). An example of a study that specifically attempts to link cultural expectations to the prevalence of ORS generally is Rogers' (1974) study of leisure behavior in the Soviet Union. On the basis of secondary analysis or research reports by Soviet sociologists, she concluded there is a prestige hierarchy of ORS activities in that country, with cultural, educational, sports, and art activities most favored. Although the correspondence between actual participation rates (aggregate data) and the cultural hierarchy is not perfect (especially for television viewing, which is rated low but a very frequent activity), there is generally a rather close relationship between an activity's prestige rank and its prevalence in the population. Where Rogers' study dealt with all kinds of leisure activities, other studies focusing more clearly on ORS have also found evidence of a prestige hierarchy of activities and changes in the prestige of different types of ORS over time in a culture (Aalto, 1971; Allardt and others, 1958b; Iso-Ahola, 1975; Luschen, 1969; Sutton-Smith and Rosenberg, 1961). Of these studies, Luschen's (1969) is particularly interesting in suggesting that the newer the sport, the higher its social prestige in a culture. Other researchers have noted this same tendency, with a gradual diffusion of new forms of ORS to middle- and lower-status individuals in a culture over time (Andersen and others, 1969; Dunning and Sheard, 1979; Gruneau, 1976; Metcalfe, 1978; Pudenz, 1960; Riesman and Denny, 1954). However, Page (1973) argues that the class to mass analysis is simplistic and masks the patterns that have characterized the changing relations of social class to sports. There is also evidence of increased participation through cultural change in the role of women in society (Robinson, 1969; Watts, 1960).

Several authors have suggested that, with movement from industrial to postindustrial society, there are corresponding cultural changes in regard to ORS. Wolfenstein (1958, p. 86) has referred to this as the "emergence of the fun morality," which is viewed as replacing an earlier achievement-oriented ethic characterizing industrial societies (Greenberg, 1958; Inkeles and Smith, 1974; Williams, 1970). Instead of being frowned upon, ORS and other expressive leisure activities become more favored generally in postindustrial (service) societies. Indeed, having fun itself tends to become an obligation in the "leisure society" (Dumazedier, 1967). Work is less likely to be a "central life interest" of individuals (Dubin, 1956) and the national ethos of leisure is evidenced by a greater tendency toward voluntary early retirement (Barfield and Morgan, 1969). There are, of course, some indications of ambivalence toward these cultural changes (Burns, 1973; Charlesworth, 1964; Riesman, 1958). What is needed now is some systematic cross-national comparative historical research as well as long-term panel survey studies to make these kinds of impressionistic suggestions of the importance of cultural factors in ORS participation more precise and to test their effects relative to other contextual factors.

The fourth type of contextual factor, *social-structural variables,* has been found to have an even clearer impact on ORS participation than cultural variables. Because the nature of the impact of such variables is clearer and probably more familiar to readers, I shall simply indicate briefly here some of the social-structural variables that have been found to be associated with greater ORS in a society or smaller territorial-political unit: (1) increasing amounts of discretionary or leisure time (Clawson, 1964; McEvoy, 1974; Pearson, 1973; Poor, 1970; Soule, 1957; Wilensky, 1961; Zeisel, 1958), although this effect may have leveled off in the past few decades after the long-term impact of industrialization ran its course and the tendency toward postindustrial service societies became increasingly pronounced (Carter, 1970); (2) decline in the market price of recreation over time, with real wages held constant, hence making ORS cheaper and more accessible to more people (Owen, 1971), though again with a leveling off in the last several decades; (3) industrialization, with increasing entry of women into the labor force (Balog, 1974; Converse, 1972b; Stockman, 1974); (4) technological innovations that favor spread of new types of ORS through all parts of society (Betts, 1954, 1969; Dargavel, 1975; McIntosh and others, 1957) as through advances in ORS equipment and facilities; (5) favorable changes in the opportunity structure (generalized access) regarding ORS participation as a result of the parks and recreation movement in the United States and elsewhere (Betts, 1974, chapter 7; Steiner, 1970); (6) general growth periods in the economy rather than recession or depression (Wagner and Donohue, 1976); (7) community or organizational structure favoring sports participation (Coleman, 1961; Eitzen, 1976).

There is evidence for the importance of all four types of contextual variables distinguished in Part One as elements of the ISSTAL model. However, the quantity and quality of research on these factors is rather poor. An overview of the many lines of possible inquiry that still remain to be examined, nearly two decades after their first being noted, has been presented by Kaplan (1960, pp. 135–136) and added to by Douglass and Crawford (1964).

Social Background and Role Characteristics

Social background and role characteristics, with their four main subtypes, have received the most attention from researchers interested in ORS participation, as has generally been the case for other kinds of informal social participation. There are, however, major variations in the degree to which the four subtypes have been studied and variations within each subtype. I shall report my generalizations based on reviewing the literature, some examples of which will be cited.

The subtype *health and physiological factors* is understudied for general populations, though physiological health and fitness factors have been extensively examined by researchers interested in the differences between outstanding and mediocre competitive athletes. Those few studies on general population samples that have been performed, however, clearly support the commonsense generalization that better physical health and the absence of handicaps or impairments are positively associated with ORS participation (Hobart, 1975; Outdoor Recreation Resource Review Commission, 1962a). In one instance, multivariate analysis was performed on a large sample of adults controlling for socioeconomic status, age, and gender, showing health still to be a significant factor after such variables were statistically controlled. There are also some studies showing specific measures of size, physical fitness, skills, and physical abilities to have significant effects in the expected directions upon ORS participation (Dowell, 1973; Engstrom, 1974; Heinila, 1964; Kane, 1970; Stebbins, 1969). Kenyon and McPherson (1974b) argue that the development of active sports participation is in part dependent on a "primary sport aptitude," a broad cluster of traits that could include various facets of health, fitness, lack of impairments, and physical abilities.

In the subtype *social position and role factors*, we find the majority of research done on ORS participation. In the synoptic presentation of results that follows, I shall begin with the ascribed and more biosocially determined positions-roles and progress toward the achieved and nonbiologically determined ones.

Birth order has only begun to be examined closely in recent years, and there is very little research relating this variable to ORS specifically. The results of this research are not very consistent, but they suggest that firstborn children are less likely to engage in dangerous ORS (Gould and Landers, 1972; Nisbett, 1968; Yiannakis, 1976) and that the effects of birth order and gender role are intertwined in complex ways not yet well understood (Landers, 1970, 1971, 1972).

For *gender*, there is a wealth of research, both from the United States and elsewhere, consistently showing that males tend to participate more in ORS generally, especially in ORS that involves substantial physical exertion or risk, competition, or danger. However, there is also some evidence that these gender differences may be changing gradually in postindustrial societies, just as in the middle stages of industrialization the extensive entry of women into the labor force was associated with initial increases in female participation in ORS (see Coffey, 1965; Gerber and others, 1974; Hall, 1973; Kenyon and McPherson, 1974a). The existing gender differences in ORS participation are probably more a result of normative expectations than of physical differences between the two sexes. The athlete role, particularly, is normatively incompatible with the traditional ideal female gender role of a passive, weak, nonassertive, noncompetitive, non-risk-taking, and emotional person. However, owing to long-term changes in the female gender role in modern societies (both industrial and postindustrial), there are some kinds of ORS in which females predominate now, though not by very much proportionately. These kinds of ORS where females may predominate are mainly the more passive types of participation that are consistent with the female gender role (for example, nature walks, picnics, and sightseeing). Leaving aside the smaller or more specialized samples that have been studied, I cite as supporting evidence for the forgoing generalizations such national sample surveys as DeGrazia (1962), Ferris (1970), Outdoor Recreation Resource Review Commission (1962a, 1962b), Robinson (1977), and Sutton-Smith (1963), for the United States; Stockman (1974) and Wonneberger (1968) for East Germany; Hobart (1975) and Curtis and Milton (1973, 1976) for Canada; Andersen and others (1969) and Kuhl, Koch-Nielsen, and Westergaard (1966) for Denmark; and Ferge and others (1972) and Robinson (1967b) for a variety of nations, mainly Western European.

Age has a generally clear and consistent relationship to ORS participation in a wide range of studies, both in the United States and elsewhere. Although there are few studies of really young children, the overwhelming conclusions from empirical research on school-age children and adults is that ORS participation tends to decline with age, perhaps from mid or late adolescence onward. The rapidity of the decline varies with the kind of activity involved. The more strenuous sports and recreational activities, requiring greater physical stamina and prowess, tend to decline with age much more rapidly than the less strenuous activities (though not necessarily because of declining physical powers). This decline with age is not uniform across countries, suggesting that normative aspects of age, besides the physical aspects, are significant. The latter point is underscored by the fact that in some special samples, such as relatively homogeneous higher-status retirement communities in the United States, there is an increase in less-strenuous ORS participation immediately after retirement (Bultena and Wood, 1970). I shall again omit the smaller and more limited sample studies. Evidence for the forgoing generalizations is found in national sample surveys such as the following from the United States and various other countries (Andersen and others, 1969; Ciccheti, 1972; Curtis and Milton, 1973, 1976; DeGrazia, 1962; Ferris, 1970; Hobart, 1975; Kuhl, Koch-Nielsen, and Westergaard, 1966; McPherson, and Kozlik, 1979; Outdoor Recreation Resource Review Commission, 1962a, 1962b; Robinson, 1967b; White, 1975). Depending on the country and the type of

ORS, participation tends to peak somewhere in the range of about fifteen to thirty-five years. Unfortunately, I know of no studies that examine age role normative expectations in regard to ORS participation; so I cannot as yet sort out the relative influence of physiological determinants from normative determinants of the observed relationships, either within or across countries.

Race-ethnicity differences have been studied very little, surprisingly, in regard to ORS participation. Historical studies of American society clarify that racism and discrimination against blacks and other minority racial categories have markedly affected their participation in ORS (McPherson, 1976). However, blacks seem to have been active in their own "separate" amateur ORS arenas rather than being cut off from participation entirely (Davis, 1966). The legacy of this long history of racism is still found in major national sample surveys in the United States, which usually show lower ORS participation by blacks than whites, even with other sociodemographic variables controlled in some studies (Ciccheti, 1972; Ferris, 1970; Kaplan, 1960; Outdoor Recreation Resource Review Commission, 1962a, 1962b; Robinson, 1977). It is likely that at least some of the apparently lower black and other racial minority participation in ORS is a result of their generally lower socioeconomic status, but this too is ultimately a result of discrimination. Only relatively small numbers of blacks with outstanding skills choose to participate in competitive ORS in order to gain social mobility, in spite of the current high proportions of blacks in certain university-level amateur ORS and in certain professional ORS. The kinds of ORS involved tend to be those where little financial investment or resource access is needed in order to participate and where there is more objective evaluation of individual performance (see Blalock, 1967; Luschen, 1967).

Religion has received even less study than race in relation to ORS participation, though there are no compelling reasons to expect major effects to appear here. In the few studies including this variable, contrary to the Protestant ethic hypothesis, Roman Catholics have tended to have higher ORS participation (Robinson, 1977; Wippler, 1968).

Employment status (employed versus unemployed or not in the labor force) has received a very modest amount of research attention in regard to ORS participation. The general results are mixed, varying according to the nature of the dependent variable ORS measure used as well as being related in an integral way to gender effects. On the whole, however, the employed tend to participate more in sports but less in other outdoor activities, with most studies comparing employed women with those not in the work force rather than dealing with unemployed men or those not in the work force (DeGrazia, 1962; Ferge and others,

1972, pp. 634–635; Robinson, 1977). There is a tendency for unemployed or not-in-the-labor-force women to engage in more passive outdoor recreation (gardening or walking for pleasure, for example). Employed women choose more active ORS pursuits (Stockman, 1974). There is also a tendency for somewhat higher total ORS among the employed (McKnelly, 1973), but results here are mixed.

Free time, in terms of time available outside obligatory work or personal activities, has received some attention in relation to ORS participation, with somewhat mixed results. On the whole, more ORS seems to be associated with more free time (Groves and Kahalas, 1975; Heinila, 1959; Hobart, 1975; Mihovilovic, 1973; Wippler, 1968), but more research is needed to determine why at times the reverse relationship is found (for example, McKnelly, 1973). Further, greater ORS participation tends to be associated with weekend days (Robinson, 1967b) and with having longer paid vacations (Outdoor Recreation Resource Review Commission, 1962b). Lack of free time clearly seems an important impeding factor in ORS participation; the majority of people give it as their reason for not participating more (as often as desired) in their favorite outdoor recreation activities (Ciccheti, 1972).

Marital status shows mixed results in relation to ORS participation, which is not surprising in view of its entanglement with such other life cycle stage variables as the number and ages of children. In summary, there is some tendency for single, never-married persons to participate more in ORS; but this relationship may be an artifact of the powerful age relationship to ORS participation noted earlier. Many studies find roughly equal levels of participation for the various marital status categories with other variables controlled. Some of the more important studies are Curtis and Milton (1976), Hobart (1975), Outdoor Recreation Resource Review Commission (1962a), Robinson (1977), and Wippler (1968).

Family size and age composition show similarly mixed results. Many studies fail to introduce adequate controls for socioeconomic status or for age and other background variables. The conclusion from various relevant studies is that there is most clearly a "child impedance" effect (a hindering of ORS participation where the youngest child in the family is under five years of age), though this effect does not appear consistently if controls for gender, employment status, and type of ORS are introduced (see Cheek, 1971a; Outdoor Recreation Resource Review Commission, 1962a; Robinson, 1977; Sessoms, 1963). Simple family size measures may or may not affect ORS participation, probably depending on the degree to which the effect of child impedance is associated with larger families in a given sample.

Educational status (level of formal education attained) shows a strong and consistent positive association with more ORS participation in a large number of studies, although there are a few exceptions where the type of ORS used as a dependent variable is an activity characteristic of lower-socioeconomic status persons. Composite measures of ORS participation almost invariably show the positive effect of education. Some of the national sample surveys from the United States and elsewhere that demonstrate this relationship include DeGrazia (1962); Sutton-Smith and others (1963); Outdoor Recreation Resource Review Commission (1962a, 1962b); Ciccheti (1972); Kuhl, Koch-Nielsen, and Westergaard (1966); Hobart (1975); White (1975); Curtis and Milton (1976); and Robinson (1967b, 1977). In some nations, the peak level of ORS comes among those with some college rather than college graduates; in a very few cases, bimodal distributions have been found with peaks at both the high and low ends of the education continuum (Robinson, 1967). Reversals of the relationship are rare, though the power of educational status as an explanatory variable is often reduced when other variables are included in a multivariate analysis, particularly if attitudinal variables are included (for example, Christensen and Yoesting, 1973, 1976).

Social class or *social stratum* position has been investigated in two ways with regard to ORS participation. The usual approach is to examine some composite measure of socioeconomic status (such as combining education, income, and occupational prestige levels) in relation to ORS participation. The clear generalization from these studies is that higher social class or socioeconomic status is positively associated with a greater amount and variety of ORS participation, although sometimes the peak participation comes in the middle- or upper-middle-class range (Havighurst, 1961; Havighurst and Feigenbaum, 1959; Hendricks, 1971; Hodges, 1964, p. 165; Luschen, 1969; McKnelly, 1973; Martindale, 1971; Stebbins, 1969). Exceptions to the forgoing generalization are apparently the result of sampling that attenuates social class variations or use of correlational statistics that mask the curvilinearity (peaking of participation in the middle range) sometimes present. The second approach to studying social class status in relation to ORS participation focuses on the modal class status of participants in one or more specific types of ORS. The results here generally show many types of ORS to be class linked, such that one could demonstrate a reversal of the usual social class positive association with more ORS participation if one chose as a dependent variable one of the relatively few types of ORS whose modal participants are of lower status (Anderson and Stone, 1979; Donald and Havighurst, 1959; Engstrom, 1974; Havighurst, 1961; Luschen, 1969, Stone, 1968). There are variations in which ORS activities are higher or lower in prestige and social class linkage across countries, but there is no clear evidence bearing on the reasons of such variations. Indeed, there are no studies I am aware of that actually investigate social class normative expectations in relation to ORS; all studies focus on the simple relationships between social class measures and ORS participation without inquiring into the matter of intervening expectation variables.

Occupational prestige level is a commonly studied component of the larger socioeconomic status complex of variables. Even more than for composite social class measures, occupational prestige level has been found to be positively associated with ORS participation generally, both in the United States and elsewhere. Some national sample surveys supporting this generalization include Ciccheti (1972), Outdoor Recreation Resource Review Commission (1962a, 1962b), Sutton-Smith and others (1963), Sillitoe (1967, 1969), Hobart (1975), and White (1975). The relationship is often diminished when controls for other social background variables or particularly, attitude variables are introduced (Christensen and Yoesting, 1973, 1976; Hobart, 1975; Outdoor Recreation Resource Review Commission, 1962a; Wippler, 1968). Such studies suggest that the apparent effects of occupational prestige may largely be a result of education and income effects, although it is possible that the entire socioeconomic status complex of variables affects ORS-relevant attitudes and normative expectations, which in turn determine ORS participation. This potential explanation of prior research results has yet to be tested. As with social class studies using composite measures, so with occupational prestige level studies of ORS participation has there been evidence that certain types of ORS are more frequent at middle or lower prestige levels, although the majority of ORS types tend to characterize higher occupational prestige level persons (for example, Bishop and Ikeda, 1970; Burdge, 1969; Clarke 1956). Again there is no research indicating how occupational prestige level normative expectations might be involved as intervening variables in these observed relationships.

Membership status in formal voluntary groups, whether with ORS or other goals, has been little studied in relation to ORS participation. The main study dealing with this issue (Hobart, 1975), however, finds voluntary organization membership in general to relate to higher ORS participation.

Geographical context roles refer to the normative expectations for behavior (including ORS participation) associated with residential status (or work place location) in a particular geographical area of whatever level of territoriality. Earlier studies reviewed under social-structural context variables, specifically urban versus rural residence, might thus be cited here. The problem is the normative expectations have not been directly measured for these or other social background variables, making it impossible to separate the effects of normative expectations of geographical context roles from opportunity structure or other contextual effects.

Many of the relevant variables in the *experiences and activities* category have been dealt with in Chapter Seven. However, not all prior activities and experiences can be properly considered part of the socialization process (for instance, idiosyncratic experiences that have no particular relationship to intended inculcation of cultural and social-structural norms). Chapter Seven shows that childhood participation in ORS is associated with later adult participation of a similar sort, particularly if there was parental encouragement of such participation. But it is also important to note that the individual's degree of felt satisfaction with prior activities is often a significant factor in subsequent ORS participation of a particular type or in general (for example, Fisher and Driscoll, 1975; Heinila, 1959, 1964; Orlick, 1974). The subsequent research to be reviewed dealing with retained information also makes clear the importance of prior experiences on later ORS participation.

There is another aspect of experiences and activities, besides the forgoing learning and socialization aspect, that is important in regard to ORS participation—namely, the covariation of ORS activities with each other and with other kinds of social participation, formal and informal. I referred to such possible positive covariation as a manifestation of the general activity syndrome in Chapter One. Although the research here is not extensive and much research that could test for the possibility of such covariation with data gathered fails to do so (for example, by failing to examine or report the results of the first principal component extracted in a factor analysis), the results are generally consistent in both areas of possible synchronic covariation. On the one hand, there is significant evidence that ORS activities tend to covary positively among themselves (Burdge, 1969; Heinila, 1959; Hendee and Burdge, 1974; McKechnie, 1974; Proctor, 1962; Ritchie, 1975). Proctor, utilizing national sample data on outdoor recreation activities of the U.S. population, is particularly convincing. His is one of the extremely rare studies of outdoor recreation that reports the results of a principal components factor analysis prior to some kind of (usually orthogonal Varimax) rotation of axes. Proctor's first principal component factor showed all fifteen outdoor recreation activities to be positively loaded .30 or higher on the first factor, and the amount of variance accounted for by the first principal components factor was substantial and far larger than the variance accounted for by the second factor. This is clear evidence of a general factor underlying outdoor recreation participation; and the fact that a Varimax rotation of the principal components factor matrix yields four meaningful factors does not vitiate this conclusion. The cluster analysis procedures used on other smaller, more territorially limited samples and narrower sets of activities also tend to show that some people are general nonparticipants while others tend to participate in a variety of activities, with only a relatively small proportion of activity "specialists" (Ditton, Goodale, and Johnsen, 1975; Romsa, 1973; Romsa and Girling, 1976; Tatham and Dornoff, 1971).

There is also significant evidence of the positive covariation of ORS activities with other forms of social participation in studies that have looked for any such possible relationships. Though their results vary, these studies generally indicate that ORS participation is positively associated with such other discretionary social participation as crafts and hobby activities; political activities; religious participation; formal voluntary group activity; interpersonal activity with friends; reading books, magazines, and newspapers; attending movies, museums, lectures, plays, and concerts; attending sports events; and visiting with relatives (Andersen and others, 1969; Curtis and Milton, 1973; Havighurst and Feigenbaum, 1959; Hobart, 1975; Kuhl, Koch-Nielsen, and Westergaard, 1966; McKechnie, 1974; Outdoor Recreation Resource Review Commission, 1962b; Torbert, 1973; Wippler, 1968). There is even some evidence of the longitudinal positive covariation of ORS participation with itself, as suggested by the general activity syndrome model (Bultena and Wood, 1970; Havighurst, 1961; Le Page and Ragain, 1974), especially for higher socioeconomic status persons.

Resource and access factors have been only very crudely studied in relation to ORS participation, as elsewhere, with family or individual income used as a proxy variable for a variety of other, more specific resource access factors likely to show stronger and more direct relationships to ORS participation. Nonetheless, the results are generally consistent, with higher individual or family income being associated with higher ORS participation in most relevant studies. National sample surveys from the United States and Canada support this generalization, as do narrower samples from North America and elsewhere (Ciccheti, 1972; DeGrazia, 1962, p. 462; Hobart, 1975; Mihovilovic, 1973; Outdoor Recreation Resource Review Commission, 1962a, 1962b; Robinson, 1977; White, 1975; Wippler, 1968). The main exception to the income relationship is, as with other aspects of the socioeconomic status complex of variables, a tendency in some studies for ORS participation to peak at upper-middle income levels rather than continuing to climb with income increases. This is most clearly seen when other social background factors are statistically controlled (Outdoor Recreation Resource Review Commission, 1962b). In cross-tabulation studies, this effect sometimes shows up as greatest ORS participation for upper-middle income persons (Reich, 1965; Stone, 1968). There are also some variations in the relationship by age, gender, employment status, and type of ORS activity; and the effect of income sometimes vanishes when other social background and attitude variables are statistically controlled (Wippler, 1968). The only specific kind of resource access factor that has been studied in relation to ORS participation is car ownership, where, as expected, the results generally show a positive association (O'Rourke, 1974; Robinson, 1977), though not always (Witt, 1971). However, aggregate recreational travel studies, using the number of recreational trips made by all persons from some area of origin to one or more recreational sites elsewhere, have shown powerful effects of distance as an impeding effect on aggregate ORS participation at a given site (Beaman, 1974, 1976; Cesario, 1975; Freund and Wilson, 1974; O'Rourke, 1974). All these studies use distance as a proxy variable for travel costs, which are almost never measured directly. When Keith and Workman (1975) did so for fishermen using a stretch of stream in the U.S. Northwest, they found significant effects of both transportation and on-site costs of users as well as opportunity costs (in the sense of forgone income for weekday, workday fishing). This study is striking because it shows only mixed relationships for individual annual income and the ORS measure used; the more refined measures of trip costs are very consistently significant predictors (lower costs positively associated with greater use of the fishing area). Such findings tend to confirm my contention that we need to go beyond standard and crude sociodemographic variable measures to more refined and specific measures of normative expectations, resources, and other intervening variables for which the former are proxy variables. For very short distances from a recreation site, resource access factors tend to be relatively unimportant (Harry, 1972; Lindsay and Ogle, 1972).

Although social background and role factors are obviously important in understanding ORS and other kinds of social participation, there has been a general tendency to overemphasize these kinds of variables to the neglect or exclusion of other ISSTAL model variables. The situation has improved since Berger (1963, p. 28) noted that leisure research has remained "little else than a reporting of survey data on what selected samples of individuals do with the time in which they are not working and the correlation of these data with conventional demographic variables." The next few sections of this chapter, though based on much less research, are consistent in suggesting the relevance of all the other personal variables suggested as potentially relevant by the ISSTAL model.

Personality Traits and Intellectual Capacities

There are few studies that attempt to examine the effects of *intellectual capacities* upon ORS participation, with the exception of

studies of very limited samples of high school or college athletes engaged
in intercollegiate or interscholastic sports and a few studies of top
professional (and sometimes amateur) athletes. The results are mixed;
some show high school and college students engaged in formal inter-
mural athletics to have lower verbal intelligence and other studies show
higher intelligence, but top athletes out of school usually have higher
verbal and reasoning abilities, whether they are amateurs or professionals (Ferris, 1970; Husman, 1969; King and Chi, 1974; Lueptow and
Kayser, 1973; Ogilvie, 1974; Otto and Alwin, 1977; Rehberg and Cohen,
1976; Slusher, 1964; Stockfelt, 1970). The relationship in the general
population between intellectual capacities and ORS participation is
unclear and no research seems to bear on this.

The situation is better regarding the relation of *personality traits*
to sports participation but not to noncompetitive outdoor recreation
participation. Most studies deal with high school or college athletes and
other students rather than with samples of the general population,
hence limiting the generalizability of the results. Review of the available
studies leads to the following tentative conclusions. Sports participation
tends to be higher for persons with (1) greater extraversion, especially
when considering team rather than individual sports (Chipman, 1968;
Davey, 1975; Edwards, 1973; Hendry, 1970; Hendry and Douglass, 1975;
Husman, 1969; Kane, 1970; King and Chi, 1974; Moore, 1969; Niblock,
1967; O'Connor, 1970; Stebbins, 1969; Warburton and Kane, 1966);
(2) greater ego strength and better adjustment (Albinson, 1971; Davey,
1975; Edwards, 1973, p. 220; Hall, 1973; Hendry and Douglass, 1975;
Husman, 1969; Kane, 1970; Kelly, 1969; King and Chi, 1974; Moore,
1969; O'Connor, 1970; Ogilvie, 1974; Sessoms and Oakley, 1969; Snyder
and Kivlin, 1975); (3) greater emotional stability (Davey, 1975; Edwards,
1973, p. 220; Hall, 1973; Hendry, 1970; Husman, 1969; Kelly, 1969;
Niblock, 1967; Ogilvie, 1974); (4) greater emotional detachment (Ogilvie, 1974); (5) greater assertiveness (Chipman, 1968; Davey, 1975;
Fletcher, 1970; Fletcher and Dowell, 1971; Hall, 1973; Husman, 1969;
Kane, 1970; Kelly, 1969; Niblock, 1967; O'Connor, 1970; Ogilvie, 1974;
Winter, 1973, p. 102); (6) greater sense of efficacy and need for achievement (Davey, 1975; Husman, 1969; Lynn, Phelan, and Kiker, 1969;
Moore, 1969; Rehberg and Cohen, 1976); (7) greater need for prominence
or prestige (Carls, 1969; O'Connor, 1970; Ogilvie, 1974); (8) greater
morality and altruism (Moore, 1969; Ogilvie, 1974); (9) greater flexibility
(Fletcher and Dowell, 1971; O'Connor, 1970); (10) greater energy level
(Niblock, 1967); (11) greater deliberateness (Davey, 1975; Edwards, 1973,
pp. 2-9-223; Fletcher, 1970; Husman, 1969; King and Chi, 1974; O'Connor, 1970; Rehberg and Cohen, 1976); (12) greater stimulation need
(Gould and Landers, 1972; Harris, 1973; Husman, 1969; Loy and Don-

nelly, 1975; McKechnie, 1974; Ogilvie, 1974; Robinson, 1977, p. 32); and (13) greater self-actualization and creativity (Harris, 1973; Ogilvie, 1974).

The foregoing conclusions are based on rather weak research support, with their relative strength indicated roughly by the number of supporting studies mentioned. There are some studies that fail to find the relationships indicated, but significant reversals of the direction of relationships occur only rarely. Investigators often use trait names other than those I used but I have categorized the results where they seemed to fit best in terms of the actual measures employed. Some personality traits in the ISSTAL model have received very little research attention (emotional detachment, need for prominence, morality, flexibility, energy level, stimulation need, and self-actualization), so these results should be viewed as most tentative. Still other traits have apparently received no attention at all in the context of ORS participation (ego defense mechanisms and ego expression styles). In sum, however, it is fair to conclude that individuals more active in sports participation tend to be characterized by more socially desirable personality traits (with the possible exception of emotional detachment—although evidence for this finding was from a single study). Much more research is clearly needed, particularly on samples of the general population with measures of outdoor recreation as well as competitive sports activity, and with proper use of statistical analysis techniques that control for other variables— something the forgoing studies very rarely do. It is also important to perform longitudinal research in order to be able to distinguish selection from socialization effects, although selection effects are probably crucial (Kane, 1970). Further, existing research fails to consider the possibility that the personality traits affecting entry into a particular kind of ORS participation role may be different from the traits affecting continuation or high activity levels in such roles, at least in terms of the patterning of weights of different traits among themselves and relative to other types of variables. Thus, future research should focus on both "stages" of ORS participation in the same study, something not done so far.

Attitudinal Dispositions

I use "attitudinal dispositions" to refer to values, general attitudes, specific attitudes, expectations, and intentions, as suggested by the ISSTAL model. A review of the literature shows the beginnings of progress with regard to the first three subtypes but very little attention at all to expectations or intentions.

There is very little research relating ORS participation to broad individual *values*. There are two main types of studies, one using a broad range of values and the other inferring values or satisfactions provided by different types of ORS (the latter kind of study might also be considered in the subsequent two sections on attitudes). An example of the first type of study is that of Lowrey (1969), who found no significant effects of individual values when social background characteristics were controlled. Other studies indicate some tendency for persons involved in ORS participation to be more conservative and socially oriented in their values, though these studies are based on student samples and hence not representative of the general population (Albinson, 1971; Rehberg and Cohen, 1976; Snyder, 1967). As for the second type of study mentioned, Steele and Zurcher (1973) review the literature on satisfactions from and motivations for leisure activities, suggesting ten major functions or values ORS and other leisure can serve. Their study of an informal sample of bowlers from two metropolitan areas indicated self-development or self-expression and affiliation values predominated. Similar findings come from some other studies, though more careful measurement on better samples is needed to be more certain about this generalization (Donald and Havighurst, 1959). When younger samples are studied, health and physical fitness values have greater importance (Andersen and others, 1969; Engstrom, 1974).

The authors of many of the studies I classify here view them as studies of needs satisfied by or motivations for ORS participation. However, several researchers have begun to develop sophisticated measures of ORS attitudes in recent years, even though they have yet to be applied to ORS participation explanation in large representative samples in general (Kenyon, 1972; McKechnie, 1974; Neulinger, 1974). However, some validation and explanatory studies have begun to be done with these and other instruments, generally showing ORS participation is greater when attitudes toward outdoor recreation, physical activity, and sports in general are more positive (Burdge, 1969; Christensen and Yoesting, 1973; Dowell, 1973; Engstrom, 1974; Fisher and Driscoll, 1975; Hall, 1973; Harris, 1970; Hendry and Douglass, 1975; Snyder and Spreitzer, 1974a; Stensaasen, 1974; Wippler, 1968). Some of the latter find positive attitudes toward ORS to have significant effects even with social background factors controlled statistically in multivariate analyses. Other researchers have focused on more general attitudes, such as positive attitudes toward nature and the environment (McKechnie, 1974), showing these to be positively associated with ORS participation. A few researchers have used measures of general attitudes to differentiate different types of ORS participants (Knopp and Tyger, 1973). Anderson (1959) helps explain the consistent finding of a decline in ORS participation with age by showing in a longitudinal study of men from age twenty to age fifty-nine that there was a marked decline with age of interest in physical skill, daring, and strenuous physical activity. Interest in solitary and more sedentary activities increased with age. Research in progress by Kenyon should make a major contribution to knowledge of the effects of general attitudes on ORS participation, based on various cross-sectional surveys that used his structured attitude instruments noted earlier.

Focusing on particular kinds of ORS activities, *specific attitude* studies have shown positive associations between participation in a given ORS activity and corresponding attitudes toward that activity (Etzkorn, 1964; Tinsley, Barrett, and Kass, 1977). More common are studies that simply ask participants in a particular ORS activity type why they engage in that activity, without attempting any sophisticated measurement, let alone relating differential self-reported attitudes to differential ORS participation (Clark, Hendee, and Campbell, 1971; Taylor and Knudson, 1973). However, Hollender (1977) has shown the degree of variety in specific attitudes that can be reliably and meaningfully measured with regard to camping. If this kind of sophisticated measurement were applied to various major types of ORS for general samples of the population, it is likely that greatly enhanced predictive-explanatory power would result (judging from the results of similar research on voluntary association participation; for instance, Smith, 1966). Attitudes toward specific ORS sites have begun to show the potential power of careful measurement of specific attitudes. The study by Murphy (1975) is particularly interesting in this regard. He shows that recreational boaters from a midwestern city are strongly influenced in their choice of which of two nearby lakes to go to for their boating by their specific attitudes toward the sites involved, controlling for socio-demographic variables, travel time to site, and the relative attractiveness of the other site. Where Murphy controlled for objective site differences, other researchers have shown in recent years that very precise attitude measurements of such aspects of specific sites as scenic beauty or quality of facilities can be measured (Carls, 1974; Lane, Byrd, and Brantley, 1975; Shafer and Tooby, 1972; Shafer, Hamilton, and Schmidt, 1969), with presence of water a primary positive factor in scenic preferences. These methods are far from perfect, as Kreimer (1977) has noted in detail; but they offer significant promise if they can be used to help distinguish among people choosing different ORS sites. It is also important to follow up on the study by Thayer and others (1976) that shows the criteria people use in judging scenic ugliness differ from those they use in judging scenic beauty (that is, one is not simply the opposite of the other on a scale). Most kinds of specific attitudes have been little studied in relation to ORS participation, but it is at least clear that specific activity (and probably site) preferences are positively associated with participation in the given type of ORS (Burdge, 1969; Hendricks, 1971; Outdoor Recreation Resource Review Commission, 1962a, pp. 172–174). Multivariate analyses using specific attitude measures as predictors of ORS participation while controlling for other factors are virtually nonexistent, especially if one adds the constraint of having a sample of the general population.

The role of specific *expectations* for satisfactions-dissatisfactions from engaging in some ORS activity in a particular time-place-situation has been ignored. An early example of the kind of research needed here is the study by Aronson and Carlsmith (1962) that showed participation expectancy to be significantly and positively associated with actual performance. More recently, Senters (1971) has studied a small number of shuffleboard players over an eighteen-month period, showing that their quality of play varied, at a given level of their skill development, according to their opponent and his or her skill level. The results fit well with Csikszentmihalyi's (1975) theory of play, in which he suggests that the individual in a specific situation of recreational activity attempts to create an optimal balance of activity opportunities (challenges) and activity capabilities (skills), altering sites, role partners, and activity levels as needed. Orlick (1973, 1974) is one of the few researchers to show that ORS participation is positively related to measured degree of positive expectancy regarding the outcome of such participation. Far more such research is needed, but the theoretical basis is substantial for considering similar results will likely be found in virtually all areas of ORS examined with regard to expectations. Normative social expectations, as contrasted with outcome expectancies in terms of satisfactions-dissatisfactions, appear to have been utterly neglected.

I know of no studies focusing on how immediate behavioral *intentions* affect ORS participation, though research from other fields suggests the importance of doing such studies.

Retained Information

There is so little research on retained information that it makes no sense to distinguish among images, beliefs, and knowledge here as suggested by the ISSTAL model. Much of what research exists bearing on retained information as a factor in ORS participation is indirect and aggregate-level study of recreational travel. As reviewed by O'Rourke (1974), for instance, such literature shows that the number of visitor trips from a given territorial unit (aggregated) is strongly affected by the distance of the recreational site from the place of origin. Only retained information about relevant site distance could readily account for this kind of relationship, in part; so these kinds of studies show the importance of retained information indirectly, even though they do not measure this variable (see also Beaman, 1974, 1976; Cesario, 1975; Cheung, 1972; Deacon, Pigman, and Dean, 1972; Freund and Wilson, 1974; Johnston and Elsner, 1972; Lentnek, Van Doren, and Trail, 1969; McKillop, 1975; Wilkinson, 1973; Wolfe, 1972). However, Mercer (1971a) notes there is evidence distance can sometimes be perceived as a positive rather than a negative factor. In his review of the role of perception in recreational travel behavior, he further notes that such ORS-related travel is a function of decision making based on preference (attitudinal dispositions, in my terminology) and information. He cites a few of the research studies that show individual retained information measures (that is, direct measures) to be related to ORS participation. For instance, Barker (1968) found the perceived nature and degree of water pollution to have a significant effect upon user evaluations and space preferences for beach goers in the Toronto region of Canada; and Hecock (1966) found similar results for Massachusetts beach goers with regard to Cape Cod. Mercer (1971b) has done research that shows individual "mental maps" (images) affect recreational travel behavior in an urban area of Australia. Adams (1971) shows the decision to travel to a New England coastal beach is related to individual evaluations of the accuracy of weather information, currently predicted and actual on-site weather conditions, and factors affecting beach users' tolerance of suboptimal weather conditions (preference or attitudinal factors). These few studies make it clear that more research on retained information in relation to ORS participation would prove fruitful. Further research supporting this point includes studies that show participants in ORS have usually determined where they will be engaging in an activity (camping, for instance) before leaving home (Lime, 1969; Taylor and Knudson, 1973) and studies that show the importance of retained childhood information (memories) regarding the particular type of ORS (W. Burch, 1969; Burch and Wenger, 1967; Hendee, 1969). And Snyder and Spreitzer (1974a) take still another approach supporting the importance of retained information, showing that individual sports participation is positively associated with knowledge of celebrity sportspersons, though no causal relation is implied here, by contrast with the previously mentioned types of studies. In sum, the very small amount of research available leaves little doubt that retained information generally tends to have a significant effect on ORS participation or at the very least is significantly associated with such participation.

Situational Variables

Situational variables have been little studied in regard to ORS participation. Most clear from the small number of relevant studies here is the fact that individual ORS participation is usually significantly affected by other persons in the situation as coparticipants. Most ORS participation types are more likely when there are friends or family available to engage in such activities with the individual (Andersen and others, 1969; Christensen and Yoesting, 1973, 1976; Connor, Johannis, and Walters, 1955; Field, 1971; Field and O'Leary, 1973; O'Rourke, 1974; Wonneberger, 1968; Yancy and Snell, 1971). The data from the twelve-nation (Szalai and others, 1972) time budget study, reported by Ferge and others (1972, p. 789) are perhaps most convincing on this point. For leisure activities in general (including sports and outdoor recreation but not mass media use), ten of twelve nations studied yielded the conclusion that 80 to 90 percent of leisure activities are done with other persons, usually friends and family (East Germany and Bulgaria being the exceptions, and even there, 40 to 60 percent of leisure activities are done with others). Both Christensen and Yoesting (1973, 1976) and Field and O'Leary (1973) have shown that the effects observed hold up when multivariate analyses are performed. The latter study shows coparticipant status to be a much stronger predictor of participation in three of four ORS activities (except fishing) than sociodemographic variables, as well as showing variations in the kinds of coparticipants most likely for different types of ORS. Other types of situational variables than coparticipants have been virtually unstudied, although there is theory (Tuan, 1974) and empirical research from other, related areas that suggest the importance of perceptual and environmental variables of the immediate situation (Craik, 1973; Mercer, 1971a). A very rare example of a study directly focusing on situational antecedents of ORS participation is that by Witt and Bishop (1970). They asked college students if they would feel like participating in thirteen different leisure activities (including three ORS activities) immediately after six different types of antecedent situations. The results showed clear evidence that leisure participation is likely to vary for the same individual according to the nature of the immediately antecedent situation, although there was also significant evidence of consistent individual activity preferences (attitudes) that vary across individuals but are similar across antecedent situations. In short, the antecedent situation can be significant, though not as important in impact as attitudinal dispositions.

Conclusions

The research reviewed in this chapter (and the larger monograph on which it is based) supports the relevance of the ISSTAL model. Although there has been very little research in some areas, wherever a particular category or subtype of variable of the ISSTAL model has been studied in relation to ORS participation, the variable type or subtype has proved significant. It should be noted, too, that the ISSTAL model as applied to ORS participation deals rather well with the kinds of criticisms leveled at ORS research by reviewers such as Brown, Dyer and Whaley (1973), while incorporating the six major methodological perspectives in leisure research delineated by Burdge and Field (1972). The ISSTAL model both takes account of the full range of factors suggested as important for understanding leisure activities by theorists such as M. Kaplan (1960) and is directed precisely at the kind of leisure research most researchers think should be done in the future (Crandall and Lewko, 1976).

Various studies here reviewed perform multivariate analyses attempting to account for ORS participation variance. Of the relatively small minority of studies performing such analyses, the majority support the ISSTAL model in showing that (1) the usual sociodemographic variables do not account for very much of the variance; (2) the strength of sociodemographic variables of the usual sort (social positions and such roles as gender, age, and educational level) tends to decline when other categories of variables of the model are included in an equation or statistical analysis; and (3) inclusion of the less usual categories of variables, such as personality, attitudinal dispositions, information, or situational variables, markedly increases the variance accounted for (Christensen and Yoesting, 1973, 1976; Curtis and Milton, 1976; Hall, 1973; Hobart, 1975; Kane, 1970; Outdoor Recreation Resource Review Commission, 1962a, 1962b; Wippler, 1968). Many more studies using multiple-regression or multiple-classification analysis techniques are needed, along with path analyses and more preferable, longitudinal statistical analyses of a multivariate nature.

Only a few studies with multivariate analyses bear on the sequential specificity aspect of the ISSTAL model in regard to a differential pattern of explanation for participation versus nonparticipation as contrasted with low versus high participation in ORS. One of the rare exceptions is the work reported by Ciccheti (1972) based on national outdoor recreation survey data from the United States. He reports very clear evidence for a "two-step" demand-supply process in regard to ORS participation by individuals. The usual sociodemographic variables are the principal explanatory variables for step one (participation versus nonparticipation), but the number of days of participation among participants is strongly affected by the relative availability and quality of recreational facilities in the individual's county or state. The impact of the latter contextual variables is doubtless partially mediated by attitudinal and information variables, as suggested in the ISSTAL model, in addition to independent resource opportunity structure effects of the context per se. Even more compelling as support for the sequential specificity aspect of the ISSTAL model is the study by Field and O'Leary (1973) of adult Americans from portions of three states. With swimming, fishing in fresh water, power boating, and visiting a beach as their dependent variables, they report the usual sociodemographic variables were powerful in explaining variance for participation versus nonparticipation but generally weak in explaining variance for degree of participation among participants (except for fishing). However, the inclusion of coparticipant status "dummy" variables representing one kind of situational variable resulted in a marked increase in the variance explained. The results of Romsa and Girling (1976), using a Canadian sample, are similar in that they find the usual contextual and sociodemographic variables do not significantly distinguish people in terms of degree of ORS participation in eighteen different activities (except for walking-hiking) when participants only are analyzed. Finally, Murphy's (1975) study of recreational boaters from the area around a midwestern U.S. city accounted for 34 percent of the variance in recreational boating trips made to a given lake in a two-month period. Even though the usual sociodemographic variables were included in the analysis, the major contributors to explained variance were attitudinal and prior activity factors, not the sociodemographic variables (which contributed only 1 percent to the explained variance). These general results held up when the sample was disaggregated on a socioeconomic status measure also. In summary, the available evidence on ORS participation confirms not only the general relevance of virtually the full range of ISSTAL model categories and major subcategories of variables but also the sequential specificity aspect of the model. No single study has yet come even close to giving the full model an adequate test, however, particularly with both "steps" or stages of the dependent ORS variables taken into account in the analysis. And the model's longitudinal aspect has been essentially untested.

The literature review on ORS participation also generally supports the general activity syndrome. The research confirms the "dominant status" thesis, with higher-status individuals being more likely to engage in ORS participation. The clearest exception is with regard to the age variable, where the apparent disconfirmation can be explained by further elaboration of the theoretical variations on the central theme of the syndrome (see Chapter Nineteen). Specifically, for some kinds of activity, a special pattern of associations may be superimposed on the usual theme of greater participation among the middle aged (thirty-five to fifty-five years old). In this case, the special pattern has to do with ORS participation being more characteristic of youth and young adults, on the whole, because it involves both physical health (which peaks during youth or early adulthood) and connotations of childlike freedom from responsibility, at least in Western culture. The general activity syndrome is also significantly confirmed in its thesis that ORS activity types will be positively associated among themselves as well as positively associated with other types of formal and informal social participation generally, according to the literature reviewed here. The syndrome's predictions regarding the directions in which psychological variables will be associated with informal social participation (see Chapter Nineteen) are also confirmed by this literature review. Namely, ORS participation tends to be higher for individuals with more socially desirable personality traits, more positive attitudinal dispositions of all types (though no data was found bearing on intentions), more of relevant retained information, and for situational variables favorable to participation. The research on intellectual capacities is too sparse to permit any conclusion. However, the summary judgment must be that the general activity syndrome variant of the ISSTAL model is well supported on the whole by the present literature review. This is particularly striking because no one has done any research specifically to test this syndrome in the ORS participation area.

Space considerations prohibit any detailed consideration of the general methodological and theoretical problems of the body of literature on ORS participation here (but see the monograph from which this chapter has been condensed). As in the other fields of social participation research reviewed in this volume, ORS participation research has many methodological inadequacies. These inadequacies somewhat vitiate the conclusions previously reached regarding confirmation of the ISSTAL model and general activity syndrome. However, there are enough adequate studies with regard to many aspects of the forgoing to make my earlier conclusions of general confirmation reasonable. The principal theoretical inadequacy of the field of ORS participation research is, as in most other areas of informal social participation, the use of a discipline-bound and generally static research paradigm. The ISSTAL model and general activity syndrome improve this basic inadequacy.

CHAPTER 9

Religious Socialization

Clyde W. Faulkner

In order for a society to survive, the life-sustaining elements of that society must be transmitted to each new generation. These elements are contained within the culture of the society and are transmitted in the socialization process "by which individuals acquire the knowledge, skills and dispositions that enable them to participate as more or less effective members of groups and the society" (Brim and Wheeler, 1966, p. 3). Socialization not only nurtures society, but it also provides opportunity for the raw material of humanity to develop in human form, to achieve a self-identity, and to acquire values. The process of learning the basic elements of social existence begins at birth and continues through life. The learner is not simply a passive object of the process. He or she responds to the multitude of stimuli encountered in the social milieu; and through that continuing interchange, the biological being becomes a socially responsive person.

The term "socialization" denotes a process about which there is some general agreement; the phrase "religious socialization" is much more difficult to define because of problems associated with the theoretical understanding of religion.

Dittes (1969) reviewed a variety of studies involving different definitions and measures of religion and concluded there are compelling arguments for multidimensionality. He also found, however, that the net effect of much research across heterogeneous populations pointed to a common factor. He concluded, "Probably both interpretations are right. The common factor as discerned in factor-analytic studies should perhaps be construed simply as religion as seen by the general population. It is based primarily on the affiliation with a highly visible institution and with a general understanding of the norms of that institution. The social scientist is still free and perhaps ought to be encouraged to discern more analytic, genotypical, and discrete variables which may elude the general population" (p. 618).

How can one possibly come to any acceptable definition in the face of the differences, disagreements, and difficulties inherent in the understanding of religion? Marty (1971, p. 68) comments, "first it is apparent that the religious reality and the need for the term (religion) are both with us and should probably remain for some time. Second, those who use 'religion' in an always pejorative and dramatically novel sense must take care to make clear their eccentric interests if they wish to be understood. Third, educators and students of religious development will have to continue to live with a sick, confusing, ambiguous term like 'religion'; no clear alternative has presented itself with enough potency to stand a chance of gaining acceptance in the culture."

The theoretical conceptualization of a problem predetermines the relevance of the social data under investigation. Religious socialization can be defined to include only orthodox Western religions with supernatural referents, or it can be defined broadly so one would have difficulty excluding any value-related socializing experience (Robertson, 1970). Because the theoretical difficulties have not been resolved, there is no clear demarcation of data relevant to religious socialization. Furthermore, research related specifically to religious socialization is rare (Westerhoff, 1973), and most of the published research on religion is cross-sectional rather than longitudinal (Strommen, 1971).

Life Stages

Paralleling previous work by Piaget and Erikson, Kohlberg (1974) and Fowler (1976) have produced theories of universal developmental structure to describe and explain the emergence of moral judgment and faith, respectively. Kohlberg posits a sequential process of moral judgment and development in which there are three levels with two stages at each level. These are shown in Table 1.

Fowler (1976, pp. 186–187) outlined six stages in the development of faith that move from the simple and undifferentiated to the complex and differentiated: intuitive-projective faith, mythic-literal faith, synthetic-conventional faith, individuating-reflexive faith, paradoxical-consolidative faith, and universalizing faith. Fowler at-

**Table 1. Classification of Moral Judgment
into Levels and Stages of Development**

Level	Basis of Moral Judgment	Stage of Development
I	Moral value resides in external, quasi-physical happenings, in bad acts, or in quasi-physical needs rather than in persons and standards.	*Stage 1:* Obedience and punishment orientation. Egocentric deference to superior power or prestige or a trouble-avoiding set. Objective responsibility. *Stage 2:* Naively egoistic orientation. Right action is that instrumentally satisfying the self's and occasionally others' needs. Awareness of relativism of value to each actor's needs perspective. Naive egalitarianism and orientation to exchange and reciprocity.
II	Moral value resides in performing good or right roles, in maintaining the conventional order and the expectancies of others.	*Stage 3:* Good boy orientation. Orientation to approval and to pleasing and helping others. Conformity to stereotypical images of majority or natural role behavior, and judgment by intentions. *Stage 4:* Authority and social order maintaining orientation. Orientation to "doing duty" and to showing respect for authority and maintaining the given social order for its own sake. Regard for earned expectations of others.
III	Moral value resides in conformity by the self to shared or shareable standards, rights, or duties.	*Stage 5:* Contractual legalistic orientation. Recognition of an arbitrary element or starting point in rules or expectations for the sake of agreement. Duty defined in terms of contract, general avoidance of violation of the will or rights of others, and majority will and welfare. *Stage 6:* Conscience or principle orientation. Orientation not only to actually ordained social rules but to principles of choice involving appeal to logical universality and consistency. Orientation to conscience as a directing agent and to mutual respect and trust.

Source: Kohlberg, 1974, p. 7.

tempted to analyze individual structuring of faith by using a series of variables as "windows or apertures into the structures underlying faith." These variables are locus of authority, criteria and modes of appropriation, symbolic and conceptual functioning, role taking and extensiveness of identification, and prototypical challenges with which faith must deal. Individual responses measured along these five variables permit identification of the respondent's stage of faith development.

Both Kohlberg and Fowler contend the stages they describe are hierarchically related, sequential, and invariant. Both report results from longitudinal studies to support their contention. Kohlberg (1971) also cited cross-cultural data on the basis of which he asserted a claim of universality for his model of the development of moral judgment. Fowler's approach is yet to be tested outside the United States. Further cross-cultural and longitudinal study of both theoretical frameworks is expected to be forthcoming.

Developmental theories assume both direction of change and existence of intrinsic stimulation or satisfaction that reinforces the directional thrust. They also have a built-in value bias clearly visible, for example, when Kohlberg described "a discussion process to help the students move in the direction of greater adequacy" (1974, p. 10). Fowler, however, cautioned against regarding stages as achievement levels and maintained each stage has its own special merit (Gilmour, 1976). The possibility of an intrinsic impetus being present in a developmental process poses challenging methodological and practical problems. According to Kohlberg (1974), the stimulus for movement to the next stage of moral development can occur during the educational process. He reported that when students at different stages of moral development discussed problems requiring moral judgments and decisions, exposure to the next stage of reasoning resulted in change to that next level of moral development, a change still present a year later when the students were retested. Reflection on this result suggests a variety of questions for study.

What factors provide necessary and sufficient conditions for one to move through the stages of develop...g moral judgment? If regression to an earlier stage does not occur generally, are there conditions under which regression will occur at all? What factors are barriers to development? To what extent can moral development be directed through planned intervention? What is the relationship between the process of developing moral judgment and other processes involved in human growth? Specifically, for our concern in this chapter, what is the relationship between moral development and faith development?

Kohlberg (1974, pp. 13-14) noted, "It is almost self-evident that they would roughly parallel one another." He further hypothesized "that development to a given moral stage precedes development to a parallel faith stage." Fowler reviewed Kohlberg's analysis of the relationship and generally agreed with the parallelism but raised questions about precedence. "The nub of my theoretical and conceptual difference with Kohlberg can be put this way: I think it is a mistake to assume that faith is or must be an *a posteriori* derivative of or justification for morality, the appeal to Kant notwithstanding. In fact, I would argue conversely, that every moral perspective, at whatever level of development, is anchored in a broader system of beliefs and loyalties" (1976, p. 208). Kohlberg and Fowler both look to further research for material to help assess the relationship between their theories.

Family Background

Family structure, the centrality of which is a major component of our cultural heritage, is basic to the communication of values, beliefs, and behavioral expectations. It is the first group with which the child has continual contact. The pattern of intimate and extensive emotional attachments in the family provides the framework for all experience and perceptions. Within that pattern, the mother has been assumed to be a more significant influence than the father in the moral development of the child, female or male (Hoffman, 1971). Recently, however, a number of researchers have suggested this is a shortsighted view and that, in fact, child development researchers have missed the importance of fathers because of our cultural habit of focusing on maternal influence. (See, for example, Biller and Meredith, 1975; Lamb, 1976; Lynn, 1974.)

That the family as a whole is important in the process of religious socialization is generally supported by research, with some exceptions. Both Moberg (1971) and Thomas and others (1974) concluded that religious socialization of the child has an impact on religious behavior and beliefs that lasts beyond childhood. Indeed, Aldous and Hill (1963) found religious affiliations endured across three generations, at least, for most people in their sample. In a study of a national sample of American Catholics focused primarily on devotional behavior, McCready (1972) reported parental influence outweighed any social class effect and there appeared to be a transmission of patterns of devotional behavior between generations. Summarizing data from three national studies, Bealer and Willets (1967, p. 442) conclude, "The adolescent tends strongly to accept rather than reject parental values." The authors of a study of confirmands of the American Lutheran Church wrote, "the postconfirmation religious activity is more closely related to individual influential persons, and especially the level of parental activity, than to the organized program of the church" (Havighurst and Keating, 1971, p.

712). The relationship between parental control and support reported among urban Catholic adolescents by Thomas and others (1974) was also generally confirmed for a sample of Mormon adolescents in a small university town (Weigert and Thomas, 1972). Adolescents had the highest self-esteem, conformed most to parental expectations, and had the highest religiosity scores when they also reported receiving a high degree of support and control from parents.

Studies of college-age students also report a positive impact for parental influence upon religion-related behavior. Johnson (1973) found that middle- to upper-middle-class college students perceive their parents as generally similar to themselves in religious commitment. Those students who were more religious reported their parents to be happier, warmer, and more accepting than less-religious students reported their parents to be. An inquiry into the religiosity of university students from six Latin American countries by Smith (n.d.) confirmed the importance of parental ideas about religion as influences upon the students' religiosity. The data showed both religious identity and attendance to be strongly correlated with parental religiosity.

There is other evidence involving a very atypical group that points to the positive impact of childhood background upon adult manifestations of religiosity (Hoge and Keeter, 1976). A study of teachers on two primarily undergraduate college faculties showed childhood religion and home culture were major influences upon religiosity. There was little evidence of a "religion of science" as a functionally equivalent competitor with traditional religion. These data do not support the "scholarly distance" theory of Lehman and Shriver (1968) that the more one's discipline includes the study of religion, the less religious one will be. Lehman (1974), however, concluded that the scholarly distance relationship holds only for large, research-oriented universities and that other types of institutions present different patterns. So perhaps the scholarly distance hypothesis is not invalidated by Hoge and Keeter's data.

There are some exceptions to this general trend of results showing religious socialization to have effects lasting into adulthood. Elifson (1976), in a study of the religious behavior of urban Southern Baptists, found that intergenerational transmission of religious values was minimal. Keeley (1976) reported that the younger generation, when compared to parents, did seem to have more difficulty with selected conditions of life: uncertainty about its meaning, low level of satisfaction, and fear of death. However, the trend in the findings reported suggests the differences between generations are probably not as great as popularly assumed. Keeley (1976) suggested some findings of generational differences may reflect differences between one parent and the offspring rather than differences between both parents and the offspring.

Gender Differences

Females are consistently reported to be more religious than males on all criteria (Argyle, 1958; Gallup, 1976). The explanation for this difference in religiosity lies not in biological difference but in the socialization process (Payne and Whittington, 1974; Westerhoff and Neville, 1974). Males and females learn the culturally approved styles of behavior for their sex. There is a major difference from the beginning of socialization. The cues for female behavior tend to lead women into roles as culture bearers for the society. This responsibility is reflected in data on the importance of mothers in communicating values to the next generation (Thomas and others, 1974; Salisbury, 1970). Females are reinforced for "appropriate" behavior in ways that may be unintentional but that are by and large very successful. The language of religion, for example, refers to the deity in male pronouns, to (male) Christian soldiers, to men of God, and such. Westerhoff and Neville (1974, p. 142) also report that "Careful examination and comparison of ethnographic data from the major subcultural groups in the United States reveal that there is a strong tendency in them all to emphasize the centrality of the mother in transmitting the cultural heritage [and] it is apparent from the data that the central role of mother as socializer is shared by the major European traditions." Conditions are changing; there are now female clergy and acolytes in many churches. But the traditional gender differences in religiosity are deeply rooted in our religious culture and are unlikely to disappear soon.

Education

Religious organizations seek to inculcate beliefs, values, and behavioral patterns through specifically religious, short-attendance-period school, usually held on Sundays or Saturdays. Although there are studies attempting to relate Sunday school experience to subsequent behavior (Argyle, 1958), there has been very little research on church youth groups as groups (Havighurst and Keating, 1971). Sunday schools and other church-based youth activities provide specifically religious education, but the consequences for participants extend beyond the religious results. Havighurst and Keating (1971) followed two groups from the fourth and sixth grade until age eighteen. They found a youth subculture existed outside the public school subculture. The church youth programs provided opportunity for some young people who were not high school leaders to take leadership roles in religious youth groups. Thus, church-sponsored programs provided general socialization opportunities for young people in addition to promoting the participants' religious development.

Research into the influence of parochial school education consistently reflects the importance of family background. Studies of Jewish (Rosen, 1965), Catholic (Greeley and Rossi, 1966), and Protestant (Johnstone, 1975) youth show that parochial schools have a strong influence on religious beliefs and rituals and are most effective with children from the most religious homes. Greeley and Rossi identified a "multiplier effect" for the combination of religious home and Catholic school that together showed stronger impact than could have been predicted from either alone. The implications of a multiplier effect in conjunction with what is known of the effectiveness of isolation from competing influences in the socialization process suggest parochial education under certain conditions might be very influential upon participants. Moberg (1971) cited evidence supporting the popular belief that isolation from the dominant culture through parochial schools and other social structures permits attention to values and beliefs that leads to intensive religious experiences. Greeley and Gockel (1971, p. 294) believe "The most useful sort of study, then, would not be one that would consider whether parochial schools have an impact on adult religious behavior. . . . Rather, the more relevant question would be how religious education interacts with the other variables which have influence on the religious socialization process. Such a research design would be far more complicated than any described herein, but in our judgment such a design is the next logical step in any theoretical consideration of religious socialization."

Personality Characteristics

Various data have shown a positive correlation between orthodox religious commitment and certain, presumably unhealthy, personality traits; but the findings have not been consistent. For example, Argyle (1958) found evidence of somewhat more neurosis for religious than for nonreligious persons between the ages of sixteen and thirty; but the trend was reversed for older people, with the more religious being better adjusted. He also reported no evidence that psychotics were either more or less religious. Dittes (1971a) found a positive correlation between measures of religiosity and low self-esteem and other indexes of pathology. However, the relationship was weak. Stark (1971) argued there is a negative relationship between commitment to conventional religious beliefs and degree of psychopathology.

If pathology were positively related to religiosity, one would expect to find particularly strong evidence for this relationship among religious professionals. However, Dittes reviewed more than a thousand reports concerning the psychological characteristics of religious professionals and concluded the relationship has not been proved and "nothing is confidently known about the distinctive personality characteristics of religious professionals" (1971b, p. 425). Simmonds, Richardson, and Harder (1976) also believe the issue remains open.

In the assessment of these diverse findings, Rokeach (1970, p. 230) commented, "results cannot be accounted for by assuming, as the anti-religionists do, that religion is an unqualified force for evil; nor by assuming, as the pro-religionists do, that religion is a force only for good. Instead, I believe that these results become more understandable if we assume that there exist simultaneously, within the organized religions of the West, psychologically conflicting moral forces for good *and* evil—teaching brotherhood with the right hand and bigotry with left, facilitating mental health in some and mental conflict, anxiety, and psychosis in others. I realize that this seems an extreme interpretation; but the research bears it out."

Readiness Factors

When an individual's behavioral patterns, for whatever reason, become less satisfying, the individual is ready to change. Readiness to change is a result of situational factors and individual responses to them. Lofland and Stark (1965) speak of "turning points," such as a move to a new town, loss of employment, business failure, divorce, and school failure. During such critical times, individuals are likely to be relatively susceptible to pressure to change. Such changes may involve only the individual and those closest to her or him or they may lead the individual to participate in efforts to bring about broad social change—to participate in a social or religious movement.

Glock (1964) saw "felt deprivation" as a necessary precondition for the rise of a social or religious movement. Deprivations may be economic, social, psychic, organismic, or ethical (the perception of evil where good should be). Yinger (1970, p. 153) pointed out that readiness to change must be accompanied by opportunity. Basing his analysis on a description by Lofland of a "doomsday cult," Yinger outlined these essential conditions for the conversion of an individual to a deviant religious group's perspectives: Members will have experienced enduring, acutely felt tensions within a religious, problem-solving perspective. They will have been led to defining themselves as religious seekers and, at a turning point in their lives, will have encountered the cult.

Affective bonds to adherents to the cult will be formed—or may have already been in existence—while extracult attachments will be weak or broken. Through the resulting intense interaction between members, they become "deployable agents" of the cult. To put this more simply, the converts to a new religious movement will be people who are ready to change, who have the opportunity to change, and who are reinforced rather than impeded in the change process.

A key factor in this process is face-to-face contact. Harrison (1974b) found that the major sources of recruitment to Catholic pentecostalism were friends and acquaintances. The frequency of interaction and the effect of the interaction on the potential convert were more important in understanding recruitment to a group than the identity of the recruiter (Gerlach and Hine, 1970). The value system, statement of goals, belief structure, and total program are all important; but they must be conveyed in a positive manner for commitment to follow. Gerlach and Hine (1970, p. 88) wrote, "We would only point out that a truth, or even The Truth, must be communicated to be believed. And it is our observation that truth is most successfully communicated in the context of a personal relationship in which a certain degree of rapport and trust has already been established."

Conclusion

There are many reasons for encouraging research in religious socialization, but I wish to emphasize only two of them. First, research in the area has barely begun and we have no comprehensive longitudinal studies. We have no real idea of what lies ahead. I believe efforts to investigate religious socialization can fruitfully focus on any facet of the process by which humans transcend themselves in order to affirm the meaning of their existence. The experience of transcendence is an area of human reality that evokes the interest of both social scientists and theologians (Brewer, 1975; Johnson, 1974). The possibility of self-transcendence is assumed to be a critical element that facilitates the transition of individuals through the life stages outlined by Kohlberg and Fowler. Thus, the study of the origins or causes of the experience of transcendence is both theoretically and empirically important.

Second, the quality of the socialization of individual members determines the effectiveness of any group in accomplishing its established goals. Religious socialization is a specific subpart of the socialization process in general, and that process is of critical importance during a time of rapid social and cultural change. A salient factor of modern American society is structurally induced frustration. In the evolving socioemotional milieu that characterizes our society, the affective needs of humans appear to receive special emphasis (Zaretsky and Leone, 1974). Part of the change has taken the form of families becoming more "humanistic" in character. But we have also observed that youth who experience that sort of socialization sometimes have difficulty adjusting to the bureaucratic, impersonal, instrumental relations of the adult occupational structure (Anthony and Robbins, 1974).

This condition of structurally induced role conflict has an analogue among religious groups that find their members being taught one thing but learning another. Rokeach (1970, p. 231) wrote, "The contradictions in religious teachings are more subtle than those in politics and would, for the most part, be denied consciously. A conflict between ideological content and ideological structure—between what is taught and *how* it is taught—must be very subtle. A particular religious institution not only must disseminate a particular religious ideology; it must also perpetuate itself and defend against outside attack. It is this dual purpose of religious institutions, I hypothesize, that leads to the contradiction between the *what* and the *how*. It leads to the paradox of a church disseminating truly religious values to the extent possible, while unwittingly communicating antireligious values to the extent necessary." Awareness of the unintentional results of the socialization process may be as important as the intended consequences of the educational or religious educational process.

As a lifelong process, socialization continues. Persons can and do change their patterns of perception and response. Of particular interest in the area of religious socialization are the new forms of informal religious participation. Failing to find themselves experiencing satisfying rewards—material, social, or psychic—many persons, especially youth, have chosen emerging patterns of religious behavior. Reich (1970) believes the new consciousness to which the new religious cults are related provides important societal opportunity for the future, and others believe the new American cult permits youth to raise questions, to entertain great ideas (Johnstone, 1975).

The processes by which these groups have emerged and are perpetuating themselves include a multitude of socializing components (Anthony and Robbins, 1974; Hill, 1975; Johnson, 1976; Moody, 1974). Techniques used include separating prospective converts from former associates, suppressing the importance of former accomplishments, emphasizing the benefits of the new experience, providing ranked positions to which the new member may aspire, rewarding conforming behavior, training through the use of models to guide behavior, communicating beliefs in an affectively supportive environment, aiding the new member in developing an orderly world view, and maintaining a "community" relationship as the context for the socializee's adaptive responses. Remembering that much of this new religious activity centers around personal quests for meaning, purpose, and roots in an unsettled and quavering if not fractured social environment (Johnstone, 1975), one would anticipate the effectiveness of a religious socialization that utilizes these components carefully. If we are to understand the social change around us, it seems imperative to understand the process of religious socialization much better than we do now.

CHAPTER 10

Nonassociational Religious Participation

Barbara Pittard-Payne

The inclusion of a chapter on religious participation in a volume on informal social participation marks a major theoretical and methodological addition to voluntary action research. Only recently have religious organizations begun to be viewed as voluntary organizations similar to other organizations (see Scherer, 1972). Social science researchers have usually excluded, by definition, membership in religious organizations (Babchuk and Booth, 1969) or have included only religious organization subgroup memberships, such as church school classes, altar guilds, service and Bible study groups, and social clubs for singles, seniors, and such. In addition to obscuring the extent of voluntary organizational memberships in society, this arbitrary operational definition excludes the millions of individuals whose major social participation outside of work organizations and the family is either in associational or nonassociational religious forms. This chapter is concerned with these forms of religious participation. More specifically, it focuses mainly on new forms of informal religious participation emerging in the past few decades.

Individual religious participation is generally equated with membership in a religious organization, and individual religiosity is therefore usually measured by attachment to some church (Demerath and Hammond, 1970). But more properly and broadly, religious participation (associational and nonassociational) includes (1) addressing the supernatural (prayer and exorcism), (2) religious music making (singing, chanting, and playing instruments) and dancing, (3) physiological religious exercise (physical manipulation of psychological states through psychedelic drugs, deprivation, and mortification), (4) religious recitation (use of the sacred written and oral literature, which contains statements regarding the pantheon, cosmology, myths, and moral injunctions), (5) religious simulation (imitating things for the purpose of control), (6) use of religious power or mana (touching things possessed of sacred power and laying on of hands), (7) observing religious taboo (avoiding things to prevent the activation of unwanted power or undesired events), (8) religious feasts (sacred meals), (9) religious sacrifices (immolation, offerings, and fees), (10) religious congregation (processions, meetings, and convocations), (11) religious inspiration, (12) manufacture and use of religiously symbolic objects, (13) extending and modifying the religious code, and (14) applying religious values in nonreligious contexts.

So strong is this assumption that religious participation and religiosity must be reflected in formal affiliation with a specific church (at least in the United States) that the antithesis of religion is held to be meaningful only in the context of formally organized religion. An organizational assumption would define religion as a system of beliefs and practices by means of which a group of people struggles with the ultimate problems of human life (Durkheim, 1954; Yinger, 1970). In contrast, a private, individual assumption includes such definition as the following: Religion is what man does in his solitariness (James, 1950) or man's attempt to enlarge and complete his own personality by finding the supreme context in which he rightly belongs. The individual religious quest is solitary because though people are socially interdependent with others in a thousand ways, no one else is able to provide an individual with a faith or prescribe one's individual pact with the cosmos (Allport, 1950, p. 161).

Paradoxically, there is an equally strong assumption, developing out of the Protestant Reformation's emphasis on the priesthood of all believers, that religion is an individual matter and therefore the private business of each person. This assumption has led gradually to the attitude that one can be a good Christian (religious person) without having anything to do with the organized church. Some researchers view the prevalence of this attitude as an empirical indicant of the penetration of institutional barriers and the beginning of noninstitutional forms of individual religious activity (Hargrove, 1974). Of course, if one takes a long historical perspective, one finds that noninstitutional participation has long been common in traditional and preliterate societies.

The duality of assumptions equating religious participation with associational membership and the privatization of religion is reflected in the domination in religion research of studies of associational forms of participation and of religiosity (Fichter, 1975; Fukuyama, 1961; Glock and Stark, 1965; King and Hunt, 1972; Pittard-Payne, 1966). Most studies have identified and measured individual religious activity in an organizational context—by church attendance or commitment to orthodox systems and goals of religious associations. In part, this is because data on the associational forms of religion are relatively plentiful, and formal adherents to religion and their specific kinds of participation are relatively visible and accessible to study. *The Yearbook of the Churches* and Gallup surveys reporting church membership, attendance, and orthodoxy of beliefs have been used as major statistical indicators of the waxing and waning of religious participation in American society. Although these data are limited methodologically, they are the only statistical indicators consistently reporting religious participation. (See Brewer, 1973, for a discussion of religious indicators used in research.)

The surfacing of many new nonassociational forms of religious participation came as a surprise to most researchers. They had, as Fichter (1975) observes, studied the so-called religious revival as a statistical phenomenon of church membership after World War II while witnessing a long-term trend toward secularism. By 1960, traditional religious forms (denominations) were being identified as marginal in modern society. Industrial urbanization, it was concluded, had created the secular city, secular church, and secular person (Cox, 1965; Wilson, 1970). While Hadden (1969) was forecasting a gathering storm in the churches and Altizer and Hamilton (1966) were pronouncing God dead, new forms of religious participation were emerging all over the world. By all previous measures, religious skies were dark. But, God (or religion) was not dead; he (she? they?) was alive and well in many places.

The researchers' overconcentration on associational forms of religious activity failed either to provide an account of the place of religion as a social form or of individual religious participation in modern industrial societies or to predict its form and place in postindustrial society. Furthermore, as Luckmann (1967, p. 28) concluded, church-oriented religious activity is perhaps not even the most important form of religious participation in modern society. The new forms represent expansion and not decline of religion and social differentiation rather than cultural uniformity. Some of the new forms of the sacred in modern and postindustrial society are very old; some are Christian; some are not. Whether they herald the beginning of the post-Christian era may be questioned, but it seems certain that an era of growing nonassociational religious participation is dawning. Greeley (1970) warns of the temptation to interpret the recent emergence of bizarre manifestations of religion and the sacred as a "resacralization." Society, he maintains, was never "desacralized" in the first place. The 1976 Gallup survey found little evidence of any widespread disenchantment with religion in the United States in the last decade and a half. Generally, church attendance and affiliation have remained constant. Ninety-four percent of the American people surveyed expressed a belief in a supreme deity; 71 percent reported membership in a church or synagogue; and 40 percent attended a church or synagogue weekly. Moreover, the widespread disenchantment with religion among youth appears to have subsided. The popular idea that religious interest is declining most likely stems from loss of membership and general decline in church going by youth in the sixties in certain denominations, such as Methodist and Catholic. Thus, Gallup (1976, p. 5) expands the interpretation of the new forms as a change and not a decline in religious participation to include the associational participation and concludes, "While some observers contend that we are entering a post-Christian era, the data presented in their report would seem to portend just the opposite—that we may be in the first stages of spiritual renewal in this country."

There has probably been more nonassociational religious participation in this country than previously identified. While formal religious organizations in the United States and other Western societies were adversely affected by the social and political upheavals of the sixties, those same upheavals spawned new religious groups and provided the stimuli for the new forms of nonassociational religious participation. As researchers, we have some new research questions: (1) What is the social structure of the new forms? (2) What is the social context for them? (3) Who are the participants and why do they participate in the new forms?

To limit this chapter to the nonassociational forms would be, of course, to recommit the church-oriented errors of preceding research. My review, then, concerns mainly nonassociational participation; but I have attempted to view the new forms within the total theoretical and social context of religious participation. Before I summarize the literature, some comments on the theoretical framework and methodological nature of the studies are in order. The theoretical framework for much of the study of collective religious behavior has been the church-sect typology (Becker, 1957; Brewer, 1952; Eister, 1972; Troeltsch, 1960). Although subjected to much valid criticism, these typologies provide a convenient framework within which to analyze new forms. But they also have yielded evidence that this theory, especially the concept of sect or cult, is not entirely adequate (Fenn, 1972; B. Johnson, 1971; Snook, 1974).

Nonassociational religious participation takes place mainly in informal groups, such as charismatic, prayer, or social action groups, and in private activities such as Bible and religious reading, meditation, listening to the radio, and viewing television programs, as distinguished from more formal participation in church programs, services, and administration. The church, ecclesia, and denominations are characterized by written constitutions or bylaws, specifically designated leaders, explicity stated goals and objectives, ritual, clear group boundaries, and established procedures for inducting new members (Brewer, 1952). In contrast, cults and sects are usually centered around a small primary group with relatively undifferentiated leadership of a charismatic character. Authority is rooted in direct religious experience. Allegiance is voluntary but individuals are admitted only on proof of conviction. Faith is first, and members order their lives accordingly.

Sects are distinguished from cults by their schismatic character—that is, opposition to the parent groups, dissatisfaction with routinized traditions, and a desire to seek their own way to religious salvation (Wilson, 1970). The cult is not schismatic but focuses on God, the Holy Spirit, and direct inward, religious, or psychic experiences. It may draw its inspiration from other than a primary religion but operates within formal religious organization (Fichter, 1975; Glock and Stark, 1965; Yinger, 1970). Because the main thrust of the new forms of religious participation is the hope of ecstatic experience, Ellenwood's (1973, p. 19) working definition of a cult is particularly appropriate for the analysis of the new groups: "A cult is a group derived from the experience of one or a few individuals who are able to enter (or fascinated by the possibility of entering) a superior, ecstatic state of consciousness in which contact and rapport with all reaches of a nonhistorical and impersonal universe are possible with the help of intermediaries (human and/or supernatural). In a cult an outer circle of members experiences the presence of the sacred in their individuals, and seeks to participate in this experience."

Ecstasy-based groups to be described here exhibit a combination of cult and mysticism. I suggest this signifies the emergence of a fourth type of religious group (neither cult, sect, nor church) capable of taking institutional form. Troeltsch's (1960, pp. 730-731) church-sect-cult-mysticism typology is relevant for defining these ecstacy-based groups and new forms of religious participation:

[M]ysticism is simply the insistence upon a direct inward and present religious experience. It takes for granted the objective forms of religious life in worship, ritual, myth, and dogma;

and it is either a reaction against these objective practices, which it tries to draw back into the living process, or it is the supplementing of traditional forms of worship by means of a personal and living stimulus. Mysticism is thus always something secondary, something which has been deliberately thought out, although this emotional condition which has been deliberately produced is characteristically connected with an immediacy of feeling which is the entire opposite of the former process. Thus it always contains a paradoxical element, a certain hostility to popular religion and its average forms of expression, and artificiality which, however, is again extinguished by its own thirst for direct communion with God. . . . The vitality of the religious sense . . . when it is faced with objectified religion, easily and often develops mystical characteristics. It expresses itself in ecstasy and frenzy, in visions and hallucinations, in subjective religious experience and "inwardness," in concentration upon the purely interior and emotional side of religious experience.

The methods used in formal participation research (especially the sample survey and religiosity scale) are not entirely appropriate for research into cults and mysticism. Researchers report difficulty in finding participants willing to be interviewed because many new groups are suspicious of outsiders. The nature of the data in most of the studies does not permit sophisticated statistical analysis, and the representativeness of any sample obtained is difficult to ascertain. Many of the existing studies utilize journalistic accounts and self-reports by members and leaders (Enroth, Breckenridge, and Ericson, 1972; Leming and Smith, 1975; Plowman, 1971; Truzzi, 1972). Newspaper and magazine feature stories of uncertain accuracy must often be used for information on the origins of these groups. Many researchers have employed interview and participant observation methods (Balswick, 1974; Hamby, 1975; Harder, Richardson, and Simonds, 1972; Hill, 1975; Hine, 1969; Judah, 1974; McGuire, 1975; Peterson and Mauss, 1973). It must be pointed out, then, that generalizations based on secondary sources, case studies, or limited or purposive samples will require caution. However, the cumulated data do show enough consistency to generate some hypotheses and/or at least suggestions for further research, and the following review will include these where possible.

Historical Context

The decades since World War II have been marked by continued industrial development, urbanization, population increase, affluence, and social and political protest. Mass phenomena in such fields as education, media, leisure, and production characterize the period. About these years Yinger (1963, p. 65) observed, "For the first time in human history there are societies within which poverty . . . (a shortage of goods and services) is no longer the central fact." There may still have been substantial poverty, but most people in the newly affluent societies were better off than they had ever been (Banfield, 1968). For persons in technologically advanced societies, life expectancy at birth had been extended from forty to over seventy years.

Roszak (1969) describes the society of the sixties as so complex that it transcends the competence of the amateur citizen and demands the attention of specially trained experts. The prime goal of such a society is to keep the productive apparatus turning effectively. Efficiency and successful management are the order of the day. Pressures to compete and succeed are often overwhelming. The sixties were the years of the youth culture, counterculture, generation gap, and protests. The restlessness and revolt of American youth, exemplified by the extremist political groups on the one hand and the bohemianism of the "hippy" on the other, became worldwide phenomena. For the first time in history, college education was for the masses. Colleges and universities experienced unprecedented growth in one decade. It was not uncommon for the student population on college and university campuses to grow from six to twenty thousand students, equal to the size of most towns in the United States. These campuses provided the arena for protesters and causes such as civil rights, ecology, and the Vietnam War. There was extensive debunking of norms and authority. Business, military, government, churches, and family institutions were attacked and found to be structurally dysfunctional, depersonalized (that is, devoid of regard for human values), and morally weak. The protests and dissent of individuals and groups progressed from nonviolent, rather peaceful sit-ins to more militant action that included occupying university buildings, burning sections of cities, and bombing and led to a national political convention being held behind barbed wire. The 1970 Cambodia–Kent State–Jackson State debacle marked the end of the politicization of the campuses and disillusionment with efforts to change society. Quieter, but still significant, manifestations of protest among the youth were the drug and hippie cultures (Boskin and Rosenstone, 1972). The hippie phenomenon subsided in the late 1960s when disastrous drug trips, rapes, murders, and other crimes in areas like New York's Greenwich Village and Atlanta's Tenth Street Strip destroyed the flower children's image of love (Peterson and Mauss, 1973).

Religious organizations did not escape the effects of these social upheavals. Public issues were hotly debated within local churches and denominational councils (Quinley, 1974). Religious leaders were involved in many of the protest movements. Even liberal leaders faced resistance from rank and file church members who began to demand and exercise more authority in their churches. Most Protestant groups responded with plans for "restructuring" and ecumenism. The Catholic church's early response was Vatican II, with changes in ritual and religious practice. The first seven years of the seventies seem to have been a period of reassessment and retrenchment in which religious leaders were not as actively involved in public issues and liberal churches were reordering their priorities in the face of serious financial crises (Quinley, 1974). This period was climaxed by the Watergate burglary and subsequent revelations of corruption in political, business, and military systems and by the economic crises of inflation and depression.

Forms of Nonassociational Religious Participation

I classify the forms of nonassociational religious participation by type of religious orientation: (1) Christian, including church- and non-church-related groups and private individual participation; (2) mysticism, especially that inspired by Eastern religions; and (3) occult, including magic and satan groups.

Christian Nonassociational Religious Participation. Church surveys in the United States and Europe consistently identify a small fraction of church membership who comprise a "hard core" or "ritual core" of people who attend weekly and participate in other religious activities (Gallup, 1976; Luckmann, 1967). Estimated weekly attendance is 40 percent in the United States and 20 to 30 percent in Europe and England (Dumazedier, 1974; Gallup, 1976; Gorer, 1967). Fichter (1952) views 60 to 70 percent of church members as "marginal," "dormant," "dead," or, in Moberg's (1962) more judgmental term, "backsliders." By whatever name they are called, occasional attenders may be seen as nonassociational participants on the grounds that their participation is no more significant to the institutional life of the church than non-members'. Research is needed to determine the patterns of religious participation of this large proportion of occasional church attenders as well as the participation patterns of the small proportion (8 percent) of nonattenders Gallup (1976) reports who participate in church activities other than formal services.

Many nonassociational activities identified by researchers as church activities are not dependent upon associational membership. These include attending neighborhood prayer groups, neighborhood or communitywide groups organized around the teaching of a Bible expert, evangelist, or charismatic leader, and continuing education classes at community religious colleges; meditating; discussing religion; reading religious materials; listening to and viewing religious programs; and providing community services (practicing the faith). In religiosity studies, these practices are usually considered measures of devotionalism related to commitment to the church (Fukuyama, 1961; Glock and Stark, 1965; King and Hunt, 1972; Pittard-Payne, 1963).

Focus on these nonassociational religious expressions broadens the definition of religious participation and includes some of the "invisible" religious activities (Lemert, 1975; Luckmann, 1967). Machalek and Martin's (1976, p. 320) research supports the "contention that people's perception of life's ultimate concern and accompanying coping mechanisms are not limited to an institutionalized religious context." Their results lend credibility to Luckmann's observations about the importance of nonpublic religious activity in modern society.

Several sociologists recognize non-church members as a significant population in religious research (Brewer and Weatherford, 1962; Cuber, 1940; Mauss, 1969; Vernon, 1968). Cuber studied marginal church members and found that 18 to 37 percent of those attending church were nonmembers and that almost every clergyman interviewed reported receiving numerous requests from nonmembers for religious ceremonies (weddings and funerals). Vernon likens these religious "nones" to "political independents" who have no organizational visibility. They have no recognized spokesperson or ready audience for their beliefs. The opinions of church members and leaders are sought on religious questions, but the opinions of the unchurched are not (Nathanson, 1955). In fact, as Lipman and Varspan (1962) conclude, the atheist, agnostic, and nonbeliever to some degree are second-class citizens.

In a southern Appalachian study, Brewer (1959) and Brewer and Weatherford (1962) found that 80 percent of the nonmembers participate in a religious activity weekly. In order of importance, these activities included (1) listening to religious radio or television programs; (2) private prayer, Bible reading, or reading other religious material in private; (3) talking about religion at work or in social groups; (4) saying a family blessing at meals; (5) helping the needy or some community project; (6) having family prayers or Bible or devotional readings; (7) attending church services; and (8) visiting a minister. Brewer interprets the high importance of talking about religion at work or in social groups as evidence that nonmembers substitute work and social groups for church groups as opportunities to discuss religion. Among the most significant activities for church and non-church members were involvement in informal religious affairs. These findings emphasize the importance of nonassociational religious participation in understanding religious life.

Jesus Movement. The Jesus movement represents the major new nonchurch group within the Christian tradition. Begun in the late 1960s in California and Texas, it is diverse, decentralized, and only loosely organized (Balswick, 1974). Its manifestations range from informal groups to Puritan communes to the extremely militant Children of God. Researchers disagree about including the Children of God as a part of the Jesus movement, and some would place them on the fringe of the movement (Leming and Smith, 1975). These groups are like sects in their antiestablishment stance. They are reacting against the organized churches and in varying degrees to other "establishments" in society. Reasons commonly given for splitting with churches are (1) liberal, institutional Christianity fails to recognize the individual's alienated state and the need to be rightly related to God before one can be rightly related to one's fellow humans; (2) conservative, institutionalized Christianity pays only lip service to the personal gospel and is often unloving, intolerant, and racially and socially discriminatory; (3) Americans are so obsessed with the church (having an "edifice complex") that the church has become an organization to be served, not to serve; (4) evangelism, when it exists, has been inside the church and not in the marketplace, where it belongs; and (5) church services are out of date and offer no opportunities for dialogue or community (Balswick, 1974, pp. 361-362).

The size of the Jesus movement has been estimated at thirty thousand. There are approximately six hundred communes, Christian houses, and colonies in North America with an average of about fifty residents each (Peterson and Mauss, 1973, p. 263). Most "Jesus people" live in these groups; but the defection and relocation rate, as high as 50 percent per year, makes it difficult to determine the exact size of the movement. The success of these groups varies from time to time and place to place. The usual pattern is formation, schism, defection, and decline. The greatest period of growth and dispersion was the first three years (1967 to 1970), and the movement seems to have peaked in the early 1970s. Even the Children of God are decreasing in number in North America, although a stable core group continues.

I found no studies on the movement beyond North America, but the only in-depth study of the Children of God (Hill, 1975) reports about 85 percent of the members and their leader, Moses David, live outside the United States. Others report the Jesus movement has spread to Europe. The largest and fastest growing segment is the Children of God, with thirty-nine colonies and a total of three thousand members in the United States and sixty other countries (Enroth, Breckenridge, and Ericson, 1972; Hill, 1975; Leming and Smith, 1975). The Christ Commune, with its thirty-five houses and six to eight hundred members, is one of the most stable groups. They operate a central agricultural commune and a small fishing fleet in a western state. Total financial assets of this commune are estimated at about $1 million (Harder, Richardson, and Simonds, 1972).

Coffeehouses, the streets, communes, houses, and colonies are the usual bases of operation. The Christian house communities and colonies are at the heart of the movement and provide a combination family, work group, and congregation. Sexual segregation is maintained and the routine is similar to that found in cooperative dormitories on college campuses. Elders, house parents, and sometimes committees provide spiritual leadership and parental supervision. The daily routine includes Bible study classes, street work (proselytizing), and prayer meetings in late afternoon and evening. The latter are the "religious meetings" and have a strong pentecostal atmosphere, including praying, testifying, preaching, speaking in tongues (glossolalia), wiggling about, and responding with clapping and interjections of "praise God" (Balswick, 1974; Peterson and Mauss, 1973). The Christ Commune and the Children of God colonies are more rigidly organized around schedules that resemble monastic orders (Hill, 1975; Leming and Smith, 1975).

The coffeehouse provides a socializing milieu for "freaks" and an outreach device for contacting young people. Here, low-pressure proselytizing in the form of "raps" with people who drop in is done against a background of Jesus rock music and free coffee. Visiting usually begins in midafternoon and includes testimonies, conversations, and exclamations of "praise God" and "Jesus loves you" (Peterson and Mauss, 1973). The publications of numerous newspapers, generally with similar format and content, provides tractlike materials for street evangelism and communication between groups and promotes group cohesion. Circulation is estimated to vary from one hundred thousand to four hundred thousand for the in-house letters.

A major difference between Children of God and mainstream Jesus movement people is the emphasis on the coming judgment of God in a world controlled by Satan (Hill, 1975; Leming and Smith, 1975). This belief increases the intensity and form of their proselytizing. The Children of God also claim to be the only faithful followers who have given up everything to live in a radical Christian community. The unifying feature of the Jesus movement is the fundamentalist Christian belief that a person can overcome alienation and find real meaning in life only through a personal relationship with Jesus Christ. The movement combines this fundamentalist Christianity with a hippie life-style that incorporates the symbols and language of the counterculture (for example, taking a trip with Jesus, having an external high, Jesus power, and the Jesus revolution). Converts are referred to as Jesus people, Jesus freaks, street Christians, God's forever family, or babes.

The Jesus movement is predominantly a youth movement. The Children of God have been exclusively under thirty, but their leaders are adults, predominantly male, authoritarian, and charismatic. Many like David Berg, now Moses David, were rock musicians, some quite well known. Theocratic in organizational form, the Christ Commune and the Children of God adhere to the most rigidly defined status-roles and hierarchy of authority. Strict literal adherence to the Bible results in a male-female hierarchy in which the "woman knows her place." The woman's role is submission to man, just as a man's role is submission to the Lord. As a result, women do not often fill positions of authority and decision making, except as an extension of the male leaders' authority. (That is, the wife of a leader may take over the management of the group in her husband's absence.) The leader rules by God's authority and direct revelation. The Children of God have a network of hierarchical leaders extending from the international leader to hemisphere leaders (shepherds), to regional shepherds, to colony elders and tribal rulers (Hill, 1975). The exclusiveness and separatism of the Children of God and their distrust of those over thirty, including parents and families (who are viewed as part of the establishment world controlled by Satan), have precipitated a counterorganization to oppose them called Free the Children of God.

Charismatic (Neo-Pentecostal) Groups. The outreach charismatic renewal, pentecostal groups in Catholic and mainline Protestant churches in the early sixties, represent the largest and most researched of the church-related forms of nonassociational participation. Pentecostalism is not new, particularly among Protestants. The current neo-Pentecostal forms, however, have newly emerged within Protestant liturgical churches and the Roman Catholic church. Charismatic Catholics are markedly different from traditional Catholics, yet most of them remain active in their church. Most of the groups are ecumenical, having both Protestant and Catholic members; but Protestants outnumber Catholics in most groups (Fichter, 1975).

There is no way of knowing the exact number of charismatics. Hine (1969) estimates that the total world membership in the neo-Pentecostal movement (including independent sects) is about eight to ten million. Harrison (1974b) estimated there were seventy-five thousand active Catholic Pentecostals. There are more than twelve hundred fifty prayer groups listed in the Directory of Notre Dame Charismatic Communication Center, with a median membership of twenty-eight. An estimated twenty thousand persons attended the Notre Dame Annual Prayer Meeting in 1973. We do know that enough groups have been formed within mainline (non-Pentecostal) Protestant churches to require the latter to develop a policy about glossolalia. There is no evidence that this movement has peaked.

The charismatic groups are cults within ecclesia—that is, small groups, informally structured, having beliefs and practices at variance with the church but contained within it (Fichter, 1975; Harrison, 1974b; Lapsley and Simpson, 1964). Members maintain separation between their usual church worship and the charismatic group (prayer) meeting. The latter is not a formal church activity, although the members do not view their participation as in conflict with their formal church participation (Fichter, 1975; Hamby, 1975; Kildahl, 1973; McGuire, 1975). On the contrary, most new charismatics report increased involvement in their churches and finding formal worship services more meaningful (Fichter, 1975; Hamby, 1975).

Although they are not schismatic, they do seek renewal of the churches (structurally and functionally) through personal renewal and through building a new society within the shell of the old. Like the Jesus people, Pentecostals are critical of the practices and failures of organized religion to deal with individual, experiential needs. Many view churches as being in a crisis of faith and society as showing a breakdown of moral and social order (McGuire, 1975).

Small, informal prayer groups are the typical format for Protestant and Catholic charismatic activity. However, there are some groups with over one hundred members (Harrison, 1974b; McGuire, 1975). Fichter (1975) and Harrison (1974b) found elements of the usual large-scale organization in the Catholic groups, including a decision-making structure, group goals, established communication channels, and differentiation of roles (division of labor through specialized ministries). Looking at the extent to which the leadership permits the general membership to influence or speak in meetings, McGuire (1975) found groups vary from open (free) to closed (controlled). Group leadership is predominantly lay but may include clergy and other religious professionals such as nuns, Christian educators, and theologians. Harrison (1974b) reports that Catholic Pentecostals are developing increasingly closer ties to the clergy.

Another form is the "intentional" community, which represents an extension of the emphasis on the community of believers, group cohesion, witnessing (putting the faith to work), and ministry to each other. From a participant observation study of the Allelulia Community, Hamby (1975) reports a structure similar to the Jesus people's Christian communes and houses, with all income held in common and most members working outside the community. Coordinators and household heads are responsible for spiritual leadership. The houses are clustered in a single neighborhood.

The fundamentalist Pentecostal beliefs include literal acceptance of the Bible as the ultimate authority for living and belief in the Holy

Spirit, the virgin birth, and miracles. Emphasis is upon the subjective religious experience—that is, upon the spirit that dwells within, the Holy Spirit that interprets past, present, and expected behavior. Stress is placed upon charismatic gifts, such as the power to do physical healing and glossolalia. The most recent convert may (but not all do) speak in tongues—an entry to significant status, at least in the Jesus community. The fit of healing is supposed to be a group phenomenon; but the leaders, who are closer to God, may serve as mediators. (The Children of God pray as a group for the health of a needy person.) Not only physical healing but also the correction of social or psychological behaviors, such as overcoming a drug or alcohol habit or sexual promiscuity, can be achieved by acccepting Jesus (Hill, 1975). Pentecostal ethics involve renunciation of things of the world and stress personal relationships. Thus, they do not see need to change evil social structures and, with the exception of the revolutionary Children of God, are apolitical. This fundamentalist, Pentecostal, and "hip" faith contains an element of religious pragmatism. Belief in Jesus "works" in one's life; converts report "kicking the drug habit," changing their life-style, and no longer feeling lonely, alienated, or unloved (Balswick, 1974). These are millennialists who believe they are a part of the movement of the Holy Spirit that heralds the end of the world and the second coming of Christ in their lifetime. The work of Jesus is their political participation.

Central to all the charismatics is the baptism of the spirit as a discrete spiritual experience. Evidence of the experience is "receiving the gifts of the spirit," which includes speaking in tongues, prophecy, and healing. The charismatics claim they are reaffirming the mystery and miracle of orthodox Christianity. They stress community and group fellowship. Members maintain a rigid time schedule for private and group prayer and Bible study, but with an antiintellectual approach. Literal interpretation of the Bible and personal religious experience are the bases of authority. All participants are expected to testify to what God has done for them, how life has changed, and to praise the Lord for these gifts. They believe God takes an active role in everyday affairs. Healing is a part of every meeting and includes petitions on behalf of sick or crippled members or friends. Fichter (1975) reported 37 percent of the 154 groups he surveyed witnessed physical healing regularly. But psychological healings (of resentments and hardened feelings) are the most frequent type. In belief and practice, these groups remain a "cult of the paraclete" (Fichter, 1975) with some sectarian organizational characteristics (Harrison, 1974b). The charismatics, then, are an internal cult of renewal rather than an external sectarian movement in that they "focus their devotion on the Paraclete, The Holy Spirit, the third divine person of the Trinity" (Fichter, 1975, p. 21).

Mysticism: Eastern Groups. Many of the new forms reflect renewed interest, influence, and appeal of Eastern religions in the Western world. Groups have been formed around emigrant Hindu gurus and swamis and variations of Buddhism. I shall describe the Krishna Consciousness Society, Meher Baba, and Nichiren Shoshu.

One of the most conspicuous of the new groups is the Krishna Consciousness movement. This ecstatic interpretation of a school of Hinduism was introduced to North America by a seventy-year-old charismatic leader, Swami Bhaktivedanta, in 1965. He originally attracted New York hippies to his beliefs while chanting in a park. By 1974, he had established the International Krishna Consciousness Society with twenty-eight of its sixty-eight temples in the United States (Ellenwood, 1973; Judah, 1974). The number of full-time devotees (converts or members) is unknown, but it is estimated at less than one or two thousand. However, the influence of Krishna goes far beyond its actual size, as indicated by the sale of more than three hundred thousand copies of each issue of their publication, *Back to the Godhead*, which is translated into French, German, Japanese, Chinese, and Hindu, and by the financial success of their art and ceramics business in India and their large incense factory in the United States.

The Krishna devotees have been described as counterculture Protestants who reject such significant elements of the establishment as (1) valuing material success achieved through competitive labor; (2) an education that promotes that end; (3) accumulation of unneeded possessions for a sense of gratification; (4) authorities, both civil and parental, who favor the status quo; (5) wars, such as the Vietnamese conflict, that are regarded as a product of a selfish economic imperialism; and (6) hypocritically supporting norms regarding civil rights and social relationships and churchgoing without practicing the ideals that give rise to them (Judah, 1974, p. 16)

The core of the Hare Krishna belief is the account of Krishna's life on earth five thousand years ago. The joyful dancing and devotions are a ritual means of participating in the bliss of those who loved him then. According to Ellenwood (1973, p. 241), they believe "the Vedar, Bhagavad Gita, and canonical lives of Krishna are literally and historically true. Krishna is the supreme personal Lord; he lives in a paradisal world. The souls of all individuals are eternal and, though intended to love Krishna, are trapped in a series of material bodies owing to ignorance and sensory illusion. By love for Krishna the soul overcomes this identification with the temporary body and lives outside of Karma. The devotee's acts are pure and no longer bring retribution. Devotionalism is higher to the Krishnaite than Yogic or Vedantic meditation . . . and definitely better than . . . impersonalistic philosophy."

Devotional practices involve dress, physical appearance, dietary regulations, dancing, and singing "Hare Krishna." Full-time devotees wear saffron robes, and men shave their heads except for a topknot in the back. For sanctification and protection, they ornament themselves with telka, a wet mixture of clay they paint on their faces and eleven other places on their bodies. The sacredness of the cow is the basis of their vegetarian diet. The Hare Krishna have established a school for devotees' children aged eight to fifteen. It aims to train Krishna-conscious children who will know they are spirit savers rather than material bodies (Judah, 1974).

Separation from and rejection of the establishment culture have forced the development of communal living. Most devotees live together at the temple and share a rigid discipline. Some live in the outside world and carry on a business, profession, or trade for Krishna. They are all very visible and audible in the world but are not of it.

Although membership is open to all regardless of age, sex, race, or class, it is open *only* to those who are seriously interested. Homosexuals and those on drugs are excluded. After following the discipline for six months or longer, the new convert becomes eligible for initiation by a spiritual master (Judah, 1974). Women are accepted and their souls are considered of equal value with men's, but they may not be presidents of temples or occupy positions of authority. Their services are confined to housekeeping roles. Women are treated as children, to be protected and given limited freedom. All devotees are lay leaders of the faith, much like monks in a monastery. They are highly mobile and may visit (and live in) two or more temples a year.

Many of the devotees do not abandon their former faiths but view Krishna (like the charismatics view their prayer groups) as a means of expanding it to perfection. They find no contradiction in chanting Hare Krishna and believing in Jesus (Judah, 1974). Devotees' street efforts have occasionally led to their arrest on charges of loitering and unlawful assembly, but the mayors of New York and San Francisco have commended the movement for its work with alienated youth.

The Meher Baba cult (also known as the Lovers of Meher Baba) has hundreds of thousands of followers in India. Its American following remained small until its revival of discovery by young people in the mid-1960s. The founder, Meher Baba, a Hindu, based his teachings on Sufi masters and the celebration of God's love expounded in his book, *God Speaks,* published in 1967 (revised edition, Baba, 1973). His followers perceive him as a universal savior, a messiah who came to inspire and lead humanity out of materialism to a higher level of consciousness (Ellenwood, 1973; Needleman, 1970; Robbins and Anthony, 1972). He was opposed to psychedelic drugs as agents for inducing different levels of consciousness. His universal message was "love," which in its purest form arises in the heart in response to the descent of grace from the master (Baba, 1973). He also emphasized a metaphysical unity among all persons. Baba is viewed as a personification of universal expressivity, which he demonstrates through his relationships with his followers, the Baba lovers. Baba's modified work ethic maintained that action in the world was important for spiritual advancement, but the spiritual aspirant must cultivate a sense of inner detachment from the results of his or her activity. Work roles are instrumental roles endowed with expressive meaning.

The cult has no formal boundaries, membership certificates, or criteria. The major social organization is a spiritual center at Myrtle Beach, South Carolina. It was established by the "lovers" on Baba's orders as a place for rest and renewal of the spiritual life. Here his teachings are personified in organizational procedures that stress informality, spontaneity, and familiar relationships. The center plays a central role in establishing and teaching the nature of the cultic beliefs. It is a place for followers to gather and for possible converts to learn about the Baba way.

Followers establish groups, but they are scattered and not formally linked. The groups may meet in a Baba bookstore or in private homes. Meetings are informal and emphasize the creation of a fellowship of coequal love. Attendees read, sing, chant, and view movies of Baba in which he is portrayed as jolly, playful, and loving. Baba functions as a model for relationships within the fellowship (Robbins and Anthony, 1972). Proselytizing is not an important function of the follower. All who are interested in Baba or the spiritual path are welcome. The acceptance of a set of beliefs is not important; interest in or becoming a Baba lover is not considered incompatible with continued belief and activity in other religions. Like many in the other new cults, Baba lovers view their efforts as expanding their basic beliefs. Robbins and Anthony (1972) view the cult as an integrating group. That is, it synthesizes expressive and instrumental role orientations, which makes it possible to maintain the cult within the larger society while maintaining the expressive (love) emphasis that gave it birth.

Nichiren Shoshu was a small sect when religious freedom came to Japan in 1944. It became the fastest growing religion in the world in the 1950s and by 1970 had a membership of more than seven and a half million families. Ellenwood (1973) observes that to lonely people, including United States servicemen transplanted to the great industrial cities of Japan, it offered participation, activity, and a sense of direction. The lay person's organization within the sect, Soka Gakkai, is best known to the Westerner. The first Soka Gakkai in America was established in 1960 with some three hundred families, mostly of Japanese origin or descent, or war brides and their American husbands. Kie-chiang Oh (1973) estimates there are now about two hundred thousand member families in the United States, with about 90 percent of recent converts being native Americans. No accurate count of individual members is available due to the practice of giving the worship object, "Gobonzon," to the convert's family. The convert is expected to persuade the rest of his or her family to join (Kie-chang Oh, 1973).

A structural form resembling a denomination has evolved. The basic unit is the district, which meets several times a week. It is divided into groups of five to ten members under the supervision of experienced individuals. There are regional chaplains, men's and women's bureaus, a student bureau, an active publications department, and a newspaper (*World Tribune*). There are two temples in the United States, one in Honolulu and one in Etiwanda, California, where major ceremonies and consecrations are held. The bureaucratic organizational form is reflected in hierarchical leadership.

The "Bible" of the Nichiren Shoshu followers consists of the twenty-eight chapters of the Lutus Sutra. Salvation in a time of religious obsolescence can be obtained only by chanting sections from the scriptures and doing the prayer service. In addition to group meetings, members carry out daily devotions and silent chanting throughout the day. The sect is militantly committed to a worldwide propagation of the "true Buddhism," and members are tireless proselytizers. Kie-chiang Oh (1973) explains that a believer must share in the worldwide propagation of Nichiren Shoshu out of charity and compassion to save the world. Members' missionary zeal resembles that of the Christian missionary dispatched to save the Asian world in the nineteenth century. It is too early in its development to predict whether the current rate of growth will be sustained.

Occult Groups. Neopagan activities are not new, but there has been recent renewal and widespread interest in them. Their popularity may be indicated by the proliferation of publications (including syndicated columns in the daily newspapers) and stores selling books and items concerning the occult. Although there is a small but significant increase in the number of serious advocates, most analysts view it as part of the popular culture that shows a playful contempt for what many once viewed seriously. Its advocates are primarily young; and as a pop religion or science, the occult seems to represent a playful side of the rejection of religious and educational institutions, in contrast to the serious rejection by the Jesus people and others. Perhaps it also represents a kind of victory over science. Truzzi (1972, p. 240) concluded, "for most Americans, the involvement in the occult is a leisure time activity and a fad of popular culture rather than a serious religious involvement in the search for new sacred elements."

Truzzi's analysis of the revival of occultism represents the most reliable and comprehensive assessment of the movement. He found little systematic research on the subject, with existing descriptions primarily by nonscientific writers and journalists. Of the four major focuses of occult interest within the youth culture Truzzi identified, only astrology, witchcraft, and satanism show a significant increase in popularity since the 1960s. Parapsychology as a popular interest seems to be declining, but scientific interest in extrasensory perception (ESP) continues. Although they are not central values in the youth occult world, parapsychology and Eastern religious ideas that were popular with the "beat" generation of the 1950s have legitimating links to broader and more generally accepted areas of science and religion, according to Truzzi. That is, respectable laboratory analyses of ESP link the occult with science, and inclusion of Eastern thought is related to Western philosophical naturalism.

Astrology accounts for most of the occult followers, who range from the pop horoscope fan to the committed believer. Estimates are that about ten thousand full-time astrologers in the United States serve some forty million persons (Truzzi, 1972, p. 229). Few believers accept astrology as a science that is a predictive framework for understanding humankind and human behavior; most believe it to be beyond legitimate science. Three levels of involvement can be distinguished. The majority of devotees participate at the superficial, newspaper horoscope level, finding there more entertainment than enlightenment. Horoscope readers usually know little about the mechanics of astrology, and its quasi-scientific character may act as a legitimizing factor for those who are not scientifically critical. Horoscope advice is always ego boosting and directive, with an element of esoteric mystery that contributes to the entertaining element. The ambiguity of the messages makes them difficult to falsify and they become self-fulfilling prophecies. Participation is usually private, not undertaken in groups; participants tend to be middle aged.

At the second level of involvement, astrology is still a faddish and fun thing but in addition is pseudoacademic. Followers, who are mostly college age and have some knowledge of astrological mechanics and language, have experts cast their horoscope. There was a relatively greater increase of followers at this level during the sixties than among the superficial or the serious.

The serious or deeply committed followers are involved in the literature and cast their own horoscope. They are less concerned with the advice or prediction than adherents at the other two levels. Astrology for them is a complex belief system more like religion than science. It offers a meaningful view of the social and physical order and gives an understanding of the individual's place in that order. Most important is its function as a means of establishing self-identity. Only a few thousand believers are this serious about astrology. The serious followers formerly consisted of a few elderly people, but new members are mostly youthful. Organizations of astrology believers vary greatly. Most are informal groups, usually of friends. Leaders (for all levels) are the most deeply committed.

Popular superficial interest in witchcraft and satanism is greater than the increase in real participation. The primary difference in these two forms of the occult is between white and black magic (that is, the uses of magic for positive versus negative social or personal ends). Witches view themselves as an offshoot of pre-Christian fertility religion rather than as heretical offshoots of Christianity, as do the satanists. They view their craft as a folk tradition of magical beliefs and view magic as value free, as the technology of the supernatural or supernormal (Truzzi, 1972; Heeman, 1973).

Most witches are women (male witches are referred to as "warlocks" usually). About one-third are individual practitioners who inherit the secrets of the art from kin. Some witches belong to covens of not more than thirteen members, which they frequently compare to convents of nuns. The self-designated individual witch is considered illegitimate by coven members, who believe a true practitioner must be initiated into a coven and learn the group secrets. Participation in the group ritual evokes or awakens magical power. It is estimated that in the United States there are 1,950 coven members and probably fewer than 3,000 witches (Truzzi, 1972, pp. 233–237). Although no organization of covens exists, a secret register of existing covens around the world is reported to be held by witch Monique Wilson. There are six witchcraft "museums" (schools) in Great Britain and the United States for the training of professional witches. Despite this measure of professionalism, most covens are cult-like groups. Ceremonial magic through ritual empowers the members to heal or help, cure or hex. Each member has the ability to develop magical powers and believes in the power of psychic forces, reincarnation, and the survival of the spirit after death.

Like witches, satanists may act as solitary agents or in groups. Little is known about the solitary satanists. The groups range from those who preceive Satan as an angel to be worshipped, to the pornographic sex club type, to the acid cult of the Charles Manson type, to the church type. The dominant group is Anton LaVey's Church of Satan in San Francisco. More churchlike than cultlike, the church claims over seven thousand members. The church, or grotto, has organized other grottos and is hierarchically governed. (See LaVey, 1969, 1972.)

Satanists believe in the supernormal and worship their own ego. They espouse an atheistic, elitist, and materialistic philosophy. Such conditions are perceived to be the forces in life necessary for the greatest magical success. It is not escape from but full control of the real world that is the satanist's goal. The most succinct summary of satanist beliefs can be found in the "nine satanic statements," a diabolical equivalent of the Ten Commandments (LaVey, 1969, p. 111):

- Satan represents indulgence, instead of abstinence!
- Satan represents vital existence, instead of spiritual pipe dreams!
- Satan represents undefiled wisdom, instead of hypocritical self-deceit!
- Satan represents kindness to those who deserve it, instead of love wasted on ingrates!
- Satan represents vengeance, instead of turning the other cheek!
- Satan represents responsibility to the responsible, instead of concern for psychic vampires!
- Satan represents man as just another animal, sometimes better, more often worse than those who walk on all fours, who, because of his "divine spiritual development," has become the most vicious animal of all!
- Satan represents all of the so-called sins, as they all lead to physical, mental, or emotional gratification!
- Satan has been the best friend the church has ever had, as he has kept it in business all these years!

Social Background and Role Characteristics

What are the participants in these nonassociational forms of religion like? Are there differences in the social background and role characteristics between those who participate in the new forms and those who do not?

Age. Most of the participants in new nonassociational religious activities are young adults, many of whom were a part of the youth counterculture. Fifty-four percent of the "nones" (adults reporting no religious preference) are under thirty years of age, and 66 percent of the under-thirty "nones" are eighteen to fourteen years of age (Gallup, 1976). The average age of the Jesus people has been estimated at twenty-one (Enroth, Breckenridge, and Ericson, 1973; Harder, Richardson, and Simonds, 1972; Peterson and Mauss, 1973; Plowman, 1971). The Children of God only recently accepted members over thirty (Hill, 1975; Leming and Smith, 1975). Eighty-five percent of Hare Krishna members interviewed by Judah (1974) were twenty-five or younger. Those attracted to other Eastern religious cults, such as Meher Baba, are mostly young people, including a fair number of drug users (Robbins and Anthony, 1972).

The neopagan cults attract both those over thirty and young adults. LaVey's reported seven thousand satanists are mostly under thirty (Ellenwood, 1973), but many outside the youth culture are interested in the occult. As Truzzi (1972) points out, empirical research on adherents to neopagan beliefs is nearly nonexistent. However, we do know that 88 percent of the ninety-four thousand monthly readers of *Fate* magazine are over thirty-four, with 37.9 percent being over fifty-five (Truzzi, 1972, p. 227). *Fate* is one of the most popular magazines dealing with paranormal and supernatural phenomena, published by Clark Publishing of Highland Park, Illinois.

Alfred's (1976) research contradicts this impression of occultism as a youth phenomenon. He reports relatively few (less than 20 percent) young persons were members of the Church of Satan during 1968–1969. Furthermore, a 1968 attempt to missionize the Berkeley campus of the University of California produced little interest and few converts. Over half (52.9 percent) the youth of the San Francisco Bay Area knew about the Church of Satan; but only 2 percent reported being strongly attracted to it, 10 percent were mildly attracted, and 64.9 percent were totally uninterested. Most attenders at the Central Grotto of the Church of Satan are middle-class whites in their late twenties to forties.

Gender. With the exception of the charismatic neo-Pentecostals, the sex distribution seems to be normal. Charismatics report more female than male members (Fichter, 1975; Harrison, 1974b; McGuire, 1975). However, the leadership in the new nonassociational religious groups is predominantly male (with the exception of witches' covens). Among members with no religious preference, 68 percent are men and 32 percent are women. Women are relegated to dependence on male authority in all social relationships, reflecting both fundamental Western and ancient Eastern orientations. For example, most communes are headed by an authoritative male leader and there are only two women on the twenty-seven-member National Catholic Renewal Advisory Committee. The occult groups are an exception here.

Education. Most of the youth in the Jesus people and Hare Krishna groups are high school or college dropouts. Judah (1974) reports that among the Hare Krishnaites the reason for dropping out was usually disillusionment with the educational system. (Only 2 percent of the devotees he interviewed had a D average at the time they dropped out of school, so poor performance is not involved.) The charismatic groups appeal to those with above-average education (college level) and those who express interest in intellectual activities, such as reading books and going to concerts and plays (Wuthnow, 1976).

Religious Background. Participants come from all types of religious and nonreligious backgrounds. There is a disproportionate number of Catholic and Jewish youth among the Jesus people (Piazza, 1976) and Hare Krishna groups (Judah, 1974). Among Protestant groups, Baptists are best represented, followed by Methodists, Lutherans, and Pentecostals. More members of the Christ Commune than of the other sects report they attended church regularly as children, but half of these report their families were not regular attenders and did not turn to God in time of crisis. Most Protestant denominations and the Catholic church have participants among the charismatics and Hare Krishna.

Occupational Roles. Participants in all the groups tend to come from families reporting middle-class occupations. The adults in the Pentecostal groups are mainly in middle-class occupations, unlike earlier Pentecostal members, who were mainly from the lower working class. Pentecostals are predominantly middle-class in education and occupation, with leaders who have college or more education. Over half of the nonstudent members have a college education and are classified as professionals.

The occupations of the younger members cannot be classified in traditional categories that denote socioeconomic background. They seek the jobs necessary to support communal life-styles or proselytizing activities rather than those necessary for status or stable lifelong employment. More significant than the class of occupations filled by these participants is their attitude toward work. They maintain a strong work ethic, but work is more expressive than instrumental; it is a means to their religious goals rather than a means to a career, success, and economic goals. Many are involved in agriculture and related occupations. They operate businesses such as bookstores, coffeehouses, and art shops and sell the artifacts and literature of their faith.

Marital Status. Family, work, and friendship commitments are negatively related to participation in the nonassociational forms; and those who have work or school commitments are not likely to be involved unless their spouse or peers are involved. The commune style of the Hare Krishnas encourages marriage within the group and child rearing then becomes a part of the life-style as well.

Race. Few blacks participate in any of the new forms described. Yet informal, cultlike religious participation is no new phenomenon for blacks in America. The emergence of many new religious groups in

urban centers since 1900 is generally regarded as a response to urbanization and segregation. Blacks attend church at about the same rate as
whites (Gallup, 1976). In the sixties, new religious groups were organized around civil rights and economic issues. At the same time that the
new groups evolved, many established black religious groups were
becoming more formal and political (while white groups were becoming more informal and apolitical). Demerath and Roof (1976) remind us
that black religion has been traditionally viewed more as an opiate than
as an inspiration for social action, but there was a substantial change in
the relationship between black militancy and religiosity during the
1960s. For example, Marx (1967a, 1967b) found most black adults in 1964
were too otherworldly to encourage civil rights and racial militancy; but
members of less "temporal" local churches or denominations were most
likely to support racial militancy. In 1969, when Alston, Peek, and
Wingrove (1972) examined the association between religiosity and militancy among black adults, they found a weak tendency for blacks high
on militancy to be low on religiosity; but this trend was not statistically
significant, as it was in the Marx (1967b) study. However, they found
that age, sex, and denominational affiliation remain strong indicators of
both religiosity and militancy. For older black men who are Baptists,
high religiosity is clearly associated with low militancy; but the opposite
tendency is seen among black women. Thus, it appears that the social
and political changes of the 1960s have had a more dramatic effect on
black religious behavior than the studies of nonassociational participation indicate.

Personality Characteristics

Following Reddy and Smith (1972), I define personality factors as
generalized and enduring dispositions individuals have toward themselves, others, and the environment. I categorize personality factors in
terms of (1) a dependency syndrome, which includes traits of submissiveness, nonaggressiveness, and rigidity; (2) a fulfillment-deprivation
cluster, which includes ego strength, anxiety, self-concept, extroversion,
introversion, achievement needs, and fatalism; and (3) a social cluster,
which includes empathy and the need to belong.

Dependency Syndrome. McGuire (1975) in a study of seven Catholic Pentecostal prayer groups during 1971–1974 found a strong expressed need for security, described as "crisis mentality," which
incorporates many of the characteristics of anomie and alienation. Participants report being highly upset by the condition of the church and the
world and feel the need for more authority than established churches
offer. McGuire relates crisis mentality to the debunking of religious

authority and norms following Vatican II and to perception of break-down in the moral and social order.

Harrison (1974b) found that Catholic Pentecostals report react-ing with feelings of ambiguity and disillusionment to the deemphasis on traditional beliefs and forms of devotion in the church in the 1960s. All the new forms I described reflect some feelings of deprivation on the part of the participants. It is not the specific changes themselves but the fact of change that destroys their old assuredness. The charismatics find the desired authority in the Holy Spirit and assurance in "gifts of the spirit" (healing, speaking in tongues, exorcism). Harrison's (1974) comparative study of Pentecostal and non-Pentecostal Catholics also supports the view that reliance upon traditional religious organizations is an expression of the need for unchanging authority. He found that strong prior commitment to personal religious devotions and to the Catholic church were associated with attraction to charismatic groups. Hine and Gerlach (1968) and Fichter (1975) report similar findings.

Social Deprivation. The social side of deprivation feelings in-volves perceived loss of social status, prestige, or social acceptance in comparison with others. Such feelings of deprivation involve a strong need to belong and a deliberate search for belonging. Lemming and Smith (1975) relate this need, particularly among those under thirty, to middle-class socialization, which employs love withdrawal to enforce normative conformity. Others relate the need to family experiences fraught with turmoil and conflict (Peterson and Mauss, 1973). This leads to the search for love, understanding, and authority and to attrac-tion to communal groups that meet this primary familial need, such as the Children of God, where members call each other "brother" and "sister."

Age is related to feelings of social deprivation. Those in their late teens or early twenties are relatively powerless and in a period of role uncertainty. The new groups provide an alternative status system and legitimation that is particularly important for those with a troubled self-concept and for those who have trouble "making it in the establish-ment" (Peterson and Mauss, 1973). The new status system legitimizes the rejection of the basic institutions of family, school, and church.

Viver (1960, pp. 432–433) described the characteristics of the crisis mentality among glossolalics as follows: Glossolalics "can be consid-ered as a group of people who have been torn by insecurity, conflict, tension, and emotional difficulties. Being troubled by doubt and fear, anxiety and stress, they have turned from the culturally accepted, tradi-tional, orthodox, and formalized to something that held out for them in unorthodox, the supernatural; to an environment of sensitiveness for emotional feelings and a group of people bound with the same purpose and clinging to each other for support." Wood (1965) found the Pentecostals exhibited more anxiety than non-Pentecostals; they seemed to be troubled, problem-ridden people who spend much time coping with life. Viver (1960) reports the glossolalics were more disturbed and had more psychopathology than nonglossolalics. Kildahl (1973) found that 85 percent of the glossolalics had experienced marital difficulties, financial concerns, ill health, and general depression. Although he found no differences in the ability to give and receive love and to take responsibility among tongue speakers and nontongue speakers, the tongue speakers expressed an exaggerated dependency reaction. In TAT tests, glossolalics appeared more suggestible and dependent and more like "followers" than nonglossolalics. Harder, Richardson, and Simonds, (1972) also found Jesus people to have high dependency needs and to be relatively willing to submit to a leader's authority.

Balswick (1974); Enroth, Breckenridge, and Ericson (1973); Harder, Richardson, and Simonds (1972); Hill (1975); Judah (1974); and Robbins and Anthony (1972) have reported that most of the Jesus people, Children of God, Hare Krishna, and Meher Baba lovers had been drug users who were disillusioned with school, organized religion, the world, and the demise of the counterculture. Lemming and Smith (1975) believe a permissive upbringing leaves many participants with a felt need for discipline. These nontraditional groups demand sacrifice, specific work, and the discipline of prayer, meditation, and the study of religious literature. Participants in these groups are said to be seeking a leader more powerful than any of the members. Millennialism also seems to be a part of their crisis mentality. That is, the end of this evil age will come, as the book of Revelations predicts; and Christ will return to rule for a thousand years with his faithful and martyred followers.

Psychic Deprivation. Psychic deprivation is much like anomie, an "absence of a meaningful system of values by which to interpret and organize one's life" (Glock, 1964, p. 212). It results in a search for a new self-concept, values, and faith; for meaning, simplicity, and closure; and in disillusionment with futile intellectual pursuits (Peterson and Mauss, 1973). Peterson and Mauss interpreted the emphasis on rebirth among the Jesus people as the need for a greater ego strength and a stronger self-identity. The spoiled identity of many with hippie backgrounds or a history of deviant or criminal behavior required a "rebirth" into a new self-concept and identity. The Children of God symbolize their "new selves" by taking on names from the Bible (Lemming and Smith, 1975). Harder, Richardson, and Simonds (1972) found the "new selves" felt less need for self-confidence, achievement, or dominance. They suggest the communes have developed a life-style that encourages cooperation and self-abasement in place of competition and dominance.

Situational Determinants

Bibby and Brinkerhoff (1974) propose three major sources of situational factors that affect participation in nonassociational religious activity: socialization, accommodation, and cognition. Most participants in the new nonassociational forms had experienced childhood religious socialization. They were children of church members; many held church memberships and found no contradiction between their new and old beliefs (Judah, 1974). For these people, Bibby and Brinkerhoff (1974, p. 74) maintain that "church involvement is often likely to be an end in itself rather than a means to a problem-solving end." Socialized into a religious milieu, they may well find God and religion simply a part of their normal activity. This prior socialization, then, may be viewed as a situational factor that predisposes many to seek or respond to nonassociational religious groups and practices in personal crisis, such as overinvolvement with drugs, alcohol, or sex; political crises, such as the Vietnam War; religious crises; and life-cycle crises that occur in youth, middle age, and old age.

Friendships and family networks are significant situational determinants. Recruits to new groups may be accommodating to social pressures, such as that from peer groups in the youth counterculture during the 1960s. Hine and Gerlach (1968), Fichter (1975), and McGuire (1974) found preexisting social relationships to be a crucial factor in joining a Pentecostal group. Nash and Berger (1962) report the three most significant social factors related to joining a religious group are accommodation to or consideration for significant others (spouse, friend, or parent), efforts to strengthen a relationship within a proposed or established family, and becoming a parent. DeJong and Faulkner (1972) found that intellectuals (university faculty) placed primary importance on church-based training in morality and ethical principals for themselves and their children.

For many, the place and social setting may also be related to recruitment into nonassociational religious activity. Hood (1977), in a study of mystical states (non–drug induced), reported that intense religious experience is more likely to occur in a noninstitutional setting. Individual experiences of mysticism are frequently triggered by a combination of anticipatory stress and sudden natural situational stress (Rosegrant, 1976). Informal or primary type groups in a variety of settings seem to be conducive to intensified religious experiences of "the presence." Furthermore, the testimony (witnessing or sharing) of Bible reading, prayers, and speaking in tongues by the Jesus people and charismatics are social-situational mechanisms that precipitate conversion and strengthen commitment (McGuire, 1975). The community provides the setting for developing new life-styles in which the religious role controls other significant roles such as work, friendship, mate selection, and family life (Bellah, 1976). And finally, there was, as Bellah (1976, p. 339) concludes, a crisis in social-philosophical beliefs and orientations: "The deepest cause, no matter what particular factors contributed to the actual timing, was in my opinion, the inability of utilitarian individualism to provide a meaningful pattern of personal and social existence, especially when its alliance with biblical religion itself has been gutted in the process. I would thus interpret the crises of the sixties above all as a crisis of meaning, a religious crisis with major political, social, and cultural consequences to be sure." Most of the participants of new forms of religious activity described here were responders to the religious crises.

Religious Participation as a Leisure Activity

Religious participation can be defined as a leisure time activity in the sense that it is not remunerative activity. Individuals in postindustrial societies have large blocks of free time and many devote much of it to some kind of voluntary action. Many affluent youth, adults, and retired persons devote that time to nonassociational religious activities (Dumazedier, 1974; Payne, 1973a). For example, the Jesus people and the Children of God and Hare Krishnas spend most of their nonwork time in individual Bible or religious study, group religious activities, and proselytizing. During the post–World War II revival of religious interest, it was predicted that the continued increase in time freed from work and family obligations would result in an increase in time devoted to religious activities. This prediction included the period (1960–1975) of the emergence of the new religious activities reviewed in this chapter. Contrary to this prediction, church attendance has shown a steady decline from 1955 to 1970 (after which the level remained unchanged at least until 1976) for all groups except the healthy elderly over seventy-five years of age (Gallup, 1976; Hadden, 1969; Payne, 1973b; Riley and Foner, 1968). At the same time, research on the new religions shows that the participants devote more uncommitted time to the new groups than the average church member does to traditional churches. Participants in charismatic groups have been found to spend more time both with the new groups and at formal church services.

Furthermore, the commitment of leisure time to the new religions marks a change in the concept of work and leisure for many, such as the Jesus people, Hare Krishnas, and Children of God. Work has lost much of its Calvinistic significance and gained more instrumental value (as a means to an end, not *the* end). Leisure is valued as time for self-fulfillment and for social and spiritual activities; and many have found their psychological, social, and spiritual needs met by the new religious groups.

Participation in these groups takes two forms. For some participants, especially those in the neopagan activities, it is a playful matter. For others, participation is both social and spiritual. Whether fad or new faith, the new forms of nonassociational religious participation are also new uses of leisure time and can be expected to continue to grow. Although current participants have been drawn primarily from the youth culture, participants in the next decades can be expected to include more middle-aged people and retired people with much free time and many years yet to fill with meaningful activity.

Conclusion

Although nonassociational religious participation in the form of Bible study; small informal Bible and prayer groups; religious discussions with neighbors, coworkers, and friends; meditation; and service to individuals and the community has always been a part of most Americans' religious behavior, it has usually been considered by researchers and society in general as an extension of commitment to the church. The new forms of participation emerging in the 1960s accompanied by the decline in church membership and participation have focused scholarly attention on the quantitative and qualitative differences between church and nonchurch religious activities. Many of the new, youth-oriented groups providing these latter (Jesus people, Children of God, and Hare Krishna) peaked in the early 1970s.

The high participation of youth and adults of middle-class background and above-average educational level indicates both strengths and weaknesses in terms of the new groups' futures. As Wuthnow (1976) points out, the present overrepresentation of youth, who will be passing into other stages of personal growth and development, makes for an uncertain future. Many may abandon their interest as they become more mature. However, these same people can be expected to continue some of the new privatized religious practices and to introduce many of the group practices learned from the new forms into the traditional churches. Change in belief emphases and practice consequently may be expected in traditional churches.

The pessimism of the 1960s about the decline in religiosity has become a sign of a new spirituality and religious consciousness. The new spirituality represents the need, or rather the demand, for present, personal, and healing religious experience and activities that are integrated in everyday life. Although it was primarily the youth who raised our consciousness in the 1960s, I suggest the next groups to raise our collective religious consciousness will most likely be the emerging elderly subculture of the 1970s. The healthy elderly are the individuals in society with the most uncommitted time, and many of them are currently experiencing crises of identity, psychic and social deprivation, and changing social situations. Furthermore, the youth-become-adult may be expected actively to support an elderly counterculture movement; the coalition of the newly mature and newly old could have a major impact on forms of religious participation in the future.

CHAPTER 11

Socialization for Mass Media Consumption

Leo W. Jeffres

Mass media consumption is such a ubiquitous activity that its origins are often taken for granted. The mass media serve as socializing agents, transmitting culture from one generation to the next; but mass media use itself is a product of the socialization process. This latter point has been relatively neglected in research because scholars have tended to concentrate on the effects of mass media messages rather than the process through which the media behaviors are developed.

In their summary of media socialization research, McLeod and O'Keefe (1972) identify five types of variables as important in the socialization process: (1) age or life cycle position of the influence, (2) social-structural constraints operating to affect learning, (3) agent or source of the influence, (4) learning processes involved in socialization, and (5) content or criterion behavior being explained as the dependent variable.

This fifth variable draws us to the problem of how to conceptualize the dependent variable of interest here—that is, media use. Researchers most often describe media participation in terms of frequency units (such as number of hours spent watching television or how often people listen to the radio). Some studies have looked at patterns in frequency data, such as the degree of similarity or difference in frequency of media use between socialization agents (parents) and influencees (children). But we should also look at other dimensions of media use, such as medium preferences, content choices, degree of specialization in usage patterns, intentions and motivations for media use, and gratifications and deprivations. The importance of a particular variable may vary over the life cycle. For example, although we expect explicit parental guidance and reinforcement to affect television watching during childhood, during late adolescence we may find parental influence operating only in some specific areas, such as evaluation of particular programs. During adulthood, a spouse may affect both amount of time spent and the type of content consumed. Differences by medium would be expected because television viewing is a group activity in most homes. Reading is a solitary matter. We also might find that attitudes toward the mass media are more successfully transmitted than actual usage patterns, which tend to be constrained by available time and media outlets. Furthermore, changes in the media delivery system, such as development of cable systems, which shift some control from senders to users, may alter existing patterns and require additional research to reestimate the parameters of media usage.

After I examine the four major classes of variables, I shall return to a discussion of research problems and prospects in the socialization area. The emphasis in socialization research has been on continuities between generations. The research questions that remain largely unasked concern why discontinuities would be expected from one generation to the next and within a single generation.

Life Cycle Variations

Childhood. Mass media consumption begins very early in a child's life. Children learn attitudes, facts, and behavior from the mass media. Television is the first medium to occupy much prominence in most contemporary children's lives in the Western world; but because young children have short attention spans, early viewing is usually only for brief periods. Preschool children are exposed to about twenty-five hours of television per week. Comstock (1975), in a summary of research on children and television, notes that children typically begin their television viewing three to four years before entering first grade. Most children watch at least some television every day and most watch for two or more hours per day. The amount of viewing increases during the elementary school years. (The average viewing times reported vary across studies because different measures are used. Roberts, 1973.)

Cartoons and situation comedies are favorite programs in these early years. Streicher and Bonney (1974) found that the popularity of cartoons decreased for both girls and boys as they got older, with interests shifting to more adult programming. Of course, what a child understands from or gets out of early television use is limited by the level of cognitive development (Wackman, Wartella, and Ward, 1977; Ward, Wackman, and Wartella, 1977). Brown (1976) looked at usage and medium preference among one thousand schoolchildren aged seven to fifteen in Scotland in 1972. The media listed for the children were television, records, other people, books, self, radio, comics, cinema, newspapers, and magazines. They were asked which they used to learn how others live, to find out about different places, to learn things one does not learn in school, to find out what it is like to be grown up, when they felt lonely, when they felt bored, when they wanted to forget something unpleasant, when they felt sad, and when there was no one to talk to or play with. They were also asked which medium was the most exciting, which made them think about things, and which they got lost in. Selection of television for purposes of mood control (sadness or unpleasantness) never exceeded 32 percent in the various age groups; use of television for social purposes (so they could talk about television with friends) never fell below 31 percent. At age seven, children peaked on television usage for diversion (getting lost), to alleviate boredom, so they could talk about it with friends, and because television makes one think about things. At age nine, two other information uses appear: using television to find out about different people and different places. Among eleven-year-olds, the most important uses are to learn about different people, to be able to talk about television with others, to relieve boredom, to get lost in viewing, and to stimulate thinking. At age thirteen, learning about different people and places, learning about things not learned in school, and talking about television with friends are the most often mentioned functions of television. Thus, it appears that informational uses become more important with advancing age. In the early years, many children say they watch television so they can join in conversations with friends about television. This function is mentioned less often as the children get older, with a rise in the selection of other media (particularly records) for purposes of having input into social conversations. Similar switches are seen in media usage for trying to forget unpleasantness and when one is feeling sad.

Use of print media also depends on cognitive development, of course—the ability to read. Reading for recreation increases steadily during school years until the end of grade school and then drops to about a book a month by the end of high school (Schramm, Lyle, and Parker, 1961). Magazine reading follows the same pattern, but the decrease begins a bit later. The last medium to attract children's attention is the newspaper. Children begin to read newspapers at about age seven and usage increases steadily as they grow older. Although movies and radio get some attention from small children, they were not found to be popular media until adolescence. In a U.S. study in the late 1950s, usage of all media combined accounted for more than 40 percent of children's leisure time when they were between the ages of five and eight. This figure rose to more than 50 percent among twelve-year-olds. A study of Swedish children by von Feilitzen (1976) yielded similar patterns to those reported in this section, which suggests these results may be generalizable across the major Western nations.

Adolescence. Television viewing (in both the United States and Sweden) reaches its peak at the beginning of adolescence and by the end of adolescence has declined by 10 percent or more (Comstock, 1975; von Feilitzen, 1976). The major decrease comes in prime time and late afternoon viewing (Lyle and Hoffman, 1971). Decreases are found for all content categories except public affairs and news programs, for which a modest increase is found for girls (Chaffee, Ward, and Tipton, 1970). Reported motives for using television remain relatively stable, according to one study. Both sixth and tenth graders watch television for relaxation, entertainment, and relief from loneliness (Lyle and Hoffman, 1971), at least in the United States. Brown (1976) found that for Scottish children, the use of television for generating conversation topics, for diversion when feeling sad, and for forgetting unpleasant things declined from age nine through age fifteen, while the importance of records and peers in meeting these needs increased.

As noted, newspaper reading increases in adolescence while use of books and comics declines. Interest in public affairs increased with age among teenage boys interviewed by Clarke (1968). Their preference for newspaper content was closely connected to age-related interests and needs. In late adolescence, reading of "teen news" decreased. Schramm, Lyle, and Parker (1961) found an increase in radio listening and record playing during adolescence, with teenagers devoting more time to radio than to any other medium except television. Motion pictures also served an important social function for teenagers.

Adulthood. Early adulthood can be said to begin with the completion of high school. As youths leave home for employment, educational, or family reasons, the socialization process undergoes a sharp change of course. The subsequent life-styles of those entering college are very different from the life-styles of those entering the labor force directly from high school. Almost no research has focused on changes in the media usage patterns of the latter group. We do know that college freshmen watch much less television than they did while in high school and are only light newspaper readers (McLeod, Becker, and Elliott, 1972; O'Keefe and Spetnagel, 1973). Radio use is high during early college years. In later college years, radio use declines while television viewing and newspaper reading increase. Jennings and Niemi (1974) found that regular use of the media for political news rises substantially after high school. McLeod, Becker, and Elliott (1972) reported that college students with liberal arts majors look toward print media and those in other fields are more oriented to the electronic media.

In general across the life span, newspaper reading and television viewing increase with age and radio listening and movie attendance decline. Patterns in magazine reading are not clear (McLeod and O'Keefe, 1972). Some studies have shown this increase in television viewing to be linear; but others show a curvilinear relationship between age and viewing, with a drop in middle age (Greenberg and Kumata, 1968; Kline, 1971; McLeod and O'Keefe, 1972; Samuelson, Carter, and Ruggles, 1963).

Gordon, Gaitz, and Scott (1976) looked at leisure activities in five age groups: twenty to twenty-nine, young adult; thirty to forty-four, early maturity; forty-five to sixty-four, full maturity; sixty-five to seventy-four, old age; and seventy-five to ninety-four, very old age. They interviewed 1,441 people in 1969 and 1970 in Houston, Texas. The rate of movie attendance fell steadily and sharply with age. A constant but less sharp decline was noted for heavy reading; and the curve for heavy television viewing rose between young adulthood and early maturity, remained fairly constant over the next two age groups, and then decreased in very old age. No sex differences were seen for attending movies and reading, but a relatively large proportion of women reported heavy television viewing.

Media usage during adulthood was also examined in a 1964 Survey Research Center cross-sectional survey reported by Jennings and Niemi (1974). Looking at use of media to gather political information, they found that in the twenty-one to twenty-four age group college graduates used an average of 3.2 media and non–high school graduates used about 1.8. This educational difference narrowed in succeeding age groups, with the less well educated increasing their usage and the better educated decreasing theirs. In the age sixty-five group, college graduates used an average of 2.9 media to gather political information and those with less than a high school education used 2.6.

Jennings and Niemi (1975) also reported results of a panel study focusing on 1,669 high school seniors and their parents interviewed in the spring of 1965 and early in 1973. Between the two sets of interviews the parents' lives changed relatively little; but the young people's lives changed greatly as they assumed new roles and became mobile. Although the researchers expected to find the life cycle effects suggested by their earlier research, they also noted there are other factors that would affect data gathered for comparison over time and between generations: There may be differences between generations and "period" effects (long-term cultural changes), and there will be some individual continuity over time. A contemporary period effect superimposed on life cycle effects is that of the long-term, populationwide increase in use of television and decrease in use of radio and newspapers.

Their data showed that television did rise dramatically in the younger generation (from under 40 percent watching television daily to almost 60 percent). Parents' viewing remained stable, between 60 percent and 70 percent. Newspaper reading was unchanged for the younger generation in 1973 and showed a small drop for the older generation. Declines of five to ten percentage points were found for magazine readership and radio listening for both generations. (Jennings and Niemi do not report whether respondents simply reduced the frequency of particular media behaviors or the total amount of time spent as well.) They concluded that the rise in television use and the fall or steady state of uses of other media constitute a period effect. The continuation of the lag in newspaper usage by the younger generation is viewed as a generation effect, but the increased use of television by this group is a life cycle effect. Note that in 1973, the filial generation was still mobile and less settled than their parents; the observed differences may vanish in time.

Another study using cross-sectional analysis to look at life cycle effects is that by Chaffee and Wilson (1975). A total of 544 Wisconsin adults was interviewed in October 1974. Television viewing time, charted from age eighteen on, showed a drop in the thirty-four to fifty-seven age groups, reaching its low point in the forty-two to forty-nine group. The amount of time spent viewing was highest for the fifty-eight to sixty-five group and dropped some for the older groups. Thus far the results are consistent with those reported by McLeod and O'Keefe (1972). But Chaffee and Wilson also found that attention to television news increased steadily across age groups, dropping only slightly for the oldest groups. (They note that the sample size for the oldest group is small, and thus, the latter result may be unreliable.) As for newspaper use, low readership was seen in early adulthood, with a gradual rise to a peak after retirement age and then an enormous drop in the oldest group (seventy-four to eighty-nine). Although attention to public affairs and political news specifically is somewhat lowered after age fifty, time spent watching television news rises at this point. The researchers caution against concluding that reading gives way to listening and watching in old age; the age-by-usage relationship for the other print medium, magazines, is similar to that for the other electronic

medium, radio, across the life span. Peaks in usage in these two media
are found at about age thirty, followed by a drop and then a second peak
later in life. Usage of both radio and magazines drops in the oldest age
group.

Chaffee and Wilson (1975) also examined the importance of the
media as sources of information about four environmental issues. About
75 percent of all respondents cited the mass media as the most important
source of information about what they felt was the most important
problem (with the other 25 percent selecting interpersonal communication and direct experience). Television and newspapers are reported to
be the most important media, with radio and magazines secondary.
These results hold at all age levels. Newspapers' importance as a source
for information on environmental issues peaks and television's bottoms
out in the young adult group (twenty-six to thirty-three). In the forty-
two to forty-nine age group, these two media change places. Among
those over fifty, the rated importance of all four media levels out.

For comparison purposes, Chaffee and Wilson included measures of voluntary participation and interpersonal communication. A
gradual increase in contacts with relatives across age groups was found,
with a parallel decline in communication with friends outside of one's
local community. Membership in formal organizations increased steadily across age groups until about age seventy, when it began to drop. The
authors noted that, with a few exceptions, variations in levels of interpersonal communication across the life cycle were quite small compared
to the variations seen for mass media usage. They suggest that individual motivation for interpersonal communication remains relatively
constant throughout most of one's life, even though the opportunity for
social contact may vary as one moves into new communities, new jobs,
and such. In contrast, changes in roles and situations have major significance for motivation for media usage. We know something of the shape
of the patterns involved as media usage changes. We do not yet, however,
know much about the significance of life cycle turning points that can
be seen reflected in these data; and we as yet can do little to disentangle
life cycle changes from period and generation changes.

Robinson and Jeffres (1979, p. 7) found a steady increase in both
newspaper reading and television news viewing with advancing age and
education. The percentages of respondents in a 1975–1976 survey who
said they read a newspaper the previous day were: by age—eighteen to
twenty-four, 51 percent; twenty-four to twenty-nine, 51 percent; thirty to
thirty-nine, 66 percent; forty to forty-nine, 67 percent; fifty to fifty-nine,
79 percent; sixty to sixty-five, 87 percent; sixty-six and older, ninety
percent; by education—grade school, 51 percent; some high school, 64
percent; high school graduates or some college, 73 percent; college

graduates, 74 percent; by income—under $5,000, 53 percent; $5,000–9,999, 65 percent; $10,000–14,999, 72 percent; $15,000–24,999, 74 percent; $25,000 and more, 75 percent. Similar trends are found for television news viewing, though the percentages are considerably less at each level. Of those age eighteen to twenty-four, 36 percent watched television news the previous day, compared to 48 percent of those age forty to forty-nine and 68 percent of those sixty to sixty-five. Some 42 percent of those with grade school educations watch television news "yesterday," compared to 53 percent of high school graduates and 54 percent of those with grade school educations watched television news viewing by income, with 51 percent watching in the following categories: under $5,000, $5,000–9,999, $15,000–24,999. Some 49 percent of those with incomes of $25,000 or greater watched television news, while 52 percent of those $10,000–14,999 watched.

Socialization Processes

Clausen (1966, p. 4) defined socialization as a process through which the child takes on the "way of life of his family and of the larger social groups in which he must relate and perform adequately in order to ultimately qualify for full adult status." How does a child acquire knowledge of rules, norms, and behavior? Developmental psychologists have suggested a number of ways in which this might be accomplished. Those most relevant for mass media socialization appear to be modeling, reinforcement, and social interaction (McLeod and O'Keefe, 1972).

Explicit research into the role of reinforcement in the development of media behavior is limited. Clarke (1969) found that similarity of father and son in reading patterns was contingent upon identification of the son with the father in the area of achievement. Presumably, this involves reinforcement of sons' behavior by fathers. Lyle and Hoffman (1971) found that few mothers restricted the amount of children's television viewing time or selection of programs. The few attempts reported on the use of reward and punishment to influence children's media behavior come before adolescence (Greenberg and Dominick, 1969; Lyle and Hoffman, 1971). Jeffres (1968), however, reports that explicit parental rewards had some effect on the child's newspaper reading behavior.

Evidence for learning in the course of social interaction is more abundant. Lyle and Hoffman (1971) found that movies and television programs were reported to be important topics of discussion with friends and parents. Clarke (1971) found the key predictors of information seeking about symphonic music to be the existence of a relationship with a peer or parent interested in symphonic music. However, Clarke also found that perception of the peer or parent as having such attitudes was a better predictor than actual interaction on the topic, indicating the importance of significant others and reference group pressures here.

Perhaps the most significant evidence that social interaction is important in the developmental aspects of media behavior comes from a series of studies done by a group at the University of Wisconsin (Chaffee and McLeod, 1972; McLeod, Atkin, and Chaffee, 1971a, 1971b). They categorized the families they interviewed along two dimensions of parent-child interaction: "socio-orientation," focusing on child-parent relations, and "concept-orientation," focusing on child-concept relations. In "protective" families, the stress was on social relations only, with little attention to conceptual development. In such families, adolescents spend the most time watching television of any adolescents interviewed and prefer entertainment to news and public affairs programs. In "pluralistic" homes, strong and varied conceptual development of their children is an important concern of the parents; insistence on obedience is relatively low. In these families, adolescents spend relatively little time viewing television and show relatively great interest in news and public affairs programs. The third type of home, "laissez-faire," is characterized by both low socio-orientation and low concept-orientation. In such homes, adolescents' television watching is moderately high, but they are disinterested in newspapers or public affairs programs on television.

The extensive research on the effects of television violence is, in large part, research into learning through modeled behavior. (For a review of some of this research, see Lefkowitz and others, 1977; Liebert, Neale, and Davidson, 1973.) Closest to the concerns of this chapter are studies that use modeling to influence reactions (approval or imitation, for example) or exposure to specific content (aggressive content, for example). Jeffres (1968) found that modeling effects are most likely to be seen under conditions of high identification between influencee and agent. Clarke's (1971) study suggests the importance of others' verbal behavior and activity, rather than explicit teaching, in the shaping of behavior. Reinforcement and social interaction may provide impetus to learning, but learning may more reliably take place if the expected behavior is modeled. Generally, research into the various processes through which media socialization takes place has not yet provided clear answers to the basic questions.

Social Context Factors

Both agents of influence and influencees' behaviors are affected by the social context in which they occur. McLeod and O'Keefe (1972) note that the variable used most often in social context studies is social class, although its relationship to socialization practices is unclear (Zigler and Child, 1969)—and may be changing. For example, social class differences in the amount of time spent viewing television seem to have decreased (Lyle and Hoffman, 1971; Schramm, Lyle, and Parker, 1961). Douvan and Adelson (1966) surveyed thirty-five hundred fourteen- to sixteen-year-olds in 1955 and 1956. They found that boys with upwardly mobile aspirations were more likely to engage in leisure reading than boys with stable or downwardly mobile aspirations. However, they found few class differences in newspaper reading. Some class differences have been found for motivation for mass media usage and for content preferences and usage patterns. Greenberg and Dominick (1969) found that working-class children were more likely than others to say they used television to learn and to see television content as true to life. Lyle and Hoffman (1971) report that adolescents from blue-collar families preferred adventure programs and those from white-collar families preferred family and comedy shows.

Educational level has been a major concern of researchers into adults' media usage (see Chapter Twelve). Samuelson, Carter, and Ruggles (1963) found a positive relationship between the amount of time spent reading the newspaper and education (with age controlled). McLeod, Ward, and Tancill (1965–66) found a negative correlation between education and the amount of time spent watching television; but Samuelson, Carter, and Ruggles (1963) reported a similar pattern in their data disappeared when number of children in the family, organizational memberships, hours worked, and hours spent on a hobby were controlled. Jennings and Niemi (1974), reporting 1965 data on high school seniors and their parents, reported that students with more education than their parents tended to read newspapers and magazines more often than their parents. The reverse was true when parents had more education than the children. However, in the case of television news, parents watched more frequently than their children regardless of educational attainment. Stronger relationships have been found in other studies between education (and other social class measures) and attention to news in the print media and public affairs news in general (Donohew and Thorp, 1966; Greenberg and Kumata, 1968; McLeod, Ward, and Tancill, 1965–66). In general, students are less attentive than their parents are to politics, particularly when education is controlled. However, Jennings and Niemi (1974) found a reversal of results among black high school students and their parents. Black youths were higher on newspaper readership and about the same as their parents in viewing television news. These data were gathered in 1965, a time of turmoil and possibly great change for the black population.

Race and socioeconomic status have typically been used as simple locater variables rather than explanatory factors in research on media usage (McLeod and O'Keefe, 1972). Socioeconomic status is a frequently used variable in socialization research, but why and how it has an impact has never been well explained (Zigler and Child, 1969). We do have some conjectures: For example, upper-class parents are most likely to provide models for the value of reading to their children because newspapers, books, and magazines may be important in their occupation, provide topics for their most important social interactions, or meet education-induced needs for information. But we know little about the relationship between role availability and actual imitation. We also need to know more about the constraints posed by children's growing but still limited capacity to process information and to perform particular behaviors; and we need to know a great deal more about media "quality" (for example, the effect of the *New York Times* versus a tabloid-style paper) on socialization outcomes.

Socialization Agents

There is a variety of agents of socialization into any behavior, not all of whom are aware of their socialization role. Learning can take place without intention to learn or to teach. Parents are a major force in the socialization process, but they are not the only force. Peer groups and siblings are also important (Clarke, 1973). Teachers, spouses, one's own children, work associates, friends, and neighbors may all also serve to influence one's media usage patterns. Furthermore, the socialization process may be reciprocal, particularly among adults. The potential importance of various agents changes as the influencee matures and grows old. From early childhood to adolescence, the parents' influence wanes and the influence of peers and teachers (and probably the media) increases. In adulthood, occupational peer groups, friends, spouses, and the various reference groups we adopt as bellwethers for our opinions should increase their power to influence media usage (see, for example, Hyman and Singer, 1968).

On the other side of the range of possibilities, there will be some lack of continuity in socialization processes. Some agents lose interest and some agents lose power—parents, for example, may attempt to influence children to do as they say, not as they do, without success; or they may encounter among their adolescent children a negativism that ensures socialization attempts will elicit mirror image behavior. Lack of interest, attention, or opportunity on the part of the influencee may also lead to discontinuity. Lippitt (1968) has suggested a major issue in socialization is this matter of discontinuity and inconsistency in the input of various socialization agents. Research into these questions as they relate to mass media socialization is nonexistent.

Problems and Prospects

I have identified a number of problems in the area of research into mass media socialization; so far, these problems have concerned mainly the lack of relevant research. In addition, there are a number of other very general problems that have to do with methodology and research strategies. First, there have been very few panel studies of media usage and none that spans more than one generation or decade. The Jennings and Niemi (1975) and Chaffee and Wilson (1975) studies are good examples of what needs to be done with a wider variety of dependent variables and diverse populations. Obvious barriers are lack of resources and the variety of technical and personal problems involved in longitudinal studies. Another problem is that much of the research has focused on simple exposure measures and very little on content preferences, attitudes and reactions, or other dependent variables that would allow us to make finer discriminations when discussing media behavior. Some studies (Chaffee and Wilson, 1975, for example) use time use measures, but even here finer discriminations would be useful.

There are some conceptual problems in the research as well. With the exception of Jennings and Niemi, researchers have not considered the possibility that parent-child similarities and dissimilarities may be due to generational or period effects rather than direct or rebound effects of socialization. The dissection of these effects is, of course, difficult with cross-sectional research; again, it is clear that long-term research efforts are needed. Another problem is that the various media have received unequal research attention. Television is the most studied, with newspapers in second place. We need more studies of book and magazine reading, radio listening, and film viewing.

Socialization is a perspective, not a theory. McLeod and O'Keefe (1972) refer to a "blueprint" of variables to which researchers should pay attention as they attempt to link culture and personality or children's and parents' characteristics. There are also a number of socialization theories that should be explored in the study of media socialization. Wackman and Wartella (1977), for example, reviewed cognitive development theory and research, examining its implications for children's television behavior. They view children's cognitive abilities as being developed across a series of stages, as becoming progressively differentiated and complex with increasing experience. Ward, Wackman, and Wartella (1977) used this theoretical structure to study children's processing of television commercials. They found, as expected, that as children grow older, their attention to television stimuli becomes more differentiated. Older children usually understand the commercial intent of television advertising; but about half the kindergarten children studied had no awareness of the selling motive of commercials, compared with 12 percent of third graders and only 3 percent of sixth graders (Ward and Wackman, 1973; see also Robertson and Rossiter, 1973).

Although the research by this group is concerned primarily with how children process media stimuli, their findings have implications for learning processes in socialization. The developmental stage a child is in places limitations on what he or she can learn from the media and how complex motivations, usage, and gratifications can be. In other words, the learning processes (modeling, reinforcement, and social interaction) that McLeod and O'Keefe suggest are most relevant to media socialization operate within the limits of each child's stage of development. Thus, we should expect to find different positive and negative reinforcements at different ages, which should in part explain age differences in use patterns. For example, Chaffee and Wilson (1975) looked at attention to public affairs content by age groups. As one would expect, the ability to understand and to find such programs reinforcing is age related.

Media usage patterns are generally supported by individual sets of needs and gratifications. (See, for example, research by Blumler and Katz, 1974; Katz, Gurevitch, and Haas, 1973). This functional perspective suggests we should be researching changes in use and gratification patterns over time if we are to understand media socialization. For example, teenagers might be expected to do much radio listening in order to keep up with peers in their knowledge of the latest in popular music; but married adults might be expected to watch television, partly as a form of spousal companionship. Generally, we might expect that when parents have a wide range of uses for and gratifications from media usage, they are highly likely to serve as models for their children's media usage, in contrast with parents with more restrictive, singular uses.

It should be clear at this point that research into media socialization is a field with many unanswered questions, as yet undeveloped theory, and only the beginnings of a solid research base. There are many policy issues that make the need for more research in media socialization an urgent matter. We have seen some voluntary policy making by television networks, for example, concerning violence on television during the times most children are watching, but this is probably just a stopgap action against the ever-increasing demand that television programming be federally regulated. Formal public policy concerning media delivery systems is probably inevitable, which means policymakers sorely need more research into media socialization if they are to fashion wise policies.

CHAPTER 12

Participation in Mass Media Consumption

Leo W. Jeffres
John P. Robinson

This chapter examines individual mass media participation as a form of informal voluntary activity. Both mass media consumption and other types of informal or formal social participation can be seen as ways people choose to use their discretionary time. Media participation or exposure may supplant other forms of voluntary participation, formal or informal, and may accompany still others. Mass media use can also stimulate participation in voluntary organizations or affect the pattern and nature of informal social participation.

Mass media perform several functions in a society. The most often cited and perhaps most powerful function is *entertainment*. But other observers have noted that the media also serve as *teacher*, helping us understand our social and political environment; as *watcher*, alerting us to important events in that environment; and as a *forum*, allowing alternative views on issues to be heard and discussed (Rao, 1966; Schramm, 1973).

Communication researchers have observed that fictionalized dramatic television programs also perform these functions for their viewers. Rather than viewers "escaping" from their environment, therefore, these "uses and gratifications" studies (see Blumler and Katz, 1974) suggest viewers use television drama to understand the nature and workings of social organizations, to orient themselves to their social and political environment, and to confront the changing elements of society in the safety of their own home (and within the television producers' traditional plot construction). Although there is a certain play or unreal dimension to this participation, a 1970 national survey found that almost 80 percent of favorite dramatic programs were described by viewers as showing "life as it really is" (Robinson, 1971a). Thus, although the accuracy and value of this instruction may be questioned, there can be little doubt that even "escapist" media usage allows some meaningful participation in one's culture and society.

After a period of claiming the mass media exerts minimal effects on audiences, communication researchers have begun to document that media participation does have demonstrable effects. We have evidence that, in the long run, attention to news media is linked to increased knowledge about the actors and events in the political environment (McCombs, 1972; O'Keefe, 1975; Robinson, 1972, 1976a, 1976b), to increased political participation (Kraus and Davis, 1976), to changes in political images (Nimmo, 1976), and to increased agreement on the priorities of issues on the national agenda (Becker, McCombs, and McLeod, 1975; McLeod, Becker, and Byrnes, 1974). On the less positive side, news media use has been linked to increased political cynicism— although perhaps this is a more realistic orientation than the previous simple trust citizens vested in public officials (Jennings and Niemi, 1975). Exposure to violent television drama has been linked to aggressive behavior (see U.S. Department of Health, Education and Welfare, 1972) and preference for "underground" music to increased drug usage (Robinson, Pilskaln, and Hirsch, 1976). These linkages have been established after controls were put into effect for other factors related to the dependent measure; in some instances, the correlations have been found to hold across time, introducing the probability of causal linkages between media participation and actual behavior.

We now have sufficient empirical evidence, then, to treat mass media participation as an activity that has demonstrable effects on its mass audience and as a form of social participation that deserves more recognition and study than it has received in the past. Participation in mass communication is usually referred to as *media use*, though several other terms, such as *media consumption, mass media exposure,* or *media behaviors,* are also used. There is no general consensus on the meaning of these terms, but operational definitions usually tap the frequency or amount of viewing, listening, or reading. Other mass media variables include attention, degree of involvement, content preferences, attitudes, and media gratification.

The following sections focus on the available research for the major classes of determinants of mass media usage, though by far the greatest attention has been given to individual sociodemographic characteristics. We start at the higher levels and move to lower levels of analysis.

Cultural and Historical Context

Relatively little attention has been paid to factors affecting media variables at the national or cultural level or across historical periods. Most of the commentary is based not on systematic quantitative studies but on isolated observations of nations, cultures, or historical periods. At this level, we would examine a variety of dependent variables such as number of mass media source units available to consumers (number of newspapers, television stations, and so forth) and usage (total or per-capita circulation, for example). Researchers have been particularly interested in the role of mass media in national development. Thus, there has been concern over the availability of mass media for development programs. UNESCO (Schramm, 1964) has set minimal media use levels as national goals: ten copies of daily newspapers, five radio receivers, and two cinema seats per hundred persons. Schramm believes media are development tools and constitute capital in which nations should invest at a rate somewhat parallel to the investment in other sectors. Lerner's (1958) modernization model includes a link between urbanization and literacy and between literacy and media participation. Lerner's central proposition is that four dimensions are systematically related to each other in the process of modernization: urbanization, literacy, media participation, and political participation. In testing the order among these four variables, Winham (1970) found support for the links from education and communication to development and from urbanization to education to development; however, for the U.S. data, there was a reciprocal causal relationship between urbanization and education. Inkeles and Smith (1974) also show mass media exposure to be important as a factor in individual modernization.

National traditions have been cited to explain differences in attitudes toward newspapers. Maslog (1971) notes that such attitudes tend to be positive in Egypt and negative in Syria. The role of women in a society is another factor. Lerner (1958, p. 177) quotes a Lebanese woman as saying she did not miss reading newspapers because "It's not for us. It's only for the men—they know how to read and they are more capable of thinking than we are." Hardt (1970) notes the improved status of women in post–World War II Europe is a far-reaching change affecting decision-making patterns in consumer purchases, including the selection of newspaper reading material. Religious factors also have affected media development; Edeani (1970) points to the influence of religion in the development of mass media in Africa. Christian missionaries brought printing presses and spread literacy and the notion of formal education.

Nixon (1976) used a combination of political, legal, and economic factors to rank countries on amount of press freedom. Specific government controls included were control of foreign exchange, government licensing, and extralegal controls such as threats and violence. Using the press freedom index developed by the University of Missouri School of Journalism, two native and two nonnative judges rated 115 countries. Jeffres (1975a) found positive correlations between this press freedom measure and the following print media usage variables: number of daily newspapers, circulation of daily newspapers per thousand population, number of nondaily newspapers, number of other periodicals, newsprint consumption (total and per capita), and number of book titles published.

Numerous physical, environmental, and technological factors have also been cited as determinants of media development (Jeffres, 1975a). For example, the introduction of Latin characters in Turkish printing in 1928 was a short-lived pseudocrisis that initiated an era of progress in the techniques of journalism and advertising. Changes in script used for writing also are important. Asian scripts, except for Chinese, usually require about half again as much space as English to cover the same material; thus, the change from Arabic to Roman script in Malaya was an important step (Lee, 1971; Yalman, 1964). Until the late 1950s, it was impossible to reproduce Chinese ideographs by automatic teletypesetting; and this inhibited development of print media (Hollstein, 1971).

Few regional differences are found in the United States. The lower amount of reading found in the South could be a function of the lower educational levels there. One interesting variation in television viewing that occurs by region stems from climate. In southern locations with the most intense summer heat, television reached its peak during the summer months; in the northern locations, viewing reaches its peak during the coldest part of winter (Nielsen, 1969).

The few rural-urban differences in media use that have been found in the United States are more likely due to the lower availability of certain media in rural areas and the lower socioeconomic status (SES) levels of rural residents than to any feature of urbanicity per se. Even if these factors are not taken into account, media use differences between

U.S. urban and rural residents are usually insignificant. However, higher newspaper readership and broadcast consumption among urban and metropolitan residents is noted in Japan (Richardson, 1973). A report summarizing a decade of studies in Poland (Bajka, 1971) found the basic group of readers was formed by workers in big towns. Looking at relatively isolated peoples in Alaskan villages, Harrison (1972) found radio to be the most important medium; language differences may have constrained reading in this case. Menanteau-Horta and Carter (1972) found radio to be the most intensely used medium among the rural population of Chile as well as the citizens of metropolitan Santiago. However, differences in how print media were used were found.

Social Background and Role Determinants

Though the field of mass communication research is relatively young, considerable information has been gathered on mass media participation by North Americans and other peoples. The most extensive U.S. data is collected by market research and advertising organizations such as Nielsen, Simmons, ARB, and Starch. Generally speaking, however, these detailed commercial studies have not been made available for secondary analysis by academic researchers. What has been made public tends to confirm what the more limited academic and polling studies of people's media usage have found. This section examines the major demographic predictors of mass media usage and summarizes the studies that have examined these factors.

Age. There appears to be a slight U-shaped relation between age and television viewing across the life cycle (Greenberg and Kumata, 1968; Mendelsohn, 1968). At about age two, the child begins a pattern of watching three or more hours of television per day that decreases only slightly as the child enters school. At around age thirteen, viewing time drops significantly (though radio listening increases significantly) and is noticeably lower through the teenage years and early twenties. As young people become settled into the routines of work and family, television viewing time climbs steadily so that by age thirty viewing time has reached a level that remains stable for the rest of one's life, with slight increases occurring when children leave home (in the forty-five to fifty-five age group) and when one retires from work (McLeod and O'Keefe, 1972).

The pattern for print media use is more linear. It is only in the mid twenties and early thirties that newspaper reading becomes part of the daily routines for most of the population. All types of reading also increase as children leave home (Sharon, 1973–74b). Bulcher (1973) noted that younger people generally prefer television and older people prefer the newspaper. Also, youth in America have adopted the radio as a major media "friend." Dominick (1974) found that youngsters not well integrated into peer groups listened to the radio more than did those who were well integrated. Also, youths with few peer group contacts used radio more for informational reasons; those with more contacts used radio more for entertainment.

Age is an important factor in changes in media use patterns. Many have thought older people used television as a means of "social disengagement." Hess (1974) found that viewing can substitute for face-to-face communication no longer available to older people, but Davis (1971) failed to support this notion. Davis found that television serves as a companion to older people. Graney and Graney (1974) suggest senior citizens may use mass media as a form of activity substitution. Adams and Groen (1975) found little differentiation in importance of media use by income, health, or ethnic group among the aged; newspapers, radio, and television all played important parts in older people's lives. Furthermore, older adults are not homogeneous in their media use. Wenner (1976) identified three types of older TV viewers: socially mobile persons to whom the "hard news" functions of television are important, socially isolated persons who use TV to compensate for lack of face-to-face social interaction with other people, and socially isolated persons who use television as a conversation topic to initiate and build face-to-face social interaction with others. Information functions of television are not important to this third type.

Age-related media research has also been conducted in other countries. In Holland, Zweers (1971) found television to be a strong competitor of movies, with older people preferring the entertainment provided by television and younger people seeking out films for experiences. Age differences in radio programming preferences also are noted in Great Britain, with younger people seeking popular music programs (British Broadcasting Corporation, 1977, pp. 83–84). The pattern of television viewing among youths in Great Britain also contrasts with that of older viewers. For example, the percentages of people watching television by age group at 6 PM on weekdays are age fifteen to twenty-four, 19 percent; twenty-five to forty-four, 18 percent; forty-five to sixty-four, 25 percent; sixty-five and older, 51 percent. In Japan, Muramatsu (1975) found Japanese youth relating television programs to the world around them more than did adults.

Occupation. Using Duncan's well-accepted occupational status scale, Robinson (1977) found significant positive correlations between occupation and media usage, particularly print media. With education controlled, the correlation between occupational status and media usage drops. Wilensky (1964) criticized this approach, focusing instead on occupational "situs," which reflects job content rather than prestige. He found, within the higher status occupations, that professors were far more likely to be consumers of sophisticated media fare than lawyers, who in turn were users of more sophisticated fare than engineers. Differences were also found within the same occupation—professors at an urban state university compared with those at a church-related university, lawyers working in a firm compared with those in individual practice, and engineers working for a firm with a diversified product line compared to those working for a firm producing a single product. Similar differences by occupational situs may be found in nonprofessional occupations.

Kando and Summers (1971) looked at compensation and spillover hypotheses that relate work to nonwork situations. Spillover hypotheses suggest work habits and interests may spill over from work into family and community life. For example, jobs requiring constant reading may make some white-collar workers who are compulsive workers feel better if they read during nonwork hours. Compensatory hypotheses suggest workers attempt to find desirable experiences insufficiently present in the work situation or seek reactive compensation, "letting off steam" in response to job tension and such. The two mechanisms are not mutually exclusive, and both may operate at the same time for the same individual.

Kline (1971) found occupation and union membership related to amount of time spent with the media. Kadushin, Hover, and Tichy (1971) suggest the status of U.S. intellectuals is not clearly defined and there is a "dearth of institutions which can certify intellectuals." Thus, certain magazines form a kind of meeting place. They identified eight magazines as the meeting place of the intellectual elite in the United States (journals such as *The New York Review of Books, Harpers,* and *Saturday Review*). Readership of these magazines was found to be strongly related to occupational status. Weiss (1974) reports on the reading behaviors of top leaders of American institutions, including industrial executives, labor leaders, congresspersons, high civil servants and political party leaders, voluntary association heads, and mass media executives and professionals. Very heavy newspaper and magazine readership was reported. Data on respondents' choices for most valuable sources of information and ideas about important national issues show that leaders rely heavily on mass media for information.

The double role of the mass media in providing leisure time activities and also directing people to other leisure behaviors is illustrated by a study that looked at changes occurring when workers went from a five-day to a four-day workweek (Nayman, Atkin, and Gillette, 1973). Time allocation data showed a modest increase in television viewing on weekends. Increases also were noted for viewing local news and for magazine reading, but only a slight change in newspaper reading was found. The authors examine the types of mass media content consumed, noting, "The four-day week provided workers an opportunity to spend more time in active leisure pursuits on long weekends. Not only should mass media exposure increase to fill the additional hours, but specific types of content should be sought out for utilitarian application to such activities as outdoor recreation, hobbies, creative cookery, and educational improvement" (p. 307). The data supporting their conclusion show many workers either beginning to watch or increasing exposure to an outdoor sports program (14 percent), a gourmet cooking program (15 percent), a show dealing with pets (12 percent), and a show dealing with sewing (5 percent). Exposure to various types of magazines also reflected a trend toward seeking media content that could be applied to free time avocations, (Nayman, Atkin, and Gillette, 1973, p. 307). Readership of general interest magazines increased only slightly, but substantial increases were found for specialized publications (sports, hobby, and homemaking magazines). (In the U.S., there has recently been increasing specialization of magazines, many designed to meet special leisure interests and hobbies; Schramm, 1973. Thus, the delivery system appears to be changing to meeting the needs of those with increased leisure time.)

Occupational differences in mass media use are also found in research conducted in countries other than the United States. In Hungary, farmers were found to spend less time on leisure than other workers and employees; however, as in other countries, the major use of leisure time at home was television viewing (Koltai, 1972). Lansbury (1974) studied people in systems analysis, computer programming, operational research, and productivity services employed by a large British corporation. A social participative pattern of leisure characterized younger staff with a career orientation, and a home-centered leisure pattern characterized specialist staff. Thus, career perspective may be as important as one's type or level of occupation. The voluminous literature on diffusion of innovations similarly points to the importance of social background and role determinants in that process around the world (Rogers and Shoemaker, 1971). Opinion leaders are often found to be voracious consumers of the mass media. One way opinion leaders gain their competency is by serving as an avenue for new ideas entering the social system. Early adopters of innovations also tend to have greater exposure to the mass media than do late adopters.

Although some strong beginnings have been made in research into the relationship between media use and occupation, we still have not moved much beyond the relatively simple linkages between frequency of mass media use and occupational characteristics. We need to know more about what features of occupations other than status are significant for mass media consumption. How important are different types of media content in various occupational groupings? Because people discuss a host of topics at work, including mass media topics, we would expect this to affect people's consumption patterns. If this is true, shifts in the work force composition should be accompanied by changes in workers' demands of the mass media. More research also is needed to determine how people in various occupations use the specialized media, such as business and labor publications and organizational papers.

Education. The most important correlate of mass media usage is usually found to be education, a finding that holds true in many countries. (Following education in terms of importance as predictors are the amount of free time available and employment status.) Robinson's (1972) multivariate analysis of television viewing showed that, other things equal, the less educated watch more television than the well educated. In comparison to college graduates, for example, the rest of the U.S. population may watch twice as much entertainment television but no more news programming—indicating the college viewer's greater selectivity in television usage (Bower, 1973). Differences in newspaper use are far less pronounced, although the college graduate reads more and gives much more attention to serious content, such as that appearing on the editorial page. But in the use of books and magazines, college graduates differ greatly from the rest of the population, being three to six times more likely to read analytical commentary or news magazines and 50 percent more likely to read *Reader's Digest* (Robinson, 1967a, 1971b). Reading is ubiquitous among American adults, with most reading time spent on newspapers, magazines, books, and job-related material (Sharon, 1973–74b). Those with more formal education tend to read more of each of these types of material than those with little or no formal education. Two studies comparing newspaper readers with nonreaders found that the latter tended to be less educated (Penrose and others, 1974; Westley and Severin, 1964). Examining Lerner's model of modernization at the individual level of analysis and within the United States, McMartin (1974) found a positive correlation between education and mass media use.

Robinson and Converse (1972) found the relationship between education and television viewing to vary by country. In Eastern European countries, where the programs are similar to U.S. educational television, the better-educated segments of the population watch more television than those with less education. In other Western countries, the relationship between education and amount of viewing is negative, as it is in the United States. Katz and Gurevitch (1976) found that people with "middle education" are the most ardent television fans in Israel, with the least and most educated watching less television. They also found that education is strongly related to book reading in Israel and point to a rising consumption of most mass media, increased participation in hobbies, and increased participation in voluntary organizations as education rises. Inkeles and Smith (1974) found education positively related to mass media exposure in six developing nations.

McLeod, Becker, and Elliott (1972) found that major in school was important: Liberal arts majors were oriented more toward the print media and vocationally oriented students stayed more with the electronic media. McLeod and O'Keefe (1972) note a complex web of interrelationships involving education, age, income, mass media use, and other factors. For example, McLeod, Ward and Tancill (1965–66) found a negative relationship between television viewing and education; but Samuelson, Carter, and Ruggles (1963) report that the negative correlation between viewing and education disappeared when number of children, job-connected hours, organizational membership, and hobby hours were controlled for. More research is needed to sort out the effects of various factors in combination. We also need to identify education-derived skills that affect mass media consumption at different ages.

Income Level. Income is strongly correlated with education and, thus, produces much the same pattern of correlations in studies of media usage. Nonetheless, correlations are stronger with education, and differences by income rather than by education are attenuated when both factors are examined simultaneously (Robinson, 1967a, 1972). Meyersohn (1968) found that low-income groups generally have fewer leisure interests other than television, belong to fewer organizations or clubs, own fewer pieces of leisure equipment, read fewer newspapers or books, and attend fewer movies than middle- and upper-income groups. They also watch more television than higher-income people. Nonreaders of newspapers tend to have low incomes, according to two other studies (Penrose and others, 1974; Westley and Severin, 1964).

Though income level is less important than education and other factors affecting mass media use today, it is likely to play a more significant part in people's use of recently developed media (video cassette systems, television disc players, and large screens, for example). The high cost of these units is likely to limit their use to upper-income families. Similarly, rising costs (relative to incomes) of some print media could have a negative impact on their use by lower-income segments of the population.

Gender. U.S. men and women do not differ greatly in their media usage habits. Far greater differences in media use are found between women in the labor force and women not in the labor force than between women and men. Women in the labor force tend to hold two jobs—the paid job and a family job—and so have little time to devote to either print or broadcast media. Women with only the family-housekeeper role watch more television than employed women. They are also more likely to combine viewing with other activities and read slightly more books and magazines than men. The biggest difference in the other direction occurs for newspapers, with men being significantly more likely to read newspapers than are women (Robinson, 1976b). In a U.S. study of all reading activity, Sharon (1973–74b) found women reading an average of 101 minutes per day, compared to the 113-minute average for men. Robinson (1971a), reporting on a national survey conducted in the fall of 1969, found 25 percent of adult men and 22 percent of adult women reporting they watched national news programs on an average day.

Race. Black Americans are generally found to be heavier television viewers and less intensive print media users than whites. However, once educational differences have been taken into account, blacks appear to be heavier users of both broadcast and print media (Robinson, 1977). Carey (1966) reported finding racial differences in preferences for television programs, but the introduction of income controls produced contradictory results (Dervin and Greenberg, 1972). Allen (1968) found that only 14 percent of black ghetto dwellers subscribed to a daily newspaper; but radio, and, to a lesser extent, television were pervasive media. Sharon (1973–74a) found racial differences in newspaper reading to be greater than those for other forms of reading. Although newspapers do not reach a large number of blacks, especially the poor, the racial difference does not stem solely from economic factors. Bogart (1972) found most of the differences in newspaper and radio exposure between blacks and whites, but not in television viewing, could be accounted for by differences in education, income, and geography. In contrast to findings for whites, upper-income blacks watched more prime-time television than did those lower on the economic scale. Using a sample of black students, Tan and Vaughn (1976) found negative correlations between use of newspapers and magazines and black nationalism.

Language can also be a factor in some areas (Jeffres, 1973). Relatively few researchers have focused on ethnic media use in the United States, though ethnic radio programs and newspapers still attract consumers across the country. The persistence of older European ethnic communities and the appearance of newer ethnic groups provides a mix and a flux that need attention by mass media researchers. Jeffres and Hur (1978) found more frequent use of ethnic mass media among those with greater ethnic identification in a survey in Cleveland in 1976. A Canadian study (Mousseau-Glaser, 1972) found few people who watched programs and read newspapers in both English and French, even among bilingual people; most people consume mass media products in the language they know best. Williams, Dordick, and Horstmann (1977) found marked differences in the pattern of information seeking in different communities. There was a bias in the black community for interpersonal networks as sources of information; in the Mexican-American community, for institutions or agencies; and in the predominantly white community, for print media and the telephone. They concluded that agencies attempting to communicate entertainment, social service, or municipal service information to the public must take these differences into account.

Religion. No systematic attempt has been made to identify religious differences in media behavior; neither does there appear to be any reason to expect any differences beyond those that are education related. Thus, one might expect to find Jews, Episcopalians, and Presbyterians (who are relatively well educated, on the average) making greater use of the print media and less of television, with these differences vanishing as education is controlled. However, there are probably religion-related variations in media content preferences.

Marital Status. Although differences are not large, married people spend more time with both broadcast and print media than do single people. Similarly, home responsibilities increase with having children, which means more time is spent with the media, particularly with television when there is a preteen in the household (Robinson, 1977).

Organizational and Political Participation. Relatively few researchers have examined the relationship between mass media usage and organizational participation. One area of research where much empirical evidence is available, however, is the political. Media usage in relation to political material is clearly related to other forms of informal political participation (Burstein, 1972; Robinson, 1972). Thus, people who contribute money, ring doorbells, wear buttons, put on bumper stickers, proselytize others, and so forth are more likely to follow a campaign in both printed and broadcast media than those who are not involved in various kinds of informal political participation. The close link between political and mass media participation accounts for the rather paradoxical finding that voters most exposed to media during the campaign (and, hence, most likely to encounter messages unfavorable to their candidate or party) are those voters likely to defect from their party (DeVries and Tarrance, 1972; Robinson, 1976a).

Organizational participation generally is also strongly linked to social status, a major predictor of patterns of mass media participation. Those with higher social status (in terms of education, income, or occupation) pay more attention to print media (particularly magazines and books) and less attention to broadcast media (particularly entertainment on television) than those with lower status. This state of affairs leads to a correlation between media use and organizational participation, with organizational participants being more likely to attend to print media content and less likely to attend to broadcast entertainment content (Robinson, 1977).

There are a few survey studies in which both media use and other organizational data were collected. Kline (1971) used path analysis to examine connections between life-style variables and other factors related to time spent reading and viewing television. Older families were more likely to read newspapers; and only organizational participation seemed to cut into reading time, with a positive relationship found between education and participating in organizations (number of meetings attended). However, organizational participation was the best predictor of both spouses' book reading. Villani (1975) found a positive relationship between participation in activities outside the home and light (versus heavy) television viewing. Graney and Graney (1974), in a panel study of elderly women, found a positive relationship between attendance at voluntary organization meetings and two media use variables, television viewing and radio listening. Organizational membership also was related to radio use in this study.

Tomeh (1976) studied full-time college students in Lebanon and found the highest rate of both club membership and mass media consumption among the last born rather than among the firstborn. She suggests this shows the other-directed orientation of the youngest group. Control of demographic characteristics did not alter the pattern. In Holland, Schilt (1969) looked at two forms of social participation, formal and informal music groups, expecting to find that formal groups exert more socializing pressure on members and informal groups emphasize the "personalization process." However, attendance at films, the theater, and sports events was higher among members of the informal group, which also showed fewer conformist tendencies. Using an analytical technique to group activities on the basis of intercorrelations, Katz and Gurevitch (1976) found television viewing to be clustered with attending lectures and belonging to organizations for older people; but for the general Israeli sample, television viewing was not closely related to other activities (60 percent of respondents owned TV sets at the time of the study). In France, Dumazedier (1973) linked participation in sports activities and media participation, finding that sports activities occupied a very small part of leisure time in areas with television.

Attitudes and Personality Traits

Attitudes toward the media have long concerned journalists and media people. Confidence in the mass media has fluctuated, but recent data show the public's decreased confidence in the mass media is accompanied by decreased trust in many American institutions (Gallup, 1977; Harris, 1976a, 1976b; Jennings and Niemi, 1975; Watts and Free, 1974).

Attitudes Toward Mass Media. Since 1961, Americans have consistently voted television their most believable medium. Newspapers follow in second place (Blumler and McQuail, 1969; Jacobson, 1969; Roper, 1969). Roper reports twice as many people prefer television as prefer newspapers over other media. Television is also the preferred medium in Finland (Starck, 1969). However, Ryan (1973) found newspaper and television credibility varies by topic. Newspapers were more credible for state affairs and science news; television was more believed in news of student protest, a highly visual topic. There was no major difference in the proportion of respondents selecting television and those selecting newspapers for other national and international public affairs topics surveyed. Shaw (1973) found media use and perceived credibility to be positively correlated. Multimedia users chose television over the other daily news media as the most believable. Wade and Schramm (1969) also noted the importance of the visual element of determining whether people considered television the more credible medium. Television tends to be preferred for visual stories and the newspaper for science and health news (Bogart, 1968–69; Wade and Schramm, 1969). However, most people use more than one source for information on any topic (Wade and Schramm, 1969).

Media Uses and Gratifications. People put the mass media to a variety of uses and derive a host of gratifications from such use. Research into uses and gratifications stems from a functional orientation that stresses the motivational factors that attract people to the media and help maintain media use patterns. There have been a number of efforts to categorize uses and gratifications in a theoretically meaningful way. One of the earliest studies, by Berelson (1949), analyzed the uses of newspaper reading—the uses identified were to keep in touch with friends and to learn of entertainment, activities, and such. Lasswell (1971) identified several social functions of communication: social radar, manipulation and decision management, instruction, and entertainment. (These functions are attributed to communication generally, not just mass media use.) Weiss (1969) categorized research on uses and gratifications under somewhat similar headings, also used by others: time filling (Himmelweit, Oppenheim, and Vince, 1958; Jeffres, 1975b); relaxation and diversion (Katz, Gurevitch, and Haas, 1973; Klapper, 1960; Schramm, Lyle, and Parker, 1961); socializing (Schramm, Lyle, and Pool, 1963; Westley and Severin, 1964); and personal uses and relationships (Forsey, 1963; Maccoby, 1954).

A rather different theoretical scheme was proposed by Atkin (1973). He categorized media uses in terms of utilitarian purposes (that is, attention to media content in order to solve practical problems). A message was defined as having utility if it provides useful input for responding to everyday stimuli. Atkin outlines four types of adaptation requirements that produce uncertainty and, thus, the need for information. In cognitive adaptation, individuals need surveillance information, which allows them to understand developments that may affect them (Kay, 1954; McLeod, Ward, and Tancill, 1965–66; Maslow, 1963). In affective adaptation, individuals need guidance information for attitude formation and decision making. Blumler and McQuail (1969, p. 85), for example, found that 51 percent of British respondents said they watch party political broadcasts "to judge what political leaders are like"; 26 percent said they watched "to help me make up my mind how to vote." Other studies finding examples of affective adaptation include Vinyard and Sigel (1971) and Blume and Lyons (1968). In behavioral adaptation, people need performance information because they are unsure how to perform some tasks. Two studies showed that party activists paid closer attention to television ads than did the general public (Atkin and others, 1973; Sheinkopf, Atkin and Bowen, 1973). In defensive adaptation, people need reinforcement information, confirmation of a previously arrived-at position. Though the evidence for selective exposure—a conscious preference for supportive material—is unconvincing (Sears, 1968; Sears and Freedman, 1967), "de facto selectivity" has been identified (Atkin, Galloway, and Nayman, 1973; Clarke and James, 1967; Schramm and Carter, 1959).

The most comprehensive treatment of uses and gratification is found in Blumler and Katz's (1974) review of perspectives on gratifications research. Katz, Blumler, and Gurevitch (1974) note that each major uses and gratifications research project has yielded its own classification of functions. For example, McQuail, Blumler, and Brown (1972, p. 155) provide the following typology of functions: diversion, personal relationships, personal identity, and surveillance. Katz, Blumler, and Gurevitch (1974, p. 27) identify five social situations (also noted by others) in which media-related needs originate: (1) social situations producing tensions and conflicts that lead to pressure media use can reduce (Katz and Foulkes, 1962); (2) situations creating awareness of problems demanding attention and, thus, information seeking (Edelstein, 1973); (3) situations offering impoverished real-life opportunities to satisfy needs, which are directed to the mass media for servicing (Rosengren and Windahl, 1972); (4) social situations that give rise to values whose affirmation and reinforcement is facilitated by appropriate media content (Dembo, 1972); and (5) group situations providing expectations of familiarity with particular media materials, which must be consumed as an aid to social integration (Atkin, 1972). McLeod and Becker (1974) found strong support for the validity of self-report measures of gratification and avoidances developed by Blumler and McQuail (1969).

Rosengren (1974) tried to place uses and gratifications, motives, and other factors into a single paradigm of function research. In contrast, Johnstone (1974) identified two basic types of mass media uses. One involves uses where the individual takes into account the social context (experiential media uses) and maintains contact with his or her own experiences and daily reality. The other pattern directs the individual's attention away from everyday experience (transcendental uses). Noting that relatively little television content specifically reflects the youth culture, Johnstone (1974) found that high school students not well integrated into the youth culture were the heaviest television users. Looking at media use in Israel during a crisis, Peled and Katz (1974) found people sought relief from anxiety in the media; they also used the media to participate in the national grief and for reinforcement of feelings of national solidarity.

In a study of schoolchildren in England, Greenberg (1974) factor analyzed reasons for watching television and found seven factors: learning, arousal, habit, companionship, relaxation, forgetting, and passing time. Several attitude measures correlated positively with most of the identified functions; talking about television with others and seeing things on television one wants to talk about were related to each of the seven functions. Using television to learn, because it is a habit, and to relax were related to talking about television frequently. Children who used television to relax or as a matter of habit tended to be the most avid viewers. They also talked about television more and tended to use its advertising as a buying guide. These seven functions accounted for 56 percent of the variance in actual viewing.

Brown, Cramond, and Wilde (1974) were able to study the functional similarity between various media behaviors in a situation where television was newly introduced. They found a reorganization of media functions rather than simple displacement. (See also Cherry, 1971.) McGuire (1974) attempted to delineate four dimensions of motivation related to communication gratification: (1) cognitive versus affective, (2) self-growth versus self-preservation, (3) active versus passive initiation, and (4) internal versus external goal orientations of human motives.

Judgments and Values. A few studies have linked ethical judgments and basic values. Shuttleworth and May (1933) looked at light and heavy movie goers and found no evidence of differences between the groups in values and ethical or moral judgments. However, a more recent study by Schramm, Lyle, and Parker (1961) found that acceptance of middle-class values regarding the importance of schoolwork and education, aspirations for high occupational status, and willingness to defer gratifications were linked to low television viewing.

Family environment can produce a set of values that lead to particular media patterns. Wisconsin communication researchers (McLeod and O'Keefe, 1972) categorized family communication patterns into four types: (1) laissez-faire families, which lack emphasis on either social or concept orientation; (2) protective families, which stress obedience and social harmony and show little concern for their children's conceptual development; (3) pluralistic families, which emphasize development of strong and varied concept relations without insisting on obedience to authority; and (4) consensual families, which stress both types of orientation. Adolescents from pluralistic homes spend far less time with television than the average child; and, when they do watch, their attention to news and public affairs content is high. Adolescents in pluralistic homes are only slightly above average in newspaper reading and attention to print news. Children in laissez-faire families show little interest in public affairs content on TV or in newspapers; adolescents in consensual homes are above average in their interest in public affairs. Adolescents from protective homes spend the most time watching television of any group, and they watch it for entertainment rather than public affairs programming (Chaffee and McLeod, 1971; McLeod, Atkin, and Chaffee, 1971a, 1971b).

Personality Traits and Moods. A number of personality traits have been found to be related to patterns of mass media use. Rees (1967) found need for achievement was positively related to reading magazines categorized as "delayed gratification" publications. Kline (1971) found that amount of television viewing was positively related to anomie. Robinson (1977) also found heavier viewing among people with high alienation, and people who felt that they often had time on their hands also tended to be heavy viewers. McLeod, Ward, and Tancill (1965–66) found alienated people less interested in nonsensational headlines than the nonalienated. Katz and Lazarsfeld (1955) reported that women who said they worried "as much as others" and were depressed occasionally were more likely than others to read popular fiction and movie magazines and to listen to daytime radio serials.

High television viewing is also associated with low self-esteem. People with high self-esteem watch an average of 3.1 hours daily; people with moderate self-esteem watch 3.6 hours; those with low self-esteem watch about 4 hours. Jeffres (1975b) dichotomized media behaviors into media seeking, where an individual moves toward a medium without regard to content, and content seeking, where the movement is toward particular content. He found that saliency of negative feelings in reasons given for engaging in media use was related to media seeking of radio and newspaper fare, and mention of boredom and the need to "kill time" was related to media seeking of television and newspaper fare. However, Scott (1957) found few relationships between personality characteristics measured by Minnesota Multiphasic Personality Inventory scales and movie preferences. Obviously, the relationship between media usage and personality or mood is complex and much exploration still needs to be done in this area.

Situational Factors

Media participation has seldom been the subject of research focused at levels of analysis other than the individual. Using longer time spans, for example, we can examine period differences for evidence of important situational factors in media participation. Dotan and Cohen (1976) found media-related needs were more pronounced during wartime. They also found that perceived helpfulness of television, radio, and (to a less extent) newspapers in providing information and helping people understand events was higher during wartime.

The situational context can also be studied in terms of group differences. An interesting example of such research can be found in the work of a Minnesota team that has conducted an ongoing program of mass communication research in various communities (Donohue, Tichenor, and Olien, 1972; Tichenor, Donohue, and Olien, 1970; Tichenor and others, 1973). They have identified a differential growth in knowledge between socioeconomic groups as the amount of public affairs information into the social system increases. Prior exposure to public affairs information is greater among upper socioeconomic groups, and thus they have an advantage in existing understanding to begin with. Other factors contribute to increasing the "knowledge gap." These include (1) formal education level, which is related to communication skill; (2) social contacts relevant to public affairs topics; and (3) reliance on print media, which publish more public affairs information than other media. Higher-status groups tend to have more formal education, more social contacts, and more exposure to print media. Tichenor and others (1973) also report that conflict and social tension stimulate information seeking and information exchange and thus may alter the relationship between class and public affairs knowledge.

Time Use Studies

With their focus on what people do across the full twenty-four-hour day, time use studies provide an appropriate framework within which to examine the totality of media use. Recent methodological research has established the fundamental reliability and validity of this approach to measuring human behavior (Robinson, 1977). Moreover, time use data point to the major weakness of other types of data on media use: The latter tend to overestimate time spent with the media. The research with time budgets supports the premise that survey questions dealing with any irregular or interrupted activity (such as media participation and participation in voluntary organizations) will produce generous estimates of actual time spent in that activity. With regard to television viewing, commercial rating services indicate the typical American spends well over three hours a day in front of his or her television set. (The often-cited six hours a day figure refers to the total time the set is on in the household.) Similar estimates can be found in some other countries; the Japanese reportedly spend an average of three hours and thirty-eight minutes each day watching television, with the figure rising to four hours and forty-nine minutes on Sundays (*The Asian Messenger*, 1976).

Time budget data from a national 1965–66 study (Robinson, 1977) detailing all the person's time uses during the day show that television viewing is a primary activity on the average just about half that amount–eighty-nine minutes per day. When viewing as a secondary activity (combined with other activities) is included, daily viewing times go up to about 50 percent; but the total is still about an hour short of that reported by the rating services. North Americans, then, do watch a great deal of television, and undoubtedly more than they should in the view of some; but the majority of their free time is still spent on activities other than television. This figure is in line with the viewing times reported for twelve other countries that took part in this time use study (once the differential ownership rates of television sets across countries are taken into account; see Szalai, 1966; Szalai and others, 1972). By this yardstick, North Americans seem more addicted to television than people in other countries only because they have more television sets and program broadcast time and variety.

The time data make quite clear, however, how television dominates mass media activity in the United States; compared to the average of ninety minutes spent with television, the newspaper takes twenty minutes; magazines, five minutes; books, five minutes; radio, four minutes; movies, three minutes; and reading (unspecified), another three minutes. Nonetheless, on a daily participation basis, newspaper reading is just about as common as television viewing (about 80 percent use each medium on a typical day); and given that many viewers avoid television news programs during the day, newspapers obviously have a greater daily news reach than television does. One rating service, in fact, puts the total audience for the national evening news at about 25 percent, making it difficult to see how over half the U.S. population can claim to get most of their news from television.

Whatever the case, Robinson's (1977) time use data for the United States show how employed men and women and nonemployed women allocated their daily time in 1965–66. Their total leisure comes to just under five hours per day or about thirty-four hours per week. Media consume proportionately more of the free time of employed men (50.5 percent) than of employed women (38.9 percent). Newspaper reading and movie attendance are considerably higher among men than women. Nonemployed women devote the same proportion of their free time to primary use of media but have 38 percent more total free time than employed women.

Robinson's data show a strong negative relationship between education and television viewing. People who have been to college have roughly the same amount of free time as the rest of the population but spend about half as much of it in front of the television set as those who have not been to high school. No educational difference appears for newspaper reading. Magazine and book reading take up relatively more time among the well educated than among the less well educated. Educational and organizational participation also take up more time among those with at least some college education. People who have been to college report almost all the adult educational activity. Although their religious participation is about equal to that of the rest of the population, college-educated women report more participation in other types of formal organizational activity. However, the total average time spent on organizational activities—six minutes out of an average day—is only a little more than the time spent reading magazines. It is also less than a tenth of the time spent in informal social interactions.

Conclusion

The imbalance between mass media use and organizational participation indicates the former deserves far more attention as a voluntary activity than it received in the past. However, it would be difficult to argue that mass media use is of the proportionately greater significance to society that these differences in time use might suggest. By that logic, sleep becomes the most important use of time in society. We have noted, however, that evidence of rather strong effects associated with media usage (such as gains in information or influence on responses to the social and political environment) is mounting.

The paucity of research noted at various points in this chapter points particularly to the need for more work investigating the historical context and situational factors in media participation. Most research has concentrated on social background and role determinants, with only secondary attention to attitudes and personality traits as determinants of

media participation (rather than as variables affected by media participation). This suggests that perhaps we need a fresh orientation in media
research. In particular, there is a need for more research that crosses
levels (for example, individual, community, or nation) of analysis and
integrates existing evidence. A relevant line of research is the "ecological
analysis" that stems largely from Robinson's (1950) influential article
describing the problem of the ecological fallacy—assuming that empirically supported relationships found between phenomena at one level
hold for another level. Dogan and Rokkan (1969, p. 17) argue that the
warning against ecological fallacies should not just be treated as another
"red light" but "should be used as a springboard" for the development
of new methods of multilevel analysis. "The level-by-level discrepancies
in the direction and strength of correlations constitute an important
field of research in its own right: individual behaviors do not vary
directly with ecological characteristics, they interact dynamically with
them." Alker (1969) generalizes the Robinson argument to show how the
ecological fallacy fits into a broader typology of level-to-level shortcuts
in analytical procedures, for example, cross-level fallacies—false generalizations from individual relations within a single region to a universe
of intercollectivity relationships. As Valkonen (1969) has noted, ecological research is concerned with several levels of social organization.
Several studies in this area can be found in Dogan and Rokkan (1969),
Blau (1960), Tannenbaum and Bachman (1964), and Hannan (1971) (the
last focuses on problems of aggregation and disaggregation, relating
observations on individuals to group-level concepts). Blau (1977) also
deals with ecological structure in his theory of social structure. Although some studies can be cited, communication researchers have
generally given only a small proportion of their attention to ecological
analysis. Though we expect media participation to be patterned behavior (as are other human behaviors—a central tenet of sociology), our
analyses have most often been limited to average frequency data and
other aggregations that are very likely to conceal the patterns of individual behavior. Sears and Freedman (1967) pointed out, for example, that
most research on selective exposure to mass media has involved
measurement at the individual level; but inferences have been drawn at
the contextual level. Przeworski and Teune (1970) suggest a method in
which analysis begins at the highest level and works downward to the
lowest point where the relationship holds. However, if we expect a
relationship to change at some level, we must have some idea of what
variable will be responsible for the change before we plan our research.
In short, whatever we do to expand the scope of our research and to avoid
falling into the ecological fallacy, it is clear we need to begin with a more
complex conceptualization of the determinants of mass media usage.
One avenue that may lead to a broader conceptualization is the integration of research from different disciplines.

Part IV

Altruistic and Helping Activities

Jacqueline Macaulay

*The chapters in Part Four depart somewhat from the style and organiza-
tion of the chapters in Parts Two and Three. They represent a form of
human behavior that is at once rare (or rarely recognized) and yet
thought to be of immense importance in human life. There is a great
volume of literature on altruism by social scientists. (The authors in this
section review a fair amount of it but do not begin to cover it all—for
this, one must go to the comprehensive reviews the contributors cite.) It
is clear from the extensiveness of this literature that researchers view
altruism as very important. It is a behavior on which neither informal or
formal philosophies of life or religions can or will remain silent. There
exist diatribes against altruism (as a brake on maximization of human
potential, for example), but even here it is not a behavior to be treated
lightly. One can also find diatribes against the folly of political participation, but the latter do not fall in the theme of behavior antithetical to
human nature, as do diatribes against altruism.*

*Another distinguishing characteristic of the activities discussed
in Part Four is that they tend to be activities with a relatively important
interaction element. That is, with the possible exception of those actions
usually defined as "philanthropic," these activities involve two groups*

of participants, the helpers and the helped. The individuality of the ultimate target of the activity is important, if not in terms of intrinsic characteristics, at least in terms of the target's reactions or of changes in his or her situation. One can play tennis, vote, work for a political candidate, even throw a bomb without concern for the effects on other individuals; but when it comes to helping others, effects on others are part of the essential definition of the behavior as actual or intended help. Thus, this section has a chapter on the help recipient.

Another distinctive characteristic of this area is that types of altruistic behavior are seldom compared and contrasted in terms of differences within the class. We have in this section separate chapters on one recognized subtype (philanthropy) and one special situation (behavior following disasters), but that leaves the rest of altruism undifferentiated in terms of intrinsic differences in the behaviors involved. We do not, for example, have ready-made divisions such as those found for political behavior (conventional versus unconventional). Instead, we begin with an amorphous two-term title, "altruism and helping activities." The second term is thrown in because some kinds of helpful behavior, such as that following natural disasters, seem more compelled by circumstances than everyday usage allows for altruism. Adequate and specific definitions of altruism can, of course, be set out—and must be in order to specify, for example, what goes into a chapter on socialization for altruism. But such definitions vary and tend to be subject to much debate. (For example, is it altruistic to do a good deed that gives you pleasure? Is the proper motivation crucial to altruism? Is altruism possible if one considers motivation?)

It is this characteristic of altruism, as a term covering a shifting ground, that led me to welcome Kemper's chapter. This review and synthesis, rather than being an exhaustive review of the literature (which is almost impossible in a single chapter anyway), tries to categorize altruistic behaviors in terms of intrinsic characteristics and to establish a baseline, much as is done without special comment in discussions of political behavior and leisure activity.

As noted in the preface to this volume, we inadvertently ended up with something of an experiment to test the hypothesis that the classes of explanatory variables would be similar across disciplines. Part Four is possibly the major test of the hypothesis. In spite of the differences between Part Four and Parts Two and Three, we believe in the end Part Four's focus converges with the focuses of other sections and so confirms the hypothesis.

CHAPTER 13

Socialization and Prosocial Behavior in Children

Ervin Staub
Helene K. Feinberg

Everyday encounters afford us opportunities to help other persons. Hunger, suffering, and injustice exist in the world and any one of us might work to eliminate them. Why does one person help on more occasions than another or in different ways than another would help? Our objective is to examine the socialization of children that might lead to a tendency to engage in voluntary social action or behavior that benefits others. To understand better the child-rearing antecedents of prosocial behavior, we first review some of the determinants of adult prosocial behavior. This provides the background against which we can view the ways certain socialization practices contribute to particular personality characteristics that enhance the likelihood of prosocial action.

Note: Some of the research reported here was supported by NIMH Grant #23886 to the first author. An elaboration and further development of some of the ideas presented here, and a more extensive review of relevant research literature can be found in Staub (1978, 1979).

Prosocial behavior, altruism, or voluntary social action of the prosocial variety refer to behavior by which actors produce benefit for someone other than themselves. Prosocial behavior is any behavior that benefits other people. The degree of benefit and the degree to which self-sacrifice is involved may vary widely. The behavior may be directed at a single individual or may serve a social cause, for example, the abolition of slavery, which would benefit many people. The actor may have varied motives, including self-serving ones (hoping to be rewarded for producing benefits); but his or her help is not coerced or accidental. In this sense, the behavior is intended to benefit another and hence may be considered voluntary action. The term altruism applies to a specific subset of prosocial behavior where actors may be judged to act without "selfish" motivation. They are not motivated by material or social gain; their sole concern is the desire to contribute to another's welfare.

Although we focus on prosocial behavior as the end product, intentions or motives underlying action are important for several reasons. First, in everyday activities, people consider others' motivations and intentions and respond to their actions in accord with the evaluations they make about them (Heider, 1958; Jones and Davis, 1965). Second, for the actor, the benefits of the act may be secondary to the anticipated personal gain. Third, individual differences in the motivation for a specific prosocial act are likely to be associated with individual differences in the willingness to help under other circumstances.

The literature strongly indicates recipients' attributions about their benefactor's motivation influence whether reciprocation of a favor will occur (Schopler, 1970; Staub, 1972b). However, the recipient's attributions about the other are liable to be colored by his or her own motivations; in order not to feel obligated to return a favor, a person may attribute selfish motivation to a benefactor. Another issue is the importance to most benefactors of their prosocial behavior appearing genuine, arising out of concern with the other's welfare, because prosocial intentions have great social value. It is partly because of the difficulty in assessing motivations and intentions underlying prosocial behavior— that is, for pragmatic reasons—that we emphasize prosocial behavior as the outcome or end product rather than prosocial intention. Further, in terms of its consequences for the beneficiary, it is prosocial behavior that is particularly important. However, in discussing both determinants and development, we emphasize personal values (leading to concern about others' welfare) and personal goals, which presumably motivate the tendency to act prosocially.

Personality determinants of helping have been somewhat neglected in the research literature. Among the reasons for this neglect is social psychologists' attention to the social-situation determinants of helping. Also influential in this regard was Hartshorne and May's (1929) findings suggesting that honesty is situationally determined. In their influential research on bystander intervention, Latane and Darley (1970) found no personality differences between helpers and nonhelpers. Several writers have recently questioned a trait approach in personality research (Jones and Nisbett, 1971; Mischel, 1968). Still more recently, emphasis has returned to person-situation interactions (Bowers, 1973; Mischel, 1973). Bowers' (1973) review suggests in studies that examine both person and situation variables, person-situation interactions account for greater proportions of variance than either personality or situation factors alone.

We will further explore the meaning of person-situation interaction in accounting for social behavior. We believe when situational forces are not extremely strong and so do not lead to uniform behavior, situational characteristics require certain person characteristics in order to activate prosocial behavior by the potential helper. That is, for helping to occur, a matching of person characteristics with situational factors must occur.

Personality Characteristics

Some of the person characteristics that are important for helping to occur are general in nature; they would contribute to an inclination to help others in many situations. Certain values or constellations of values and the tendency to react empathically to others (to experience others' emotions vicariously) have been the most frequently suggested personality characteristics that might motivate prosocial behavior across a variety of situations. Such characteristics might make helping others a desirable outcome, leading to efforts to bring about that outcome. However, in order for helping to occur, several conditions in addition to the presence of such personality characteristics have to exist. One of them is that no conflicting values or goals that counteract the influence of the goal of helping another person be activated.

Another is that a person possess an action tendency or, more specifically, the characteristics required for taking action in a particular situation in order to bring about the goal. An action tendency probably has several elements; a sense of control over events, leading to confidence about one's ability to bring about desired outcomes, might be the most important one. Courage, adventurousness, and other characteristics might be preconditions for action in some situations. Such characteristics are general; but with regard to prosocial behavior, they are specific in that they are required in some helping situations but not in others. Even more specific characteristics are specific competencies, such as first aid skills or the ability to swim, that might be required from a would-be helper in certain situations.

In order to predict whether a person will behave prosocially in a particular situation, it is necessary to understand the kind of values or goals the situation might activate. Only those goals an individual already possesses can be activated. The extent to which the activated values combine or conflict with each other and the resulting dominance of one value (for example, helping another person or trying to achieve personal success) will help determine helping behavior. Knowing the specific characteristics the situation demands from a would-be helper and the degree to which a person possesses them should improve behavior prediction.

The fact that helping is not a unitary phenomenon becomes explainable in this framework. Helping situations may activate different combinations of goals and make widely varying demands, calling forth any of several possible combinations of person characteristics from potential helpers. Few individuals are likely to possess all the person characteristics required for action by varied helping situations, which explains why low correlations might occur among different types of prosocial behavior across different settings.

Role Taking. The capacity for taking another's role, perceiving feelings and the probable or actual consequences of events on his or her internal or physical states, has frequently been suggested as an important influence on helping behavior. Although some psychologists consider role taking the equivalent of empathy, the capacity to take others' roles does not guarantee a person will take the role in any particular instance. Moreover, having taken another person's role and thus having come to understand his or her feelings, one may still not experience the other's distress or joy; one might even come to feel the opposite way. Role taking might be a precondition of but not a guarantee for experiencing empathy or for activating prosocial values or goals in many situations. An interesting question concerns the extent to which another's role will itself arouse the inclination to help a person in need versus the extent to which other characteristics, such as prosocial values, have to be present for this to happen.

Awareness of Consequences. S. Schwartz (1970b) suggested a person's tendency to analyze and thus be aware of the probable consequences for others of his or her behavior is an important determinant, in combination with other characteristics, of helping behavior. He found fraternity members scoring high on his measure of this characteristic were perceived as more helpful by their peers.

Perhaps the awareness of consequences measure is, to some extent, a measure of a person's concern with and tendency to think about the direction events may take, particularly where other people's welfare is involved. Thus, awareness of consequences might be part of the ability and tendency to plan, a form of cognitive competence that extends role taking to the realm of the consequences of one's actions on others. It might be related, therefore, to action tendency in the domain of helping behavior.

Assuming Responsibility. S. Schwartz (1970b) has also suggested that individual differences in the tendency to assume responsibility for others' welfare is an important determinant of helping behavior, in combination with personal norms and awareness of consequences of one's actions on others. Ascribing responsibility to the self for others' welfare might be regarded, on the one nand, as a manifestation of a personal value. On the other hand, it might indicate the strength or intensity of a person's values that refer to others' welfare and thus indicate value-behavior consistency in the realm of helping behavior. Perhaps some individuals who strongly value others' welfare have formulated more clearly, and believe to a greater degree in, their own responsibility to contribute to others' welfare.

Personal Goals. Values, beliefs, and social norms are generally regarded as important motivators of moral behavior, behavior that affects other people's welfare. Internalized values and norms might best be thought of as personal characteristics that make it important for a person to behave in certain ways, primarily because they bring about certain outcomes. Preference for outcomes or end states might be regarded as personal goals.

Personal goals are activated in many situations. In situations where someone needs help, the goal of improving others' welfare may be aroused. For some people, the primary goal might be to engage in a certain activity, such as being helpful, rather than the beneficial consequences of the helpful behavior. Depending on the specifics of the situation, other goals may be aroused as well, perhaps in conflict or in support of a helpfulness goal. For example, the need for approval might motivate prosocial action.

Personal goals vary in their importance. People have a rank ordering of goals they develop and maintain with a certain degree of stability. Although we may assume most individuals have many of the same goals, their order of importance may vary widely. This assumption of the rank ordering of goals is similar to Rokeach's (1973) discussion of the rank ordering of values. In fact, we consider values and goals interchangeable terms. A value, as defined by Rokeach (1973), is a belief that is prescriptive or proscriptive. According to Allport (1961, p. 454), "A value is a belief upon which a man acts by preferences." We consider a personal goal a preference for a certain outcome or end state or an aversion to an outcome. The definition of value implies such preference or aversion. We prefer to talk in terms of personal goals because of our belief in the importance of the motivating power of certain end states or outcomes, which this term more clearly implies.

The reliability (test-retest) of rank ordering values on Rokeach's measure (a subject assigns a rank to each of eighteen values relative to each other) averages about .63 with a year and a half interval and about .73 with a three- to seven-week interval. It is reasonable to expect one's ordering of values and goals to be somewhat flexible. It is likely to be the case, in fact, that in different situations only a subset of goals is aroused and that their rank orderings will vary, perhaps as a function of particular characteristics of the situation leading to the activation of some goals with greater power, force, or urgency than of others.

One potential basis for the degree to which a goal is activated and for the determination of its relation to other goals is a person's perception of its applicability to the situation. Range of applicability refers to the nature of stimulus conditions to which a personal value or goal is applicable. For example, for some individuals, the value of consideration for others may apply only to friends and be irrelevant in relation to employees or strangers. When rank orderings of values are obtained in the abstract (Rokeach, 1973), it is not possible to ascertain how wide or narrow the range of applicability of the subjects' values are. Thus, the ability to predict behavior from these rank orderings is somewhat limited. (For a more elaborate discussion of the range of applicability concept and of the theory of social behavior here described, see Staub, 1975b.)

Norms are generalized social expectations or rules that specify the kind of behavior expected of people in specific situations (Thibaut and Kelley, 1959). Like values, norms ideally become internalized so people behave the same way when they are not under surveillance by others as they would when they are (Kelman, 1961). The sanctions for behavior also become internalized. Norms and values are similar in nature; but values are more likely to imply a desired end state, and norms are more means related, specifying the expected behavior but only implying the desired end. Rokeach (1973) distinguished between terminal values and instrumental values. The latter (helpfulness, for example) can be relatively easily stated in normative terms; but the former (a comfortable life, for example) are more difficult to define that way because they imply an end state without the means by which it is to be achieved. Thus, goals, which emphasize end states, are closer to (terminal) values in meaning than they are to norms. Norms usually specify, to some degree, the conditions under which specific behaviors are expected. Although the meanings of these terms overlap, values and goals might be regarded as more general and abstract and may be used to deduce the correct norms (behavioral manifestation) for given situations.

Empathy. Empathy is also frequently referred to in the literature on prosocial behavior and altruism as an important motive for helping. Studies have found that subjects witnessing another person in pain or failing on a task respond affectively, as measured physiologically or by verbal reports (Berger, 1962; Craig and Weinstein, 1965; Lazarus and others, 1962; Murphy, 1937; Stotland, 1969). Adults are clearly affectively responsive to the emotional states of others, but there is little evidence as yet that empathic reactions really motivate prosocial acts. Moreover, the existing studies measure the capacity to respond affectively, not the predisposition. The instructions that elicit affective arousal in the observers ask subjects to pay close attention to the victim (Berkowitz, 1970b; Stotland, 1969). In daily life, the opportunity to avoid the others' state is often available. Lazarus (1968) found that providing subjects with different sets (different interpretations of events in a movie) altered both their verbal reports of disturbance and their physiological reactions to the disturbing stimuli presented in the movie. Thus, the tendency (in contrast to the capacity) to empathize and actual emotional reactions to others' feelings may be a function of cognitive-evaluative sets individuals possess, including their beliefs and values. In other words, values and empathic reactivity may not be independent.

Murphy (1937) found in an extensive study of nursery school children that those children who became visibly upset in response to another's distress and acted to relieve the other's distress experienced emotional upset of shorter duration than those children who did not act on the other's behalf. It is possible that children who learn to cope with others' distress quickly may increasingly shorten their empathic emotional response. The reduction of their own negative state may reinforce their helpful behavior. Perhaps empathy is an important motivator of children learning to help others as a means of reducing their own negative affect. One might speculate that individuals who do not learn actively to alleviate others' distress may eventually learn to reinterpret empathy-evoking situations, thereby reducing their negative empathic experience without acting on the other's behalf. To the extent that empathy is generated and maintained purely by situational cues, it might often be easier to deal with empathic reactions by escaping from stimuli that cause unpleasant empathic reactions (Staub and Baer, 1974) rather than by helping. When a person comes to represent external stimulus cues internally, so they continue to have an impact even after the stimulus disappears, the likelihood of taking action in response to empathic reactions might increase. In such persons, a relationship between prosocial values and an empathic tendency is particularly likely to exist.

Personality and Helping Behavior. Staub (1974) found a variety of personality characteristics, most of them appearing to reflect personal values or goals, related both to helping a person in response to sounds of distress from an adjoining room and to various forms of helping behavior in the course of subsequent interaction. Some forms of helping were related to scores on a variety of personality measures, including Kohlberg's (1964) measure of moral stages, Christie's (Christie and Geis, 1968) test of Machiavellian orientation, S. Schwartz' (1970a) test of ascription of responsibility for others' welfare to the self, and the degree of importance assigned to a variety of Rokeach's (1973) values. The relationship between personality characteristics and helping differed as a function of the nature of the situation; that is, personality-situation interactions were found. To some extent, these differences in relationships indicated that values activated by the situation conflicted with each other, as suggested before, and that certain values decreased helping because they activated a goal incompatible with helping. For example, when subjects were told to work uninterruptedly on their task because it was a timed task, those who ranked ambition high were not less helpful in other treatment groups where the conditions activating ambition were presumably less pronounced. It was also found that many of the value-related personality tests loaded high on one factor and that scores derived on the basis of that factor were highly correlated with most measures of help, which further suggests "beyond the specific aspects of personality measured by each test there is a more general prosocial orientation that is characteristic of individuals, which may predict helping behavior of different kinds" (Staub, 1974, p. 333). If such a general prosocial orientation exists, its components are likely to include personal values related to helping and a sense of personal responsibility for others' welfare, as well as the other general characteristics previously discussed.

It is worth considering the consequences of somewhat different value orientations. Durkheim (1961) differentiated between individuals who are "good" (concerned with others' welfare) and those who are "responsible" (concerned with the maintenance of societal rules). Hoffman (1970) made a similar distinction, referring to some seventh-grade boys in his study as "humanistic-flexible" and to others as "conventional-rigid," the latter being concerned with rules of propriety and with controlling undesirable impulses. Rokeach (1973) found activists, who may be considered willing to correct a perceived wrong, to differ from nonactivists: The former ranked equality and helpfulness as important; the latter ranked responsibility and a comfortable life as important. There is also speculation about and suggestive evidence for a prescriptive-proscriptive dimension in moral values (McKinney, 1971). The primary distinction might be between an orientation to what one personally considers right and to what relates to others' welfare, in contrast to an avoidance of doing what is socially considered wrong and/or toward doing what is prescribed by social norms and conventions. Staub's (1974) subjects' ranking of the value "clean" was associated with significantly less helpful behavior on several measures of help. Possibly, contemporary college undergraduates who think of cleanliness as an important value are rather conventional, more responsible than good, in Durkheim's terms. This is also suggested by the significant correlates of ranking of clean, such as religiosity. A good and responsible value orientation is in some regards prosocial but would have different behavioral consequences under many conditions.

Situation Characteristics

Frederickson (1972, p. 115) suggested that with a "systematic way of conceptualizing the domain of situations and situational variables we could make rapid progress in studying the role of situations in determining behavior." We will describe a number of stimulus dimensions suggested by the findings of research on people helping others in physical distress or danger that seem important in determining helping behavior. Most of these dimensions seem also relevant to other areas of helping behavior. Specifying the location of a particular situation along such dimensions may be a way of specifying the degree of force with which the situation elicits or inhibits helping behavior and the likelihood of influence by various kinds of personality characteristics.

Ambiguity of Perception of Help Need. Both clarity in contrast to ambiguity of need and variations in the definition of the situation by other people as one in which help is or is not needed have been found to affect prosocial behavior (Bickman, 1972; Clark and Word, 1972; Staub, 1974; Yakimovich and Saltz, 1971).

Subdividing this dimension into action components yields circumstances that require responsive versus self-initiated helping. In the former case, stimuli indicate clearly both the need and the kind of action required; and a person may even be specifically asked to perform an act. At other times, under conditions of uncertainty or ambiguity, decisions need to be made and initiative is therefore required to help. To the extent that helping behavior will be a function of variation in personality in the latter situation, an interesting question involves the extent to which general prosocial characteristics versus specific ones might be important.

Focused Versus Diffused Responsibility. Research has shown that when a person is alone, he or she is more likely to help than when other people are present; that when someone is with a blind person, he or she is more likely to take action than when with a sighted person; and so on (Latané and Darley, 1970; Ross, 1971).

Costs of Helping. There is a variety of costs of helping or not helping, including material costs (such as physical injury), loss of time and other resources, and social costs (such as the degree to which one might suffer disapproval for not helping or for helping). Having to forgo the satisfaction of conflicting goals and motives aroused by the circumstances should also be included among costs.

Activation of Social Norms or Personal Goals. To some extent, all the previous dimensions are relevant here: ambiguity, focusing of responsibility, and costs. In addition, the severity of a person's need, the immediacy of the impact of the distress cues (for example, how near or far they are), and their duration might also be relevant (Staub and Baer, 1974). In addition, the degree to which conditions focus attention on the self, particularly creating self-concern or concern about others' reactions to one's behavior (Berkowitz, 1970b; Isen, 1970; Staub, 1974) or simply lead to preoccupation with a task and thus decrease attention to the external world (Darley and Batson, 1973) is likely to decrease the activation of relevant norms, values, and goals.

Preexisting Relationship. Finally, scattered in the research literature are indications, particularly in research not related to physical distress, that the existence of a relationship to a person in need, even as minimal as the belief that a stranger is similar to oneself, or expecting to spend some time in the future with a stranger enhances the likelihood of empathic reactions and of prosocial behavior (Hornstein, 1972; Stotland, 1969).

A retrospective analysis of a helping situation might be useful to demonstrate our conception of the match between the situation and individual characteristics that is required for help to occur. London (1970) concluded on the basis of extensive interviews with "rescuers" (people involved in an underground system of saving Jews and others persecuted in Nazi Germany) that they had three characteristics in common. These were a strong conscious identification with moral parents, adventurousness, and a sense of marginality in relation to the community. Presumably, strong moral identification leads to personal values promoting helping behavior and thus to the motivation to help. The costs of helping in this situation were potentially extremely high, loss of life being probable and loss of liberty being certain if they were discovered. The sense of adventurousness, that is, gaining satisfaction from dangerous activities and perceiving them as exciting, which apparently led these individuals to participate in other dangerous activities in the course of their lives, seems important. This characteristic might not only have enhanced their action tendency in carrying out their prosocial goals but might be thought of as an additional goal that could be satisfied by helping. Finally, marginality might have helped rescuers in not accepting the definition by their environment of the persecution of Jews and others, a definition that most likely would have minimized the perception of need or at least the justification for involvement. Even when a person possesses the characteristics that seem to be needed for help, when helping is so potentially costly, circumstances might be required that allow gradual rather than precipitous involvement. Most of the rescuers got involved in order to help a specific person they knew. Once involved, they continued their rescue activities. Similarly, circumstances that could lead to gradually increasing involvement characterized the people who fought for the abolition of slavery in the first part of the nineteenth century (Tompkins, 1965).

Socialization and Prosocial Behavior

The remainder of this chapter examines different socializing practices or parental behaviors and explores how they might contribute to the development of a tendency to behave prosocially. We are primarily concerned with the antecedents of general, not specific, prosocial characteristics. The parental behaviors considered might affect the relationship between the parent and child as well as constitute both direct and indirect instruction of the child in prosocial values, behavior, and other components of a prosocial orientation.

Parental Nurturance. Nurturance or parental warmth emerges repeatedly in both laboratory and naturalistic studies as an essential contributor to children's prosocial behavior (Staub, 1975c). Parental nurturance may contribute to prosocial behavior in several ways. It may create in the child a positive orientation toward others. First, the child's interactions with his or her parents have been positive, so the child comes to anticipate positive and rewarding interactions with others. Second, the child has learned from his or her parents some skills for positive interaction with others. Further, nurturance might increase the desire to be like the parent and thus enhance imitation and identification. In the case of parents who themselves are prosocial, this would further increase prosocial behavior.

Another consequence of parental warmth might be a positive orientation toward oneself. Self-concern, negative affect, or preoccupation with the self, which might result from negative experiences in interaction with parents, might be important inhibitors of prosocial behavior. They are likely to decrease attention to others and activation of prosocial values and goals and to increase concern about negative evaluation by others, thus decreasing the willingness to initiate action.

The influence of nurturance by itself on helping behavior has not been widely studied experimentally; most of the research has concentrated on the capacity of nurturance to enhance modeling. There is, however, evidence that a nurturant interaction with an adult enhances the likelihood of helping attempts by kindergarten children in response to another child's sounds of distress (Staub, 1971a). The evidence that prior nurturance by a model enhances imitation of the model's donation of previously acquired rewards for needy children is somewhat inconsistent (Staub, 1975c). It appears that prior nurturance does not enhance such modeling, presumably because the nurturance suggests greater tolerance by the model for children keeping their rewards for themselves. However, extensive interaction by nursery school children with nurturant and nonnurturant adult models over a period of weeks resulted in significantly greater subsequent imitation of the model's helpfulness of children who interacted with nurturant models (Yarrow, Scott, and Waxler, 1973).

Yarrow and Scott (1972, p. 263) found the types of behavior imitated by young children exposed to a nurturant in contrast to a nonnurturant adult differed: "Under low nurturance, 18 children imitated exclusively nonnurturant themes, and only 6 imitated exclusively nurturant themes. Under high nurturance, 18 imitated exclusively nurturant themes, 6 imitated exclusively nonnurturant themes, and 11 had mixed themes ($X^2 = 7.0$, df = 2, $p < .02$)." Clearly, the content of the modeled behavior interacted with model nurturance. The modeling took place in five sessions over a span of two and one-half weeks. Behavior was either modeled in a task setting where there was low competition for the children's attention or, in the case of "embedded" modeling, no special attention was called to the modeled behavior. In the task context, 85 percent of the children imitated. In the embedded situation, 71 percent of the children imitated the model. Model nurturance had no impact on the immediate matching behavior by the children, but there was "significantly more delayed imitation with high nurturant than with low nurturant models" (p. 265).

Thus, from experimental studies, there is some evidence that nurturance alone enhances subsequent helping behavior and that it enhances the modeling of helpful or prosocial behavior. Further evidence comes from research relating child-rearing practices or information about parent characteristics to prosocial behavior. Parent's reports, children's reports, and retrospective reports by adults of parent characteristics or behavior were the sources of data about parents.

In one study, Hoffman and Saltzstein (1967) found a positive correlation between reports of maternal affection and peer ratings of seventh-grade boys' consideration for others. In another study, Hoffman

(1975a) found a similar relationship for fifth-grade boys. In neither study was there a relationship between father's affection and peer's perception of the children's prosocial behavior or any relationship between maternal affection and peer ratings of girls' prosocial behavior. Rutherford and Mussen (1968) found that preschool boys who perceived their fathers as more nurturant shared more candy with their peers than those who viewed their fathers as less nurturant.

A number of studies have explored the background of participants in social action. Cowdry, Kenniston, and Cabin (1970) found that Yale students who acted in accordance with their previously stated beliefs, whether for or against the Vietnam War, reported significantly more affection in parental relationships than those whose actions were not consistent with their beliefs. Antiwar students who acted in accord with their beliefs by signing an antiwar petition differed from antiwar nonsigners on several variables. Antiwar nonsigners reported relatively less happiness in their parent's marriage, fewer shared interests and values between their parents, lower respect for parents, less acceptance by their fathers, and a low emotional bond to their fathers. It seems there was less warmth in these families and specifically less warmth extended by fathers to sons and vice versa. The prowar nonsigners who acted consistently with their prowar beliefs by not signing the petition reported family dynamics similar to those of antiwar signers. Both prowar nonsigners and antiwar signers saw themselves as more similar to their fathers whom they saw as optimistic, generally involved, and outgoing.

Perhaps parental warmth or nurturance increases the likelihood of attitudinal and behavioral consistency. As Cowdry, Kenniston, and Cabin (1970, p. 548) hypothesize, "the disposition to act publicly in support of private attitudes is a separate variable, which may be independent of the content and intensity of attitudes." Nurturance or, more generally, a family atmosphere conducive to the child's experience of security and satisfaction may provide the sense of personal security that lessens self-concern and so enhances the ability to take action in support of one's beliefs.

Complications arise, however, in that nurturance or the lack of it might often be associated with other conditions; so whatever consequences ensue might be the result of a number of correlated variables. Rosenhan (1970) provides a good example of this in an interview study of civil rights workers. Those individuals who were more committed, as evidenced by participation in civil rights activities for periods lasting at least one year, reported warmer, closer, and more loving relationships with their parents than less committed individuals, who participated in only one or two marches. In addition, the more committed individuals reported their parents had worked for important causes. The less-committed individuals reported their parents ascribed to altruistic values but had not acted upon them. Rosenhan described them as having a crisis of hypocrisy arising out of the inconsistency of parental values and behavior. It is unclear from these findings what combination of variations in love and affection from parents and in parental hypocrisy (apart from correlated factors) might have been at work. There is evidence that although hypocrisy by models seems to have no direct effects on subjects' behavior (Bryan, 1975), hypocrisy decreases the model's influence on children. Reinforcement for prosocial behavior by a previously hypocritical model was found to decrease prosocial behavior (Midlarsky, Bryan, and Brickman, 1973).

A set of consistent findings that positive moods contribute to both greater helping (Isen, 1970; Isen and Levin, 1972) and sharing behavior (Isen, Horn, and Rosenhan, 1973; Moore, Underwood, and Rosenhan, 1972) and negative moods decrease both helping and sharing may be relevant to the role of parental nurturance. As previously suggested, parental nurturance may lead to a positive orientation to oneself and to low self-concern; this might manifest itself in a relatively persistent (although, of course, still variable) tendency toward positive moods. Although the implications are interesting, they are speculative; neither the association of greater prosocial behavior with characteristically more positive moods nor the association of parental nurturance with a greater tendency for positive moods has as yet been demonstrated. Less self-concern and more positive moods might enable people to turn their attention to other people's needs. One consequence of this might be, as previously suggested, a greater likelihood of activation of prosocial personal goals. Less concern about others' negative evaluation might also lead to a greater willingness to initiate helpful action.

Modeling and Values. Parental affection and nurturance might affect the development of the child in a variety of ways. One reason for its influence might be that by being nurturant, parents act as prosocial models who teach their children the value of kindness.

Several experimental studies have investigated the influence of others' behavioral examples on children's subsequent helping behavior (Staub, 1971a; Yarrow, Scott, and Waxler, 1973), and many explored the influence of models on children's willingness to donate rewards they earned for needy children (Bryan, 1972, 1975; Bryan and Walbek, 1970a, 1970b; Grusec, 1972; Harris, 1971; Rosenhan and White, 1967). Mostly, the findings can be taken as a strong demonstration that the example of how another person behaves, which was found to influence many types of behavior, also affects prosocial behavior. Most of these experiments, however, only demonstrate that modeling enhances prosocial behavior in the same setting and at the same time; so they provide clear evidence only for the effectiveness of modeling in setting situational rules and in exerting immediate social influence. A few experiments demonstrated long-term or generalized effects (Rushton, 1975; Yarrow, Scott, and Waxler, 1973), suggesting that modeling can have long-lasting educational influence, as generally believed.

As suggested, parental example might be an important means by which children learn parental values. From another perspective, parents who hold prosocial values will probably in some manner impress upon their children the importance of those values. Hoffman (1975a), for example, found a significant positive relationship between altruistic values reported by parents and the perception of their children by peers as prosocial. The degree to which parents successfully impress their values on their children, and its manner, whether by parental example, verbalization to children, reinforcement for prosocial behavior, or focusing responsibility on children, and the degree to which these various forms of parental influences are consistent or discrepant, will probably vary. Modeling, however, is likely to be both a highly important form of transmitting values and an indicator of their appropriate behavioral manifestations.

In this connection, again, research on the effects of hypocrisy is relevant. Unfortunately, much of this research shows only the immediate consequences on children of discrepancies between what an adult model does and what he or she says. Bryan (1975) reports that such discrepancies do not affect the immediately following behavior of children or the evaluation of the model. It might be of extreme importance, however, that they diminish the later capacity of the model to reinforce children's prosocial behavior (Midlarsky, Bryan, and Brickman, 1973). The finding that reinforcement for donating by previously hypocritical models leads to a decrease in children's donating behavior might indicate either that negativism develops toward a hypocritical person or that interaction with a hypocritical person serves to justify children being more selfish. More research about the effects of hypocrisy on the power of adults to socialize children is needed.

McKinney (1971) found an association between prescriptive value orientation by parents (values emphasizing what one "ought to do") and the use of relatively more rewards than punishments. Parents with a proscriptive ("ought not") value orientation use relatively more punishment as perceived by their college student children. Olejnik and McKinney (1973) also found that the emphasis upon prescriptive rather than proscriptive values by parents was associated with greater generosity by four- to five-year-old children (anonymous donations of M & M candies).

As suggested, parental value orientation might be communicated to children in a variety of ways, perhaps by how parents themselves behave as well as by how they discipline or interact with their children. Differences in parental value orientations might result in different value orientations of children (for example, "good" versus "responsible").

Responsibility Assignment and Prosocial Behavior. Focusing responsibility on children to behave prosocially and actually having them engage in prosocial behavior might be an important way for children to develop personality characteristics that will enhance later prosocial behavior (Staub, 1970a, 1975a, 1975c). However, focusing responsibility is likely to have such effects only if it leads to actual engagement in prosocial behavior.

Responsibility assignments might be differentiated according to the degree of structure involved. It is less structured when the opportunity to act prosocially occurs in the context of ongoing events and when an adult communicates to the child that he or she is expected to behave considerately. In contrast, assigning regular duties to children, such as household chores, care of other siblings, or duties that involve the maintenance of the family, or demanding that children regularly engage in specific prosocial behavior that would benefit other people might be regarded as structured responsibility assignment.

Focusing responsibility on children may teach them several things: (1) that others consider such behavior important, that parents, teachers, or other people approve and encourage such behavior, thereby teaching a prosocial norm; (2) that others' welfare is to be valued; and (3) that the child has a personal responsibility to act prosocially. Participation in important, meaningful activities, such as those contributing to the welfare of the family or helping another child learn and develop (tutoring) may give the child both a sense of ability to do important things and a sense of importance, enhancing self-esteem. The conditions surrounding the child's prosocial activity, such as explanation from others of the beneficial consequences of behavior or various forms of reinforcement, also seem important.

In several studies of the modeling of donating behavior, when children either voluntarily donated in the adult's presence (Rosenhan and White, 1967) or were induced by an adult to donate (White, 1972), they subsequently came to donate more than subjects who only observed a model but did not practice the behavior.

In cross-cultural research, Whiting and Whiting (1969) found differences in the extent to which children in six cultures acted altruistically versus egoistically, the former characterized by high incidence of offering help, offering responsible suggestions, and being helpful, the latter characterized by frequent requests for help and support. Although these cultures differed in a number of ways, on the basis of the correlation pattern, the authors concluded the source of these differences was the difference in children's participation in activities important for family maintenance. The more children had to tend animals, care for siblings, and the like, the more altruistic they were. In the "Yankee" town they studied, the children were only responsible for the neatness of their own rooms, a task that does not seem essential to the family's welfare. These children were the least altruistic.

One culture that seems to use responsibility assignment extensively is the Soviet Union (Bronfenbrenner, 1970). For example, elementary school children are assigned a younger schoolmate for whom they are responsible; they walk the younger child to school and are expected to help the child with any problems, particularly schoolwork. Their responsibility for the younger child is part of the curriculum; they receive a grade. Classwork is done in terms of five or so peers, with each member responsible for all others. These seem examples of structured responsibility assignment.

Bronfenbrenner (1970) noted the relatively low occurrence of disruptive or inconsiderate behavior among children and considered it largely due to the importance the Soviets assign to child rearing and the values they propagate. It is considered a major goal of child rearing that the children be prosocial and careful attention is given to methods that foster prosocial behavior. Parental child-rearing practices and parental education in these practices have high priority and are not left to chance; manuals are prepared for parents and teachers alike.

One question of interest, with little actual data, is the effect of children's experience in Russian schools on their prosocial behavior toward individuals in everyday settings. Although Bronfenbrenner (1970) described instances in which teachers encouraged prosocial behavior in interaction among individual children or discouraged negative behavior, the primary aim of Russian education seems to be to instill a sense of responsibility toward the group and the collective society (Tschudnowski, 1974). Even if successful, it would be important to know to what extent this sense of responsibility is also evoked when there is no accountability to an authority such as the teacher.

Other information relevant to learning prosocial behavior by participation in prosocial activity comes from reports, generally anecdotal, about the apparently nationwide movement of using cross-age tutors (Lippitt, 1968; Thelen, 1969). Several writers indicate, on the basis of their informal observations, that the consequences of older children tutoring younger children results in benefits to the tutors that are as great if not greater than benefits to the tutees. Tutors initially considered behavior problems, when given the responsibility of helping younger students with learning problems, often show dramatic increase in self-esteem and substantial positive behavior change.

Acting as a teacher and benefiting someone by teaching him or her might be an important form of learning by participation in prosocial behavior. This activity could give children a sense of importance and thus enhance their self-esteem while it is benefiting others. Staub (1975c) found that fifth- and sixth-grade subjects who teach second and third graders in an experimental setting are subsequently more likely than control subjects to engage in prosocial behavior, either by donating gift certificates for other children or by writing letters to hospitalized children. Interestingly, when the activity the children teach is not obviously prosocial, such as teaching puzzle making or teaching another child to make toys to help an art teacher determine the best activities (Feinberg and Staub, 1975), children's subsequent prosocial behavior is greater than when the activity is clearly prosocial, such as teaching first aid or teaching another child to make toys for hospitalized children.

Further support for the influence of responsibility assignment on helping behavior is that oldest siblings tend to be the most helpful and youngest siblings the least helpful in response to distress sounds by another child (Staub, 1970, 1971b). Oldest siblings tend to be less certain of themselves in social situations and less popular with peers (Hartup, 1970), which, one might expect, would lead to less taking of initiative. Perhaps, then, the greater responsibility placed on them, for example, in caring for younger siblings, accounts for their greater initiative in attempting to help.

A number of research studies have shown that subjects who on a paper and pencil test ascribe responsibility to themselves for others' welfare are more likely to be perceived as helpful individuals (S. Schwartz, 1970a) as well as more likely to respond in a helpful manner in another person's apparent physical distress (Schwartz and Clausen, 1970; Staub, 1974). Although we have no data on the origins of this personality characteristic, we may speculate that focusing responsibility on children and participation in prosocial behavior contribute to its development.

Parental Control. If focusing responsibility on a child or other types of parental influence attempts are to enhance later prosocial behavior, effective means of control or follow-through will be important. Parental control ensures the child pays attention to parental demands and verbalizations and acts according to them. Firm parental enforcement of the behavior expected from children was strongly related to indexes of social responsibility and achievement among nursery school children (Baumrind, 1971).

Several types of parental control have been investigated. Hoffman (1970) classified the basic types as power assertion, love withdrawal, and induction techniques. Power assertion involves the parent's use of physical punishment, deprivation of material objects or privileges, direct applications of force, or threat of any of these. Love withdrawal techniques rely on the parent giving direct but nonphysical expression of anger or disapproval of the child for his or her behavior. For example, the parent ignores the child, refuses to speak or listen to him or her, explicitly states a dislike for the child, or threatens to leave him or her. Induction refers to the parent's explanations or reasons the child should not behave in certain ways or requirement that the child change his or her behavior. The parent may point out the possible harmful consequences to the child and others or the physical requirements of the situation. "Other-oriented induction" (Hoffman, 1970) points out to the child the implications of his or her behavior for another person: explaining the other's intentions, motivations, or needs to the child and showing the child how he or she is responsible for the other's present state.

Although each of these basic methods of parental control may obtain the child's compliance, what the child learns in each case may be different. For example, children whose parents frequently use physical punishment as a means of control are aggressive with peers (Eron, Walder, and Lefkowitz, 1971). Physical punishment may enhance children's negative feelings toward others and affect how they evaluate others and themselves. Also, the parent serves as an aggressive model from whom the child learns the skills of aggression and its value in achieving goals. Infrequent use of physical punishment does not seem to have these effects; it does not seem to interfere with the development of moral values and concern for others' welfare and its effect seems to be a function of the whole pattern of parental practices (Staub, 1975a).

The effectiveness of love withdrawal for internalization of moral values has been questioned. Hoffman (1970) suggested that love withdrawal is a form of aggression that is more controlled than power assertion but less controlled than induction. These techniques use the affectionate relationship between parent and child, but in a way likely to produce anxiety. Too much arousal interferes with the child's awareness of wrongdoing and ability to generalize to other appropriate situations.

Among the three types of parental control, induction appears most logically related to the development of values conducive to considerate behavior toward others, assignment of responsibility to oneself for others' welfare, and empathy, all of which were previously discussed as personality characteristics contributing to prosocial behavior. Induction focuses the child's attention on the internal state, feelings, or degree of well-being of another person and through minimal arousal of anxiety or anger permits the child to develop a cognitive understanding of the consequences of his or her behavior for others. Arousal of the child's approval needs may be sufficiently motivating for him or her to cease behaving negatively and to attend to the information content of the reasoning. Clearly, however, this will not always be so; and most parents are likely to use all three types of controlling techniques at various times but to differ in the relative frequency of their use.

Research supporting the importance of induction, particularly other-oriented induction for prosocial behavior, is limited. Hoffman's (1970) study of seventh-grade boys distinguished them on the basis of whether their primary concern about wrongdoing was the possibility of punishment, deviation from societal rules, or harming another person. The first group of boys (punishment oriented) had parents who emphasized power assertive discipline; the latter two groups had parents with relatively higher scores for induction (and affection) than for power assertion. The second group (conventional-rigid) experienced more frequent love withdrawal as a discipline technique than the third group (humanistic-flexible). Perhaps love withdrawal produced children concerned with avoiding wrongdoing rather than with the welfare of others. Hoffman (1975a) found that children who are perceived as altruistic by their peers have at least one parent (usually the same sex) who communicates altruistic values and one (usually the opposite sex) who uses victim-centered discipline. Victim-centered discipline is a specific form of other-oriented induction that involves pointing out to the child the consequences of his or her harmful behavior on another person and/or requiring the child to compensate for the action.

Positive induction (Staub, 1971b, 1975a) or pointing out to the child the benefits of his or her behavior for another person, appears logically related to the enhancement of behavior that is considerate of others. Positive induction may be a component of a constellation of different forms of parental reasoning with the child. Unfortunately, there is relatively little research evidence about the influence of such verbal communication. Research exploring the influence of verbalized exhortations (for example "giving to charity is a good thing to do"), which may or may not be related to induction, shows they have no effect on how much children donate to needy children immediately after they experience the exhortation (Bryan, 1975). However, exhortations to share lead to positive, and "preaching" selfishness leads to negative evaluation of adult models (Bryan, 1975), which may mean the former would enhance and the latter would decrease the subsequent effectiveness of the adult as a socializer. Rushton (1975) found no effect of exhortations on children's donations on a test that immediately followed modeling but a positive effect in a two-month follow-up test. Perhaps reactance (Brehm, 1966) is aroused in the immediate situation; children may be sensitive to adult pressures and perceive the exhortations as limiting their freedom (Staub, 1975a). After some time has elapsed, the reactance effect may be diminished. The children later recall the exhortations and are willing to donate to charity, now perceiving their donating as self-imposed.

Although experimental studies have generally found variable effects of verbalizations by adults on children's helping and sharing behavior and overall less effect than originally expected (Bryan, 1972, 1975; Grusec, 1972; Staub, 1971b, 1975a, 1975c), there is evidence that under certain conditions positive induction will enhance subsequent prosocial behavior, leading to both delayed and generalized effects. This, however, seems to be true of girls only. A requirement for the effectiveness of positive induction seems to be that the induction be integrated with relevant concurrent experiences of children (with participation in a prosocial activity). In one study, for example (Staub, 1975c) girls who participated in four forty-minute sessions making puzzles for hospitalized children and who had various positive consequences of their activity pointed out to them in each session wrote significantly more letters to hospitalized children about a week later than girls who only made puzzles, participated in a neutral activity, or received induction only. In another experiment, pointing out to children the positive consequences of making toys for hospitalized children in conjunction with participation in such an activity enhanced some types of subsequent prosocial behavior of girls, particularly making toys again for hospitalized children; but it had a slightly negative effect on boys' behavior (Feinberg and Staub, 1975). This sex difference in the effect of verbalization on boys and girls is consistent with previous findings in other behavioral (Staub, 1972a) or in attitudinal (Hovland and Janis, 1959) domains.

At least two explanations of this sex difference seem plausible. First, boys may learn to a greater degree than girls to disregard adult verbalizations, particularly those that aim to instruct them in the social-behavioral domain. Children might come to regard what adults say and what they do as two parallel, relatively unrelated systems, partly because of adult hypocrisy, partly because of frequent lack of enforcement of demands made on children. If boys are more resistant to authority and less obedient, they might often experience unenforced verbal communication of different kinds. Second, boys might be more sensitive than girls to verbal instructions and other influence attempts that might limit their behavioral freedom; so they may more often disregard such influences or act contrary to them.

Role Taking and Empathy. The discussion so far has focused on how certain child-rearing practices might lead to the learning of values, beliefs, and norms and to affective components involved in positive orientation to others and self. Given prosocial values, behavior might be motivated by the satisfaction experienced either upon reaching outcomes made desirable by those values or by engaging in behavior consistent with those values. Being helpful might itself be a personal goal, apart from the welfare of others it might promote.

Little of the discussion has dealt with the identification of antecedents of empathy with others in need or with groups of people who might suffer. Part of the reason for this is that procedures to measure empathy are highly inadequate; as a result, one can use empathy as an explanation of conduct but cannot demonstrate that the empathic experience was really evoked. The difficulty is to show that people are actually experiencing an empathic emotion rather than that they simply know how to describe an empathic emotional reaction and choose to do so. The problem is that the act of measurement during the course of ongoing events would presumably have an interfering effect on the arousal and emotion being measured. Nonetheless, a paradigm for measuring empathy will have to be worked out if progress in this research area is to occur.

The use of induction as a child-rearing technique may enhance role taking (the ability to view events from another person's position and to infer another's motivations). Having the ability to take roles in this way may be a precondition for empathy, at least in those cases where subtle emotions must be discriminated if empathy is to occur. But the ability to take roles does not ensure a tendency to do so. It certainly does not seem necessarily true that one who can recognize others' distress will experience similar, vicarious distress; one might even enjoy another's suffering.

What child-rearing experiences might lead to the development of a tendency to experience other's emotions vicariously? Aronfreed (1968) suggested a classical conditioning paradigm of empathy development. The child is punished by parents who are upset with his or her behavior and so is made to experience discomfort or distress. As a result, the child frequently experiences feelings parallel to those of the parents, and the parents' feelings become conditioned stimuli that evoke parallel feelings in the child. When parents are distressed for other reasons, their discomfort might also distress the child. Considering verbal parental communications, such as criticisms and negative evaluation at the time of punishment, the resulting cognitions become conditioned stimuli and elicit emotions that guide behavior. Thus, parent verbalizations contribute to the child's ability to guide her or himself. If we apply this reasoning to the development of positive empathic reactions, it would seem that when parents experience pleasure with or satisfaction in relation to the child (and probably when they experience good feelings due to unrelated reasons), their behavior toward the child makes him or her also experience positive feelings. In this manner, other people's positive feelings become conditioned stimuli for parallel feelings of satisfaction by the child. As part of such learning, the child may also learn instrumental activities that will minimize others' negative feelings and bring about positive feelings in others. For a child to learn to be helpful, he or she has to learn to react with vicarious emotions to others' experiences, through conditioning, and to learn instrumental competence in affecting others' experience.

This view seems reasonable, but cognitions most likely not only function as conditioned stimuli that elicit emotional reactions but also have the capacity to elicit varied feelings because of their meaning. Moreover, children probably have many conditioning experiences in interaction with people other than their parents: When other people feel good, they frequently behave in a manner that makes interaction with them satisfying; and when they feel bad, interaction with them might often be upsetting or uncomfortable. Thus, there might be many opportunities for others' emotions to acquire the properties of conditioned stimuli.

In a different approach, Hoffman (1975b) presented a developmental view of how empathy unfolds through several stages of development. Primarily through conditioning, a primitive form of empathic distress is present in the child at a very early age, between infancy and age two. A second level appears after this age as the child develops a more stable sense of self and a sense of others as distinct from self. Empathic distress is now to a larger degree than earlier a function of the experience of the other, independent of the impact of events on the child. At the third level, around age eight or nine, the child becomes better able to consider the other person in the overall context of his or her life and to understand what that person's general level of well-being and deviations from it are. At this age, the child can consider not only another's actual emotional reactions but also situational cues that have meaning for the others' potential or actual well-being. Hoffman, like Aronfreed (1968), sees empathic distress as the motivator of altruism.

Although most writers have discussed empathy and values as separate determinants of behavior, such a separation is probably somewhat misguided. Current theories of emotions strongly emphasize the role of cognitions in determining emotional reactions. As some writers (Arnold, 1960; Lazarus, 1966) suggest, perhaps the manner in which an event is assessed determines whether arousal will occur in response to it. The assessment, which is an interpretation, would also determine the quality of emotion that will occur. Thus, prior cognitions that are brought to bear on a situation might determine whether and what kind of emotional reaction will occur. A value orientation that involves concern about human welfare (such as the "good" or "humanistic-flexible" orientations previously discussed) represents a set of interrelated cognitions and might be an important determinant of whether other people's needs evoke empathic emotional reactions. An interesting and important question is whether a history of conditioning experiences is necessary for a strong value orientation of this kind to develop. A first, although in itself not conclusive, approach to answering this question might be a careful analysis of parent-child interactions in the course of parents exercising control, providing nurturance, or reasoning with the child. We might find that many parent-child interactions conform to the requirements of a classical conditioning paradigm. Subsequently, the necessity of this for the development of a strong prosocial value orientation of any kind could be explored. Such a careful analysis is also necessary if we are to determine how much similarity our experimental procedures have to real life (their ecological validity). Thus it would be useful to ascertain the degree to which associative learning experiences contribute to the development of personal values and important to establish the relationship of certain values and beliefs to empathic reactivity. After all, if a person is to react empathically to others, the capacity to do so must be present and one source of this capacity might be specific value orientation.

Child-Rearing Practices. In our discussion, we have considered several child-rearing practices that were postulated, and to some extent shown by evidence, to enhance children's prosocial behavior. It is probable that these practices cluster together into a few basic patterns or constellations, some promoting and others undermining the tendency toward prosocial behavior.

Baumrind (1967) has studied child care practices related to three patterns of preschool behavior. Pattern I children ranked high on mood (more positive adjustment and happy, energetic involvement in activities), self-reliance, and approach to others in unfamiliar situations. Pattern II children ranked low on peer affiliation and mood dimensions and did not rank high on the approach dimension. Pattern III children ranked low on self-reliance, self-control, or tendency to approach others. Parent behaviors selected for study were nurturance, control, maturity demands, and parent-child communication. Although helping behavior was not a focus of this study, one child behavior rated was "helps other children adapt." Pattern I children were rated significantly higher on this item than either pattern II (p<.001) or pattern III children (p<.01). Child-rearing practices associated with pattern I behavior included significantly higher levels of parental nurturance, control, communication, and maturity demands than for the other patterns. These parents also "tended to accompany a directive with a reason." They were more "supportive and communicated more clearly with their children than did parents of children in patterns II and III" (p. 80).

Pattern II children were significantly less content, more insecure, and less affiliative toward peers. They functioned at a higher cognitive level than pattern III children. Their parents were, by comparison with parents of the other two groups, less nurturant and involved with their children. They used power freely but offered little support of affection. "They did *not* attempt to convince the child through the use of reason to obey a directive" (p. 81). Overall, these parents were high on control and maturity demands and low on communication and nurturance.

Pattern III children were lacking in self-control and self-reliance by comparison with children in other groups. Their parents demanded little from them. "Mothers used withdrawal of love and ridicule rather than power or reason as incentives" (p. 82). Although more nurturant than pattern II parents, they were less controlling. Parents of the more withdrawn pattern II children were controlling and not warm; parents of pattern III children were comparatively warm and not controlling.

Parental nurturance, firm but reasonable control, and the use of verbal communication and reasoning with the child, practices our review has suggested are important as antecedents of prosocial behavior, were associated in Baumrind's research with self-reliance by children and an outgong orientation toward others. Some additional practices (not studied by Baumrind) are also probably important for the development of a tendency to behave prosocially. These include parental values that are prescriptive and emphasize concern for others' welfare, parental focusing of responsibility on the child, opportunities for the child to behave prosocially, and parental modeling of prosocial behavior. Whether all these parental practices need to occur together in a single pattern or whether the presence of particular subgroups is sufficient is an interesting question.

We have focused here on the development of general personality characteristics that may contribute to prosocial behavior under varied conditions. These characteristics are primarily motivational in nature; that is, they tend to lead to the desire to behave prosocially or to contribute to others' welfare. Some of the socializing influences discussed seem also to contribute to the development of competence, a sense of control over events, and a relative lack of self-concern. These characteristics, which we called specific, might be important for prosocial behavior under certain conditions and less important under others. Our review did not specifically consider the antecedents of such characteristics.

Socialization that takes place among peers is probably very important but has not been discussed in this chapter. Although we know a great deal about peers' influence on each others' immediate behavior

(Hartup, 1970), we know little about the manner in which peers shape each others' personality characteristics. That such peer socialization does take place is highly likely. It is known, for example, that children greatly vary in popularity among their peers and that a child's popularity or unpopularity can be quite persistent. Popular and unpopular children are likely to have different behaviors directed at them by others, which in turn is likely to shape their behavior differentially. According to the limited evidence, interaction among peers is reciprocal. Children who experience positive behavior behave positively, and those who behave negatively have negative behavior directed at them. Persistent differences in popularity and in related interactive patterns are likely to shape a child's feelings about other people and about herself or himself and to train him or her in certain types of interactive patterns. Whether such developments actually occur is a question that needs further research. Experiences with peers are probably not independent of parental input. Some research suggests children with greater role-taking ability and greater sensitivity and responsiveness to others, characteristics presumably affected by parental socialization, are more popular (Hartup, 1970). This is a domain in which more information would be important.

CHAPTER 14

Altruism and Voluntary Action

Theodore D. Kemper

Although voluntary action embraces more than altruistic behavior (Smith, 1973a) and may even be positively "evil" (Smith, 1973c), its proponents believe it is broadly capable of "coping with human and social problems [and] making our society more humane, just, open, nonviolent, and uncoerced" (Center for a Voluntary Society, 1973). Because the latter goals of voluntary action certainly overlap those of altruism, the success of voluntarism will depend partly on how many members of society can be mobilized for humane causes and purposes. It is of interest, therefore, to assess the sheer number of altruists ordinarily available in society, and doing so is one purpose of this chapter. The data suggest a strikingly narrow range in the baseline percentage of persons who select the altruistic alternative in a variety of situations. Additional evidence shows it is often possible to increase the baseline rate by special manipulations, situational conditions, and prior socializations or in emergencies.

Note: I wish to thank Edgar W. Mills, Jr., Roslyn Bologh, Christine Gaylor, Nicholas Katsoulis, and Jan Matlak for helpful comments on this chapter.

A second purpose of this chapter is to present a typology of altruistic behavior. Just as voluntary action is not a unitary concept in regard to the volunteers' particular goals and interests, altruism is not unidimensional. Some of the different components of altruism are suggested in the previous statement of the Center for a Voluntary Society: "humane, just, open, nonviolent, and uncoerced." This ad hoc list of desiderata has virtually no theoretical justification or grounding. In order to promote a better understanding of the altruistic potential of voluntary action, I derive four types of altruism from a more general social relational scheme, thus permitting a more satisfactory articulation with ongoing research and theory in social science. The practical ends of both altruism and voluntary action may be served by this improved theoretical foundation.

The literature on altruism I reviewed is not exhaustive of the field. I attempted to canvas the evidence, but I certainly have omitted some studies through oversight. I have included many of the more frequently cited research reports, however. I have purposely excluded two categories of studies from the analysis: (1) those dealing with children (reviews are found in Bryan and London, 1970; Hoffman, 1970; Krebs, 1970; and Chapter Thirteen of this book) and (2) those in which altruism was measured as an average or proportion of behavior responses instead of as a percentage of the sample emitting the altruistic response. Interest here is the number of altruists in samples of persons rather than the amount of altruism in behavior samples. This interest ipso facto has excluded from consideration some of the most prominent work on altruism (such as that by Berkowitz and his colleagues). Only in a small part of his work does Berkowitz report percentages of altruists rather than scores on a behavioral measure.

It is of some interest that, in his review of some studies of altruism that do report percentages of altruists, Berkowitz (1972, p. 67) concludes, "the exact proportion of help-giving in these studies does not really matter, of course . . . what is important about the figures . . . is that they are far from zero."

The first question addressed here is "How far from zero?" From the point of view of voluntary action, at least to the extent that such action is devoted to attaining altruistic goals, the proportion of altruists in the population is a significant factor for both recruitment and goal attainment. To fish in a poorly stocked pond is to go home empty-handed. To attempt to mobilize a mass movement in the population for an altruistic purpose when there is but a scant number of altruists is to fail, yet not merely to fail; the outcome of failed ideals is often cynicism and a possibly more retrograde outlook than before. The calculus of social movements oriented to humane goals must take into account the limits of altruism.

I shall discuss studies of altruism under three major headings. The first is those reporting data that can be interpreted more or less as operant responses. This means there has been no special manipulations, appeals, experimental inductions, sample self-selection, or social role requirements to influence the baseline rate of altruistic responses. Data discussed under this heading are designed to show what proportion of a population responds altruistically in circumstances that minimally tamper or interfere with ordinary response dispositions. The second heading is studies in which some special manipulation or condition can be expected to change the proportion of altruists from the baseline level. The third is studies of emergency situations, in which there is usually a real or experimentally posed victim who requires assistance.

Baseline Level

The attitude-behavior dichotomy used in this section is important because it is well known that attitudes do not adequately predict behavior (Fishbein, 1966; Liska, 1974). Attitudinal data are of interest, however, because they indicate probable maxima with respect to voluntary behavior. Attitudinal percentages of altruism are somewhat like upper bounds of likelihood of performance—all other things being equal. One of the notable outcomes of the analysis here is that proportions of altruists measured either by attitudinal or behavioral indexes are about the same. A conceivable artifact involves possible differences in difficulty of items sampled from the separate domains of attitude and behavior. If the items selected for the attitudinal responses were harder to answer altruistically, this would keep the proportion of attitudinal altruists somewhat low. If the items selected for behavioral response were somewhat easy to respond to altruistically, this would keep the proportion of behavioral altruists somewhat high. The result might be to cause the attitudinal and behavioral proportions to converge. Resolution of this matter must await research that examines both attitudinal and behavioral altruism for the same items.

Behavioral Data. One of the most extensive surveys of altruistic activity in American society was conducted by the U.S. Department of Labor in 1965. Data were obtained on the number of types of persons who "contributed their labor to some form of health, education or welfare services for the general good during 1965" (U.S. Department of Labor, 1969). The results show that about twenty-two million persons over fourteen years of age performed such volunteer services during the year. Taking the whole year as the unit of analysis yields a figure of about 16 percent. Because half this group worked fewer than five times during the year, a smaller percentage was actually engaged in volunteer work during any single week. For example, during the week of November 7, 1965, only seven million people (or about 5 percent) were involved in volunteer activity. Despite this marked drop in the proportion of those contributing effort on a volunteer basis, we have no basis for assuming a week is the natural time unit for tallying altruistic behavior. The yearly figure of 16 percent will continue to engage our interest.

Some indication of the stability of the 16 percent figure of community service involvement is found in the comparison of the 1965 results with those of an earlier Detroit Area Study (1953) sample. Combining charitable and welfare organization membership with youth service group membership in Detroit for 1952 produces a figure of 15 percent involved in formal organizations with identifiable altruistic programs.

With the emergence of college campuses in the 1960s as sources of activity directed toward meliorative social change, data on the proportion of altruists among college students is of special interest. In an extensive longitudinal study of students at Stanford and the University of California (Berkeley) between 1962 and 1965, Katz (1968) found that only 8 percent of students described themselves as engaging "frequently" in service activities off campus. When "occasional" participants in these activities are added, the percentages rise to 21 percent for men and 40 percent for women for the 1965 responses. If we aggregate men and women students, the percentage of frequent occasional participants in service activities is 29.8 percent.

Despite the crescendo of attention to social problems and social solutions that enveloped the campuses in the latter part of the decade, later data show student involvement in altruistic organizational activity does not appear to go beyond the 30 percent Katz found. In one of the more ambitious campus efforts, at Michigan State University in 1969, a concerted program of community assistance managed to enlist the efforts of about a quarter of the students enrolled (Theodore, 1973, p. 319). Overall, the level of social service by college students was lower than this. Peterson (1973, p. 138) reports data collected by the National Student Volunteer Program that show out of 5.676 million students 400,000 were engaged in "service oriented volunteer programs," that is, 7.1 percent, a figure very close to the 8 percent reporting "frequent" involvement in Katz (1968).

We see from these figures that despite local peaks of altruistic service, the overall proportion of student volunteers is only about half that for the population at large. It is of some interest, however, that the low figures for altruism in the college years are somewhat amplified in adulthood. This is evidenced by the fact that a disproportionately large part of the adult volunteer corps are college educated (U.S. Department of Labor, 1969). We must assume some overlap between those who volunteer while in college and those college graduates who volunteer as adults. Given traditional women's roles in the family, it is likely that a substantial portion of the women college graduates who give volunteer service today do so in lieu of holding a job. The trend toward part-time and even full-time employment among educated women should have some bearing on the pool of educated women available for altruistic community service. Other things being equal, the proportion of such women should fall and the number of volunteers therefore decline as employment rates among educated women rise.

Data from a roster of international nongovernmental organizations provide another view of the question of what proportion of the population is altruistically inclined. Skjelsbaek (1973, p. 110) reports results assembled by Speeckaert on the types of organizations, by field of activity, founded between 1693 and 1954. Adopting a broad definition of altruistic activity, in which organizations in two categories are joined— those in "philosophy, ethics, and peace" and those in "relief education, youth, and women's movement"—we find a remarkably stable proportion of the total number of organizations founded to foster these interests: between 1693 and 1914, 15.7 percent of organizations; between 1915 and 1944, 16.6; percent and between 1945 and 1954, 16.1 percent.

Although the proportion of organizations is a different measure than the proportion of individuals, there is a rough correlation between them; and these data, international in scope, provide some basis for thinking that the baseline level of voluntarism with an altruistic intent is more than a national phenomenon.

Bryan and Test (1967) placed a disabled car at a roadside and observed how many motorists out of the first two thousand passing cars stopped to offer assistance to the ostensible driver, a woman. The periods of observation were two Saturday afternoons between about 2 and 6 PM in two different locations along a stretch of road in a residential section of Los Angeles. Thirty-five of the two thousand cars, or 1.75 percent, stopped to offer assistance.

It is clear that a considerable effort was required to stop and provide the required assistance (fixing a flat tire) and that there is relatively little time to observe the situation, make the decision, and pull over safely within a reasonable stopping distance to give aid. In addition, women drivers, who usually do not have experience replacing flat tires and who may not be confident of their strength to do so, ought to be eliminated from consideration. Bryan and Test (1967, p. 403) do not report the proportion of women drivers; but they do say, "virtually all offers of aid were from men." Thus, it would appear that the experimental conditions and some of the measures (the inclusion of women drivers) warrant the conclusion that the observed proportion of altruistic responses in this situation is inordinately low. As it happens, Bryan and Test were interested not in the actual percentage of helping responses but in whether the presence of a helping model would affect the proportion of drivers who stop to give aid.

A second experiment Bryan and Test report dealt with contribution to a Salvation Army kettle during the Christmas season. The kettle was posted outside a large department store in Trenton, New Jersey. It was possible to calculate the proportion of shoppers over a two-day period who donated some (undetermined) amount of money. Because the purpose of the experiment was to test the effect on mainly white shoppers of white and black Salvation Army solicitors, two estimates of donation behavior are available. With the white solicitor, approximately 6 percent of shoppers made donations; with the black solicitor, only about 3 percent donated. These quite low figures probably underestimate the proportion of contributors in the population of shoppers. Some of the 3,703 persons who were tallied as passing the kettle on the two days of the experiment may very well have been repeat passersby or people who had already contributed or who would become contributors subsequently. Donors probably increase as Christmas Day approaches. Although there is no way of ascertaining the cumulative proportion of donors, we can assume the obtained percentages constitute a minimum estimate. It is also of interest that altruism is more severely tested when the Salvation Army solicitor is black instead of white.

Titmuss (1972) considers a relatively difficult task—the giving of blood—and finds in his comparative study of the United States and Great Britain that in England approximately 6 percent of the population within the pertinent age categories are blood donors. The proportion of donors in the United States is 3 percent. In both countries, the figures are low and are certainly related to the "costs" of giving. Even in regard to the donors themselves, there are national differences in altruistic intent. Apparently only 9 percent of U.S. donors are wholly voluntary, that is, they are not simply replacing blood in behalf of a relative or friend; the proportion of voluntary donors in England is about 72 percent. This makes the purely voluntary, baseline U.S. rate just over 0.25 percent; the comparable figure for Great Britain is 4.2 percent. It is clear that there are certain conditions—as in the case of the black and white solicitors in the Salvation Army study—that will affect the proportion of altruists. Although the modifying conditions may be relatively powerful, the percentage of altruists does not seem to go beyond a certain magnitude.

That percentage is brought into focus by a seasoned, if not experimentally reasoned, comment on the nature of political campaign donations. A *New York Times* report (September 24, 1972) on polling that appeared during the 1972 election campaign included the following: "Polls can damage financially the candidate on the short end of the findings. As a Democratic adviser commented, 'People want to invest in a winner. Only about $1 in $5 is altruistic.'" It is important to note that the statement was not about contributors but about dollars. As in the case of the percentages of different types of international organizations previously discussed, I assume a positive correlation between the percentage of altruistic contributors and the percentage of altruistic dollars. There is, of course, no way of knowing how the politician's judgment was arrived at. This is indeed one of the sharp differences between inferences based on a scientific procedure and inferences based on intuitive judgment. The value of the inference in this case is that it conforms to a frequently recurring pattern with regard to the percentage of altruists.

Another case of money donation is reported by Latané and Darley (1970). When solicited by an (apparent) college student in Grand Central Station, 34 percent of passersby gave a dime, even though no explanation of need was proffered. This is a relatively high percent of altruistic responses, certainly higher than any yet noted. Assuming that donating a dime under the conditions specified, where no explanation is given for the request, is indeed altruistic, we must also acknowledge that very little is being asked for and that the appeal is being made directly by the apparent beneficiary. This study is included here in the nonmanipulation category because, even though there is a direct, face-to-face appeal, there is no further experimental induction, as will be the case in the variations to be discussed.

A number of studies conducted in the research laboratory can be evaluated for altruistic responses at the operant level. This means the research subjects select an altruistic behavioral alternative when other choices, more clearly congruent with immediate self-interest, are available. In a typical study (Sermat and Gregorovich, 1966), research subjects are involved in an experimental game such as prisoner's dilemma, in which certain behavioral options are clearly cooperative and (by definition here) altruistic and others are clearly competitive and nonaltruistic. Participants are usually allowed to behave in either an altruistic or nonaltruistic fashion on a number of experimental trials. In the Sermat and Gregorovich study, out of eighty experimental subjects, twenty-four (30 percent) chose to play the game in a cooperative way. In a similar experiment, Deutsch (1958) found that 36 percent of his subjects selected the cooperative alternative in the face of instructions that indicated they should look out for their own interests. These instructions are of special significance because the results obtained suggest some subjects saw the cooperative choice as maximizing self-interest, apart from the effect of the choice on the interests of the other. Thus, in effect, there is probably an overestimate in the 36 percent figure of the proportion of those who would be prone to select the option that maximized the other's interest, especially if it entailed some cost to the self. Because a purely altruistic choice is not an option in the prisoner's dilemma game, I retain the percent cooperative choice—which comes closest to altruism—as an upper-bound estimate.

Kelley and Stahelski (1970b) introduced a somewhat finer distinction in cooperativeness. Players of a joint game played against the experimenter could select from among four options: work for him- or herself, cooperate with the experimenter, cooperate with the other player, and strongly cooperate with the other player. The wording of the last alternative was as follows: "I will actively work to establish strong cooperation with the other player against the experimenter. I will be concerned with my own chips and the other player's chips." Twenty percent of 338 UCLA female undergraduates who participated in the experiment selected this way to play the game. An additional 36 percent selected the weaker cooperation mode. Because the participants were made aware of all four possible ways of playing the game before making their selection, I assume the 20 percent who chose the strong cooperation mode are more altruistic and the 36 percent who chose the weaker form of cooperation refrained from choosing the alternative that would have been more costly to themselves. As for the somewhat jarring note of working "against the experimenter," which on the face of it appears to be far from altruistic, we must appreciate that the limited alternatives of the game permitted only the kind of ingroup altruism of players working for joint gain against a "hostile" environment (Campbell, 1965).

Gyman (1971) reports on an experiment in which research subjects were placed singly in two separate rooms. By pressing a button, each subject could turn on the light in the other person's room. When both subjects pressed their buttons, each subject sat in light. When neither did, both subjects sat in darkness. When only one pressed, only the other subject had light. After a number of trials, both subjects established a steady pattern of button pressing, each providing light to the other. One of the circuits was then disconnected; thus, only one button produced light. In a short while, thirty-one of forty subjects in the room no longer being lighted stopped pressing their button to provide light for the other subject. Only nine out of forty or 22.5 percent of the subjects continued to press the button to give light to the other person, even though they received nothing (no light) in return for it.

This study adds additional weight to the view that reciprocity and altruism are different phenomena (Berkowitz and Freidman, 1967).

Attitudinal Data. There are numerous studies of value orientations, some of which ask for preferred values in very general terms (for example, Morris, 1956), others of which ask for preferred behavior that reflects values in very concrete topical terms (for example, Meux, 1973). The research results reviewed here are not in any sense a representative sample of value studies, but they cover a broad spectrum of populations.

One of the most extensive and broadly comparative studies of values was undertaken by Morris (1956). He collected data from college students in the United States, Canada, China, India, Japan, and Norway. He asked respondents to rank thirteen ways to live according to how they liked each way. He assumed the preference order according to liking also indicated degree of preference for living accordingly. Ways to live included (1) preserve the best humanity has attained; (2) cultivate independence of persons and things; (3) show sympathetic concern for others; (4) experience festivity and solitude in alternation; (5) act and enjoy life through group participation; (6) constantly master changing conditions; (7) integrate action, enjoyment, and contemplation; (8) live with wholesome, carefree enjoyment; (9) wait in quiet receptivity; (10) control the self stoically; (11) meditate on the inner life; (12) chance adventuresome deeds; and (13) obey the cosmic purpose.

The third way is clearly the altruistic alternative. Its full statement says, "This way of life makes central the sympathetic concern for other persons. Affection should be the main thing in life, affection that is free from all traces of the imposition of oneself upon others or of using others for one's own purposes" (Morris, 1956, p. 16). The percentage of first choices for the altruistic way ranged from about 6 percent to 18 percent for men in the five countries. (Morris does not report data on percentage of first choices for women for any country other than the United States. This percentage is relatively small: 4.55 percent. The percentage for U.S. men is 6.06 percent.) In addition, Morris reports the data from Canada are very much like the U.S. data and thus are not reported in detail. Of great interest here are the Chinese data. Unfortunately, these were collected in 1948, when China was still largely under Nationalist control. The Chinese figures are thus unaffected by the Communist takeover and the institution of a collectivist orientation. One of the most important and useful sources of data in the study of altruism would be from societies where the sociopolitical system is specifically directed toward collective interests. Data from such societies are lacking, however.

In contrast with the highly abstract formulation of altruism values Morris provides, many studies deal with specific alternatives.

Meux (1973) posed four questions to University of Utah students, dealing with behavior that might affect the "common good": (1) Would the person reduce his or her use of the automobile in order to minimize air pollution? (2) Would the person delay an expensive vacation in order to reduce economic pressures of inflation? (3) Would the person refrain from taking paper clips where it was known that university expenditures to replace stolen items eliminated two scholarships for needy students? (4) How many children did the respondent prefer? (The last question assumed the more altruistic response would be for somewhat smaller family size in order to reduce the population growth rate.)

Meux reports that only three of one hundred eighty respondents answered in ways that conformed to the "ideal" higher pattern. But it was possible to select twenty-one men and thirty women respondents who were distinctively higher than the remainder of the group. Pooling the sexes produces an altruistic percentage of 30 percent (fifty-one out of one hundred seventy).

Katz (1968) asked Stanford University students to rank a number of personal and career interests. About 15 percent of the men and about 5 percent of the women ranked "participation in activity toward national and international betterment" among their first three interests. The category "helping other people" was ranked among the first three interests by approximately 15 percent of both men and women students. Katz does not indicate the degree of overlap among respondents choosing these two categories, but it is likely they are not totally independent. Aggregating the responses, under the unreasonable assumption of total independence, produces about 30 percent of the men and 20 percent of the women.

Gallimore, Weiss, and Finney (1974) posed a hypothetical question to two samples of Hawaiian and Japanese high school students in Hawaii concerning how they might spend a $1,500 windfall. The results show that 21 percent of the Hawaiians and 18 percent of the Japanese elected to spend money on friends and charities. In addition, 32 percent of the Hawaiians and 17 percent of the Japanese students chose to spend money on their families. If we treat only the friends and charities responses as altruistic, we find a startlingly similar response for the Japanese of this study with the Japanese of Morris's (1956) study of value. In the latter case, 17.7 percent of the Japanese ranked the altruistic (third) way as their first choice. Although it would be interesting to know what proportion of respondents would spend the money exclusively on charities, this figure is not available in the data presented by Gallimore, Weiss, and Finney (1974).

Another perspective on how to allocate money is given by potential recipients in response to a question contained in a New York City

Office for the Aging (1970) study of 1,551 older persons. One survey question reads, "A family should be willing to sacrifice some of the things they want for their children in order to help support their aged parents." Because the research respondents are in most cases "aged parents," they would have had to disagree with the statement in order to make the altruistic response; 22.4 percent disagreed. The respondents are overwhelmingly of low income—only 10 percent had incomes over $4,500 in 1969—so their willingness to forgo certain benefits in favor of their grandchildren is a measure of concern directed toward others.

In another study of values, Fallding (1965, pp. 228–229) defines five types of values, of which one, membership, can be understood as altruistic. Fallding asserts that membership values entail "altruism, service, loyalty, truth, reasonableness, sacrifice, forgiveness . . . [toward] as many things and people in [the] field of experience as possible." Although the definition includes areas not usually associated with altruism, (such as reasonableness), there is obviously strong altruistic intent in membership values. Fallding, who disparages his method somewhat, judged the value commitment of the Australian families from four types of indicators: Allport-Vernon Value Profiles; direct questions on what aims and interests the parents wanted their children to have; spontaneously expressed maxims, proverbs, and *weltanschauung*; and accounts of activities during the "normal" day and on weekends, holidays, and such. Thus, Fallding used three attitudinal and one behavioral indicator. Applying these measures to a small sample of families, he found that seven of thirty-eight or 18.4 percent "followed membership values alone, while twenty-five (of thirty-eight or 65.8 percent) followed membership values in association with other values" (p. 231).

One of the fringe benefits of Fallding's research, which compensates in part for the small sample, is that it provides comparative data from a rarely examined population, namely, Australia. It is, however, a highly industrialized society with high per-capita income and thus may not differ much in regard to the structural sources of values from the United States or Canada. But the availability of comparative data does affect our capacity to generalize about the phenomena in question, even if only to modern, industrialized societies.

Wexler (1972) provides another comparative view. Israel is distinguished by both individualistic and collective communities (kibbutzim); but unfortunately, Wexler did not draw his sample from a kibbutz. In his survey, Wexler asked high school students the following open-ended question: "A young man works in a factory. With difficulty he managed to save a little money. One day his cousin came to him and said: 'I have no job and no money and I really need some (money). You're my cousin. Share your savings with me.' To what extent is the young man obligated to share his savings with his cousin?" According to the content analysis of the essay responses, Wexler found that 27.6 percent indicated an "obligation to give substantial help." The question confounds kinship obligation with altruism of a more general kind; but it does, again, permit an upper-bound estimate.

A somewhat different attitudinal view of altruism is seen in the question Sorokin (1950) asked 465 Harvard and Radcliffe students in 1949. He asked whether the respondent disliked anyone or had an enemy. The responses showed 15.15 percent had no enemy or disliked person. Because the ordinary course of social life can lead to abrasions and collisions in which the consequence is a developed sense of dislike for particular persons, it requires extraordinary good fortune to have avoided such encounters. This suggests the individuals who emerged from them without a residue of negative affect are in general either sufficiently giving to others so as to preclude their more punishing behavior or are themselves not punitive when others have acted in an offensive or reprehensible way. This consideration affords a view of altruism that has not been explored very frequently in the research literature or appeared in any developed way in conceptual discussions of altruism (Wispé, 1972). I shall offer a comprehensive theoretical analysis in which withholding a punitive response is incorporated into the general domain of altruistic behavior.

Nettler (1959, p. 377) deals directly with the issue in his assertion that "those individuals have most 'respect for human personality and human dignity' who, among other things, are most resistant to revenge and who are loath to inflict pain." With this orientation in mind, Nettler collected data from nearly a thousand persons in Houston who were members of welfare agency boards, committees, and professional staffs, teachers, and other educational personnel. Four items measuring preferred sanctions for juvenile offenders were employed to construct a scale score of punitiveness. Because the items formed a Guttman scale, each score bespeaks a particular configuration of responses. The following is an example of the type of item used: "If there are 'problem children' who drop out of school or are suspended from school for long periods of time, what do you believe should be done about them? 1. Establish special schools for them—schools with a heavy vocational bent. 2. Provide a caseworker to help adjust their problems. 3. Force them to attend the regular schools by punishing them for nonobedience. 4. Nothing. 5. Other _____ (specify)." Among the 778 respondents for whom complete data were available, 141 or 18.2 percent obtained scale scores indicating relatively nonpunitive alternatives on the four items. A substantial number in the Nettler sample are persons with special socialization that might affect their responses, so the study might more properly be included in the section covering manipulation. However, I mention it here in conjunction with the Sorokin data because both reflect a kind of altruism rarely dealt with in the literature, namely, the withholding of punitiveness to others.

Several studies enable us to evaluate attitudes of trust toward others. They should be viewed as cognate with the behavioral studies in which behavior options that indicate cooperation or trust are selected. Kelley and Stahelski (1970a) undertook a series of comparative studies at five universities in the United States and at universities in Belgium, France, and the Netherlands in which they asked respondents to evaluate the cooperativeness in bargaining processes of the "typical person." Aggregated over all samples and individual bargaining orientations (that is, whether the person responding chooses to act cooperatively or competitively in bargaining), the number of those who judged the typical person to be cooperative was 107 out of 550 or 19.5 percent.

I assume the more altruistic orientation judges others to be cooperative and, therefore, more dependable and trusting. Deutsch (1960) has shown a relationship between trusting others and trustworthiness. We are prone to believe that those who judge others to be more trusting are more trustworthy themselves, that this suggests interest in the well-being of others and, therefore, altruism.

Another set of questions on trust is found in the New York City Office for the Aging (1970) study. Respondents were asked to agree or disagree with questions about whether one can trust most people and whether one does not know whom he can count on these days. The altruistic response to the first question (agreement) was 32.1 percent; the parallel response to the second question (disagreement) was 26.8 percent.

A considerably higher percentage of affirmative responses in the estimate of the trustworthiness of others is reported in Michigan Survey Research Center national opinion polls of 1960, 1964, and 1968 (Survey Research Center, 1960, 1964, 1968). In response to the statement "Some people say that most people can be trusted. Others say that you can't be too careful in your dealings with people," the percentages who asserted most people can be trusted were 55 percent, 54 percent, and 56 percent for the three different surveys. Yet another question from the 1960 survey that reflects very much higher levels of trust was the 80 percent affirmative response to the statement "Human nature is fundamentally cooperative." This high rate of altruistic orientation stands in virtually antipodal contrast with the estimates obtained in other studies (such as Kelley and others, 1969). Because the respondents were members of a national United States random sample, the result must be regarded as important. But its discrepant magnitude from the trend of such studies creates a reluctance to accept it at face value.

The final attitudinal variable I shall consider involves explanations of one's own behavior or presentation of one's own motives. Such studies must be evaluated in the light of two factors. First, there may be large areas of ignorance and defensiveness about one's own motives and behavior. Second, the motive of behavior that has already taken place or is in progress may suffer from the bias that, rather than the stated motive inspiring the behavior, the behavior may have inspired the stated motive. Because most research into behavioral motivation is cross-sectional and usually undertaken at a late stage in the sequence, it is not possible to clarify this issue. The results of the three studies reviewed here, however, are suggestive.

Gannon (1967) interviewed members of the Harlem Domestic Peace Corps in 1962, 1963, and 1965 as to their reasons for joining the corps. If one aggregates responses over the three years, precisely 20 percent gave reasons coded under the category "helping others." Other categories included interest in Harlem, understanding people, career advancement, and other self-oriented explanations.

In Moberg's (1962) study of the clergy, in which more than seventeen hundred students from seventeen seminaries were surveyed, 26 percent gave as their chief reason for entering the ministry that they "wanted to serve mankind." This was in contrast to such other major response categories as "need of man and society for Chirst" (31 percent) and "a call from God" (35 percent). Moberg points out that these other, ostensibly nonaltruistic reasons for entering the ministry also contain some component of wanting to serve others. It is not surprising, therefore, to find that in a depth interview study of twenty-nine clergymen by G. Burch (1969), 72 percent indicated they entered the ministry because of a desire to help people. Despite obvious socialization and social role influences that might affect the responses of both Gannon's volunteers and Moberg's seminary students, the data are viewed as baseline responses because they presume to report motives and intent prior to entry into the role.

From another occupational sector, science and engineering, in response to the question "What are some of the things you would most like to accomplish during your lifetime?" 17 percent of the sample provided answers in the category "contribute to the betterment of mankind" (Schevitz, 1970). This would clearly be the type of response that would fall under the altruistic rubric.

Most striking about the results of the studies discussed so far is the heavy concentration of the percentage of altruists at around 20 percent. A frequency distribution of all the relevant percentages reported in the studies reviewed is found in the second column of Table 1. The average percentage of altruists in these studies is 21.48 percent. It is evident that a very broad definition of altruistic action (or attitude) has governed the

Table 1. Distributions of Percentages of Altruists in Baseline, Manipulation, and Emergency Studies

Percent	Baseline Studies	Manipulation Studies	Emergency Studies
0–5	5	2	0
6–10	5	2	1
11–15	1	1	0
16–20	12	4	0
21–25	3	2	1
26–30	5	2	2
31–35	4	2	1
36–40	1	2	0
41–45	0	1	2
46–50	0	4	0
51–55	1	4	0
56–60	2	1	0
61–65	0	4	1
66–70	0	0	1
71–75	0	3	3
76–80	0	1	1
81–85	1	0	1
86–90	0	0	1
91–95	0	0	0
96–100	0	0	2
Average	21.48 (N=40)	39.16 (N=35)	57.47 (N=17)

inclusion of studies in this section. Ordinarily, such looseness of definitional scope could be expected to increase (error) variation, thus diffusing the obtained percentages very widely. That this is not the case bids us consider the serious possibility that there exists a relatively fixed baseline percentage of altruists in the general population of noncollective societies (where the studies reviewed here were done). If such a baseline percentage is relatively stable and more than a statistical artifact—a mean can reflect a number of different distributions—then the implications for voluntary action are quite stringent: Movements oriented toward the common good or the welfare of others are severely handicapped in the matter of recruitment. Not everyone is a potential member. Nor, if the relative constancy of the coefficient of altruism found here is to be trusted, is this a matter simply of differential interest in "issues." There is, indeed, a limited consituency for any given issue. The message of these data is that the total of those who can be involved in any issue is limited to about 20 percent. Yet this is not the entire picture. There are special populations, already self-selected or socialized, within which the percentage of altruists rises much higher than 20 percent. And there are special conditions, inductions, or emergencies where the percentage of altruists is shown to rise above the baseline level.

Altruism Subsequent to Manipulation

I define manipulation very broadly as any special conditions of experimental design or preparation of the respondent by prior information, explanation, or other inducement or by virtue of specialized socialization or of social role considerations in which specialized norms are applicable.

Interactional Solicitation or Explanation. Although it is difficult in the case of some of the baseline studies reviewed to determine that no special interactional inductions of altruism were involved, interactional solicitation of altruistic behavior is a manifest aspect of the situation in the studies reviewed here. S. Schwartz (1970a) indicates the importance of direct solicitation: "The probability that most people will experience a sense of moral obligation is increased by drawing their attention to the consequences. . . . The person who presents the request provides a social validation for the particular consequences he mentions, which makes denial of their reality or significance more difficult."

We see this effect in the results obtained by Latané and Darley (1970, pp. 10–11). When a college student merely solicited passersby for a dime, 34 percent gave the dime. When explanation of the need was included in the solicitation, the percentage of those giving a dime increased to 38 percent. When the student said he had spent all his money, 64 percent gave when he said he needed it to make a phone call. When he said his wallet had been stolen, 72 percent gave.

In a similar experiment, Berkowitz and Macaulay (reported in Berkowitz, 1972, p. 66) found that more than 50 percent of women shoppers gave a male university student forty cents for bus fare when the student explained that his wallet had disappeared. These results are compatible with those of Latané and Darley, and both instances show a level of altruism higher than what has generally emerged in the large number of studies reviewed in the no-manipulation condition.

Successful solicitation of altruistic behavior may be accomplished in several modes. Telephone solicitation in the experiment by Freedman and Fraser (1966) obtained a 22 percent assent by housewives to permit a team of researchers from a consumer service agency to come to the home for a couple of hours to list all their household products. The altruistic nature of the assent is indicated by the fact that the results were presumably to appear in a "public service publication." In other experimental conditions, where previous contacts had been made with the experimental subject, rates of agreement to a request to post a large safe driving sign on the front lawn were as high as 76 percent (Freedman and Fraser, 1966).

In another telephone solicitation experiment, Schwartz (1974) asked female students at the University of Wisconsin to volunteer to assist at a Head Start cake sale. When considerable information on the need for volunteers was given, 53 percent of the seventy students volunteered. An additional facilitative factor, which is difficult to assess in this study, is that fifty-eight of the seventy women had been tested about a year earlier on several dimensions that have been prominent in Schwartz' research, namely responsibility, awareness of consequences of helping or not helping, and sense of internal or external control over circumstances. We may assume a year is a sufficiently long period to eradicate the possible instigation of social responsibility by this prior testing, but this is only a surmise and awaits demonstration. In addition, the other twelve subjects had been tested for responsibility, awareness, and internal versus external control only a month prior to the telephone solicitation. No information is given as to the difference in rates of volunteering between the two subgroups.

Models. There is a large literature dealing with the effects of modeling (see Bandura and Walters, 1963), and numerous studies of altruism have examined the impact of models on this behavior. Most studies employing models have been done with children, perhaps because it is easier to create an apparently natural situation in which a model is observed to act in an altruistic fashion. For adults, the modeling must be almost incidentally observable, as it were, to avoid making the experimental status of the situation transparent to the subjects. Bryan and Test (1967) have undertaken a number of "naturalistic" studies involving models. Their study of persons who stopped to help a woman whose car was apparently disabled by a flat tire has been described. In an experimental variation, Bryan and Test stationed another disabled car about one-quarter mile before the test car, one at which a motorist had apparently stopped to give aid. This was the "model." In contrast with the 1.75 percent of passing motorists who stopped to help when there was no model, 3 percent stopped when there was a previously observable model. The helping rates in either case are not very high, but the model's effect is pronounced.

In an ingenious experiment involving the return of apparently lost wallets (Hornstein, 1970), the model was not physically observable; but the model's sentiments were available through a letter ostensibly written to the owner of the wallet. The model had apparently lost the wallet, too; thus, the model's letter was available to the experimental subjects. Several different experimental treatments were imposed on the basic situation and the rate of return ran from as low as 10 percent (when the model's letter was critical of the person who had ostensibly lost the wallet) to a high of 70 percent (when the model's letter was sympathetic). The striking variations in return rate under the different experimental conditions suggest the potency of the various types of models. The 10 percent rate, however, comes close to the original operant level in the studies reviewed in the first section of this chapter. It seems to represent a minimum level of social responsibility in this situation because it apparently overcame the effect of a negative model.

Special Samples or Social Roles. An important condition that tends to elevate altruism rates involves the selection of special samples. S. Schwartz (1970a) found that 59 percent of the sample volunteered as blood marrow donors. Because the donation requires a brief period of hospitalization, the high percentage of volunteers is amazing until it is learned that the sample was obtained at a blood donor center from among people who had just given or were about to give blood. Schwartz realizes the peculiar nature of the sample may have affected the rate of volunteering, but he chooses to dismiss this explanation and views it instead as a result of compliance with the earlier request to come to speak with the solicitor. This is the explanation, known as the "foot in the door technique," offered by Freedman and Fraser (1966) for some of their experimental findings. Specifically, higher rates of compliance were found among those who had already acceded to an earlier request.

It may be true to some extent that the bone marrow volunteers were acceding due to their previous compliance, but the arduousness of what was requested of them seems to militate against so simple an explanation. A later experiment by S. Schwartz (1973) sheds some light on the matter. The dependent variable was again volunteering to be a blood marrow donor. Those solicited to be donors had, as in S. Schwartz (1970a), complied with a previous request. The principal differences between the two studies are in the later study, donors were solicited by mail instead of in person and names were obtained from a list of civil service employees without further indication of their propensity to altruistic behavior, instead of from among blood donors whose involvement in a life-supporting altruistic activity was already known. The results are as one might expect, given the two different samples. Instead of a 59 percent volunteer rate, only 24 percent indicated any interest at all; only 9 percent actually volunteered for the donor pool. The previous request in the second study was not the same as in the first, but if the foot in the door technique is in fact the explanation of the high rate of responding in the original study, then it ought not to prove itself so weak in the later study.

Another way volunteers or other altruists may represent a special population is when their behavior is governed by social role considerations. If a social role entails certain behaviors, we would expect higher proportions of persons occupying the role to perform in the manner specified. "Fireman, save my child!" would sound ridiculous changed to "Accountant, save my child!" Darley and Batson (1973, pp. 104–105) found that 40 percent of a group of forty seminarians, for whom social role considerations involve ministering to others, stopped to offer help to a man who was apparently ill—sitting in a doorway, head slumped down, and groaning. Yet even social role effects could be mitigated by considerations of time pressure. Three different time urgencies were experimentally induced: In the "low hurry" condition, 63 percent stopped; in the "intermediate hurry" condition, 45 percent stopped; and in the "high hurry" condition, only 10 percent stopped. This strong effect of time pressure may also cast some light on the very low percentage of motorists who stopped to help the woman whose car had the flat tire in the study by Bryan and Test (1967). It may be imagined that the driver is virtually always in a hurry. Conditions of urban life place a premium, when one is driving, on getting there as soon as posssible.

In an attitudinal study of Boston priests, Neal (1965, p. 53) found that about 35 percent agreed with social change–oriented values as expressed in such items as "Concerns about caution have little place when the issue is one of social justice." Although there are no comparable data on this item with a lay population, the 35 percent level of agreement with an apparently altruistic item is a little higher than the customary level of agreement with altruistic attitudinal items by general populations. (The pertinent data were reviewed in the first section of this chapter.)

Yet another demonstration of social role effects was obtained in the comparison between civilians and police officers in their likelihood of returning an apparently lost wallet (*New York Times*, September 6, 1974). The data pertaining to the comparison are ambiguous with regard to experimental control, and the results are part of a controversy between the New York City Police Department and Patrolmen's Benevolent Association (a quasiunion). Nevertheless, they are suggestive. The police department study, undertaken to put police officers on notice that the department was concerned with their honesty, found that 30 percent of a sample of police who were seen to find an apparently lost wallet did not return it or kept its content. The subsequent study by the patrolmen's group reported that 84 percent of a civilian sample did not turn in wallets they were observed to have found. Thus, the putative altruism rating of the civilians was 16 percent and the altruism rating of the police was ostensibly 70 percent. With the caveat concerning the polemical nature of at least the study by the patrolmen's group, it is of some interest that the 16 percent figure conforms very closely to the pattern of altruism in general populations when there are no prior manipulations. From social role considerations, as indicated, we would expect a higher rate of return from the police officers.

The distribution of all pertinent percentages derived from studies in which special manipulations, inductions, and socializations were applied to the population sampled is shown in the third column of Table 1. The average is 39.16 percent, almost double the figure for the baseline studies. The dispersion of percentages is much greater than for the baseline studies. The practical lesson to be derived from these findings for altruistically oriented voluntary action is that special subpopulations, appealed to in special circumstances, are most likely to provide recruits than the general population. Limited-scope, high-intensity recruitment strategies directed at specific groups should be more effective than diffuse strategies in any effort to broaden the membership base. Perhaps any smart market researcher or political campaign manager could have told us as much without reviewing research results. It is useful, however, to confirm even the most apparent intuitions.

Helping in Emergencies

When a person is ill or a life is endangered, the need for altruistic response is greatest but so is the possible cost to the helper. In some cases, actual danger to oneself may be the issue (for example, plunging into the surf to save a drowning swimmer or coming to the aid of a victim in an ongoing robbery). In other cases, the cost of helping may be interruption of one's schedule or an assigned task. Due to ethical considerations, there are no controlled experimental studies in which danger level to the helper has been evaluated as a possible barrier to altruistic action. Most studies, have involved low costs.

In a series of studies dealing with the effects of group size on the likelihood of helping in an emergency situation, Latané and Darley (1970) found considerable variation in the proportions of helpers, depending on group size. Most of the time they found a higher proportion of persons who offer aid when they are alone than when they receive the appeal for help in the actual or implied presence of others. In the case of a woman who had apparently fallen from a chair in an adjoining room, 70 percent of subjects in the alone condition and as few as 7 percent in a group condition offered aid (Latané and Rodin, 1969, p. 193). In a situation where a fellow student apparently suffered an epileptic fit, 85 percent of the students who were alone attempted to give aid; only 31 percent and 62 percent of persons in groups of four and six, respectively, offered help. The only anomaly from the point of view of diffusion of responsibility is that 100 percent of the pairs of persons tried to help (Latané and Darley, 1970, p. 97).

In other experiments, Latané and Darley (1970) found that location, which may bear on time urgency of the passersby, as well as familiarity, may influence helping in emergencies. A person with an apparent knee injury was offered help by 41 percent of passersby at an airport; 83 percent offered help in a subway location (Latané and Darley, 1970, p. 118). Even higher rates of helping in the subway are reported by Piliavin, Rodin, and Piliavin (1969). As many as 100 percent of passengers within a defined physical distance from the apparent victim offered aid when the person fell to the floor, and as many as 70 percent did when the victim appeared to be drunk rather than ill.

In similar experiments designed to test help giving in emergencies, Staub and Baer (1974) found that varying percentages of people helped an apparently ill person, depending on whether they could "escape" the victim. In the maximum escape potential condition, 28 percent offered assistance. This figure suggests the baseline level. In the minimum escape condition, as many as 78 percent of passersby offered assistance to the apparently ill person.

Natural disasters—tornadoes or floods, for example—create another type of emergency situation. Studies of helping behavior in disasters show wide variation in the percentages of those who help. Wallace (reported by Midlarsky, 1968) found that 67 percent of a group of victims undertook to aid other victims. In their review of disaster studies, Dynes and Quarantelli cite helping percentages ranging from a low of 10 percent to a high of 88 percent (among persons with high rates of predisaster helping activity) in Chapter Fifteen. It is important to note that natural disasters are widely variable in intensity and scope of community impact. These factors will affect both the type and amount of aid required and available and by whom. These sources of variability make it difficult to compare percentage of helping in disasters (as a category) with results in other types of situations. In general, however, conforming to the expected increase of aid in emergencies, the percentage of helpers is higher than in nondisaster situations.

Milgram's (1965) study involved an emergency created in large part by the potential helper. He asked subjects to assist the experimenter by ostensibly shocking a person for his learning errors; thus, the subjects are inducing the emergency conditions. Altruism in such a case would involve withdrawal from the experiment and no longer shocking the "victim." As part of the experiment, the subject turned a switch to shock the learner when he or she made an error. If errors continued, however, the subject was instructed to elevate the voltage level of the shock. At the seventy-five volt level, the learner (supposedly on the other side of a wall) began to grunt and moan. At the one hundred fifty-volt level, the learner demanded to be let out of the seat; and at one hundred eighty volts, the victim claimed to be able to stand the pain no longer. The full series of shocks reached a terminal point at four hundred fifty volts. Only 16 percent of the experimental subjects terminated their participation by the hundred and fifty-volt level. By one hundred and eighty volts, only another 4 percent had withdrawn. No more refusals occurred until the two hundred eighty-five-volt level. Thus, we have a marked break between those who withdraw relatively early from further hurting another person, even under conditions of experimenter approval and the sanction of "science," and those who would not withdraw until a late phase of apparently painful shock administration, if they withdrew at all.

The fourth column of Table 1 shows the frequency distribution of the relevant percentages from the studies of altruistic behavior in emergency conditions. The average for this type of study is 57.47 percent, nearly three times the average of the baseline percentages and about half again higher than the special manipulation studies. Despite the fact that relatively low-cost emergencies were involved, we can see emergency conditions evoke higher proportions of altruists from the population than either ordinary (baseline) or special manipulation conditions. This is encouraging. But it should be noted that, by definition, there can be no permanent emergencies. This means that altruistically oriented voluntary action organizations that come into existence during emergencies are doomed to decline as normal conditions reassert themselves. If the percentages obtained here are any guide, membership should decline by about two-thirds after the emergency has passed.

Altruism Coefficient

The forgoing review of studies of altruistic behavior or attitudes points to a striking conclusion: There is an operant or baseline level of altruism that appears to hover about 20 percent. Special conditions or emergencies can elevate this percentage; but the baseline level is the "normal" state of matters, and it invites some effort to explain it.

Any relatively stable feature of human action must be evaluated in terms of its possible genetic origin. Campbell (1965, 1972) has offered interesting arguments for the evolutionary significance of altruism. In particular, Campbell stresses the idea that self sacrifice enhances the likelihood of group survival. Death in battle or while protecting others against wild beasts or doing without food so others may eat are altruistic acts that certainly promote group survival at the altruist's expense. The evolutionary-genetic argument, however, soon encounters a logical quandary. If altruism is a genetic quality, the self-sacrificing altruists would fail in many instances to pass along their genes. Thus, the proportion of altruists in the population ought always to be decreasing. Campbell (1972) recognizes the problem in his second consideration of altruism but does not consider the logical outcome of self-sacrifice, namely, the end of altruism in the population. The same logic, working in the reverse direction, would lead to the conclusion that at one time the proportion of altruists was very high. If this is the case, we must wonder at the panorama of human cruelty that has been deeded to us in the historical record. Because the proportion of altruists appears to rise with increases in education or social status (S. Schwartz, 1970a; U.S. Department of Labor, 1969), the genetic hypothesis is questionable on this score as well, for education and social status levels have increased in recent generations. Increased altruism is directly contrary to the logic of the genetic explanation.

If there is a genetic component to altruistic behavior, it appears obvious that situational and socialization modification are also possible. The most telling evidence against the genetic hypothesis is that in situations where there has been prior manipulation or where there is an emergency, the proportion of altruists is higher than the proportion at the baseline or operant level.

Social Organizational Determinants

In lieu of a genetic explanation, I propose the social organization of general populations is such as to dispose a certain proportion to altruism. The very existence of the division of labor entails the idea of exchange and cooperation. In this regard, Durkheim (1933, p. 228) said, "Altruism is not . . . an agreeable ornament to social life, but it will forever be its fundamental basis. How can we really dispense with it? Men cannot live together without acknowledging, and, consequently, making mutual sacrifices, without tying themselves to one another with strong durable bonds." Although exchange in the division of labor does not directly imply altruism, because the exchanger may be disposed to "help" only his or her trading partners (see Berkowitz and Friedman, 1967), it does imply doing something of immediate benefit to another that is not of direct utility for oneself. In the Durkheimian sense, then, we all have practice, because of our participation in the division of labor, in undertaking behavior that benefits others. Thus, many persons are able to respond to others' need because such behavior is in their response repertoires. But this does not yet answer the question of why the baseline rate tends to hover around 20 percent. I shall consider two possibilities.

Socialization is a process by which certain conversions are undertaken, depending on one's theory, from a "pleasure principle" to a "reality principle" (Freud, 1922) or from "premoral" to "self-accepted moral principles" (Kohlberg, 1964). The outcomes of socialization can be considered inefficient in that parents, even with the best intentions, fail to socialize their children to altruism. Brim (1960) has reviewed several bases for socialization failures: inadequate knowledge of how to inculcate certain behavioral and motivational principles, inadequate motivation or simply wrong motives with regard to the socialization of children to altruistic motives and behavior, and simply inability to do so, as in the case of parents who too quickly lose patience with their children's errors or who are so moralistic they cannot help elevating minor trespasses into major sins, thus providing poor models for their children. Only very recently, considering the long history of human interest in altruistic action, has systematic attention been given to the techniques of socializing altruistic motives and behavior. The matter is susceptible to quite subtle nuances, as found in the work of Hoffman and Saltzstein (Hoffman, 1970) who differentiated two types of "moral" behavior among children—one a somewhat legalistic, correct kind and the other a more flexible, spontaneous kind. Hoffman also tries to sort out the differences in parental treatment that lead to differences in the two types of ostensibly altruistic orientation in the children. Parents of children with the more conventional type of moral orientation frequently resort to techniques of love withdrawal; but parents of the children with the more flexible orientations employ a broader range of techniques, from outright power assertion to outright permissiveness. Hoffman's work is only suggestive and obviously a good deal more effort must be given to understanding how to raise the efficiency level of socialization for altruistic action. (See also Chapter Thirteen).

One of the enduring contributions of the social sciences is the understanding that forms of social organization dispose populations to accentuate certain value patterns. Despite a lively controversy over the issue of whether values can also determine forms of social organization (for example, Weber, 1958), there is little debate about the impact of patterns of social organization on values. In this regard—though I am oversimplifying—I suggest two broad patterns of social organization: individualistic and collectivistic. Societies organized according to these two different patterns should reveal different forms of the major social institutions from the economy and polity to the family. In order to ensure the availability of persons who can successfully play roles in the respective systems, socialization in the two systems would entail two different sets of values. Values, here, will be understood as in Parsons (1967) as conceptions of the "good society."

Although the data for the review of baseline studies were collected from widely dispersed populations, all were obtained from societies organized more or less on individualistic principles, engendering, therefore, individualistic value orientations. It would be of great interest, for a proper evaluation of the baseline rate of altruism, to have data from societies with a collectivist orientation. Marxist and other socialist theory strongly suggests the emergence of altruism as a characteristic of societies with socialized productive forces, but I am unaware of data from existing socialist societies that permit a test of the hypothesis.

One of the ironic dangers that besets the latter hypothesis is that the availability of institutionalized structures devoted to altruistic goals may lead to a reduction of individual interest in altruism and thus to a reduction in the proportion of altruists. Put otherwise, altruistic action would become the standardized social role responsibility of a defined set of actors, such as social workers. Although this would elevate the general level of well-being (one assumes), it might depress the baseline rate of altruism because there would be less need and opportunity for it to be manifested. There is, again, no evidence for this outcome; but we can speculate that the development of welfare institutions in American society has removed to a certain extent the need for individual contribution to the welfare of others. This may have caused some diminution in the expression of altruism and, therefore, its availability in the response repertory of Americans. Were this speculative hypothesis to be true, we would also have to surmise—other things equal—that the proportion of altruists in American society once may have been higher than it presently is. But, again, the availability of data showing increasing proportions of altruists with increasing amounts of education casts doubt on the last surmise because education levels have increased concomitant with the increase of the bureaucratized welfare institutions that have displaced the more personal pattern of giving to those in need.

Thus, it may be seen that a number of factors with perhaps opposite effects may be at stake in determining the baseline rate of altruism in any population. At any given time, those factors have a particular configuration; to the extent that they change in given directions, the result may be either increase or decrease in the baseline percentage.

Altruistic Action Typology

The discussion so far has assumed altruism is a well-understood, unitary concept. Wispé (1972), for example, discusses such cognate concepts as sympathy, aid, cooperation, helping, and donating. Although each of these shares the core meaning of action or attitude that embraces the situation of others, each also has a distinctive, nonoverlapping significance. To make matters even more complex, attempts to locate a single explanatory theory for altruistic behavior at the level of personality have not succeeded. This has led Gergen, Gergen, and Meter (1972, p. 117) to admitted "pessimism" with regard to the possibility of such a theory: "Various types of prosocial activities will appeal to or motivate people for different reasons. The complex of payoffs for reporting a fire, rescuing the dying, sending lost letters, giving away candy, returning wallets, contributing to charity, helping people of other ethnic origins, and so on are [sic] all different. The types of persons who will choose to engage in such activities can be expected to differ in each case."

The search for a single underlying motive is probably doomed to failure, but altruistic action can probably be successfully brought within the analytical framework of a single theory and its subtypes specified. Furthermore, pessimism about locating the motives of altruistic action does not close the doors of inquiry, either in regard to motives or in areas where motives are of little interest. Weber (1968, pp. 946–947) treated the question of motives in a somewhat parallel case—the matter of obedience to the command or orders of an authority: "In a concrete case the performance of the command may have been motivated by the ruled's own conviction of its propriety, or by his sense of duty, or by fear, or by 'dull' custom, or by desire to obtain some benefit for himself. Sociologically, these differences are not necessarily relevant."

Mutatis mutandis, we may draw a similar conclusion about explanations of altruistic action. Whether the motive is selfish or compassionate, conformist or individualistic, exchangist or self-sacrificing is not always a question of interest. Indeed, in the studies reviewed earlier, there is very little evidence of what motives guided the altruists' behavior. In virtually all the studies, altruism was either explicitly or implicitly defined in terms of the effects of the attitude or behavior rather than the motives of the action. The typology of altruistic action I propose concentrates on one type of effect, namely, change in the relationship between actors.

I approach altruistic action as a form of relational behavior. This presupposes that actors are in some relationship with each other to begin with or, of necessity, get into such a relationship. Relationship implies one actor directs his or her behavior toward another, as opposed to a task where the other is not directly involved. More systematically, it is conceived that actors are very frequently engaged in a division of labor where there are certain technical activities for which each actor is responsible. The technical activities—driving a truck, designing a space vehicle, collecting trash, or writing chapters for books—are augmented by relational activity. That is, the actors also undertake action toward each other—giving emotional support, firing from a job, raising salary, ignoring at a party, kissing, killing, or whatever. Sometimes the relational and the technical activity overlap, as in the case of child care, psychotherapy, and custodial care in prisons. The distinction between technical and relational activity is deemed primarily of analytical significance because, in concrete instances, the behavior is all of a piece.

A large body of empirical literature (reviewed and discussed by Kemper, 1973) suggests relational activity can be viewed in terms of two major dimensions. The first involves a complex of behaviors that entail force, punishment, coercion, threat, hurt, domination of one actor by another, and the like. It has been convenient to label this relational dimension *power*, following Weber's (1946, p. 180) definition. The second dimension entails behaviors that are rewarding, supportive, gratifying, friendly, nurturing—ultimately, loving (Kemper, 1972). Following a certain tradition of sociological usage, this relational dimension has been labeled the giving of *status.*

The implications of this two-dimensional relational scheme include the following: Actors acquire what they wish to acquire from other actors either by means of power relations—forcing the other to give—or by means of status relations—in which the other gives voluntarily. Any single episode of interaction can be analyzed according to the power-status formulation. Did actor A give X to actor B because B forced him to (power) or because actor A wanted to give (status)? Over the course of many episodes, relationships become stabilized; and, for analytical purposes, it is possible to characterize the structure or customary (probability) pattern of a relationship, as depicted in Figure 1. Each actor has a certain position in the power-status space vis-a-vis the other actor. The space is itself created by orthogonal axes because the power-status dimensions emerge as orthogonal factors in many factor analyses of social interaction. There are four relational links between the actors: the respective power of each over the other and the respective status that each gives to the other.

I propose that altruistic action can be understood in terms of these four relational dimensions. Adopting the stance of actor A in Figure 1, we see that this actor can operate altruistically in each of the relational channels. First, he can act in behalf of the other in the channel of his own power by withholding the use of it when there is an opportunity to use it—as in retribution, revenge, or punishment. It is the withholding of power that Nettler (1959, p. 377) had in mind when he wrote, "Those individuals have most 'respect for human personality and human dig-

Figure 1. The Four Relational Channels for Altruism
Between Two Actors (A and B)

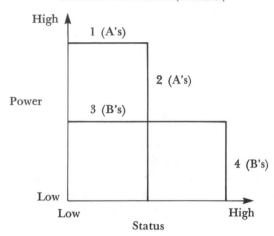

nity' who, among other things, are most resistant to revenge and who are loath to inflict pain." It is precisely this type of altruistic action that is reflected in the withholding of one's own power. It is also the withholding of power that is implied by inclusion of the goals "nonviolent" and "uncoerced" in the statement of the Center for a Voluntary Society (1973). Another altruistic mode within the channel of one's own power is to reduce the materials and resources of one's power. Here we would find such (rare) acts as unilateral disarmament or presidential signature of a "war powers" bill that sharply limits the president's power to involve the nation in a war against its will. Reduction of one's own control or capacity to threaten or give pain to others can be classified as action in behalf of others, as altruistic (regardless of motive).

The second mode of altruism involves actor A acting to augment the power of B, that is, operating in the channel of B's power. Although power is often treated as a zero-sum concept (what A loses, B gains and vice versa) and in certain instances this is a correct formulation, the power of A and B to coerce, threaten, punish, or dominate each other are considered somewhat independent capacities. If we look at international relations, the case of the United States and the Soviet Union provides a clear instance of how each nation has a great deal of power relative to the other but the exercise of that power is held strictly in abeyance. Each nation acts toward the other not only with its own power in mind but also keeping in mind the power of the other. Indeed, international relations are a useful arena for discussing the operation of altruism within the channel of raising the other's power. It is clear that the several rounds of negotiations between the United States and the Soviet Union on the topic of nuclear arms limitations have been premised on the notion that approximate parity between the superpowers in nuclear destructive capacity is the most certain guarantee of continuing nonnuclear confrontation between them. Each of the two nations, therefore, must ultimately agree to the increase of the other's power, should a disparity become evident.

Another example includes the several programs in the area of civil rights and the war on poverty of the late 1960s that were designed to increase the power of deprived minorities. Legal aid to combat economic exploitation in the community, provision for inclusion of minority members on community decision-making boards dealing with the allocation of antipoverty funds, and the Equal Rights Amendment backed by the enforcement power of the federal or state government are cases where the more powerful sector of the community (white and male) has attempted to increase the power of less-powerful sectors of the community (black and female).

It may be argued that A's action in these cases to increase B's power is not very great and is not "truly" altruism but results either from self-interest or from B's power. These are indeed serious objections, but only to the cases and not to the analytical category whereby action in behalf of others is taken by increasing their power relative to one's own. As far as the specific cases go, it can be said that even small increments to the other's power are evidence that such action can be taken. Furthermore, I postulated at the outset that I would not be concerned with the motives of the actor who acts in behalf of others. This is not entirely satisfactory as an answer. Therefore, it will be useful to partition the whole dominant group into those who are responding on the basis of self-interest or to the power of the nondominant group and those who are responding on any other basis. This partition should provide at least an intuitive sense that there are some (20 percent?) who are willing to augment others' power relative to themselves not merely in self-interest or as a response to the power of these others.

Moving out of the power dimension, we come to the third mode of altruistic action, namely, where A reduced his status in behalf of B. Status is understood as what A receives from B as part of B's voluntary contribution and compensation to A in the social division of benefits. Any reduction in what B gives to A is included here. By a broad understanding of status and what is involved in reducing it, we can view progressive taxation as a form of status reduction in behalf of others—again keeping in mind that only some of those who will be taxed at higher rates (altruistically) accept such a tax formula in principle.

Yet another complication with this form of altruistic action involves the fact that resources at actor A's disposal could have been obtained from B either as a result of B's voluntary giving and compliance (that is, as a result of status, as previously defined) or could have been obtained from B by A's use of coercion, force, or threat (that is, power, as previously defined). Thus, when we speak here of a form of altruistic action in which A reduces his status, a strict construction would mean he reduces what he gets from B when B gives voluntarily. A broader construction would include, within A's reduction of status, not only reducing what B gives voluntarily but also what B gives (or gave) involuntarily. This broadening of the formulation allows us to view any charitable behavior as a reduction in one's own status, regardless of how the resources that eventually go into the charitable contribution were actually acquired. If we think of the many American fortunes acquired in the nineteenth and early twentieth centuries that have been subsequently transformed into charitable funds and foundations (Rockefeller, Guggenheim, Ford), we have some examples of status reduction in which we can judge that the original fortunes were acquired in part as status, in part by power.

Another question in relation to status reduction in behalf of others is that such action is often not distinct from elevating the status of others, which is the fourth relational channel for altruistic action to be discussed. As in the matter of power relations, reducing one's own status adds to the stock of resources available to the other and, to that extent, raises the other's status. That is to say, A, by reducing what B gives him, has in effect raised what he gives to B.

This is not, however, the universal case. Thus, A can act to raise B's status without lowering his own. Sometimes, in fact, acting to raise B's status leads to increments in one's own status. The two cases can be illustrated by the following economic options: (1) Shares of income can be redistributed so that, in effect, A receives less and B receives more. (2) A can work for increased productivity so that B will benefit. Incidentally, A will also benefit. We must imagine that at least some As who work for increased productivity do so because they believe this is the best way to provide benefits for B and any gain to themselves is incidental. Although this is concerned with motives, which I have proposed to ignore, I introduce the distinction to underscore the point that the case under discussion is not implausible.

We can see, then, that the fourth relational channel, where A acts to increase B's status, is at least sometimes distinct from the third type of altruistic action, in which A reduces his own status. Of course, in some instances, the two are linked by the zero-sum notion.

If the power-status analytical scheme proposed here has value for understanding altruistic action, then the many studies of altruism reviewed should be classifiable according to the four types of altruistic action proposed. Table 2 classifies the studies according to the scheme.

Table 2. Studies of Altruism Classified According to Relational Channels

	Power	*Status*	
Reduce Own	Deutsch (1958) Fallding (1965) Hornstein (1970) Kelley and others (1969) Kelley and Stahelski (1970a) Milgram (1965) Morris (1956) Nettler (1959) Sermat and Gregorovich (1966) Skjelsback (1973, p. 110) Survey Research Center (1960, 1964, 1968)	Berkowitz (1972) Bryan and Test (1967) Deutsch (1958) Fallding (1965) Gallimore, Weiss, and Finney (1974) Kelley and Stahelski (1970a) Latané and Darley (1970) New York City Office for the Aging (1970) *New York Times* (1972) S. Schwartz (1973) Schwartz (1974) Sermat and Gregorovich (1966) Wexler (1972)	
Enhance Others	Kelley and others (1969) Neal (1965) New York City Office for the Aging (1970) Survey Research Center (1960, 1964, 1968)	Berkowitz (1972) Bryan and Test (1967) Darley and Batson (1973) Detroit Area Study (1953) Deutsch (1958) Fallding (1965) Freedman and Fraser (1966) Gallimore, Weiss, and Finney (1974) Gannon (1967) Gyman (1971) Hornstein (1970) Katz (1968) Kelley and Stahelski (1970a) Latané and Darley (1970) Latané and Rodin (1969) Meux (1973) Midlarsky (1968) Moberg (1962)	Morris (1956) Neal (1965) New York City Office for the Aging (1970) *New York Times* (1972) *New York Times* (1974) Peterson (1973, p. 138) Piliavin, Rodin, and Piliavin (1969) Schevitz (1970) S. Schwartz (1970a) S. Schwartz (1973) S. Schwartz (1974) Sermat and Gregorovich (1966) Skjelsback (1973, p. 110) Staub and Baer (1974) Theodore (1973, p. 319) Titmuss (1972) U.S. Department of Labor (1969) Wexler (1972)

Note: Some studies appear in more than one cell due to an estimate that more than a single relational channel is involved.

In some cases, the assignment of a study to a particular cell is made difficult by the unavailability of evidence that would permit unambiguous assignment. Nonetheless, the results are suggestive with regard to the distribution of research interests according to the different types of altruistic action. We see a large deficit of studies of altruistic action involving power, especially the reduction or withholding of one's own power. In the enhancement of other's power, we see attitudinal studies. For example, the concept of "trust" implies one will put oneself in the power of the other. The studies are overwhelmingly concentrated in the status-giving channel. All emergency aid situations entail elevation of the status of the other. Those who pass by or ignore victims are indeed not providing the victims with support, help, relief, or comfort, the elements of status as here defined.

A final point in regard to the four relational channels of altruistic action is that although different channels may be more pertinent in different situations, we may ponder whether there is any differential difficulty in undertaking altruistic action in the different channels. Is it harder, for example, to raise the other's status than to reduce one's own? Is it more difficult to reduce one's own power than to increase the other's status? No comparison studies have been undertaken and the situations are not always comparable, but Maslow's (1954) hierarchy of needs at least suggests an answer. Maslow ordered five types of needs according to their demand for satisfaction. Only when a lower-order need is satisfied can a higher-order need engage the actor's attention. The needs, from lower to higher, are (1) physiological (hunger, thirst), (2) safety (security, order), (3) belongingness and love (affection, identification), (4) esteem (prestige, success, self-respect), and (5) self-actualization (self-fulfillment).

The first need after the basic physiological needs is for safety and security. This is clearly a need whose fulfillment is related to power, both one's own power to deter others from harming one and the level of power available to the others that can be used to harm oneself. If Maslow's placement of this need so early in the hierarchy is correct, we see it is a more difficult need about which to be altruistic. Giving away a dime is one thing; giving up one's defenses and making oneself vulnerable to another's power is something else again.

To pose the question of differential difficulty in achieving different dimensions of altruistic action is to return to the statement of the Center for a Voluntary Society previously cited. A "humane, just, open, nonviolent, and uncoerced society" entails each of the relational channels. Thus, the goals and programs of voluntary action organization invite analysis as to their interest and commitment to altruistic orientation in each channel. Over and above the plentitude of topical issues, organizations can develop programs along the lines of the relational channels. An awareness of the relational channels of altruistic action can perhaps assist voluntary action organizations to develop more coherent goals. Topical issues will always abound. To fit them into a large theoretical framework of awareness and intention appears to be a way to mobilize organizational efforts more effectively. If, further, it is true that the baseline rate of altruistic action is about 20 percent, more effective organizational adaptation is one way to compensate for the relatively small recruitment base.

CHAPTER 15

Helping Behavior in Large-Scale Disasters

Russell R. Dynes
E. L. Quarantelli

Disasters are a significant and persistent theme in the mass media presentations in every modern society. Newspapers give them banner headlines. Radio presents on-the-spot reports of such events. Television uses them to set the tone for the evening news. Movies use such incidents as a basis for plots to feature well-known stars. The reasons for the media preoccupation are perhaps not as clear as the image they present (but see Kueneman and Wright, 1976; Waxman, 1973). The image usually focuses on the suddenness of human need, followed by the struggle to mobilize assistance. There is a duality to the image—one part focuses on damage, loss, tragedy, and destruction; and the other part focuses on heroism, optimism, healing, recovery, altruism, and rebuilding. Because of this duality, disasters can become a collective projective test, providing an ambiguous form into which society members project their own meanings. Some see only loss; others see opportunity. Some see only the end of aspirations; others see the beginnings of hope and change. Some see the need to help; others see the helping that is needed.

In addition to offering projective possibilities, disaster situations provide the opportunity for examining types of behavior variously labeled helping, altruism, or voluntary action. There is a research tradition on disasters that can be utilized for both empirical observations and ways of conceptualizing such behavior. Most studies of helping behavior in other contexts focus on individuals, looking at ways they exhibit such behavior in a wide variety of situations. Such studies are usually concerned with the incidence and conditions of helping behavior. Differential rates of involvement are often explained by traditional demographic variables, situational factors, and personality or motivational factors. In examining help in disasters, however, we have chosen to view such behavior in social-organizational terms. We assume that because behavior is guided by norms and occurs within the context of certain social relationships (Weller and Quarantelli, 1973), helping behavior in disaster situations is no different than any other behavior.

Preliminary Considerations

It is necessary to provide some initial comments about disasters in order to identify the context surrounding the helping behavior under discussion. Our interest here is on disaster as a social, rather than just a physical, occurrence. Because the term disaster has many different connotations, it needs to be delimited. We will be concerned primarily with those events caused by "natural" agents, occurring relatively suddenly, and creating rather diffuse damage. Excluded from consideration are disasters outside the context of American society or other kinds of mass emergencies, such as civil disturbances. Thus, the prototype disaster for this discussion is an earthquake or tornado that strikes a U.S. community and produces extensive damage, creating a situation wherein helping behavior is both possible and necessary.

Sociologically, a disaster is an event, located in time and space, that produces the conditions whereby the continuity of the structure and processes of social units becomes problematic. Disaster agents may differ as to their cause, frequency, controllability, speed of onset, length of forewarning, duration, scope of impact, and destructive potential (Dynes, 1975). Some of these characteristics have consequences for the types of tasks created and also affect the social unit's ability to respond to the tasks.

Disasters have a time dimension with a sequence that starts with warning, proceeds to threat, impact, damage assessment, rescue, immediate remedy, initial recovery, and, finally, to longer term rehabilitation. Some tasks, and the need for particular types of helping action, are more critical at some periods than at others. We will concentrate here on the middle phases, from impact through initial recovery.

Disaster impact can also be represented in space as a series of concentric circles (Wallace, 1956). At the center is the *total impact zone,* the area of primary destruction to property, life, resources, and organization. Immediately surrounding it is the *fringe impact area,* where partial damage exists. Surrounding this is the *filter zone,* through which resources going to the impact area have to pass. The *exterior circles* consist of the space where community aid is organized, and immediately beyond that is an area characterized by organized regional assistance. This spatial pattern provides clues to the differential behavior of populations that have different kinds and degrees of involvement with impact.

As events in time and space, disasters provide a useful context in which to study helping behavior. However, an initial caution should be provided here. Popular images of disasters usually suggest they create dramatic need for all forms of assistance. This need is seen as stemming from extensive losses and destruction that overwhelm the few who have survived. The source of this kind of image of disasters is in the media failure to relate accurately the extent of losses to existing resources. The impact and resulting losses are characteristically overestimated and the resources still available to the community after impact are usually underestimated. One reason for this trend is the common lack of procedures or mechanisms for inventorying sudden changes in resources. Another reason is the inclination to become preoccupied with immediate problems and to assume they are widespread. There is also a tendency to imagine the worst in the absence of information to the contrary. Resources tend to be underestimated because immediate losses are obvious and the taken for granted nature of customary resources tends to blind people to available substitutes.

As an illustration, initial estimates of casualties might be 200. If 50 people initially receive medical attention, it is assumed there must be more. Of course, even 50 casualties might be "many"; but if the event is in a community of half a million, there are 499,950 noncasualties. Even if there were double the casualties, it would not increase the casualty rate substantially. In another case, 500 damaged homes make considerable debris; but in a community with 10,000 houses still standing plus many other public and private buildings also available, this hardly constitutes "total" destruction.

The usual overestimate of impact and the underestimate of still available resources by survivors is important in this context because it is usually assumed that disaster losses automatically create shortages of personnel that makes extensive helping behavior essential if the organized community is to survive. Natural disasters seldom result in near total losses. A much more frequent problem is that so much personnel is available for disaster tasks it is difficult to utilize it effectively. This suggests that, prior to impact, organized communities utilize their residents very inefficiently in their day-to-day activities. It also implies that communities could, when necessary, mobilize tremendous personnel reserves in relatively short periods of time. This, in turn, suggests there is an extensive reserve of helpfulness among individuals and traditional social-structural arrangements can be modified quickly to channel such behavior toward new activities.

Disaster Research

Disasters are often written about but are less frequently studied. In addition to the immense popular literature based on anecdotes, there is, fortunately, a considerable and ever increasing body of social-scientific work on which to base our examination. The beginnings of the social-scientific interest in disaster can be traced to Prince's (1920) study of the Halifax explosion. During the 1930s and 1940s, there was very little work done; but after World War II, concern for the consequences of nuclear attack provided impetus to disaster studies. In the 1950s, field studies were carried out by groups at Johns Hopkins University, Michigan State University, University of Texas, University of Oklahoma and the National Opinion Research Corporation connected with the University of Chicago. In the late 1950s, a Disaster Research Group was formed in the National Academy of Sciences. Initially a clearinghouse, this group later conducted its own research program and made a number of valuable contributions to our understanding of disaster sequelae (for example, see Fritz and Mathewson, 1957). It ceased to exist in the early 1960s; but in 1963, the Disaster Research Center (DRC) at Ohio State University came into existence. DRC has focused primarily on organizational response to disaster. Because of the continuity of its operations and its extensive field experience, DRC has become a major research center on social aspects of natural and technological disasters in the world. However, there are other field research programs in the United States, notably at the University of Denver (Drabek and Key, 1975; Drabek and Stephenson, 1971). Other centers have developed in Italy, Sweden, France, England, and Japan (Quarantelli, 1977). The research tradition developed in these centers covers a variety of types of disaster events as well as a diverse research focus. Useful summaries of some of this research can be found in Barton (1969), Dynes (1975), Quarantelli (1977), and Quarantelli and Dynes (1977). Furthermore, a comprehensive inventory of disaster field studies is being compiled (Disaster Research Center, forthcoming); it builds on an older one produced by the Disaster Research Group of the National Academy of Sciences (1961). This article is based on this body of research as well as on our own observations in fieldwork in a variety of disasters.

Helping Behavior in Emergencies.

It is difficult to separate helping behavior, even conceptually, from the whole set of responses communities make to disaster impact (Shaskolsky, 1967). In fact, one might view the total community response as an emergent system of helping behavior (Taylor, Zurcher, and Key, 1970). However, we will try to separate helping behavior out here by restricting its meaning to actions that have as their purpose improving the status of disaster victims and that are not performed as part of a normal occupational role in an everyday social-organizational context.

It might be useful at this point to provide a description of a typical emergency behavior pattern so the context of helping behavior can be understood. We are assuming here an event of sudden impact with extensive, diffuse damage in a middle-sized city. Even if warning has been possible, when impact occurs, its actual dimensions and the nature of its damage are unknown. The initial activities are concerned with developing information as to what happened as well as response to the most obvious consequences. In the total impact zone, immediate search and rescue are initiated by those already there who are uninjured or have only minimal injuries. Outside the total impact zone, emergency organizations have received initial notification that something has "happened" and begin to inventory and mobilize their resources. Maintaining access to the impact zone becomes the focus of attention of a number of efforts. Some individuals engage in debris clearance while security forces establish traffic and perimeter control around the impact area. Attention is given to the damage to utilities; and efforts are made to restore these services, particularly those that will be needed for emergency operations. After the immediate consequences of impact are recognized and acted upon, attention shifts to long-term consequences of impact. If considerable damage has occurred to residential housing, there is activity on every level, by victims, neighbors, and agency officials, to provide some type of shelter and food for those displaced. After initial accommodation is made for the immediate needs of the victim population, there is time to direct attention toward the long-range recovery problems.

At every stage, the activity going on is an amalgam of individual responses, responses on the part of small groups, such as families, search and rescue groups, and debris clearance crews as well as action by emergency organizations within the community, such as police departments and hospitals. Together, these responses compose an emergency system. After the initial impact period, individual helping behavior is closely tied to other, more organized community activities; so it is essential to see this behavior in a social-organizational context.

Studies

There are several systematic studies of disasters that provide empirical information concerning helping behavior. These studies involved random samples of the population in the impact zone and the surrounding areas and focused on situations of massive impact where extensive helping activity was necessary. The field research was conducted in connection with a tornado in White County, Arkansas, in 1952 (Marks and others, 1954); a tornado in Lubbock, Texas, in 1970 (Nelson, 1971, 1973); a flood in Wilkes-Barre, Pennsylvania, in 1972 (Disaster Research Center, 1973); and a tornado in Xenia, Ohio, in 1974 (Disaster Research Center, 1974). Other studies of helping behavior have been undertaken, but they have not involved the gathering of similar quantitative data (see, for example, Bates and others, 1963; Form and Nosow, 1958; Taylor, Zurcher, and Key, 1970).

After the tornado in Arkansas, 27 percent of all adults and about half of the men in the impacted area took part in rescue work (Marks and others, 1954). Their rescue effort was directed primarily at acquaintances or strangers rather than kin or close friends. In contrast, only 10 percent of the impacted households participated in formal relief activities. However, 26 percent of the nonimpact households were so engaged.

Because the Arkansas tornado affected a cluster of small towns rather severely, a nearby untouched city became a medical headquarters for the area. Although few in the impacted localities donated labor or other assistance to the medical effort, 13 percent of the nonimpact population did. Within the community where the medical activity was centered, 26 percent of the adults engaged in some form of aid or offered to help. Of this 26 percent, 6 percent used related skills such as nursing; most of the rest were "general" volunteers. Most of the volunteers put in from one to six hours of work, mainly at the time of greatest need.

There is another aspect of helping behavior expressed in terms of providing shelter for victims displaced from their housing because of disaster impact. In Xenia, Ohio (Disaster Research Center, 1974), with massive damage to housing because of a tornado, 34 percent of the population provided shelter for persons the first evening. Of those who provided shelter, 56 percent sheltered relatives, 47 percent sheltered friends, and 12 percent sheltered acquaintances. (Several families sheltered both friends and relatives.) The need for shelter was massive because 47.5 percent of the families had to leave their houses overnight as a result of the tornado. Some who left, however, did not necessarily have damage to their own homes but evacuated because of loss of utilities. Of those who left, almost 75 percent went to relatives' homes and 19 percent went to friends' homes. About 5 percent went to motels, less than 3 percent went to public shelters, and 2 percent went to acquaintances' homes. (Again, members of certain families may have been in more than one location.) These figures indicate the massive amount of help given informally in such situations. It is important to note that most of the shelter was given to relatives and friends rather than to persons not known previous to the disaster. It is also important to note the almost complete lack of dependence on public shelters. In the absence of close friends and relatives, those needing shelter chose motels rather than public shelters.

Helping activity after impact may be channeled through formal organizations as well as undertaken informally. Extensive rainfall as an aftermath of tropical storm Agnes in 1972 created a massive flood that moved down the Wyoming Valley and flooded Wilkes-Barre, Pennsylvania (Mussari, 1974). Although there were few casualties, there was extensive damage to housing and other property. In a random sample of the area a year later, it was found that about 24 percent of the population had been involved in some type of volunteer work for various community organizations—15.5 percent were unpaid volunteers and 7.2 percent were paid volunteers (Disaster Research Center, 1973). The paid volunteers were primarily utilized in federal and state government programs that emerged in the recovery period. The unpaid volunteers were found most frequently in local government offices, such as civil defense; in voluntary groups, such as Red Cross and Salvation Army; and in religious entities, such as individual church organizations and interfaith groups. In 4.5 percent of the households, there were multiple volunteers, and these households supplied almost 20 percent of all volunteers. This suggests there may be "volunteer families."

In examining the Wilkes-Barre data, based on a sample size of 964, certain inferences can be made relating to individual participation in organized voluntary action in this particular situation. In terms of the model developed by Smith and Reddy (1972a), the factors reported here from the Wilkes-Barre study would be primarily categorized as relating to individual social background and social roles. If one compares volunteers with nonvolunteers, the following pattern emerges.

Volunteers tended to come from larger households, primarily families with children. They were likely to be young and male. Most of them had full-time jobs, primarily at high skill levels—professional and managerial. They tended to work for large organizations as opposed to being self-employed or working for small organizations. Whether their volunteering was compensated for in the sense that their salary was not docked for lost time at work could not be determined from the data. It is possible that large organizations might facilitate emergency volunteering. Not reported here is a category for "paid volunteers." In terms of individual characteristics, paid volunteers seem to fall between volunteers and nonvolunteers.

Emergency volunteers seem to be people with high status in the community. Those who identified themselves as being upper-middle and middle class were more likely to be volunteers than those who identified themselves as working class. Higher status was also indicated by volunteers' high levels of education—college and college graduate—and high levels of occupational prestige—professional and managerial.

The volunteers seemed to be well integrated into the community. This was indicated by family status, relatively long residence in the community, involvement in religious activities, and employment status. Social integration was also suggested by the fact that they tended to have sheltered people in their own homes after the flood. (The volunteers' average flood loss, however, tended to be low; so they also had more opportunity as a class of persons to open their homes to others.) One interesting finding was that volunteers had a relatively positive attitude toward the total impact of the flood on their community, suggesting they were proud of their community's response and felt the experience had produced a valuable sense of community closeness. Whether this more positive attitude was a result of their voluntary activity after the flood or whether it indicates a preexisting positive attitude toward the community that led to their involvement cannot be determined here.

Types of emergency helping behavior were compared in a study made in Lubbock, Texas, subsequent to a tornado that struck the city in 1970 (Nelson, 1971, 1973). In a probability sample of adult male residents drawn early in 1971, four types of emergency helping behavior were examined: donation of funds, provision of goods, performance of services (that is, services not related to regular occupational duties), and volunteering to perform disaster services (that is, many people volunteered but were not needed to help). Two-thirds provided goods; less than half provided funds; and a third provided some type of disaster service. Individuals characterized by high rates of predisaster helping activity also showed high rates of helping activity after the disaster. However, for those respondents who lived within the impact area, there was a negative correlation between predisaster helping indexes and formal postdisaster related activity, except furnishing disaster services. This suggests those in the impact area were very involved with immediate informal helping activity and those outside the area became involved later in activity channeled through conventional community organizations.

Social-Organizational Perspective

Studies based on probability samples of individuals or households can provide information concerning rates of helping behavior and make possible the establishing of statistical relationships with other variables. Such studies, however, tend to "summarize" and "average" many types of behavior with different origins and meanings. By focusing on rates of individual behavior, one is tempted to look for psychological explanations for behavior that may be explained more adequately in other ways. At the very least, we think there is value in utilizing a social-organizational perspective to understand helping behavior rather than assuming it can be viewed only within a social-psychological framework. The latter approach, of course, is a traditional one some have found useful (for example, Latané and Wheeler, 1966). However, we believe our perspective provides insights and explanations not possible in the typical way the problem has been approached.

The social-organizational view suggests behavior is best explained as being guided by norms embedded in roles. This is true for behavior in disaster situations as well as behavior in ordinary situations. Disasters do not modify the factors affecting behavior but rather create a series of tasks with which the existing social organization of the community must cope. Some of these tasks are already familiar and differ from everyday tasks only in their urgency and frequency (Forrest, 1974). Every community deals with a few casualties daily but not with as many at one time as a disaster may produce (Tierney and Taylor, 1977). Some tasks are new, having never been encountered previously in quite the same way. Most nondisaster casualties are obvious and do not have to be the object of search and rescue efforts, but the task of finding the casualties of a disaster may be one never faced before in quite the same way.

In coping with these new tasks, a community primary resource is its predisaster social organization. Helping behavior channeled through this organization is likely to be more effective than unsystematic individual efforts. The community has four options open to it in attempting to cope with new problems (Dynes and Quarantelli, 1968):

1. The community can supplement predisaster patterns of organization that would customarily deal with the problems if they had occurred in a predisaster context. For example, hospitals handle routine casualties; so with supplementation, they can handle an unanticipated overload (Stallings, 1970; 1977).
2. The community can redirect predisaster organizations that would customarily have marginal relevance to the disaster-created problems. Some aspects of community structure lose their saliency and utility; they can be utilized as resources in an emergency social system. For example, the school system may provide teachers and buildings as resources (Dynes and Quarantelli, 1976).

3. The community can utilize individuals who might not normally offer emergency help. This helping behavior may occur in conventional relationships as well as in ad hoc roles that expand the personnel resources of organizations attempting to deal with disaster impact. For example, housewives not normally working outside the home might be utilized in social service agencies, or adolescents can be used as the prime labor force in building levies or clearing debris.

4. The community may have to create new roles to cope with tasks lacking predisaster equivalents or critical tasks for which existing social organization cannot be quickly adapted. For example, search and rescue on a large scale may have to be initiated or large numbers of dead bodies may have to be quickly identified and prepared for burial (Blanshan, 1977).

The help given through these four types of community adaptation is, of course, that of individual volunteers. We have devised a typology of volunteers based on field observations of helping behavior in a wide variety of disaster situations: (1) whether their behavior is guided by emergent norms or by norms operative in the predisaster situation and (2) whether the behavior occurs mainly in the context of emergent social relationships or would also occur in predisaster relationships. This classification (Figure 1) yields four different types of volunteering.

Figure 1. Types of Disaster Volunteering

	Established relationships	Emergent relationships
Enduring norms	Organizational volunteers	Volunteers in expanded roles
Emergent norms	Group volunteers	Volunteers in new roles

Note: The emphasis here is on behavior rather than persons. Any one individual may fall into more than one category.

This first type is organizational volunteers. These individuals express their helping behavior through conventional social organization. They are members or participants in an organization that has emergency responsibility in its charter and so has developed plans that call for the addition of personnel to meet disaster needs. These organizations have a latent structure that is activated when emergencies occur. This latent emergency structure has, in its preplanning, already specified the necessary roles and relationships. When such a plan is activated, those who have positions in the emergency organization are notified by a call-up system or may report to assist simply by their recognition of the presence of conditions on which the plan is based.

Such a system of channeling helping behavior is characteristic of most traditional emergency organizations, such as police and fire departments, civil defense offices, Salvation Army units, public works organizations, hospitals, and local Red Cross chapters. For example, a police department may have an auxiliary police unit that is activated under certain conditions. The norms that guide helping behavior already exist within the predisaster organizational structure and, in addition, the volunteer is placed in preplanned social relationships. For example, the volunteer fits into a rank structure within the auxiliary police unit, and the relation of the auxiliary unit to the regular departmental authority structure has already been established. These structures allow for relatively efficient matching of personnel to tasks at hand in an emergency.

The second type, the group volunteer, is a member of some organization that has no specific emergency-related purposes. However, such groups may be concerned broadly with community service and so, when a disaster occurs, see disaster-related activities as a logical extension of their previous orientation. The group member does not volunteer; the organization does. The member's involvement is an extension of group membership. The behavior, then, follows predisaster patterns of social relationship while new norms that focus group activity on new, disaster-related tasks emerge.

Examples in this category include mobilization of a scout troop by the scoutmaster to act as messengers for an emergency operation center, utilization of a church building as a shelter staffed with church members or of a parochial school with the parent-teacher organization as staff, and assumption of the responsibility for feeding disaster workers by a Veterans of Foreign Wars post. In all these instances, considerable personnel can be mobilized quickly and channeled toward tasks created by the emergency. In addition to personnel, such groups and organizations have at their command many other types of resources—buildings, supplies, money, and information.

It is important to emphasize that the behavior of the two types of volunteers described follows lines of already established social relationships. These are not spontaneous, random acts of generosity on the part of isolated individuals but are extensions of predisaster relationships. It is difficult to make a quantitative assessment, but we can assume it is likely that these two types of volunteers contribute at least a substantial portion of the help seen following disasters. The Lubbock and the Wilkes-Barre studies suggest that over a quarter of the nonimpact population may become involved in such types of helping behavior in extensive disaster situations. The Lubbock data and other studies also suggest that many more persons than are actually needed volunteer. The other two types of volunteering have less of an organizational base but still stem from existing patterns of predisaster social organization.

The third type is volunteers in expanded roles. Some volunteers assume roles similar but not identical to some predisaster role or one that involves training not currently in use. For example, a physician in a private practice may go to a local hospital to offer emergency medical care. Perhaps even the psychiatrist may be assigned to some nondemanding surgical task that calls for skills not practiced since internship days. Engineers, security personnel, pharmacists, cooks, truckers, or drivers may similarly assume roles they are capable of enacting but are not involved in until the disaster. From the organization's viewpoint, these are "walk-ons" who may present some problems because they have not had previous organizational connections. Thus, some physicians without prior hospital affiliations may have difficulty fitting into the ongoing social structure because the addition of new roles requires an adaptation on the part of the organization. In the Arkansas tornado study, 6 percent of the population in the community where the medical help center developed had such job-related skills and volunteered them to the emergency medical effort.

It is useful to extend this analysis of formal and occupational roles to more informal roles existing in the community. These would include such roles as relative, friend, and even to the more abstract role of community member. Each of these roles carries with it certain obligations activated by a disaster. The obligations may be as diffuse as a generalized one to help others in need. Those who provide shelter see this as a diffuse obligation to relatives and close friends. The Xenia study shows that those who offered shelter offered it mainly to relatives and to friends and those who sought shelter went mainly to accommodations provided by friends and relatives. Only a very small percentage utilized public shelter, a finding consistently observed in American disasters (Drabek and Boggs, 1969; Erickson and others, 1976).

It is possible to interpret some helping behavior as the extension of a more abstract role of community member with certain "citizenship" obligations. One of the consequences of a disaster is the heightened morale that stems from widespread involvement with disaster tasks. Pride develops in community ability to cope, and this provides the occasion for the reaffirmation of community obligations. There are individuals who lack social ties, either to service organizations or social groups, who lack occupational roles that might be relevant to disaster activity, or who lack relatives and friends in need of help. These individuals may become involved in more impersonal forms of helping, such as giving blood, providing certain types of relief goods or funds, or other forms of input into active organizations to which they do not belong.

In all these instances, the normative obligations are already present, at least in a latent sense, in existing role obligations. These role obligations are extended as the basis for helping action. Much of this action has little organizational consequence because it follows interpersonal ties or it takes the form of impersonal donations of disaster assistance. If the role expansion comes from an occupational role, however, the helping action changes social relationships by adding roles to an existing structure.

The fourth type is volunteers in emergent roles. Volunteers sometime step into new roles created by the exigencies of the disaster situation (Quarantelli, 1970). This type of helping behavior is relatively rare but nonetheless occurs. Perhaps the clearest example is development of search and rescue teams or debris clearance groups. Those who join together may be workmates, neighbors, or friends who are joined by other individuals or groups. In their activity, they institute certain procedures and may develop some role specialization or division of labor and finally a certain esprit de corps that binds them together for some time after the disaster. In one situation, four persons drinking at a bar when an earthquake occurred acquired maps and in a few hours developed a damage assessment team. In this time, they accumulated information essential to subsequent community emergency activity. None of the individuals had predisaster or role responsibilities that would have directed their activity along these lines. To a large extent, they created new roles for themselves as damage assessors, which they carried out for several days. Similarly, Zurcher (1968) has described how a debris clearance crew emerged after a tornado in Topeka. This crew, composed of individuals with little previous experience in construction, operated for several days and developed such social cohesion that they found it difficult to disband when they worked themselves out of a job.

Another distinctive case of the creation of new roles is found in a study by Fritz, Rayner, and Guskin (1958) of a shelter operation involving eight hundred people stranded by a snowstorm at a highway restaurant on the Pennsylvania Turnpike in 1958. In this incident, a number of cars was immobilized during the night along the turnpike. In the morning, many of the travelers made their way to the restaurant. Early that afternoon, they began to organize themselves for their indefinite stay. Those who had been stranded were a cross section of a population—physicians, nurses, ministers, truck drivers, college students, soldiers, and a rock and roll music group. They were of all ages, with forty children under twelve and seven infants. Starting with the preexisting restaurant pattern of operations, they developed a more extensive organization to deal with the special problems of very crowded quarters with limited facilities. A division of labor developed based on skills related to occupation or associated with age and sex. The activities dealt with problems of physical comfort, activity, emotional support, information, privacy, and special consideration for dependent persons. The organization dealt adequately with the problems for the twenty-four to thirty-six hours of the group's confinement. About noon the following day, the road opened and within a few hours almost everyone had gone.

Organizational Consequences of Helping Behavior

In our discussion of types of volunteers, we pointed out how help is channeled through various community organizations. Such inputs have organizational consequences, leading to the four different types of organizational adaptations represented in Figure 2.

Figure 2. Types of Emergency Organizations

	Established relationships	Emergent relationships
Enduring norms	1. Existing organizations	3. Expanded organizations
Emergent norms	2. Extended organizations	4. Emergent groups

The first type is existing organizations. The helping behavior exhibited by some existing organizations is preplanned and the operative work relationships are anticipated. The mobilization of those who will help is systematic because they primarily use people who are already members of the organization. This is exemplified by a police force directing traffic around the impact zones (Kennedy, 1970).

The second type is extended organizations. Some organizations' helping behavior is unplanned and perhaps even unanticipated, but the fact that the group or organization enters the emergency system as a unit minimizes mobilization problems. These groups can direct their activities toward new disaster-related tasks using preexisting organizational patterns as the basis of mobilization. This is illustrated by a construction company using their personnel and equipment to move debris during a rescue operation.

Expanded organizations are the third type. Some voluntary formal associations have a latent emergency function separate from their usual activity. When a disaster occurs, the core group of the association organizes the efforts of other members acting in expanded roles. For example, in one disaster DRC studied (Dynes and Quarantelli, 1968), the ratio of volunteers to full- and part-time professional Red Cross workers was at least ten to one and at times twenty to one. These organizations usually have the most difficulty in disaster operations because they have to depend on unsystematic expansion. With expansion, these organizations change both structure and function because expanded operations create problems of coordination with existing emergency groups. This would characterize most civil defense offices (Anderson, 1969) and relief agencies that operate in emergency periods (Adams, 1970).

The fourth type is emergent groups. Some groups develop from scratch in the disaster situation. They tend to have a loose structure and often are without a name. They emerge in situations where obvious needs develop and are not met by existing organized effort. For example, they come into being in situations such as that created by the snowstorm described earlier where people are isolated from established emergency groups. They also emerge in situations that demand immediate search and rescue, debris clearance, or damage assessment. Such emergent groups fill in the gaps in the emergency social system. Such gaps, however, are rarely noted in studies of disasters and thus emergent disaster-based groups have been studied relatively rarely (Quarantelli, 1970; Stallings, 1977).

Conclusion

We have argued that the primary mechanisms that channel helping behavior into the emergency social system subsequent to disaster impact are social-organizational. Based upon a review of the relevant disaster literature, we identified four forms of adaptations commonly utilized to deal with the tasks created by disaster. The first of these is planned adaptations of predisaster patterns that bring organizational volunteers into emergency organizations. A second adaptation is the supplementation provided by extending organizations into the emergency system, which, in effect, provides group volunteers. The third is the utilization, in new organizational form, of role behavior relevant to the disaster tasks. This provides volunteers by role expansion. The fourth involves the creation and organization of new roles to deal with tasks that are new or overlooked by other forms of organization. These become volunteers by role creation. These inputs of helping behavior are mediated through the various organizational components of the emergency social system—existing, extending, expanding, and emergent organizations. Through these mechanisms, communities are able to utilize their resources to meet the problems that emerge from disaster impact. In all but massive disasters, these resources are sufficient without drawing on helping behavior from outside the community. Although a community's ability to utilize its potential resources in this fashion suggests predisaster community organization is inefficient in normal use of resources, it is comforting to know the immediate helping behavior needed in mass emergencies is usually available in impacted American communities.

CHAPTER 16

The Help Recipient's Perspective

Alan E. Gross
Barbara S. Wallston
Irving M. Piliavin

Affluent Americans apparently subscribe to a norm of social responsibility (Berkowitz and Daniels, 1963) that prescribes they should help those who are dependent on them. Individually, they donate billions of dollars to hundreds of charitable causes, some not even tax deductible. Collectively, their society has instituted and accepted massive formal helping arrangements, such as foreign aid and welfare systems.

Note: This chapter, originally written for this volume, is adapted from a substantially similar version, "Reactance, Attributions, Equity, and the Help Recipient," which appeared in the *Journal of Applied Social Psychology*, 1979, *9*, 297-313. Some of the research reported here was supported by NIMH Grant No. 19762 to Gross and Piliavin. We appreciate the comments of Susan K. Green, Martin Greenberg, Jane Piliavin, and Lawrence Wrightsman on earlier versions of this chapter.

At first glance, U.S. helping systems appear to testify to American people's compassion and their desire to accept responsibility for less-fortunate or less-able people. Although helping structures may reflect some degree of altruistic intent, close scrutiny of U.S. helping systems reveals they are often insensitive to the best psychological interests of the constituency they profess to serve.

For example, most welfare agencies seem to be funded at a level sufficient to "handle" the embarrassing problem of poverty in a rich society at minimal cost. Typically, they function more to distribute the money, goods, and services the society or its agencies believe the disadvantaged are entitled to receive rather than to distribute what the disadvantaged want or need to receive in order to maintain physical and mental well-being. And institutionalized helping arrangements—the manner in which help is delivered—are usually determined by the requisites of those who pay for and supply the service rather than by those of the needy client. It is hardly surprising, then, that in a society that treats the disadvantaged person largely as an administrative and financial problem, little attention has been paid to the psychology of the help recipient—to how he or she feels about seeking and receiving aid.

In the past decade, social psychologists have intensively investigated helping behavior; but most of their research has been concerned with variables that facilitate or inhibit potential helpers' acts (see Berkowitz, 1972; Krebs, 1970; Macaulay and Berkowitz, 1970, for reviews). Little attention has been paid to the recipients. Thus, although we have learned a great deal about the conditions that determine if and when people will help the distressed or unfortunate, we still know very little about psychological conditions that lead people to seek help or the variables that affect how the help recipient reacts to receiving aid.

Researchers have recently begun to collect a body of data related to the psychology of help receiving, and an entire issue of the *Journal of Applied Social Psychology* (Gergen, 1974) was devoted to bringing together a handful of empirical studies that deal with the psychology of receiving help. Although we will review some of these studies in this chapter, our main purpose is to examine the relevance of social-psychological theory in suggesting research that will lead to better understanding of the helping relationship from the recipient's perspective and eventually to the design of efficient, economical and humane helping systems.

How as well as how much aid is delivered may be an important determinant of what attitudes help recipients develop toward help givers and toward themselves. It is clear that the amount of benefit delivered accounts for most of the variation in recipient reactions. It is also apparent that the manner in which aid is delivered often has psychological side effects. Historically, social agencies and other help givers have been almost exclusively concerned with how much aid or service is delivered and have largely ignored questions of how aid is rendered. Recently, however, Greenley and Mechanic (1976) have shown that although psychological distress (the need for help) plays a major role in seeking help for psychological problems, social-psychological factors independently influence help seeking. We shall discuss and document some of the negative effects that may result from receiving aid and explore the relevance of three social-psychological theories in explaining these possible negative effects.

Social-Psychological Theory and Receiving Aid

Simple reinforcement theories emphasize the positive aspects of receiving aid; and because material benefits usually do result from seeking and receiving help, obtaining help is probably a positive experience for most people, at least when the alternatives are failure or starvation. But it is obvious that there are also negative factors associated with seeking and receiving help.

Foreign nations do not routinely express thanks to Uncle Sam for monetary aid and neither do student subjects who role play aid recipients (Gergen and others, 1975; Morse and Gergen, 1971). And, to the dismay of some novice caseworkers, a welfare recipient may display resentment instead of the expected gratitude for advice or service (Bredemeir, 1964, p. 97).

Several writers have indicated that recipients of habitual help develop negative attitudes. For example, Alger and Rusk (1955, p. 277) in a study of the rehabilitation process conclude, "many people in our society find it a humiliating experience to receive help." Goldin and others (1972) also maintain that adverse dependency reactions occur in the institutionalized patient: "There are not infrequent instances in which the patient's efforts to do things for himself are discouraged, blocked, or openly prohibited" (p. 22). In these authors' view, some of the helping behavior in this setting not only impeded physical rehabilitation but was also instrumental in reinforcing dependency rather than the capacity for self-help. Lipman and Sterne (1962), who discuss similar problems among the aged, depict elderly help recipients as struggling to maintain respectable status in an unfriendly society. And in a somewhat parallel discussion of the poor, Haggstrom (1964) documents instances where professional helpers, who are seen as morally and materially superior, elicit feelings of unworthiness and inferiority among their poor clients.

Derivations from at least three social-psychological theories—reactance (Brehm, 1966), attribution (Jones and Davis, 1965; Kelley, 1967), and equity-reciprocity-indebtedness (Adams, 1965; Blau, 1964, Gouldner, 1960; Greenberg, forthcoming; Homans, 1961; Walster, Walster, and Berscheid, 1978) lead to the hypothesis that in some circumstances people who seek and receive help will develop negative attitudes toward themselves, the helper, and the society. Each of these theories offers plausible explanations for negative attitudes associated with routinely receiving help.

Reactance. Brehm (1966) postulates that people are motivated to maximize their own freedom of choice. Applied to the phenomenon of help, the reactance formulation suggests that dependence on a source of help may limit freedom and lead to negative feelings toward would-be helpers as well as resistance toward their efforts to help. Although no laboratory studies that directly relate receipt of help with negative feelings are known to us, Morse and Gergen (1971) found attraction for the aid giver decreased when aid was denied and increased very little when aid was granted. In addition, three studies have been reported that link the receiving of a favor to subsequent behavior. Brehm and Cole (1966) found subjects who receive an unrequested favor are in some circumstances less likely to do a favor for the helper than are subjects who receive no favors. Schopler and Thompson (1968) reported that subjects who receive inappropriate favors are less likely to aid the helper than are subjects who receive appropriate favors; and Morse and others (1977) found that subjects receiving expected help volunteer less time to the helper than subjects receiving unexpected help.

The circumstances of the disabled, nursing home residents, and welfare recipients—individuals whose autonomy and control over their lives are reduced by dependence on professional helpers (doctors, nurses, social workers)—offer real-world parallels to laboratory subjects whose circumstances lead them to experience reactance. These recipients not only lose autonomy and control over their lives by virtue of the program the helper prescribes but also as a condition for receipt of the program. For example, Briar (1966), in summarizing extensive interviews with more than a hundred welfare families, states that aid recipients do indeed give up freedom as part of the helping contract. When these families were asked about the legitimacy of refusing entry to a social worker at night, more than two-thirds of them acknowledged that a search warrant was legally necessary; but only half felt they had the right to refuse entry. Briar's data include other examples of experienced loss of freedom—the majority of the respondents in his study felt obligated to follow social worker suggestions on budget, psychiatric visits, and marriage counseling. Even when freedom is not actually threatened, the act of receiving help can be perceived as part of a contract that implies loss of freedom (Brehm, 1966).

Help recipients may experience reactance because, although they may initially request assistance, they are later placed in a position where continued help is initiated by a professional or an agency. In various forms of classic psychotherapy, for example, the patient initiates the service contact; but once the helping relationship begins, it is usually only the therapist who can pronounce the patient cured and no longer in need of help. It is often the case that continuance of help is unwanted or unneeded, limiting the recipient's freedom and leading to reactance, which may be expressed in several ways, including negative feelings toward the helper, the agency, and the self. Reactance as a consequence of such circumstances has not been experimentally documented, but some nonexperimental studies have disclosed help recipients' negative attitudes that might be attributed to reactance. For example, in a series of interviews with disabled and handicapped persons, Ladieu and others (1947) found that when the help did not expand the freedom of movement of the injured person or further his or her goals, help was resented; and the helper was viewed as incompetent and interfering.

In summary, then, reactance and associated negative feelings toward assistance should be greatest when help is arbitrarily and externally imposed and least when the recipients have maximum choice regarding when, where, and how they are helped. The reactance model, however, does not attend to other relevant considerations in the helping situation. These other considerations, which deal with help recipients' perceptions of the basis on which help is rendered and the implications of these perceptions, are more relevant to attribution theory.

Attribution Theory. According to attribution theory (Jones and Davis, 1965; Kelley, 1967), help recipients will be more or less likely to interpret seeking and receiving aid as negative information about their abilities and capacities, depending on the motives attributed to the help giver and the manner in which help is offered.

The knowledge that a person has applied or asked for help may have significance in itself. And once a basic helping relationship is initiated, a help recipient may attach further meaning to the helper's actions especially to the extent the helper is seen as acting independently of role requirements (for example, Kiesler, 1966). Helpers may administer more or less help than prescribed by their roles; for example, a nurse may spend many off-duty hours comforting a hospitalized patient or a teacher may refuse to assist a student with difficult problems.

Aid recipients obtain the least information about themselves when the helper's behavior can be attributed to rigid role requirements and the most information when the helper is free to respond to individual situations. Even within role requirements, helpers may have freedom to determine when, where, and how much they help. The recipients' interpretations of the general situation and of the help givers' actions lead to their determination of the extent to which the help is contingent on their own individual characteristics.

In addition to interpreting the helper's actions, recipients may take their own help-seeking behavior as evidence about themselves. An important factor in determining self-attributions is the normativeness of receiving help. To the extent that recipients make an external attribution such that they believe anyone, even a competent individual, would need help in a similar situation, it is not necessary for them to make inferences about their own adequacy or competence. When the help seeking is not perceived as normative they may infer from the fact that they are seeking or receiving help that they are inadequate, incompetent, or unable to cope successfully. In Kelley's (1967) attribution model terms, if consensus is low (that is, others in the same situation do not seek help), then the help seekers may attribute their own acts to internal characteristics such as weakness. For example, Tessler and Schwartz (1972) found more help seeking when it was normative to receive help and where the need for help was easily attributed to the difficult situation rather than to personal inadequacy. This effect may extend to others' perceptions of recipients; for example, Calhoun, Dawes, and Lewis (1972) report questionnaire findings indicating that subjects perceive people who seek help for an "internally" caused problem as more likely to be rejected than people who seek aid for an "externally" caused problem. A helper who initiates the aid may create the attribution that help is normative in the situation. In addition to normativeness, centrality of the task may determine self-attributions, although the Kelley model does not specify this. In the Tessler and Schwartz (1972) study, high self-esteem women sought less help on an important central task than on a peripheral task. Using a sex-role centrality manipulation, Wallston (1976) replicated this finding for traditional male subjects.

Fisher and Nadler (1974) have demonstrated that there are times when subjects may attribute failure to themselves and hence suffer loss of self-esteem, even in a situation where help is offered rather than requested. They found lower self-esteem ratings in situations where aid was received from a helper similar to the subjects than when aid was rendered by a non-social-comparison other. In a second study, Fisher and Nadler (1976) found that receiving aid from a high-resource donor constituted a greater threat to self-esteem than receiving aid from a low-resource donor.

In summary, an attribution framework suggests recipients who perceive their need for help as internally motivated rather than produced by external circumstances may come to attribute negative characteristics, such as incompetence and inadequacy, to themselves. Such negative internal attributions are more likely when recipients are constrained to request help directly than when aid is helper initiated. Thus, attribution theory predictions differ somewhat from those of reactance theory. First, they focus on the recipients' feelings toward themselves rather than on reactions to the help or helper. Second, they suggest that externally initiated help or help that anyone in the same situation would receive would be less likely to produce negative reactions. In contrast, reactance theory implies that externally imposed help would be more likely to produce negative reactions.

Equity Theory. Whereas reactance and attribution notions usually focus on the recipient's perceptions, several equity theories (for example, Adams, 1965; Blau, 1964; Homans, 1961; Walster, Walster and Berscheid, 1978) consider the helper-beneficiary relationship as a continuing social interaction. These theories postulate a negative or uncomfortable state when an individual's social receipts and expenditures are not about equal. Greenberg's (forthcoming) theory of indebtedness is an attempt to apply these equity-balance conceptions to help-receiving reactions. Greenberg argues, primarily on the basis of Gouldner's (1960) reciprocity norm, that indebtedness, or the felt obligation to repay a benefit, has motivational properties similar to cognitive dissonance in that it is an unpleasant psychological state. Thus, whenever possible, people will attempt to reduce feelings of indebtedness. Several writers (Kalish, 1967; Lipman and Sterne, 1962) have discussed how the elderly wish to avoid indebtedness and to retain feelings of independence. Lipman and Sterne (1962, p. 200) define independence in terms of fulfilling reciprocal obligations and point out that the aged demand that retirement support be construed not as help to a dependent nor as a "dole to a troublesome mendicant" but as "due payment for a job well done."

Indebtedness may produce either gratitude or resentment. Resentment is more likely when the recipient is unable to repay the debt and thus risks losing status in the eyes of the donor. Greenberg (1968) suggests that resentment is especially great when helping involves expertise, as in the case of the disabled individual or nursing home resident (especially those not paying for their care) who receives "expert" assistance from doctors, nurses, and occupational therapists. According to equity notions, any such help recipient who does not have opportunities or sufficient resources to return help may reduce the resulting inequity either by resenting the help or derogating the helper, that is, coming to believe the helper is not worthy of or entitled to reciprocal behavior. For example, Bredemeir (1964) comments that welfare clients often feel hostility toward caseworkers, especially toward those who expect the client to demonstrate progress and gratitude.

Additional documentation for the aversive qualities or nonreciprocal help is provided in a study by Greenberg and Shapiro (1971). They report that subjects who anticipate difficulties in reciprocating aid may be less willing to request help in the first place. Subjects who believed they would be unable to reciprocate waited significantly longer before making a request for aid. Morris and Rosen (1973) have pointed out that methods used in the Greenberg and Shapiro study may have confounded the lack of opportunity to reciprocate variable with feelings of inadequacy. Using the Greenberg and Shapiro paradigm, Morris and Rosen (1973) found that subjects who were made to feel "quite inadequate" in performing a task were significantly more reluctant to ask for help than were subjects whose performance was rated as "quite superior." However, the Morris and Rosen study also provided partial support for the reciprocity prediction advanced by Greenberg and Shapiro (1971).

We would expect that under conditions where it is necessary to accept aid with little repayment possibility, or when the motives of the helper are suspect (Nadler, Fisher, and Streufert, 1974), the helper will be resented. But in many situations, the reputation and motives of the helper are unassailable (for example, the doctor, nurse, social worker, or best friend). In such cases, where derogation of the helper is difficult or impossible, help recipients might then lower their own self-esteem. A relationship in which a person with little merit, power, ability, or resources receives help from a person with greater resources can be considered psychologically equitable. But a similar nonreciprocal relationship between equals may be perceived as inequitable.

An important exception to this expected pattern is that in which the helper is paid or rewarded through a third party. Under these circumstances, the help receiver is not usually put into a situation of indebtedness and the helper's motives are not easily questioned. Third-party sponsors of help, however, may be subject to suspicions and resentments similar to those experienced by direct helpers. A well-known example of this is the negative relationship sometimes developed between public assistance recipients and people who set and administer public policy. In this situation, recipients may see their workers as helpful but regard policymakers and fund managers as repressive. Furthermore, those in a position to view their public assistance benefits as a pension in return for work and taxes paid (the elderly) make more positive assessments of public assistance than those not in this position (AFDC recipients). See Briar (1966) for a fuller discussion.

In one reciprocity study, Gross and Lubell (1970) demonstrated that subjects who had no opportunity to repay a favor liked the helper considerably less than subjects in two reciprocity and three control conditions. The study also showed that intended reciprocal help is functionally equivalent to actual reciprocity in reducing presumed resentment. Subjects who were offered a chance to provide reciprocal aid but were interrupted by the experimenter before being able to perform the helping act liked the other person as well as those who were allowed to complete the reciprocal help.

Another reciprocity study (Gross and Latané, 1974) also indicates that a benefactor is liked more if the beneficiary is allowed to reciprocate or if the recipient subsequently is able to offer aid to a third person. But in contrast to the Gross and Lubell study, subjects who were not helped at all also liked a confederate better if they were allowed to help him or her. The pattern of means in the Gross and Latané study generally indicates that the college student subjects feel more positive toward people who help them and more positive toward people they help. In a similar experiment, Castro (1974) found the highest liking scores for the helper when subjects were able to reciprocate to the original helper, the next highest when the subject helped a third person, and the lowest when the subject was unable to help anyone. Gergen and others (1975) obtained findings in the United States, Sweden, and Japan that indicate subjects are more attracted to a donor who requires reciprocity than to donors who ask nothing or who charge interest.

Gross and Somersan (1974) measured the number of help units sought as a function of the helper's costs and benefits. They found, in accord with equity notions, that subjects requested more help when the potential helper's perceived input or effort was lower; and under one set of conditions, subjects requested help sooner when the helper's perceived benefits were higher.

In summary, equity theory has implications for help-receiving behavior that relate to the recipients' ongoing relationship with help givers. Equity formulations suggest that when individuals receive help, they incur indebtedness that needs to be reduced through such means as reciprocal helping, derogation of the helper, or self-depreciation. Under certain conditions, such as when the recipient engages in self-derogation to restore equity, this model suggests, similar to attribution predictions, that negative self-perceptions on the part of the recipient can occur as a result of receiving help.

Social-Psychological Research

In the forgoing discussion, we have mentioned negative consequences that may occur when help recipients feel threatened with loss of freedom, consider themselves inadequate or dependent, or are in a state of indebtedness: They may derogate the helper, their own self-esteem may suffer, or they may avoid seeking needed help. We have also cited a number of studies which follow notions derived from reactance, attribution, or equity theories. In this section, we will describe some experiments from our research program that were derived from the previously discussed social psychology theories and are also potentially applicable to real-world helping systems. The specific applied question this part of our research program addressed is, "What form of help delivery—helper-initiated help or self-requested help—leads to more usage of service, enhanced helper attractiveness, and better recipient feelings?" Our first attempts at answering this question were guided by reactance theory, but it soon became apparent that reactance and attribution theories can lead to contrasting predictions.

Brehm's (1966) notion of reactance suggests dependence on a source of help may lead to perceptions of limited freedom and to negative feelings toward the helper as well as to resistance to the helper's efforts. In accord with reactance theory, negative feelings toward assistance should be greatest when help is externally imposed and least when recipients can choose when, where, and how they are helped. One possible means of mitigating negative reactions to aid, then, may be to allow the help recipient to play a more active role in the helping relationship. A first step in this direction would be to allow the recipient to decide if and when to initiate a helping interaction. To test this derivation from reactance theory—that recipient-requested help would be more positively viewed than helper-initiated help—several studies were designed in which subjects were assigned a problem to solve and were either (1) free to decide if and when they would request aid or (2) constrained to wait until the helper initiated aid.

For example, in one study (Berman, Piliavin, and Gross, 1971), forty-four undergraduate business majors were recruited to participate in a computer game in which they made a series of financial decisions. Because the game was difficult and related to the students' majors, involvement was assumed to be high. Approximately half the students were visited by a consultant who offered assistance at regular intervals (helper-initiated condition); the remainder could receive help only by signaling it was required (recipient-initiated condition). Contrary to expectation, acceptance of help offers in helper-initiated condition occurred more frequently than did requests for help in recipient-initiated condition. Second, and more important, prior to receiving feedback from the first set of decisions, request subjects indicated significantly greater anxiety and negative self-ratings on a self-concept test than did helper-initiated subjects. The higher anxiousness ratings in request conditions may have reflected the threatening aspects of active confession of need for help as contrasted to more passive acceptance of regularly available aid.

Three additional studies (Gross and others, 1971) in which locus of help initiated was varied also failed to provide support for the reactance hypothesis. Freedom to initiate requests (for assistance in building a molecular model) in these studies did not result in more help seeking or in more positive recipient reactions to receiving help. On the contrary, there were tendencies for more help to be obtained and for the helper to be better liked in helper-initiated conditions. Thus, these studies suggest that having the opportunity to request help may not only fail to make the experience a more positive one but indeed may lead to more negative effects than does passively receiving help. The unexpected data resulting from these laboratory studies and corroborative information gathered in field interviews with welfare recipients led us to focus more on negative aspects of self-requested help associated with attribution theory.

According to attribution theory concepts, the potential helper and other witnesses can infer from an open admission of need that the help requester is inadequate, incompetent, or unable to cope. But people who can accept available offers of help avoid public admission of need and the associated perceptions of inadequacy. In addition, in helper-initiated conditions, people are usually free to refuse offers and may not experience reactance-related negative feelings.

Broll, Gross, and Piliavin (1974) attempted to replicate the findings that helper-initiated aid results in more aid and better recipient feelings. Subjects were instructed to complete an extremely difficult logic problem. Pretesting had indicated it was virtually impossible to complete the problem within the allotted time; however, subjects were allowed to enlist the aid of a trained consultant. Half the subjects were allowed to request help whenever they wished; the other half could accept the consultant's help when it was offered periodically. Subjects in offer conditions received 47 percent more units of help than subjects in request conditions, and the consultants were liked more when they offered assistance than when they responded to subject-initiated requests. Because the task was equally difficult in both treatments, these data emphasize that asking for help may lead to negative attitudes toward the helper and inhibit potentially beneficial help requests. More positive reactions in the offer conditions may also have resulted from reduced perceptions of indebtedness and hence lessened need to restore equity.

Greenberg and Saxe (1975) attempted to relate this locus of help initiation variable directly to equity theory. They asked their subjects to read a story about a male student who needed assistance. The authors predicted and found that subjects estimated the fictitious needy student would feel most obligated in situations when he initiated a request compared with situations in which help was offered to him or imposed on him.

In the Broll, Gross, and Piliavin (1974) study, help was not imposed by the consultant; it was merely offered. This offer technique may have the double benefit of reducing reactance (to the extent that freedom to refuse is perceived) and of making it possible to receive benefits without actively seeking them. Easy acceptance of a helper-initiated benefit is captured in the familiar phrase, "Well, as long as you're here (up), you might as well . . . " In fact, it may be possible to offer aid in a manner such that recipients believe they are pleasing or benefiting helpers by accepting the offer. Such tactics could reduce negative feelings produced by reactance, self-attributions of inadequacy, and feelings of indebtedness and a need to restore equity.

Although these laboratory data shed some light on the processes involved in help seeking, the variables in the Broll, Gross, and Piliavin (1974) study were selected because it was believed they were relevant for understanding psychological processes involved in institutional helping arrangements as well. Because the external validity of data collected from college students would be strained by direct application to a field helping setting, these lab data were considered more suggestive than definitive; and related field studies were being planned concurrently with the laboratory work.

A pilot field study set in a medium-sized welfare agency in a midwestern county (service catchment area population two hundred thousand) was designed to contrast caseworker-client relationships that require the client to initiate home or phone service contacts versus those in which the service worker arranges contacts. The research procedures did not generate sufficient service contacts during the pilot year to allow reliable comparisons between the two kinds of relationships, but the feasibility of conducting experimental research within a host welfare agency was demonstrated and we moved to a research site with a much larger client population.

During our early negotiations with the agency administrators at the larger site (a midwestern county agency with catchment area population in excess of one million), it became clear that data relating to self-requested help were germane to recent federal changes in welfare policy. Federal guidelines now mandate (with threat of financial cutoff for noncompliance) that financial aid for welfare clients should be separated from provision of other services. This policy change means a caseworker typically becomes involved in a helping relationship only when the client requests it. In the past, social workers who provided both financial aid and social services were able to offer social services on the occasion of making a contact to deal with financial matters. But clients in a separated system must initiate contact with service caseworkers, and this act of initiation may make salient any real or perceived inadequacies that led to the contact.

What emerged from consultation between our research team and agency personnel was a large-scale field study that not only allowed a further test of the client-initiated versus worker-initiated questions posed in the pilot field study but that also directly investigated the effect of the new policy of separation of aid and service.

Subjects for the project were new female clients for Aid to Families with Dependent Children (AFDC). Only mothers who had just been granted eligibility for AFDC, who had not previously received AFDC benefits, and who did not require the provision of social services by law were selected. The total sample consisted of 210 women, of whom 112 were assigned to a no-treatment control group and the remainder were assigned to one of four experimental conditions of a two (client or worker-initiated) by two (separated or combined aid and service) factorial design.

Regular agency social workers were employed by the project and were paid overtime for their research activities, which included instructing the clients at an initial interview and recording data from each phone or home contact. At the initial interview, client-initiated subjects were told they were free to request social services at any time by phoning the worker. A calling card including the worker's phone number was left with the client and reminder postcards including the phone number were mailed to clients every three to four months. In worker-initiated conditions, clients were visited at their homes at approximately three- to four-month intervals.

In separated conditions, clients were assigned to a case aide, who handled financial matters via telephone, in addition to the caseworker. In combined conditions, the caseworker informed the client he or she would handle both financial and nonfinancial matters related to her case. This treatment essentially parallels conditions existing for delivery of social services to AFDC recipients prior to 1970. Clients in all four treatments were assigned to each caseworker.

Recipients were provided with services for a year or until they terminated AFDC eligibility. At the end of this period, all recipients received a questionnaire that asked them to rate their satisfaction with the services they had received and with the caseworker. During the project, a count of service requests and visits was maintained. Additional details appear in Piliavin and Gross (1977).

In general, the results revealed that AFDC recipients in the combined conditions were approximately one and one-half times more likely to request and/or receive all kinds of services and that they expressed more satisfaction with caseworkers. Across all types of worker-client contacts, clients in the worker-initiated condition were more likely to request nonfinancial services from their workers. Thus, main effects on service usage were demonstrated for the client versus worker-initiated and for the separated-combined variables.

Increased help seeking under worker-initiated conditions replicates findings in our laboratory studies, especially Broll, Gross, and Piliavin (1974). As noted, an attributional analysis of these data focuses on the negative consequences of explicitly acknowledging a need for assistance by making a request. Such acknowledgment may lead to attributions of personal failure and inadequacy. Additionally, potential recipients may be aware that other people consider requests for aid a stigma that can lead these others to perceive them as failures. It is also possible to interpret the separate-combined differences in an attributional framework. In the combined conditions, clients were often able to request nonfinancial services when they were dealing with a worker on a financial matter. Financial needs might have been perceived as more "legitimate" in that they are less likely to reflect personal failures. In any event, the combined conditions of service delivery often make it unnecessary for a person in need of counseling or other personal service to ask separately for such help.

Conclusion

The experimenting society of the 1960s spawned a great many research projects aimed at identifying social problems and suggesting amelioration. The majority of these projects (for example, the negative income tax experiment) concentrated largely on economic variables. Even today, welfare and other helping agencies usually focus on monetary measures in program evaluation. Of course, economic indicators are of primary importance in considering how optimally to distribute goods and services; but we have argued in this chapter that social-psychological variables also have important consequences and the effects of psychological variables on the potential help seeker or help recipient are especially salient.

As social scientists, we recognize the necessity for considering social psychology along with economics in our attempts to analyze and understand helping relationships and systems. As concerned citizens, we believe a truly empathic, humanitarian society must respond sensitively to the attitudes of its distressed or needy individuals. The attitudes, feelings, and reactions of the needy should be a critical factor in designing helping system and procedures. Questions about the conditions under which help will be accepted or refused, the kinds of helping arrangements that lead to eventual independence or dependence, and when seeking help causes resentment and negative self-attitudes must be investigated and answered and the results implemented.

CHAPTER 17

Individual Philanthropy and Giving Behavior

Richard D. Reddy

This chapter is concerned with philanthropy and voluntary giving to groups and individuals in settings other than communes or intentional communities or disaster situations. It does not deal with direct, person-to-person charity; sharing among friends and neighbors; or short-term, immediate, personal aid to strangers. This chapter's mandate to review individual philanthropy and giving behavior does not include consideration of foundation giving because all foundation activity is, at least in a legal sense, "mediated"—the foundation being a mechanism through which the wishes or intentions of the individual(s) who created it are carried out. However, individual acts of establishing or contributing to a foundation are within its purview. (Corporate or other groups establishing or contributing to foundations are not.)

My concern is with a very substantial activity, one that in monetary terms in the United States alone entails tens of billions of dollars annually and has had a profound effect on a number of our most important institutions, especially those centering around religious expression, education, health, and welfare. For example, information published in the *New York Times* (May 6, 1975, p. 53, and May 30, 1976,

p. 24) showed that total giving in this country was $25.23 billion in 1974 and $26.88 billion in 1975. Churches and religious organizations received the largest share of contributions, $10.85 and $11.68 billion, respectively, in 1974 and 1975. Health-related charities garnered $3.9 and $4.01 billion; schools had contributions of $3.72 and $3.59 billion, respectively. Social welfare organizations (including the United Way) received over $2 billion. Arts and humanities groups raised over $1 billion. These totals reflect giving by individuals, corporations, and foundations. However, adverse economic conditions would appear to affect corporate and foundation giving more than it does individual giving. During the economic decline in 1975, corporate and foundation giving declined by about 3 percent from 1974 while private donations and bequests increased by about 8 percent. Private donations and bequests make up the bulk of giving in the United States. Corporations and foundations give only about 12 percent of the total. Moreover, the overwhelming bulk of foundation assets (ranging somewhere between $25 and $35 billion, depending on market conditions) is the product of individual giving.

I have used the term "giving behavior," which is a more generic concept than "philanthropic behavior." "Philanthropy" has two different levels of meaning. It may be broadly understood as entailing an active effort to promote human well-being arising out of a love of mankind. At this level, philanthropy includes many forms of voluntary action, from membership in voluntary associations to volunteer work to involvement in social movements, some political participation, and such. Philanthropy includes giving of time, talents, supplies, blood, body organs, and so forth. It might involve supporting homeless children, aiding in the resettlement of refugees, going around the neighborhood soliciting donations for charities, giving benefit performances, and raising money for scholarships, disaster relief, and a myriad of other causes. At this level, philanthropy and altruism are virtually synonymous, although the latter implies a greater degree of selflessness or sacrifice. (See, for example, dictionary definitions of the two terms.)

Philanthropy's second level of meaning is narrower. It is often taken as referring to contributions to good causes by the very wealthy. These contributions may be in cash or in items of very high value such as stocks, art works, or mansions. The motivation behind such gifts may be altruistic or it may reflect tax concern and estate planning. When I use "philanthropy" in the following pages, it may or may not refer to truly altruistic giving. Determination of whether a specific instance of giving is philanthropy in the first sense depends on an assessment of the giver's motivation. Because I am not making such motivational assessment, I will normally use the term "giving behavior." This area has, perhaps surprisingly, drawn less concerned and sustained scholarly interest than a number of other aspects of voluntary action. It deserves fuller and more systematic attention, not only because of its extent and impact but also because the pattern of results that emerges from the existing research on philanthropic and giving behavior bears a marked resemblance to the pattern of findings on other aspects of voluntary action.

Contextual Variables

Contextual variables are external to the individual. As described by Smith and Reddy (1972b, p. 299), contextual variables "form a matrix within which the social background, personality, and attitudinal characteristics of individuals originate, develop, and change. Indeed, more 'internal' individual characteristics have their essential meaning and interpretation in light of and with respect to the complex set of social expectations, norms, structures, cultural patterns, human population, and biophysical environmental variables comprising the category of contextual characteristics."

I review two classes of contextual variables (cultural and social-structural variables). For completeness, I also mention human population variables and biophysical environmental variables. However, there is little or no social-scientific research on the nature of the effects (if any) of these latter two types of variables upon giving behavior.

Cultural Variables. Smith and Fisher (1971, p. 11) define cultural norms as "all of the socially transmitted and created content and patterns of values, ideas, and other meaningful symbolic system elements that are associated with membership in a given society, ethnic group, or very widespread social roles within such systems." This concept of culture involves basic, powerful patterns of values and ideas that are widespread and general in nature. Thus, a cultural norm has proper application to all or nearly all the members of a given society. Cultural norms are sources of relative homogeneity within a large group.

Cultural norms are significant for the understanding of philanthropic and giving behavior in a number of ways. They determine the meaning of giving behavior for oneself and others within the society. They provide motivational bases for giving and not giving by defining if, when, and why this behavior might be appropriate. These norms identify possible beneficiaries in terms of personal or socially perceived needs. They also help specify what can or should be given.

Before turning to the literature on the relationship between cultural variables and philanthropy, I shall make some observations on the nature of that literature. With some exceptions (such as Mauss, 1966), most of what we know of how cultural factors affect giving behavior comes from two sources: (1) studies of giving behavior in significant eras in Western European history (Ancient Greece and Rome, Medieval England and France) and United States history and (2) general, relatively brief commentaries on how a variety of historical influences have created current conditions in the United States. Detailed, contemporary, comparative studies of a variety of nations do not now exist. Some scholars suggest the U.S. experience is unique, but we do not know the extent of this uniqueness or the historical basis and contemporary supports for it. We do know that individual philanthropy, as we understand it, did not and currently does not exist in some societies and that giving behavior in a number of societies is markedly different from that discussed here. Hands (1968, p. 26) says, "In the vast majority of texts and documents relating to gifts in the classical world, it is quite clear that the giver's action is self-regarding, in the sense that he anticipates from the recipient of his gift some sort of return. To the modern mind such 'giving' may seem more like an economic transaction than an altruistic gesture. Yet as anthropologists, such as Marcel Mauss, have pointed out, simple societies can be found even today in which such giving, far from being amoral, let alone immoral, is the whole basis of friendly intercourse and exchange of *any* kind." In Mauss' (1966, p. 11) words on the mutual obligations of giving and receiving in primitive societies, "to refuse to give, or to fail to invite, is—like refusing to accept—the equivalent of a declaration of war; it is a refusal of friendship and intercourse." What Mauss terms the "obligation of worthy return" compels the gift recipient to make an equivalent gift under pain of losing status within the community or, in extreme cases, losing freedom and becoming the slave of the giver.

Philanthropy of a certain type did exist among ancient Greeks and Romans. Weaver (1967, p. 7) points out that "among the Greeks and Romans . . . the object of the giving was not really individual needy people, but rather the public at large. The intent was not so much to relieve suffering as to enrich life." Weaver goes on to quote Bertrand Russell on Aristotle: There was "an almost complete absence of what may be called benevolence or philanthropy. The sufferings of mankind, in so far as he is aware of them, do not move him emotionally; he holds them, intellectually, to be an evil, but there is no evidence that they cause him unhappiness except when the sufferers happen to be his friends." A good deal of Greek and Roman acts of giving (and a good deal even in the Christian Era until governments assumed responsibility for them) were "public works": aqueducts, theaters, stadia, baths, roads, and bridges.

As was the case of culture's influence on individual participation in organized voluntary action (see Smith and Reddy, 1972b), it is likely that values such as pluralism and freedom of thought, expression, and action encourage the development of philanthropy. Similarly, an important series of values may be those relating to persons' basic perception of and disposition toward their world, be it one of "doing" or of "being," of "mastery" or of "subjugation," of "active confrontation" or of "passive acceptance of fate or destiny." Moreover, as Crawford (1974) points out, some values serve to specify what is important, what matters, and what counts.

If individual private action is permitted or even encouraged, another series of values may define desirable recipients by highlighting the direct support of governmental needs (this sometimes occurring in times before systematic taxation has developed), the direct support of general public benefit projects (facilitating public transportation or sanitation), or by drawing attention to identified "problem" areas. Finally, another series of broad cultural values that may serve to delimit responsibilities are those that define responsibilities as familial, governmental, or religious or as those of the wealthy or of the general population.

Religion's impact on the development and articulation of values relating to individual philanthropy can be considerable. It has been said that religion is the mother of philanthropy. Jewish doctrines and practices regarding philanthropy and giving behavior have drawn the attention of scholars (for example, Chetkow, 1957; Cronbach, 1951; Curti, 1958; Frisch, 1969; Kahan, 1967; Kaplan, 1930; Keith-Lucas, 1972; Marts, 1966; Mead, 1957; Shapiro, 1966; Weaver, 1967), not only because of their profound impact on Christian philanthropy but also because Jewish approaches and Jewish philanthropic institutions were markedly different from those of ancient Greece and Rome and of other primitive societies as described by researchers such as Mauss (1966) and Hands (1968). In Jewish doctrine, those who could help had a duty to give and those in need had a right to receive. Although the giver might merit deference and respect, because the giver was being rewarded in that fashion and merit was its own reward, special obligations of reciprocity between the recipient and the giver did not develop. Indeed, synagogues frequently had rooms in which those who were able to give could secretly leave money and in which those in need could secretly receive.

The impact of early Christian doctrine on the development of philanthropy has also been a popular topic among scholars (for example, Constantelos, 1965, 1968; Curti, 1958; Hands, 1968; Keith-Lucas, 1972; Marts, 1966; Mayer, 1973; Ross, 1968; Troeltsch, 1950; Ulhorn, 1883; Weaver, 1967). The spread of the concept of charitable giving throughout the "civilized" world followed the spread of Christianity, especially after A.D. 321. In contrast to ancient Greeks and Romans, for whom the poor were not special objects of attention or concern, Christians were actively concerned about the poor and those with special needs (the sick, travelers, the aged, orphans, prisoners, and so forth). Charity was universal, but it was originally largely personal in nature. As Christianity grew, charitable institutions were established to routinely provide the appropriate aid: homes for the poor and the aged, hospitals, orphanages, and such. Charity in the broadest sense was incumbent on all, but themes regarding the spiritual riches that came from "good works" on the part of the well-to-do and the Pauline doctrine of "stewardship" (accountability for the proper use of one's wealth) also emerged.

Concern over the storing up of spiritual riches through good works was a major theme throughout the Middle Ages and into the twentieth century (see Carnegie, 1900). As Keith-Lucas (1972, p. 189) put it, "The major perversion of the helping impulse in the Middle Ages was the growth of the idea that the purpose of giving was to ensure salvation for the soul of the giver. Even St. Chrysostom believed that the poor were useful to the rich so that the rich might get rid of their abundance and win treasure in heaven." Keith-Lucas reports that until the end of the Middle Ages, there was little to indicate a concern with what those in trouble needed, the emphasis being on what helping could do for the helper. Rosenthal (1972, p. 130) confirms Keith-Lucas' observations, saying, "Medieval charity was primarily aimed at the spiritual welfare of the donor, rather than improving the worldly condition of the recipient. Philanthropy directed toward social reform was singularly absent from the late medieval world, both in theory and in practice." Despite that emphasis on what charity could do for the donor, it is not proper to conclude that recipients were neglected by the church's ministrations. Usually adequate, and not infrequently heroic, work was done.

Weaver (1967, p. 15) notes, "A great deal of the individual giving of the Middle Ages was an indiscriminate sentimental type of charity, such as the alms to beggars at the monastery gate. . . . But this pattern began to change as the recognition emerged of intense and persistent poverty as a social evil rather than an individual misfortune, and an attempt was made to change the pauperism of large segments of the population."

Historians have recently been concerned with the major transition period in England from 1300 to 1660 as that nation emerged from the Middle Ages (Auffenberg, 1973; Crowther, 1954; Jordan, 1959, 1960, 1961a, 1961b; Leonard, 1965; Marts, 1966; Rosenthal, 1972; Thompson, 1965). Jordan (1959, p. 16) terms this period "one of the few great cultural revolutions in Western history: the momentous shift from men's primarily religious preoccupations to the secular concerns that have moulded the thought and institutions of the past three centuries." As a result of that shift, funds previously given to the church or at least channeled through its auspices were increasingly being put to a secular war on poverty, misery, and ignorance. In Jordan's (1959, p. 17) words, "The medieval system of alms, administered principally by the monastic foundation, was at once casual and ineffective in its incidence, never seeking to do more than relieve conspicuous and abject suffering. . . . Poverty was first systematically attacked in the sixteenth century with gifts for the outright relief of the poor and then later, with the really massive endowments designed to eradicate its causes by a variety of undertakings, among which the extension of educational opportunities was not the least." Although religious motives remained, a strong trend toward humanism was coming to the fore in England. A similar pattern can be found in France (Fairchilds, 1973; Lallemand, 1902–1906); except with the French Revolution, there was in addition a substantial shift in responsibilities for the care of the poor from both the religious and private sectors to the public sector.

A number of scholars have reviewed the development of philanthropy in the United States (see Andrews, 1953; Bremner, 1960; Curti, 1961, 1963; Cutlip, 1965; Enck, 1970; Gettleman, 1963; Hosay, 1969; Huggins, 1971; Lubove, 1965; Marts, 1953; Weaver, 1967). The roots of American philanthropy lie in European patterns, but a distinctly American philanthropy eventually emerged. The philanthropy that established (and continues to establish) churches and schools and later contributions that provided museums, concert halls, libraries, hospitals, parks, medical and scientific research, and such are documented. Recipients include the poor, widows, orphans, immigrants, and sailors. Although governments, through their tax codes, may encourage and subsidize philanthropy, they are themselves very rarely the object of philanthropy. Good causes include emancipation of slaves; prison reform; teacher education; education of the deaf, the blind, and the retarded; and pension funds for teachers and preachers. The heroes given their due include Carnegie, the Rockefellers, the Vanderbilts, Ford, Russell Sage, and Stanford.

Historical developments of particular interest include the Charity Organization Society movement and the ethic of "scientific philanthropy," which permeated the early major foundations (Bremner, 1956; Lubove, 1965). The former arose out of a concern that charity would corrupt the poor, making them dependent and irresponsible. The latter, although also concerned that only worthy causes be supported, arose chiefly out of the recognition that large sums would produce more substantial benefits when they were given according to a careful plan rather than merely in reaction to a myriad of demands as they arose. Thus, although occasionally some "seed money" might be offered to the "worthy poor," the emphasis in these developments was on providing encouragement, guidance, moral guardianship, and general leadership rather than money to the needy. Further, the separation of church and state influenced the creation of a large number of independent, but religiously oriented, philanthropic agencies. Giving behavior is often seen to be religiously motivated but tempered by the "steward's" concern that only "worthy" recipients be the object of philanthropy.

Social-Structural Variables. Smith and Fisher (1971, p. 14) define social-structural variables as "normatively patterned social and individual behaviors that are associated with and learned through special roles, settings, organizations, groups, and institutional contexts." Thus within a given culture or subculture (and in contrast with cultural norms), social-structural elements are sources of diversity. Because we do not yet have systematic, comparative studies of patterns of philanthropic and giving behavior in societies with differing social structures, we have speculative possibilities rather than confirmed relationships.

Societies clearly vary in structural openness to voluntary action of any type. In some nations, notably the more closed societies of Eastern Europe and Asia, the realm of voluntary action as we understand it is narrow, circumscribed, and controlled. Individual philanthropy virtually does not exist in many countries. The state and its agencies support and provide education, cultural activities, and medical and scientific research and take whatever care of the poor is seen as necessary. Despite the increasing role, in these realms, of local, state, and federal governments in the United States, the extent and scope of the influence of individual philanthropy is greater in the United States than in most of the other countries of the world (Marts, 1966; Ross, 1968).

The legal status of philanthropy and giving behavior is another significant social-structural variable. The application of the law and its utilization varies across societies. The United States acquired many of its basic legal principles from English common law, but its law relevant to philanthropy is uniquely American now. Although scholars have paid some attention to the development of law in both England and the United States concerning philanthropy (Andrews, 1958; Kutner, 1970; Miller, 1961; Newman, 1955), we are far from a precise knowledge of how laws and legal precedents and decisions affect giving behavior.

The same may well be said about the impact of the special category of tax laws. Philanthropic and giving behavior is sometimes discouraged by being taxed and sometimes encouraged through tax exemptions. (For American examples, see Bittker, 1955; Casey, Lasser, and Lord, 1953; Harriss, 1939; Hunter, 1968; Kutner, 1970; Lasser, 1948; Lasser and Casey, 1951; Merritt, 1961; and Skilling, 1970; and for European examples, see the International Bureau of Fiscal Documentation, 1965; Nebolsine, 1963; and Rhys-Williams, 1953.) Empirical investigations of the actual impact of tax provisions on contributions include Barlow, Brazer, and Morgan (1966); Brannon (1974); Kahn (1959, 1960); McNees (1973); Morgan, Dye, and Hybels (1975); S. Schwartz (1970b), Taussig (1965, 1967); and Thiessen (1968). Feldstein (1975) estimated that eliminating the present tax deduction provisions would create about a 20-percent decline in total charitable contributions and a 50-percent decline in gifts to educational institutions, hospitals, and the arts. The more affluent taxpayers, those who itemize deductions, would be most affected by provision changes.

Those private and semiprivate institutions with philanthropic purposes (such as hospitals, schools, social welfare agencies, cultural facilities, and scientific research organizations) have been the product not only of tax laws but also of the belief by some that individual "investment" in a special-purpose institution is a suitable way to deal with a particular social problem. These institutions normally need constant support to continue their activities, so they develop various fund-raising techniques. They must create habits of giving as well as efficient means of collecting funds. As needs or the number of competing organizations increase, donors must be encouraged to give more and/or new donors must be found. If successful, these efforts create more people who are accustomed to giving or to giving more and organizations learn how to get more.

When funds are successfully channeled to address a real problem, both the problem and the possibilities of coping with it through funding are dramatized. It becomes clear that something can be done; and to the extent that the problem is real and the effort viable, allocating resources to the effort becomes increasingly legitimate. Precisely how that claim on funds may be met (through private auspices, a mixture of private and public auspices, or through public auspices) may, however, be subject to shifting emphases over time. Yet, to the extent that the efforts of private or semiprivate groups are successful in meeting real social needs, their claim for continuing support becomes stronger and the likelihood of expanded efforts by existing organizations or the creation of new organizations to meet emerging but related needs is enhanced.

Other social-structural factors, as yet unstudied, that may be related to individual participation in organized voluntary action have been suggested by Smith and Reddy (1972b). A nation's level of modernization may be influential because in less-developed nations, there is a greater tendency to rely on familial resources to provide services typically rendered by philanthropically supported groups in more-developed countries. With modernization, the voluntary sector grows and philanthropically supported institutions are developed to meet new problems created by the modernization and to confront old problems (Smith, 1973c).

The socioeconomic level of the community will also be a factor in giving behavior—the affluent, of course, usually give more. In addition, the size of a contribution is also often determined by what the individual perceives as being standard in the community (Lutterman, 1962; Thiessen, 1968).

Patterns of regional variation exist in the amount and types of donations. Lamale and Clorety (1959), using national data, found southerners more likely to contribute to religious than to welfare causes, northerners about equally likely to contribute to each, westerners more likely to contribute to welfare than to religious causes. Bremner (1960, p. 109) reports what he calls an "interesting, although not reliable" survey of the giving habits of millionaires conducted by the *Review of Reviews* in 1893. This survey found: "The percentage of millionaires who 'recognized their obligations' varied from city to city. Baltimore, with 49 percent of her millionaires listed as active givers, ranked highest on the list and New York, where millionaires were most numerous but apparently least generous, was at the bottom. Donors in different cities had distinct preferences: Cincinnati's millionaires supported musical and artistic ventures; those in Minneapolis gave to the state university and the public library; and Philadelphians were interested in overseas relief, arctic exploration, and the education of Indians and Negroes." Lamale and Clorety (1959) also found some evidence for variation according to city size. Those in small cities gave larger percentages of their income in total giving and proportionately more to religious causes and less to welfare causes than those in large cities.

Personal Variables

Personal factors are characteristics or tendencies that may typify or serve to classify an individual in any given context. I divide them into four types: background and social role characteristics, personality traits, general attitudes toward philanthropy, and specific attitudes toward philanthropy.

Background and Social Role Characteristics. Background and social role characteristics provide behavioral expectations, models for role behavior, and experiences that affect the breadth and specificity of knowledge of one's world. These characteristics stem from the individual's sociocultural status and geographical context (local, regional, and national). Singly and in combination, these factors facilitate the development of various attitudinal and personality tendencies or may limit the direction this development may take. The relationship between background and social role characteristics and individual participation in organized voluntary action has been covered in Payne, Payne, and Reddy (1972). I use their categorization of these characteristics.

The *life cycle variables* include factors of age, marital status, and number and age of children. The impact of age on giving behavior affords a very mixed and complex picture. Long (1975) found that age had an insignificant effect. Roistacher, Morgan, and Juster (1974); Roistacher and Morgan (1974); and Morgan, Dye, and Hybels (1975) reported that age had a major, and essentially linear, impact on giving, with the elderly giving more. This was true especially for religious contributions and for those over seventy-five years of age. Roistacher and Morgan (1974) and Roistacher, Morgan, and Juster (1974) discovered that age was a more powerful variable than income on whether those over seventy-five would make a contribution. Age's effect on secular contributions tended to diminish for those beyond their forties. However, most other researchers (Borsky and Banacki, 1961; Lutterman, 1962; Marcus, 1973; Morgan and others, 1962; Thiessen, 1968) report a curvilinear relationship between age and contributions, with younger persons and the elderly contributing less and contributions peaking in the middle years. Economic factors are behind much of this reported curvilinear relationship. For example, Thiessen (1968) found that secular giving was highest where income potential was highest. The lowest-status group showed peak giving in their thirties, reflecting peak productivity for manual workers; middle- and upper-income groups peaked in their forties. Morgan and others (1962, p. 266) note, "the decline in contributions among older (family) units is entirely the result of declining income, and disappears if only the high income (family) units are examined." However, Lamale and Clorety (1959) and Thiessen (1968) found the elderly are likely to contribute at a relatively high rate (though not necessarily in large amounts) to at least religious causes.

Because most people in their middle years are married, marital status should be related to philanthropy. Lamale and Clorety (1959), Thiessen (1968), and Roistacher and Morgan (1974) found that in some instances singles contribute less than do the married. Yet Morgan, Dye, and Hybels (1975) reported that single women contribute more and

Long (1975) indicated that both single women and men contribute more than the married.

On the whole, the effects of marital status on contributions is surprisingly weak (Lutterman, 1962; Sennott, 1971). Lutterman (1962) found that couples who are members of different churches contribute substantially less in total to both their churches than do same-faith spouses.

One might expect that within various income categories, the larger the size of the family, the smaller the size of the contribution (the larger family having less discretionary income). Borsky and Banacki (1961) reported that larger givers were more likely to have no children under eighteen years of age. Lutterman (1962) found the expected negative relationship for religious contributions, but Morgan and others (1962), Thiessen (1968), and Sennott (1971) report no such relationship. Lamale and Clorety (1959) found a curvilinear relationship with increases in philanthropy as family size increased to six and declines for larger families. The relationship was stronger for secular giving. Kirstein (1968) observed that those with children tend to give more during their lifetimes, leaving whatever remains to their children; and those without children give less during their lifetimes and bequeath more to charity upon their death. It may be that the effects of having children or family size on giving are limited to nonwealthy families. This possibility has not been studied.

Socioeconomic status may be measured by income, education, occupation, subjective social class, or earning potential. Income is the most studied variable here. It will not come as a surprise to learn that the prime requisite for giving is having. Those who have larger incomes contribute more (Andrews, 1950; Barlow, Brazer, and Morgan, 1966; Borsky and Banacki, 1961; Jenkins, 1950; Jones, 1954; Lamale and Clorety, 1959; Long, 1975; Lutterman, 1962; Marcus, 1973; Morgan and others, 1962; Morgan, Dye, and Hybels, 1975; Rositacher, Morgan, and Juster, 1974; Schwartz, 1966; Seeley and others, 1957; Sennott, 1971; Sills, 1957; Thiessen, 1968). However, both those with the largest and the smallest incomes contribute at higher rates than the middle-income groups (Andrews, 1950; Lamale and Clorety, 1959; Lutterman, 1962; Morgan and others, 1962; Morgan, Dye, and Hybels, 1975; Roistacher, Morgan, and Juster, 1974; Thiessen, 1968). Lutterman (1962) found a strong negative relationship between income and the rate of religious contributions to the church. Less-wealthy members of the congregation contributed at a substantially higher rate than their fellow communicants. Thiessen (1968) reported similar findings for religious charity; but for secular contributions, upper-income groups were seen to contribute at the highest rates, and the average amount of secular contributions increased rapidly for incomes over $15,000. Thiessen concluded that substantial support for secular charities was to be found only among the very rich. He pointed out that over two-thirds of the secular contributions made by high-income persons represents indirect government support; the real cost of their contributions was substantially less than the amount given because they are deducted from income for tax purposes. Feldstein (1975) and Morgan, Dye, and Hybels (1975) reported findings similar to Lutterman's and Thiessen's. Feldstein also found that lower-income persons are more likely to concentrate their contributions to religious groups and to social welfare, health, and community service groups such as the United Way; upper-income persons are more drawn to higher education, health, and cultural institutions.

Data on the education variable are provided by Thiessen (1968). He found that education was not a powerful variable in religious giving, but it has a strong effect on secular contributions. Within each of his three income samples (below $4,000; $4,000 to $19,999; and $20,000 and above), he found a strong positive relationship between education level and amount of secular contributions. Long (1975) reported a positive relationship for his sample of religious groups. Roistacher and Morgan (1974) and Morgan, Dye, and Hybels (1975) found education's impact to be strongest on the amount of giving, especially for the college educated. Borsky and Banacki's (1961) study of giving to the United Jewish Appeal of Essex County, New Jersey, illustrates the intimate relationship between education, occupation, and income. The donor group contributing the smallest amounts had the highest proportion of those who had no more than a high school education, but the next lowest donor group had the highest educational level. This group had a substantial number of doctors, lawyers, and accountants; whereas the groups that donated the largest amounts of money were overwhelmingly comprised of business executives ("proprietors and managers") who were self-employed. Although this study does not correlate education and occupation or education and income or occupation and income, it is likely that the self-employed business executives were wealthier and less educated than the bulk of the doctors, lawyers, and accountants.

The relationship between occupational status and contributions has been investigated by Lamale and Clorety (1959) and by Thiessen (1968). Lamale and Clorety reported that the urban families giving the highest percentage of their income were families whose heads were not employed. They believe these were likely to be families with a retired head. These were followed very closely by salaried professionals and the self-employed. Thiessen found that people in different occupations contribute at substantially different rates. Operatives, supervisors, craftspersons, and clerical workers contributed at the lowest rate; farmers, sales representatives, and professionals contributed at the highest rate. Controlling for income level did not erase occupational differences. Lamale and Clorety (1959) and Lutterman (1962) discovered strong relationships between occupation and rates of religious contributions. Lamale and Clorety found that families whose heads were not employed were especially likely to donate a large percentage of their incomes to religious organizations. Thiessen's (1968) data showed weaker occupational effects on rates of religious contributions than did the other two researchers, with what "important" effects that did appear occurring in the lower-income sample. However, assessing his results for the middle- and upper-income samples, Thiessen observed that some occupational categories (the more prestigious and remunerative) tend to be more visible to church leaders than are other occupations. Churches have a tendency to choose those in these more visible occupations as leaders, with those chosen usually expected to contribute at a higher rate. Borsky and Banacki (1961) report similar findings.

Turning to secular giving, Lamale and Clorety (1959) found the self-employed and the salaried professionals gave the highest percentages of their income to welfare organizations and were twice as likely as any other group to make secular contributions. Thiessen (1968) also reported that occupational differences were stronger in the upper-income categories than in the lower one. Thiessen surmised that those in high-visibility, high-income occupations tend to be sought out at work for contributions and noted that the bulk of all secular contributions were made by professionals and business executives.

Thiessen (1968) also used subjective social class as a predictor of giving behavior. It was positively but weakly related to amount of secular contributions but not to religious contributions. The effect of this variable was found mainly in the middle- and upper-income categories.

Morgan and others (1962) created an index of earning potential on the bases of ethnicity, physical condition, occupation, age, and education. A white man in good health, in a nonfarm occupation, in his middle years, with a high level of education would have the highest earning potential. They found curvilinear relationships for the index as a whole, except among the wealthy. Earning potential could reflect mainly the effect of age because age shows the same pattern (Lamale and Clorety, 1959). When the family's gross disposable income is controlled, the longer-run measure of family head's earning potential continues to affect the family's contributions. Apparently, then, both short-term and long-term financial considerations are involved in giving behavior.

Thiessen (1968), in a multivariate analysis of socioeconomic variables, found that income, education, occupation, and subjective social class together had the greatest impact on middle-income giving. Substantially less variance was accounted for in the other two samples. The greatest variance accounted for (25 percent) was for secular contributions by this middle-income group ($4,000 to $19,999).

Sociophysical characteristics include sex, race, ethnicity, health, and physical abilities and disabilities. Because the social definition and personal perception of these physical characteristics tend to be as important as the physical characteristics themselves, "sociophysical" is used here.

I know of no research on philanthropic and giving behavior utilizing any of these variables. The review by Payne, Payne, and Reddy (1972) suggests that little variance would be accounted for by many of these variables. Contributions by married couples are likely to be joint contributions, so the question of sex differences may be moot. Men have been assumed to be dominant in financial decision making. However, because more women now have independent incomes, the question of sex differences may be important for future research.

Race and ethnicity have not been found to be important factors in studies of participation in voluntary associations in the United States when controls have been introduced for socioeconomic status. The studies of giving in the general population have had too few cases of minority group members for meaningful analysis. However, the findings for socioeconomic status coupled with the fact that substantial segments of various U.S. minority groups are of low socioeconomic status suggest that their rates of giving, especially to churches, may be high in comparison to other groups. A good many secular contributions by middle- and upper-income individuals are made to formal, well-established organizations. Lower-income persons have often been found to be uncomfortable with formal organizations and so may be unlikely to give to establishment-oriented charities, even if the personnel of such organizations felt comfortable about asking them for donations.

I know of no research on the role of health in giving behavior. Poor physical health will affect earnings and discretionary income (due to medical care costs) and thus should reduce giving. However, a history of major illness or handicap of a certain type for a family or person might well lead to heightened charitable giving to organizations attempting to deal with that problem. Such questions require future research.

It is becoming increasingly evident, based on the work of scholars such as Ahtik (1962), Allardt (1961), and Smith (1969), that there is a *general activity syndrome*—that activity and involvement in one sphere of life is often positively related to activity and involvement in a variety of others. Research in philanthropic and giving behavior, especially that of Thiessen (1968), has found the expected positive relationships between these variables and participation in voluntary associations and political and religious involvements.

Several researchers have noted relationships between aspects of participation in voluntary associations and giving behavior. For example, Sills (1957), in his study of the National Foundation, noted that seven out of ten March of Dimes volunteers belong to at least three organizations other than the foundation and many belong to six or more. Barlow, Brazer, and Morgan (1966) reported a relationship between active participation in voluntary associations and charitable donations. Borsky and Banacki (1961) reported that the largest donors to the Essex County United Jewish Appeal also tended to have the highest rates of voluntary association membership. Marcus (1973) found that those most involved in voluntary associations were most likely to contribute. Morgan, Dye, and Hybels (1975) noted that "concerned citizens" give more. Sennott (1971) found that membership in voluntary associations was positively related to giving of time to and giving of money for philanthropic causes.

Thiessen (1968), in a systematic accounting of the relationship of voluntary-association-related variables to philanthropic and giving behavior, found that total amount of contributions was positively related to the number of memberships in secular organizations, to being an officer or committee member in such groups, to having collected funds for an organization, and to frequency of attendance at meetings. Similar results were found when contributions were divided into religious and secular categories and when rates, rather than amounts, were examined, with the exception of rate for religious giving, which was not related to any of the voluntary association variables. Multiple-correlation coefficient results for the relationships between number of memberships and officerships and the amounts and rates of giving show the bulk of the variance is accounted for by relationships in the middle-income sample (incomes between $4,000 and $19,999). For that sample, membership and officership levels together accounted for 19 percent of the variance in the amount of total contributions for the middle-income sample but only 8 percent for the lower-income sample and 7 percent for the upper-income sample (Thiessen, 1968, p. IV-38). The lower-income sample tended to show stronger relationships between secular giving and the voluntary association variables than the upper-income sample. In addition, Andrews (1953), Long (1975), and Thiessen (1968) report finding positive relationships between volunteer work and the amount of contributions.

As to the variable of political involvement, Morgan and others (1962) and Thiessen (1968) found that Republicans contribute more than Democrats. However, Morgan and others (1962) report that in low- and high- (but not middle-) income samples, Republicans contributed at a lower rate than Democrats. Controlling for income and age, they found that independents contributed more than members of either party; but without those controls, Thiessen found they contributed less than the members of either party. Thiessen (1968, pp. VI-46–VI-49) suggests, "while it may be true that Republicans emphasize voluntary charitable efforts, rather than governmental efforts to meet our social problems, this ideology is not behaviorally demonstrated by an acceptance of greater personal responsibility."

Thiessen's (1968) study employed three measures of political activity: doing work for a political party, voting in the most recent gubernatorial election, and voting in the most recent presidential election. The correlations between amount of total donations and these variables were low but positive. The variables of "political work" and "voting in the presidential election," in an adjusted multiple-correlation analysis, accounted for no variance whatsoever in the amount or rate of total, religious, or secular contributions for the upper-income sample. In the middle-income sample, they accounted for 7 percent (Thiessen, 1968, p. IV-64) of the variance in amount of total contributions; in the lower-income sample, they accounted for 15 percent (p. VI-45) of the variance in the amount of secular contributions and 13 percent (p. VI-129) of the variance in the rate of secular contributions. No effect was found for the upper-middle sample.

As to the variable of religious involvement, Andrews (1953) reports that Jews and Catholics contribute more than Protestants; and Morgan and others (1962) report that Jews contribute more than the other religious groups. But most researchers have found that denominational differences tend to be slight (Barlow, Brazer, and Morgan, 1966; Lutterman, 1962; Thiessen, 1968), especially in the low- and middle-income groups. Morgan, Dye, and Hybels (1975) confirmed this pattern of relatively small differences. However, they also showed Jews giving slightly less than might be "expected" at given income levels and less than any other category when their "expected" pattern was adjusted in regression analyses. Thiessen's (1968, pp. V-162a, VI-154) data showed from 12 to 18 percent of the variance in giving was accounted for by religious affiliation in his upper-income sample, largely because Jews and those with no religious affiliation donated relatively less to religious causes and more to secular causes. However, the distinction between religious and secular contributions by American Jews is often somewhat arbitrary. The Roman Catholic church directly operates many religiously oriented facilities, as do various Protestant denominations; but many Jewish philanthropies are not under the direct control of religious leaders. Yet contributions to Jewish philanthropies may often not be as strictly secular as some researchers would have it. For example, Borsky and Banacki (1961) have shown that a substantial number of past and current measures of Jewish religious and sociocultural identification are related to giving more to the United Jewish Appeal and other Jewish causes (and to giving less to more clearly secular causes).

The level of giving, religious and secular, falls well below the biblical tithe. Individuals or groups who come close to the tithing norm have not been adequately studied by those interested in giving behavior.

Participation in church activities has been found to be strongly related to the amount and rate of religious contributions, with some slight spillover effect sometimes found into secular contributions. (Barlow, Brazer, and Morgan, 1966; Borsky and Banacki, 1961; Long, 1975; Lutterman, 1962; Morgan and others, 1962; Morgan, Dye, and Hybels, 1975; Thiessen, 1968). Relationships between various measures of religious involvements and rates of giving are stronger than relationships between those measures and amounts given.

Of special interest are Thiessen's (1968) findings, expressed in terms of adjusted multiple-correlation coefficients, for the effects of "church officer" and "frequency of church attendance" on giving. Virtually no variance in either amount or rate of secular contributions is accounted for by these two variables; but substantial amounts of variance, ranging from 19 to 22 percent, in both amount and rate of religious contributions are accounted for in all three income samples. These two measures of religious behavior and activity proved to be more predictive of giving behavior than was self-assessed personal "religiosity."

Investigations of the relationship of other interpersonal roles and experiences to philanthropic and giving behavior have not been very fruitful. Only actual fund-raising and contributing experience has been found, not surprisingly, to be a significant factor in philanthropy. Although Borsky and Banacki's (1961) larger givers reported socialization to giving, Thiessen (1968) found the religiosity of one's parents made little difference in any kind of giving. The only effects observed in the upper-income sample were where the rate of secular contributions was positively related to father's religiosity and negatively related to mother's religiosity. Other Thiessen data suggest that only for some upper-income families is contributing to charitable organizations a tradition passed from father to offspring. Jordan (1959, 1960, 1961a, 1961b) has documented inheritance of specific beneficiaries as well in medieval England. The extent to which such patterns exist today is unknown. Thiessen also found his respondents' contemporary interaction patterns were little related to philanthropy. Visiting with relatives made no difference in any aspect of giving behavior, and meeting with friends had only a slight impact. Gift giving to relatives and friends was also seen to be only minimally related to general philanthropy.

Studies of the relationship between *mass media exposure* and voluntary action have involved a limited set of variables, such as the number of newspapers a person reads, whether the person regularly reads a nonlocal newspaper, the number of magazines read, and going to movies. Research on the relationship between these mass media variables and involvement in voluntary associations shows those with the highest exposure to mass media are the most extensively and actively involved in voluntary associations (Ahtik, 1962; Allardt, 1961; Smith, 1972).

Thiessen (1968) provides the only evidence concerning the relationship between mass media behavior and philanthropic behavior. Using newspaper and magazine reading as media variables, he found only a weak relationship in the upper-income sample. However, in the middle-income sample ($4,000 to $19,999), 3.4 percent (p. IV–57) of the variance in the amount of total contributions and 6.6 percent (p. V–39) of the variance in the amount of secular contributions was accounted for; in the lower-income group (incomes below $4,000), 10.7 percent (p. IV–57) of the variance in total contributions and 12.1 percent (p. V–40) of the variance in religious contributions was accounted for. In other words, exposure to what is likely to have been predominantly secular media has virtually no effect for the upper-income sample and a substantial relation to secular contributions in the middle-income sample and to religious contributions in the lower-income sample. These results are interesting, but I must note that the mass media variables studied have not yet included television or radio and have not been specified in terms of type of content respondents were exposed to.

Individual membership and participation in voluntary associations have been found to be related to *residential mobility* and *length of time resident in the community*. Philanthropy may often be community based and community oriented, and community involvement and community integration take time to develop. Also, the resettlement process in and of itself takes time and costs money. For these reasons, one would expect philanthropy to be positively related to length of time in a community. Marcus (1973) found the expected relationship, but Thiessen (1968) did not. Residential mobility and length of time resident in a community were only weakly related to giving behavior in Thiessen's sample. No effect was found for the upper-income sample. Slightly curvilinear relationships emerged for the lower- and middle-income groups, with those who just moved into a community and those who have lived in it for a long time (and who therefore may be older) giving somewhat less. Morgan, Dye, and Hybels (1975) noted those living in the same neighborhood for twenty or more years gave more; but when they introduced controls, the effect was insignificant.

Personality Traits. Personality traits are relatively enduring, transsituational dispositions that are relevant to a large variety of situations. Reddy and Smith (1972, pp. 294–295) note, "personality traits and capacities have frequently had low interest priorities for sociologists and other social scientists . . . on the other hand, psychologists have tended to show greater interest in personality and attitudes, but only a secondary interest in relating these to participation in voluntary groups." That statement also applies to study of the relationship between personality traits and philanthropy.

Only Thiessen (1968) has given serious, systematic attention to the relation between personality factors and giving. His analysis showed that trust was a relatively weak predictor of giving behavior. More-trusting individuals (especially in middle- or upper-income groups) were only slightly more likely to give large amounts or to give at higher rates than less-trusting people. The alienation variable was a stronger predictor of the total amount of giving, accounting for 5 to 11 percent of the variance in types of giving. Less-alienated persons in the lower- and middle-income groups tended to contribute more. However, alienation proved to have a negligible effect on the rate of giving. Thiessen also studied the relationship between self-reported religious disposition and giving. Not surprisingly, this variable was most strongly related to religious giving, particularly in the upper-income group. This trait was not related to secular giving. Furthermore, it was less predictive of religious giving than were church attendance, activism, or membership.

Much research clearly remains to be done relating personality traits to giving behavior. It seems especially important to know how giving is affected by such traits as extraversion, adjustment, optimism, efficacy (internal control), empathy, moral orientation, and superego strength. No research has been done on how capacities or intelligence might affect giving, either.

General Attitudes Toward Philanthropy. The differences between personality characteristics and general attitudes are matters of degree rather than of kind. Although general attitudes are also transsituational dispositions, they are relevant and salient in a narrower range of situations than a personality trait would be.

One general attitude that might be expected to be related to private, individual giving is toward the nature of responsibility for providing help: Does the basic responsibility in any area belong to individuals or to the government? Presumably, those who feel responsibility belongs to governments will feel largely absolved of personal responsibility and so less inclined to personal charity. The evidence on this question is sparse. Morgan and others (1962, p. 262) found, "Those who think the government should have primary responsibility for the aged are less likely to be contributing, not only to other individuals but also to church and to charity." Thiessen's (1968) data show those in the upper-income sample who thought the government was not doing enough for the poor tended to contribute more than others in that sample. However, he found the reverse in the middle- and lower-income data. In addition, he found interest in politics to be weakly but positively related to the amount of contributions, especially in his lower- and middle-income samples. Attitudes toward foreign aid were virtually unrelated to any of the measures of giving. Marcus (1973) reported that a belief in the desirability of private donations as opposed to taxation was associated with giving to a local United Way campaign. In that same study, he found a positive attitude toward the community and a belief in the importance of local areas studying local need and finding local solutions for local problems was associated with giving to the local United Way campaign.

Thiessen (1968) included in his study several indicators of racial attitudes, including attitudes toward open hotel accommodations, interracial marriage, and school integration, and the perception of the seriousness of lack of equal opportunities for blacks. Singly these variables accounted for very little variance. An adjusted multiple-correlation analysis of their combined impact showed an effect only for rate of religious contributions, and that only in the upper-income samples, accounting for 9 percent of the variance. Surprisingly, this result shows those with relatively negative attitudes toward minorities in that upper-income sample contributed at a relatively high rate. Perhaps giving to religious causes rather than to secular causes reflects something of the same general attitude toward society as do negative racial attitudes.

Some (see Kirstein, 1968) think a desire to repay society for one's good fortune motivates much giving. A related theme is that many donors are motivated by the desire to reduce guilt (Freedman, 1970; Goulden, 1971; Ross, 1965), which arises out of success itself or from the perception that their success entailed cost to others. Thiessen's (1968) data showed those who feel they owe some debt to society are only a little more interested in repaying their debts than those who feel they have none. Knowing someone who benefited from an organization to which the person contributed made no difference in any of the measures of total, religious, and secular giving.

In contrast to the negligible effects of these do-good motives, the motivation to reduce taxes is the most powerful single variable in those studies that have included it (Barlow, Brazer, and Morgan, 1966; Hawes, 1967; Thiessen, 1968). As Kirstein (1968, pp. 235–236) pointed out, "If we think of the word generosity as connoting some sacrifice on the part of the giver, philanthropy, as it is organized today in America, has little if anything to do with generosity. The amount to be donated is frequently dictated by an accountant who is thoroughly familiar with the Internal Revenue Code's encouragement of charitable giving."

Thiessen (1968) found that tax consciousness was very strongly related to the amount of total religious and of secular contributions (accounting for 17 percent (p. IV-32) to 26 percent (p. VI-25) of the variance). Tax consciousness, of course, is basically a factor for those whose incomes are large enough to require itemized deductions. Thiessen reports that in his middle- and upper-income samples, those who say they are influenced by tax considerations give about three times as much as those respondents within the same income bracket who do not claim tax benefits to be a motivation for their contribution. Morgan, Dye, and Hybels (1975, p. 11) said, "relatively few people except at the highest income levels believe that they would give a lot less without the tax advantages of giving." Yet these respondents were willing to believe others were likely to be influenced; and, protestations to the contrary and despite a general lack of knowledge of their own marginal tax rates, the respondents who itemized did tend to give substantially more. Barlow, Brazer, and Morgan (1966, pp. 104–107) reported that for those with incomes under $75,000 who had a large stock portfolio, 5 percent of those with no tax consciousness gave an appreciated asset to charity and 26 percent of those with some tax consciousness did. For those with incomes of $75,000 or more and common stock worth more than $500,000, 62 percent of those with unrealized capital gains gave an appreciated asset to charity. Hawes (1967) reported that thirty persons who made single contributions of $1 million or more in 1965 ranked tax considerations fifth on a list of twelve factors that had influenced them. However, when asked if loss of tax deductibility would affect their giving, they indicated an average reduction of 43 percent would result.

Thiessen (1968) found expecting to benefit in any way (other than tax breaks) from specific contributions to be only a weak predictor of giving. The question concerned specific contributions, but the dependent variables were not amounts or rates of contributions to the specific groups from which one expected to gain personal benefits.

Curti (1958, p. 429) notes, "having spent untold effort in getting rich, having tasted the sweets and boredom of extravagent spending, some, driven by a never-ceasing lust to achieve, turned to philanthropy."

Kirstein (1968) similarly suggested that the self-made man's pride in personal accomplishment gives rise to a desire to establish clear evidence of that success through impressive gifts. One fund raiser quoted by Kirstein claimed it is a rare major gift that is anonymous. Possibly the choice of the recipient of any large donation is determined more by available glory for the donor than by the cause itself.

However, although researchers are often skeptical, we cannot dismiss the possibility that some philanthropy arises out of or is encouraged by genuine desires to do good or because it is an interesting and pleasurable activity (Andrews, 1953; Barlow, Brazer, and Morgan, 1966). According to Andrews (1953), donors who are actually grateful for the opportunity to give are sometimes encountered. Whatever other motives might be important, many large donors do undoubtedly sincerely believe they are altruistic. At the very least, some hope to profit from others' recognition and respect for their altruism (Borsky and Banacki, 1961; Goulden, 1971), a motive that probably should not be regarded as venal as the tax avoidance motive. Ross (1954), as an example, points to younger businessmen and professionals who become active in philanthropic and charitable work because of a desire to become better known and more respected in their communities and thus to advance their careers. Expectation of respect or praise from significant others (parents, relatives, spouse, and friends) toward philanthropy may also be very significant in philanthropy, though research evidence is lacking here. Other sources of general attitudes to philanthropy may be specific experiences with groups that seek funds from the public. These experiences can be positive or, when pressures to contribute are too pressing and too frequent, the net effect can be negative.

Borsky and Banacki (1961) discovered a number of general attitudes related to larger contributions to the United Jewish Appeal. Among them were the beliefs that good Jews must contribute to charity and good Jews must support Israel (some of the UJA's funds go to Israeli organizations). In addition, positive dispositions toward and a general identification with Jewish groups and causes were associated with giving to the UJA. Similarly, Marcus (1973) found that positive attitudes toward the community prompted larger gifts to the United Way.

The work of both Borsky and Banacki (1961) and of Morgan, Dye, and Hybels (1975) point to social desirability tendencies in reporting general attitudes. For example, both groups of researchers observed respondents were much more likely to indicate others were probably affected by tax considerations than were willing to indicate they themselves were. Borsky and Banacki (1961, p. 44) also found respondents were more likely to see others giving to avoid criticism and social pressure and because they feared divine disfavor in this world (a decline in wealth and good fortune) or in the next. As they aptly put it, "Most of the so-called 'selfish motives' are attributed to others but denied for oneself." Finally, regardless of motivation, be it noble or base, some donors have positive attitudes toward philanthropic and giving behavior because they find it pleasurable or satisfying either in itself or through perceived effect (Andrews, 1953; Barlow, Brazer, and Morgan, 1966).

Specific Attitudes Toward Philanthropy. Less social-scientific research has been done on the effect of attitudes toward specific causes on giving behavior than might be expected. Most researchers have been interested in the total amounts given or the rates at which people give rather than why some groups get more or less than others. Specific attitudes are more relevant for the latter question than for the former. Yet, because fund raisers are raising money for specific groups, there are many practical suggestions from observers and practitioners concerning donor attitudes, even though there is little published research. Also, when organizations do study why people contribute to them and what people's attitudes toward them are, the data are usually kept confidential.

Funds are usually donated to groups the giver knows something about and is positively disposed toward and to groups that can effectively claim a genuine need for those funds. Borsky and Banacki (1961) have shown that those who gave the smallest amounts to the United Jewish Appeal had the fewest direct or indirect contacts with the groups the UJA supported. The logic here would seem to be that "sales resistance" is high when it comes to making contributions and that although donors will make token contributions to groups they are unfamiliar with, anything more than such a contribution requires greater familiarity and positive assessments about what is known. This desire for knowledge often arises out of a concern about being "taken" or "fleeced" in the giving process by unworthy and/or unscrupulous potential recipients—the stewardship theme repeating itself here. *Caveat donor* may very well be taken more seriously by Americans than the better known warning, *caveat emptor.*

Positive dispositions toward an organization can be generated and may be reflected in a number of ways. Perceived program efficacy has been found to be positively related to giving in several studies (Andrews, 1953; Borsky and Banacki, 1961; Marcus, 1973; Sills, 1957). For example, Marcus found that United Way givers were more likely than nongivers to believe the United Way did a good job of distributing the money and the social service agencies it supported were providing the most important services to local citizens, thus making the community a good place for a family to live.

Perceived program efficiency also appears to prompt giving behavior. Recurrent exposés of charities with excessive administrative costs probably have raised donor concern about how much of the dollar given actually goes into program activities. Marcus (1973) reported that donors tended to see the United Way as being a more efficient and economical way to help local people; that expenses, salaries, and overhead were reasonable; and that they had enough information on how the money was spent. Borsky and Banacki (1961) noted that, when prompted to cite things they did not like about the United Jewish Appeal, one common complaint concerned administrative expenses. However, on the whole, they found the larger contributors tended to underestimate administrative expenses and smaller contributors tended to overestimate them.

Another spur to philanthropy to specific organizations is that of perceived personal benefit, direct or indirect. Kennedy (1968), for example, in discussing the early years of the American Museum of Natural History, indicates its founders not only had a personal interest in natural history but also saw the museum adding to New York City's prestige. Crawford (1974), in a report prepared for the Filer Commission, suggested a variety of personal benefits that might come through contributions: being able to influence or control the use of donated money, being able to gratify personal tastes, being able to receive something of value in return for the contribution, and being able to ratify and support one's own values.

Attitudes toward the beneficiaries of the group's efforts (Andrews, 1953) may also play an important role in determining decisions to contribute. For example, Auffenberg (1973) noted that "charity briefs" in seventeenth-century England permitted fund drives for any number of good causes; but the most successful briefs tended to be for the aid of foreign Protestant victims of religious persecution. For a contemporary example, witness the outpouring of support for Israel on the part of American Jews during the Yom Kippur War. In a similar vein, Borsky and Banacki (1961) observed that donors expressed pleasure that the United Jewish Appeal helps Jews, assists Israel, and helps local groups. Marcus (1973) also found that the United Way received support because it helps local people. The other side of the coin, noted by Kirstein (1968), is that however good the ultimate cause may seem to be, the perception of that beneficiary as controversial or disreputable may put off potential donors. Similarly, Marcus (1973) suggests that agencies serving "stigmatized" clients (the poor, the aged, and minority groups) tend not to do as well as those serving the general public.

An important correlate of giving behavior is identification with and approval of the group's programs (Barlow, Brazer, and Morgan,

1966; Sills, 1957). As Crawford (1974) noted, personal identification with the group's programs may be prompted by the positive attitudes of significant others and/or by positive prior personal experiences with the group. Borsky and Banacki (1961) also point to the importance for giving behavior of personal and/or familial involvement with the group's activities.

Finally, funds are donated to groups that can effectively claim a genuine need for those funds (Borsky and Banacki, 1961; Marcus, 1973). Emphasis has to be placed on "effectively claim" and on "genuine need." Some groups have in the past received a great deal of money when the need was relatively slight because they could make their claims effectively, and other groups with genuine need have failed to raise funds because they could not press their claims effectively. An interesting example of this is described by Carter (1961) in his study of an ill-fated voluntary health organization of the 1950s named the Common Cold Foundation.

Situational Variables

In addition to general contextual variables, there are characteristics of the immediate situation that influence the potential giver. Although it is at the situational level that both contextual and personal variables have their direct effect, because it is difficult to study the setting of individual voluntary actions and the moments just prior to a charitable act, situational variables have not been adequately studied.

Perhaps the most common aspect of the situation in which most givers find themselves is that they are being asked to give. Contributions are sought by a myriad of groups for a myriad of causes in American society. Spontaneous, unsolicited, freewill offerings do, of course, occur; but the vast majority of groups that depend on philanthropy must systematically and relentlessly mount fund-raising campaigns on an annual basis.

Some groups pursue powerful, massive, public relations and publicity campaigns; and virtually all groups attempt to create a positive climate for their appeals. The campaigns are aimed at making potential donors more knowledgeable about the group, its programs, and activities as well as at raising funds. The campaign's appeal is often carefully orchestrated for maximum impact by illustrating and emphasizing the needs that exist and the group's effectiveness (actual or promised) in meeting them. To the extent the campaign is doing its job, people give and give more generously than they might have originally. In essence, the entire effort is an attempt to create a new situation, an intensified situation, a more favorable situation within which giving decisions may be made.

Although the value of these "stage-setting" efforts appears to be important, what matters most is probably the translation of a general appeal into a personal decision to respond. "Who, *me?*" and "Why *me?*" are the two questions that must be answered effectively if more than a token contribution is to be forthcoming. Three factors appear to be important as answers to those questions: the personal perception of the need, the personal desire to give, and the personal ability to give.

The importance of the individual's perception of the need and of its personal relevance is attested to by virtually all professional fund raisers. Glowing accounts are to be found in their writings of being able to say the right thing at the right time; of being able to tap successfully the personally relevant themes that bring forth positive responses; of being in accord with concerns and dispositions; or articulating desires, dreams, and aspirations; and of reflecting religious and humanistic beliefs and principles.

These themes are also confirmed in the research that has been done on specific organizations (see, for example, Sills, 1957). A desire to give may be prompted by evoking images of the personal, social, community, and societal beliefs of giving. But a significant aspect of the giving situation that is often deliberately created is the "encouragement" of desire by use of personal influence or social pressure creating a context within which image, status, and prestige can be maintained, gained, or lost, depending on the nature of the person's response to the invitation to give. All fund raisers (see, for example, Gamble, 1942, or comments in Long, 1975) agree that personal solicitation by close friends or close associates yields the most substantial contributions; the closer the relationship, the better the results. Mail solicitations come a very distant second. In the personal solicitation, the friend is seen as being able to frame the most effective appeal; but he or she is also able to, through persistence, insist on (or at least strongly recommend) a worthy and appropriate norm for giving in light of the organization's needs, the individual's perceived capacity to give, and the amount typically given by others of similar circumstances and means. Research confirms fund raisers' views about the importance of personal influence (Borsky and Banacki, 1961; Crawford, 1974; Marcus, 1973) and social pressure (Borsky and Banacki, 1961; Crawford, 1974; Johnson, 1968; Long, 1975; Marcus, 1973). Nevertheless, it appears that respondents are reluctant to admit they are or could be influenced or pressured. For example, Long (1975) and Morgan, Dye, and Hybels (1975) found that respondents reported being little influenced by the prospect of the amount of their pledge or contribution being made public. Marcus (1973) and Morgan,

Dye, and Hybels (1975) observed that subjects insisted they made their decisions to give independent of others. Indeed, in Marcus' study, only about one-quarter were even willing to state their decision was influenced by their spouse. At the same time, however, Marcus found givers did experience more pressure to give than nongivers. Nongivers had lower estimates of the average contribution to the United Way and were more likely to say they were not asked, they were unaffected by company expectations that they give, and group pressures at work did not influence them. These results might be accounted for by the donor's tendency to see his or her decision as spontaneous. For example, Borsky and Banacki (1961) found that although those who gave large amounts to the United Jewish Appeal were likely to plan their giving ahead of time, many even in this group reported their decisions to give and how much to give were made spontaneously.

Finally, the individual's understanding of his or her current and near future ability to give (see Andrews, 1953) is yet another situational factor that deserves more attention. Although all but the most destitute could make a token contribution whenever asked, the amount given to any specific group is likely to be a function of one's present financial state and other charitable commitments.

The decision to give may also be influenced by the perception of group norms for giving. As mentioned in the discussion of the impact of income on giving, Lutterman (1962) and Thiessen (1968) found that various religious congregations tend to have norms concerning the appropriate amount to be given for the support of the church. Here, a fixed dollar amount, largely without regard to the donor's income, was common. However, in other studies, such as Borsky and Banacki (1961), the reference group for deciding on the appropriate norm may be those with similar incomes within similar occupations in the community. Borsky and Banacki (1961) found that such reference groups were especially important for those who gave the largest amounts of money to the United Jewish Appeal. In a conflicting finding, Thiessen (1968) reported that in his study dealing with general giving behavior, sensitivity to one's own giving behavior (giving more or less than friends do) was especially keen among the middle-income sample. Although the choice of which reference group the person centers his or her giving decision around and the person's perceptions of what that group's giving norms are may be important factors in the ultimate giving decision, Butners and Buntaine (1973, p. vii), in the overview of their annotated bibliography, caution, "There is little evidence that people actually think of social norms when choosing a course of action. That is, when an individual gives, he may be guided by his first reactions to the stimulus in the situation, and not by a complicated choice among a variety of norms."

Conclusions

The literature reviewed here is far more suggestive than definitive. It is rare to have three or more researchers investigate the same
relationship. Most studies have employed only a few variables and have
been relatively unsophisticated methodologically and statistically.
Thus, virtually all relationships call for considerable investigation and
a substantial number of questions have not yet been explored.

Those few multivariate studies done have sometimes included
variables from the background and personality and/or attitude realms,
but they have not done so in any adequate test of the explanatory-
predictive strength of these different realms. For example, Thiessen
(1968) combined in his analysis of the effects of alienation measures,
background characteristics such as income, number of organizational
memberships, and being an officer of an organization, along with an
index that measures alienation as a personality trait and the general
attitude of feeling a debt to society. However, he never analyzed any of
his realms taken as a whole. Although he does have some personality
and general attitude variables in his data, the measures chosen do not
effectively cover either realm. So little multivariate work has been done
in general that no reliable estimate can be made of the predictive power
of any one of the major realms of independent variables or of the total
variance in giving behavior explainable by these various realms in
combination.

However, several needs suggest themselves:

Because much of our current research knowledge is limited to the
United States, it is culture bound. We need cross-cultural comparative
research to sharpen and refine our understanding.

Multivariate, multirealm studies are also called for. They are a
major hope for understanding the relative importance of various realms
of independent variables (background, personality, general attitudes,
and specific attitudes) and for understanding patterns of influence
among the various independent variables.

Careful, systematic work needs to be done with a variety of specific (in contrast to composite, multifaceted) dependent variables. We
have some evidence that composite measures of giving to religious
causes have different correlates than do composite measures of giving to
secular causes. But there are many kinds of giving within those two
broad categories (such as giving for routine support of the activity or
contributions for special, one-time needs or projects). We need to know
more about whether or how giving varies along this dimension.

Similarly, we ought to learn more about the dynamics of giving
decision points. Is the first contribution made to a group subject to

different influences than more routine contributions made thereafter? Are the factors that influence giving the "regular amount" different from those that play an important role in decisions to give more or less? How are decisions to give less different from decisions to give no longer?

In a society whose members spend a good deal of leisure time watching game shows in which the fortunate contestants win several thousand dollars and perhaps a car, it borders on the incredible that scholars have shown so little interest in that same public giving tens of billions of dollars a year of their own money away to causes they believe in.

In retrospect, one may choose to be saddened by how little we know or stimulated by how much there is to learn. In an era that knows from intimate experience the darker aspects of people's character, it may be encouraging that there is much to learn about people's willingness to share their wealth with others for causes they believe are good.

PART V

Theoretical Models of Informal Social Activity

David Horton Smith

In this concluding Part, I draw together the various threads of research consistency and theoretical development into an integrated whole. In this introduction, I review briefly some evidence of "crisis" and malaise in the social and behavioral sciences that others have perceived, having stated my views at length in the first Part of this volume and elsewhere (Smith, 1979c). This section concludes with a brief discussion of the probable direction of resolution I see and its potential advantages. Chapter Eighteen presents a compact version of the ISSTAL model, followed by a more expanded version, citing argument and, where possible, empirical evidence for the various aspects of the model. Chapter Nineteen performs the same task for the general activity (GA) model variant of the ISSTAL model. The final section of the last chapter presents without elaboration a brief equation that expresses very crudely the nature of the ISSTAL model. This equation sets the stage for the next phase of development of my theoretical formulations, to be dealt with in future works. Finally, in Chapter Twenty, I attempt to present the most important and/or distinctive testable propositions of the ISSTAL model and the GA model and to suggest a variety of lines of needed future research that follow from these formulations.

All is not well in the social and behavioral sciences, if one is to take seriously the conclusions of a variety of knowledgeable members and leaders of this broad scientific community. Sometimes the malaise is manifested by explicit statements of crisis or by flat contradictions between alternative perspectives on the same phenomena. In other cases, I infer the existence of a widespread problem or "crisis" from repeated statements about the need for more research in most areas, from statements about the apparent lack of progress in many important research areas, or from statements about the great need for some kind of integrative theory that will help make sense of a welter of often conflicting findings in well-worked research areas. In the best of situations, there are elaborate models for some kind of phenomenon but little or no testing of these models as wholes and as alternatives. Because I am by training a sociologist and social psychologist, I am most familiar with the statements of crisis in these fields, though I have made some cursory attempts to identify similar indications in political science and economics. I assume a careful search in any of the established social and behavioral sciences would lead to similar indications of crisis, at least in our understanding of individual behavior (and generally also at the level of collective, aggregate, and social system behavior).

Taking sociology first, there have been a notable number of explicit statements of crisis in recent years (Bottomore, 1975; Boudon, 1972; Eisenstadt and Curelaru, 1976; Gouldner, 1970; Ritzer, 1975; Zeitlin, 1973). These authors see the crisis from various perspectives, to be sure, but the root perception in all cases seems to be a kind of irreducible conflict among schools of thought and research perspectives in sociology. Several suggest what is needed is some new paradigm that integrates the major approaches to some degree (for example, Eisenstadt and Curelaru, 1976; Ritzer, 1975; Zeitlin, 1973), although some residual conflict is to be expected and is often healthy for intellectual development of the discipline. Other evidence of crisis comes from the apparent lack of substantial cumulation of knowledge in sociology. This is noted explicitly by Freese (1972) and implicitly by comparison of the more sociological sections of Berelson and Steiner (1964) or more purely sociological reviews like Merton, Broom, and Cottrell (1959) or Faris (1964), dating from fifteen to twenty years ago, with the contents of the recently begun Annual Review of Sociology *(Inkeles, Coleman, and Smelser, 1975, 1976, 1977; Turner, Coleman, and Fox, 1978). Many more things are being studied now than fifteen or twenty years ago, let alone than thirty or forty years ago. Yet in virtually every field of study there is a sense of numerous and often conflicting facts, conflicting research orientations, and few or no empirically grounded integrative theories worthy of this label. As DiRenzo (1966) notes, part of the problem is the widespread lack of clarity and specification in sociology and most of the other social and behavioral sciences (see also Homans, 1967).*

Turning to social psychology and the study of personality (two related and often difficult to separate fields of psychology), the picture is similar. There are again a number of explicit statements of crisis in these fields (Byrne, 1971; Elms, 1975; Hathaway, 1972; Neel, 1977; Petrinovich, 1979; Phares and Lamiell, 1977; Sechrest, 1976; Silverman, 1976). Again there are references to the lack of cumulation of research, to the continuing contradictions in much research, and to the need for some resolution of the viewpoints of competing schools of thought and research perspectives. The very presence of "schools of thought" suggests, according to T. Kuhn (1963), that the field of study is in a preparadigmatic or even prescientific phase of development. The continuation of competition among schools of thought here can be seen by examining the similarities of these schools over time (Deutsch and Krauss, 1965; Hall and Lindzey, 1957, 1970, 1978; Lindzey and Aronson, 1968–1969; Neel, 1977; Woodworth, 1948). The lack of direction and theoretical synthesis has been well stated by Byrne (1971, p. 15): "This random fact-finding has been summarized by psychoanalyst Leslie Shaffer as embodying the wisdom of an ancient Patagonian proverb, 'He who collects enough chamberpots will one day come to possess the Holy Grail.'" It has also been said that "One thousand studies do not a theory make." All of which leads me to agree with Hall and Lindzey (1978, p. 15) who state explicitly that, if one uses the perspective of T. Kuhn (1964), then personality theory—a kind of general theory of behavior—is in the preparadigmatic stage of development. So, too, is social psychology, I would argue.

The situation is no better in the other social and behavioral sciences, however. For instance, in comparing the state of knowledge about political participation in 1965 and a dozen years later, Milbrath and Goel (1977) find remarkable stability in the conclusions reached. And yet at neither time is there more than suggestive evidence for any empirically grounded comprehensive model, let alone full-fledged theory of individual political participation. In the realm of economic behavior, K. Smith's (1962, pp. 1–4) conclusion still seems relevant, namely, that the usual economic analysis is flawed not only because it inadequately understands human behavior but also because it misunderstands fundamental human needs. It similarly fails, in his view, to understand and specify meaningfully the complex motivational dynamics of everyday behavior patterns. And even though, as a result of growing interest in "micro-micro economies," there are today several quite complex and comprehensive models for individual consumer behavior, these models are essentially untested in a comparative manner (pitting one against the other in examining the same data set with appropriate methodology) and in some cases little tested even by themselves (Schiffman and Kanuk, 1978, p. 455). Interdisciplinary social science fields, such as the study of leisure (Brown, Dyer, and Whaley, 1973), or suicide (Lester, 1972), lead to similar conclusions regarding inadequate integrative theoretical perspectives of a compelling sort.

Human behavior is clearly far more complex in nature than are the phenomena of the biological and physical sciences (see Smith, 1980). The number of relevant variables affecting human behavior is vastly greater than the number affecting most, if not all, biological and physical processes and events, and our objects of study, human beings, have a far more complex response or action repertory and are more affected by the process of being studied than are the objects and processes studied by the biological and physical sciences, generally. But this greater complexity does not necessarily rule out the possibility of eventually developing a truly precise science of human behavior. As Richard D. Reddy said to me, we must test the limits for a truly precise science of human behavior rather than assuming them at the outset. To do so, however, will require substantial improvements in the most common methodological approaches of the social and behavioral sciences. There is enough evidence now regarding the frequent systematic biases and random ("noise"-producing) errors inherent in both laboratory and field research as performed in the social and behavioral sciences to make it clear that better data-collection methodology is imperative (Friedman, 1967; Naroll and Cohen, 1973; Phillips, 1971; Rosenthal and Rosnow, 1969; Silverman, 1976; Webb and others, 1966). And avoidance of use of "primary data" in favor of use of "secondary data" routinely collected by various administrative agencies is no solution, as the extensive controversy over statistical data on deviance illustrates (see Gibbs and Erickson, 1975), though aggregate gross income or unemployment figures can be as readily criticized. I suggest the most pandemic methodological problems, as discussed at length in Chapters One and Two, are the extreme paucity of adequate longitudinal and time budget research data (though the many more general problems discussed nearly two decades ago by Nagel, 1961, still hamper the human sciences), and the narrowness of the range of predictor and dependent variables commonly used. Financial support for large, complex, lengthy projects utilizing a synanthrometric approach is crucial if human sciences are to make optimal progress—just as very expensive equipment and facilities have been crucial to major progress in the physical and biological sciences when they reached a certain stage of intellectual development.

The crisis, if it should indeed be termed such, is neither solely theoretical-conceptual nor solely methodological. The fundamental problem is both theoretical and methodological. Ritzer (1975) has shown how major schools of thought or perspectives within sociology are conventionally linked with a particular methodological approach. Similar analyses could be made of the major schools of thought or perspectives in the other social and behavioral sciences. In none of these disciplines has a particular perspective come to be dominant. In terms of T. Kuhn's (1964, p. 4) analysis of the intellectual and social history of modern science, "the early developmental stages of most sciences have been characterized by continual competition between a number of distinct views of nature, each partially derived from, and all roughly compatible with, the dictates of scientific observation and method." The differentiating features of the various perspectives were their incompatible world views and ways of doing science. In this "preparadigmatic" stage of science, T. Kuhn (1964, p. 15) argues, "all of the facts that could possibly pertain to the development of a given science are likely to seem equally relevant. As a result, early fact-gathering is a far more nearly random activity than the one that subsequent scientific development makes familiar." Kuhn's characterizations are striking because they seem to echo so clearly what is being said at present by a number of astute social and behavioral scientists about their own disciplines.

Kuhn has been taken to task for the multiple uses he made in his classic work of the term "paradigm." Masterman (1970), for instance, distinguishes three separate uses of the term by Kuhn: metaphysical (or world view) paradigms, which involve an entire world view in regard to some set of phenomena; sociological paradigms, involving a widely recognized scientific achievement held up for emulation and admiration within a discipline or field; and construct or artifact paradigms, which consist of problem-solving devices or methods for the study of some phenomena. In discussing this and other criticisms of Kuhn, Crane (1972, p. 30) concludes that the growth of scientific knowledge in a field or discipline is stimulated by both paradigms as world views or perspectives and paradigms as problem-solving devices. She suggests large numbers of fields and entire disciplines can share the former; but the latter tend to be more confined to particular fields or research areas. Insofar as social and behavioral science disciplines lack paradigms, it is in the first sense distinguished by Masterman. There are many paradigms in the sense of problem-solving devices or approaches; and, indeed, these differentiate the various schools of thought that are so common (and conflicting or contentious) in the social and behavioral sciences. When the individual scientist can take a fundamental world view type of paradigm for granted in his or her discipline, according to

T. Kuhn (1964, pp. 19–20), it is no longer necessary in major works to attempt to build the field anew, "starting from first principles and justifying the use of each concept introduced. That can be left to the writer of textbooks." Kuhn goes on to argue, "Today in the sciences, books are usually either texts or retrospective reflections upon one aspect or another of the scientific life. The scientist who writes one is more likely to find his professional reputation impaired than enhanced. Only in the earlier, preparadigm, stages of the development of the various sciences did the book ordinarily possess the same relation to professional achievement that it still retains in other creative fields." Though articles and papers are increasingly important, books and monographs are still vital, so that once again, Kuhn's observations seem to fit well with characterizing the human sciences as essentially preparadigmatic at the level of integrative world views. Such observations also help to explain why I have written at such length in Parts One and Five.

These disciplines indeed have their problem-solving paradigms of one sort or another, but each of these paradigms in the narrowest sense gives only a partial perspective on the phenomena of interest. And what is worse, the schools of thought or "theory groups" (to use Mullins and Mullins', 1973, terminology) generally tend either to ignore or attack each other rather than seeking some broader integrative synthesis (see Crane, 1972, chap. 5; Krantz, 1969; Ritzer, 1975). This situation is the most fundamental crisis that faces the human sciences today. It is a crisis of fragmentation of research and theoretical perspectives in these disciplines, described aptly for science in general by Oppenheimer (1958). The roots of this fragmentation lie in the compartmentalization and reward structures of the human sciences, as discussed in Parts One and Five of this volume. But if fragmentation is the basic underlying problem, then efforts toward synthesis both within and across the social and behavioral sciences must be a major part of the solution, however imperfect these attempts may be and however much they may be resisted (Smith, 1979c).

A mapping of relevant variables or development of an accounting scheme seems to be a reasonable step toward broad synthesis, as M. Smith (1968) and others have pointed out. One value of this approach is that, even though the precise nature of the interrelationships among the variables may be unclear, use of a mapping model will make it more likely that the interested and persistent researcher, using appropriate techniques, will be able to explain to a more substantial degree the phenomena studied than if narrower, less comprehensive research perspectives are used. Effective integrative syntheses not only induce inclusion of more of the relevant variables in research but also have a variety of other virtues: They can help to summarize and make sense of prior research in their domain of focus; they can help to resolve apparently opposing or competing schools of thought and theoretical approaches; they can suggest directions of future research that will lead to rapid qualitative progress in scientific knowledge where stagnation or slow growth has been common; they can stimulate greater quantities of research in their domain of focus by attracting new attention to and providing new perspectives on old questions and phenomena; they can bring greater precision of understanding and explanation to the domain of inquiry; they can highlight the crucial questions that most need research or theoretical attention in order to advance knowledge further; they can have practical and policy implications that are far clearer and more important than great masses of fragmentary, unsynthesized research; they can serve as a standard for judging more wisely the relative importance of different lines of research, past or future; and they can stimulate other scientists to theoretical elaborations and alternatives that might well otherwise not have been pursued.

I do not claim that the ISSTAL model and general activity model, as parts of the integrative synthesis I am calling "synanthrometrics," will perform all of the foregoing. I hope they will, but only time will tell, and much more work remains to be done in theory and model elaboration, testing, and refinement. The magnitude of the task I have undertaken is great, perhaps more than my own powers can handle. What I present in the subsequent two chapters is a first attempt at the kind of integrative synthesis or synanthrometric theory that I believe is needed and that will be effective in the senses just mentioned. As J. Miller MacPherson, a colleague who read an earlier draft of Part Five, commented, these chapters tend to circle around the central problems, skirmishing with them, rather than dealing with them by a direct frontal attack that resolves them once and for all. He added that existing research does not yet permit the latter approach. I agree on both counts. And I think the skirmishes (if only sketchy outlines now) are a necessary prelude to the frontal attack (in the form of a fully developed theory) that will, it is to be hoped, follow in not too many years. I offer in Chapter Twenty a fairly extensive set of suggestions for undertaking future theorizing and research that will move us closer to launching that frontal attack successfully. The ISSTAL and GA models can and should be pushed as far as possible in the directions suggested there, particularly by testing further and elaborating the major propositions of these models.

CHAPTER 18

ISSTAL Model

David Horton Smith

In essence, the ISSTAL model is a codification of the kinds of variables that need to be taken simultaneously into account when attempting a comprehensive and interdisciplinary explanation of individual human discretionary behavior. By extension beyond the research literature previously reviewed, the ISSTAL model can also be viewed as a proposed model for the explanation of *all* conscious individual behavior, both conforming and deviant, though such extension is not considered in this volume. In its present form, the model is intended to be a kind of world view paradigm for the social and behavioral sciences, not a formal, axiomatized, and mathematicized theory. It is a theoretical orientation and research perspective, a type of conceptual formulation that Bunge (1972) would term a natural or semiformalized theory. As such, the model possesses only some of the crucial elements of a fully developed theory as distinguished by Hage (1972, p. 173), namely, concept names, verbal statements, some theoretical definitions, some operational definitions, and some theoretical linkages and operational linkages. Hence, it lacks completeness in terms of several of the forgoing elements and presently makes no attempt to provide an ordering into primitive and defined terms or to provide an ordering into premises and equations, as demanded by a complete theory. In conjunction with the material on the model presented in Part One, this chapter presents both background

assumptions about the domain of inquiry and some explicitly formulated assumptions or postulations (see Gouldner, 1970, p. 29, regarding
"background assumptions"), so the context out of which the model
emerges can be seen. And in terms of Mullins' (1974) discussion of the
four types of properties of relationships in a theory, the model makes
some clear statements of association and asymmetry but only weak quan-
tification statements in terms of signs (directions of relationship) rather
than precise degree of effect. And it ignores, for the present, explicit
statements of interdependence through multiple causation, though
suggesting the existence of such relationships as a necessary part of the
further elaboration of the model.

Brief Version

The following set of abstract propositions is a compact and
highly simplified statement of the ISSTAL model content:

1. Human individual discretionary behavior can be adequately understood (explained and predicted with great precision and consistency
   using a dynamic, time process model) only by utilizing a comprehensive interdisciplinary set of predictor state and process variables;
   although one can study and explain small segments or specific types
   of behavior, this can be done adequately only in the larger synanthrometric theoretical context because otherwise the effects of crucial and
   potentially confounding variables will be ignored, leading to spurious results.
2. Such understanding requires an interdisciplinary and comprehensive
   view of the states and processes within and the relationships between
   psychological systems, the human physiological system, and major
   features of the external context or environment of the individual, even
   when narrow goals of research or theory are sought.
3. The most appropriate dependent variable unit of behavior for such
   understanding is behavior in situation or behavior in role (combined
   as behavior in situation/role), viewing any such behavior in situa-
   tion/role unit as having potentially six successive time phases, each
   of which may be differently related with the predictor state and process variables; failure to distinguish these different phases leads to
   conflicting empirical results.
4. Full understanding of any individual behavior requires viewing it in
   an individual life span perspective as part of an ongoing hourly and
   daily stream of behavior units with corresponding continual changes
   in both state and process variables, leading generally through humanization and social control processes to conformity but sometimes
   to deviance.

5. The independent and dependent variables that must be taken into account for such understanding even in narrowly defined research contexts manifest an important asymmetry termed "sequential specificity," a pattern that is to be found in the ordering of the independent variables in terms of their behavior unit generality and long-term time sequence, as well as in their differential relationships with the short-term potential time phases of a behavior unit.

6. Additional patterns of consistent relationships are probable among the variables of the model previously indicated, including patterns of common direction in independent-dependent variable relationships, patterns of relative strength of such relationships, and patterns of paradoxical and difficult to accept intrinsic, fundamental duality of relationships among variables. ("Intrinsic, fundamental duality" refers here to a situation or configuration of phenomena where apparently paradoxical features of the same phenomenon are simultaneously present in reality, as in the well known wave-particle duality of electromagnetic radiation in quantum physics.)

7. Mathematical representations of the forgoing will be fruitful in terms of both discrete and continuous dynamic formulations (that is, both in terms of stochastic process finite mathematics and in terms of deterministic mathematics such as structural equal models or simultaneous differential equation systems). This fact is a social and behavioral science analogue of the particle-wave duality of quantum mechanics.

8. For the understanding of nondeviant and socioculturally preferred (valued) discretionary individual human behavior, a general activity model variant of the more general ISSTAL model will be found as an underlying pattern of consistent relationships among the forgoing variables, coexisting with major and minor variants of this pattern. These facts also will constitute intrinsic, fundamental duality in the nature of human individual behavior.

Expanded Version and Evidence

The ISSTAL model can also be stated in a more developed and elaborated form, indicating either the theoretical or empirical justification or both for each of its major points as well as making them more specific and concrete where possible. Space limitations necessitate giving only a rough outline of many of the major theoretical justifications and merely citing the empirical support for various points rather than discussing them in adequate depth. In some instances, I do little more than refer to future work developing the ISSTAL model further when attempting to justify the inclusion of a particular point. Hence, all of my propositions here can be viewed essentially as hypotheses, some having much greater degrees of existing confirmation and testing than others that have been essentially untested or poorly tested. Nonetheless, there has been evidence in the preceding chapters and their references for most key points of the model. In the more expanded version of the ISSTAL model that follows, I use letters to represent the major propositions, presenting them in the same order as in the brief version just given. In the process of elaboration, however, there is a more than threefold expansion in the number of propositions. I make no attempt to specify explicitly which of these are primary postulates and which are derivative, although this will sometimes be obvious. Such differentiation must await future axiomatization and mathematization of the model.

A. Human individual discretionary behavior can be adequately understood only in the context of a highly interdisciplinary model drawing on all the social and behavioral sciences (hereinafter termed "the human sciences"). Discipline-bound models and problem-solving paradigms have not been adequate to the task, because they ignore variables crucial to the dynamics of behavior and hence generally produce misleading or weak results. Indeed, the sense of crisis or malaise in the various social and behavioral science disciplines and their subfields can be directly traced, in the views of many "human scientists" (using this label as synonymous with "social and behavioral scientists"), to the lack of even adequate problem-solving paradigms, let alone integrative world view paradigms, that will synthesize the warring, or ignoring but competing, conceptual perspectives and research traditions within these disciplines. The Introduction to Part Five cites evidence supporting this point, as do some of the earlier chapters (such as Chapter Eight). But there have also been numerous attempts over the past few decades to push for or present versions of interdisciplinary synthesis in the human sciences, and these constitute even more compelling evidence for the present proposition (for example, Anderson and Carter, 1974; Buckley, 1968; Campbell, 1969; A. Kuhn, 1963; Laszlo, 1972; March, 1970; Sherif and Sherif, 1969; Sutherland, 1973), attempts to dismiss them as futile notwithstanding (Lilienfeld, 1978). Lodahl and Gordon's (1972) survey of over a thousand scientists from the social and physical sciences adds further support, with its finding that the human sciences are viewed by both their own members and other scientists as having consistently lower degrees of consensus on paradigms ("laws, theory, and methodology"). I could cite much further evidence of pleas for and attempts to provide interdisciplinary syntheses because they are believed to be necessary, but the forgoing is sufficient to support my general proposition.

This first proposition does not deny the value of research or theory that focuses primarily on some small portion of the larger enterprise of explaining human behavior in general, especially discretionary behavior. There is nothing intrinsically trivial or worthless about research that investigates the nature of relationships among a handful of variables without even attempting to account for the full range of variance of the behavior being studied. If such narrowly focused research is to make a contribution to the real growth of knowledge, it is essential that the study somehow take adequate account of the large number of variables, variable subtypes, and variable types of the ISSTAL model that are *not* of primary interest in the given study but are crucial to understanding behavior dynamics. If the ISSTAL model is basically correct in the present proposition, failure to take account of this larger theoretical context of important variables even in studies with narrow research aims will lead generally to weak results that are misleading, spurious and inconsistent across apparently similar studies because of inadequate understanding of behavior dynamics.

Such a failure to take account of the larger theoretical context in human science research is analogous to an early physicist attempting to study the acceleration of falling objects of different kinds without taking into account the crucial variables of air resistance and the density and flow of matter in the medium through which the objects of study must fall. In retrospect, we can readily see the folly of those early physicists (though they did not call themselves such), but in terms of the theoretical world view paradigm they were operating with, if any, these unmeasured variables were largely irrelevant. Given a more adequate world view paradigm for the study of "mechanics" or the motion of objects, no physicist today would begin to study even a minor aspect of "mechanics" without taking account of air (or more broadly, medium) resistance and the density and flow of the medium. Many, if not most, human scientists today are making errors of omission in unmeasured variables and variable types and subtypes that are as gross as the example just given.

Thus, an essential aspect of the first ISSTAL model proposition is that most human scientists doing research today and in the past cannot possibly contribute much to the real growth of knowledge because of the very nature of their discipline-bound research paradigms. The boundaries of disciplines and of even subfield compartmentalization overlap with the boundaries of important types and subtypes of ISSTAL model variables; otherwise it would not be so important and so limiting. Behavior dynamics cannot be understood because important variable types and subtypes are neither measured nor controlled for by sampling and if noticed at all by most researchers are dismissed as irrelevant to their narrowly defined and discipline-bound, often subfield-bound, task in a given study. Only by taking seriously to a significant degree the larger, synanthrometric, interdisciplinary and dynamic time process perspective suggested by the ISSTAL model can worthwhile research generally result, even when other aspects of methodology are adequate and the principal focus is on a narrowly defined research topic dealing with individual discretionary behavior rather than on maximizing explained variance for that behavior.

B. An adequately interdisciplinary synthesis must include at least the following major types and subtypes of predictor "state" variables: (1) external contextual factors (with such major subtypes as biophysical environmental factors, human population factors, cultural factors, and social-structural factors); (2) individual social background and social role factors (with such major subtypes as physical and physiological characteristics, ascribed social positions and roles, achieved social positions and roles, experience and activity history, and possessions, resources, and access to resources); (3) personality and intellectual capacity factors (with a wide range here of content, process, and structure subtypes included); (4) attitudinal dispositions (with values, general and specific attitudes, expectations, and intentions as subtypes); (5) retained information (with images, beliefs, knowledge, and plans as subtypes); and (6) situational variables (with definition of the situation and immediate awareness as subtypes). All of these will be representatively associated with individual behavior as classes and subtypes (that is, without every variable of every class and subtype being involved) to a statistically significant degree, and in special cases any single variable type or subtype can override the effects of all others. These associations will be at times direct and at times indirect, mediated by other variables included in the total set indicated. Assigning relative weights and even directions to variables in relationships is a task that requires additional research. The more detailed, specific content of the various classes and subtypes of variables previously noted is presented in Chapter One. But, even there, space limitations prohibited indicating specific operational measures for the variables, though in most cases these kinds of measures are sufficiently well known to need no such specification in this volume. All of these are essentially "state-variables," rather than "process-variables," in the sense that they are viewed as having meaningful effects and measurements at a given time. Process variables, by contrast, necessarily deal with events taking place over several points in time and can be measured meaningfully and understood only over a period of time. Process variables transform state variables.

A major source of evidence for the necessity of these classes and subtypes of variables in an adequate interdisciplinary model is the fact that, when examined with appropriate methodology in research reviewed in the preceding chapters, they have generally shown themselves to have significant associations with one or more (usually several) types of informal discretionary participation. For the sake of brevity, I shall present a selective version of evidence bearing on this proposition of the ISSTAL model. Table 1 presents in simple form one or two examples of variables from each of the six major classes of explanatory variables mentioned as (statistically) significant for the explanation of each of the major types of informal social participation reviewed earlier in this volume. In a few cases, where the earlier chapter failed to mention a particular type of variable as significant but where some other major literature review does mention it, the variable is included in the table as if it had been mentioned, for the sake of intellectual closure. The additional sources so used are indicated at the bottom of Table 1. The particular subtype of variable selected from each of the six major classes reflects roughly the frequency of attention given by social and behavioral scientists to the various subtypes within a major class, if they pay attention to the class at all. Thus, most common subtypes are presented.

Table 1 shows clearly that, without exception, one or more variable subtypes in each of the six major variable classes has been found to be significantly related (in statistical terms) to each of the major types of informal social participation reviewed in this volume. This gives one broad kind of confirmation to the ISSTAL model, but it is only a first step. Perforce it covers only a small proportion of the total set of variables. A more detailed examination of each subtype of the six major classes of explanatory variables against each type of informal social participation reviewed further confirms the impression table 1 conveys. In spite of the fact that several variable subtypes have received little or no adequate research attention in relation to most types of informal discretionary participation (that is, cultural variables, human population variables, nature of the nonhuman natural and artifactual environment, health and physiological factors, life cycle stage variables other than age and marital status, intellectual capacities, values, expectations, intentions, and all subtypes of information variables), when examined with anything approaching adequate methodology, all variable subtypes the ISSTAL model distinguishes show a preponderant tendency to have significant relationships with each type of informal social participation.

The gaps in research are so great for some of the subtypes noted that only one or two participation types have been examined in a few instances (for example, intentions, human population variables, nature of the nonhuman environment, family size and children's ages, and images). Hence, more research is needed before the relevance of all explanatory variable subtypes can be tested for all types of informal social participation. Yet the showing of the ISSTAL model so far, at least on this first simple test of utility, is strong. In the majority of cases,

Table 1. Selective Indication of Statistically Significant Variables from Six Major Classes as Positive Correlates of Various Types of Informal Social Participation

Types of Behavior and Participation

	PP Political Participation	UPP Unconventional Political Participation	CP Citizen Participation	URP Unconventional Religious Participation	MMP Mass Media Participation	ORP Outdoor Recreation Participation	AB Altruistic Behavior	GB Giving Behavior	DHB Disaster Helping Behavior
Class One: Social and historical context. *Example:* Social structure of context of individual	Multiparty system; parliamentary democracy	Rapid social change; local of government regime illegitimacy; moderate degree of government reaction to dissent	High degree of government support for CP; presence of worker management schemes	Structural modernity of society; financial problems of established churches	High degree of press & broadcast freedom; high development of MM sources in society	Technological advances relating to ORP; societal role differentiation in leisure realm	High parental role norms for AB socialization; low org. of society & roles for formal AB	Favorable tax laws re: GB; low degree of government philanthropy. Welfare state benefits for needy & disadvantaged	High degree of predisaster formal org. prepared for disasters; ability of local auths. & orgs. to use informal DHB effectively
Class Two: Social background variables									
Example: Education of individual	High	High	High	Above average	High	High	High	High	High
Example: Age of individual	Middle years	Young adult	Middle years	Young adult	Middle & older years	Youth	Middle years	Middle years	Young adult
Class Three: Personality and intellectual	High ego strength;	High personal	High personal	High introversion; low need for	High in need for	High extraversion;	High trust in people	High trust; high opti-	High empathy

capacities *Example:* **Key personality traits of individual**	high socia-bility/extra-version	efficacy	efficacy	ego strength	achievement	high per-sonal efficacy			mism
Class Four: **Attitudinal variables** *Example:* **General attitudes toward realm of participation by individual**	High politi-cal efficacy; high identi-fication with own politi-cal party	High dis-trust of political auths.; high political efficacy	High inter-est in neighb. problems; high politi-cal efficacy	High disil-lusion with world & established religion; felt social iso-lation	High trust in media; preference for multiple sources of info. on topics of interest	High OR & sports inter-est; positive attitude to given ac-tivities	High moral attitudes toward help-ing others	High posi-tive attitude to charity groups; felt moral obli-gation to give	High posi-tive attitude to commu-nity; less subjective sense of rela-tive depri-vation
Class Five: **Retained information** *Example:* **Relevant in-formation known by individual**	High level of political information re: leaders	High knowl-edge of techs. of political action & in-dividual protest	High under-standing of specific is-sues of CP area	High knowl-edge that established R faiths/be-liefs are false or in-adequate	High knowl-edge of where to get needed in-formation from MM	High knowl-edge of sports/OR figures & sites for per-sonal in-volvement	High knowl-edge of need for AB at present	High knowl-edge of group & how it spends GB money	High aware-ness that others accept GB moral stan-dards re-quired for DHB
Class Six: **Situational variables** *Example:* **Definition of situation by individual**	Solicitation by person on phone or in person in situation	High envi-ronment cues for vio-lence & aggression in situation	(Asked to join CP board per-sonally in situation)	Active social pressure from others in situation to get in-volved	Felt bore-dom or bad feelings in situation	Felt free time and perceived opportunity for S/ORP in situation	Perceived pressure of AB model in situation	Convinced of genuine need for GB and money in situation	Less per-ceived loss by self in situation
Additional Sources:	Milbrath & Goel, 1977.						Krebs, 1970; Latané & Darley, 1970; Staub, 1978.		Barton, 1969.

where someone bothers to examine the possible relevance of one of the main variable classes or any of its subtypes to any specific kind of informal social participation, some significant relationships are found. In many cases, results are mixed, according to which variable falling into a subtype is examined; and there are variations from study to study in the significance of a given variable within a subtype, according to differences in samples and other aspects of methodology and analysis.

The literature reviews of this volume can be further supplemented, seeking additional testing of the ISSTAL model, by other sources. In part, this is necessary to round out the set of types of informal social participation. For instance, the category of informal interpersonal relations, upon which we had intended to have a review chapter, is second only to mass media use in its absorption of individual free time and hence as informal discretionary participation. Robinson's (1977) national time budget survey data indicate the relevance of the ISSTAL model in this realm of activity. From the data in his Tables 2.2, 5.2, and 5.5, it is clear that there are significant relationships for some subtypes of variables from each of the five major classes of variables examined to some degree in the data (no data being present on information variables). These same survey data also indicate the relevance of the ISSTAL model to such other types of informal discretionary activity as study, religion, entertainment, cultural events, and resting. Other sources, such as Johnstone and Rivera (1965) and Smith (1979a), further support the relevance of some variable classes and subtypes to participation in adult education and to conventional church attendance, respectively. The latter review is a necessary supplement to Chapter Ten, which focuses upon participation in sects and cults—nontraditional religious participation—rather than upon conventional church attendance and related church organizational activity. Both additional sources just noted indicate the relevance of the information class of variables, not present in the Robinson (1977) survey data. Finally, the second part of Smith, Reddy, and Baldwin (1972b) and Smith (1975) further confirm the significance of the ISSTAL model variable classes and most of their subtypes for voluntary association participation.

At this point it is appropriate to ask whether there is similar evidence for the relevance and significance of the ISSTAL model in nondiscretionary realms of individual behavior. The answer here is again affirmative. Robinson (1977) thus shows the significance of five of the major variable classes to a variety of nondiscretionary activity types in his national time budget data. Other studies (often national sample surveys) and literature reviews present similar evidence for several or sometimes all six main classes of predictor variables of the model, though very rarely for all subtypes as well. Examples of such supportive material include Ritchey (1976) on migration; Mann (1973), Pierson (1973), Pred (1967), and Rossi (1955) on residential moving; Fried, Havens, and Thrall (1977) on travel behavior from one's residence; Bollman, Moxley, and Elliott (1975), Dutton (1978), Foley (1950), Kelly and Schieber (1972), and Michelson (1971) on use of community facilities, including health facilities; Britt (1966), Engel, Kollat, and Blackwell (1973), Howard and Sheth (1969), Nicosia (1966), Schiffman and Kanuk (1978), Sheth (1974), and Zaltman, Pinson, and Angelman (1973) on consumer buying and decision making. The latter set of models is particularly striking in its inclusion of all major predictor variable classes of the ISSTAL model with virtually all the subtypes of variables as well.

The literatures on educational attainment, occupational selection, and mate selection are very extensive; but there, too, one generally finds represented the six major variable classes and their subtypes (see the references in Spenner and Featherman, 1978; Weiss, 1975; Winch, 1958). Finally, even the literature on social deviance, crime, delinquency, suicide, accidents, mental illness, and the sick role suggests the relevance of the full range of variables of the ISSTAL model, though as usual they are seldom if ever included simultaneously in the same study (see Dohrenwend and Dohrenwend, 1974; Douglas, 1967; Iskrant and Joliet, 1968; Langner and Michael, 1963; Lemert, 1972; Lester, 1972; Levine and Kozloff, 1978; Malikin, 1973; Matza, 1969; Resnick, 1968; Scott and Douglas, 1972; Suchman, 1970; Sutherland and Cressey, 1970; Wolfgang, Figlio, and Sellin, 1972). Several prior models for individual behavior of a particular type (for instance, Allport, 1954; Campbell and others, 1960) or in general (Fishbein and Ajzen, 1975, for example) also confirm the ISSTAL model, by being essentially incorporated in it, though I shall postpone a discussion of them until a later volume.

C. If, as I suggest, only a model of individual human behavior that seeks to understand dynamics and essentially takes account of all the predictor variable classes and subtypes just distinguished will be adequate, assuming also adequate treatment of dependent variables and other methodology, then it follows that human science research that fails to take adequate account of the six main classes of predictor variables and their subtypes (presented in detail in Chapter Two) will not explain very much of the variance in human individual discretionary behavior. Because of the inadequacy of most human science research on individual behavior, proportional reduction of error variance (PRE) measures of the explanatory power of the variables included in a given study are seldom used. If they are used, they generally show low to moderate proportions of variance explained, correcting for degrees of statistical freedom, except when the particular behavior being studied is special by virtue of being powerfully affected by a single type of variable and that type is included in the study (for example, powerful effects of a social norm) or, alternatively, when an appropriately wide range of classes and subtypes of explanatory variables is included. Hence, much of social science research is of only marginal utility in understanding the complexities of individual behavior because it fails to take account of (by sampling, statistical control, or use as a variable) or have an adequate representation of the major realms of variables.

Although I have not yet performed the content analysis to demonstrate this proposition systematically (and hence it is still a major hypothesis), the research on individual behavior, especially discretionary behavior of individuals treating individual (rather than aggregate) behavior units as dependent variables, rather consistently confirms my contention, on the whole. In the previous literature review chapters, it is notable that the research reviewed rarely indicates the amount of variance in individual behavior accounted for. When there is such indication, either explicitly in the review or implicitly in the documents being reviewed, the amount of variance accounted for is almost invariably only low to moderate, seldom over 30 to 40 percent and usually no more than 10 to 20 percent. The very fact that most of the review chapters had little or nothing to present in the way of data on proportional reduction of error variance indicates this perspective on the kind of discretionary behavior research being reviewed was a rare one. Yet in those rare instances when multiple classes of explanatory variables are taken into account in a multivariate analysis procedure, the results show consistently better and often strikingly better reduction of error variance (that is, better explanation-prediction of discretionary behavior). Space prohibits a detailed review, but Knoke (1974) is a good example of my point. He notes the research literature on voting has generally been split into two relatively separate traditions, the sociological (using what are mainly social background variables of the ISSTAL model) and the psychological (using mainly attitudinal variables, general and specific, in our terms). When the two classes of variables are combined in the appropriate temporal-causal order, first social background and then psychological variables (like party identification, issue orientations, and candidate evaluation), just over 50 percent of the variance is accounted for. Here the psychological variables add two-thirds or more of the total after social background variables have been taken into account in attempting to predict a dependent variable that ranges from voted (in the 1964 or 1968 presidential elections, analyzed separately with national sample data) for the Democratic candidate, did not vote but preferred the Democrat, did not vote and has no preference or voted for other candidates, did not vote but preferred the Republican candidate, and voted for the Republican candidate. Earlier work by Campbell and others (1960) similarly supports my point. For a different type of political participation, volunteer time working with a health planning council, Parkum (1973) found similar results—greater variance accounted for when both social background and another class of variables was used (in this case, information or cognitive variables).

In the studies of altruistic, helping, and giving behavior, multivariate analyses with more than one class of variables represented have been extremely rare. The study by Thiessen (1968) is almost unique in this regard. He combines in his analysis measures of social background characteristics, the personality characteristic of alienation, and the general attitudes of "debt toward society" and "tax consciousness" (awareness of tax implications and positive attitude toward the effect of giving on one's taxes) in his study of giving behavior. Although he does not perform analyses with all the variables in each of the three major classes included, first separately and then in full combination, his analyses are nonetheless highly indicative that the combination of the three classes of variables he dealt with would explain significantly more of the variance in combination than could be explained by any one separately.

In the area of expressive leisure, there are again very few multivariate analyses that attempt to represent adequately more than one class of the explanatory factors identified by the ISSTAL model. Part of the problem, from the present perspective, is that contemporary researchers studying religion, for instance, are inclined to view certain types of religious behavior (for example, church attendance, church-related organizational participation, private prayer and devotional behavior, or friendship activities with other members of the congregation) as dependent variables along with religious orthodoxy, which is part of the class of information variables in terms of this model. Thus, religious belief measures are seldom included as predictor variables for religious behavior. Nonetheless, it is clear from the few studies that do perform some multivariate analyses including variables from more than one explanatory variable class that the variance explained when multiple classes (or representative variables from them) are used is significantly greater than when only a single class is used. For example, Roof (1976) shows that 30 percent of the variance in church attendance can be accounted for by education (a social background variable) and local community reference (an attitude index), essentially. If he had added religious orthodoxy (a belief or knowledge type of information variable) to the analysis as an independent variable, it is likely the variance explained would have been still greater, given the latter variable's zero-order correlation with church attendance. In another realm of expressive leisure participation, several studies I reviewed in Chapter Eight show

clearly that the adequate representation of multiple classes of explanatory variables significantly enhances the amount of variance accounted
for (for example, Christensen and Yoesting, 1976; Murphy, 1975).

The use of multiple classes of explanatory variables is also rare in
the study of formal participation in voluntary associations, another type
of discretionary activity. This being my principal past area of specialization, it strikes me, perhaps more than others, as exceedingly anomalous
—if enhanced intellectual understanding be the main aim of researchers
studying participation—that so few studies in the past dozen years or so
have been performed using a broad set of predictor variable classes. My
study of voluntary association participation in Chile (Smith, 1966)
showed conclusively for the data involved that there were independent
contributions to be made to the variance accounted for by attitudinal,
personality, and social background variables (with some situational
variables, by my present definitions, included in the attitudinal realm).
That study also showed substantially higher amounts of the variance
could be accounted for than had hitherto been possible when such
multiple classes were used (71 percent of the variance in differentiating
members from matched nonmembers and 56 percent when differentiating rated active from rated inactive members). Rogers' (1971) partial
replication of the study, on a U.S. sample of members of several farm-
related voluntary associations, showed attitudinal measures made a
great improvement over social background variables alone in explaining participation levels among members. Studies by Crigler (1973),
Grupp and Newman (1973), Reddy (1974), Townsend (1973), and others
have shown similar results in the sense of higher levels of variance
explained when multiple classes of the ISSTAL model predictor variables were used in attempts to explain individual participation. Conversely, lack of multiple classes of variables leads to low levels of
explained variance (Smith, 1973b).

Again without systematic empirical data from a thorough survey
of the literature, I would argue that similar results will be found in other
areas of individual human behavior. This follows as a likely
probability from the results of the previous section and the proposition they supported. Because the full range of variable classes and
subtypes of the ISSTAL model have been found to be significant in a
wide variety of studies of both formal and informal discretionary
behavior, as well as in nondiscretionary behavior, only extreme multi-
collinearity and lack of independence of the several variable types or
subtypes could prevent their combination from making a greater
contribution to the variance explained than their use alone. My impressions of the literature on nondiscretionary individual behavior
confirm that, as expected, the use of multiple classes and subtypes of

variables of the ISSTAL model also enhances significantly the variance explained there. In some systematic future research, I shall attempt to demonstrate this more convincingly for a variety of realms of individual behavior. But even given the existing evidence, rare as it is, in the realm of discretionary behavior and the fact that such evidence has been available for many years now, the lack of more such research seems to me to require explanation. The conventional norms of science suggest scientists, human scientists included, will pursue "the truth" or the best possible explanations for the phenomena they choose to study, whatever those phenomena may be. In the human sciences, it is reasonable to expect researchers, if following such norms, would seek to explain the greatest possible amounts of variance (corrected for statistical degrees of freedom) possible. Therefore, in view of the demonstrated (if only rarely tested) superiority of utilizing multiple variable classes and subtypes, they might reasonably be expected to make very frequent use of something approximating the ISSTAL model. In fact, this is not the case; and I suggest at least two reasons for it.

D. Contrary to their customary pretensions, explicit or implicit, the great majority of human scientists are antiscientific in the broadest sense while presumably well-intentioned and acting in accord with scientific norms in a narrower sense. This proposition will doubtless arouse hostility and denials from many human scientists; at the very least many readers will consider it peripheral to the main thrust of my argument. Unfortunately, such reactions are part of the problem I am pointing to; they are a real and important barrier to scientific advancement. In economic terminology, there is a massive degree of suboptimization of scientific activity owing to the fact that most human scientists are constrained in their inquiry by two factors that militate against the maximum understanding, explanation, and prediction of the phenomena they study. One such factor, discussed earlier, deals with the discipline-bound nature of the human science disciplines and even many of their subfields in terms of acceptable variables and study methods, particularly a lack of concern for behavior dynamics. A second factor relates to the kind of "Gresham's law of human science inquiry" I discussed briefly in Chapter One. Alternatively, it is a symptom of the alienation of human scientists from their ostensible collective aim—the understanding of human behavior in all its facets and intricacies. Speaking specifically of studies of individual behavior, it seems fair to say the phenomena have been so complex and difficult to explain with any degree of precision that most human scientists have effectively retreated from the basic problem in one of two ways. Either they have retreated to the stance that such behavior is so complex one can never understand it in a quantitatively precise manner (hence calling for and using very subjective and imprecise qualitative methods), or they have retreated to the stance that such behavior can be understood only in very tiny pieces or narrowly defined circumstances—and even then only partially, in terms of the influence of one or a few variables. The former stance leads to interesting qualitative accounts of individual behavior that give the sensitive reader the impression of understanding what has happened. The level of intersubjective confirmability of such accounts, however, is low; and their use in predicting future behavior is usually negligible. The second stance leads to usually less interesting quantitative research on highly circumscribed phenomena with only a few variables, seldom variables from more than one ISSTAL class or even more than one or two subtypes of a given class.

The alienation involved in both stances is demonstrated by the fact that many human scientists seem to be mainly concerned with "going through the motions" of science rather than actually contributing to the accumulation of scientific knowledge. Both qualitative and quantitative methodologies have their virtues and defects in the human sciences, as do both broad scope and narrower modes of inquiry. But most human scientists produce publications that are at best marginally cumulative (because of failures of methodology and description thereof) and that are primarily concerned not with behavior dynamics but with demonstrating the significance (whether statistical or impressionistic) of only a small set of variables, perhaps just one or two, on a limited aspect of human behavior or on some factors thought to influence such behavior for a nonrepresentative sample of humans. And if examined carefully, most inquiry by human scientists will turn out to be more concerned with getting reports of the results published in as prestigious a professional publication as possible than with contributing to real knowledge, though the two are not incompatible. This desire to publish is reinforced by the current reward system of the human sciences, which promotes career success for those who conform to the norms of discipline-bound science, whether or not the research results contribute to a general understanding of human behavior. For human scientists in nonacademic settings, matters are even worse; they are mainly rewarded for delivering a reasonably competent report of their inquiry to their research sponsors, whether or not it enhances the understanding of human behavior and irrespective of adherence to the norms of discipline-bound human science. Thus, it should be no surprise that the production of documents reporting the results of human science inquiries far outstrips any increases in our understanding (ability to explain and predict precisely at will) human behavior (see Smith, 1979c, for some related arguments and elaboration).

E. An adequate interdisciplinary synthesis for the explanation of individual human behavior requires not only an appropriate set of state-variables (referring to states or configurations of circumstances at a particular time), as presented earlier, but also an appropriate set of process-variables (referring to processes or how transitions, transformations, interactions, reactions, and other changes through time occur for the various possible state variables). This proposition follows from the nature of scientific theory in general and is so well accepted and confirmed in its utility that there is little need for adducing evidence here (see, for instance, Blalock, 1969; Hage, 1972; Hempel, 1952). Postulating, describing, and understanding these processes (as "process variables" are more usually termed) takes place at two different levels: Some processes cannot be observed directly and hence are hypothetical constructs, just as are many state variables. Other processes can be observed, and hence measured, directly, usually with substantial precision if this is desired. Both types of processes lead to some observable relationships between or among state variables at different times or at the same time. However, some human scientists (for instance, most "behaviorist" psychologists) believe the postulation of unobservable process variables is inappropriate. Because there is some disagreement among human scientists on this issue, the present model states explicitly the necessity for inclusion of process variables. Not to include such variables leaves unexamined the dynamics or underlying reasons for relationships between state variables over time that may be regularly observed and hence fails in the fullest pursuit of understanding human behavior. Such an approach thus forgoes the possibility of an adequate understanding of change of all kinds.

F. There are a number of psychological, psychobiochemical, psychophysical, biological, chemical, and physical processes that must be postulated in order to understand human individual behavior. Assuming the biological, chemical, and physical processes (blood circulation, stomach chemistry, and physics of arm movement, for example) to be relatively well understood and well described in standard textbooks, it is most appropriate to specify here only the more problematic psychological, psychobiochemical, and psychophysical processes that must be taken into account. Unfortunately, there are not clear lines of demarcation among these three types of processes; so any such categorization must be arbitrary to some degree. At the very least, there must be postulated psychobiochemical activity as the class of processes in which biochemical factors such as hormones, drugs, and disease organisms affect the psychological states and processes of the individual and vice versa. Similarly, there must be postulated at least two broad classes of psychophysical processes, namely, sensation (sight, hearing, smell, and such) and psychomotoric activity (individual conscious and unconscious motoric responses affected by or affecting the individual's psychological states and processes). Those processes I am categorizing as more "purely" psychological all have biochemical and physical substrates; but they are distinguished by being readily viewed as components of the individual's psychological system, by having their effects and causes almost solely understood therein, in contrast to the psychobiochemical and psychophysical processes, generally speaking. Moreover, for all the psychological processes (though least so for perception and emotional activation), the connections between these processes and psychobiochemical or psychophysical processes is far from clear at present.

One must postulate at least the following psychological processes: (1) perception (as the seeking of critical features and forming of consistent patterns from the stream of sensations), (2) emotional activation (as the mood, feeling, or affective changes of the individual's psychological system, conscious and unconscious), (3) learning (as the acquisition of information and response tendencies), (4) remembering (as the retrieval of retained information into conscious awareness), (5) thought processing or thinking (as the relating of items of information, the reviewing of such items, and the formation of new items of information as a patterned synthesis), (6) focusing of the questing center of attention of the mind (as attending to or allocating a plurality of cognitive resources to some aspect[s] of the conscious awareness), (7) cognitive synthesis of a definition of the situation (as a special thought process, always active in noncomatose or non-brain-dead individuals, which establishes the basic parameters of physical danger or other high-priority features of the person's situation as a frame of reference within which other psychological processes take place), (8) psychodynamic synthesis (as a process whereby the person's full range of competing motivational dispositions, both personality and attitudinal, are synthesized into a net resultant motivational tendency, often complex in nature, at a given time), (9) maintenance of the self-organization (as a process of developing and maintaining a central structural and content integration of the psychological system with reference to the person as a unique being), (10) sensory-perceptual adaptation (as the process of getting used to, expecting regularly and subconsciously, a certain configuration of sensation and perception over time), (11) experiencing (as the process whereby all or any combination of the forgoing processes are recognized, consciously or unconsciously, by the person's psychological system or "mind"), and (12) forgetting (as the loss of access, in one degree or another, of the conscious awareness and especially the questing focus of attention, to some previously or presently retained information). This listing attempts to be comprehensive after careful review of the literature, but it may omit some important additional processes.

The evidence supporting the existence of all the forgoing psychological, psychophysical, and psychobiochemical processes can be found in the appropriate chapters (on sensation, perception, thinking, decision making, motivation, emotion, and so on) in the past three decades of the *Annual Review of Psychology* and in the numerous sources cited therein. I have also found helpful in formulating the forgoing set of processes such review monographs as those by Allport (1955), Blumer (1969), Boulding (1956), Cofer (1972), DeCharms (1968), Freud (1932), Guilford (1967), Hall and Lindzey (1978), Joffe (1969), Lindzey and Aronson (1968–1969), McHugh (1968), Miller, Galanter, and Pribram (1960), and Rummelhart (1977), among others. There is a variety of theoretical arguments that can be presented in support of the necessity for considering each of the process variables previously delineated, but space prevents doing this here. In a future volume, where a dynamic version of the ISSTAL model is presented, such arguments will be presented and illustrated, with more extensive documentation from prior research regarding the necessity of including them.

This general proposition of the ISSTAL model provides for the full range of interactions between the individual's psychological system, the physiological organism of the individual, longer-term genetic and evolutionary influences upon the individual, and the general influence of the individual's external environment (see Baldassare, 1978; Barchas, 1976a, 1976b; Barker, 1968; Campbell, 1974; Craik, 1973; DiRenzo, 1977; Huntington, 1945; Inkeles, 1959; Moos, 1974; Proshansky, Ittelson, and Rivlin, 1970; Shapiro and Crider, 1969; Sommer, 1969; Wilson, 1975, 1978). This proposition forces the interdisciplinary synthesis of the human sciences to reach even beyond these broad boundaries into the adjacent biological and physical sciences. Such interfaces are clearly there and clearly important, so it is sheer narrow-mindedness to dismiss them simply because they involve interdisciplinary research and theory.

G. An adequate way of conceptualizing the dependent variable unit of behavior is crucial if interdisciplinary synthesis is to be achieved. The most appropriate such conceptualization, according to the present model, is to associate socially significant sequences of overt behavior (as the smallest behavioral units of analysis) with situations or roles in which they are performed. In brief form, the dependent variable unit of behavior can be termed, thus, "behavior in situation/role," where the term "situation/role" implies that the situation involved may or may not have sufficient normative expectations attached to it by others to involve a clearly developed role or that the role involved may or may not be clearly connected to a particular situation. A behavior unit can be anything from picking up a hitchhiker for a few minutes to a lifelong career, depending on one's analytic purpose. An early theorist to suggest something analogous to the present behavior unit was Coutu (1949), who emphasized that motivation and personality should be viewed not as tendencies in the abstract but rather as tendencies in situations or "tinsits," as he termed them. I am pushing this notion a step further to insist on viewing (or at least seeking) the intrinsic connectedness of behavior sequences and the situations/roles in which they take place. Barker and his associates have done a great deal of work over the past twenty-five years to clarify the necessary methodology for measuring such behavior sequences or "behavior episodes," as Barker and Wright (1955) first termed them (see also Barker, 1963, 1968; Barker and Schoggen, 1973). This work has also shown that certain characteristic kinds of behavior tend to be associated with particular situations or behavior settings in a patterned way. The work of time budget researchers also supports the importance of connections between particular types of behavior and particular situations, where the term "situation" includes such factors as physical setting, time of day and week, and presence or absence of other persons and their relationship to the individual (see Szalai and others, 1972).

Finally, there has been a lengthy controversy in psychology regarding the relative importance of personality traits, attitudes, and other dispositions as determinants of behavior as contrasted with situational cues, pressures, and other factors as determinants. Although there are dogmatic advocates of the extreme view of either position, there seems to be some growing recognition that both are simultaneously important. Carlson (1975), for instance, argues on the basis of the research literature that the best view now is person-situation interaction; and Bowers (1973), in a somewhat earlier review of this specific controversy, drew a similar conclusion. One cannot ignore either personal constructs or the situation in attempting to understand individual behavior. I again extrapolate from this conclusion to the proposition that, therefore, the dependent variable unit of behavior should be similarly situation or role connected. Let such connections be assumed, and let empirical research indicate the kinds of behavior that have no such culturally or socially normative connections. Zero "situation/role connection" of a particular type of behavior sequence or episode is quite as readily imaginable theoretically as perfect behavior in situation/role connection.

Conceptualizing the dependent variable behavior unit in the interactive or connected form subtly changes one's theoretical and research perspective on individual behavior in an important way. Now one assumes such connections from the outset and sees lack of them as unusual, with some degree of connection clearly the most usual occurrence. In the common assumption of many social and behavioral scientists, behavior is seen in the abstract as nonsituation or nonrole connected; and such connections are viewed mainly as special cases or exceptions. Thus, this proposition of the ISSTAL model requires a paradigm change at the level of problem-solving devices or construct paradigms (see Masterman, 1970). If this proposition is correct, an examination of the existing literature on individual behavior should indicate behavior that is more situation/role connected, other things equal, is more readily explicable and predictable than less situation/ role connected behavior. Indeed, Chapter Eight and the larger monograph of which it is a condensation provide direct evidence of this. Similarly, Smith (1975) concluded that more specific attitudes toward participation (which involve reference to a particular association as the context of participation behavior) are usually more powerful than general attitudes toward participation. This can be interpreted as resulting as much from the specificity of the dependent participation variable (situation or role connectedness) as from the specificity of the independent attitude variables.

H. Adequate interdisciplinary synthesis and understanding of individual behavior can occur only if the dependent variable unit of behavior in situation/role is viewed as having potentially six sequentially ordered time phases, each of which may have a markedly different pattern of relationships with the major classes and subtypes of explanatory variables. These six time-ordered phases are entry consideration, entry, performance, exit consideration, and exit, plus the subsequent phase of reflection (which may or may not instigate repetition of the cycle in some other similar situation or at another time). In this sequence, the terms "entry" and "exit" are broadly defined to encompass simply starting and stopping some behavior as well as more complex stages where entry into a situation or role, or exit therefrom, involves a series of interrelated behaviors by both the individual and others (for example, as in joining an organization or quitting a job). This formulation draws on the standard perspective of role entry, role performance, and role exit but adds some additional stages that have emerged as potentially important in recent theory or research. Further, this formulation extends the role involvement sequence to apply also to situation involvement, even where there is no formal role involved, and still further to the basic dependent variable unit of behavior in situation/role. Some theoretical justification for the general role entry-performance-exit sequence can be found in such standard sources as Sarbin and Allen (1968) or Biddle and Thomas (1966). More recent work bearing on my extension of the usual sequences can be seen in Thornton and Nardi (1975), who propose a four-stage model of role acquisition. Their "anticipatory" stage is essentially the same as the present consideration phase. The term "consideration" seems more appropriate because one may or may not decide to enter a particular behavior in situation/role. The additional three stages they suggest (formal, informal, and personal) may be viewed as further specifications of the entry phase in my sequence. These stages usefully explicate aspects of the entry process, and the fourth stage gradates over into the performance phase of my sequence, having to do with the process of accommodation between the individual personality and the situation/role (and corresponding expected behaviors) in question.

The empirical justification for the presently postulated six phases is so far weak, though not insignificant. At a commonsense level, such justification comes from studies of reasons individuals give for joining versus participating versus leaving some organization or role. Comparison of the response frequencies in such simple descriptive studies generally shows a different pattern of responses to some extent for the different phases (see, for example, ACTION, 1974, regarding reasons given in regard to volunteering by a national sample of U.S. adults). More sophisticated empirical justification for several of the phases comes from research on consumer purchasing behavior, where there is often extensive prepurchase search as well as postpurchase evaluation, corresponding to the consideration and reflection phases of the present phase sequence (see Schiffman and Kanuk, 1978, chap. 15). Additional support for the utility of the time phase sequence proposed here comes from the (admittedly scanty but intriguing) evidence of differential relationships of explanatory variables to the dependent behavior in situation/role unit according to the time phase of the latter involved. This evidence will be examined later in the chapter when the various aspects of sequential specificity of the ISSTAL model are considered.

I. *Only* by the inclusion of a time allocation-life span perspective in an interdisciplinary integrative model can social and behavioral scientists hope to explain human individual discretionary behavior precisely, consistently, and in a manner that permits the resulting research and theory to be applied to problems of public policy and everyday practical human affairs. There are several subaspects to this proposition. First, there is the assertion that failure to consider the full range of daily time allocation and the full life span of the individual in any given piece of human science research or theory takes that research out of its proper interpretive context. Individual events, situations, and behaviors have their most central meaning for the individual only in the context of that individual's everyday life and the larger context of the person's life span. I have no systematic evidence here, but an example should make my point clear. If one is doing research on some form of informal social participation, for instance, on a sample of people, some of whom have recently been subjected to particularly stressful life events (see Coelho, Hamburg, and Adams, 1974; Dohrenwend and Dohrenwend, 1974), the results obtained for the sample may be markedly unrepresentative if the subset exposed to stressful, unusual events is relatively large. Or, on a smaller time scale, if one is doing research that involves interviewing people either in the morning or in the afternoon or evening after work, when the interview is performed can markedly affect the results if there are major intraday mood fluctuations owing to fatigue or other factors.

Another aspect is the assertion that the methodology of time budgets and longitudinal (multiple points of data collection) studies constitute necessary adjuncts at the least and preferably central modes of empirical research for the social and behavioral sciences. Work by Juster (forthcoming), Robinson (1977, chap. 1), and their colleagues has shown that time-diary research methods yield estimates of individual behavior and participation that are significantly more accurate than the estimates derived from the usual survey type interview or questionnaire. Hence, error variance in the dependent variable is reduced and more precise explanation is made probable. However, use of such methods is no cure-all, for they have their defects as well, especially when not performed for a series of different days at different times of year in order to reduce various possible cyclical biases and "unusual" days of the respondents. Time budget methods do, however, when combined with state variable measures, have a number of additional advantages, such as permitting more certain determination of the time sequence and hence probable direction of causality in relationships between different states and behaviors of the individual.

Longer-term longitudinal panel studies (collecting data at several different times from the same set of persons) over periods of years or decades have even more utility in this sense, if properly performed. But again, there are also special difficulties, for historical period factors can become easily confounded with life span developmental factors for individuals unless age cohorts (sets of respondents or "panels") with different birthdates are studied simultaneously for different lengthy time periods. If one were studying U.S. adolescence in a longitudinal panel study during the 1960s, for instance, how could one separate the effects of that historically special decade from "normal" aspects of adolescent development? An analysis of some of these problems and possible resolutions thereof can be found in such sources as Elder (1975) and Glenn (1977). Hannan and Tuma (1979) discuss methods of temporal analysis more generally, showing that there are many analysis problems to be overcome even with longitudinal data (especially if the data are collected at only two points in time).

A third assertion about the utility of a time allocation-life span perspective is that it can clarify tradeoffs and irreversibilities that may not be clear from cross-sectional data (see Gutenschwager, 1973). It may also highlight long-term trends (Elder, 1975; Hogan, 1978) or short-term daily patterns and cycles (Szalai and others, 1972) that otherwise might go unnoticed. Perhaps most important, a fourth assertion about the utility of the present perspective is that, when applied assiduously to both the independent and dependent variables of individual behavior, it is likely to permit scientifically grounded rational choice among competing models and construct paradigms in various areas of individual behavior. The "crisis" of competing schools of thought in all the human sciences that study individual behavior could well be resolved in each discipline and interdisciplinary synthesis could be fostered if there were sufficient and adequate time allocation-life span research of the sort just mentioned. Many of the assumed causal relationships found in cross-sectional studies may be overturned by appropriate longitudinal analyses, as Meyer (1972) shows for the relation of size and organizational structure in work organizations and as MacPherson (forthcoming) shows for the stability and change in voluntary association memberships (see Babchuk and Booth, 1969). More generally, though they are not panaceas, time budget and longitudinal studies of individual behavior are likely to eliminate many of the overwhelming number of alternative hypotheses consistent with any complex set of cross-sectional data, thus helping to reduce publications "inflation" in the human sciences and to produce greater real growth in knowledge in these fields.

Another assertion about this proposition is that the incorporation of a time allocation-life span perspective into human science models and hypotheses is likely to help increase understanding of individual behavior by spurring the search and demand for adequate resources to perform the kinds of research called for. I dwell at some length in Chapter One on the dearth of this kind of research and the problems contributing to this dearth, both in terms of funding and in terms of the social structure of human sciences (reward systems geared to frequent publications, principally). My point here is that if sufficient numbers of high-prestige researchers were to work at developing models and theories that could only be tested by time budget and long-term longitudinal research, however expensive this might be, more such research would be likely to result. Fortunately, there seem to be some significant recent trends toward "acceptance of a life span framework in studies of human development, socialization, and role or status sequences (in contrast to age specific models); and . . . increasing interest in the relation between historical change and life patterns, as seen in comparative study of cohorts" (Elder, 1975, p. 186). The latter point is one final assertion that can be made about this proposition, namely, that it will enhance the relationship of human science research and theory not only to everyday life but also to the long-term sweep of historical change, a matter of no small importance.

J. The time allocation-life span perspective needs to be an integral part of any adequate interdisciplinary model of human individual behavior, not just in terms of the measurement of and relationships among state and behavior variables, independent and dependent; it must be applied to the full range of relevant process variables as well. More specifically, it is postulated that adequate understanding of individual behavior cannot result from isolated studies of psychological, psychobiochemical, and psychophysical processes at times that are merely convenient to the investigators. Such processes can be expected to vary both in the short term (in terms of daily, weekly, monthly, and seasonal cycles, as well as in response to special life stress events or unusual occurrences) and over the longer term of the individual life span (as a result of maturation, aging, disease of a progressive or chronic nature, or chronic impairment). By far, the majority of attention has been focused in prior research on variations in human state variables over time (see Bloom, 1964, for instance); but in recent years, there has been increasing attention to variations in human process variables as well (for example, Datan and Ginsberg, 1975; Goulet and Baltes, 1970; Mortimer and Simmons, 1978). The bulk of such attention has been to changes in these process variables during the early years of maturation into adulthood and the declining years of old age (Birren, 1964; Birren and Schaie, 1977; Clausen, 1968, chaps. 2 and 4; Elder, 1968; Goslin, 1969; Kagan and Moss, 1962; Maas and Kuypers, 1974; Palmore, 1970; Riley and others, 1972; Zigler and Child, 1969). However, there has also been a marked increase in the past decade in research on adult socialization and psychological state and process variable changes during the middle years, approximately from twenty to fifty years of age (DiRenzo, 1977; Mortimer and Simmons, 1978; Riley and others, 1969b). But by far the bulk of attention has been on the changes in state variables and the external factors thought to be responsible, with only a minimum of attention to the internal processes involved and their variation over time.

In terms of the various psychological processes listed (under point F), there is a major dichotomy in research attention from a life span perspective. One subset has received a good deal of attention in terms of how the processes vary over the life span, especially at the extremes of youth and old age. Included in this category of reasonably well studied processes are psychobiochemical activity (see the *Annual Reviews of Medicine* and the *Annual Reviews of Physiology*); psychomotoric activity and sensation (see the *Annual Reviews of Physiology* and the *Annual Reviews of Psychology*), which are processes closely related to the biological or physical sciences; and a few of the more purely psychological processes, like learning, remembering, and forgetting (see the *Annual Reviews of Psychology*). But most of the latter type of psychological processes have been studied mainly among adults as if there were no important changes in their nature over the life span after the attainment of adulthood. Of course, several of these processes have been examined for variation over the period from birth to adulthood; but even here the record is spotty (see chapters on developmental psychology in the *Annual Reviews of Psychology* and, to a lesser extent, chapters on perception, cognition, and feelings and emotions). There has been little or no life span–oriented study of the variations in such processes as the focusing of attention, cognitive synthesis of a definition of the situation, psychodynamic synthesis of a resultant motivation, sensory-perceptual adaptation, or experiencing. Some attention has been given to longer-term life span variations in the maintenance of self-organization, but even here the focus is more on the state variable of self-concept (including self-esteem, body image, and such) than on the psychodynamic processes involved (see Gordon, 1972; Gordon and Gergen, 1968; Loevinger, Wessler, and Redmore, 1970; Spitzer, Couch, and Stratton, 1971; Wells and Marwell, 1976; Wylie, 1968, 1974). However, changing self-concept and self-organization processes over the life span have received attention from various researchers (Becker, 1968; Coopersmith, 1967; Gergen, 1971; Gordon, 1976; Lifton, 1976; Strauss, 1959; Turner, 1975; Webster and Sobieszek, 1974; Ziller, 1972; Zurcher, 1977). The principal exception to the earlier statement about the lack of attention to changing cognitive processes over the life span is the seminal work of Piaget and his colleagues (see Ginsberg and Opper, 1979; Phillips, 1969, for an overview) on the development of and changes in cognitive processes from birth to adulthood. At the other end of the life span, there has been some corresponding work on the effects of senility and disease upon cognition by the aged (see chapters dealing with cognition and brain activity in the *Annual Reviews of Medicine,* the *Annual Reviews of Physiology,* and the *Annual Reviews of Psychology*). Yet it remains generally true that a full life span perspective on the nature of psychological processes has been applied only rarely. There is far less research that takes an everyday time allocation perspective on these processes, attempting to examine how shorter-term variations in human behavior in situation/role affect such processes.

To sum up, the ISSTAL model postulates that only by examining psychobiochemical, psychophysical, and psychological processes of all types with a time allocation-life span dynamic perspective will it be possible fully to understand human individual behavior. This is true whether one has a broad or narrow research aim and focus. Application of this perspective means not assuming the only changes in the nature (versus content or resulting state) of such processes occur during physiological maturation from birth to adulthood or during physiological decline in old age or in cases of chronic terminal illness. Application of this perspective also means not assuming during any given short-term period of life—childhood, youth some part of adulthood, or old age—that these processes are essentially stable in nature for the individual and unaffected by day-to-day factors. This latter fine grain of variations in the nature of individual psychological and related processes has generally been ignored, except for a somewhat isolated set of researchers dealing with psychopharmacology and the effects of alcohol, hallucinogens, and other drugs or a still more isolated and smaller set of researchers who have studied "altered states of consciousness" (see relevant chapters in the *Annual Reviews of Pharmacology and Toxicology* on the former point and, with some overlap, the following on the latter point: Bucke, 1961; Laski, 1961; Lee and others, 1977; Mishlove, 1975; Ornstein, 1973, 1977; Reed, 1974; Smith, 1976; Soyka and Edmunds, 1977; Tart, 1972, 1975). The ISSTAL model asserts the relevance of these and other kinds of inquiry to an adequate interdisciplinary understanding of human individual behavior, especially discretionary behavior. Material from some of the review chapters in this volume supports the significance of such considerations (particularly the chapters on religion and outdoor recreation and sports, though presumably certain aspects of mass media exposure are also highly relevant as well as informal interpersonal relations, including sexual activity).

K. Although a time allocation-life span perspective is crucial for understanding all psychological and related processes, it is particularly relevant and crucial for an understanding of the relationship among humanization, social conformity, and social deviance, all of which must be incorporated into an adequate interdisciplinary integrative model. "Humanization" (see Hamblin, 1971; Zigler and Child, 1969) has been defined by DiRenzo (1977, p. 265) as a generic process of human development and social learning made up of four separate subprocesses: maturation (development of the biological organism), culturation (learning a primary or secondary culture or subculture), socialization (learning the social-structural and social process aspects of society and social relations), and personality development (psychological development of a unique character in terms of the nature and pattern of state and process attributes). All four of these subprocesses are affected by the nature of the individual's genetic inheritance, postconception nonhuman environment, and postconception human environment, both before and after birth. The relative importance of the latter types of determinants of the four subprocesses varies by subprocess (for example, with maturation most affected by genetic factors) and by time location within the life span. The ISSTAL model asserts all four subprocesses are interacting with each other at all times from birth until brain death (except for comatose periods, but including sleep periods). It also asserts the behavior and psychological states of the individual at any point in the life span are strongly affected by these humanization processes, with there being a powerful tendency for accommodation over time between the requirements of the culturation and socialization processes and the nature of the personality or character development process. The reverse direction of causality is also possible but far less frequent—individual character development affecting the culturation and socialization processes. Yet, as Wrong (1961) has pointed out, there are many ways culturation and socialization can be imperfect, from the standpoint of the larger human sociocultural system, owing both to variations in the manner in which the processes are presented to and enforced upon the individual as well as to the developing uniqueness of the individual character and psychological makeup.

The net result of the humanization processes for most individuals in any sociocultural system at any time, according to the ISSTAL model, is general conformity to the social and cultural norms and values, in terms of both overt behavior and covert psychological states and processes. There are clear and well-documented variations among sociocultural systems, as well as additional variations within subcultures and social substructures of a given sociocultural system, which in turn lead to variations for particular individuals from the general pattern of conformity just referred to. But the model also asserts there will inevitably be some deviance from the general pattern of individual conformity. This deviance will be of at least two broad theoretical varieties: recognized (and hence socioculturally labeled or otherwise reacted to by negative sanctioning) and unrecognized (and hence not labeled or otherwise negatively sanctioned by the sociocultural system). There is controversy in the literature on deviance regarding whether and to what extent deviance is a progressive reaction over time to being recognized and labeled as deviant and regarding the extent to which this recognition and labeling is a result of actual behavioral deviance from sociocultural system norms and values for various reasons (see Gibbs, 1972; Gibbs and Erickson, 1975; Lemert, 1972; Matza, 1969; Quinney, 1970; Turk, 1969). In its present state of development, the ISSTAL model makes no positive statement regarding the precise extent to which recognized deviance is a result of incidental or accidental factors unrelated to the actual frequency of deviant behavior relative to the larger sociocultural system. However, the model does assert that most recognized and labeled deviance will be the result of actual deviant behavior of one degree or another from the norms and values of the larger sociocultural system, although additional deviant behavior ("secondary deviance") will often result from such labeling. Arbitrary and accidental recognition and labeling of deviance when the behavior of the individual involved was not in fact deviant will occur in only a minority of instances, but this too will often result in secondary deviance. However, only by the study of individuals' life span deviance, both recognized and unrecognized, will the process of becoming deviant, remaining deviant, escalating deviance, reducing deviance, or ceasing deviant behavior become fully understandable, studied in the context of extent of recognition and a variety of other factors specified by the larger ISSTAL model. Of particular importance, the model postulates, will be the relationships between deviance and the maintenance and change of the self-concept or self-organization (see Kaplan, 1974, 1975a, 1975b; Schwartz and Stryker, 1971). The classic hypotheses regarding the reasons for becoming deviant are all incorporated into the ISSTAL model in one way or another. Thus, Merton's (1957) view of deviance as a reaction to anomie, now seen as relating more to official or recognized deviance than to all deviance, can be readily derived from such factors as relative individual access to resources, differences in the educational and occupational opportunity structure for higher- versus lower-prestige individuals, differential social system reactions to evidence of deviant behavior by individuals according to their wealth and prestige status, personality differences in risk taking and aggressiveness, frustration tolerance differences, and differential awareness of and expectations of recognition of deviant behavior by sociocultural system sanctioning agents and processes. Similarly, Sutherland's (1939) differential association theory can be seen as the result of accumulating deviant information, particularly beliefs and plans, from significant others who have themselves been deviant or acquired such information previously. Or Cohen's (1955) subcultural hypothesis about the origins of delinquent behavior, even though it has been largely discredited (Gibbs and Erickson, 1975), can be seen as the result simply of culturation to a subculture in the present model. In a sense, each of these alternative approaches to explaining deviance that is subsumable by the model gives additional support to the model's proposed set of state and process variables and their interaction through the life span.

Not least of the evidence for the validity of this general proposition of the ISSTAL model regarding the importance of humanization processes are the various chapters in this volume that have reviewed prior research on socialization related to various kinds of informal social participation. Collectively, these chapters and the respective literatures they represent clearly demonstrate several points. First, every type of informal social participation examined in any depth with regard to humanization processes, particularly culturation and socialization, have shown themselves to be significantly influenced by such processes. Second, such humanization research on informal social participation is generally in its infancy (though political humanization research might be said to be in early childhood) and shows wide variation in the methodological approaches and theoretical perspectives emphasized. The chapter authors for these reviews were given no general pattern to follow because no appropriate one came readily to mind; and the resulting variation in emphases, which is substantial, may thus be taken to represent wide variations in the types of such research being performed, both in terms of quantity and quality. Third, the maturation process is relatively little studied in relation to informal social participation, with the exception of significant amounts of such research in regard to outdoor sports and recreation. Similarly, the personality or character development process is also rather poorly studied, except in regard to political participation and, to a lesser extent, helping behavior. Further, the difficulty that many times emerges in keeping the content of the socialization chapters separate from the content of the participation chapters confirms the ISSTAL model's postulation of an integral relationship between state and process variables over the life span as necessary for understanding individual behavior. Finally, the various strands of research on humanization in regard to informal social participation clearly indicate the relevance of adult socialization, or humanization through the life cycle, as well as the occasional relevance of resocialization (Kennedy and Kerber, 1973)—as in the case of converts to a new religious sect or cult or to a new political or protest group, again confirming the necessity of a life span perspective on humanization processes. Although, as Bloom (1964) noted, some individual characteristics seem to stabilize, as a result of humanization, rather early in the life span, nearly any human characteristic (state variable or process variable) can change during any portion of the life span when the relevant intervening experience occurs. However, this change may or may not be probable in certain directions and may or may not be desirable from the standpoint of the norms and values of the sociocultual system or individual long-term quality of life.

L. The ISSTAL model postulates, through its time allocation-life span perspective, that behavior is the result of a continuing process of lifelong decision making as well as lifelong learning and change. Another way to state this is to say that the ISSTAL model is intrinsically voluntaristic—emphasizing a kind of constrained free will whereby the individual is able to make choices, if so desired, among the range (often limited, sometimes very wide) of possible behaviors in situations or roles available at a given time. The options available to an infant or prisoner in solitary confinement are very much more limited than the options available to a white, twenty-five-year-old, independently wealthy, non-institutionalized, healthy, intelligent, nonhandicapped, male Anglo-Saxon, Protestant of presentable appearance who is an American citizen. At the same time, the ISSTAL model suggests the decision alternatives among which the individual is continually choosing be conceptualized in terms of behavior in situation/role options. Sometimes, indeed often, these options refer to situations or roles of a highly consensual sort where normative expectations of the larger sociocultural context are major constraints on the range of behavior that can be chosen without negative sanctions. This is true nearly as often in discretionary behavior situations/roles as in more obligatory roles. Yet there is always some degree of freedom, except in the rarest instances. If a life span perspective is taken, the individual has the greatest amount of freedom of choice in choosing voluntary or achieved roles (stages one and two of the six potential stages of behavior in situation/role), least in performing behavior in situation/role, and a moderate amount in considering exit or actual exit from behavior in situation/role, generally speaking. This follows from the fact that sociocultural normative expectations are presented to and enforced for role incumbents of all kinds of roles (or situations) with substantial success by role/situation partners in virtually all roles/situations. Whether internalized or not, these normative expectations have a major impact in limiting the options during the performance stage of behavior in situation/role. And very often the reward and punishment systems, combined with other socialization and culturation mechanisms, are successful in bringing about internalization, whether or not the situation/role incumbent is initially willing.

A corollary of the present proposition is that the full range of theory and research on behavioral decision making is relevant to and can fruitfully be applied to the study of informal social participation, as to other types of individual behavior. Although there has been extensive work applying behavioral decision theory in the realm of consumer economic behavior (Schiffman and Kanuk, 1978), the review chapters in this volume show little or no evidence of such applications to the study of informal social participation. Slovic, Fischhoff, and Lichtenstein's (1977) extensive review of behavioral decision theory further confirms the forgoing assertions, both as to the lack of applications in regard to informal social participation generally and in regard to the overall promise of utility this approach holds. But the ISSTAL model goes quite a bit further than the usual approaches to behavioral decision making; the latter tend to focus on a particular decision or class of decisions at a single point in time. The ISSTAL model, by contrast, postulates the necessity of a life span perspective on individual decision making, stating that individual behavior can be understood adequately only by looking at the "stream of individual decisions" that flow in parallel and just prior to the stream of individual behavior (see Barker, 1963, for an early use of the phrase "stream of behavior"). When particular decisions are isolated from the larger stream of decisions, they are likely to be less readily understood because they are integrally linked to the decisions that precede and that follow them. Put another way, isolation of a particular individual decision from the larger decision stream of which it is a part inevitably distorts the interpretation of that decision because it removes it from its proper context for the given individual. It may further be postulated that there is some inertia of individual decision-making processes (for example, when they become habitual), but that there are also many instabilities, rapid changes of direction, and widely varying degrees of commitment by the individual to particular outcomes or even to the type of decision-making process the same individual uses at different times. Finally, the ISSTAL model postulates that the best way to view individual decision making is in terms of two separate analytical components, one cognitive and one psychodynamic or motivational. The process of arriving at a decision involves, at base, the creation or selection of a plan for behavior and the synthesis of competing and often conflicting motivational dispositions (personality traits and the full range of attitudinal variables distinguished) into a resultant motivation at a given time. As Miller, Galanter, and Pribram (1960) suggest, behavior then emerges from the resultant motivation as the equivalent of an order by the brain to put into operation (execute) the plan that has been created or selected, with behavior continuing in feedback units until the plan and its intended goal have been reached. Of course, as Simon (1967) has noted, goal attainment per se is not the only behavior termination mechanism. Also important are satisficing (achieving a goal well enough though not as originally planned), impatience (taking the best alternative outcome available so far), and discouragement (giving up because of the negative emotions aroused by trial and failure, possibly repeated several or many times). Use of the behavioral decision theory perspective, in one of its varieties, is ultimately essential because it permits the application of reasonably precise methods and mathematics or statistics to the processes and states of the individual that most proximally cause behavior.

M. As one of a larger class of possible models involving the same independent and dependent variables and a time allocation-life span perspective, the ISSTAL model differs in postulating sequential specificity patterns will be found and exist as kinds of asymmetry of relationships among the variables, particularly the independent variables. The ISSTAL model has already postulated one kind of asymmetry in stating explicitly an extensive set of independent explanatory variables that are causally prior to the dependent variable units of behavior in situation/role. The essence of this postulate is the presence of a further set of types of asymmetry that are held to be necessary for adequate interdisciplinary understanding of human individual behavior. There are three main forms of sequential specificity postulations of the model: an ordering of the independent variables in terms of their behavior unit generality; an ordering in terms of their longer-term time sequence going beyond any particular behavior unit and, in part, beyond any given individual; and an ordering in terms of their shorter-term time sequence in relation to a particular behavior unit or type of behavior unit for the individual. I shall now consider each one of these asymmetries in turn.

N. One aspect of sequential specificity postulated by the model is principally a formal rather than substantive property of the patterning of the independent variables, although there are causal implications (see Allport, 1954; Campbell and others, 1960). There is asymmetry in the breadth of relevance of the six classes of explanatory variables and their subtypes with regard to dependent behavior in situation/role. External contextual variables are most generally relevant to many situations, many individuals, and many behaviors. The immediate awareness and situational variables of a certain individual in a particular situation at some time are the most specific class of variables, perhaps being relevant only to the given situation, individual, and behavior. The other classes of variables fall between these extremes, but with a clear progression toward increasing situational specificity present and explicated in the case of personality and attitudinal dispositions. Similar explication of a progression from more general to more situationally and individually specific relevance could be performed for the class of social background variables and the class of retained information, though in the interests of brevity I have not done so. Thus, some background factors, like gender and physical health, have very general relevance; and other background factors, like prior experience in playing a given role with given role partners under certain circumstances, can be highly specific to an individual, situation, time, and behavior. Similarly, some kinds of retained information are very general in their relevance to individuals, situations, and behaviors (for example, basic knowledge about how others are likely to react to violence or aggression directed toward them); and other information is highly idiosyncratic to an individual, situation, time, and behavior.

The importance of this formal variation in the sequential specificity of ISSTAL model explanatory variables is that the desired precision of explanation-prediction is permitted, and the application of the model to behavior units of highly varied degrees of generality is permitted to the user. Thus, if the user desires only a rather crude level of explanation, only the more general and abstract levels of variables within the six classes need be used, with more use of the classes that are intrinsically more general (social and historical context and social background) and little or no use of the classes that are intrinsically more specific (immediate awareness, situational, and attitudinal variables, especially specific attitudes, expectations, and intentions). Indeed, it is this crude level of explanation that is most common in most of the social and behavioral sciences today, with the possible exception of psychology. If full precision is desired, the model user can measure and include in explanatory or predictive analysis the full range of independent variables from most general to most specific, both across and within classes. Naturally, employing the full power of the model involves more resources and more effort; so for many uses, it will not be reasonable to do so. When the latter is the case, the formal aspect of sequential specificity indicates to the model user which of the numerous classes and subtypes of independent variables should be omitted and which retained in order to have a given level of precision.

O. A second type of asymmetry of the sequential specificity aspect of the model is the postulation of some degree of long term temporal sequence in which the various classes of variables have their effects upon behavior (see Figure 1). Thus, external context factors are taken as most usually prior, and in the study of individual behavior, exogenous in a

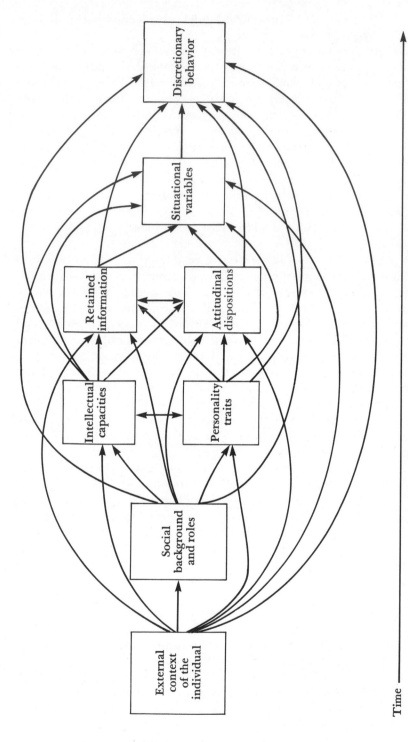

Time ⟶

Figure 1. Crude Temporal Sequence of Main ISSTAL Model Variable Types

temporally ordered view of the model. Individual social background characteristics are viewed as, on the whole, consequences of these external (particularly social and historical) context variables, although there are definite feedback effects from "later" classes of variables in the model (particularly personality, capacity, attitudinal, and information variables affecting achieved roles, possessions, or resources to which access is gained by accomplishment, many prior experiences and activities, and to some degree health and physiological variables). Social role and resource access variables, as subtypes of social background variables in general, take on their principal meanings for the individual from the external context, and conversely, the social and historical context take on meaning for the individual from his or her social roles and access to resources.

However, there is also some degree of temporal sequence within the class of social background variables, with genetic and constitutional aspects of health and physiological variables being earliest in the sequence, affecting both later health and physiological variables (although not revising genetic composition) and other classes of social background variables. After birth, the subtypes of ascribed social positions/roles and of experiences and activities become important earlier in the sequence than other subtypes, though again each of these subtypes affects both later states of variables within its own subtype as well as other subtypes of variables. Subsequently, individual achieved social positions/roles and possessions and access to resources begin to have significant and lasting effects, both on their own later states and upon other subtypes and classes of variables.

The class of personality traits and intellectual capacities is viewed as being largely determined by the two earlier broad classes of explanatory variables, through the interaction of genetic and physiological factors with experiences and learning processes of the individual in the situations, roles, and social and historical contexts to which the person has been exposed. Moreover, it is postulated, on the basis of a good deal of research, that the basic parameters of both personality and intellectual capacities are formed in the first two decades or so of an individual's life, usually, even though subsequent experiences and events can cause changes within (or in rarer cases, outside) these initial parameters (see Berelson and Steiner, 1964; Bloom, 1964; Borgatta and Lambert, 1968; Buss and Plomin, 1975; Clausen, 1968; Fiske and Maddi, 1961; Ginsberg and Opper, 1979; Goslin, 1969; Hall and Lindzey, 1978; Kagan and Moss, 1962; Maas and Kuypers, 1974; Phillips, 1969; Sanford, 1970; Wilson, 1978). But this special importance of the earlier years of life, especially in the case ot personality, does not mean substantial development and change are absent in subsequent periods of the life span. It has become increasingly apparent in the past decade or so that there are important personality changes as well as significant continuity throughout the life span (Bloom, 1964; Hunt, 1965; Levinson, 1978; Mischel, 1969; Neugarten, 1973).

Variables in the next two major classes of variables begin to be relevant a year or two after birth, but it is the acquisition of language, beginning in the second year of life, that really makes information and attitude acquisition take place rapidly. And although there are basic kinds of attitudes and information that nearly every individual in a given sociocultural system is pressured to learn by culturation and socialization processes, there is also an idiosyncratic pattern to the acquisition of information and attitudes guided by the specific person's configuration of social background, personality, and intellectual capacity characteristics. Hence, the three prior classes of explanatory variables generally have temporal and causal priority for any particular instance of attitudinal or informational acquisition and its outcome. There is no special temporal priority or causal priority postulated for information and attitudinal variables with respect to each other because there is so much interaction and feedback between the variables in these two classes. However, if an ordering were to be forced, I would argue for the priority of the information class of variables because the balance of retained information is crucial in the development of attitudinal dispositions of all kinds, although there are other factors as well (Bem, 1970; Fishbein and Ajzen, 1975, chap. 6; Zimbardo, Ebbesen, and Maslach, 1977).

Finally, one's immediate awareness and situational variables are seen to be the result of all prior classes of variables and their subtypes. Immediate awareness is influenced by both the residue of prior experiences in the form of personality traits, intellectual capacities, attitudinal variables, and information and current stimuli from the body and the external environment, all within the context of the individual's genetic composition and the larger social and historical context. But this whole temporal and causal ordering of sequential specificity is seen as only a generally accurate pattern of interrelationships and asymmetry, not as an exclusive statement of recursive causality that is invariably linear and lacks any feedback effects. There will be variations from the general pattern of temporal and causal ordering and numerous instances of feedback effects as modifications of the general pattern in more precise versions. And there will be particular individuals, situations, times, and behaviors for which such variations are more frequent than for others. For instance, there are rare individuals who seem to have more influence on their social and historical context than it has on them (for instance, Hitler, Stalin, and Alexander the Great). Or alternatively, there will be rare situations of such overpowering impact upon the individual that all (or nearly all) residues of prior experience tend toward zero in their importance for understanding individual behavior (for example, extreme torture or extremely damaging and painful illness). The empirical demonstration of the validity of the present aspect of sequential specificity ordering in terms of time and causality postulated here would be a massive task (some will say impossible), requiring reference to and review of all aspects of social and behavioral science. Hence, I attempt no more than a statement of the postulate and some argument in support of it, with a few examples.

P. The third type of sequential specificity postulated by the model also involves temporal and causal asymmetry, but in this case with a finer degree of focus on the dependent variable unit of behavior in situation/role: The ISSTAL model postulates that the more personally superficial classes of variables and subtypes within them will have stronger effects in determining individual behavior (of a nonobligatory sort) in regard to the first two potential time phases of a behavior unit (that is, entry consideration and entry); but the more specific and personally central (deeper) classes and subtypes of variables will have stronger effects in determining (nonobligatory) behavior in regard to the latter four time phases (that is, performance, exit consideration, exit, and reflection), and conversely. Thus, contextual and social background variables are postulated to have more powerful effects on individual consideration of and actual entry into a behavior in situation/role than they will have on performance, exit consideration, exit, and reflection for a given behavior unit. The reasoning here is that entry consideration and entry are strongly affected by the eligibility requirements for a behavior unit, by the individual's propinquity to an appropriate opportunity for engaging in the behavior unit, and by the very existence of the situation/role of a given sort in the larger sociocultural system; and all these are mainly determined by contextual and social background factors. The first two time phases of a behavior unit will also, it is postulated, be more affected by such general subtypes of variables as values, general attitudes, general images, and general beliefs about the behavior in situation/role than will the subsequent four time phases of the behavior unit. In this case, the reasoning is that human individual (and probably collective) decision making tends to be made in terms of incomplete knowledge about behavior units in the first two time phases. Usually the mental image is vague and superficial, and hence general attitudes, favorable or unfavorable, along with relevant values, tend to be powerful motivating forces. Again because of the lack of strongly held specific attitudes and direct personal experience with the behavior unit initially, the individual is also postulated to be more susceptible to direct personal influence by any other person during the entry consideration and entry phases of the behavior unit. In this case, the "superficiality" of the determinant (which falls into the situational variables category) involves the general suggestibility of human beings by other persons, especially significant others.

In the latter four time phases of the behavior unit (performance, exit consideration, exit, and reflection), the forgoing patterns of relative strength change markedly, it is postulated. Instead of the more superficial variables (in terms of relevance to individual accommodation to the behavior in situation/role) being more powerful, the more central variable classes and subtypes become more powerful. The more general aspects of contextual and social background variables that strongly influence entry aspects fade in significance in most cases because they have already "filtered out" most of the population from a particular behavior unit performance and possible subsequent time phases. The individuals who eventually pass through the entry phase of a behavior unit tend to be quite homogenous relative to the total population, when nonobligatory behavior is considered. The evidence on this point is unequivocal, on the whole, for the various review chapters on types of informal participation in this volume. The characteristics of active participants in any of the kinds of informal social participation reviewed tend to be relatively similar among themselves and to differ significantly from the pattern of characteristics of the general population.

During this performance time phase of the behavior unit, general images, values, attitudes, and personal influences no longer have the same power they had in determining entry phases. Instead, as a result of direct personal experience and knowledge of the behavior in situation/role, more central informational and attitudinal variables are formed or previous superficial informational and attitudinal variables (whose levels were determined by stereotypes and mediated acquaintance with the behavior unit) are changed to fit the reality the individual perceives. Simultaneously, general values toward the behavior unit decline in importance relative to the accommodation or matching of the specific demands of performing the behavior in situation/role with the personality traits, intellectual capacities, physical capacities, and affective states of the individual.

If the accommodation (perhaps with adjustment of both the individual self-organization and the situation/role demands) is reasonably good, performance is likely to be satisfying and the individual may well seek to become more active or to engage in the behavior unit more frequently. If the perceived reality of the behavior in situation/role is far from the general image the person initially held and the reality is perceived as unpleasant or if the accommodation between the individual self-organization and the behavior unit is poor, performance is likely to be unsatisfying, activity level is likely to decrease and become less frequent, and exit consideration and actual exit phases are likely to follow soon after entry. And instead of superficial situational variables, such as any personal influence pressure, being important during the performance and subsequent time phases of the behavior unit, more self-central situational variables, such as the relationships with others in the situation or role or the opinions of one's friends and close relatives, become far more important. Indeed, the whole class of situational variables becomes more important as it relates specifically to the behavior unit. Thus, specific qualities of both the human and the nonhuman environment where the behavior in situation/role takes place become particularly important determinants of performance and subsequent phases, as do internal stimuli.

Because the present aspect of the sequential specificity model has been little examined empirically, there is not a great deal of support in the literature; but what support there is seems significant (see Smith, 1979d). There were only a few instances in the review chapters of this book where some test of this proposition was possible, but here the results were generally supportive. Ciccheti (1972) and his colleagues analyzed data from national outdoor recreation surveys using a two-step demand-supply model, which essentially involved analyzing separately the entry and the performance phases, in the present terminology. The results showed the usual sociodemographic variables where the principal explanatory variables for entry or participation in a particular kind of activity at all, and the performance in terms of number of days of participation in a given activity depended very significantly on the availability and quality of recreational facilities in the individual's county or state. Although the latter are contextual variables, they are very specific ones, measured relative to each individual; hence, their impact is likely mediated by attitudinal, information, and immediate awareness variables. Other supporting evidence includes the study by Field and O'Leary (1973), who sampled adults eighteen or older from portions of three states in the U.S. Pacific Northwest. With swimming, freshwater fishing, power boating, and visiting a beach as their dependent variables, they report the usual sociodemographic variables were powerful in explaining variance for participation versus nonparticipation (entry) but generally weak in explaining variance for the degree of participation (performance) among participants (except for fishing). However, the inclusion of immediate situation coparticipant status variables (dummy variables regarding participation with friends, with family, or with both versus not with anyone) resulted in a marked increase in the variance explained, generally rising from the 3 to 5 percent range to 20 percent or more. On the basis of a Chi-square analysis, Romsa and Girling (1976) found similar results for a national Canadian sample. Analyzing only participants in eighteen different outdoor recreation activities (that is, focusing on the performance phase), they found the usual broad contextual (province, community size) and sociodemographic variables did not significantly distinguish people in terms of degree of participation for the eighteen activities (except for walking-hiking), contrary to earlier results on the same data when participation versus nonparticipation had been studied (entry).

Perhaps the clearest evidence I am aware of in the area of informal social participation is again from the type of participation I reviewed, namely, the study by Murphy (1975) of recreational boaters from the Columbus, Ohio, area. He found 34 percent of the variance for his full sample could be accounted for in a multiple-regression analysis of the number of boating trips (performance) people had made to a given lake during a two-month period. The usual sociodemographic variables (age, gender, socioeconomic status, and such) were present in the analysis but made virtually no contribution to accounting for the variance. Instead, the major predictors were one's specific attitude toward an alternative lake in the area, one's prior frequency of visits there, and one's travel time and specific attitudes toward the given lake. Further multiple-regression analysis with subsamples disaggregated on a socioeconomic status measure gave similar results. Because other studies on these kinds of outdoor recreational activity focusing on participants versus nonparticipants (entry) have consistently shown significant effects of sociodemographic and contextual variables of a general sort (for example, Outdoor Recreation Resource Review Commission, 1962a, 1962b), the basic pattern difference in explanation of behavior unit entry versus subsequent phases is thus confirmed here.

In other areas of informal social participation, some additional support may be found for this proposition in what otherwise appear to be deviant cases or anomalous results. In most studies of informal social participation previously reviewed, the focus has either been on the entry phase (engaging or not engaging in some kind of participation) or on a kind of dependent variable behavior measure that does not permit distinguishing the entry phase from the performance phase of the behavior unit (that combines the participant versus nonparticipant distinction with variations in amount of participation). When particularly anomalous results in regard to the usual sociodemographic variables have appeared in the reviews, this has sometimes been attributable to the use of a performance-type dependent variable measure for which such predictor variables may be expected (in terms of the ISSTAL model) to have less impact. However, I have not been able to examine in full detail the original sources of all the reviews in this volume, so my suggestion about the interpretation of some anomalous results is more a hypothesis than a conclusion.

I am on firmer ground when I turn to another kind of social-discretionary participation—participation in formal voluntary associations. When I put an earlier version of the sequential specificity model to the test (Smith, 1966), I compared the relative strength of different major classes of predictors (social background, general attitudes, specific attitudes, and personality traits) for members versus matched nonmembers of several Chilean voluntary associations of different types and socioeconomic status levels (entry phase), as contrasted with samples of inactive versus highly active members (according to ratings by leaders or actual participation records) of these same associations (performance phase). The results strongly confirmed the present proposition; indeed, they first led me to note it, although the nature of my sampling involved a search for some differential patterning of the results. Personality variables were far more significant predictors of performance than entry, and general attitudes were far more important predictors of entry than performance. No valid comparison of the strength of demographic social background variables could be made because the sampling process involved matching of members and nonmembers on such variables. However, when included in the multivariate analysis of performance (where respondents were not matched on social background variables), sociodemographic variables were the weakest by far of the four types of variables included. Specific attitudes toward a given association were strongest of all types for the entry comparison and second in strength for the performance comparison (personality traits being strongest). This suggests such attitudes are important for either of these two phases and presumably the others as well; it also suggests the essence of the present aspect of sequential specificity is superficiality versus depth or centrality of the variable type in relation to the individual's self. More superficial factors are likely to affect more strongly the entry phase behavior; factors more central to the self-organization, such as personality traits and self-esteem considerations, are likely to be more powerful in affecting performance and subsequent phases of a behavior unit.

Some other studies from the voluntary association participation literature further support this proposition. Most studies reviewed by Smith (1975) using an entry-type or combined entry-and-performance measure of participation show the sociodemographic variables to have consistent significance in predicting participation. However, those few studies that examine performance per se among the members of an association (or several) tend consistently to find such variables less important than attitude or personality variables, especially specific attitude variables (see Marsland and Perry, 1973; Reddy, 1974; Rogers, 1971; Smith, 1979b; Townsend, 1973; Warner and Rogers, 1971). And Mac-Pherson (forthcoming) uses longitudinal data to show, among other results, that sociodemographic variables predict adding new affiliations with associations (that is, entry) more strongly than they predict dropping existing affiliations (that is, exit). Yet the overall conclusion must remain that the research bearing on this proposition is too sparse at present to permit the statement that it is well confirmed by empirical research for a variety of types of discretionary social behavior. Perhaps less than 1 percent of research on discretionary behavior has any direct bearing on this proposition because the vast majority of researchers fail even to assume the possibility that this proposition of the ISSTAL model is true.

Unless and until more researchers are willing to consider it as a possibility, gathering and analyzing their data to test its validity, no more progress toward empirical confirmation is likely to be made in the future than has been made since the notion was first suggested. However, it would be useful to examine other research literatures dealing with the obligatory types of social behavior (for example, educational achievement, occupational attainment, marriage, and divorce) to seek evidence of the proposition. For instance, the work of Winch (1958) in the area of mate selection is quite consistent with this proposition. He argues there are stages of the mate-selection process, with the first stage affected largely by such contextual and social background factors as propinquity of two individuals of the opposite sex, similarity of social class background, and age similarity but with the male a few years older (see also Berelson and Steiner, 1964, chap. 7). General value and attitude similarities are also important at this stage. However, Winch argues that the complementarity of personality needs is important for actual entry into marriage and particularly for satisfaction and permanence in the marriage relationship (the performance phase).

The latter point raises an important issue requiring at least brief elaboration here. The essential reason for the discrepancy between the usual patterning of explanatory variables for entry phases versus performance and subsequent phases is the degree of direct, personal knowledge the individual has of the behavior unit in question. It follows, therefore, that in those circumstances where an individual takes great care and sufficient time during the entry consideration phase to gain direct, personal knowledge of the relevant behavior in situation/role, more central and specific personality, emotional, attitudinal, informational, and situational variables will have a stronger impact on entry than where, as is more usual, the entry consideration phase is less careful or thorough. This proposition of the ISSTAL model is thus in large part an explanation for the truth of the adage, "Marry in haste, repent at leisure," as a generalization. Or, based on the research literature, the proposition is part of the general explanation for why there is greater proneness to divorce where there is short acquaintanceship before marriage, a short engagement, or none, where there are very different definitions of husband and wife mutual role obligations, and where disapproval by kin and friends of the marriage is significant (Goode, 1961; Weiss, 1975). Exit from the marriage role is thus rather consistently greater where the entry consideration was superficial and where the accommodation is poor between centrally important aspects of the self (including self-esteem in the eyes of kith and kin and support from one's spouse for the manner in which one is performing the marital role) and behavior in situation/role. This same body of research also shows less proneness to divorce where there is general similarity of background of the two spouses, indicating the initial entry consideration "filtering" on the basis of sociodemographic variables leads to more satisfaction during the performance phase (that is, a "happy marriage" or at least a satisfactory one).

There is one final issue to be raised in relation to the present aspect of sequential specificity. I have so far avoided the question of repetition of behavior unit cycles and the matter of differentiating continued but intermittent performance from exit and reentry. In the present stage of development of the ISSTAL model, this issue is not clearly resolved. All that is clear is the following: The present proposition regarding sequential specificity will apply to repeated cycles of behavior units unless and until the individual learns to spend more time and care in the entry consideration phase so as to raise the probability of satisfaction in performance. When the individual begins to engage in close, direct, and careful consideration of behavior unit entry (or applies retained information during the reflection phase to entry phases), then the pattern of explanation usually characterizing performance and subsequent phases will come to characterize the entry and perhaps even the entry consideration phases as well. And as for the definitional problems, let it suffice for the moment to define behavior unit "exit consideration" and "exit" in both a temporary and a permanent manner. The temporary definition of behavior unit exit refers to cessation of the behavior in situation/role temporarily with the implicit or explicit assumption of continuing with performance again at some time in the future. The permanent definition of behavior unit exit refers to cessation of the behavior unit with the explicit intent not to resume performance of that behavior in situation/role ever again. There will be gradations between the two, according to variations in aspects of the behavior or the situation/role in question (one can give up tennis forever, give it up on clay courts, give it up with opponents of inferior skill or superior skill, or give it up for the day expecting to play again soon). Explanation patterns will vary for temporary versus permanent exit consideration and later phases.

Q. The ISSTAL model postulates there will be consistent patterns of relationships found across research studies that use the same class or classes of independent (explanatory) variables in examining different types of human individual discretionary behavior. Similarly, the model postulates there will be consistent patterns of relationships found across research studies that use the same type of human individual discretionary behavior as a dependent variable in examining the effects of different types and classes of independent variables. These postulates suggest the search for consistent patterns of relationships across both independent and dependent variable types will be fruitful. In its "strongest form" with regard to consistency, the ISSTAL model hypothesizes there will be found both types of consistency patterns simultaneously, at least to some significant degree. That is, this version of the model suggests the same classes and subtypes of independent variables will have generally similar effects on most or all kinds of human individual discretionary behavior. However, there will also be one or more (probably several) variations on the general pattern that will be explicable within the ISSTAL model and will themselves constitute subpatterns. Such subpatterns can be viewed as modifications of or overlays of influence upon the more general underlying pattern. More fine-grained analysis may well reveal still more subtle subsubpatterns as variations on certain subpatterns. The analogy of superimposition of modulating variable wave forms upon a more stable, basic "carrier wave" form may help one to grasp the idea here being proposed. A variety of consistent patterns of relationships among the variables of the ISSTAL model are postulated, as follows.

R. Implicit in the sequential specificity aspect of the ISSTAL model, particularly in that aspect that postulates a long-term temporal ordering of the major classes and subtypes of variables, is the postulate that many contextual effects upon human individual behavior are generally mediated by variables of the other five major classes of variables and their subtypes. This means that, aside from direct physical or chemical limitations of the environment upon the individual (for example, immersion in sand, snow, or water or subjection to electromagnetic radiation, gravitational forces, or fire), the common types of contextual variables used in the social and behavioral sciences will cease to have any direct effects upon individual behavior when the appropriate mediating variables of the other five classes are entered into the analysis. Contextual variables such as region of the country, city size, urban versus rural residence, population density, social structure, culture and subculture, population morbidity rates in terms of different diseases and types of impairment or injury, and even opportunity structures and behavior niches will all be essentially explicable through their effects on other mediating variables, which in turn will have direct or indirect effects on individual behavior. This may seem like a minor achievement (and certainly the technique is not new), but it is more than that because it means the ISSTAL model will indicate the processes and mechanisms whereby most current contextual variables in use by human scientists actually affect individual behavior. No longer will such contextual variables be proxy variables for a melange of other, unmeasured variables. Rather, their importance will be clearly defined in terms of their relationships to other more proximal variables affecting individual behavior more directly.

    S. Similarly implicit in the postulate of long-term temporal/ causal ordering of the variable classes and subtypes in terms of sequential specificity is the postulate that the explanatory power of the usual sociodemographic variables (particularly ascribed and achieved roles, and to a lesser extent possessions or access to resources) in regard to discretionary social behavior, and perhaps human individual behavior in general, will be shown generally to have only indirect and mediated effects upon behavior. Again, here, the ISSTAL model will show in detail how the usual sociodemographic variables are proxy variables for other, more sequentially specific, and usually unmeasured variables that are specified as important in the model. In the model, the social position and role types of variables are viewed as having two components, either or both of which may be responsible for the apparent strength of the sociodemographic variable as a crude proxy variable for underlying components. One underlying component is the set of normative expectations associated with the particular role and social positions, as presented to and enforced by the individual's sociocultural milieu and as learned, internalized, or rejected by the particular individual. The second underlying component is a set of other psychological or physical characteristics that tend to be associated with being an incumbent of the particular social position and role.

    The wealth, income, and possessions type of common sociodemographic variable is viewed in the model as having two underlying components, only one of which is similar to the forgoing. The first underlying component is again the normative expectations associated with the possession of a certain amount of wealth, income, or property. The second underlying component is the actual access to resources of all kinds that wealth, income, and possessions or their equivalents (for example, usage rights) give an individual. The ISSTAL model hypothesizes that both kinds of common sociodemographic variables will decline in importance in a multivariate analysis of individual discretionary behavior when the appropriate underlying components are properly measured and entered into the analysis, especially when dealing with the post-entry stages of the dependent variable, behavior in situation/role. In this sense, the ISSTAL model critiques most social and behavioral scientists for working too long and too compulsively with natural language social position and role names as if they were sophisticated variables when in fact they are crude proxies for underlying variables seldom measured directly and used properly in multivariate analyses. This is not to say the social positions and roles involved are unimportant, but merely that they are being dealt with simplistically.

As for the previous proposition of the ISSTAL model, so too for the present one it is difficult to present solid empirical support here. One reason for the difficulty is simply space limitations. Another is that the appropriate interdisciplinary research using sufficient variable subtypes and classes in order to permit testing of these two propositions is exceedingly rare. A third reason is that I have not yet had time to review the literature thoroughly to find all such relevant "needles in a haystack." Let me, therefore, offer some examples. The first is a study by Bronfenbrenner (1960), who was examining participation in community associations as his dependent variable with a sample from a small U.S. community. He included a number of important attitude and personality variables and even a measure of intellectual capacities along with standard sociodemographic variables in his analysis. When he performed a multivariate analysis, the sociodemographic variables dropped out as important predictor variables. This so puzzled the author that he subtitled his article "The Case of the Vanishing Variables." In terms of the ISSTAL model, there is no puzzle in his results at all: He was simply clever enough to include sufficient relevant mediating variables from the explanatory variable classes of personality and capacities, attitudinal variables, and perhaps information, to eliminate any direct effects of the sociodemographic variables upon participation in his analysis. Had he performed a path analysis, it is likely he would have found direct effects of the sociodemographic variables upon the mediating variables of his study because the zero-order relationships of several of the sociodemographic variables were of the usual direction and statistical significance.

The second example of the kind of study that supports this proposition is by Christensen and Yoesting (1973, 1976), based on a study of the use of outdoor recreation facilities among north central Iowa adults. Using as predictor variables measures of coparticipant status (a situational variable indicating whether or not anyone, and if so who, is accompanying the individual in participation), early childhood experience with similar participation (a social background variable not of the usual sociodemographic type), general attitudes toward leisure activities, and various usual sociodemographic variables, his multiple-regression analysis showed the latter variables to have very little explanatory power once the former variables were taken into account.

A final example, drawn from my review of the church attendance and participation literature (Smith, 1979a), is a study by Roof (1976), that indicates how contextual variables can decline to negligible importance in a multivariate analysis if the proper intervening social-psychological variables are included. Using data from a sample of North Carolina Episcopalians, Roof performs a multiple-regression analysis on both church attendance and church organizational participation, separately, in which he shows that community size and length of residence lose their zero-order significance in relation to church attendance when an attitude scale of "local community reference" and years of formal education (itself a sociodemographic variable) are included in the analysis. For the church organizational participation dependent variable, the results are similar, but community size was not initially statistically significant in its relationship. (See also Smith, 1979b.)

T. Another form of patterned consistency of relationships the ISSTAL model postulates involves the sequential specificity aspect of the model: Relationships between types of instances of human individual discretionary behavior, as dependent variables, and particular classes or subtypes of explanatory variables are expected to be generally stronger for the more specific variable classes and subtypes of variables. This greater strength of relationship with behavior is expected and hypothesized for all three types of sequential specificity distinguished earlier—abstractness or generality, longer-term temporal sequence, and shorter-term time phase sequence for behavior in situation/role. The general argument for expecting such a pattern is that the greater the relevance of an explanatory variable spatiotemporally to a given instance of dependent variable behavior, the stronger the causal linkage is likely to be. Another part of the argument is that human behavior is extremely complex and variable; so more general and spatiotemporally distant factors tend to have less explanatory power for behavior units because of the variety of more specific and proximal events that tend to intervene and cause variations within larger or longer-term patterns. Finally, there is also an argument based on levels of system reference, suggesting that variables closest to a given level of system reference (for example, humans as psychobiophysical systems versus organizational or role systems versus societal or cultural systems versus the total world system) are most likely to be influential causally at a given level of system reference. Thus, in studying human individual behavior, those more sequentially specific classes and subtypes of explanatory variables are likely to have the strongest relationships to the dependent variable of individual system behavior because such explanatory variables are closest in level of system reference. Were one studying the behavior or operation of organizations, variables relating to social structure and roles characterizing the organization and variables relating to the organization's environment would be closest in level of system reference and hence most likely to have strong relationships with the dependent variable (see McGrath and Altman, 1966). And so on for the study of whole societies or institutional subsystems thereof or for the study of the world system.

There is a good deal of empirical support for this proposition in the research reviewed in most of the review chapters on informal social participation in this volume, though not in a readily usable form. Again, space and time limitations prevent more than the giving of an example or two here from the types of discretionary participation literature I have reviewed. More specific variables (attitudinal and situational) in terms of the sequential specificity aspect of the ISSTAL model have thus been found to have stronger relationships with outdoor recreation and sports participation than more general (sociodemographic and contextual) variables (Christensen and Yoesting, 1973, 1976; Hobart, 1975; Murphy, 1975; Outdoor Recreation Resource Review Commission, 1962a, 1962b; Snyder and Spreitzer, 1974a). Ajzen and Fishbein (1969) have shown similar relationships for a variety of leisure and recreational activities, including mass media exposure, cultural and entertainment events, and indoor social and games activities. My supplementary review of the church attendance and participation literature (Smith, 1979a) also supports the proposition from various studies, as does my review of the voluntary association participation literature (Smith 1975).

U. The ISSTAL model postulates that the process of humanization and particularly culturation, socialization, and personality or character development, can be best understood as occurring in a time-ordered sequence of phases potentially, though not every phase may be of significant duration or occur in the usual order for every individual. These phases represent both continuity (in the sense of progression through time) and discontinuity (in the sense of discrete phases, stages, or even "plateaus" that punctuate the developmental progression). The central progression of humanization will vary by culture, subculture, social-structural location of the individual, individual genetics and physiology, nonhuman environmental factors, and uniqueness of the individual character. However, a basic underlying pattern consistent across all these variations will eventually be discernible, with the variations being seen as modifications of it.

This proposition asserts the fundamental similarity of all members of species *homo sapiens* in terms of the processes that produce "humans" rather than just another one of the higher primates. Evidence for this fundamental similarity comes from anthropological studies of large numbers and a wide variety of types of cultures and societies. Murdock (1949), for instance, presents a partial list of over seventy features that seem to occur in all human cultures. Hall (1959) and others present alternative sets of such "cultural universals." For any of them to be universal aspects of culture implies there are universal similarities in the culturation process. Similar evidence can be presented from the realm of social structure, viewed especially from the perspective of age positions and roles. Thus, Eisenstadt (1956), Ariel (1965), Glaser and Strauss (1971), and others have shown social-structural consistencies across societies in the kinds of demands placed upon human individuals according to their ages. From the standpoint of maturation and character development, numerous authors have delineated important stages or phases of growth, without necessarily specifying *discrete* life phases or stages (for example, Baltes and Schaie, 1973; Brim, 1966; Bruner, Oliver, and Greenfield, 1966; Buhler and Massarik, 1968; Cain, 1964; Cumming and Henry, 1961; Datan and Ginsberg, 1975; Elder, 1975; Flavell, 1963; Goslin, 1969; Goulet and Baltes, 1970; Lidz, 1968; Mortimer and Simmons, 1978; Phillips, 1969; Riley and others, 1972).

However, a number of authors have been working in the past decade or so to extend and revise discrete life phase theory or models, sparked initially by Freud and more recently by Erikson (1959). These researchers hypothesize varying numbers of discrete phases, sometimes for the entire life span of the individual and sometimes for particular portions of it (for example, Gordon, 1976; Gould, 1972; Kohlberg, 1969; Levinson, 1978; Lowenthal and others, 1975; Sheehy, 1974; Spierer, 1977). Lack of adequate longitudinal comparative research makes it impossible to determine which, if any, of these various formulations best approximates the basic underlying pattern of relatively discrete but progressive stages of the humanization of an individual through the life span. But collectively, these works suggest strongly that some such pattern probably exists, as postulated by the ISSTAL model, along with variations from it.

V. Inherent in the ISSTAL model is a perspective that accepts not only the possibility but the probability of intrinsic and fundamental "dualities" in the nature of human individual behavior. Such dualities are the equivalent in the human sciences of the wave-particle duality in quantum physics, the latter referring to the fact that light and other electromagnetic phenomena (and perhaps other phenomena as well, such as gravitation) can only be adequately understood, predicted, and explained by viewing them as operating simultaneously as waves and as particles, in spite of the apparent contradictoriness of the two views. I believe there is a variety of such intrinsic and fundamental dualities that applies to human behavior and an adequate integrative interdisciplinary model of individual human discretionary behavior must take these dualities into account and accept them. However, it is also clear from an examination of human science literature that there is great resistance by the majority, indeed nearly all, human scientists to accepting such dualities, as I have argued at length elsewhere (Smith, 1979e). A simple example of the kind of duality postulated as necessary to this model is the simultaneous presence of both a basic underlying pattern of consistency in the relationships between the independent and dependent variables of the ISSTAL model, as suggested in its "strongest form" previously, and at the same time the presence of major and minor variations on that basic pattern. A more concrete example, presented later, is the simultaneous presence of a primary pattern of positive covariation of valued discretionary activities, as postulated by the general activity model, and major and minor variations from it. Other examples abound in social and behavioral science literature, including, for instance, the fundamental and intrinsic duality that there usually appears to be some kind of "general intelligence" factor coexisting with a variety of major and minor variations in the form of more specific types of intellectual capacities (see Smith, 1979e, for further elaboration and additional examples).

W. Although there are many possible patterns of basic consistency that might exist and be compatible with the strongest form of the ISSTAL model, I postulate that the most likely pattern of basic consistency between the classes and subtypes of predictor variables, on the one hand, and the various major types of human individual discretionary behavior, on the other hand, is the accommodation of body, context, and character to one's sociocultural system postulated as the central causal explanation of the general activity model. I emphasize this pattern is but *one* of many possible underlying patterns so that the ISSTAL model more generally can be clearly distinguished from and hence assessed separately from the general activity model, the essence of which is presented in the next chapter.

X. In terms of mathematical-statistical representation, the ISSTAL model postulates that human individual discretionary behavior in both the short and long term can be fruitfully conceptualized as the result of stochastic processes, with the series of states involved being types of behavior in situations/roles or, more crudely, simply situations/roles or behavior types. A situation/role simplified view of a person's life span would describe it as a series of situations/roles that characterized the individual actively throughout the life span. Similarly, a simplified behavior type view of a person's life span would describe it as a series of behavior types that characterized the individual over the time from birth (or even from "quickening" in the womb) to death. In any of the three approaches, there is a transition probability matrix that reflects for some specified population the likelihood of an individual in that population moving from a given state (behavior in situation/role, situation/role, or behavior type) to another state. It is an empirical question whether some type of Markov model is most appropriate to characterizing the transition probability matrix or whether some more complex stochastic process model is more appropriate (see, for example, Tuma and Hannan, 1979; Tuma, Hannan, and Groeneveld, 1979). The patterns of probabilities of transition for a given population are largely determined by the nature of the social and historical context, that is, by aggregate data and global characteristics of a particular society, culture, and its population. However, the pattern of probabilities of transition for a given individual is determined, at any point in the life span, by a combination of the population transition matrix of probabilities and the individual's own unique variation of that transition matrix.

Analogically, one may think of the population transition matrix as a kind of sociocultural "carrier wave" of transition probabilities; the individual's unique variant transition matrix modulates or modifies the general population probabilities carrier wave to produce a resultant transition probability matrix equivalent to the total broadcast signal emitted from a particular radio station at a particular time. Alternatively, one may view the population transition matrix as a major variance component and the individual's unique transition matrix as a minor variance component, the two of which combine to account for much of the total variation in actual role transitions for the individual. The full range of individual characteristics of social background and more psychological characteristics determine an individual's particular variant transition matrix. Multiple-classification analysis or multiple-regression analysis could be applied alternatively to the forgoing, with different analyses performed for different end states of interest (behavior types, situations/roles, behaviors in situations/roles). The virtue of the stochastic process approach is its greater simplicity and ability to encompass massive amounts of information very compactly.

Y. Although at one level of analysis, stochastic process models seem likely to provide highly parsimonious and useful mathematical mappings of behavior in situations/roles in everyday life and the entire life span, other more deterministic (versus probabilistic) types of mathematical mappings are also likely to be useful in various circumstances. It will be particularly important to develop an adequate dynamic form of the ISSTAL model, which might be termed a DISSTAL model (where "D" is for "Dynamic"), or a dynamic version of synanthrometrics. Such a dynamic model is necessary to do justice to the complexity of human individual behavior. It cannot be a simple, recursive, linear model; it must be nonrecursive and perhaps nonlinear. It will involve mediated effects, sometimes through multivariable linkages and feedback effects of both a positive and negative kind. Given the number of variables that has been shown to be relevant to individual human behavior, the model must necessarily be highly multivariate and probably will involve a complex set of differential equations. Systems of linear equations may well not be adequate. Human behavior is far more complex than the phenomena of the physical or biological sciences (Smith, 1980), both of which often use nonlinear mathematics, including nonlinear differential equation systems, to provide adequate mathematical mappings. How then can human scientists reasonably expect the phenomena they study to be amenable to adequate mapping by the simple linear and recursive mathematics that is almost universally applied (with economics and geography being major exceptions, but still often fitting the forgoing shoe)? Techniques such as those discussed by Blalock (1969, especially chap. 6), Asher (1976), Bielby and Hauser (1977), Goldberger and Duncan (1973), and numerous others in annual volumes of *Sociological Methodology* need to be applied to the overall ISSTAL model and its subcomponents. This is one of the major tasks for further development of the model, as noted earlier.

Z. The postulated fruitfulness of representing a dynamic version of the ISSTAL model mathematically and statistically both in terms of discrete, probabilistic, finite mathematics of stochastic processes *and* in terms of continuous, deterministic, nonfinite mathematics of differential equation systems and structural models of a nonrecursive and perhaps nonlinear sort is itself a direct example of the kind of intrinsic fundamental dualities postulated to be necessary for adequate understanding of individual human discretionary behavior, indeed, of all human individual behavior. It is particularly interesting that this duality may turn out to be the human science equivalent of the mathematical wave-particle duality in quantum mechanics, which also turns on the necessity of mathematical representation, at times in discrete forms and at times in continuous forms, in order to understand the phenomena of interest. Human behavior, like electromagnetic radiation, has simultaneously both continuous wave and discrete particle aspects much in need of further study.

Conclusion

Detailed presentation of the content of the ISSTAL model along with arguments and evidence supporting its validity lead to the conclusion that this theoretical framework has genuine promise for providing a kind of much-needed interdisciplinary integration in the study of human individual discretionary (and possibly obligatory) social behavior. Far more research is needed before the forgoing conclusion can become anything approaching a widely accepted human science world view paradigm, but at least I have now asked this question and shown why it should be given serious consideration.

CHAPTER 19

General Activity Model

David Horton Smith

As suggested in the previous chapter, the general activity model can be viewed as a particular variant of the ISSTAL model. As such, it indicates some special underlying patterns of relationship that are postulated to exist among variables of the ISSTAL model, in addition to the general patterns indicated in the previous chapter along with supporting evidence or argument. A rough sketch of the general activity (GA) model was given in Part One in order to sensitize the reader to possible patterns that might emerge in the various chapters of Parts Two, Three, and Four. Now a more systematic presentation is in order, along with a summary of the most important evidence bearing on its validity.

Content of the General Activity Model

The GA model refers to several important kinds of patterns postulated to exist in the variables that are part of or describe human individual discretionary behavior: (1) The pattern of activity types (such as those distinguished in time budget studies) in which individuals engage in everyday life and over the life span is nonrandom. (2) Although there are other factors that affect or determine this nonrandomness, such as the biophysical environment (for example, daily cycles of light and darkness) and human genetics and physiology (for example, the necessity for substantial amounts of sleep on a regular basis

461

throughout the life span), one very important factor is a kind of mutual accommodation of the individual's sociocultural system and body, character, and context. (3) This accommodation, made primarily by the individual in most cases, is fundamental to the operation of human society because it permits and indeed encourages the optimal accomplishment of activities (by individuals) that are considered good, useful, or proper in the framework of the sociocultural system involved. (4) The main reasons for this accommodation's occurring are, from the standpoint of the sociocultural system, the survival value to the system when encouraging such accommodation and, from the standpoint of the individual, the survival value and quality of life of the individual that results from accepting such accommodation. (5) The process of humanization, particularly socialization and culturation, of the individual is the principal means by which the accommodation is *established*. But this process is never perfect (Wrong, 1961), so the process of sociocultural control (monitoring and rewarding conformity and punishing deviance) is necessary for the *maintenance* of accommodation of the individual to the sociocultural system.

(6) *One central thesis of the GA model, then, is that as a result of this accommodation, discretionary social participation activities of all kinds tend to fall into cumulative patterns* (as do also obligatory activities and probably deviant discretionary activities, though this volume is not concerned directly with these points) *such that socioculturally encouraged* (valued, acceptable) *discretionary activity exhibits significant positive covariation or correlation across types of activity, across subtypes of activity, and through time for both types and subtypes of activity*. Thus, individuals active in one type of discretionary activity of a socioculturally encouraged sort are also likely to be active in other types of encouraged discretionary activity. Similarly, individuals active in one subtype of activity are likely to be active in other subtypes within the given type. And individuals who are particularly active in discretionary activity at one point in their life span are also likely to be active at any other point in their life span, although with a socioculturally encouraged age-related secondary pattern of discretionary activity and life cycle stage effects superimposed upon the general continuity of discretionary activity levels, within and across types. Role linkages and behavior type similarities both contribute to the pattern of positive covariation of activities.

(7) The cumulativeness or positive covariation of discretionary activities encouraged by the sociocultural system applies at all levels of activity such that those of moderate activity level within a given activity type or subtype may be expected to be only moderately active in other activity types or subtypes and to engage in only a moderate number of

other types or subtypes of discretionary activity. And those low in activity levels in socioculturally encouraged discretionary activity of one sort may be expected (probabilistically) to be low in their levels of activity in other types or subtypes of activity and to engage in very few discretionary activities of an encouraged sort, generally. Further, those who are socioculturally deviant in being low in their general discretionary activity levels for encouraged activities will also be more likely to engage in specifically socioculturally deviant (discouraged) discretionary activities.

(8) Because individual activity is most properly viewed as occurring in a particular situation or role that has socioculturally defined normative expectations associated with it, the positive covariation of discretionary activity types and subtypes, both synchronically and diachronically, can best be viewed as a covariation of behavior in situation/role, as indicated by the more general ISSTAL model. (9) A major manifestation of this positive covariation, thus, is the probabilistic linkage between different roles and segments of roles (the latter referring to socioculturally meaningful clusters of activity expectations within a given role); some of this probabilistic role linkage is the result of socioculturally encouraged or normative role linkage expectations. (10) Because of the special nature of very highly active individuals and their value to the sociocultural system due to their high degree of interchangeability among roles and behaviors in situation/role, the postulated positive covariation of discretionary activities is hypothesized to be nonlinear, with stronger tendencies for such covariation among very active individuals.

(11) Individual character, body, and context are also significant determinants of the four types of activity positive covariation identified and postulated (synchronic and diachronic inter- and intraactivity type positive covariation) as most basic manifestations of the general activity model in behavior. The term "character" here refers to the entire set of psychological states and processes uniquely characterizing an individual at a given time. The term "body" refers to the entire set of physical, chemical, and biological processes and states uniquely characterizing an individual human being at a given time. The term "context" refers to all states and processes characterizing the universe external to the individual human being at a given time.

(12) The individual's body has an obvious direct causal role in producing overt behavior or individual activities through the movement of muscles, limbs, vocal cords, lips, tongue, and so forth. But more important here is the manner in which the longer-term nature of an individual's body (for example, health; physical fitness; strength; motoric and psychomotoric skills, habits, and capacities; and sensory

acuity and impairments) is accommodated to the patterns that facilitate performance of the most socioculturally acceptable activities, both discretionary and obligatory, within the limits set by the individual's genetic composition and externally induced impairments and constraints (for example, from injury, disease organisms, and intrauterine biochemical environment). Sociocultural systems vary in what is the preferred or acceptable nature of the body, especially emphasizing physical fitness, strength, endurance, psychomotoric coordination, and sensory acuity in preliterate, peasant, and underdeveloped societies where most members' main occupational activities (hunting, gathering, agriculture, food preparation, shelter construction and maintenance, and child rearing) require such bodily characteristics for optimal performance. In industrial and postindustrial (service) societies, many, if not all, of the forgoing become much less important, where most people's main occupational activities (manufacturing, service, child care, and household work with the aid of electromechanical devices) do not require such bodily characteristics for optimal performance, or at least for satisfactory performance.

However, sheer good physical health and normal functioning of sensory and motoric capacities are generally preferred for most people in almost all sociocultural systems. Hence, good health and lack of sensory or motoric impairment are postulated as being positively associated with higher levels of general discretionary (and obligatory social) activity by individuals, both synchronically and diachronically. Other aspects of the body in modern industrial or postindustrial society are postulated as being important only for those types of physical activity that involve extremes of strength, effort, or endurance (for example, special fitness and motoric skills optimal for outdoor recreation and sports activities).

(13) Although the sociocultural system is itself a crucial part of the individual's context, as indicated earlier in the ISSTAL model, the individual accommodates his or her personal context to specific and personally relevant aspects of the sociocultural system and other aspects of the environment, both in daily life and over the life span. For example, the individual accommodates his or her microcontext in daily life by living, sleeping, working, and engaging in valued discretionary activities in socioculturally preferred and acceptable locations and buildings, as well as by commuting or traveling as expected in order to engage in socioculturally preferred activities in the proper locations. Over the life span, the individual also adapts by changing residences, migrating, and changing activity locations and sites to meet life cycle–related, occupational, and other sociocultural system expectations. Here, too, there is much variation among sociocultural systems in

preferred and acceptable aspects of the individual's microcontext, even in such apparently minor aspects as the preferred distance from another person in having a conversation (see Baldassare, 1978; Hall, 1966, pp. 172-173) or personal interaction of some other sort.

The accommodation is not all one way, of course, and individuals can and do to some extent choose and make their contexts to suit their characters. Within this larger set of accommodation processes, it is postulated that higher levels of general discretionary (and obligatory social) activity by individuals, both synchronically and diachronically, will be positively associated with individual access to what are socioculturally defined as the proper or acceptable environments for such activities. More specifically, individuals with greater wealth, income, possessions, and general access to resources and facilities are postulated as being more likely to be generally active because of such access relationships. But irrespective of general wealth and resource access, individuals with greater specific access to appropriate (in sociocultural system terms) facilities for various discretionary activities are postulated as more likely to be generally active in such activities, particularly in those discretionary activity types and subtypes to which they have relevant specific access relationships.

For example, higher general discretionary activity levels are likely to be associated positively with access to a variety of leisure and recreational equipment and facilities, with having access to a car or inexpensive public transportation for travel to discretionary activity sites away from one's residence, with having more leisure and recreational facilities in or near one's work place or home, and such. Further, individuals' higher general activity levels are postulated to be positively associated with the presence of socioculturally favorable or preferred microsocial settings (for example, being asked by a friend to participate or having friends or relatives as coparticipants), preferred human population configurations (for example, absence of a disease epidemic in one's general locality or absence of overcrowding of discretionary activity sites), preferred natural environmental conditions (for example, moderate weather relative to local standards for the season or variety of types of natural settings in one's locality or region of ready access), preferred social-structural conditions (for example, social-structural conduciveness and pressure toward participation or lack of actual or imminent widespread emergency or major problems affecting normal social structure and processes—war, economic depression, and revolution), and preferred cultural conditions (for example, general cultural approbation of leisure, play, and discretionary activities of all kinds, particularly active and social discretionary activities).

(14) The greatest degree of individual accommodation to the sociocultural system is, aside from social behavior itself, in terms of individual character. Including as it does all individual psychological states and processes, character comprises the unique pattern of motivation (personality traits and the full range of attitudinal variables), intellectual capacities, retained information, as well as psychological and related processes characterizing an individual. *It is another central thesis of the GA model that, shaped by and highly variable among sociocultural systems* (DiRenzo, 1977; Inkeles and Levinson, 1969), *socioculturally preferred individual character is postulated to be positively associated with higher levels of socioculturally preferred discretionary* (and possibly obligatory social) *activity by individuals, both synchronically and diachronically.* This general postulate includes and implies several major corollaries, not all of which were mentioned in Chapter One, though the logic for them all is generally the same. Each of these corollaries makes a specific statement of relationship for a different major aspect of human individual character. After stating these corollaries, I will present three additional postulates that are attempts to identify some patterning of socioculturally preferred character types across sociocultural systems in space and time. As such, these postulates give some more specific content to the general assertions implied by this postulate. Note, however, that the present postulate could be true without the next one being true. This means that my specifications of socioculturally preferred character types should be tested independently of the broader assertion of the further postulates.

(15) The active-effective character is defined as a socioculturally preferred character that is, relative to the average positions of the population of a sociocultural system of an essentially autonomous sort (a society or nation-state), *above* average on a series of socioculturally valued dimensions and subdimensions relevant to social participation, to be specified. As an "ideal type" hypothetical construct, this character type might be defined as involving positions near the poles of the various dimensions involved (for example, the highest deciles) relative to a given sociocultural system's distributions along such dimensions. And in the world historical context, the ideal type construct would involve positions near the theoretical (absolute) poles of the various dimensions. The active-effective character is specifically higher than average (or very high) on the following psychological state and process variables:

(a) Intellectual capacities, particularly those involving verbal and social content, and to a lesser extent numerical-symbolic content (see Guilford, 1967).

(b) Certain personality traits, including extraversion, ego strength, emotional stability, intimacy, assertiveness, efficacy, prominence need, practicality, morality, flexibility, energy/activation, deliberateness, stimulation need, curiosity, self-actualization need, effective ego defense, and effective ego expression (as presented in Chapter One). Among these, particularly central are extraversion, ego strength, assertiveness, efficacy, energy activation, and stimulation.

(c) Certain values, such as those "terminal values" identified by Rokeach (1973, p. 28) as a sense of accomplishment, an exciting life, a comfortable life, equality, freedom, self-respect, social recognition, and true friendship. The other terminal values he distinguished, insofar as they are socioculturally valued (normatively expected), are also likely to be peripheral parts of the active-effective character. And individuals who are activity "specialists" in one type of discretionary activity (such as religious activity) are likely to have a special configuration of values, emphasizing one or more of the general set of values (salvation, for example), as preeminent.

(d) Certain general attitudes, such as a positive concern for and interest in community affairs, in politics and political life at various territorial levels, in religion and religious affairs, in the mass media as sources of information, in social welfare and the common good, in recreational and sports activities, in esthetic and artistic-musical activities, in interpersonal contacts and relationships, in organizations as means to accomplish ends, in education and educational activities, in economic and financial matters, in international affairs and relationships, and in other aspects of what is going on in the larger society that are considered important by the sociocultural system. Where kinship institutions are particularly powerful in a sociocultural system (or subsystem), positive general concern for and interest in kinship matters will be an important part of the active-effective character; but in modern society, this is less the case. Thus, at the level of general attitudes, the active-effective character is defined here as being relatively more extrafamilial than familial in orientation, more cosmopolitan than local in orientation (though concerned with community affairs), and more organizational than nonorganizational in orientation (that is, having positive general attitudes toward formal organizations as means of accomplishing goals of all kinds). All these kinds of general attitudes promote, in a modern society, involvement in or engagement with preferred social structures and processes of the larger sociocultural system in which an individual lives rather than withdrawal into oneself or a narrow circle of other people (nuclear family and a few close friends, for instance).

(e) Certain specific attitudes, such as specific positive concern for and interest in various subtypes of conventional political activity (for example, voting for the Republican candidate for governor in the next state election), in various subtypes of nonviolent unconventional political activity (for example, participating in a national boycott of nonunion lettuce when buying at one's local grocery store), in various subtypes of mass media exposure of a less passive sort (for example, reading several newspapers each day at breakfast or around dinner time), in various types of outdoor recreation and sports (for example, playing tennis once or twice a week at one's local tennis club or public courts), in various types of established or nonestablishment subtypes of religious activity (for example, attending one's church or synagogue weekly or proselytizing potential new members of one's sect whenever feasible), in various types of indoor games and hobbies (for example, playing bridge with friends every week or two), in various subtypes of educational and "cultural" activities (for example, taking a course at evening school at a nearby high school or college or attending a concert when a famous musician is featured), in various subtypes of informal interpersonal relations (for example, talking with close friends by telephone after their residences become too distant for in-person conversation, except infrequently, as a result of residential mobility or migration), in various subtypes of giving behavior (for example, giving to the local Black United Fund during its annual campaign), in various subtypes of emergency or disaster helping behavior (for example, helping in informal group volunteer search and rescue activities in the center of one's town after a flood), in various subtypes of nonemergency helping behavior to strangers or acquaintances (for example, helping a stranger with directions when approached in the downtown area of one's place of work or residence), in various subtypes of formal voluntary group activity (for example, participating actively in one's local Red Cross chapter), and in various other types of discretionary time activities. The essence of this set of specific attitudes is individual favorability toward a wide variety of particular subtypes of discretionary time activities or at least toward several subtypes of activity within most major types, particularly those subtypes that involve other people rather than being solitary, that are organized and socially structured rather than being informal and unstructured, and that involve some type of instrumental accomplishment, some overt activity of significant duration-complexity-effort, or some useful or potentially useful outcomes in terms of information, social contacts, social recognition, and resources.

(f) Certain expectations, such as perceived normative expectations of one's sociocultural system (and relevant subsystems) and significant others that involvement in various types and subtypes of discretionary time activities is the preferred and proper way to spend free time, plus personal expectancies that involvement in such types and subtypes of discretionary activities in particular situations/roles will probably provide net satisfactions to the individual. Examples are still more specific versions of the examples given for the category of specific attitudes (for example, that the individual is to a significant degree socially obligated or expected to attend church or synagogue weekly and that some significant intrinsic satisfactions will result therefrom in addition to the avoidance of negative sanctions from one's spouse or friends). The expectations here are more highly situationally specific than specific attitudes and involve details of a particular time, place, set of coparticipants, alternative uses of the discretionary time, probable consequences, and such.

(g) Certain intentions, particularly an extensive set of intentions to participate in a wide variety of types and subtypes of discretionary time activities when the opportunities present themselves or can be created or sought out. This multitude of intentions favoring high levels of discretionary activity in general, across activity types and subtypes and across time, can be viewed as part of the individual's "latent intention structure." It involves a consistent pattern of actual and potential (hence "latent") individual intentions that are highly probable to lead to involvement in extensive discretionary time activity. Persons low in terms of this aspect of the active-effective character tend to have latent intention structures that are *in*consistent in being likely to lead to extensive discretionary time activity or intention structures that are consistent in *not* being likely to lead to such activity. An example of the latter would be an individual whose latent intention structure in regard to discretionary time activity centered on resting, drinking alcohol alone, and watching television extensively for entertainment at home either alone or with a spouse.

(h) Greater amounts of retained information, particularly beliefs and knowledge relevant to and favorable toward discretionary activities of various types and subtypes—access to them, their nature, how best to do or engage in them, when and where best to participate, who best to participate in them with, preparation needed and requirements for optimal participation, optimal means of terminating participation temporarily or permanently, how best to optimize satisfaction from participation, memories of prior participation by oneself and significant others, probable consequences of different modes-styles-situations of participation, outstanding present and prior participants in the activity, standards of excellence, taboo or proscribed aspects potentially related to the type of activity, and so forth. Greater numbers of (nonsymbolic) images regarding various types and subtypes of discretionary activities will also be conducive to greater general participation and hence a peripheral part of the active-effective character. More important, however, are plans relevant to participation in various types and subtypes of discretionary activities, with plans viewed as hypothetical constructs that involve both symbolic and nonsymbolic information about how to engage in such activities. Collectively, the individual's set of actual and potential plans for discretionary time activities are part of that person's "latent plan structure" or pattern. Potential plans are here understood as plans implicit in the individual's retained information but either vague or largely subconscious (unconscious). Following Miller, Galanter, and Pribram (1960), discretionary activity may be viewed in large part as the result of the individual's latent *intention* structure causing execution of elements of the individual's latent *plan* structure through time, though other important determinants have also been delineated here.

(i) Effectively functioning psychological processes, including definition of the situation, perception, sensory-perceptual adaptation, maintenance of self-organization, psychodynamic synthesis, emotional activation, remembering, thought processing, learning, forgetting, focusing of attention, and experiencing or immediate awareness. Each of these processes contributes in its own way to the active-effective character, and inability to function adequately in terms of any one of them tends to make the individual less close to the ideal type of such character for his or her sociocultural system at a given time. Yet these processes are so basic to the nature of human psychological systems in all times and places that it is postulated there will be relatively little variation among sociocultural systems and historical periods in the importance of effective functioning in terms of these processes as significant components of the active-effective character.

(j) Certain preferred or socioculturally "dominant" social positions and roles, both ascribed and achieved, viewed as composites of motivational, informational, intellectual capacity, and psychological process variables that are, from the standpoint of the individual, clustered and interrelated into meaningful larger wholes (sets) as a result of the humanization process. Though there is substantial variability among sociocultural systems and among historical periods in which social positions/roles are most preferred or dominant, it is postulated that in most literate (nonprimitive) societies and during most historical periods the following have been preferred or "dominant" positions and roles: male gender, middle age (relative to the usual life expectancy), married, parent of several "legitimate" children, parent of children who are mainly in the age range of about five to fifteen years, friend of several persons of both sexes, acquaintance of many people of both sexes, member of several formal voluntary groups, nonsick, nonimpaired (nonhandicapped), attractive in facial features, strong, moderately tall, well proportioned for one's sex, nondeviant behaviorally (noncriminal and sane), long-term resident, native (nonimmigrant), urban or suburban resident (nonrural or "backcountry" resident), capital or major city resident (nonprovincial), high in income and wealth (however measured in the sociocultural system), employed in paid work (not unemployed or working for payment in kind, as apprentices, servants, housewives), free (nonindentured and nonenslaved), employed in a large organization or powerful type of social institution, high in responsibility for or control over other people, high in occupational prestige, high in formal educational level, member of the most powerful and prestigious religion (or one of them in a highly multireligious society), member of (one of) the most powerful and prestigious ethnic-racial category (categories), member of one or more high prestige voluntary associations, leader in nonwork organizations one belongs to, firstborn among one's siblings (at least firstborn of one's sex among siblings), born of legitimate parents (nonillegitimate), citizen (nonforeigner or resident noncitizen), enfranchised, born of a well-known and respected family, having many kin who are wealthy-powerful-prestigious, high in social class-estate-caste or equivalent, and having high discretionary powers over the use of one's time.

For certain sociocultural subsystems, there are major variations from these tendencies; and there are often complexities of identifying accurately the "dominant" or preferred social position or role of a given type because "lip service" may be given to (that is, a verbal fiction maintained consensually regarding) the importance of a particular position or role when the facts of actual choice behavior and deference relationships belie the fiction (for example, fictional dominance of religious positions and roles in secular societies). Further, the nature of a particular type or subtype of discretionary behavior-in-situation/role may be sufficiently different from most other discretionary activities in its requirements for optimal participation that the usual socioculturally dominant or preferred social positions or roles do not characterize the modal participant. This makes for variations on the central theme of relationship between dominant roles and high general levels of discretionary activity. The next proposition deals with this point more generally.

There are two important qualifications that must be added to the forgoing presentation of the preferred or "dominant" status relationships with discretionary (and obligatory social) activity. First, for every social position or role that can be ranked relative to similar or related roles (for example, slave versus free person, male versus female, doctoral degree holder versus various lower levels of formal education), the *degree* of difference between the two or more differentially ranked positions is crucial. Thus, ranking per se is really an inadequate measurement method for the purpose; instead, some sort of interval or metric measurement method is needed that can capture the degree of difference in preference, valuation, or prestige of the two or more positions being considered. The greater the absolute degree of difference between the more or most preferred position and the subordinate but related positions on the same dimension or ranking, the more strongly will the preferred status be associated positively with socioculturally preferred discretionary (and obligatory social) activities. For example, the difference between free person and slave is vast, where both are present in a society; but the difference in preference between male and female gender is relatively small and declining in modern, especially postindustrial, society. Hence, one may expect male-female gender role effects on social participation to be small in modern society generally and slave-nonslave effects to be very great where present.

Similarly, the differential valuation of two or more similar or related positions can change in absolute magnitude over time, markedly affecting the strength of relationship of such positions to social participation. Again, gender roles are a good example. In primitive (preliterate) and traditional peasant societies, where agriculture or hunting-gathering are the predominant occupations, the absolute magnitude of the male-female gender role difference in prestige and valuation is usually far greater than in modern industrial and postindustrial society. Hence, the effects of gender role on social participation can be expected to be far greater in preindustrial than in industrial or postindustrial (service) societies.

The second important qualification to the "dominant" status presentation has to do with permanence. The effects of differential sociocultural prestige-preference-valuation of similar or related roles will be much stronger for relatively stable and enduring social positions than for more unstable, changeable, and temporary ones. This follows from the fact that more enduring social positions and roles tend to be more completely internalized by the individual and more consistently socioculturally controlled (monitored and conformity enforced) than more temporary roles in a sociocultural system. As a result, where ascribed and achieved roles have equal sociocultural system preference value, the former may be expected to show more effects on social participation. And among achieved roles, those that are more permanent once achieved (for example, formal educational status) may be expected to show more effects on participation than more temporary ones (voluntary group membership status in modern society, for instance). As with the previous qualification, so too here it is important to attempt to measure differential role valuations with an interval or metric approach in order to test the present generalization, with similar measurement for role permanence.

(16) The more active-effective character is postulated to have a positive association with higher general socioculturally valued discretionary (and obligatory social) activity by individuals both synchronically and diachronically. Thus, this character type is viewed by the GA model as socioculturally preferred. Although there are variations in details and absolute levels on various dimensions across historical periods and across sociocultural systems, this generalization is held to be true for all sociocultural systems and historical time periods, subject to two reservations. First, the more active-effective character is generally assessed relative to modal or average positions of the population of a given sociocultural system at a given time. An active-effective character in the United States today (see Johnson, 1972; Jourard, 1974, for some examples of this ideal type) will be much higher on most of the relevant dimensions of character than either the active-effective character of two hundred years ago in this nation or the active-effective character of ancient Greece, let alone of a preliterate society. Yet the differences will mainly involve relative locations along the character dimensions involved, not the direction of relationships generally.

A second reservation is that there are kinds of sociocultural subsystems with deviant preferred characters—relative to the larger society and its sociocultural system or relative to the vast majority of societies of human beings. The norms of such deviant subsystems are usually superimposed upon individuals humanized in a larger sociocultural system of the common sort, though in some cases individuals may be humanized from birth in these deviant sociocultural subsystems. In either case, some basic elements of the active-effective character model may be changed in direction when members of such deviant sociocultural subsystems are considered. This will be the case particularly, it is postulated, when the subsystem in question emphasizes (a) lack of normal interpersonal relations or minimization of such relationships; (b) lack of normal physical activity or minimization of such activity; (c) nonaccomplishment of normal physical, mental, artistic, or other tasks, with focus on meditation and "being" rather than doing or becoming; (d) extreme specialization of daily and life span individual activity on one or a few types and subtypes (that is, minimization of variation and variety in individual activity); (e) expression of psychological abnormality, whether induced psychologically, biochemically (drugs), or organically (genetics, physiological constitution, disease, or traumatic injury), relative to the larger sociocultural system; or (f) manifestation of collective or individual behavioral deviance from larger sociocultural system norms.

Some examples of such deviant subsystems include, usually, cloistered monasteries and convents, "nonestablishment" ideologically oriented or religious communes, mental hospitals, prisons, concentration camps, violent gangs, terrorist underground groups and other extremist groups and groups in "total environments" (see Goffman, 1961). Space does not permit specification here of the changes in the active-effective character model that would be needed in order to take account of such deviant sociocultural subsystems, but one example may suffice to indicate how and why such changes might be made. In a cloistered monastery or convent, where close, exclusive interpersonal relations are minimized and obedience is emphasized, the direction of relationships of personality variables concerned with interpersonal relations and assertiveness are likely to be altered from that of the general model for the active-effective character. The latter model suggests (as we have indicated) that such personality variables as high need for relational closeness and high assertiveness will be associated positively with higher general activity, but these relationships may fall to zero or even turn negative in a cloistered monastery or convent, where the norms require and reward essentially low closeness and low assertiveness. Thus, for each specific deviant sociocultural subsystem, the norms bearing on character and behavior would have to be examined and appropriate adjustments to the more general model made accordingly. Only in the rarest of instances, however, would more than a small proportion of the total set of postulated aspects of the active-effective character need to be changed in direction, it is postulated. Most changes will be attentuation, at times to zero, of otherwise significant relationships and will affect only a few dimensions of the active-effective character as here defined.

(17) As a historical trend, particularly as a result of the influence of the industrial revolution and the effects of societal modernization upon the individuals (see Inkeles and Smith, 1974), the state-variables (but not the process-variables) of the active-effective character are becoming more prevalent in the world and will continue to do so, it is postulated, barring major and prolonged world sociocultural system disasters or disruptions (barring thermonuclear World War III, ecological breakdown of food production or protection from the sun's ultraviolet rays, pandemic plague or other disease, or a new Ice Age). The active-effective character state-variables would have to be measured in an absolute and worldwide, historically valid sense, rather than relative to a particular sociocultural system at a given time, in order to test and make sense of the present proposition. Hence, unlike prior propositions of the general activity model, this postulate is likely to be extremely difficult and expensive to test. The active-effective character is not identical with the type of character defined by the overall modernity (OM) scale (Smith and Inkeles, 1966), but the two constructs share many

elements, particularly in terms of the attitudinal and retained information aspects of the latter. Some of the modernizing experiences (such as formal education) studied as independent or causally prior variables by Inkeles and Smith (1974; also Smith and Inkeles, 1975) are seen here in terms of social positions or roles that are integral parts of the general activity model. However, it is these modernizing experiences, among others, that lead to the development of the active-effective character as well as to overall modernity, as suggested by the sequential specificity aspect of the ISSTAL model.

Cross-nationally similar changes in social structure, culture, human population variables, and other contextual variables are postulated to be the broader determinants of the long-term historical trend indicated in this general proposition. The social-structural changes involved at the societal level that fall under the broad rubric of "modernization" (for instance, educational upgrading and spread of literacy, industrialization, growth and spread of mass media, and urbanization) are an important part of the determinants of the historical trend; hence, the research of Inkeles and Smith (1974) and others (see the review by Form, 1979, and by Meyer, Boli-Bennett, and Chase-Dunn, 1975) can be viewed as partial support for this proposition, even though I argue here that other contextual changes are also involved.

(18) The general activity model can be viewed as a part of a larger and more generalized ecodynamic theory (see Boulding, 1978, for introduction of this term in a related context) of the adaptation or accommodation of organisms, individually and collectively, to their environments. The GA model is based on and rooted in the accommodation of individual human beings (body, character, and personal context) to their larger social, cultural, biological, and physical contexts. In turn, social and cultural systems can be viewed as adapting to their biological and physical contexts, to other sociocultural systems in their environment, and to outstanding individuals, ideas, artifacts, and subsystems within themselves. And biological populations of organisms, including the human species, also adapt to external biological and physical features of the environment as well as to internal pressures brought to bear by sociocultural systems and outstanding individuals, ideas, and artifacts. Boulding (1978) presents one view of the way much of this may fit together, though without attention to the notion of a general activity model. Where he speaks of three major evolutionary patterns—physical biological, and societal—I would add that a fourth—the psychological —is necessary.

By psychological evolution I mean not a change in the nature of the psychological processes that are part of the active-effective character model but rather a long-term change in the nature of the psychological state-variables (using absolute, cross-culturally and historically valid dimensions) that constitute part of the active-effective character pattern. This psychological evolution is the previously postulated trend for individuals to reach higher average levels on such active-effective character dimensions as the intellectual capacity of interpersonal skill, the personality trait of efficacy, the value of equality, the attitude that political participation is worthwhile, and an interest in worldwide current events. With regard to socioculturally preferred social positions, psychological evolution involves a trend for the elimination of some of the major perceived normative variations in "dominance" entirely (such as the abolition of slavery) and for the diminution of other variations (such as the increasing equality of men and women). The result is that in absolute terms greater numbers of people and a greater proportion of people are high rather than low on these sociocultural preference dimensions of social positions and roles.

All of these trends of psychological evolution refer to the past 10,000 years or so, with particular emphasis on the past 250 years. Still longer term trends are far harder to find evidence for, although they may indeed have occurred. Moreover, the psychological evolution involved is not necessarily unilinear or irreversible, since virtually all of the principal aspects of the active-effective character referred to in this context are learned, consciously or unconsciously, intentionally or unintentionally. If sociocultural systems regress or vary markedly from the evolutionary development of other sociocultural systems, the members of these systems will tend to undergo corresponding psychological devolution (return to an earlier stage of psychological evolution) on the average. At the least they will show variation from the psychological evolution patterns of members of other sociocultural systems of the "mainstream" of societal evolution.

In keeping with the general principle of accommodation of an individual's body, context, and character to the larger sociocultural system, sociocultural system evolution is the primary cause of the psychological system evolution of its members. The evolution of human societies from hunting and gathering nomads to more settled agriculturalists, which occurred about 10,000 years ago, is postulated to have led to corresponding important changes in psychological systems. The settled agriculturalists are considered more active-effective in their character state-variables than the nomads. I know of no tests of this hypothesis, but some of the existing anthropological materials on preliterate societies (for instance, the Human Relations Area Files, created at Yale University, and now available at numerous universities) might be used to make a crude test.

The evolution of psychological *process*-variables of the active-effective character is unclear. The perceptual processes or thought processes of modern individuals may differ not only in the content they deal with but in their actual nature from the corresponding processes of more traditional or even primitive individuals. Certainly one can postulate with some confidence that psychological evolution of psychological process variables has accompanied biological evolution of genus *homo*, with the psychological processes of species *homo sapiens* being higher in terms of the active-effective character process dimensions than earlier species of our genus. But it is quite a different question to ask whether there have been similar if qualitatively less important increases in the effectiveness of psychological processes over the time span of our species' life on earth. Initial reflection and examination of relevant data suggests that many aspects of the sensory and perceptual acuity processes of modern individuals are less effective in an absolute sense, because they are less dependent for their lives and livelihoods on sensory and perceptual acuity than traditional or primitive individuals. However, mass education and literacy in highly developed languages may well have increased the effectiveness of modern individuals' thought processing. If there is an imbalance of net change in one direction in this mixed pattern of greater and lesser effectiveness, it is probably toward the psychological evolution of active-effective character process-variables on the whole.

Future development of the ISSTAL model and its general activity model variant should pay careful attention to the interesting and potentially fruitful possibilities inherent in an ecodynamic analytic approach that includes constructs such as "ecological niche expansion" not only in relation to populations of biological organisms in general but also in relation to the members of sociocultural systems and to sociocultural systems as wholes. However much in disfavor evolutionism may be in the human sciences these days, a more sophisticated approach to long-term historical development of both sociocultural and psychological systems of human individuals using certain evolutionary concepts may prove valuable in the development of human science and a syanthrometric paradigm that does justice to all the complexities of human individual and collective development over the past hundred thousand years or more.

(19) Although the general activity model represents an overarching general type of accommodation between the sociocultural system and an individual's context, body, and character, several other important types of secondary accommodation often superimposed upon this primary type of accommodation are postulated. These secondary types of accommodation account for major variations or deviance patterns from the general activity model, both in terms of types or subtypes of discretionary activity that do not covary with the majority of discretionary activities as well as in terms of independent variable characteris-

tics of the individual that do not covary with discretionary activities as postulated by the GA model. Such secondary variations can be viewed as modifications (modulations) of the primary pattern ("carrier wave") that can amplify, dampen, or otherwise distort the latter under specified conditions. But these variations can be distinguished precisely, it is argued, if sufficiently accurate measurement and sufficiently sophisticated analysis (such as Fourier analysis) are applied. Some of the most important secondary variations or deviance patterns postulated to exist in different combinations, according to the individual, are the following:

(a) A life cycle stage engagement-disengagement pattern (see Cumming and Henry, 1961) is postulated as a major secondary variation modifying the general activity model. In terms of this pattern, the earliest stages of the individual life cycle will deviate from the primary pattern because the individual is in the process of being humanized into the primary pattern of "engagement" with, or involvement in, his or her sociocultural system and subsystems. Similarly, at the latter stages of the normal individual life cycle, there will be deviation from the primary pattern because the individual is in the process of being forced or induced out of the normal engagement mode and into a relatively "disengaged" mode (relatively lower involvement with many aspects of his or her sociocultural system and subsystems). Corresponding to the early engagement phase of this secondary pattern will be greater involvement of the very young in physical sports and recreation as well as in purely expressive play and games. Such types of discretionary activity involve minimal instrumental accomplishment and social responsibility, but gain in the latter qualities with increasing age of the individual. Religious activity of an overt sort is also characteristic of early stages of the life cycle, after infancy and early childhood; but this activity is essentially compulsory for the young child as the parents attempt to ensure proper humanization of their children in this realm. In societies where television and radio are prevalent and where there are entertainment programs specifically directed at young children, extensive passive involvement in such mass media is also common, often at the expense (in time budget terms) of games and play involvement.

Corresponding to the later disengagement phase of the secondary, life cycle pattern superimposed on the primary pattern of the GA model will be general reductions in interaction and the loss of many central life roles (Cumming and Henry, 1961, chap. 12), with corresponding changes in "the quality of relationship in the remaining roles." In addition to disengagement from obligatory work roles, there tends to be disengagement from much discretionary activity in situations/roles of a formally organized, instrumental, active or relatively impersonal sort, with more emphasis on informal, expressive, passive, and personal or solitary discretionary activity. The latter include passive entertainment mass media exposure (radio and television, where available), kin interactions, informal interpersonal relations with friends, religious activity, and resting, dozing, and daydreaming. Discretionary time activities requiring vigorous physical activity and extensive travel tend toward a minimum, on the average with increasing age because of sociobiological, opportunity structure, and normative constraints on the aged.

(b) A psychobiological deviance pattern (see Phillips, 1968) is postulated as a major secondary variation modifying the primary pattern of the GA model. In terms of this pattern, individuals who are very abnormal, relative to the standards of their sociocultural system, in their biological or psychobiological characteristics will show extreme and accelerated disengagement and low levels of general discretionary activity of the sort with which the general activity model is concerned. Because these sorts of individuals are very low in having aspects of the active-effective character, they are already taken account of to some extent by the primary pattern described earlier. Hence, this postulate emphasizes that extreme biological or psychobiological deviance tends to cause more than a linear degree of noninvolvement, or disengagement from involvement, in socioculturally preferred discretionary activity types and subtypes.

If the psychobiological deviance is congenital, adequate initial humanization usually fails to take place and full societal engagement never occurs (for example, in the case of mongoloids or spastic individuals). If the psychobiological deviance is postnatal and traumatic in origin, whether from disease or injury, the disengagement from socioculturally normal levels of discretionary activity is likely to be very sudden and severe in degree, paralleling the suddenness and severity of the psychobiological deviance. The nature of the disengagement and the number and types of activities in situations/roles affected will often be equivalent to the disengagement of the latter stages of the life cycle but may be more severe and widespread. The disengagement may also be temporary and reversible, at least to some degree. In normal individuals who suffer traumatic injury or disease, disengagement may be followed by adjustment and partial or "alternative" reengagement stages or even complete reengagement if the physical problem is totally cured. The extreme disengagement of many elderly individuals is itself a result of the present psychobiological deviance pattern being superimposed upon the normal life cycle stage disengagement pattern of physically and mentally healthy elderly persons. Included in this type of psychobiological deviance pattern are various forms of apparently "purely" psychological deviance of an extreme sort, where no biological determinants are currently known. Certain forms of neuroses (perhaps all), suicidal depressions or despair, and other types of powerful psychological strain are thus included here as probable causes of deviance from the primary pattern of the GA model. Such psychological strains may be thus caused by generally stressful life events (Dohrenwend and Dohrenwend, 1974; Langner and Michael, 1963), by cross pressures or conflicting sociocultural system or subsystem role demands, or by more biologically based phenomena (including drugs and chemically induced psychological reactions as well as disease- or injury-induced psychological reactions).

(c) A psychosocial behavioral deviance pattern (see Malikin, 1973) is postulated as a major secondary variation modifying the primary pattern of the GA model. In terms of this pattern, individuals who act or are labeled as very deviant (in a negative sense) in their behavior patterns, relative to the standards of their sociocultural system, will often show extreme and accelerated disengagement and low levels of valued discretionary activity of the sort with which the primary pattern is concerned. The pattern here will apply to both "primary" and "secondary" deviants. This kind of secondary pattern gradates into the previous one at the point where one considers drug- and alcohol-induced behavioral deviance, as well as psychological strains resulting from conflicting sociocultural system, subsystem, or role demands that lead to behavioral deviance. In its purest form, this secondary pattern results from relatively freely chosen individual behavioral deviance and from sociocultural system reactions to such deviance, or labeling the individual as behaviorally deviant on the basis of minimal cues (usually as a result of normative prejudice toward some characteristic[s] of the individual so labeled). The latter is often referred to as "secondary deviance." Because of subsequent societal withdrawal from, negative sanctioning of, and frequent incarceration of general behavioral deviants, individuals so labeled by their sociocultural systems (or subsystems) tend to show extreme and accelerated disengagement from socioculturally preferred discretionary activities, paced according to the severity and speed of the sanctions meted out to them by their society (or subsystem within it).

Again the central thrust of this postulate is a nonlinearity of the disengagement and social isolation process affecting discretionary activities as well as more socially obligatory activities. People labeled as general behavioral deviants by their society have great difficulties in subsequently engaging in either preferred obligatory or discretionary social activity types. They are driven by a limited opportunity structure to the more passive, escapist, solitary, noninstrumental, and socioculturally deviant discretionary time activities, on the whole. In a sense, this proposition complements an earlier one stressing the nonlinearity of general discretionary (and obligatory social) activity by the most highly societally involved individuals. But where the latter participate more than would otherwise be expected, the general behavioral deviants of a society participate less than would otherwise be expected from their characteristics.

(d) A deprivation-affluence resource access deviance pattern is postulated as a major secondary variation modifying the primary GA model pattern. In terms of this pattern, individuals who are either extremely affluent or extremely deprived in terms of access to valued resources in their sociocultural system (or subsystems) will tend to show less than the otherwise expected levels of involvement in preferred discretionary (and obligatory social) activity types and subtypes. The argument for this secondary variation is that at both extremes of the affluence-deprivation continuum in a society (or subsystem), individuals have fewer incentives to conform to the socioculturally preferred patterns of activity of that society. The very deprived have little to lose by deviating according to their personal preferences because they have few or no valued resources. The very affluent have so much they can literally afford to take the chances of losing significant amounts of their valued resources in deviating according to their personal preferences. And the very fact of their access to so many valued resources makes the likelihood of severe sanctions by society for their deviance much lower, other things equal, than would be the case for individuals elsewhere on the continuum of access to valued resources.

Hence, the pressure of societal (or subsystem) norms regarding preferred activity types and subtypes is stronger in the middle range of the resource continuum; weaker at either extreme, relatively speaking; and weakest in an absolute sense at the lower extreme. This maximum absolute weakness of sociocultural system normative control at the lower extreme of the continuum of valued resource access is postulated as a result of non-institutionalized individuals at this extreme being lowest in their perceived dependence on the society for and probability of valued resource access, and in any event being most likely to be labeled as deviant generally for their behavior (as a result of normative prejudice against them by most members of the society). The very affluent, by contrast, are ultimately quite dependent upon maintenance of the structure of the larger society for continuation of their extremely high level of resource access. Hence, they must still conform publicly to a variety of *basic* societal norms in order to maintain their favored positions, even though they can much better afford deviance than less affluent people. Moreover, they can more readily engage in visible, token conformity while making use of their greater opportunities for privacy, isolation, and exclusivity to engage in private or quasi-private deviance.

(e) A contextual historical change deviance pattern is postulated as a major secondary variation modifying the primary pattern of the GA model. In terms of this pattern, relatively rapid historical (long-term and relatively enduring) change in the context of an individual will tend to produce anomie, defined as conflicting or ambiguous indications of what are socioculturally preferred and valued discretionary (and obligatory) social activity types and subtypes. Such conflicts and ambiguities, owing to historical changes in the sociocultural system, in the human population, or in the natural and artifactual environment, will cause greater variability in patterns of discretionary (and obligatory) social activities and their determinants during the period of rapid change than during more stable periods. This greater variability results from the conflicts and ambiguities regarding socioculturally preferred activities being reflected in both ongoing humanization and sociocultural system control processes as they impinge on individuals in the society (or subsystem). Yet it is also postulated that sociocultural systems tend to adapt themselves to such rapid historical changes in context (including their own nature) within relatively short periods of historical time, so that new moving equilibrium states are established in which there is once again general consensus on preferred discretionary (and obligatory social) activity types and subtypes and hence greater consistency with the primary pattern of the general activity model for that society.

(f) An emergency-disaster-social disruption pattern is postulated as, by definition of "disruption," a major secondary variation modifying the primary general activity model pattern. In terms of this pattern, the actual or imminent presence of a major and widespread emergency, disaster, or other type of social disruption (for example, revolution, civil war, coup d'etat, or invasion) will tend to produce temporary variations from the normal primary pattern such that most usual types of socioculturally preferred discretionary (and obligatory) social activity types occur less frequently and interpersonal helping behavior is generally heightened (see Chapter Fourteen), as in unconventional political participation (see Chapter Five), if the emergency has political connotations of a major sort (as contrasted with a famine, flood, or other weather disaster, for instance). The usual preferred types of discretionary (and obligatory) social activity types and subtypes are reduced because the society or subsystem mobilizes much of its efforts to deal with the emergency-disaster-disruption, sweeping people out of their normal activity patterns and into one that takes major account of the special circumstances. The active-effective character type of person is likely to become at least temporarily involved in extensive helping behavior, unconventional political participation, or both; the individual low on the dimensions of this character type will tend to withdraw even more than usual from social participation. Amount of helping behavior will also depend heavily on the capacity to help; those with appropriate equipment, vehicles, shelter, supplies, and so forth are more likely to be able to help significantly than are those lacking in such special resources or resource access. Involvement in unconventional political participation will tend to occur where a substantial proportion of the population perceives the political effects of the emergency-social disruption to be very important to their own and their families' future general welfare (for example, an invasion that is likely to lead to loss of one's wealth and prestige or a revolution or civil war that is likely to lead to improvement of one's living conditions and job opportunities).

(g) A behavior in situation/role specialization deviance pattern is postulated as a major secondary variation modifying the primary pattern of the general activity model. In terms of this pattern, certain individuals in any sociocultural system (or subsystem) will become "specialists" and highly active in only one or two preferred discretionary (and obligatory) social activity types but inactive in nearly all other preferred activity types and subtypes. This deviates from the primary pattern of the general activity model and is viewed here as resulting from inadequacies of humanization and sociocultural control processes impinging on the individual, on the one hand, as well as from extreme accommodation of the individual to the particular activity types, situations, and roles in question, on the other. Either way, the result will generally be an individual who, in spite of being outstanding in some type of behavior in situation/role, is considered somewhat deviant, lacking in a sense of balance and priorities, and, although perhaps praised, still not really valued by others in the sociocultural system as much as if that individual followed the primary pattern more closely. In the realm of work an example is the so-called "workaholic" or fanatic worker-achiever who has or makes no time for normal discretionary time activities. In the realm of discretionary time, an example is the fanatic and single-minded devotee of any particular type or subtype of discretionary activity, from hang-gliding to chess, from local politics to evangelical religion. Such excessive zeal for any single type or subtype of preferred discretionary activity will tend to be relatively short in duration on the average, given the total life span of the individual, because the humanization and sociocultural control processes of the society will usually be successful in eventually shaping the individual into a more normal pattern, given the constraints of body, context, and character of the person. Only rarely will individuals be able to maintain their specialization for most of their adult years; and such specialization is more likely to characterize youth or the aged, where life cycle patterned deviance from the general activity model is more tolerated and expected in any event.

(h) A secondary deviance pattern of sociocultural subsystems cross pressures is postulated as a major substantive modification of the primary GA model pattern. Variation from the primary pattern will occur in this pattern because individuals are sometimes members of subsystems whose norms differ markedly from those of their larger sociocultural system or who bring the norms of entire other sociocultural systems with them as they immigrate into a new system. In either case, the norms of a second sociocultural system or subsystem may create cross pressures (to use political science terminology) or role or normative conflict (sociological terminology). If there is intrinsic normative conflict regarding valued discretionary activities or valued aspects of the active-effective character, such conflict will tend to result in deviance from the primary GA model pattern when the alternative norms are strongly held or enforced in a special sociocultural subsystem (an ethnic community, for instance).

(i) An artifactual population base rate deviance pattern is postulated as a major methodological rather than substantive, secondary variation modifying the primary pattern of the general activity model. In terms of this pattern, variation from the primary pattern will occur purely as an artifact of measurement and population base rates when the latter rates are very high or very low, thus attentuating the observed statistical relationships. This problem can be handled, in many cases, by appropriate refinement of the measures used so they show more variation for the particular population studied. But if crude dichotomous measures of activity (especially measures of activity in an infrequent or very frequent situation/role) are used, then apparent deviance of the individuals studied from the primary general activity syndrome pattern is likely. The main thrust of this proposition thus is to urge the investigator examining evidence bearing on the general activity model to take account of population base rates, adjusting measurement instruments or procedures so as to maximize population variability on both independent and dependent variable measures to the extent feasible for the given sociocultural system (or subsystem). Otherwise, the actual presence of the primary general activity model pattern will be masked and perhaps even eliminated as an artifact of the measurement procedures used. Use of statistical analysis procedures of little power to detect existing differences and covariation, or use of small samples of individuals, will lead to similarly biased and artifactual results even in the presence of the primary pattern here postulated. Exclusive dependence upon orthogonal rotations of factor matrices, to the neglect of oblique rotations and of the reporting of principal components factor results, is still another kind of methodological bias that will tend artifactually to mask the validity of the general activity model when applied to a variety of measures of activity types or subtypes.

(20) In the broadest sense, the general activity model involves a general theory of social integration of the individual and hence can incorporate a variety of narrower theories dealing with particular types of social behavior (the Durkheimian theory of suicide, for instance). Because of the generalizability of the logic underlying the general activity model, it is postulated that (like the ISSTAL model of which it is a specific variant) the GA model can be fruitfully applied to more obligatory social behavior as well as to discretionary time activity of individuals. However, no direct evidence on the latter point will be presented here because of space constraints. Similarly, it is postulated that the general activity model as presented here will be able to deal adequately with both sociocultural deviance and with sociocultural change, even though it is primarily directed toward nondeviant social behavior during periods of relative sociocultural stability in historical terms. This too remains to be demonstrated elsewhere and subsequently to this volume.

Evidence Bearing on the GA Model

Space limitations prevent, again, more than a relatively brief review of the evidence bearing on the general activity model just outlined. Rather than proceeding to adduce evidence point by point for the various major propositions, I have chosen to focus primarily on two key points suggested in Chapter One as particularly crucial tests of the existence of the GA model. The most essential of these tests can now be stated rather simply, given the forgoing elaboration of the model: Do the data and generalizations from the research review chapters of this volume support the existence of an accommodation process between the sociocultural system and the individual's body, personal context, and character and support the diachronic and synchronic positive covariation of major types and subtypes of socioculturally valued individual discretionary activity? I argue that the answer to both parts of this question must be generally affirmative, taking account of the several kinds of secondary variations from the primary pattern noted in the forgoing section of this chapter. In summary form, the evidence is as follows.

Correlates of Discretionary Activity. First, consider the results of research on various types of discretionary social participation regarding the nature and direction of relationships between independent and dependent variables. The dependent variables here are the various types and subtypes of discretionary participation reviewed in the three forgoing parts of this volume. The independent variables are the various categories of the ISSTAL model for which research existed and was reviewed in those chapters, plus some additional research and research review work that supplements those chapters. If we examine the postulated relationship of general health and nonimpairment of normal sensory-motoric functioning to valued discretionary activity, we find there is insufficient data in nearly every major activity category reviewed here to permit any conclusion (but see Smith, 1975). Only in regard to sports and outdoor recreation participation has there been even a modicum of adequate research. Here the research strongly supports the postulated relationship, with better health and nonimpairment (lack of handicaps, especially severe handicaps) significantly and positively associated with greater outdoor recreation and sports participation, especially of the active physical variety (as contrasted, for instance, with picnicking or driving for pleasure). Clearly, a great deal more research is necessary (or needs to be found, if already existing) bearing on this aspect of the GA model.

There is more research bearing on the matter of accommodation of the individual's personal context to the sociocultural system as postulated by the general activity model, but even here the evidence is rather scant for lack of relevant research studies—with one principal exception. That exception is research bearing on the postulated greater valued discretionary activity of individuals with greater amounts of wealth, income, possessions, and general access to resources and facilities. Research reviewed earlier in this volume on conventional political participation, unconventional political participation, citizen participation in local decision making, mass media exposure, outdoor recreation and sports participation, charitable giving by individuals, and disaster helping behavior generally confirms this relationship; and the research on other types of discretionary participation reviewed does not bear on the question. The review of research on church attendance by Smith (1979a) as well as the national survey by Johnstone and Rivera (1965) on adult education participation and the national survey data reported by Robinson (1977) on adult education, "cultural" activities, and away from home public entertainment participation all lend further support to the present generalization, though Robinson's data fail to support it in the case of religious activity, informal interpersonal relations (visiting and conversation), and resting. The latter exceptions, particularly, come as no surprise because they require little in the way of resources, generally, in order to permit participation.

Study of the effects of more specific types of resource access on participation in the activity type or subtype directly relevant to such resource access has been rare (and no one has studied disuse of available resource access adequately), so this aspect of the GA model remains largely untested. There are a few exceptions, and these studies generally confirm the postulated positive relationship. Thus, in Chapter Eight, I noted that distance from outdoor recreation facilities, once beyond ready access distance (roughly thirty miles or less), was a major determinant of use of such facilities by individuals in a number of studies. Also, a few studies suggest specifically that possessing a TV is associated with amount of television viewing, that possession of an automobile (or more than one auto) is associated with active sports and outdoor recreation, and that possession of sports equipment is associated with participation in the related sport or recreational activity (see Chapter Eight and Robinson, 1977). A related kind of support is the finding that presence of household help (paid domestic workers, at least part time) is associated with more interpersonal visiting (Robinson, 1977). Relatively little attention has been given specific resource access factors in regard to political participation, but some studies have shown that provision of transportation to interested voters who lack it increases voting participation (Milbrath and Goel, 1977). It would, of course, be interesting to determine the strength of other variable classes, controlling resource access.

Other aspects of the individual's personal context held to be conducive to greater participation by the general activity model also have been little studied. The relevance of microsocial settings such as the nature of coparticipants has received attention in only a few studies, principally focusing on sports and outdoor recreation participation. As Chapter Eight indicated, the presence of friends or relatives as coparticipants is strongly associated with such discretionary sports and outdoor recreation activity, consistent with the syndrome postulates. However, there has been more research attention given to other kinds of favorable microsetting situational variables, particularly being asked personally (by telephone or in person) to participate in some kind of discretionary activity. Although Chapter Four does not mention it, Milbrath and Goel (1977) refer to research showing that in-person and telephone solicitation of voting and that accompanying people to vote increases voting participation. Chapter Ten similarly indicated that participation in informal, unconventional religious activity was made more probable where there was active current social pressure, especially from friends and acquaintances, for such participation. Chapter Seventeen indicated that giving behavior was more likely if the individual was personally asked to give, particularly where social influence and pressure via friends and associates are involved or where there is perceived social pressure at work. Further, Chapter Fifteen showed more disaster helping behavior was likely where the individual had more personal contact with victims or with local informal leaders who had information and relevant resources. Chapter Nine indicated conversion to a new religion was much affected by the active recruitment efforts of friends and acquaintances interacting with the individual. In the realm of formal associational participation, the reviews by Mulford and Klonglan (1972) and by Smith (1975) indicated some similar findings, with people more likely to join associations if personally asked to do so and more likely to remain active if they have friends in the association. Other review chapters in this volume have noted that various other situational variables (cues, pressures, and lack of constraints or excuses of nonactivity) favorable to one or another kind of discretionary activity have tended to foster and maintain such activity, as the GA model postulate suggests.

A few kinds of human population variables have also been examined, mainly in regard to the same kind of discretionary activity (though only very few relevant studies exist), showing that overcrowding of discretionary sports and outdoor recreation sites tends to decrease individual participation at such sites. Disaster helping behavior, as reviewed earlier, occurs by definition during a time when the human population in one's context has suffered major loss or damage or is about to do so; hence, it is consistent with the "emergency-disaster" secondary variation of the primary GA model. Similarly, the tendency toward more unconventional political participation during times of severe population pressure and little chance for outward migration is consistent with the secondary variation just mentioned. The quality of the natural and artifactual environment shows up in few studies of discretionary behavior reviewed in this volume, except by definition as a circumstance precipitating disaster helping behavior. Yet Hunt and Goel (Chapter Five) note that unconventional political participation is more frequent during times of disaster, famines, and such, again consistent with the emergency-disaster secondary variation of the general activity model. Chapters Eight and Twelve note the effects of weather, including seasonal effects. The minuscule amount of research available does confirm that outdoor recreation and sports participation is greater when the weather is better, seasonally adjusted, as well as being greater when the weather is better by season (that is, usually in the summer). There are, of course, sports and outdoor recreation activities appropriate to nearly all forms of weather except the most extreme. The effects of the weather and season on mass media activity are quite variable, according to the subtype of activity (Michelson, 1971; Robinson, 1977); but bad weather seems to be associated with greater television viewing among women (Robinson, 1977). This suggests that extreme bad weather, like emergencies-disasters, may depress the usual more active and sociocul-turally valued forms of discretionary activities and substitute more passive and less valued types by decreasing the ecosocial niches for valued activities (cancelled events, closed organizations) and partly by requiring more time and energy simply to cope with the obligations of daily life.

More research is available on some aspects of preferred social-structural conditions for discretionary activities. In the large majority of cases, the results confirm the general activity model, not surprisingly, because the latter merely suggests here that social-structural conditions will be conducive to discretionary activity in a variety of ways. The details of specifically conducive conditions must be indicated separately, for the most part, for each major type of discretionary activity. In another place, this has been done for social-structural conditions facilitating voluntary group participation (Smith and Reddy, 1972b), where it was indicated that individual participation in such discretionary activity of an organized variety is generally greater for greater social-structural openness (nontotalitarian and nonauthoritarian regimes), for greater social-structural societal modernization, for high community socioeconomic level, for greater degrees of organizational development of a community (per-capita number of formal organizations of all kinds), for low population and especially small towns, and for certain organizational characteristics of the group in which participation is being examined (for example, higher required minimum levels of participation, broader distribution of organizational control and decision making, higher ratio of perceived member benefits to costs of membership, greater proportion of association members holding office, smaller size of association, and lesser degree of formalization of the association). Various of the review chapters in this book present some related findings from studies of informal social participation.

As indicated briefly in Chapter Four and more extensively in Milbrath and Goel (1977, chap. 5), conventional political participation by individuals has been found to be facilitated by such social-structurally conducive factors as the presence of parliamentary democracy, voting rights, a developed party system, broad and open eligibility requirements for voting and office holding, more socioeconomically developed societies, and other factors. Parkum and Parkum indicated in Chapter Six that citizen participation in community decisions was facilitated by the presence of extensive federal funding for such citizen participation programs, by urban violence (riots) in the recent past of a given city, and by worker management and employee participation schemes in major business firms in the community. Hunt and Goel, in reviewing unconventional political participation in Chapter Five, suggest this kind of discretionary political activity is facilitated by rapid socioeconomic development and social change, by the uneven spread of commerce and industry within a society so major geographical discrepancies result, by the development of political institutions for parliamentary democracy lagging behind aggregate popular aspirations and demands for them, by low levels of political party system development and few mediating voluntary organizations between the elites and the masses, by lack of national or local government regime legitimacy, by lack of regime flexibility and adaptability to changing conditions in the society, by indiscriminate government repression of dissent and disproportionate response to unconventional political activity, by inconsistency in government coercion, by the presence of effective protest organizations (see Gamson, 1975), and by other factors.

Though encompassing a wide variety of social-structural factors, the forgoing are all consistent with the general activity model postulate on structural conduciveness, although the latter requires a great deal more specification itself (elsewhere and subsequently) to avoid sometimes being a tautologous catchall. For the moment, space limitations prevent doing more than indicating that all the previously mentioned social-structural conditions found to be associated with discretionary political activity tend to share a very important characteristic that may be taken, for the present, as the essential or defining aspect of a "social-structurally conducive" factor: The forgoing factors or conditions all tend to expand existing social-structural opportunities for political participation, to create new opportunities, or to make the creation of such opportunities likely to result in collective goods for significant numbers of people in the society. In a sense, then, the common factor is the creation or expansion of a social-structural "niche" for conventional or unconventional political participation and community decision-making participation, analogous to the creation of ecological niches for new species or genuses of biological organisms (though even niche theory in biology has its problems). In both cases, the concept of niche refers to a configuration of circumstances in the environment that is potentially utilizable for the development and maintenance of a certain pattern of activities over time by a population of living organisms.

Part Three further confirms the relevance of social-structurally conducive factors, so defined. Pittard-Payne, for instance, suggests in Chapter Ten that the development of new, informal sects and cults and corresponding individual religious participation in them results in part from increased leisure time in postindustrial society and from the increasing problems (especially financial, moral, and organizational) of established or conventional churches. Together with the general pressure of modernization and increasing organizational complexity, with many alternatives for formal religious participation (or even alternatives to religious participation at all to meet personal needs), the forgoing social-structural changes have opened new social-structural niches for more informal and personal kinds of religious groups and individual religious participation. The formerly extremely powerful social pressures on individuals to participate in one or more established or conventional religions of their society have been weakening, so that not only does informal sect or cult religious participation become a viable niche, but also totally non-group-related religious activity and lack of any religious affiliation at all.

Turning to mass media participation, the creation of new or expanded niches social structurally becomes even more obvious as a type of important determinant of individual participation. Jeffres and Robinson note in Chapter Twelve that greater mass media participation has been found to be related to differences among and within societies in the presence of mass media sources (for example, radio and television stations, newspaper publishers, book publishers, and magazine publishers). The presence of a broadcast mass media source in a particular area (that is, reaching a particular population) creates social-structural conduciveness or a social-structural niche for individual participation in that broadcast medium within the particular population. The greater the number and types of mass media sources available to a given population, the greater will be the social-structural conduciveness to individual participation and the greater the observed participation, other things being equal. The prevalence and variety of mass media sources in a society or area are in turn affected by such variables as degree of freedom allowed to the mass media by the government, economic development levels, degree of urbanization, average education and literacy levels, and related factors. The more modern the society social structurally and the greater the freedom of operation allowed mass media sources, the more social-structural conduciveness toward mass media participation there is. Such conduciveness is not an equivalent of the dependent variable, though some readers might consider it so, incorrectly.

The social-structural factors reviewed in Chapter Eight also fit the niche creation-expansion hypothesis suggested. Because the evidence is quite consistent, we need only consider a few examples here. One important social-structural change over the past few hundred years has been an increase in the amount of free or discretionary time available to individuals. Although this increase seems to have leveled off for the past several decades, the change from earlier centuries is quite marked. The result is the creation of an extensive variety and number of social-structural niches for all kinds of discretionary individual participation, sports and outdoor recreational activity included. A second social-structural change affecting sports and outdoor recreational participation has been the development of new types of sports and recreational activities, each one constituting a new social-structural niche for individual participation. And as noted in Chapter Eight, new types or subtypes of sports and recreational activities have tended to be developed among the upper ("leisure") classes and then spread throughout other parts of the society, extending the participation niches to ever broader portions of the population. In many ways, the invention and development of new subtypes of sports and recreational activities was facilitated by technological advances involving equipment, sites, means of access to sites, and other artifacts. One of the simplest but most pervasive examples is the invention and widespread use of the electric light, which opened up great quantities of time for indoor and outdoor sports and recreational activities that were not feasible with gas, oil, or candle lights. The full realization of the use of night time has only begun, argues Melbin (1978). Another example of social-structural change that has facilitated more sports and outdoor recreational participation is the changing role of women in society. As the traditional passive, weak, nonassertive, fragile stereotype of women has declined gradually with modernization (though still dominant in most societies), sports and outdoor recreational participation niches have been greatly expanded for women, however limited they may still be. With further change in the direction of greater gender role equality of opportunity in societies, even greater increases in female participation in sports and outdoor recreation can be expected in the future. Two final examples, little studied so far, have been the impact of commercial mass media sources (such as television networks) in causing sports to develop and be of more interest to people, and the impact of sports and recreation businesses in fostering sport and recreation development to create large mass markets for their equipment or services.

       Part Four can also be seen as supporting the social-structural conduciveness aspect of the general activity model. Taking the case of individual giving behavior, as reviewed in Chapter Seventeen, we find that such behavior is more frequent and extensive when the social-structural niches for it are larger and more numerous by virtue of tax laws that favor charitable giving through exemptions for gifts by individuals and exemptions of income of charitable organizations and corporation or association laws that favor or permit the easy formation of charitable organizations with special legal status. Another type of niche facilitation Reddy noted was relative lack of duplication of the use of philanthropic funds from individual gifts with the activities of government agencies; that is, if charitable organizations have no viable niche in terms of their use of individual gifts, relative to government philanthropy in the welfare state, then individual giving behavior is far less likely. Similarly, individual giving behavior was found to be enhanced by other indications of the existence of a viable social-structural niche for charitable organizations—effective, noncorrupt, nonwasteful use of charitable funds; less dependence of individuals in need upon family sources of philanthropic giving, characteristic of more traditional societies; and community norms supportive of individual charitable giving, which are particularly likely in higher socioeconomic status community settings.

The role of social-structural facilitation is even clearer in disaster helping behavior, for much such behavior is informal and short term but widespread, according to Chapter Fifteen. Most of this behavior is shaped by predisaster social structure and norms; but an essential distinguishing feature of much disaster helping behavior is that, insofar as it is informal, it is performed by volunteers in emergent roles and with emergent norms. Thus, the existence of a disaster can be viewed as creating or inducing creation of, at least temporarily (indeed, usually only temporarily), special social-structural niches for informal disaster helping behavior that do not normally exist. When there is no disaster or impending disaster, established institutions and formal organizations, along with more normal levels of interpersonal helping behavior (see Chapter Fourteen on this point), are sufficient to meet widespread socially recognized human needs in the community or society. And even for those individuals whose disaster helping behavior is more formally organized, much of this activity takes place in the context of extended or expanded groups and roles—all of which extension and expansion can be viewed as the creation of new though temporary social-structural niches for disaster helping behavior. Finally, though no thorough review of the determinants of individual helping behavior in normal social circumstances has been included in this volume, it is clear on the face of it that the existence of a potential "helping behavior situation" as a social-structural "microniche" is virtually essential to actual helping behavior. There must be one or more persons the individual can perceive as being in need of some help (that is, a helping behavior situation) in order to create a social-structural, though ephemeral, niche for individual helping behavior to take place. Such situational variables are not sufficient to determine the helping behavior but nonetheless play an important part in the joint determination of such behavior (see Latané and Darley, 1970, for instance).

The special literature review of conventional church attendance by Smith (1979a) further supports the social-structural conduciveness thesis. There is evidence from empirical studies that such participation is greater in smaller communities, in rural rather than urban areas, in more sectlike rather than more established churches, in communities where the prevalence of churches is higher per capita, in churches with more conservative theology and where the norms requiring attendance are greater, and in churches where there are more church attendance opportunities per week. Church attendance is also characteristic of complex industrial societies; but as societies develop into postindustrial stages with corresponding proliferation of alternative organizations and widely accepted secular belief systems as alternatives to sacred belief systems, church attendance and other forms of participation in formal and established, conventional religious bodies tend to decline. All these relationships lend themselves to being interpreted more generally in terms of the number-extensiveness of church attendance niches available to the individual, combined with the strength of sociocultural system and subsystem norms (including the norms of specific religions or branch units of them) requiring involvement in such niches (situations/roles), all taken in the larger context of competing opportunities and demands for discretionary time use.

Smith and Reddy (1972b) and Smith (1975) also confirm the present postulate of the general activity model and the interpretation in terms of social-structural niche creation, maintenance, or expansion. The major social-structural factors favoring greater individual participation in this form of discretionary activity included social-structural openness (versus repression) with regard to voluntary groups, greater social-structural modernization of a society, higher socioeconomic level of a community or neighborhood, greater general level of organizational complexity and development of the community, smaller size of town or city, and possibly other social-structural factors. The connection to more social-structural niches for associational participation is clear for some of these, but others require more subtle interpretation. Thus, the manner in which societal modernization, particularly as a result of the industrial revolution, expanded the niches for formal associations and hence formal association participation is discussed by Smith (1973c) in some detail. It is suggested that the basic roots of the increase in associational participation lie in an expanded variety of values and goals that become widespread within the population (for example, through mass education and literacy and through the mass media), an expanded and more developed transportation and communication structure permitting more kinds and numbers of interpersonal relationships, and a general increase in the collective action orientation of the population (including, among other factors, more permission and instigation of voluntary groups by government and more objective payoffs for their formation).

The preferred cultural conditions that facilitate high levels of general discretionary activity are rather sadly lacking in systematic comparative research, so the review chapters in this volume have relatively little solid evidence bearing on the very simple thesis of the general activity model in this realm. That thesis was that general discretionary activity, especially active and preferred social-discretionary activities, would be more prevalent where there was general cultural approbation of such activities as well as of play and leisure time activity in general. Chapter Eight touched briefly on the literature that deals most generally with this point. That literature, more impressionistic and illustrative than systematically comparative or quantitative, suggests that cultural values regarding play and leisure in general have something of a curvilinear relationship with level of societal and sociocultural system developmental complexity. Thus, preindustrial and postindustrial societies are viewed as having value systems more generally favorable to leisure and discretionary activities generally than is industrial society. In the latter type or stage of sociocultural system development, instrumental accomplishment and not "wasting time" predominate. At the level of more specific major types of discretionary activity, there is also impressionistic and qualitative historical evidence of major variations in such relevant cultural values and traditions as political freedom and individual participativeness in the sociocultural system decisions; acceptability of protest and dissent in search of reform or reddress of grievances; degree of religiosity (versus secularism) of world view and the application of religious concepts to everyday life; freedom of speech, the press, and the broadcast media; emphasis on active sports and outdoor recreation participation (versus passive leisure and spectatorship, if leisure is acceptable at all); emphasis on mutual aid and collective-altruistic values in all phases of life and work, including everyday helping behavior, whether in normal or emergency situations; emphasis on lifelong learning and the value of education and knowledge; freedom of association and the value of formal voluntary groups to accomplish a wide variety of goals; emphasis on close and warm interpersonal relations among individuals rather than superficial or distant relationships; and emphasis on exposure to the most valued achievements of "high culture" in the form of music, painting, dance, sculpture, and so on. The greater the extent to which any or all of the forgoing are present in a sociocultural system, the greater the corresponding types of discretionary social activity and the greater the discretionary social activity in general, strands of research reviewed here and elsewhere (Smith and Reddy, 1972b) suggest.

Having examined the available evidence bearing on the body and personal context aspects of the general activity model, I now consider the evidence for the most central part of the thesis, namely, the relationship of the active-effective character to discretionary social activity. Here the review chapters in this volume provide a great deal more evidence because these kinds of personal characteristics have attracted the bulk of research attention in the study of discretionary social participation by individuals. This attention, however, is far from uniformly spread among the various classes and subtypes of variables of the ISSTAL model relevant here. There is insufficient data on the impact of intellectual capacity variables, for instance, to permit any general judgment to be drawn. Staub and Feinberg, in Chapter Thirteen, suggest that prosocial behavior involves more capacity to take the role of the other and more awareness of the consequences of one's own behavior for others, which suggests higher social content capacities (social skills). A small amount of research, largely on college and high school students, shows mixed results for grades and verbal intelligence in relation to sports participation in Chapter Eight. But Smith (1979a) found some evidence that for the general population, higher intelligence generally is associated with less religious behavior. Unfortunately, these and the other meager results noted seldom come from studies that properly control for potentially confounding variables especially age and education. In an earlier review of the research on individual participation in formal voluntary groups, (Smith, Reddy, and Baldwin, 1972b), however, at least a few studies of more general populations using multivariate analysis procedures showed verbal and social intelligence to be associated with greater association participation by individuals. Moreover, because of the generally substantial association between level of formal education and verbal intelligence in the population of a society as a whole, and because of the generally substantial association between level of formal education and verbal intelligence in the population of a society as a whole, and because of the generally positive and substantial relationship between formal educational level and active social discretionary behavior (as will be discussed later), it seems likely that future research will confirm the positive association between intellectual capacities, especially those involving verbal and social content, and various major types of discretionary activity of a socioculturally preferred sort. The apparent discrepancy with regard to conventional church participation may vanish with proper controls for other variables (such as whether the participation is viewed as intellectually or emotionally compelling) or may be a manifestation of the lesser sociocultural value of such activity in modern society relative to other discretionary activity.

With respect to personality traits, there is some significant research, but only in a few areas of discretionary activity and mainly for a small subset of traits relative to the larger set that the general activity model postulates as relevant. Thus, in Chapter Four, Goel was able to find evidence bearing on the present kind of relationship for only a few traits. Generally, these studies showed more political participation for higher sociability, for greater ego strength, for less dogmatism (more flexibility, less authoritarianism, and less closed-mindedness), and for greater psychic self-actualization needs. Parkum and Parkum, in Chapter Six, find evidence bearing on only one trait: Greater participation is positively associated with a greater sense of personal efficacy. Some of the studies Goel classified as attitude studies measure this variable with sufficient generality that they too can be viewed as further confirmation of the positive association of felt efficacy with conventional political participation. Hunt and Goel, in Chapter Five, find similar support for the positive association of felt personal efficacy and participation, as well as a positive association between personal optimism (ego strength) and participation. But unconventional political participants differ from the primary general activity model pattern in tending to be poorer in general mental health (ego strength, effective ego defense, and emotional stability) and higher in dogmatism than average. These variations from the primary pattern, if supported by sufficient future research to prove themselves stable generalizations, may be interpreted as instances of the psychobiological deviance or the psychosocial behavioral deviance secondary pattern modifying that primary pattern (see Smith, 1975). Hunt and Goel note, however, that the research to date is meager and seems to be biased toward showing unconventional political participants to be psychological deviants, as well as focusing mainly on leaders rather than comparing rank-and-file participants with nonparticipants.

Little research relates personality traits to mass media participation, either in terms of general media types or specific media content according to Chapter Twelve. What little there is suggests that magazine reading (and perhaps, by implication, use of other print media with primarily informational rather than entertainment content) is positively associated with need for achievement (efficacy and prominence needs). Television viewing, which is seen as a passive, relatively nonsocial form of discretionary activity and hence not a part of the set of preferred discretionary activities in modern Western society (especially entertainment television generally versus informative television), is associated with low ego strength of various forms (low self-esteem, high anomie, and high alienation). Chapter Ten makes it clear that, just as this form of social participation is generally socioculturally deviant and nonpreferred, so too are the usual personality traits of its participants the nonpreferred ones, generally opposite to the poles of the dimensions that define the active-effective character. Thus, greater nonconventional informal religious participation is found in the research literature to be associated with greater general dependency (submissiveness, nonassertiveness, and rigidity); more social deprivation and need to belong; more anxiety, suggestibility, anomie; less self-esteem, self-confidence, or ego strength; introversion; and low sense of personal efficacy (fatalism) and low need for achievement (low prominence need). Because the kind of participation involved here is not socioculturally preferred, the findings are consistent with the general activity model, particularly with the psychobiological deviance and the psychosocial behavioral deviance secondary patterns thereof and possibly also with the behavior in role/situation specialization deviance secondary pattern. More information on the individuals is needed in order to be able to determine what mix of these secondary patterns applies. My impressions of the literature and personal observations suggest the third pattern just noted ("specialization") may be most prominent.

Smith's (1979a) review of conventional church attendance research reveals some similar findings for younger frequent church attenders—more personal maladjustment, more dogmatism (closed-mindedness, authoritarianism, and suggestibility), more introversion, less self-esteem, and less emotional stability. These traits tend to characterize the most conservative, fundamentalist, and orthodox church attenders of other ages as well, all being relatively disvalued types of church participants in our society. Hence, if high church attendance among postchildhood younger persons and attendance at very conservative, fundamentalist churches are viewed as nonpreferred in modern, secular society, these kinds of discretionary activity also can be expected to fall outside the primary pattern of the general activity model and into one or more of the three secondary patterns just noted for nonconventional, informal sect and cult activity. However, in a society where conventional church attendance (at least for a particular religion or set of denominations) is socioculturally preferred, adequate national sample survey research including personality trait measures (none of which has been performed in any modern society, to my knowledge) would tend to show the pattern of trait-attendance relationships suggested by the general activity model. The fact that most of the small quantity of research in this area has been done on smaller and special samples, usually without measuring a full range of personality traits, may account for the fact that frequent church attenders seem to be low on dimensions of the active-effective character in the United States, Britain, and a few similar societies where most of this research has been done. If more adequate research studies in these societies show both that conventional church attendance (or some types of such activity) is part of the cluster of socioculturally preferred discretionary activities and that high attenders, or attenders versus nonattenders, are low in the active-effective character, this will be a disconfirmation of the general activity model. Care will have to be taken to determine not only what type but also precisely what level of religious participation is socioculturally valued, however; for it could well be that in modern secular society, the most valued or preferred level is a low to moderate one, with nonattenders and high attenders of conventional churches both being somewhat deviant. In this case, the active-effective character should apply most closely to those individuals who engage in the low to moderate levels of attendance preferred; and special statistical analysis techniques would be required to test for this possibility (that is, not simple correlations or Chi-square statistics).

In Chapter Eight, Smith found that a relatively substantial number of studies on personality and participation (none of them being of particularly high research quality in themselves) indicated participation was generally higher for persons (high school and college students being the usual individuals studied) who showed greater extraversion, greater ego strength and adjustment, greater emotional stability, greater assertiveness, greater efficacy, greater need for prominence, achievement, and prestige, greater morality and altruism, greater flexibility, higher energy levels, greater deliberateness, greater stimulation need, greater self-actualization and creativity, greater emotional detachment, and greater practicality and reality sense. Except for emotional detachment, all the forgoing traits are related as postulated by the active-effective character model to participation, so the results as a whole are strongly confirmatory. The reversal of emotional detachment (versus emotional closeness) may result from a secondary behavior specialization pattern required for skillful, active physical activity. However, there is again much need for better research here that uses larger samples of the general population and a full range of potentially relevant personality traits, with adequate statistical analysis and control procedures. It is no accident that virtually all the aspects of the ideal type active-effective character would qualify as socioculturally preferred or desirable in modern society, as was noted earlier in regard to these traits of the active sports and outdoor recreation participant. This fact is viewed in the context of the general activity model as but one more manifestation of the basic root of the GA model's validity, namely, the accommodation between the sociocultural system and the individual's body, personal context, and character, with individual behavior being basically a function of the latter three factors. Robinson's (1977) data on a national U.S. urban sample indicates participation in visiting, conversation, and away from home public entertainment are positively associated with the personality trait of extraversion (measured by an item asking about interest in meeting new people). This suggests other forms of socioculturally preferred discretionary behavior not reviewed in this volume also conform to the pattern of the GA model, though much more evidence is needed to be very confident of this thesis.

Finally, Part Four revealed virtually no research on the relationship between personality traits and altruism and helping behavior. Reddy noted only one study in Chapter Seventeen showing more individual giving behavior where there was high trust and low alienation. Dynes and Quarantelli noted no relevant studies in Chapter Fifteen, though Barton's (1969) review of disaster behavior indicates disaster helping behavior is more likely where the individual shows more sympathetic identification with the victim (which may be interpreted as reflecting intimacy, extraversion, and morality as personality traits). And Chapter Thirteen in this volume notes that prosocial or altruistic behavior in general is positively associated with greater empathy regarding the other person's emotions, with need for approval, with greater sense of responsibility for others' welfare (morality), with a general factor of value-related personality tests, and, in high-risk potential situations, with more adventurousness (need for stimulation). Hence, the small amount of research in this area of discretionary behavior also confirms the relevance of the active-effective character model for the prediction-explanation of discretionary activity participation.

Available research (however meager and inadequate so far) on various kinds of informal social participation generally supports the general activity model. Either the personality traits suggested by the active-effective character model are associated as expected with the various types and subtypes of discretionary activity or the discretionary activity involved can be readily viewed as not socioculturally valued and preferred in modern Western society. Principal exceptions of the latter sort have been television viewing (and, though no data was presented, presumably radio listening) and both informal, unconventional as well as formal, conventional religious participation. These exceptional types of discretionary activity can be viewed as either passive, world rejecting, or both; socioculturally valued and preferred discretionary activities in modern society tend to be more active and world accepting. Both exceptions also tend to be primarily expressive rather than instrumental in nature and to have (generally but not always) little or no emphasis on utility or accomplishment in one's life in "this world"; but modern society again favors the opposite—utility and accomplishment. It may be predicted from the general activity model that participation in those aspects of television viewing (for example, news and educational programs) and religious participation (for example, helping one's children receive appropriate religious education; helping the needy through religious group activity; and helping to organize, maintain, or develop one's religious group) that have active, world-accepting, useful, and instrumental primary components will tend to attract persons approximating the active-effective character type as participants.

Going beyond the research on informal social participation that has been the focus of this volume, the earlier research reviews by Reddy and Smith (1972) and by Smith (1975) provide relatively strong support for the general activity model, particularly with regard to the most central personality traits of the active-effective character. Thus, Reddy and Smith (1972, p. 293) found highly consistent results from their research review, indicating that formal association participation was positively associated with extraversion variables; with ego strength, emotional stability, and deliberateness (impulse control) variables; with assertiveness variables; and with efficacy and achievement motivation variables. The findings regarding the flexibility trait were inconsistent and inconclusive, and the traits of intimacy (relational closeness) and morality have shown similarly positive though weaker associations with association participation. Other potentially relevant personality traits have gone essentially unstudied. Smith (1975) could add only a few more pieces of research, but these too tended to confirm the relevance of the active-effective character model as a basis of prediction-explanation for association participation. Higher participation in formally organized voluntary action was found for individuals with greater ego strength, morality, efficacy, assertiveness, intimacy, prominence, and extraversion (affiliation need, social conformity, and social desirability). Thus, there is support for the significance of most of the personality traits studied in relation to valued discretionary activities, whether formally or informally structured, as postulated by the active-effective character aspect of the general activity model.

The study of attitudinal variables in relation to informal social participation permits additional testing of the general activity model, but only in some of the subcategories of attitudinal variables. Values individuals hold have been very little studied, for instance, in relation to informal discretionary activities; but the review chapters in this volume have indicated a few bits of relevant evidence. Goel noted in Chapter Four that the value or highly general attitude of civic obligations (valuing participation in the polity) has been found related to conventional political participation in several studies, always with the expected positive association, though this research comes almost wholly from stable democracies. Parkum and Parkum conclude in Chapter Six that citizen participation in local decision making is greater where individuals hold the value or general attitude of community involvement (valuing participation in decisions of the local polity). Hunt and Goel, by contrast, view material values (perhaps Rokeach's "comfortable life") and moral values (perhaps Rokeach's "quality," "freedom," and "self-respect") as leading to relative deprivation attitudes, which in turn are associated with unconventional political participation, in Chapter Five. With regard to mass media participation, Jeffres and Robinson in Chapter Twelve found little relevant research on values, only the finding that individuals holding the common middle-class value of accomplishment or success (educational and occupational achievement) were less likely to engage in extensive television viewing. This is consistent with my earlier point that television viewing is generally a passive, expressive, withdrawing kind of discretionary behavior not overtly and publicly valued as a high prestige discretionary activity by modern society where television is prevalent (though certain aspects of such viewing may fit with other aspects of the socioculturally preferred general discretionary activity primary pattern). It is likely that the accomplishment value is positively associated with some television viewing and other forms of mass media participation, particularly print media and informational or educational broadcast media.

Pittard-Payne, reviewing informal, unconventional religious participation in Chapter Ten, found more participation to be associated with a general search for new values and meaning in life. Lacking any kind of quantitative measure, we cannot be sure what value or values are involved; but the value of "salvation" is likely to be part of the complex here. Smith in Chapter Eight found little relevant research but some indication of greater participation where individuals held the value of accomplishment (valuing education) but not high intellectual or esthetic values (wisdom or beauty). More important were social values and social involvement-conformity, including more conservative religious, political, and social values. However, the few studies involved here were performed on high school or college students rather than on a more general population sample. Perhaps the best study in this context was that by Steele and Zurcher (1973), which reviewed the literature on types of satisfactions obtained from leisure activities and studied the principal values mentioned by a haphazard sample of bowlers from cities in two states. Their findings indicated that identity generation, reinforcement, expression ("self-respect"), and affiliation ("true friendship") were the most frequently stated values for the kind of sports participation involved. Again, a national study focusing on a full range of sports and outdoor recreation in relation to a variety of potentially relevant values is necessary to gain a sense of confidence in the pattern of relationships here.

The same holds true for altruistic and prosocial behavior, where the review chapters in this volume could present but few pieces of research bearing on the effects of values. Reddy in Chapter Seventeen found some evidence of greater giving behavior where both religious and political values were higher for individuals. Kemper suggests in Chapter Fourteen that experimental manipulations that arouse values of altruism, caring for others, morality, and such lead to more helping behavior. Barton's (1969) review of disaster behavior similarly indicates an (indirect) effect of altruistic values and idealism upon the frequency of disaster helping behavior. And Staub and Feinberg in Chapter Thirteen found prosocial behavior to be higher for individuals who generally attached more importance to the whole set of Rokeach's values, who were higher in terms of their level of moral development, and who valued the improvement of others' welfare. Finally, Smith's (1979a) review of conventional church attendance research indicates such participation is positively associated with religious values and conservative values in the social and political realms. In our modern, secular, change-oriented society, such values are probably relatively nonpreferred, hence fitting in terms of the general activity model with the relatively nonpreferred discretionary activity of church participation. All in all, the research on values in relation to discretionary social participation is weak but generally supports the general activity model.

Research on *general attitudes* is more extensive and also more clearly supportive of the general activity model. A main postulate of the model here is that discretionary activity of the socioculturally preferred sort is positively associated with general attitudes that promote involvement in or engagement with preferred social structures and processes of the larger sociocultural system in which the individual lives. The particular type of preferred informal social activity involved affects the kinds of general attitudes that are relevant. In the political realm, Chapter Four showed such preferred discretionary activity to be greater for individuals with higher general interest in and concern with political affairs, higher trust in general political system responsiveness to attempts to influence it, higher personal feelings of political efficacy (ability to have some effects on the political system), and lower political alienation (rejection of system political norms and generalized political cynicism). Parkum and Parkum in Chapter Six find some evidence that participation in community decision making is greater where individuals are higher in general interest in neighborhood problems, more positive in general attitudes toward consumer control of public services (for example, health service delivery), higher in general community interest, and higher in felt political efficacy at the local level. Hunt and Goel in Chapter Five find that unconventional political participation is generally greater for individuals higher in political alienation and distrust but also higher in personal political efficacy (see Gamson, 1968, for elaboration here). Thus, the general political efficacy attitude motivates both conventional and unconventional political participation; but general attitudes toward the larger political system and its responsiveness to conventional political activities seem to determine whether the individual participates in conventional or unconventional (nonpre-ferred) political activities. Individuals active in unconventional politi-cal activities have a higher general sense of inefficacy in terms of conventional political activities, more political sophistication, and greater sense of relative or absolute deprivation (though the evidence is mixed on this latter point, in spite of much theory suggesting its importance).

In the realm of expressive leisure activities, Jeffres and Robinson in Chapter Twelve found evidence of some significant effects on mass media participation of general attitudes toward the credibility of the various media and toward the need for multiple sources of media infor-mation on crucial topics. Pittard-Payne found unconventional informal religious participation to be greater where individuals have general attitudes of social isolation and disillusionment with their society and the world at large in Chapter Ten. Because this type of discretionary participation is not socioculturally preferred, it is consistent with the general activity model that the general attitudes associated with it in-volve withdrawal from, rather than engagement with, the larger society (that is, an example of the psychosocial behavioral deviance secondary pattern is present here). Smith found in Chapter Eight that sports and outdoor recreational participation (as dependent variables) were asso-ciated positively with various measures of positive general attitudes toward leisure, sports, and outdoor recreation. These results were par-ticularly convincing because they held up when social background variables were controlled in a few studies although measures of other types of variables were rarely included. Smith (1979a) indicates, further, that conventional church attendance is greater where individuals have more positive general attitudes toward the local community, lower general political interest, more conservative political attitudes, and stronger general attitudes toward the importance of worship versus church organization activities.

Turning to the realm of helping behavior, Dynes and Quarantelli found in Chapter Fifteen greater disaster helping behavior where individuals felt more general closeness to their community, more posi-tive attitudes toward the community, and more pride in their communi-ty's response to the crisis. Barton's (1969) review of disaster behavior further indicated greater individual helping behavior where people showed stronger general moral standards requiring helping victims, less general blaming of the victims, and less general sense of relative depriva-tion compared with other individuals. Chapter Seventeen showed greater individual giving behavior where there were more general feel-ings of obligation to give funds present, more positive attitudes toward self-reliance rather than governmental dependence in helping the needy, more positive attitudes toward private donations (rather than taxes) to meet human needs, more positive attitudes toward community self-reliance in dealing with its problems, more general interest in politics, and more positive general community attitudes. Finally, Johnstone and Rivera's (1965) national survey of adult education showed greater participation in such activities where general interest in learning and education was greater.

Although there are exceptions, the forgoing research on general attitudes is broadly consistent with the relevant postulate of the general activity model as far as informal discretionary social participation is concerned. The earlier reviews by Mulford and Klonglan (1972) and by Smith (1975) are further confirmation of the GA model postulate in the realm of formal association participation. These reviews indicated more association participation where individuals showed such general attitudes as more general obligation to participate in such associations, more positive attitudes toward the general instrumental value of associations in accomplishing goals, more general preference for formal groups (versus informal or unorganized activities), more of a service orientation to use of leisure time, more positive concern for the community, more sense of duty to the community, more general interest in local and national affairs, more general commitment to solve community problems, less anomie and alienation from society, and more sense of political efficacy. All these findings are consistent with the active-effective character model predictions of more preferred discretionary activity where individuals have general attitudes that promote extrafamilial rather than familial, cosmopolitan rather than merely local (though still locally concerned), and more organizational than nonorganizational discretionary activities.

The essential postulate of the active-effective character model (as part of the general activity model) with regard to *specific attitudes* is that discretionary activity will be greater where individuals have favorable attitudes toward a variety of specific types and subtypes of preferred discretionary activity. The research review chapters in this volume generally support this postulate, as do other reviews and research on discretionary activity. For conventional political participation, Goel showed in Chapter Four that much research supports greater activity by individuals who are characterized by such favorable specific attitudes as political party identification and specific candidate and issue preferences. Similarly, Parkum and Parkum in Chapter Six found evidence of greater participation in community decision making where individuals felt they had more influence in specific decision-making committees, more relevant skills to help in such activities, more of a sense of habitual involvement, and more similarity of attitudes to the attitudes of citizen participation committee staff. Hunt and Goel in Chapter Five found essentially no research involving specific attitudes in relation to unconventional political participation. Pittard-Payne's review of informal, unconventional religious participation in Chapter Ten was similarly devoid of results for specific attitudes, although there is an implication that such participation is greater where individuals perceive a particular sect or cult will provide strong leadership. Jeffres and Robinson in Chapter Twelve indicated a variety of media preference specific attitudes given by individuals as reasons for media participation, but the level of measurement and statistical analysis make the results more suggestive than supportive. Smith's review of sports and outdoor recreation participation in Chapter Eight strongly supports the importance of specific attitudes, which have been recently studied in great detail for certain areas of activity such as camping. That review shows the importance, moreover, of attitudes toward specific activities, styles of participation, and even sites of participation. For instance, national survey research on U.S. outdoor recreation participation revealed that major reasons given for nonparticipation were overcrowding of specific facilities, lack of money or the relevant equipment, lack of time, and lack of the relevant ability to participate well (in the view of the individual).

In the realm of helping behavior, Reddy's review in Chapter Seventeen showed individual giving behavior was greater where the recipient group is known better, receives favorable publicity, has a good claim to the need for charitable funds, has lower overhead costs, is more efficient in spending charitable funds, has an effective program, has beneficiaries of higher repute (lower stigma), is more favorably viewed by one's significant others, and makes more effective claims for charitable funds—all as viewed by the individual. The other helping behavior review chapters provide little or no evidence of the impact of specific attitude factors, except that one might assume the specific attitude of individuals toward whether or not an emergency or disaster exists is vital to the degree of disaster helping behavior. Smith (1979a) mentions a few strands of research on specific attitudes, with greater conventional church participation associated with having more close friends perceived as being in the church and more satisfaction being received from such participation. Robinson (1977) reports similar effects of higher satisfaction upon visiting behavior (as well as religious activity). And Johnstone and Rivera (1965) report that their national survey shows adult education participation in the United States is influenced by specific attitudes toward the utility of such activity in preparation for a new job or enhancing one's skills for one's present job. Other important specific attitudes reported were costs perceived, time required, and the drain on one's energy at the end of the day, all of which were major barriers to participation.

The forgoing material supports the relevance of favorable specific attitudes toward participation (including its site, coparticipants, timing, style, and requirements) as factors facilitating informal discretionary participation. Reviews by Mulford and Klonglan (1972) and by Smith (1975) lend still further support to the general activity model by showing a variety of specific attitudes are also important for predicting and explaining formal associational participation in discretionary time. Thus, such participation has been shown to be greater for individuals with more positive specific attitudes toward a given voluntary group, with more positive attitudes regarding their friends' perceptions of that group, with more sense of influence in the group's activities and decisions, with more felt responsibility for the group's success or failure, with higher levels of satisfaction with the group, with higher levels of personal identification with the group, with more positive attitudes toward the specific purpose of the group and its necessity for existence, with greater perceived efficacy of the group to accomplish its goals (past and future), with greater perceived attractiveness of the group in prestige terms, with higher felt obligation to participate in the group, with higher levels of perceived friendliness with group members, with greater perceived rewards relative to costs of group participation, with greater positive attitudes toward the group's leaders and their behavior in relation to members, with higher perceived decentralization or spread of power in the group, with greater loyalty or commitment to the group, and with a greater sense of personal fit with the group and its members (these attitudes tend to be positively interrelated). In addition to these kinds of specific attitudes that can be applied to prediction-explanation of individual participation across most types of nondeviant voluntary groups, there are also specific attitudes more limited in their applicability that have been found to affect participation in particular groups or kinds of groups (see Smith, 1975). Here one finds perceived political stance of a group affecting participation in a political group, perceived degree of sophistication of members affecting participation in an artistic or intellectual discussion group, and perceived degree of militancy affecting participation in a women's liberation group. Hence, in the realm of formal association participation where specific attitudes have been studied more than in many areas of informal discretionary participation, the active-effective character aspect of the general activity model finds substantial confirmation, even though again the research literature here is thin.

The research literature on the impact of *expectations* upon informal discretionary participation is very meager indeed. Neither Chapter Four nor Chapter Five refers to studies dealing with this subtype of variable, though Milbrath and Goel (1977) note a small amount of evidence that conventional political participation (specifically voting) has been shown to be higher where the individual expects a particular political act (that is, a vote) to have some significant effect on the outcome of a political process. Chapter Six indicated that participation in community decision making was higher where individuals had expectations of greater emotional rewards, more economic or career rewards, more opportunity to make their influence felt in a meeting, and greater probability of success in dealing with a community problem. However, it is not really clear whether the measurement procedures used were getting at specific attitudes or at still more specific expectations here. Chapters Ten and Twelve indicated no research on the impact of expectations, nor did the review by Smith (1979a) of conventional church attendance. But Chapter Eight did indicate a few studies where expectations concerning participation in a particular sports or outdoor recreation activity at a given time and place under certain conditions were examined. These studies showed individuals attempt to balance their skills and the challenge of the situation to maximize expected enjoyment from participation. It was also shown that sports and recreational participation is a function of positive (for higher participation) and negative (for lower or nonparticipation) expectancies regarding the consequences of participation, of the perceived expectations of others for one's own participation, and of the expected reactions of others to one's own performance.

In the realm of helping behavior, Reddy in Chapter Seventeen found some evidence of more individual giving behavior where individuals had greater expectations to benefit from a tax deduction for such giving, greater expected intrinsic satisfaction from giving, greater expected career advancement (among executives and professionals), and greater expected direct or indirect benefits from the specific organization receiving the funds. Similarly, Staub and Feinberg in Chapter Thirteen found evidence that prosocial behavior was greater where individuals expected lower costs of their behavior in terms of time, money, goods, or disapproval. And in his review of disaster behavior, Barton (1969) found evidence of more disaster helping behavior where individuals expect others will negatively sanction a lack of such behavior in the given situation. The earlier reviews of formal association participation by Mulford and Klonglan (1972) and by Smith (1975) are only supportive to a modest extent because so few studies deal with expectations as contrasted with specific attitudes. Nevertheless, there is some further support in that research literature for significant positive effects on association participation of such expectations as a greater ratio of benefits to costs of participation and normative expectations of significant others regarding one's participation. Hence, in spite of very little research attention to the matter, expectations relating to preferred kinds of discretionary participation, both formally and informally structured, tend to have significant effects on actual participation in the direction postulated by the general activity model and its active-effective character aspect.

With regard to the effects of behavioral *intentions* upon discretionary participation by individuals, the cupboard is almost bare of research. This should not come as too great a surprise because the study of behavioral intentions as hypothetical motivational constructs different from attitudes and beliefs is only in its infancy generally (see Fishbein and Ajzen, 1975). The study of the effects of intentions upon behavior well deserves great expansion from its modest beginnings. It is not easy to distinguish such highly specific intentions from somewhat less specific expectations, however, when it comes to empirical measurement. Thus, the study by Ajzen and Fishbein (1969) that shows powerful relations between stated individual "intentions" and subsequent discretionary behavior of various kinds, primarily informal social participation, may be viewed as a study of expectations rather than intentions. But the literature regarding intentions and other psychological variables as predictors of behavior in Fishbein and Ajzen (1975, chap. 8) cites several studies of discretionary behavior that demonstrate clearly the importance of intentions as predictors of religious activity, attendance at sports events, voting behavior, sexual activity, voluntary group joining, indoor game behavior, and other activity. As the authors point out, such behavioral intentions are powerful predictors of behavior insofar as they are measured at the same level of specificity as the behavior or activity to be predicted and insofar as they reflect the person's intention just prior to engaging in the activity. Much of the purported failure of attitudes to predict behavior results from failure to take account of these latter points and from failure to see more nonspecific attitudes measured much earlier than a given individual activity as partial determinants of immediate behavioral intentions. In any event, the available research on the role of immediate behavioral intentions strongly supports the general activity model and its active-effective character aspect in regard to individual discretionary activity.

The entire class of variables I have termed *retained information* has received very scant research attention in relation to most types and subtypes of discretionary behavior. This lack of research is not a result of the unimportance of such variables in explaining informal discretionary behavior; it reflects the inadequacy of theoretical models guiding most research in this field and a tendency to overlook or denigrate the importance of "obvious" variables. Yet what could be clearer theoretically than the fact that individual differences in knowledge of how, when, and where to engage in desired discretionary activity must affect the degree of individual participation in such activity? Milbrath and Goel (1977) cite evidence that higher levels of political information are associated with greater conventional participation in political affairs, and Hunt and Goel in Chapter Five note that unconventional political participation is greater where individuals have more political sophistication (knowledge) as well as stronger belief in the effectiveness of prior unconventional activity. Chapter Six is similar in reporting more community decision-making participation for individuals who understand the issues better, who believe there are local problems needing solutions, and who believe community citizen participation of this sort has improved the local situation in the past.

In the expressive leisure realm, Chapter Twelve does not mention retained information, though at the very least such information based on prior experiences must affect mass media participation, particularly selection among alternative media and media contents. Thus, the differences in media content preferences briefly noted in Chapter Twelve can be taken as indirect evidence of the impact of differences in retained information. Chapter Ten and Smith's (1979a) review of conventional church attendance both make clear the important role of religious beliefs and faith (knowledge, in my terminology) in affecting such participation. Continuing strong conventional religious beliefs and knowledge are positively associated with church attendance and conventional participation; and decline in or loss of belief and knowledge of the basic tenets of conventional religion is associated with either low religious participation in general or the search for a new, often unconventional religious belief and knowledge system. Once the latter is found, active participation in informal, unconventional religious activity is likely to be associated positively with high levels of belief and knowledge of the newly found, unconventional sort. For individuals socialized into an unconventional religious belief-knowledge system, participation in the corresponding activities is likely to be in part a positive function of the individual's degree of belief-knowledge.

Chapter Eight turned up quite a few indications of the importance of retained information of various types. Most obvious and clear has been the research on recreational travel, which demonstrates that the location of one's outdoor recreation is strongly affected by distance to the site (hence, implicitly, knowledge or belief regarding that distance), by the attractiveness of the site, and by the attractiveness of alternative sites within the probable range of travel. However, direct measures of retained information, symbolic and nonsymbolic, are generally lacking in these studies, with the role of such information as an intervening variable generally inferred. Only a few pieces of research directly measure relevant retained information in regard to outdoor recreational activity,

but nearly all of these show such information measures to have a significant effect on participation, as expected by the general activity model.
For instance, not only has research shown recreation site quality information to affect participation, but also the scenic nature of the travel route
and weather information have been shown to affect such participation.
There is growing evidence that outdoor recreation participants develop
mental maps, containing both images and symbolic information, that
guide participation decisions. These mental maps are based on prior .
personal acquaintance or experience of recreation sites as well as upon
mediated, indirect information. Some studies have emphasized that
participation in a particular type of outdoor recreation, regardless of
where, is influenced significantly by pleasant (versus unpleasant) childhood memories of such participation. Other evidence shows sports
participation to be associated positively with broad knowledge about
major professional sports figures, though the relation here is not likely
to be causal.

In the realm of helping behavior, the evidence is again very thin.
Chapter Seventeen showed more giving behavior with greater individual
familiarity with the group to which funds are given and greater knowledge of how that group spends the funds it receives. Barton's (1969)
review of disaster behavior indicated there is greater disaster helping
behavior where the individual believes others in the local environment
accept moral standards requiring it. In another realm of discretionary
behavior, Johnstone and Rivera's (1965) national survey of adult education showed there was much variation in individual awareness of adult
education opportunities, with actual facilities held constant, and such
variations had signficantly affected the actual participation. When
there was a variety of potential facilities in the community, the individual was more likely to participate in the most well known or prominent
of them.

Finally, Mulford and Klonglan (1972) and Smith (1975) also
provide some support for the importance of retained information in
affecting individual participation in discretionary activity, in this instance, formal association participation. Again there are only a few bits
of relevant data, but greater information about the existence, purposes,
nature, membership composition, and activities of a voluntary group
generally shows a positive association with participation in the group
unless the information is unfavorable. Hence, the general conclusion
here must be that retained information relevant and favorable to discretionary activities of a preferred sort tends to be positively associated with
participation in such activities, as postulated by the active-effective
character aspect of the general activity model. However, research bearing directly on this generalization has been barely begun.

The relationship of the individual's *effectively functioning psychological processes* to discretionary activity of various preferred types and subtypes has essentially been unexamined. At most, one can refer to the meager research on the relationship between discretionary participation and bodily health and nonimpairment. Yet that small body of research does not touch on most of the psychological processes specified as important by the active-effective character aspect of the general activity model. Hence, no reasonable conclusion can be reached with regard to this aspect of the GA model, except that much research is needed.

A final important aspect of the active-effective character model is the postulated positive association between preferred discretionary activity participation and *dominant or preferred social positions and roles* in a given society or sociocultural system. In its stronger form, this postulate indicates which particular social positions and roles are most likely to be preferred in literate societies generally, particularly peasant and industrial societies. Because social role characteristics are the most commonly investigated correlates of discretionary participation of nearly every kind, there is a wealth of data here for many of the types of social roles the active-effective character model specifies, though some roles (friendship status, acquaintanceship status, sickness role, handicapped role, behavioral deviant role, slave role, religious role, birth order role, birth legitimacy role, citizen role, enfranchisement role, and kin prestige-power-wealth role, for example) have received little or no research attention. I view most measures of social positions and roles as inadequate proxy variables for more detailed measures of the relevant normative expectations associated with these positions and making up these roles. Hence, it is to be expected that measurement error will attenuate many if not all the postulated relationships involving social positions and roles observed in the empirical literature on discretionary behavior. And where empirically consistent relationships do emerge within and across major types and subtypes of discretionary behavior in spite of the measurement problems, such relationships must be very powerful and important ones for the sociocultural systems studied.

Perhaps the best example of the latter type of consistently powerful relationship involves the complex of variables related to or composing socioeconomic status. By definition, these variables are directly concerned with socioculturally preferred and valued social positions and roles. The principal roles included in this small set are, in modern society, educational attainment role, occupational prestige role, wealth-income role, and general social class or social stratum role. Wealth-income role is here distinguished from actual wealth, income, possessions, and resource access, which were dealt with earlier as aspects of the individual's personal context. In preindustrial societies, caste, estate, and family lineage are also part of this complex of variables, as is achieved or ascribed "nobility" (in the sense of lords, knights, duchesses, and such rather than in terms of character) in some modern societies. The results of research on informal discretionary activity of various types reviewed in this volume are relatively unequivocal in regard to the formal educational attainment variable.

Preferred informal discretionary activities tend to be consistently associated with high levels of *formal education*, relative to the average for the society as a whole. The review chapters of this volume have found this to be true for conventional political participation (except voting, in some cases), unconventional political participation (especially for leaders relative to their constituency), participation on community boards and committees (again, especially relative to the constituency), secular giving behavior, disaster helping behavior, mass media participation (except television viewing, usually), and sports and outdoor recreational behavior. The relationship seems also to hold moderately well for informal, unconventional religious participation, but with some major exceptions—as might be expected because this kind of discretionary behavior is nonpreferred. Smith's (1979a) review of conventional church attendance shows the standard relationship with formal education, at least for the United States. Johnstone and Rivera (1965) as well as Robinson (1977) find the same relationship for participation in adult education discretionary activity, and the latter national survey data also find this relationship for participation in away from home public entertainment and in cultural events.

The earlier reviews of formal association participation by Payne, Payne, and Reddy (1972) and by Smith (1975) indicate great consistency in this same kind of relationship. The exceptions seem to be of the kind that "prove the rule," for they are nonpreferred discretionary activities like television viewing (at least in Western, modern, and non–centrally controlled nations; the relation with education is the standard one in Eastern European countries, where most television programming is educational), some unconventional political activity, some unconventional religious activity, and passive leisure like resting. There are obviously retained information and motivational components to the effects of high formal educational attainment besides the effect of this being a dominant or preferred status. However, such effects have yet to be separately investigated, in keeping with the crudeness of measurement of social position and role variables already noted.

Preferred discretionary activities, informal and formal, also tend to be consistently positively associated with higher *wealth-income-resource access status*. Because the normative expectations of different levels on this dimension have not been adequately investigated, as contrasted with the sheer contextual resource access factors reviewed earlier, it is virtually impossible to determine the relative strength of the two effects for different kinds of discretionary activity. This same lack of differentiation in measurement also makes it unnecessary to repeat here the confirmatory evidence given earlier. There are exceptions to the generalization, but these are usually interpretable as resulting from the affluence-deprivation secondary deviance pattern, from very high base rates of the type of activity involved, or from the psychosocial behavioral deviance secondary pattern (where the discretionary activities in question are nonpreferred and hence the usual dominant status-role relationship is not expected to hold).

Occupational prestige position further confirms the general pattern for the socioeconomic status complex of variables, with high occupational prestige positions being consistently associated with higher conventional political participation (except in some modern, status-political-party polarized societies), higher community citizen participation in decisions, more individual giving behavior, more disaster helping behavior, more mass media participation (except television viewing), and more sports and outdoor recreation participation, according to the review chapters in this volume. Smith's (1979a) review of research on conventional church attendance, Johnstone and Rivera's (1965) national survey of adult education participation, and the reviews of Payne, Payne, and Reddy (1972) and Smith (1975) on formal associational participation are likewise generally confirmatory. By contrast, participation in unconventional religious activity and in unconventional political activity is associated more with middle or upper-lower occupational prestige positions of individuals, consistent with the psychosocial behavioral deviance secondary pattern of the general activity model. The exception to the general relationship found in societies where there are two or more social and occupational prestige position polarized political parties can be interpreted either as a manifestation of the secondary pattern just noted or as a manifestation of a major split in society regarding consensus on preferred occupational roles. Where Marxist-Leninist ideology is very strong among the working classes and rejected by the usually higher occupational prestige strata, separate definitions of preferred or dominant occupational prestige positions may emerge in the two broad segments of society, with higher political participation to be found among the individuals with more preferred occupational prestige positions in *either* segment insofar as participation in and for that segment is concerned.

The broader composite measures of social class or *socioeconomic status* show results consistent with those just reviewed for the various major components of such status. Hence, in terms of the clearest test of the preferred or dominant social position-role postulate of the active-effective character aspect of the general activity model, the results support the thesis presented. More than this, however, the results link in a theoretically meaningful way a variety of strong and consistent relationships with different forms of discretionary behavior that have hitherto not been seen as connected. As for other elements of the active-effective character model, the results of the literature reviews in this volume force the open-minded reader to consider the nature of the larger whole of which previously isolated but consistently significant generalizations may be a part. But if the dominant-preferred social position-role thesis is correct, other types of social positions-roles should also confirm it at least to a modest degree.

Consider *gender* roles, for instance, though in modern post-industrial society the absolute difference between male and female gender roles has narrowed considerably from what was and is normal in industrial and preindustrial societies especially. The literature reviews in this volume generally support both the postulate of preferred male gender role being positively associated with discretionary behavior and the qualification that such differences have declined markedly in post-industrial society. Chapter Four shows, thus, that male gender is positively associated with higher conventional political participation in most studies around the world, particularly in less-developed nations, with the gap greatest at lower socioeconomic status levels, and with relatively little gap present in male versus female participation rates in the United States. Indeed, time series data on the male-female participation differential in India over the past three decades show that the narrowing gap in that developing country is roughly in step with the societal modernization that has taken place. While male-female gender role differentials have generally narrowed or vanished in informal discretionary participation in the United States, as in total mass media participation, there are still residues of the earlier male dominance relationship in the most socioculturally preferred types of mass media participation, such as newspaper and general reading per day and in viewing educational television. The reviews of formal associational participation by Payne, Payne, and Reddy (1972) and by Smith (1975) further confirm the general pattern indicated, with its qualifications.

But there are more major exceptions in a few areas of discretionary behavior. First, there are some kinds of discretionary activity that have become female gender role specialties, representing the behavior in situation/role specialization secondary deviance pattern relative to the primary general activity model. Conventional church attendance (see Smith, 1979a) and to a lesser extent other religious activity, conventional and unconventional, constitute good examples of a major type of discretionary activity where women are more active in modern society. In the long sweep of history, this can be seen as evidence of the lessened importance of religious activity of all kinds in industrial and postindustrial society. In preindustrial societies, males tended to predominate in religious activity because religious activity has more importance in such societies and hence the preferred gender role of male is associated with it. The remnants of this ancient legacy can be seen today in modern societies, where by far the majority of religious leaders, of conventional and unconventional religious groups, are men. There are other areas of discretionary activity, usually subtypes of broader types where men predominate, in which women tend to be more active. Thus, there are certain sports, hobbies, helping activities, aspects of community citizen participation, and formal associational activities in which women predominate. But virtually without exception, these discretionary activity subtypes tend to be less valued or even nonpreferred by society in terms of their prestige. And there are other types or subtypes of discretionary activity in which women predominate, perhaps as a manifestation of the psychosocial behavioral deviance secondary pattern (for example, occultism and astrology, visiting and conversation, and resting; see Robinson, 1977, for evidence on the latter two categories).

The relation of *age* role to discretionary participation is another area in which the dominant social position-role thesis can be readily examined, though again the relationships are complex. The most general pattern of results is consistent with the active-effective character thesis of highest participation in middle age in literate societies, so curvilinear relationships between age and preferred discretionary participation are frequently observed. This is found for conventional political participation, for community decision-making participation, for most mass media participation, for giving behavior, and for formal association participation (Smith, 1975). However, there is also a strong engagement-disengagement secondary deviance pattern that occurs frequently in the relationships between age and discretionary activity. As noted earlier, highest religious activity and television viewing are characteristic of the very young and the very old, with both activities serving as humanizing influences for the young and means of disengagement or withdrawal from society for the old. This bimodal age pattern with regard to religion holds mainly for conventional church participation (Smith, 1979a); unconventional religious activity is more characteristic of youth, according to Chapter Ten. Further evidence of the engagement-disengagement secondary deviance pattern is seen in the greater involvement of youth and younger adults in adult education activities (Johnstone and Rivera, 1965; Robinson, 1977) and in sports and outdoor recreational activities of an active sort, as Smith indicated in

Chapter Eight. There are manifestations of the behavior in situation/ role specialization secondary deviance pattern here as well, both for sports and outdoor recreation participation and for disaster helping behavior, each of which is most characteristic of youth or young adults and involves elements of physical strength and fitness. These latter strength and fitness requirements for optimal performance of the behavior in situation/role involved can be viewed as causing the normal preferred middle-age status to become secondary to a preferred youth or young adult status.

Racial-ethnic roles are another frequently studied type of social background characteristic. Because of the relativity of racial-ethnic rankings by society and over time, however, and the close connection between low ethnic-racial position and low socioeconomic status in a society, the empirical results of research here are complex and often difficult to fit into a meaningful larger theoretical pattern. Hence, here is a special challenge to the active-effective character thesis and the general activity model to provide integrative theory where it will otherwise be lacking. The most general finding from research on preferred discretionary participation, both informal (as reviewed in chapters in this volume) and formal (as reviewed in Payne, Payne, and Reddy, 1972; Smith, 1975), is less such participation for individuals of low racial-ethnic status, such as U.S. blacks. But this differential tends to narrow or vanish when socioeconomic status controls are introduced. In absolute terms, then, low racial-ethnic status individuals participate less actively in most preferred forms of discretionary activity (see Robinson, 1977, p. 32, for an overview from his national survey data on various types of discretionary activity), at least in the United States. Such individuals are higher, however, on certain less-preferred or nonpreferred types or subtypes of discretionary activity, such as conventional church participation (Smith, 1979a), television viewing, radio listening (Chapter Twelve), and resting (Robinson, 1977, p. 32, provides data supporting all three of the forgoing points). These results are consistent with the affluence-deprivation resource access secondary deviance pattern relative to the primary pattern of the general activity model.

Deprived and discriminated against, blacks in American society tend to participate less on the average in the socioculturally preferred discretionary activities while participating relatively more in the less-preferred or nonpreferred types and subtypes of activity. The psychosocial behavioral deviance secondary pattern also applies here because blacks are stigmatized on the whole in American society. Only when there is special emphasis on development of racial pride and self-consciousness and awareness of the roots of their disadvantaged status in American society do blacks tend to become particularly active in preferred discretionary activity, as in certain forms of conventional political activity, in ethnic mass media participation, and in black formal associational participation. Here we see examples of the behavior in situation/role specialization secondary deviance pattern from the primary general activity model pattern. In all, the general activity model and three of its major secondary variations seem to make fairly good sense of the patterns of relationship between racial-ethnic status in the United States and discretionary participation. Research from other societies is insufficient to draw any reasonable conclusions; but impressionistic data from certain white-controlled African nations and from European origin-controlled Latin American nations suggest blacks and native Indian peoples in the two continents, respectively, are likely to be subject to the same patterns of discretionary activity, but with even more gap in the participation levels of the high- versus low-status racial-ethnic categories. Hispano-Americans and Native Americans (Amer-Indians) in the United States are likely to show similar patterns, as are oriental-origin individuals to a lesser extent relative to European-origin whites. But the crucial test of the present aspect of dominant status theory would be to examine how European-origin whites participate in sovereign and powerful societies with oriental or black racial-ethnic status as clearly dominant and preferred. In such settings, the general activity model would predict lower participation rates for the whites, if they are truly socioculturally nonpreferred, than for the dominant Orientals or blacks, other things equal.

There is a complex of *life cycle stage* variables in addition to age that sometimes has been studied in relation to discretionary activity. Most common of these other variables is *marital status*, where some of the review chapters in this volume have turned up relevant data. Thus, married individuals seem to participate more in conventional political activities, in disaster helping behavior, and in mass media consumption. Johnstone and Rivera (1965) find some tendency for greater adult education participation among the married, and earlier reviews of formal associational participation show similar results (Knoke and Thomson, 1977; Payne, Payne, and Reddy, 1972; Smith, 1975). Unfortunately, these studies very rarely control for age effects. If they do, they usually fail to do so in terms of the relevant normative expectations for age roles versus marital status roles; so the statistical controls end up more of a hindrance than a help. The secondary pattern of engagement-disengagement deviance from the primary general activity model pattern is observed for conventional church attendance (Smith, 1979a), where married persons participate less than the single (young) or widowed (old), and for sports and outdoor recreational participation, where the never married young participate most actively (Chapter Eight). Two other life cycle stage variables, *family size* and *ages of children*, have received less attention. But what little evidence there is suggests that participation is greater in both informal and formally organized discretionary activities where family size is moderate and where children are all of school age or older. There is a great deal of variability in the results here, however, according to the type of discretionary activity involved; so more research with direct measurement of the norms and constraints of life cycle stage variables is needed—especially research that attempts through multivariate analysis to assess the relative effects of the various interrelated aspects of this complex.

Another set of social position-role variables of interest has to do with nonprestige aspects of occupations, namely, sheer *employment status* (employed versus not) and *occupational types* or situs. The data are sparse and the results ambiguous, so no conclusion is attempted here other than to state that effects of such variables have been observed but rarely if ever have they been disentangled from possible confounding effects of other variables (for example, gender, marital status, age, and occupational prestige level). A final set of social position-role variables to be considered here is *locational roles*—those dealing with where one resides or works and how long one has done so. The only one of these variables that has received sufficient, if very modest, research attention to permit the drawing of reasonable conclusions is the length of time an individual has been a resident in his or her present dwelling or community. Both for several of the types of informal social participation reviewed in this volume and for conventional church attendance (Smith, 1979a) and formal associational participation (Payne, Payne, and Reddy, 1972; Smith, 1975), longer local residence has been found to be positively associated with higher participation. As usual, there are exceptions to this generalization and a need for more research with appropriate controls for other factors. Moreover, there is great need for some exploration of the norms associated with urban versus suburban versus rural residence, with capital or major city residence versus residence elsewhere, and with residence in a particular state, province, or region of a country —all in relation to discretionary activity. At present, the research on urban versus rural residence and regional differences does not permit distinguishing contextual effects from social position-role effects, owing to inadequate measurement procedures.

Summing up the research bearing on the dominant or preferred social position-role postulate of the active-effective character model, it seems fair to say the empirical support is rather impressive but not thoroughly convincing. As in so many other aspects of the general activity model, and the active-effective character model in particular, many necessary types of research have not been performed and much existing research has methodological flaws that vitiate its usefulness. This is particularly true in the study of social positions and roles in relation to discretionary activity, where specific normative expectations associated with the positions and making up the roles are very rarely measured, instead using simply the social position incumbency as a proxy variable. Nonetheless, the dominant status postulate seems to have genuine promise and is worthy of much further attention. As suggested by Smith (1975), this thesis seems to have relevance far beyond the study of formal associational participation, where it was first introduced by Lemon, Palisi, and Jacobson (1972).

So far in this chapter, the evidence reviewed has dealt solely with the relationship of independent variables of individual body, personal context, and character in relation to various types and subtypes of discretionary activity. The second main test of the general activity model is direct evidence regarding the interrelationships of major types and subtypes of discretionary activities, particularly preferred activities in a given sociocultural system. According to the general activity model, there should be both synchronic and diachronic positive covariation (correlation, association) both among and within major types of preferred discretionary activity in a society or sociocultural system. The general failure of social science to generate much longitudinal research will make it impossible to test adequately the diachronic aspect of the forgoing postulate. But there are several pieces of research that will permit testing of the synchronic covariation thesis, and some cross-sectional research involving retrospective self-report data will allow at least some tentative conclusions regarding diachronic covariation.

Synchronic Covariation of Discretionary Activities. As Milbrath and Goel (1977) and Verba, Nie, and Kim (1971) showed, there is significant positive covariation among nearly all types of conventional political participation (with voting in national elections weakest in the cluster) and even broader covariation among both conventional and unconventional political activity subtypes (with the exception of the most violent types of the latter). Verba and Nie (1972, p. 62) present very convincing evidence of the positive covariation for conventional political activities in their principal components factor analysis of thirteen types of participation. The resulting first factor accounted for 31 percent of the total variance, and the second factor accounted for only 14 percent. This indicates the presence of a fairly powerful general underlying factor in the data, according to accepted methodological criteria. Further support is seen in the fact that all the factor loadings of the thirteen forms of participation on the first factor are positive in direction and have a magnitude of .45 or greater. Orthogonal rotation of this factor matrix shows the various items also fall into subclusters, with higher intracluster covariation than intercluster covariation. This is an example of the intrinsic, fundamental duality postulated as characteristic of human behavior by the ISSTAL model. Chapter Four shows that various forms of political participation also covary with participation in formal associations. Indeed, most researchers who have looked into this matter tend to view associational participation as a partial cause of higher-level conventional political participation, though adequate longitudinal studies have yet to be performed to settle the matter. Hunt and Goel in Chapter Five find evidence that formal associational participation is positively associated with unconventional political participation as well, at least in well-differentiated (presumably literate, possibly modern) societies. And Parkum and Parkum in Chapter Six find that formal associational participation is positively associated with citizen participation in community boards and committees, just as the latter is also positively associated with conventional political participation. Thus, all the research review chapters in this volume bearing on political participation have found evidence that significantly supports the intratype and intertype synchronic positive covariation thesis of the general activity model, though many major types of activity seem not to have been studied in relation to political participation.

In the realm of expressive leisure, Smith in Chapter Eight found strong evidence from national survey data in the United States and smaller samples that there is significant positive covariation among outdoor recreation and sports activities, even though most investigators fail to analyze their data in such a way that this covariation can be seen. In the large national sample referred to, fifteen different kinds of outdoor recreation activities were factor analyzed with a resulting first principal components factor that was very large, relative to the next and subsequent factors, and hence that indicated a general underlying common factor. Further, all fifteen activities had uniformly positive factor loadings on this first general factor with a magnitude of .30 or larger. Again, the fact that subsequent rotation of the factor matrix by the orthogonal Varimax procedure produced four interpretable factors is also meaningful but does not deny the importance of the general factor revealed by the positive covariation among the total set of activities. As with the similar results for political participation, this is a case of what I have termed intrinsic, fundamental duality where both seemingly incompatible views of the phenomenon must be accepted at the same time. Any incompatibility of the two views is in fact in the eyes or mind of the beholder, not in reality.

In addition to several studies finding such internal positive covariation among outdoor recreation and sports activities when such covariation was appropriately looked for, still other studies reviewed in

Chapter Eight have found evidence of the positive covariation of out-door recreation and sports activities with other major types of preferred discretionary activities. Thus, formal associational participation; crafts and hobby activities; conventional political participation; mass print media exposure; religious participation; attending movies, plays, concerts, museums, lectures; attending sports events; interpersonal activity with friends; and visiting relatives all have been found to be positively associated with outdoor recreation and sports activity. The main exceptions among common discretionary activities seem to be television viewing and radio listening, which do not usually positively covary with outdoor recreation and sports activity.

Only one of the studies with data bearing on this kind of positive covariation among preferred discretionary activities shows some clear recognition of its importance. Curtis and Milton (1973), performing a secondary analysis of national sample Canadian data on individuals aged fourteen and older, introduced the term "centrality" to make sense of the positive covariation among the clearly different types of discretionary activities they found. They defined this term as an individual's degree of integration into the community and the number of ties the person has to the wider community. The availability of resources of all kinds was seen to make for higher centrality, although there were probable ceiling effects noted as well as the possibility of activity specialists. Most important, the authors showed sports and physical recreational activity to be significantly positively associated with community event attendance and other discretionary activities, even with statistical controls for education, sex, age, and marital status. This indicates that aspects of the active-effective character other than social position-role factors must account in part for the observed covariation. The authors saw their general results as stemming not only from differential opportunities but also from differential socialization and differences in personality and attitudes. They made no reference to my earlier work on the general activity model (Smith, 1969; Smith and Reddy, 1972a), so we have here an instance of independent "discovery" or theory formulation.

In studying mass media participation, Jeffres and Robinson in Chapter Twelve did not present any evidence regarding the positive covariation of subtypes of mass media participation. However, such evidence does exist and has existed for many years, as Berelson and Steiner (1964, p. 532) indicate. Researchers in the mass media field apparently take it for granted and see no larger theoretical significance in it as suggested here. The main exception to the positive covariation of subtypes of mass media participation is, as might now be expected, television viewing (and to a lesser extent, radio listening). Chapter Twelve does indicate positive covariation between mass media participation and other forms of preferred discretionary activity, such as formal associational participation, hobby activity, and conventional political participation, with television viewing again being the exception. The positive covariation with other kinds of preferred discretionary participation is stronger for print media participation than nonprint media (including movies, radio, and especially television). Thus, mass media participation shows, on the whole, the kind of synchronic positive covariation postulated by the general activity model.

Chapter Ten presents no evidence on this point. But Smith (1979a) reviews a number of relevant studies. It seems there is a great deal of controversy among researchers and theorists in the field of religion regarding whether religiosity is unidimensional or multidimensional. The problem is almost invariably put in terms of an "either-or," mutually exclusive dichotomy, giving further evidence for my point that social scientists seem generally unable or unwilling to accept intrinsic, fundamental dualities in the phenomena they study. Yet the empirical data are quite clear and have been for many years. There is a great deal of powerful evidence for the significant positive covariation of different kinds of conventional religious activity when samples of the general population are examined with appropriate statistical techniques to permit such covariation to emerge if present (for example, principal components factor analysis and higher-order factoring of obliquely rotated principal components factor matrices). Thus, conventional church attendance is positively associated with involvement in religious voluntary groups, with prayer and religious devotions, and with interaction with friends of the same religion; and each aspect of the latter set is positively correlated with others of this set. Yet at the same time, it is true that some subtypes of religious activity (including here covert activity such as silent prayer, and perhaps religious belief or faith) form clusters that show stronger positive covariation within the clusters than among different clusters.

Such results led Dittes (1969) to conclude there is much evidence for the unidimensionality of religious activity, though the multidimensional approach is also valid. Here there is clear and unusual acceptance of the intrinsic, fundamental duality of religious activity, and more generally clear confirmation of the synchronic positive covariation postulated by the general activity model. Additional research reviewed by Smith (1979a) further confirms the existence of covariation between church participation and other kinds of discretionary behavior, but this positive covariation occurs mainly for religiously related activities such as participation in religious formal associations or interpersonal activity with friends of the same religion. Thus, in keeping with my earlier suggestion that even conventional religious participation may be non-preferred, when extreme, in modern secular society, the more secular aspects of religious participation seem to fit more generally with the expected pattern of positive covariation with preferred discretionary activities while the more sacred, other-worldly aspects do not.

In the realm of helping behavior as discretionary activity, there is little relevant research literature. Chapter Seventeen found clear evidence of the positive covariation of secular giving behavior with both conventional political participation and formal associational participation, as well as with greater mass media participation. Religious giving behavior seems to fit with the rather separate cluster of conventional religious participation subtypes just discussed, for such giving is positively associated with other subtypes of religious participation but not with formal associational participation generally. Informal interpersonal relations do not seem to covary significantly with giving behavior. As for internal covariation, there is some tendency for secular and religious giving to be positively associated, but this seems mainly a result of secular givers who also give to religious organizations or causes. Many religious givers seem to be "specialists," not involved in secular giving. Within the category of secular givers, there is little research on covariation; but what there is tends to support the positive covariation thesis: Individuals who give to one type of secular group or campaign are more likely to give to most other types of groups and campaigns than are nongivers. Such a relationship is a fundamental premise of practical fund raising by professional fund raisers, of course. There is also evidence from a recent national sample survey (Morgan, Dye, and Hybels, 1975) that individuals who give money to a group are also more likely to give goods and to give volunteer time. Thus, positive covariation of money-giving behavior with other subtypes of giving behavior as well as with other forms of preferred discretionary behavior is generally confirmed, with religious giving behavior being a special case that often covaries mainly or only with other religious participation, depending on the sample and measures involved. This confirms the general activity model postulate of synchronic positive covariation once again. The other review chapters on helping behavior, unfortunately, do not present much, if anything, in the way of relevant data for the current issue. Dynes and Quarantelli in Chapter Fifteen simply mention in passing that disaster helping behavior seems to be positively associated with other helping and altruistic behavior in general, as well as with religious participation. Clearly a good deal more evidence on helping behavior other than giving of funds is needed before a firm conclusion can reasonably be drawn.

Reviews by Payne, Payne, and Reddy (1972), Smith and Reddy (1972a), and Smith (1975) on formal association participation provide quite a bit of relevant evidence on this issue. Indeed, it was the study of formal association participation and its consistent positive covariation with other forms of preferred discretionary activity that first led me to consider and then seek extensive evidence to demonstrate the nature and existence of a general activity model (see Smith, 1966, 1969). The earlier reviews just noted show formal associational participation to covary positively and significantly in many studies with conventional political participation; and the same positive covariation was shown in a smaller number of studies for mass media participation, for informal interpersonal activity (with friends, neighbors, and coworkers), for recreational activity, for adult education activity, and even for church participation and social protest activity to some extent.

Smith and Fried (1979a, 1979b) and primary data they report from a national sample survey of U.S. adults in metropolitan areas further confirm the postulated existence of synchronic positive covariation as part of a general activity model. Using data from over 2,600 interviews, they created several scales each based on two or more separate questions about a given type of individual discretionary behavior. The principal types involved were informal neighboring activity (including helping behavior), informal interactions with friends ("close persons"), voluntary association participation, conventional political participation, and recreational activity. Note that these types cut across all three major content categories in Parts Two, Three, and Four of this volume. The results showed that within each type of activity and among the five subtypes of discretionary behavior there was significant positive covariation of different specific forms of reported activity, confirming the GA model in intratype covariation. All the latter Pearsonian correlation coefficients were positive and greater than or equal to $r = .12$ in a weighted version of the data analysis, with a mean positive intercorrelation of $r = .23$ among the five types of discretionary behavior.

The Smith and Fried (1979a) study also shows that informal family or kin interaction as a type of behavior is not a significant part of the larger pattern postulated by the GA model. In fact, kin interactions correlated positively and significantly only with friend interactions ($r = .15$), probably as an artifactual result of the measurement approach that permitted the respondents to perceive some (or, if desired, all) kin also as friends. The lack of any significant correlation generally between kin interactions and the other four types of discretionary behavior has several possible interpretations, none of them inconsistent with the GA model. For instance, a substantial amount of kin interaction may be viewed as socioculturally obligatory and hence nondiscretionary behavior. As such, the present version of the GA model need not be considered as directly applicable without future modifications. Alternatively, for discretionary interactions the usual frequency of performance may well be so high that its failure to correlate with other valued discretionary behavior may be considered a pattern of population base rate secondary deviance from the GA model's primary pattern. The extent to which this is likely is being analyzed.

Although the positive covariation of preferred discretionary activities has been examined most frequently between formal associational participation and conventional political participation (almost invariably finding the expected result in terms of the general activity model), one or both of these major types of preferred discretionary activity has also been found to covary positively with religious participation of a conventional kind, with mass media participation (except television and usually radio exposure), with outdoor recreation participation, with helping behavior, with giving behavior, with informal interpersonal relations (friends and neighbors), with participation in "cultural" activities (concerts, museums, theater, and such), with community resource use (for example, use of local health or welfare service organizations), and even sometimes with family and kin interactions. In several studies, various of the forgoing kinds of preferred discretionary activities are shown to be positively interrelated with each other, not just related positively to associational and political participation.

There are certainly exceptions to this postulated pattern, but they tend to be few relative to the total number of tests of such covariation. And the most frequent exceptions are by now familiar—voting in national elections, religious participation, (most) television viewing and radio listening, unconventional political participation (especially where extreme or violent), and kin interactions. There are two principal types of exceptions in the forgoing list, in my view: First, voting and kin interactions are so widespread and generally normative in society that they are subject to the population base rate secondary deviance pattern or to the behavior in situation/role specialization secondary deviance pattern. More careful statistical analysis will be necessary to determine whether and to what extent the latter explanations for these exceptions are correct. Second, the remaining exceptions tend to be either low in sociocultural system preference when performed to a high degree (religious participation and television and radio exposure) or simply nonpreferred (unconventional political participation, especially when extreme or violent). Hence, the latter exceptions can be, in principle, readily explained in terms of the primary general activity model pattern, which specifies positive covariation among *preferred* discretionary activities for a given sociocultural system. The psychosocial behavioral deviance secondary pattern and the behavior in situation/role specialization secondary deviance pattern, and possibly other secondary patterns (engagement-disengagement, psychobiological deviance, affluence-deprivation resource access and population base rate), may well exacerbate the deviance pattern of these activities from the postulated covariation of preferred discretionary activities. Again, careful measurement and analysis on large samples of the general population will be necessary to resolve these matters.

Thus, as the GA model suggests, for virtually every major type of socioculturally preferred discretionary activity, there is significant evidence of positive internal covariation among *subtypes* of that activity when such covariation is examined appropriately. And, similarly, for virtually all types and subtypes of socioculturally preferred discretionary activity, there is significant positive covariation among different *major types* of activity. The exceptions are relatively few and seem to fit with deviant secondary patterns specified by the general activity model itself, although this fit is at present more hypothetical than empirically demonstrated in a convincing manner. Nonetheless, the central thrust of the majority of relevant studies convincingly demonstrates empirically that there is significant positive covariation synchronically both within and among major socioculturally preferred types of discretionary activity. The internal covariation is present even for some types and subtypes of relatively nonpreferred discretionary activities (such as nonextreme protest activities) which show up as part of the GA model primary pattern in some studies. In all, then, there is rather strong support for this aspect of the postulated general activity model. The strength of this support is all the more surprising in view of the fact that only a few researchers have been the least bit concerned with the possible validity of such a model, let alone trying to demonstrate its validity broadly.

As far as I know, my study (Smith, 1969) that demonstrated the validity of a general activity model within and among association participation, informal interpersonal activity, and mass media activity has not been intentionally replicated, except by a few of my students and by Marc Fried and myself (Smith and Fried, 1979a, 1979b). And that earlier work followed by over a decade the earlier suggestions by Allardt and others (1958b), by Mayntz (1960), and by Ahtik (1962) that something like the general activity model might be valid and a corresponding "socially active personality" might exist. More recently, Marks (1977) has discussed the cumulativeness of roles. One can only speculate that the interdisciplinary nature of the theory involved, together with the necessity for accepting a kind of intrinsic and fundamental duality in human individual discretionary behavior, have served to prevent more resesrchers from examining these matters (see Smith, 1979c, 1979e). Now that enough evidence of the GA model has more or less haphazardly accumulated in the human sciences, and bolstered by the literature reviews and attempted theoretical and empirical synthesis in the first and last parts of this volume, it is hoped the possible validity and importance of the general activity model will be harder to ignore successfully in the future.

Diachronic Covariation of Discretionary Activities. As noted earlier, the dearth of longitudinal studies makes solid evidence regarding diachronic positive covariation within and among preferred discretionary activity types extremely rare. There are only a few strands of relevant research in the substantive review chapters in this volume. Kemper in Chapter Fourteen finds altruistic behavior to be more frequent if the individual has previously engaged in such behavior. Dynes and Quarantelli in Chapter Fifteen note the same kind of diachronic positive covariation for disaster helping behavior. Pittard-Payne in Chapter Ten found informal, unconventional religious activity to follow earlier active conventional religious participation. And Smith in Chapter Eight found a good deal of evidence for current outdoor recreation and sports activity levels to reflect earlier levels. As might be expected, however, the various chapters on socialization have a good deal more to say about diachronic covariation. Each of the five review chapters, dealing with the socialization antecedents of the major types of discretionary behavior reviewed in the several substantive chapters, gives at least some evidence that early or at least prior experiences and activities of a given type have an important influence on subsequent discretionary activity of that same type. The positive covariation over time is definitely present, as indicated by retrospective cross-sectional research for all major types of discretionary activities; and in some instances, there is relevant longitudinal research confirming this relationship. But the amount of sheer positive covariation of types of discretionary activities for individuals has only rarely been measured with much precision, so the level of confirmation of the present postulate of the general activity model is very modest though significant.

Because of the variety of influences on individual behavior at any time and because of the important secondary pattern of societal engagement-disengagement over the life span, I suggest the diachronic positive covariation found generally for various types of discretionary activities, when more adequate future research is performed, will be in the low to moderate range, though highly statistically significant in samples of reasonable size (that is, a few hundred persons or more). The engagement-disengagement secondary pattern suggests the covariation will be greater for time intervals during the long middle period of adulthood rather than for youth or the elderly, where discontinuities will be greater. And, of course, the importance of intervening influences, noted by Bloom (1964), as factors affecting the size of any diachronic covariation means the postulated positive covariation over time of the general activity model will likely be greater for short rather than long time intervals. An important matter for future theory and research is precisely what kinds of intervening experiences between two points in an individual's life span cause major changes in the levels of discretionary activity engaged in at those times. For the present, we must be content on this issue with the meager evidence of this volume and of research on formal associational participation (see Babchuk and Booth, 1969) that indicates some significant positive diachronic covariation in preferred discretionary activity. However weak it may be, it still constitutes significant confirmation for this aspect of the general activity model.

Conclusion

Just as the previous chapter showed consistent and substantial confirmation for the validity of the ISSTAL model, this chapter has shown consistent and substantial confirmation for the validity of the general activity model as a variation of that model. The implications of both chapters are indeed far-reaching. Both suggest the necessity as well as the possibility of a powerful interdisciplinary human science integrative paradigm or set of paradigms for the study of human individual discretionary behavior. There is also the suggestion, based both on the nature of the theory involved and on empirical results, that the ISSTAL model and perhaps its general activity model variant will also be applicable to more obligatory forms of social activity. Testing of the latter suggestion in detail remains a task for future research and synthesis activities. But even if the present models apply mainly or only to preferred discretionary activity, the magnitude of the theoretical integration of otherwise apparently disparate research on individual discretionary social participation studies in different social and behavioral science fields and disciplines is substantial.

Particularly important is the manner in which the ISSTAL model and its general activity model variant push researchers beyond the customary reliance on standard sociodemographic characteristics as independent variables for the prediction and explanation of discretionary activity. Almost equally important is the pressure for more precise measurement of the normative expectations (roles) associated with various social positions, rather than being content with using social position incumbency as a proxy variable for them. And though far from really precise in its present formulation, the ISSTAL model and its general activity model variant provide an extensive set of propositions about the nature of human individual behavior that are subject to testing and falsification as well as confirmation. If some significant future research can be directed toward the more explicit testing of these propositions and refinement of either or both of the models presented here, possibly they will emerge as a new, nondiscipline-bound paradigm for social and behavioral science research on individual social behavior. At the very least, further testing of these models holds the promise of our being able to explain more and more about the broad quality and quantity of human individual social activity rather than getting ever more bogged down in massive quantities of detailed but often unrelated and non-cumulative findings in different narrow areas of study that have no linkages with other areas of study. Instead of explaining more and more about less and less, we shall perhaps be able to explain more and more about the broadest patterns of human individual behavior over the life span and in everyday life. This is both the challenge and the promise of the theoretical thrust of this volume.

CHAPTER 20

Future Directions in Theory and Research

David Horton Smith

Although the amount of research reviewed in this volume is considerable, much future research is needed to test more directly and extensively the central propositions of the ISSTAL and GA models as parts of a larger synanthrometric theory. Some of the propositions presented are already well accepted parts of one or another of the human sciences, so that these require less additional attention. However, many other propositions are either new or are variations or expansions of accepted propositions. These propositions are most in need of future testing, elaboration, and, where necessary, revision. In some cases they mainly need to be acted upon rather than merely given perfunctory assent. Rather than recapitulate all of them here in detail, Tables 1 and 2 present brief versions of key propositions of the ISSTAL and GA models that require substantial future testing.

As with any complex model or theory, neither the ISSTAL nor GA model stands or falls on any single proposition, let alone on any single empirical attempt to test a proposition. But the propositions that I consider most central to each model are marked with asterisks in the two tables. If future research fails in directly relevant and adequate

Table 1. Selected ISSTAL Model Propositions
Especially Requiring Further Testing

- Discipline-bound approaches to research in the human sciences substantially hamper real knowledge growth regarding human informal social participation (ISP)/discretionary time behavior (DB).*
- Most current and past ISP/DB research has been discipline bound in both choice of methods and choice of variables.*
- The average amount of variance in ISP/DB of various types and subtypes currently accounted for in discipline-bound research is low to moderate, very rarely exceeding 50 percent.
- Most current and past research on ISP/DB has failed even to test for proportional reduction of error variance by an appropriate sort of multivariate analysis.
- Although it has been clear for at least the past twenty-five years that multivariate analysis using multiple classes of predictor variables substantially increases explained variance and understanding of ISP/DB dependent variables, there has been little, if any, proportionate increase in the use of such an approach.
- Most human scientists in fact engage in "antiscientific" behavior from the standpoint of real growth in knowledge, because of the suboptimization that occurs by following the most broadly consensual norms of one of the human science disciplines (and subfields within it) while ignoring the larger goal of increasing understanding of human behavior.*
- Two principal aspects of the suboptimization of human science research stemming from discipline-bound research paradigms are (1) the retreat into qualitative impressionism of a relatively nonreplicatable sort, or (2) the retreat into quantitative narrowness of a relatively irrelevant or trivial sort—with respect to the larger goal of understanding human behavior.
- Most human scientists lack sufficient awareness of relevant research and theory in disciplines other than their own or even outside their specialties within their own disciplines; this limits optimal real knowledge growth.
- The established human science disciplines (sociology, psychology, political science, economics, anthropology, and others) generally treat interdisciplinary research and theory as deviant, ignoring or punishing such activity rather than rewarding and recognizing it.*
- There is an equivalent of the economic Gresham's Law in the realm of human science inquiry generally, such that "bad" (inadequate, discipline-bound) research tends to drive "good" (adequate, non-discipline-bound) research out of the knowledge marketplace, particularly in terms of publication and use.
- The real growth of knowledge in the human sciences over the past several decades has greatly lagged the apparent growth; the information and publications "explosion" in this realm is partly the result of the prevalence of trivial, spurious, and inadequate research being published as "contributions to knowledge."
- The rate of real growth of knowledge in the human sciences, particularly in regard to ISP/DB, is significantly hampered by the very social structure and culture of the human science disciplines themselves. Change in the current social structure and culture of the human science disciplines is required for optimal growth.*
- ISP/DB can be better understood using a six stage behavior in situation/

Table 1 (continued)

role dependent variable approach rather than the usual combined (multistage) dependent variable or single stage variable approaches.*

- Attempting to understand or analyze ISP/DB out of its life span and daily time allocation context leads to spurious conclusions and misinterpretations and to less explained variance.*
- Although longitudinal (time series) and time budget (time allocation in daily life) methodologies have been present in the human sciences for half a century, their proportionate use in research remains very low in the study of ISP/DB in nonlaboratory situations.
- Resources invested in longitudinal (life span) and time budget (time allocation) research average greater contributions to the real growth of human science knowledge than equivalent investments in the more usual approaches to research, especially for ISP/DB.
- The six main ISSTAL model types or classes of predictor state variables and their principal subtypes are both necessary and sufficient for static (versus dynamic) explanation and understanding of ISP/DB.*
- Although all of these main types and subtypes of ISSTAL model predictor variables are needed to understand ISP/DB, not all of them, let alone every specific variable within every type and subtype, will have significant direct effects on ISP/DB; some will be important mainly or only because of indirect effects.*
- When all of the main types and subtypes of ISSTAL model predictors are used with adequate methodology, significantly more of the variance in ISP/DB can be accounted for than if any of the main types or subtypes are excluded from the analysis; the principal exception is in the case of substantial multicolinearity among variables representing the different types or subtypes.*
- ISP/DB can be better understood and explained in multistage time sequence models or path analyses when all of the main types and subtypes of ISSTAL model predictors are included; increase in understanding will be roughly proportionate to the completeness of the set of ISSTAL predictor types and subtypes used properly.*
- The general long-term temporal sequence of ISSTAL model predictor variable types suggested in Figure 1 of Chapter Eighteen is correct and useful for understanding the determinants of ISP/DB; this temporal sequence is one aspect of sequential specificity.
- The temporal sequence suggested for predictor variable types of the ISSTAL model is best understood as a complete path model, with each temporally prior variable type having some impact upon each later variable type. However, the earlier variable types will generally have much weaker direct effects on ISP/DB than their direct effects, so that psychological variable types mediate the effects of context, body, and social roles upon behavior.*
- Social role or social position variables will decline in strength of direct effects on ISP/DB to the degree that appropriate normative expectations and other psychological aspects of these roles or positions are measured and analyzed as mediating predictor (intervening) variables.
- Resources and resource access variables will similarly decline in the strength of their direct effects on ISP/DB to the degree that relevant psychological aspects and more specific opportunity structure factors are measured and analyzed as intervening predictors.

Table 1 (continued)

- For any of the ISSTAL model predictor variable types or subtypes, there will be a sequential specificity tendency such that more specific variables *within* a given category in terms of spatio-temporal closeness or situation-behavior relevance will have a stronger direct effect on ISP/DB. Among the various predictor variable types and subtypes, there will also be a stronger direct effect on ISP/DB of those categories that have more direct spatio-temporal relevance to the given behavior being studied.*
- Abstract or general ISSTAL model predictor variable types or subtypes will tend to have less powerful direct effects on ISP/DB than more concrete or specific variable types and subtypes, especially when categories of variables or specific variables with different levels of system reference are compared.
- The more personally central variables and variable types or subtypes of the ISSTAL model will tend to have greater direct effects on ISP/DB for postentry time phases of such behavior (performance, exit consideration, exit, and reflection) than on entry consideration or entry phases. The converse will be true for more personally superficial predictors, assuming eligibility requirements set by the sociocultural system are not very weak for the ISP/DB and that the ISP/DB in question is not well known by the individual (as from prior entry and exit).*
- One ISSTAL model predictor state-variable type or subtype can override the importance of any and all other predictors of ISP/DB in circumstances where the overriding predictor involves extreme psychological relevance and importance for the individual or extremes of physiological states or of the context of the individual.*
- There will be greater consistency across studies of a given type, subtype, or specific measure of a social role variable in relation to some particular ISP/DB and ISP/DB in general where there is greater sociocultural system consensus and few cross-pressures (conflicting normative expectations) on the role variable; many apparent inconsistencies in the relationships of social role variables with ISP/DB can be explained by variations in such consensus.
- With adequate methodology, there will be significant consistencies in the relationships between ISSTAL model predictor variable types or subtypes and dependent ISP/DB variables across types of ISP/DB. These consistencies are analogues of a basic pattern being modulated by different variations from that pattern, according to the specific kind of ISP/DB being examined.
- Although the present version of the ISSTAL model does not indicate short-term time sequence and feedback effects among its main predictor variable types and subtypes, some feedback effects are expected; differences between participants and nonparticipants in various kinds of ISP/DB will result in part from both selection effects and socialization or humanization effects. The socialization effects are likely to occur throughout the individual's life.*
- There are several fundamental, intrinsic dualities involved in understanding ISP/DB, among them the simultaneous (1) *existence* of stochastic process and simultaneous differential equation mappings adequate for understanding ISP/DB, (2) *presence* of discrete stages and general continuities in the lifelong humanization process, and (3) *relevance* of a primary general activity pattern of positive covariation among ISP/DB types and subtypes, along with major secondary deviance patterns of various types.

Table 1 (continued)

- Resources invested in large-scale projects that utilize the ISSTAL model to investigate ISP/DB will make significantly greater contributions to real knowledge growth than equivalent amounts of resources invested in numerous small-scale projects or equivalent large-scale projects that fail to use the model.*
- Although derived from and applied principally to ISP/DB in this volume, the most central ISSTAL model propositions are likely to have some validity for nondiscretionary activities, especially insofar as such activities have elements of discretion according to individual preferences and characteristics.

---

*Propositions marked with asterisks are particularly central to and distinctive of the ISSTAL model in contrast to other human science models and belief systems.

**Table 2. Selected GA Model Propositions
Especially Requiring Further Testing**

- Synchronic and diachronic positive covariation (association) of socioculturally valued discretionary activities exist both within and across subtypes of discretionary behavior (DB).*
- Positive covariation among different DBs will be generally stronger where the activities in question are similar, socioculturally preferred, and closer in time within the individual life span.
- The positive covariation of valued DB is nonlinearly stronger for individuals at high valued DB levels; the degree of such covariation approximates an increasing power function mathematically.
- Individuals low in their average participation in valued DB are likely to be high in their average participation in disvalued and deviant DB; positive covariation among socioculturally disvalued DB is likely, mainly among those who are low in valued DB.*
- Simultaneous, sequential, and lifetime normative role linkage patterns (which strongly affect total role linkage probabilities) within a sociocultural system (SCS) are a major source of the primary pattern of DB positive covariation; such normative role linkages are generally much stronger at middle and higher socioeconomic status (SES) levels than at lower levels.
- Higher than average SES individuals have a greater number and variety of valued DB roles represented among their friends and acquaintances than do lower SES level individuals. Such variation in familiarity with DB roles and types creates corresponding variations in the interpersonal pressure on an individual to get involved in valued DB types, as a result of normative conformity pressures (including role modeling) and opportunity structure effects (differential access to valued DB sites, equipment, and role partners).
- Individuals who are publicly labeled as deviants, especially as criminals, in an SCS are likely to be low in their valued DB of most kinds and high in their disvalued or deviant DB; thus, SCS deviance in obligatory behavior spills over into DB.
- The most general explanation for the primary DB positive covariation pattern is the mutual accommodation of individual body, context, and especially character to his or her SCS, such accommodation being accomplished largely

Table 2 (continued)

by humanization and SCS control processes and having both survival value to the SCS and to the individual.*

- The primary general activity model pattern of DB positive covariation (primary GA-DB pattern) results partly from individuals' accommodating their bodies to SCS prescriptions and preferences; usually such accommodation involves good physical and mental health, including a variety of specific physical capacities (walking, seeing, and tasting, for example).*

- In more traditional or even preliterate SCS types, physical capacities such as strength, speed, physical endurance, and high sensory-perceptual acuity are more important as valued body characteristics. In such SCS types the accommodation of the body to the SCS plays a much larger role than in modern SCS types in producing a primary GA-DB pattern.

- The primary GA-DB pattern results partly from individuals accommodating their contexts to SCS prescriptions and preferences; usually such accommodation involves access to proper DB sites, use of proper clothing and equipment, identifying and involving appropriate others in DB (especially where the DB type is intrinsically social rather than solitary in performance) at the proper time, obtaining training materials or experiences that will foster proper performance of the DB, and so forth.*

- The most powerful effects of inadequate body-SCS accommodation on DB and the primary GA-DB pattern will result from significant body impairments that are directly relevant to most types of DB or at least to a given DB type.

- The most powerful effects of inadequate context-SCS accommodation on DB and the primary GA-DB pattern will result from significant limitations on an individual's opportunity structure for DB generally or at least for a given DB type; wealth and income are primary determinants of one's general opportunity structure, but specific resources, opportunities, or limitations can overcome their importance for a given type of DB.

- The primary GA-DB pattern results *mainly* from individuals accommodating their characters to SCS prescriptions and preferences; such accommodation generally involves personality traits, intellectual capacities, attitudinal dispositions of differing levels of transsituational relevance, retained information, situational variables, and psychological processes that are valued in modern (industrial and postindustrial) societies.*

- The SCS-valued or preferred character in modern societies varies but the core elements of this character pattern tend to be similar in different SCSs and across time in the same SCS; I call this core of similar character aspects the *active-effective character*. (Its specific dimensions are described in some detail in Chapter Nineteen.)*

- Individuals high on the dimensions of the active-effective character (and having other SCS-valued aspects of character) tend to be attracted to and well suited for participation in larger numbers of and a wider variety of SCS-valued DB types and subtypes. This relation is the principal explanation for the primary GA-DB pattern and it represents an accommodation of individuals' characters to their SCSs.*

- Although social positions or roles are usually hypostatized by human scientists as if they had some existence independent of human minds, social roles are essentially psychological at base, rooted in collectively shared normative

Table 2 (continued)

(psychological) expectations; as such, social roles also form a part of the active-effective character and the accommodation of individuals' characters to their SCSs.

- The roles most valued and preferred by an SCS—termed *dominant or preferred* roles—show substantial similarity over time and across different SCSs, as do other elements of the active-effective character. Dominant roles generally correlate positively with higher levels of DB and with the primary GA-DB pattern, again accommodating the individual character to the SCS.*
- SCS-valued roles are more likely to show strong positive associations with DB and the primary GA-DB pattern where they are more stable, ascribed, and more highly valued in absolute terms relative to alternative roles (for instance, males versus females, healthy versus severely handicapped, and free versus enslaved).
- Variations in SCS valuation of social roles over time and across SCSs at a given time will account for a substantial amount of the variability of research results that investigate the associations of social roles and DB; variations in the opportunity structures and expectations associated with a given social position (for instance, male, black person, college graduate, Roman Catholic, farmer) constitute a related but different source of variability in such research results.
- Because of the accommodation of individuals' characters to the SCS generally, there is a substantial positive covariation of the various aspects of the active-effective character both synchronically and diachronically. This covariation pattern is imperfect, however, and there can be significant inconsistencies at a given time as well as major changes in different elements through time.*
- Although the opportunity structure of the larger SCS plays a crucial permissive role as a determinant of SCS mobility, the principal dynamic factor in such mobility is longer term change in important SCS-valued aspects of the active-effective character when considered for an individual as a level of system reference. The DB pattern of an individual will tend to change over time to maintain the SCS-preferred relationship between DB, SES, and other aspects of the active-effective character.
- Individuals with dominant ascribed statuses in an SCS are socialized into approximating as closely as possible the active-effective character, with variations from this general character pattern as prescribed by their particular SCS; such individuals are also socialized to seek dominant achieved statuses and roles in their SCS, for which they are better suited by their characters than are others, on the average. These achieved roles include DB roles.
- Socialization effects are the primary sources of the positive association of dominant ascribed roles and other aspects of the active-effective character, while selection effects are the primary sources of the positive association of dominant achieved roles and other aspects of the active-effective character, whether one is focusing on DB roles or not.
- Individuals with dominant ascribed statuses and roles in an SCS are generally given a kind of meta-socialization for seeking and performing SCS-valued achieved roles in their SCS—an important aspect of the intergenerational consistency in SES roles and other SCS-valued roles, including DB roles. It is a partial determinant of the primary GA-DB pattern.*

Table 2 (continued)

- The active-effective character pattern will differ from the one presented in Chapter Nineteen when SCSs or subsystems differ significantly from modern Western society in general. In these cases, adjustments must be made principally for those dimensions where a SCS values or prefers some characteristic other than the corresponding one in the present pattern of character. The resulting "adjusted version" of the active-effective character will be positively associated with the primary GA-DB pattern.*
- Aside from variations in the content of the active-effective character pattern just noted, there will be a variety of secondary deviance patterns from the primary GA-DB pattern of the GA model, including a life cycle stage engagement-disengagement pattern, a psychobiological deviance pattern, a psychosocial deviance pattern, a deprivation-affluence resource access deviance pattern, a contextual historical change pattern, an emergency-disaster-social disruption pattern, a behavior in situation/role specialization pattern, a sociocultural subsystems cross-pressures pattern, and an artifactual population base rate pattern. Variations from the primary GA-DB pattern can all be traced to one or more of these sources.*
- There has been a long-term historical trend toward a greater prevalence of individuals with active-effective characters in absolute terms (with regard to state if not process variables), because of such major social structural changes as the neolithic revolution and more recently the industrial revolution and its concomitants. Such a trend can be called *psychological evolution*, corresponding to societal evolution trends.*
- The active-effective character pattern is likely to lead to high levels of participation in SCS-valued obligatory activities, particularly work and work related activities (and for school-age youth, education and education related activities).
- The cross-cultural (cross-SCS) similarity of the active-effective character pattern is likely to be greatest at the higher (not the highest) SES and elite leadership levels, owing to greatest SCS-character accommodation at such levels; the primary GA-DB pattern will generally be highest at such levels.
- Some kind of components of variance mathematics is most appropriate to understanding the determinants of any kind of SCS-valued DB, taking into account first the general effects of the active-effective character and other GA model variables upon DB and then examining special factors accounting for a particular type or subtype of DB.
- Because nearly all extant DB research fails to take account of the effects of the basic underlying active-effective character pattern and other aspects of the GA model in studying DB, such research is generally likely to have pervasive spurious results, misleading or false conclusions, unnoticed multicolinearity and interaction effects, incorrect attributions of causality, and other defects. Such flaws, inevitably, place limitations on the strength of confirmation of the GA model itself as examined in this book, though perhaps enough adequate research has been done to give the model significant, if not substantial, confirmation.*

---

*Propositions marked with asterisks are particularly central and distinctive to the GA model in contrast to other human science models.

empirical research to confirm them, such propositions will not only have to be revised and reconsidered but the larger models of which they form a part may have to be scrapped in their present forms. Indeed, the value of my broader synanthrometric paradigm and approach will be called into serious question, at least insofar as it applies to discretionary behavior of individuals.

The ISSTAL model can be readily criticized by any human scientist on the grounds that it classifies variables or labels them in a manner contrary to one's own preferences. Such inevitable differences in style and approach at this stage of human science development are far less important than the larger questions raised by the model and the synanthrometric approach more generally. If the various main propositions of the ISSTAL model as a stage-setting device for future research and theory are genuinely new and fruitful in this version, then one should be able to locate few existing studies that use this general approach; those studies that use this approach should show superior results that contribute to real growth in our knowledge of individual discretionary behavior. Here I have had the resources only to do an impressionistic test of prior studies, which confirms quite clearly that, when the ISSTAL approach is taken, the results are superior when measured against the usual amount of variance in discretionary behavior explained meaningfully or against the amount that would be explained if predictor variables from only a single category or fewer categories had been included in the analysis.

The GA model likewise can be criticized on the grounds that the primary pattern of positive covariation among preferred discretionary activities is often weak in absolute magnitude, even though it may be significant statistically. Although technically correct, such a criticism would manifest substantial theoretical naiveté. The strength of the postulated primary pattern is expected to vary, according to the degree of sociocultural preference and similarity of the kinds of discretionary behavior involved and according to whether or not secondary deviance patterns come into play. The variation in strength of the primary pattern is an important matter for inquiry. Positive covariation is only quite strong in absolute terms within various narrowly defined, closely related, and highly valued areas of discretionary behavior, but consider the analogy that physical gravity is only quite strong in absolute terms within various narrowly defined areas of space (occupied by large planetary, stellar, or galactic masses). And the fact that physical gravity is very weak in absolute terms throughout most of the space in the universe does not decrease the importance of gravity as a pattern or phenomenon.

The pattern of accommodation among body, character, and context postulated by the GA model may also be criticized as either not new or as generally weak or highly variable. Again, this kind of criticism is rather uninformed. The degree of specification I have given to this accommodation process is new, particularly for the active-effective character and the relationships of such character dimensions to the primary pattern of positive covariation of socioculturally preferred discretionary activities. And the absolute weakness (though usually with statistical significance) and variability of the relationships between any given predictor variable and some specific type and stage of discretionary behavior as a dependent variable are expected by the model itself, because of its highly multivariate nature and its secondary deviance variations from the primary pattern of relationships.

A future empirical volume using the ISSTAL and GA models in the study of voluntary association participation, as well as other planned publications, will consider how elements of these models can be measured and tested. The kinds of studies cited in this volume do provide a wide range of potentially appropriate measurement approaches. My complaints about methodology in many cases have to do with failure to measure certain variables at all, to measure them over time properly, or to include them properly in a multivariate analysis, rather than with poor measurement of a given variable at a given time. However, I am dissatisfied with the customary measurement of sociodemographic variables which fail to measure simultaneously the normative expectations and opportunity structures accompanying social positions such as gender, age, occupational prestige level, income level, or religion. Similarly, more work is needed on the measurement of expectations, intentions, and situational variables in ways that permit such variables to be readily included in nonlaboratory studies of discretionary behavior.

The full range of detailed implications for policy making and practice of the ISSTAL and GA models cannot be spelled out here. These models could be quite readily used to design a practical program for national energy conservation and use of alternatives to fossil fuel derived energy. The two models and synanthrometrics generally also permit one to design and implement national or local programs in the realm of discretionary behavior, ranging from increasing the average levels of participation in physical recreation and fitness activities to decreasing the consumption of entertainment television, from increasing citizen participation in political processes to decreasing the failure of people to help strangers in need. Government leaders and officials need sufficient political will (to provide a legal mandate and funding) or sufficient commitment from major institutions of society and a careful application of the ISSTAL and GA models to analyze the present situation and to design and implement plans to change this situation. Some development and demonstration research projects would doubtless be helpful, if not necessary, along the way, as would intensive monitoring or evaluation of the progress being made in the implementation phase. And additional basic research on the synanthrometric approach, both to discretionary behavior and nondiscretionary behavior, would be another helpful auxiliary. The capacity for societal mobilization in any of a wide variety of directions is astounding and never more clear than in times of war and revolution or of political or religious upheaval. I find it unfortunate that this capacity is not utilized more consciously in peacetime in pursuit of the general welfare.

Aside from the future directions of theory testing and practical application, it is vital to push further in the development of synanthrometric theory itself. With regard to the ISSTAL and GA models and a focus on individual discretionary behavior, an important future direction (as noted in Tables 1 and 2) is the assignment of precise weights to each of the variable types and subtypes, even to specific variables where possible, when these are used to predict and explain various types of discretionary behavior and different stages of the dependent variable behavior in situation/role unit. Such weights will greatly improve the general precision of the models by going beyond the present specifications of asymmetries. The present models explain why *particular* activities will tend to covary positively in a sociocultural system and why *certain* individual characteristics will tend to be positively associated with socioculturally preferred discretionary activities. But not all kinds of discretionary activities covary positively, and the degree of positive covariation varies; usually it is statistically significant but imperfect. More direct research on the degree of sociocultural system preference for various discretionary activities and for various individual characteristics is needed to help test and refine this aspect of the models, particularly the GA model.

Even in the realm of discretionary behavior, there are more difficult tasks to be performed in elaborating and developing the ISSTAL and GA models. In their present forms, these models are rather static, in spite of the emphasis they place on understanding human behavior through time. Development of more dynamic forms of these models, or of a larger dynamic synanthrometric theory, based in part on the progress made in this volume, is a major task for the future. The use of time budget and life span research methodologies does not guarantee adequate causal dynamic understanding or explanation. The dynamic interaction of an individual's psychological, physical, and contextual characteristics with individual behavior represents a complex web of relationships with feedback effects we have barely begun to recognize, let alone understand. A combination of research methods will doubtless be necessary to disentangle this web. Longitudinal, time series, or panel studies, both short and long term, are likely to form a crucial cornerstone to our collective efforts.

Until further research studies test and elaborate the ISSTAL and GA models, we need to seek dynamic insights from reanalysis of the data of existing longitudinal studies and time budget studies. Because prior studies are unlikely to have measured the full range of important variables in the ISSTAL and GA models, this is far from a satisfactory procedure. Nonetheless, some of the longitudinal studies mentioned in Chapter One are likely to be quite useful for future development work, not only for the ISSTAL and GA models but also for synanthrometric theory generally.

Synanthrometrics can potentially incorporate middle range and narrower theories or models from various social and behavioral sciences. Demonstrating this potential is a task for a future volume, but I can at least suggest here some of the kinds of theoretical models I believe can be integrated into an expanded dynamic version of synanthrometric theory. I am speaking here of theoretical models of individual behavior, such as the several models of consumer behavior reviewed by Schiffman and Kanuk (1978, Chap. 15); the model of individual political behavior suggested originally by Milbrath (1965); sociological models of individual behavior, such as those of Homans (1950, 1961); social-psychological models, such as that of Fishbein (1967) and Fishbein and Ajzen (1975); and some more interdisciplinary models, such as those of Robinson (1977), Triandis, Malpass, and Davidson (1973), or Zipf (1949). Such models from different human science disciplines contain no variables I have ignored, as far as I know. Some are highly multivariate; others are rather simple; and all vary markedly in the degree of complexity of interrelationships among the variables in the models explicitly specified. Clearly, a general synanthrometric model, if it is to include and integrate such a variety of other models of individual behavior, must present a complex and dynamic set of interrelationships among variables. This brings me to a further point.

It is obvious that the present verbal formulations of the ISSTAL and GA models leave much to be desired in the way of precision as well as comprehensiveness. Not only do they fail to cover all the necessary interrelationships among variables to do justice to the complexities of individual behavior, but they are also still imprecise in failing to state accurate mathematical relationships among the variables involved. They are not fully developed and axiomatized theories. In their present form, the statements composing these models are more than the "nonoperating definitions" and "orienting statements" that Homans (1967, Chap. 1) argues are too much the preoccupation of social and behavioral science. Using variables whose definitions and, by inference and references, measurement were dealt with in Chapter Two, these models make a number of statements about human individual behavior that are testable (and often already partly confirmed) propositions about more of some measureable quantity covarying in a specified direction with more or less of some other measureable quantity.

But the most precise kinds of testing require more accurate specification of operational definitions and mathematical relationships among the variables involved. Again, this is a matter that must await a future volume, though some preliminary work done on a dynamic, general synanthrometric theory has led me to the tentative conclusion that the appropriate general form of the equation for individual behavior (B) is as follows (omitting constants):

$$B = f(M'^{.\tau}I'^{.\tau}d'^{.\tau}C^{.\tau}E),$$

where M' = Individual Motivation at time t' just prior to behavior B at time t,
$^{\tau}I'$ = Intellectual capacities relevant to B at time t',
$^{\tau}d'$ = Derived plans relevant to B at time t',
$^{\tau}C$ = Physical Capacities relevant to B at time t,
$^{\tau}E$ = Environment of the individual relevant at time t of B.

This basic equation states that individual human behavior is a multiplicative function of five major variables such that if any one of the variables falls to zero magnitude, individual behavior will effectively cease. Thus, if an individual completely lacks resultant or net motivation (based on algebraic combination of personality traits and attitudinal variables at a given time), lacks relevant intellectual capacities (required for the performance of the behavior the individual is motivated to perform), lacks relevant derived plans (required if the resultant motivation is to be able to cause the individual to carry out some behavior or activity, just as a computer requires a program that is to be executed as well as the command for execution of that activity in order to operate), lacks relevant physical capacities (required to effectuate the motivated and planned overt behavior), or lacks a relevant environment (required as a context that will permit the individual's behavior to occur), no behavior will occur for the individual at time t.

The equation also states that nonzero values of all these five variables constitute a sufficient as well as necessary condition for behavior to occur. The effects of social structure and culture, as well as many aspects of the biophysical environment and human population, are thus postulated to have only mediated effects upon individual behavior—

mainly through the motivation variable but also through each of the others as well. To see this clearly, one would have to examine the other simplified equations of the relatively extensive set of differential equations and nondifferential equations that constitute the dynamic and general synanthrometric theory in progress. These involve feedback effects of each of the variables in the forgoing equation on itself as well as some effects of variables on the righthand side of the equation on each other, which are necessary to capture the complexity of individual human behavior in mathematical form. Existing mathematical representations of human behavior are either too narrow in scope where sufficiently sophisticated or too simplistic where broad in scope, in my view, as I shall attempt to demonstrate in later work. This future development will attempt to introduce concepts, theories, and equations that suggest the possible integration of inquiry on human *individual* behavior (micro-synanthrometrics) with inquiry on *collective* human behavior (midi- and macro-synanthrometrics) and perhaps other system levels of inquiry (along different but related lines to those suggested by Boulding, 1978, and by Miller, 1978). In my future work, attention will of course be given to socially obligatory activity of various types as well as to the more discretionary activities that are the focus of this volume.

The "Catch-22" (inherent self-perpetuating problem) of developing synanthrometric theory is that further codification of the theory depends on future research testing and building on it with adequate methodology and an appropriate worldview research paradigm. Such future research is dependent on significant acceptance of the synanthrometric approach before there is solid empirical evidence for its validity. It is to be hoped the weight of evidence and argument in this volume will help some researchers to recognize this bind and break out of it.

References

Aalto, R. "Research Into How the Finn Spends His Leisure Time." In *Sport and Leisure*, the Fourth International Seminar of ICSPE in Helsinki and Jyväskylä. Jyväskylä, Finland: Finnish Society for Research in Sport and Physical Education, Publication No. 25, 1971.

Aberbach, J. D. "Alienation and Political Behavior." *American Political Science Review*, 1969, *63*, 86–99.

Aberbach, J. D., and Walker, J. L. "Political Trust and Racial Ideology." *American Political Science Review*, 1970, *64*, 1199–1219.

Abramson, P. "Political Efficacy and Political Trust Among Black School Children." *Journal of Politics*, 1972, *34*, 1243–1272.

ACTION. *Americans Volunteer*. Washington, D.C.: ACTION Agency, 1974.

Adams, D. "The Red Cross: Organizational Sources of Operational Problems." *American Behavioral Scientist*, 1970, *13*, 293–403.

Adams, J. S. "Injustice in Social Exchange." In L. Berkowitz (Ed.), *Advances in Experimental Social Psychology*. Vol. 2. New York: Academic Press, 1965.

Adams, M., and Groen, R. "Media Habits and Preferences of the Elderly." *Journal of Leisurability*, 1975, *2*, 25–30.

Adams, R.L.A. "Weather, Weather Information, and Outdoor Recreation Decisions: A Case Study of the New England Beach Trip." Unpublished doctoral dissertation, Department of Geography, Clark University, 1971.

Adelson, J. "The Political Imagination of the Young Adolescent." In J. Kogan and R. Coles (Eds.), *12 to 16 Early Adolescence*. New York: Norton, 1971.

Adelson, J., and O'Neill, R. P. "Growth of Political Ideas in Adolescence: The Sense of Community." *Journal of Personality and Social Psychology*, 1966, *4*, 295–307.

Adizes, I., and Borgese, E. M. (Eds.). *Self-Management: New Dimensions to Democracy*. Santa Barbara, Calif.: ABC-Clio Press, 1975.

Adorno, T. W., and others. *The Authoritarian Personality*. New York: Harper & Row, 1950.

Agger, R. E., and Goldrich, D. "Community Power Structures and Partisanship." *American Sociological Review*, 1958, *23*, 383–392.

Agger, R. E., Goldrich, D., and Swanson, B. E. *The Rulers and the Ruled: Political Power and Impotence in American Communities*. New York: Wiley, 1964.

Agger, R. E., Goldstein, M., and Pearl, S. "Political Cynicism: Measurement and Meaning." *The Journal of Politics*, 1961, *23*, 477–506.

Agger, R. E., and Ostrom, V. "Political Participation in a Small Community." In H. Eulau, S. J. Eldersveld, and M. Janowitz (Eds.), *Political Behavior*. New York: Free Press, 1956.

Ahtik, V. "Industrial Worker's Participation in Cultural, Social and Physical Leisure Activities. In The International Study Group on the Social Sciences of Leisure (Ed.), *Evolution of the Forms and Needs of Leisure*. Hamburg, Germany: UNESCO Institute for Education, 1962.

Ajzen, I., and Fishbein, M. "The Prediction of Behavioral Intentions in a Choice Situation." *Journal of Experimental Social Psychology*, 1969, *5*, 400–416.

Albinson, J. G. "Life Style of Physically Inactive College Males." Paper presented at Third International Symposium on the Sociology of Sport, University of Waterloo, Waterloo, Ontario, 1971.

Albrecht, S. L., and Carpenter, K. E. "Attitudes as Predictors of Behavior Intentions: A Convergence of Research Traditions." *Sociometry*, 1976, *39* 1–10.

Aldous, J., and Hill, R. "Family Continuities Through Socialization Over Three Generations." Paper presented at annual meeting of the American Sociological Association, Los Angeles, 1963.

Alford, R., and Friedland, R. "Political Participation and Public Policy." *Annual Review of Sociology*, 1975, *1*, 429–479.

Alford, R., and Lee, E. C. "Voting Turnout in American Cities." *American Political Science Review*, 1968, *62*, 796–813.

Alford, R., and Scoble, H. "Sources of Local Political Involvement." *American Political Science Review*, 1968, *62*, 1192–1206.

Alfred, R. H. "The Church of Satan." In C. Y. Glock and R. N. Bellah (Eds.), *The New Religious Consciousness.* Berkeley: University of California Press, 1976.

Alger, I., and Rusk, H. "The Rejection of Help by Some Disabled People." *Archives of Physical Medicine Rehabilitation*, 1955, *36*, 277–281.

Alker, H. R., Jr. "A Typology of Ecological Fallacies." In M. Dogan and S. Rokkan (Eds.), *Quantitative Ecological Analysis in the Social Sciences.* Cambridge, Mass.: M.I.T. Press, 1969.

Alland, A., Jr. *The Human Imperative.* New York: Columbia University Press, 1972.

Allardt, E. *Social Structure of Political Activity.* Helsinki: W. Söderström, 1956.

Allardt, E. "Community Activity, Leisure Use and Social Structure." *Acta Sociologica*, 1961, *6*, 67–82.

Allardt, E. "Types of Protest and Alienation." In E. Allardt and S. Rokkan (Eds.), *Mass Politics: Studies in Political Sociology.* New York: Free Press, 1970.

Allardt, E., and Pesonen, P. "Citizen Participation in Political Life in Finland." *International Social Science Journal*, 1960, *12*, 27–39.

Allardt, E., and others. *Youth's Interests and the Social Structure.* Porvoo, Finland: W. Söderström, 1958a.

Allardt, E., and others. "On the Cumulative Nature of Leisure Activities." *Acta Sociologica*, 1958b, *3*, 165–172.

Allen, T. H. "Mass Media Use Patterns in a Negro Ghetto." *Journalism Quarterly*, 1968, *45*, 525–527.

Allport, G. W. *The Individual and His Religion.* New York: Macmillan, 1950.

Allport, G. W. *The Nature of Prejudice.* Boston: Beacon, 1954.

Allport, G. W. *Becoming: Basic Considerations for a Psychology of Personality.* New Haven, Conn.: Yale University Press, 1955.

Allport, G. W. *Pattern and Growth in Personality.* New York: Holt, Rinehart and Winston, 1961.

Allport, G. W., and Odbert, H. S. "Trait-Names: A Psycho-Lexical Study." *Psychological Monographs*, 1936, *47*, 211.

Allport, G. W., and Vernon, P. E. *A Study of Values.* Boston: Houghton Mifflin, 1931.

Almond, G., and Coleman, J. S. (Eds.). *The Politics of the Developing Areas.* Princeton, N.J.: Princeton University Press, 1960.

Almond, G., and Verba, S. *The Civic Culture.* Princeton, N.J.: Princeton University Press, 1963.

Alston, J. P., Peek, C. W., and Wingrove, C. R. "Religiosity and Black Militants: A Re-Appraisal." *Journal for the Scientific Study of Religion,* 1972, *11,* 252–269.

Alston, W. P. "Traits, Consistency and Conceptual Alternatives for Personality Theory." *Journal for the Theory of Social Behavior,* 1975, *5,* 17–48.

Altbach, P. G. "Students and Politics." *Comparative Education Review,* 1966, *10,* 185.

Altizer, T., and Hamilton, W. "Radical Theology and the Death of God." Indianapolis, Ind.: Bobbs-Merrill, 1966.

American Public Health Association. "Community Participation and Control in Health Affairs." *American Journal of Public Health,* 1970, *60,* 180–181.

Andersen, H., and others. "Sport and Games in Denmark in the Light of Sociology." In J. W. Loy, Jr., and G. S. Kenyon (Eds.), *Sport, Culture and Society.* London: Macmillan, 1969. (Originally published 1956.)

Andersen, K. "Working Women and Political Participation, 1952-1972," *American Journal of Political Science,* 1975, *19,* 439–454.

Anderson, D. F., and Stone, G. P. "A Fifteen Year Analysis of Socio-Economic Strata Differences in the Meaning Given to Sport by Metropolitans." In M. L. Krotee (Ed.), *The Dimensions of Sport Sociology.* West Point, N.Y.: Leisure Press, 1979.

Anderson, J. E. "The Use of Time and Energy." In J. E. Birren (Ed.), *Handbook of Aging and the Individual: Psychological and Biological Aspects.* Chicago: University of Chicago Press, 1959.

Anderson, N. H. "Likeableness Ratings of 555 Personality-Trait Words." *Journal of Personality and Social Psychology,* 1968, *9,* 272–279.

Anderson, R. E., and Carter, I. E. *Human Behavior in the Social Environment.* Chicago: Aldine, 1974.

Anderson, W. "Local Civil Defense in Natural Disaster: From Office to Organization." Columbus, Ohio: Disaster Research Center, 1969.

Andreano, R. *No Joy in Mudville.* Cambridge, Mass.: Schenkman, 1965.

Andrews, F. E. *Philanthropic Giving.* New York: Russell Sage Foundation, 1950.

Andrews, F. E. *Attitudes Toward Giving.* New York: Russell Sage Foundation, 1953.

Andrews, F. E. *Legal Instruments in Foundations.* New York: Russell Sage Foundation, 1958.

Andrews, F. M., and Withey, S. B. *Social Indicators of Well-Being: Americans' Perception of Life Quality.* New York: Plenum, 1976.

Anthony, D., and Robbins, T. "The Meher Baba Movement: Its Effect on Post-Adolescent Social Alienation." In I. I. Zaretsky and M. P. Leone (Eds.), *Religious Movements in Contemporary America.* Princeton, N.J.: Princeton University Press, 1974.

Ardrey, R. *Territorial Imperative.* New York: Atheneum, 1966.

Argyle, M. *Religious Behavior.* London: Routledge & Kegan Paul, 1958.

Ariel, P. *Centuries of Childhood.* New York: Vintage, 1965.

Arnold, M. *Emotion and Personality.* New York: Columbia University Press, 1960.

Arnstein, S. R. "A Ladder of Citizen Participation," *Journal of the American Institute of Planners,* 1969, *35,* 216-224.

Aronfreed, J. *Conduct and Conscience.* New York: Academic Press, 1968.

Aronson, E., and Carlsmith, J. M. "Performance Expectancy as a Determinant of Actual Performance." *Journal of Abnormal and Social Psychology,* 1962, *65,* 178-182.

Arterton, F. C. "The Impact of Watergate on Children's Attitudes Toward Political Authority." *Political Science Quarterly,* 1974, *89,* 269-288.

Asher, H. B. *Causal Modeling.* In E. M. Uslaner (Ed.), Sage University Papers Series: *Quantitative Applications in the Social Sciences.* Beverly Hills, Calif.: Sage, 1976.

The Asian Messenger. "3 Hours and 38 Minutes." Spring 1976, p. 10.

Atkin, C. K. "Anticipated Communication and Mass Media Information-Seeking." *Public Opinion Quarterly,* 1972, *36,* 188-199.

Atkin, C. K. "Instrumental Utilities and Information Seeking." In P. Clarke (Ed.), *New Models for Mass Communication Research.* Beverly Hills, Calif.: Sage, 1973.

Atkin, C. K., Galloway, J., and Nayman, O. "Mass Communication and Political Socialization Among College Student Voters." Paper presented at annual convention of American Association for Public Opinion Research, Asheville, N.C., 1973.

Atkin, C. K., and others. "Quantity vs. Quality in Televised Political Advertising: Patterns of Reception and Response in Two Gubernatorial Campaigns." *Public Opinion Quarterly,* 1973, *37,* 209-224.

Auffenberg, T. L. *Organized English Benevolence: Charity Briefs 1625-1705.* Unpublished doctoral dissertation, Department of History, Vanderbilt University, 1973.

Axelrod, M. "Urban Structures and Social Participation." *American Sociological Review,* 1956, *21,* 13-18.

Baba, M. *God Speaks.* (rev. ed.) New York: Dodd, Mead, 1973.

Babchuk, N., and Booth, A. "Voluntary Association Membership: A Longitudinal Analysis." *American Sociological Review*, 1969, *34*, 31–45.

Bailey, J. *Social Theory for Planning*. Boston: Routledge & Kegan Paul, 1975.

Bailey, K. D. "Development of Political Orientations in Children: A 'Telescoped' Longitudinal Approach." Paper presented at the annual meeting of the Association for Public Opinion Research, Buck Hill Falls, Penn., 1977.

Bajka, Z. "Czytelnicy Dziennikow Popoludniowych" ["Readers of the Polish Afternoon Newspapers"], *Zeszyty Prasoznawcze*, 1971, *12*, 23–36.

Baker, K. L. "Political Participation, Political Efficacy, and Socialization in Germany." *Comparative Politics*, 1973, *6*, 73–98.

Baldassare, M. "Human Spatial Behavior." In R. H. Turner, J. Coleman, and R. Fox (Eds.), *Annual Review of Sociology*. Vol. 4. Palo Alto, Calif.: Annual Reviews, 1978.

Balog, M. "The Development of Leisure Time of Married Women with Children in Hungary and Their Possibilities of Acquiring Further Education." *Society and Leisure*, 1974, *6*, 29–43.

Balswick, J. "The Jesus People Movement: A Sociological Movement." In P. H. McNamara (Ed.), *Religion American Style*. New York: Harper & Row, 1974.

Baltes, P. B., and Schaie, K. W. (Eds.). *Life-Span Developmental Psychology: Personality and Socialization*. New York: Academic Press, 1973.

Bandura, A., and Walters, R. H. *Adolescent Aggression*. New York: Ronald Press, 1959.

Bandura, A., and Walters, R. H. *Social Learning and Personality Development*. New York: Holt, Rinehart and Winston, 1963.

Banfield, E. C. *The Unheavenly City*. Boston: Little, Brown, 1968.

Banton, M. *Roles*. New York: Basic Books, 1965.

Barber, J. D. *Citizen Politics*. Chicago: Markham, 1969.

Barchas, P. R. "Physiological Sociology: Interface of Sociological and Biological Processes." In A. Inkeles, J. Coleman, and N. Smelser (Eds.), *Annual Review of Sociology*. Vol. 2. Palto Alto, Calif.: Annual Reviews, 1976a.

Barchas, P. R. *Sociobiology and Behavior*. New York: Elsevier, 1976b.

Bardwick, J. M., and Douvan, E. "Ambivalence: The Socialization of Women." In V. Gornick and B. K. Moran (Eds.), *Women in a Sexist Society*. New York: New American Library, 1972.

Barfield, R., and Morgan, J. *Early Retirement: The Decision and the Experience*. Ann Arbor: Institute for Social Research, University of Michigan, 1969.

Barker, M. L. "The Perception of Water Quality as a Factor in Common Attitudes and Space Preferences in Outdoor Recreation." Paper presented at the annual meeting of the Association of American Geographers, Washington, D.C., 1968.

Barker, R. G. (Ed.). *The Stream of Behavior.* New York: Appleton-Century-Crofts, 1963.

Barker, R. G. *Ecological Psychology: Concepts and Methods for Studying the Environment of Human Behavior.* Stanford, Calif.: Stanford University Press, 1968.

Barker, R. G., and Schoggen, P. *Qualities of Community Life: Methods of Measuring Environment and Behavior Applied to an American and an English Town.* San Francisco: Jossey-Bass, 1973.

Barker, R. G., and Wright, H. F. *Midwest and Its Children.* New York: Harper & Row, 1955. (Reprinted by Archon Books, Hamden, Conn. 1971.)

Barlow, R., Brazer, H., and Morgan, J. *Economic Behavior of the Affluent.* Washington, D.C.: Brookings Institution, 1966.

Barnes, S. H. "Participation, Education and Political Competence: Evidence from a Sample of Italian Socialists." *American Political Science Review*, 1966, *60*, 348–353.

Bartlett, A. *Baseball and Mr. Spaulding: The History and Romance of Baseball.* New York: Farrar, Straus & Giroux, 1951.

Barton, A. *Communities in Disaster.* New York: Doubleday, 1969.

Bates, F., and others. *The Social and Psychological Consequences of a Natural Disaster.* Washington, D.C.: National Academy of Sciences, 1963.

Battle, E. S., and Rotter, J. "Children's Feelings of Personal Control as Related to Social Class and Ethnic Groups." *Journal of Personality*, 1963, *31*, 482–490.

Baumrind, D. "Child Care Practices Anteceding 3 Patterns of Preschool Behavior." *Genetic Psychology Monographs*, 1967, *75*, 43–88.

Baumrind, D. "Current Patterns of Parental Authority." *Developmental Psychology Monographs*, 1971, *4*, 1–101.

Bealer, R. C., and Willets, F. K. "Religious Interests of American High School Youth." *Religious Education*, 1967, *62*, 435–444.

Beaman, J. "Distance and the 'Reaction' to Distance as a Function of Distance." *Journal of Leisure Research*, 1974, *6*, 220–231.

Beaman, J. "Comments on the Paper 'The Substitutability Concept: Implications for Recreation Research and Management' by Hendee and Burdge." *Journal of Leisure Research*, 1975, *7*, 146–152.

Beaman, J. "Corrections Regarding the Impedance of Distance Functions for Several g(d) Functions." *Journal of Leisure Research*, 1976, *8*, 49–52.

Becker, H. S. "Current Sacred-Secular Theory and Its Development." In H. Becker and A. Boskoff (Eds.), *Modern Sociological Theory in Continuity and Change.* New York: Holt, Rinehart and Winston, 1957.

Becker, H. S. "The Self and Adult Socialization." In E. Norbeck, D. Price-Williams, and W. M. McCord (Eds.), *The Study of Personality.* New York: Holt, Rinehart and Winston, 1968.

Becker, L. B., McCombs, M. E., and McLeod, J. M. "The Development of Political Cognitions." In S. H. Chaffee (Ed.), *Political Communication.* Beverly Hills, Calif.: Sage, 1975.

Bell, D.V.J. *Resistance and Revolution.* Boston: Houghton Mifflin, 1973.

Bellah, R. N. "New Religious Consciousness and the Crisis in Modernity." In C. Y. Glock and R. N. Bellah (Eds.), *The New Religious Consciousness.* Berkeley: University of California Press, 1976.

Bem, D. J. *Beliefs, Attitudes and Human Affairs.* Monterey, Calif.: Brooks/Cole, 1970.

Benello, C. G., and Roussopoulos, D. *The Case for Participatory Democracy.* New York: Grossman, 1971.

Bennett, S. E., and Klecka, W. R. "Social Status and Political Participation: A Multivariate Analysis of Predictive Power." *Midwest Journal of Political Science,* 1970, *14,* 355–382.

Benny, M., Gray, A. P., and Pear, R. H. *How People Vote: A Study of Electoral Behavior in Greenwich.* London: Routledge & Kegan Paul, 1956.

Berelson, B. R. "What 'Missing the Newspaper' Means." In P. F. Lazarsfeld and F. N. Stanton (Eds.), *Communications Research 1948–1949.* New York: Harper & Row, 1949.

Berelson, B. R., Lazarsfeld, P. F., and McPhee, W. N. *Voting.* Chicago: University of Chicago Press, 1954.

Berelson, B. R., and Steiner, G. A. *Human Behavior: An Inventory of Scientific Findings.* New York: Harcourt Brace Jovanovich, 1964.

Berger, B. M. "The Sociology of Leisure." In E. O. Smigel (Ed.), *Work and Leisure.* New Haven, Conn.: College and University Press, 1963.

Berger, S. M. "Conditioning Through Vicarious Instigation." *Psychological Review,* 1962, *29,* 450–466.

Berkowitz, L. "The Study of Urban Violence: Some Implications of Laboratory Studies of Frustration and Aggression." *American Behavioral Scientist,* 1968, *11,* 14–19.

Berkowitz, L. "The Frustration-Aggression Hypothesis Revisited." In L. Berkowitz (Ed.), *Roots of Aggression: A Re-Examination of the Frustration-Aggression Hypothesis.* New York: Atherton, 1969.

Berkowitz, L. "Impulse, Aggression and the Gun." In J. V. McConnell

(Ed.), *Readings in Social Psychology Today.* Del Mar, Calif.: CRM Books, 1970a.

Berkowitz, L. "The Self, Selfishness, and Altruism." In J. R. Macaulay and L. Berkowitz (Eds.), *Altruism and Helping Behavior.* New York: Academic Press, 1970b.

Berkowitz, L. "Social Norms, Feelings, and Other Factors Affecting Helping and Altruism." In L. Berkowitz (Ed.), *Advances in Experimental Social Psychology.* Vol. 6. New York: Academic Press, 1972.

Berkowitz, L., and Daniels, L. R. "Responsibility and Dependency." *Journal of Abnormal and Social Psychology,* 1963, *66,* 429–436.

Berkowitz, L., and Friedman, P. "Some Social Class Differences in Helping Behavior." *Journal of Personality and Social Psychology,* 1967, *6,* 217–225.

Berkowitz, L., and Macaulay, J. R. "The Contagion of Criminal Violence." *Sociometry,* 1971, *34,* 238–260.

Berman, A., Piliavin, I. M., and Gross, A. E. "Some Effects of Imposed Versus Requested Help." Unpublished senior honors thesis, Department of Psychology, University of Wisconsin, 1971.

Betts, J. R. "The Technological Revolution and the Rise of Sport, 1850–1900." *The Mississippi Valley Historical Review,* 1954, *40,* 231–256.

Betts, J. R. "The Impact of Technology on Sport in the Nineteenth Century." *Journal of Health, Physical Education and Recreation,* 1969, *40,* 87–90.

Betts, J. R. *America's Sporting Heritage: 1850-1950.* Reading, Mass.: Addison-Wesley, 1974.

Bibby, R. W., and Brinkerhoff, M. B. "Sources of Religious Involvement: Issues for Future Empirical Investigation." *Review of Religious Research,* 1974, *15,* 71–79.

Bickman, L. "Social Influence and Diffusion of Responsibility in an Emergency." *Journal of Experimental Social Psychology,* 1972, *8,* 438–445.

Biddle, B. J., and Thomas, E. J. (Eds). *Role Theory: Concepts and Research.* New York: Wiley, 1966.

Bielby, W. T., and Hauser, R. M. "Structural Equation Models." In A. Inkeles, J. Coleman, and N. Smelser (Eds.), *Annual Review of Sociology.* Vol. 3. Palo Alto, Calif.: Annual Reviews, 1977.

Biller, H., and Meredith, D. *Father Power.* New York: McKay, 1975.

Binder, L., and others (Eds.). *Crises and Sequences in Political Development.* Princeton, N.J.: Princeton University Press, 1971.

Birch, A. H. "The Habit of Voting." *Journal of the Manchester School of Economic and Social Studies,* 1950, *18,* 75–82.

Birnie, A. *An Economic History of the British Isles.* London: Methuen, 1961.

Birren, J. E. *The Psychology of Aging*. Englewood Cliffs, N.J.: Prentice-Hall, 1964.

Birren, J. E., and Schaie, K. W. (Eds.). *Handbook of the Psychology of Aging*. New York: D. Van Nostrand, 1977.

Bishop, D. W., and Ikeda, M. "Status and Role Factor in the Leisure Behavior of Different Occupations." *Sociology and Social Research*, 1970, *54*, 190–208.

Bishop, P. C., and Beck, A. A. *The Consumer Support Group*. Lansing, Mich.: Capitol Area Comprehensive Health Planning Association, 1973.

Bittker, B. *Federal Income, Estate, and Gift Taxation*. Englewood Cliffs, N.J.: Prentice-Hall, 1955.

Blalock, H. M., Jr. *Toward a Theory of Minority Group Relations*. New York: Wiley, 1967.

Blalock, H. M., Jr. *Theory Construction: From Verbal to Mathematical Formulations*. Englewood Cliffs, N.J.: Prentice-Hall, 1969.

Blanshan, S. "Disaster Body Handling." *Mass Emergencies*, 1977, *2*, 215–225.

Blau, P. M. "Structural Effects." *American Sociological Review*, 1960, *25*, 178–193.

Blau, P. M. *Exchange and Power in Social Life*. New York: Wiley, 1964.

Blau, P. M. *Inequality and Heterogeneity*. New York: Free Press, 1977.

Bloom, B. *Stability and Change in Human Characteristics*. New York: Wiley, 1964.

Bloomberg, W., Jr., and Rosenstock, F. W. "Who can Activate the Poor? One Assessment of 'Maximum Feasible Participation.'" In W. Bloomberg, Jr., and H. J. Schmandt (Eds.), *Power, Poverty and Urban Policy*. Beverly Hills, Calif.: Sage, 1968.

Blume, N., and Lyons, S. "The Monopoly Newspaper in a Local Election: The Toledo Blade." *Journalism Quarterly*, 1968, *45*, 286–292.

Blumer, H. "Collective Behavior." In R. E. Park (Ed.), *An Outline of the Principles of Sociology*. New York: Barnes & Noble, 1939.

Blumer, H. *Symbolic Interactionism: Perspective and Method*. Englewood Cliffs, N.J.: Prentice-Hall, 1969.

Blumler, J. G., and Katz, E. (Eds.). *The Uses of Mass Communications*. Sage Annual Reviews of Communication Research. Vol. 3. Beverly Hills, Calif.: Sage, 1974.

Blumler, J. G., and McQuail, D. *Television in Politics*. Chicago: University of Chicago Press, 1969.

Bogart, L. "Changing News Interests and the News Media." *Public Opinion Quarterly*, 1968–69, *32*, 560–574.

Bogart, L. "Negro and White Media Exposure: New Evidence." *Journalism Quarterly*, 1972, *49*, 15–21.

Bollman, S. R., Moxley, V. M., and Elliott, N. C. "Family and Community Activities of Rural Nonfarm Families with Children." *Journal of Leisure Research*, 1975, 7, 53–62.

Bonjean, C. M., Hill, R. J., and McLemore, S. D. *Sociological Measurement: An Inventory of Scales and Indices.* San Francisco: Chandler, 1967.

Booker, D. E. *Citizen Participation in Planning.* Monticello, Ill.: Council of Planning Librarians, Exchange Bibliography No. 718, 1975.

Borgatta, E., and Lambert, W. W. (Eds.) *Handbook of Personality Theory and Research.* Chicago: Rand McNally, 1968.

Borsky, P. N., and Banacki, J. R. *Motivations for Charitable Giving: A Case Study of an Eastern Metropolitan Area.* Chicago: National Opinion Research Center, 1961.

Boskin, J., and Rosenstone, R. A. *Seasons of Rebellion, Protest and Radicalism in Recent America.* New York: Holt, Rinehart and Winston, 1972.

Bottomore, T. (Ed.). *Crisis and Contention in Sociology.* Sage Studies in International Sociology. Vol. 1. Beverly Hills, Calif.: Sage, 1975.

Boudon, R. "The Sociology Crisis." *Social Science Information*, 1972, *11*, 109–139.

Boulding, K. E. *The Image.* Ann Arbor: University of Michigan Press, 1956.

Boulding, K. E. *Ecodynamics: A New Theory of Societal Evolution.* Beverly Hills, Calif.: Sage, 1978.

Bower, R. T. *Television and the Public.* New York: Holt, Rinehart and Winston, 1973.

Bowers, K. S. "Situationism in Psychology: An Analysis and a Critique." *Psychological Review*, 1973, *80*, 307–336.

Bowman, L., and Boynton, G. R. (Eds.). *Political Behavior and Public Opinion.* Englewood Cliffs, N.J.: Prentice-Hall, 1974.

Bradburn, N. M. *The Structure of Psychological Well-Being.* Chicago: Aldine, 1969.

Bradburn, N. M., and Caplovitz, D. *Reports on Happiness.* Chicago: Aldine, 1965.

Bramel, D., and Friend, R. *Marxism and Social Psychology.* Lexington, Mass.: Heath, forthcoming.

Brannon, G. *The Effect of Tax Deductibility on the Level of Charitable Contribution and Variations on the Theme.* Washington, D.C.: Fund for Policy Research, 1974.

Bredemeir, H. C. "The Socially Handicapped and the Agencies: A Market Analysis." In F. Reissman, J. Cohen, and A. Pearl (Eds.), *The Mental Health of the Poor.* New York: Free Press, 1964.

Brehm, J. W. *A Theory of Psychological Reactance*. New York: Academic Press, 1966.

Brehm, J. W., and Cole, A. H. "Effect of a Favor Which Reduces Freedom." *Journal of Personality and Social Psychology*, 1966, *3*, 420–426.

Bremner, R. H. "'Scientific Philanthropy' 1873–93." *Social Service Review*, 1956, *30*, 168–173.

Bremner, R. H. *American Philanthropy*. Chicago: University of Chicago Press, 1960.

Brewer, D. C. "Church and Sect in Methodism." *Social Forces*, 1952, *30*, 400–408.

Brewer, E.D.C. Unpublished data, personal communication, 1959.

Brewer, E.D.C. "Social Indicators and Religious Indicators." *Review of Religious Research*, 1973, *14*, 77–90.

Brewer, E.D.C. (Ed.). *Transcendence and Mystery*. New York: IDOC/North America, 1975.

Brewer, E.D.C., and Weatherford, W. C. *Life and Religion in Southern Appalachia*. New York: Friendship Press, 1962.

Briar, S. "Welfare from Below: Recipients' Views of the Public Welfare System." In J. Brock (Ed.), *The Law of the Poor*. San Francisco: Chandler, 1966.

Brim, O. G., Jr. "Personality Development as Role Learning." In I. Iscoe and H. Stevenson (Eds.), *Personality Development in Children*. Austin: University of Texas Press, 1960.

Brim, O. G., Jr. "Socialization Through the Life Cycle." In O. G. Brim, Jr., and S. Wheeler (Eds.), *Socialization After Childhood: Two Essays*. New York: Wiley, 1966.

Brim, O. G., Jr. "Adult Socialization." In J. H. Clausen (Ed.), *Socialization and Society*. Boston: Little, Brown, 1967.

Brim, O. G., Jr., and Wheeler, S. *Socialization After Childhood*. New York: Wiley, 1966.

British Broadcasting Corporation. *Annual Review of BBC Audience Research Findings, 1975–76*. London: British Broadcasting Corporation, 1977.

Britt, S. H. (Ed.). *Consumer Behavior and the Behavioral Sciences*. New York: Wiley, 1966.

Britton, J. H., and Britton, J. O. *Personality Changes in Aging: A Longitudinal Study of Community Residents*. New York: Springer-Verlag, 1972.

Broll, L. A., Gross, A. E., and Piliavin, I. "Effects of Offered and Requested Help on Help Seeking and Reactions to Being Helped." *Journal of Applied Social Psychology*, 1974, *4*, 244–258.

Bronfenbrenner, U. "Personality and Participation: The Case of the Vanishing Variables." *Journal of Social Issues*, 1960, *16*, 54–63.

Bronfenbrenner, U. *Two Worlds of Childhood: U.S. and U.S.S.R.* New York: Russell Sage Foundation, 1970.

Brown, J. R. "Children's Uses of Television." In R. Brown (Ed.), *Children and Television.* Beverly Hills, Calif: Sage, 1976.

Brown, J. R., Cramond, J. K., and Wilde, R. J. "Displacement Effects of Television and the Child's Functional Orientation to Media." In J. G. Blumler and E. Katz (Eds.), *The Uses of Mass Communications.* Beverly Hills, Calif.: Sage, 1974.

Brown, P. J., Dyer, A., and Whaley, R. S. "Recreation Research—So What?" *Journal of Leisure Research,* 1973, *5,* 16–24.

Browne, E., Jr., and Rehfuss, J. "Policy Evaluation, Citizen Participation, and Revenue Sharing in Aurora, Illinois." *Public Administration Review,* 1975, *35,* 150–157.

Browning, R. P., and Jacob, H. "Power Motivation and the Political Personality." *Public Opinion Quarterly,* 1964, *28,* 75–90.

Bruner, J. S., Oliver, R. R., and Greenfield, P. M. *Studies in Cognitive Growth.* New York: Wiley, 1966.

Bryan, J. H. "Why Children Help: A Review." *Journal of Social Issues,* 1972, *28,* 87–105.

Bryan, J. H. "You will be Advised to Watch What We Do, Instead of What We Say." In D. DePalma and J. Folley (Eds.), *Moral Development.* New York: Halstead Press, 1975.

Bryan, J. H., and London, P. "Altruistic Behavior by Children." *Psychological Bulletin,* 1970, *73,* 200–211.

Bryan, J. H., and Test, M. A. "Models and Helping: Naturalistic Studies in Aiding Behavior." *Journal of Personality and Social Psychology,* 1967, *6,* 400–407.

Bryan, J. H., and Walbek, N. H. "The Impact of Words, Deeds and Power Upon Children's Altruistic Behavior." *Child Development,* 1970a, *41,* 747–757.

Bryan, J. H., and Walbek, N. H. "Preaching and Practicing Self-Sacrifice: Children's Actions and Reactions." *Child Development,* 1970b, *41,* 329–353.

Buchanan, W. "An Inquiry into Purposive Voting." *The Journal of Politics,* 1956, *18,* 281–291. (Also in Bobbs-Merrill Reprint Series No. PS-34.)

Buck, R., Miller, R. E., and Caul, W. F. "Sex, Personality, and Physiological Variables in the Communications of Affect via Facial Expression." *Journal of Personality and Social Psychology,* 1974, *30,* 587–596.

Bucke, R. M. *Cosmic Consciousness.* New York: University Books, 1961.

Buckley, W. (Ed.). *Modern Systems Research for the Behavioral Scientist.* Chicago: Aldine, 1968.

Buhler, C., and Massarik, F. (Eds.). *The Course of Human Life.* New York: Springer-Verlag, 1968.

Bulcher, G. "Informacion: De Donde Saca el Ciudadano su Informacion?" ["Information: Where Does the Citizen Obtain His Information?"] *Revista Espanola de la Opinion Publica,* 1973, *32,* 249–265.

Bull, C. N. "One Measure for Defining a Leisure Activity." *Journal of Leisure Research,* 1971, *3,* 120–126.

Bull, C. N. "Prediction of Daily Behaviors: An Empirical Measure of Leisure." *Journal of Leisure Research,* 1972, *4,* 119–128.

Bultena, G., and Wood, V. "Leisure Orientation and Recreational Activities of Retirement Community Residents." *Journal of Leisure Research,* 1970, *2,* 3–15.

Bunge, M. "Metatheory." In UNESCO (Ed.), *Scientific Thought: Some Underlying Concepts, Methods, and Procedures.* The Hague: Mouton/UNESCO, 1972.

Burch, G. "Career Change of Clergy to Secular Occupations: Development of a Theoretical Framework. Unpublished master's thesis, Department of Sociology, University of Maryland, 1969.

Burch, W. R., Jr. "The Social Circles of Leisure: Competing Explanations." *Journal of Leisure Research,* 1969, *1,* 125–147.

Burch, W. R., Jr., and Wenger, W. D., Jr. *The Social Characteristics of Participants in Three Styles of Camping.* Washington, D.C.: U.S. Forest Service Research Paper, 1967, PNW-48.

Burdge, R. J. "Levels of Occupational Prestige and Leisure Activity." *Journal of Leisure Research,* 1969, *1,* 262–274.

Burdge, R. J. "A Comparison of Black-White Differences in Leisure Behavior." Unpublished paper, Department of Leisure Studies, University of Illinois, 1975.

Burdge, R. J., and Field, D. R. "Methodological Perspectives for the Study of Outdoor Recreation." *Journal of Leisure Research,* 1972, *4,* 63–72.

Burnham, W. D. "The Changing Shape of the American Political Universe." *American Political Science Review,* 1965, *59,* 7–28.

Burns, T. "Leisure in Industrial Society." In M. A. Smith, S. Parker, and C. S. Smith, (Eds.), *Leisure and Society in Britain.* London: Allen Lane, 1973.

Burstein, P. "Social Structure and Individual Political Participation in Five Countries." *American Journal of Sociology,* 1972, 77, 1087–1110.

Buss, A. M., and Plomin, R. *A Temperament Theory of Personality Development.* New York: Wiley, 1975

Buss, A. R. "The Trait-Situation Controversy and the Concept of Interaction." *Personality and Social Psychology Bulletin,* 1977, *3,* 196–201.

Butler, D., and Stokes, D. *Political Change in Britain.* New York: St. Martin's, 1971.

Butners, A., and Buntaine, N. *Motivations for Charitable Giving: A Reference Guide.* Washington, D.C.: The 501(c)(3) Group, 1973.

Byrne, D. *The Attraction Paradigm.* New York: Academic Press, 1971.

Cahn, E. S., and Cahn, J. C. "Maximum Feasible Participation—A General Overview." In E. S. Cahn and B. A. Passett (Eds.), *Citizen Participation: Effecting Community Change.* New York: Praeger, 1971.

Cain, L. D., Jr. "Life Course and Social Structure." In R.E.L. Faris (Ed.), *Handbook of Modern Sociology.* Chicago: Rand McNally, 1964.

Calhoun, L. G., Dawes, A. S., and Lewis, P. M. "Correlates of Attitudes Toward Help Seeking in Outpatients." *Journal of Consulting and Clinical Psychology*, 1972, *38*, 153.

Cameron, D. R., Hendericks, J. S., and Hofferbert, R. I. "Urbanization, Social Structure, and Mass Politics: A Comparison Within Five Nations." *Comparative Political Studies*, 1972, *5*, 259–290.

Campbell, A. "The Passive Citizen." *Acta Sociologica*, 1962, *6*, 9–21.

Campbell, A., Converse, P. E., and Rodgers, W. L. *The Quality of American Life.* New York: Russell Sage Foundation, 1976.

Campbell, A., and Cooper, H. C. *Group Differences in Attitudes and Votes.* Ann Arbor: Institute for Social Research, Survey Research Center, University of Michigan, 1956.

Campbell, A., Gurin, G., and Miller, W. *The Voter Decides.* New York: Harper & Row, 1954.

Campbell, A., and Kahn, R. L. *The People Elect a President.* Ann Arbor: Institute for Social Research, Survey Research Center, University of Michigan, 1952.

Campbell, A., and Valen, H. "Party Identification in Norway and the United States." *Public Opinion Quarterly*, 1961, *25*, 505–525.

Campbell, A., and others. *The American Voter.* New York: Wiley, 1960.

Campbell, A., and others. *Elections and Political Order.* New York: Wiley, 1966.

Campbell, B. G. *Human Evolution.* (3rd ed.) Chicago: Aldine, 1974.

Campbell, D. T. "Ethnocentric and Other Altruistic Motives." In D. Levine (Ed.), *Nebraska Symposium on Motivation.* Lincoln: University of Nebraska Press, 1965.

Campbell, D. T. "Ethnocentrism of Disciplines and the Fish-Scale Model of Omniscience." In M. Sherif and C. Sherif (Eds.), *Interdisciplinary Relationships in the Social Sciences.* Chicago: Aldine, 1969.

Campbell, D. T. "On the Genetics of Altruism and the Counter-Hedonic Components in Human Culture." *Journal of Social Issues*, 1972, *28*, 21–37.

Campbell, F. L. "Participant Observation in Outdoor Recreation." *Journal of Leisure Research,* 1970, *2,* 226-235.

Caplan, N. "The New Ghetto Man: A Review of Recent Empirical Studies." *Journal of Social Issues,* 1970, *26,* 59-73.

Carey, J. W. "Variations in Negro/White Television Preferences." *Journal of Broadcasting,* 1966, *10,* 199-212.

Carls, E. G. *A Study of Social Motives and Patterns of Leisure Behavior.* Unpublished doctoral dissertation, Department of Recreation, University of Illinois, Urbana, 1969.

Carls, E. G. "The Effects of People and Man-Induced Conditions on Preferences for Outdoor Recreation Landscapes." *Journal of Leisure Research,* 1974, *6,* 113-124.

Carlson, R. "Personality." In M. R. Rosenzweig and L. W. Porter (Eds.), *Annual Review of Psychology.* Vol. 26. Palo Alto, Calif.: Annual Reviews, 1975.

Carnegie, A. *The Gospel of Wealth and Other Timely Essays.* New York: Century, 1900.

Carson, D. H. "Population Concentration and Human Stress." In B. P. Rourke (Ed.), *Explorations in the Psychology of Stress and Anxiety.* London: Longmans, 1969.

Carter, A. *Direct Action and Liberal Democracy.* New York: Harper & Row, 1973.

Carter, R. *The Gentle Legions.* New York: Doubleday, 1961.

Carter, R. "The Myth of Increasing Non-Work vs. Work Activities." *Social Problems,* 1970, *18,* 52-67.

Cartwright, D., and Zander, A. *Group Dynamics: Research and Theory.* New York: Harper & Row, 1960.

Casey, W. J., Lasser, J. K., and Lord, W. *Tax Planning for Foundations and Charitable Giving.* New York: Business Reports, 1953.

Castine, S. C., and Roberts, G. C. "Modeling in the Socialization Process of the Black Athlete." *International Review of Sport Sociology,* 1974, *9,* 59-74.

Castro, M. A. "Reactions to Receiving Aid as a Function of Cost to Donor and Opportunity to Aid." *Journal of Applied Social Psychology,* 1974, *4,* 194-209.

Cataldo, E., and Kellstedt, L. "Conceptualizing and Measuring Political Involvement Over Time: A Study of Buffalo's Urban Poor." Paper delivered at the 1968 Joint Statistical Meetings, Pittsburgh, 1968.

Center for a Voluntary Society. "Frontispiece." In D. H. Smith (Ed.), *Voluntary Action Research: 1973.* Lexington, Mass.: Heath, 1973.

Cesario, F. J. " A New Method for Analyzing Outdoor Recreation Trip Data." *Journal of Leisure Research,* 1975, *7,* 200-215.

Chaffee, H., and McLeod, J. M. "Adolescent Television Use in the Family Context." In B. A. Comstock and E. A. Rubinstein (Eds.), *Television and Adolescent Aggressiveness*. Vol. 3. Washington, D.C.: National Institute of Mental Health, 1971.

Chaffee, S. H., Ward, L. S., and Tipton, L. P. "Mass Communication and Political Socialization." *Journalism Quarterly*, 1970, *47*, 647–659.

Chaffee, S. H., and Wilson, D. "Adult Life Cycle Changes in Mass Media Use." Paper presented to Communication Theory and Methodology Division, Association for Education in Journalism, Ottawa, Ontario, 1975.

Chapin, F. S., Jr. *Human Activity Patterns in the City*. New York: Wiley, 1974.

Charlesworth, J. C. (Ed.). *Leisure in America: Blessing or Curse?* Philadelphia: American Academy of Political and Social Science, 1964.

Cheek, N. H. "On the Sociology of Leisure Places: The Zoological Park." Paper presented at annual meeting of the American Sociological Association, Denver, Colo., 1971a.

Cheek, N. H. "Toward a Sociology of Not-Work." *Pacific Sociological Review*, 1971b, *14*, 245–258.

Cherry, C. *World Communication: Threat or Promise?* New York: Wiley-Interscience, 1971.

Chetkow, B. H. "Religion and Social Work in the North-American Jewish Community." *Journal of Jewish Communal Service*, 1957, *33*, 359–365.

Cheung, H. K. "A Day-Use Park Visitation Model." *Journal of Leisure Research*, 1972, *4*, 139–156.

Chipman, L. P. "A Comparison of Participants and Non-Participants in Intercollegiate Athletics with Respect to Selected Personality Traits." Unpublished doctoral dissertation, Department of Physical Education, Springfield College, 1968.

Christensen, J. E., and Yoesting, D. R. "Social and Attitudinal Variants in High and Low Use of Outdoor Recreation Facilities." *Journal of Leisure Research*, 1973, *5*, 6–15.

Christensen, J. E., and Yoesting, D. R. "Statistical and Substantive Implications of the Use of Stepwise Regression to Order Predictions of Leisure Behavior." *Journal of Leisure Research*, 1976, *8*, 59–65.

Christie, R, and Cook, P. "A Guide to Published Literature Relating to the Authoritarian Personality Through 1956." *Journal of Psychology*, 1958, *45*, 171–199.

Christie, R., and Geis, F. (Eds.) *Studies in Machiavellianism*. New York: Academic Press, 1968.

Christie, R., and Jahoda, M. (Eds.). *Studies in the Scope and Method of 'The Authoritarian Personality.'* New York: Free Press, 1954.

Chun, K., Cobb, S., and French, J.R.P., Jr. *Measures for Psychological Assessment: A Guide to 3000 Original Sources and Their Applications.* Ann Arbor: Institute of Social Research, University of Michigan, 1975.

Ciccheti, C. J. "A Review of the Empirical Analyses That Have Been Based Upon the National Recreation Surveys." *Journal of Leisure Research,* 1972, *4,* 90–107.

Citrin, J. and others. "Personal and Political Sources of Political Alienation." *British Journal of Political Science,* 1975, *5,* 1–31.

Clark, R., Hendee, J., and Campbell, F. "Values, Behavior and Conflict in Modern Camping Culture." *Journal of Leisure Research,* 1971, *3,* 143–159.

Clark, R. D., and Word, L. E. "Why Don't Bystanders Help? Because of Ambiguity?" *Journal of Personality and Social Psychology,* 1972, *24,* 392–401.

Clarke, A. C. "The Use of Leisure and Its Relation to Levels of Occupational Prestige." *American Sociological Review,* 1956, *21,* 301–307.

Clarke, P. "Does Teen News Attract Boys to Newspapers?" *Journalism Quarterly,* 1968, *45,* 7–13.

Clarke, P. "Identification with Father and Father-Son Similarities in Reading Behavior." Paper presented at annual meeting of the Association for Education in Journalism, Berkeley, Calif.: 1969.

Clarke, P. "Some Proposals for Continuing Research on Youth and the Mass Media." *American Behavioral Scientist,* 1971, *14,* 313–322.

Clarke, P. "Teenagers' Coorientation and Information-Seeking About Pop Music." *American Behavioral Scientist,* 1973, *16,* 551–556.

Clarke, P., and James, J. "The Effects of Situation, Attitude Intensity and Personality on Information Seeking." *Sociometry,* 1967, *30,* 235–245.

Clausen, J. A. "Family Structure, Socialization and Personality." In L. W. Hoffman and M. L. Hoffman (Eds.), *Review of Child Development Research.* Vol. 2. New York: Russell Sage Foundation, 1966.

Clausen, J. A. (Ed.). *Socialization and Society.* Boston: Little, Brown, 1968.

Clawson, M. "How Much Leisure, Now and in the Future?" In J. C. Charlesworth (Ed.), *Leisure in America: Blessing or Curse?* Philadelphia: American Academy of Political and Social Science, 1964.

Clinard, M., and Abbott, D. *Crime in Developing Countries: A Comparative Perspective.* New York: Wiley, 1973.

Coelho, G. V., Hamburg, D. A., and Adams, J. E. *Coping and Adaptation.* New York: Basic Books, 1974.

Cofer, C. N. *Motivation and Emotion.* Glenview, Ill.: Scott, Foresman, 1972.

Coffey, M. A. "The Sportswoman—Then and Now." *Journal of Health, Physical Education, and Recreation,* 1965, *36,* 38–41, 50.

Cohen, A. K. *Delinquent Boys: The Culture of the Gang.* New York: Free Press, 1955.

Cole, R. L. *Citizen Participation and the Urban Policy Process.* Lexington, Mass.: Heath, 1974.

Coleman, J. *The Adolescent Society.* New York: Free Press, 1961.

Comer, J. P. "The Dynamics of Black and White Violence." In H. D. Graham and T. R. Gurr (Eds.), *Violence in America.* New York: Bantam, 1969.

Comstock, G. "The Effects of Television on Children and Adolescents: The Evidence So Far." *Journal of Communication,* 1975, *25,* 25–34.

Connelly, G. M., and Field, H. H. "The Non-Voter: Who He Is, What He Thinks." *Public Opinion Quarterly,* 1944, *8,* 175–187.

Connor, R., Johannis, T. B., Jr., and Walters, J. "Family Recreation in Relation to Role Conceptions of Family Members." *Marriage and Family Living,* 1955, *17,* 306–309.

Constantelos, D. *Philanthropia and Philanthropic Institutions in the Byzantine Empire, A.D. 330–1204.* Unpublished doctoral dissertation, Department of History, Rutgers University, 1965.

Constantelos, D. *Byzantine Philanthropy and Social Welfare.* New Brunswick, N.J.: Rutgers University Press, 1968.

Converse, P. E. "Of Time and Partisan Stability." *Comparative Political Studies,* 1969, *2,* 139–171.

Converse, P. E. "Change in the American Electorate." In A. Campbell and P. E. Converse (Eds.), *The Human Meaning of Social Change.* New York: Russell Sage Foundation, 1972a.

Converse, P. E. "Country Differences in Time Use." In A. Szalai and others (Eds.), *The Use of Time.* The Hague, Netherlands: Mouton, 1972b.

Converse, P. E., and Dupeux, G. "Some Comparative Notes on French and American Political Behavior." Bergen, Norway: UNESCO Seminar, June 1961 (mimeographed).

Converse, P. E., and Dupeux, G. "Politicization of the Electorate in France and the United States." *Public Opinion Quarterly,* 1962, *26,* 1–24.

Cooper, J. M., Jr. "Neo-Progressivism and 'Slack-Water Politics.'" In M. D. Hancock and G. Sjoberg (Eds.), *Politics in the Post-Welfare State.* New York: Columbia University Press, 1972.

Coopersmith, S. *The Antecedents of Self-Esteem.* San Francisco: W. H. Freeman, 1967.

Coser, L. A. "Sociological Theory from the Chicago Dominance to 1965." In A. Inkeles, J. Coleman, and N. Smelser (Eds.), *Annual Review of Sociology.* Vol. 2. Palo Alto, Calif.: Annual Reviews, 1976.

Couto, R. A. *Poverty, Politics and Health Care: An Appalachian Experience.* New York: Praeger, 1975.

Coutu, W. *Emergent Human Nature: A Symbolic Field Interpretation.* New York: Knopf, 1949.

Cowdry, R. W., Kenniston, K., and Cabin, S. "The War and Military Obligation: Private Attitudes and Public Actions." *Journal of Personality,* 1970, *38,* 525–549.

Cox, H. *The Secular City.* New York: Macmillan, 1965.

Craig, K. D., and Weinstein, M. S. "Conditioning Vicarious Affective Arousal." *Psychological Reports,* 1965, *17,* 955–963.

Craik, K. H. "Environmental Psychology." In P. H. Mussen and M. R. Rosenzweig (Eds.), *Annual Review of Psychology.* Vol. 24. Palo Alto, Calif.: Annual Reviews, 1973.

Crandall, R., and Lewko, J. "Leisure Research, Past and Future: Who, What, Where?" *Journal of Leisure Research,* 1976, *8,* 150–159.

Crandall, R., and others. "A General Bibliography of Leisure Publications." *Journal of Leisure Research,* 1977, *9,* 15–54.

Crane, D. *Invisible Colleges: Diffusion of Knowledge in Scientific Communities.* Chicago: University of Chicago Press, 1972.

Crawford, F. P. "Non-Economic Motivational Factors in Philanthropic Behavior," Report presented to the Filer Commission. Atlanta, Ga.: Emory University, 1974.

Crawford, T. J., and Naditch, M. "Relative Deprivation, Powerlessness and Militancy: The Psychology of Social Protest." *Psychiatry,* 1970, *33,* 208–223.

Crigler, P. W. "Significant Variables Indicative of Commitment to the Women's Movement." Unpublished doctoral dissertation, Department of Sociology, Northwestern University, 1973.

Cronbach, A. "Jewish Pioneering in American Social Welfare." *American Jewish Archives,* 1951, *3,* 51–80.

Crowther, C. *Religious Trusts—Their Development, Scope and Meaning.* Oxford, England: G. Ronald, 1954.

Crozier, M., Huntington, S. P., and Watanuki, J. *The Crisis of Democracy.* New York: New York University Press, 1975.

Csikszentmihalyi, M. "Play and Intrinsic Rewards." *Journal of Humanistic Psychology,* 1975, *15,* 41–63.

Cuber, J. F. "Marginal Church Participation." *Sociology and Social Research,* 1940, *26,* 57–62.

Cumming, E., and Henry, W. E. *Growing Old: The Process of Disengagement.* New York: Basic Books, 1961.

Cunningham, M. "Community Control and Neighborhood Health Centers." Paper presented at the annual meeting of the American Public Health Association, Atlantic City, N.J., 1972.

Curti, M. "American Philanthropy and the National Character." *American Quarterly,* 1958, *10,* 420–437.

Curti, M. "Tradition and Innovation in American Philanthropy." *Proceedings of the American Philosophical Society*, 1961, *105*, 146–156.

Curti, M. *American Philanthropy Abroad: A History*. New Brunswick, N.J.: Rutgers University Press, 1963.

Curtis, J. E., and Milton, B. G. "Social Status and the Active vs. Sedentary Societies: National Data on Leisure-Time Physical and Sports Activities in Canada." Paper presented at Southern Sociological Society Annual Meetings, Atlanta, Ga., 1973.

Curtis, J. E., and Milton, B. G. "Social Status and the 'Active' Society: National Data on Correlates of Leisure-Time Physical and Sport Activities." In R. S. Gruneau and J. G. Albinson (Eds.), *Canadian Sport Sociological Perspectives*. Don Mills, Canada: Addison-Wesley, 1976.

Cutlip, S. *Fund Raising in the United States: Its Role in America's Philanthropy*. New Brunswick, N.J.: Rutgers University Press, 1965.

Dahl, R. A. *Who Governs? Democracy and Power in an American City*. New Haven, Conn.: Yale University Press, 1961.

Dahl, R. A. *After the Revolution?* New Haven, Conn.: Yale University Press, 1970.

Dahrendorf, R. *Class and Class Conflict in Industrial Society*. Stanford, Calif.: Stanford University Press, 1959.

Dargavel, G. J. *The Development and Test of a Causal Model of Innovativeness: The Case of the Ten-Speed Bicycle*. Unpublished master's thesis, Department of Kinesiology, University of Waterloo, Ontario, 1975.

Darley, J. M., and Batson, C. D. "From Jerusalem to Jerico: A Study of Situational Helping and Dispositional Variables in Helping Behavior." *Journal of Personality and Social Psychology*, 1973, *27*, 100–108.

Dasgupta, B. "Naxalite Armed Struggles and the Annihilation Campaign in Rural Areas." *Economic and Political Weekly*, 1973, *8*, 4–6.

Datan, N., and Ginsberg, L. H. *Life-Span Developmental Psychology: Normative Life Crises*. New York: Academic Press, 1975.

Davey, C. P. "Personality and Motivation of Australian Participants in Sport." Paper presented at Conference on Sport, Society and Personality, Bundoora, Australia, 1975.

Davies, D. *Citizen Participation in Education: Annotated Bibliography*. New Haven, Conn.: Institute for Responsive Education, 1974.

Davies, J. C. *Human Nature in Politics*. New York: Wiley, 1973.

Davies, J. C. "Toward a Theory of Revolution." In I. K. Feierabend and others (Eds.), *Anger, Violence and Politics: Theories and Research*. Englewood Cliffs, N.J.: Prentice-Hall, 1972.

Davies, J. C. "Aggression, Violence, Revolution, and War." In J. N. Knutson (Ed.), *Handbook of Political Psychology*. San Francisco: Jossey-Bass, 1973a.

Davies, J. C. "Political Violence: The Dominance-Submission Nexus."

In H. Hirsch and D. C. Perry (Eds.), *Violence As Politics.* New York: Harper & Row, 1973b.

Davis, A., and Dollard, J. *Children of Bondage.* Washington, D.C.: American Council on Education, 1940.

Davis, J. P. "The Negro in American Sports." In J. P. Davis (Ed.), *The American Negro Reference Book.* Englewood Cliffs, N.J.: Prentice-Hall, 1966.

Davis, P. H. *Football, the American Intercollegiate Game.* New York: Scribner's, 1911.

Davis, R. H. "Television and the Older Adult." *Journal of Broadcasting,* 1971, *15,* 153–159.

Dawson, R. E., Prewitt, K., and Dawson, K. S. *Political Socialization.* (2nd ed.) Boston: Little, Brown, 1977.

Deacon, J. A., Pigman, J. G., and Dean, R. C. "Travel to Outdoor Recreation Areas in Kentucky." *Journal of Leisure Research,* 1972, *4,* 312–331.

Dean, D. G. "Alienation and Political Apathy." *Social Forces,* 1960, *38,* 185–189.

Dean, D. G. "Alienation: Its Meaning and Measurement." *American Sociological Review,* 1961, *26,* 753–758.

DeCharms, R. *Personal Causation: The Internal Affective Determinants of Behavior.* New York: Academic Press, 1968.

DeGrazia, S. *Of Time, Work and Leisure.* New York: Twentieth Century Fund, 1962.

DeJong, G. S., and Faulkner, J. "Religion and Intellectuals: Findings From a Sample of University Faculty." *Review of Religious Research,* 1972, *14,* 15–24.

Dembo, R. "Life Style and Media Use Among English Working-Class Youths." *Gazette,* 1972, *18,* 24–36.

Demerath, N. J., III, and Hammond, P. E. *Religion in Social Context: Tradition and Transition.* New York: Random House, 1970.

Demerath, N. J., III, and Roof, W. C. "Religion—Recent Strands in Research." In A. Inkeles, J. Coleman, and N. Smelser (Eds.), *Annual Review of Sociology.* Vol. 2. Palo Alto, Calif.: Annual Reviews, 1976.

Dennis, J. "Support for the Institution of Elections by the Mass Public." *American Political Science Review,* 1970, *64,* 819–835.

Dennis, J. *Political Socialization Research: A Bibliography.* Beverly Hills, Calif.: Sage, 1973.

Dervin, B., and Greenberg, B. S. "The Communication Environment of the Urban Poor." In F. G. Kline and P. J. Tichenor (Eds.), *Current Perspectives in Mass Communication Research.* Beverly Hills, Calif.: Sage, 1972.

de Tocqueville, A. *The Old Regime and the French Revolution.* (S. Gilbert, Trans.) New York: Doubleday, 1955.

Detroit Area Study. "Some Patterns of Group Association in the Detroit Area." Ann Arbor, Mich.: Detroit Area Study, Report 5271, 1953.

Deutsch, K. "Social Mobilization and Political Development." *American Political Science Review*, 1961, *55*, 493–514.

Deutsch, K. W. *Nationalism and Social Communication: An Inquiry into the Foundations of Nationality.* Cambridge, Mass.: M.I.T. Press-Wiley, 1962.

Deutsch, M. "Trust and Suspicion." *Journal of Conflict Resolution*, 1958, *2*, 265–279.

Deutsch, M. "Trust, Trustworthiness, and the F-Scale." *Journal of Abnormal and Social Psychology*, 1960, *61*, 138–140.

Deutsch, M., and Krauss, R. M. *Theories in Social Psychology.* New York: Basic Books, 1965.

Deutscher, I. "Words and Deeds: Social Science and Social Policy." *Social Problems*, 1966, *13*, 235–254.

DeVries, W., and Tarrance, V. L. *The Ticket-Splitter: A New Force in American Politics.* Grand Rapids, Mich.: Eerdmans, 1972.

Diamant, A. "Democratizing the Work Place: The Myth and Reality of Mitbestimmung in the Federal Republic of Germany." Paper delivered at annual meeting of the American Political Science Association, Chicago, 1976.

Dickson, P. "Humanizing the Work Place." *MBA*, 1975, *3*, 31–36.

Diem, C. *Weltgeschichte des Sports* [*Universal History of Sport*]. Stuttgart, Germany: Cotter, 1960.

DiPalma, G. *Apathy and Participation.* New York: Free Press, 1970.

DiRenzo, G. J. (Ed.). *Concepts, Theory and Explanation in the Behavioral Sciences.* New York: Random House, 1966.

DiRenzo, G. J. *Personality, Power and Politics: A Social Psychological Analysis of the Italian Deputy and his Parliamentary System.* Notre Dame, Ind.: University of Notre Dame Press, 1967.

DiRenzo, G. J. "Socialization, Personality and Social Systems." In A. Inkeles, J. Coleman, and N. Smelser (Eds.), *Annual Review of Sociology.* Vol. 3. Palo Alto, Calif.: Annual Reviews, 1977.

Disaster Research Center. "The Wilkes-Barre Survey." Unpublished study. Columbus, Ohio: Disaster Research Center, 1973.

Disaster Research Center. "The Xenia Survey." Unpublished study. Columbus, Ohio: Disaster Research Center, 1974.

Disaster Research Center. "Field Studies of Disaster: A Bibliography." Columbus, Ohio: Disaster Research Center, forthcoming.

Disaster Research Group. "Field Studies of Disaster Behavior." Washington, D.C.: National Academy of Sciences, 1961.

Dittes, J. E. "The Psychology of Religion." In G. Lindzey and E. Aronson (Eds.), *The Handbook of Social Psychology.* Vol. 5. Reading, Mass.: Addison-Wesley, 1969.

Dittes, J. E. "Religion, Prejudice, and Personality." In M. P. Strommen

(Ed.), *Research on Religious Development: A Comprehensive Handbook*. New York: Hawthorn Books, 1971a.

Dittes, J. E. "Psychological Characteristics of Religous Professionals." In M. P. Strommen (Ed.), *Research on Religious Development: A Comprehensive Handbook*. New York: Hawthorn Books, 1971b.

Ditton, R. B., Goodale, T. L., and Johnsen, P. K. "A Cluster Analysis of Activity Frequency and Environment Variables to Identify Water-Based Recreation Types." *Journal of Leisure Research*, 1975, *7*, 282–295.

Dogan, M., and Narbonne, J. *Les Françaises Face à la Politique [The French Face Politics]*. Paris: Armand Colin, 1955.

Dogan, M., and Rokkan, S. (Eds.). *Quantitative Ecological Analysis in the Social Sciences*. Cambridge, Mass.: M.I.T. Press, 1969.

Dohrenwend, B. S., and Dohrenwend, B. P. (Eds.). *Stressful Life Events: Their Nature and Effects*. New York: Wiley, 1974.

Dollard, J., and others. *Frustration and Aggression*. New Haven, Conn.: Yale University Press, 1939.

Dominick, J. R. "The Portable Friend: Peer Group Membership and Radio Usage." *Journal of Broadcasting*, 1974, *18*, 161–170.

Donald, M. N., and Havighurst, R. J. "The Meanings of Leisure." *Social Forces*, 1959, *37*, 355–360.

Donohew, L., and Thorp, R. "An Approach to the Study of Mass Media Within a State." *Journalism Quarterly*, 1966, *43*, 264–268.

Donohue, G. A., Tichenor, P. J., and Olien, C. N. "Gatekeeping: Mass Media Systems and Information Control." In F. G. Kline and P. J. Tichenor (Eds.), *Current Perspectives in Mass Communication Research*. Beverly Hills, Calif.: Sage, 1972.

Dotan, J., and Cohen, A. A. "Mass Media Use in the Family During War and Peace, Israel 1973–1974." *Communication Research*, 1976, *3*, 393–402.

Doty, W. G. *Meaningful Leisure*. New York: National Council of Churches, 1963.

Douglas, J. D. *The Social Meaning of Suicide*. Princeton, N.J.: Princeton University Press, 1967.

Douglass, P. F., and Crawford, R. W. "Implementation of a Comprehensive Plan for the Wise Use of Leisure." In J. C. Charlesworth (Ed.), *Leisure in America: Blessing or Curse?* Philadelphia: American Academy of Political and Social Science, 1964.

Douvan, E., and Adelson, J. *The Adolescent Experience*. New York: Wiley, 1966.

Dowell, L. J. "Attitudes of Parents of Athletes and Non-Athletes Toward Physical Activity." *Psychological Reports*, 1973, *32*, 813–814.

Downton, J. V., Jr. *Rebel Leadership*. New York: Free Press, 1973.

Drabek, T., and Boggs, K. "Social Processes in Disaster: Family Evacuation." *Social Problems*, 1969, *16*, 336–349.

Drabek, T., and Key, W. "The Impact of Disaster on Primary Group Linkages." *Mass Emergencies*, 1975, *1*, 89–106.

Drabek, T., and Stephenson, J. "When Disaster Strikes." *Journal of Applied Social Psychology*, 1971, *1*, 187–203.

Drakeford, J. W. *Children of Doom*. Nashville: Broadman Press, 1972.

Draper, D. *Public Participation in Environmental Decision-Making*. Monticello, Ill.: Council of Planning Librarians, No. 396, 1973.

Dubin, R. "Industrial Workers' Worlds." *Social Problems*, 1956, *3*, 131–142.

Dumazedier, J. *Towards a Society of Leisure*. New York: Free Press, 1967.

Dumazedier, J. "Sport and Sports Activities." *International Review of Sport Sociology*, 1973, *8*, 7–34.

Dumazedier, J. *Sociology of Leisure*. New York: Elsevier, 1974.

Dunning, E. and Sheard, K. *Barbarians, Gentlemen and Players*. Oxford: Martin Robertson, 1979.

Durkheim, E. *The Division of Labor in Society*. New York: Macmillan, 1933.

Durkheim, E. *The Elementary Forms of the Religious Life*. New York: Free Press, 1954. (Originally published 1912).

Durkheim, E. *Moral Education*. New York: Free Press, 1961.

Dutton, D. B. "Explaining the Low Use of Health Services by the Poor: Costs, Attitudes or Delivery Systems?" *American Sociological Review*, 1978, *43*, 348–368.

Duverger, M. *The Political Role of Women*. Paris: UNESCO, 1955.

Dynes, R. R. *Organized Behavior in Disaster*. Columbus, Ohio: Disaster Research Center, 1975.

Dynes, R. R., and Quarantelli, E. L. "Group Behavior Under Stress: A Required Convergence of Organizational and Collective Behavior Perspectives." *Sociology and Social Research*, 1968, *52*, 416–429.

Dynes, R. R., and Quarantelli, E. L. "Emergency Disaster Plans for Vocational Schools." In D. Koble and M. Newton (Eds.), *Developing the Leadership Potential of Urban Vocational Education Administrators: 1976 National Leadership Seminar*. Columbus, Ohio: Center for Vocational Education, 1976.

Easton, D. "An Approach to the Analysis of Political Sytems." *World Politics*, 1956–57, *65*, 383–400.

Easton, D. *A Framework for Political Analysis*. Englewood Cliffs, N.J.: Prentice-Hall, 1965.

Easton, D., and Dennis, J. "The Child's Acquisition of Regime Norms:

Political Efficacy." *American Political Science Review*, 1967, *61*, 25–38.

Easton, D., and Dennis, J. *Children in the Political System: Origins of Political Legitimacy.* New York: McGraw-Hill, 1969.

Easton, D., and Hess, R. D. "The Child's Political World." *Midwest Journal of Political Science*, 1962, *6*, 237–238.

Ebbin, S., and Kasper, R. *Citizen Groups and the Nuclear Power Controversy: Uses of Scientific and Technological Information.* Cambridge, Mass.: M.I.T. Press, 1974.

Ecklein, J. L., and Lauffer, A. A. *Community Organizers and Social Planners.* New York: Wiley, and the Council on Social Work Education, 1972.

Eckstein, H. "On the Etiology of Internal Wars." In I. K. Feierabend (Ed.) *Anger, Violence and Politics: Theories and Research.* Englewood Cliffs, N.J.: Prentice-Hall, 1972.

Edeani, D. O. "Ownership and Control of the Press in Africa." *Gazette*, 1970, *16*, 55–56.

Edelstein, A. "An Alternative Approach to the Study of Source Effects in Mass Communication." *Studies of Broadcasting*, 1973, *9*, 1–10.

Edwards, A. L., and Abbott, R. D. "Measurement of Personality Traits, Theory and Technique." In P. H. Mussen and M. R. Rosenzweig (Eds.), *Annual Review of Psychology.* Vol. 24. Palo Alto, Calif.: Annual Reviews, 1973.

Edwards, H. *The Sociology of Sport.* Homewood, Ill.: Dorsey Press, 1973.

Ehrenreich, B., and Ehrenreich, J. *The American Health Empire: Power, Profits and Politics.* New York: Vintage, 1971.

Ehrlich, H. J. "Attitudes, Behavior and the Intervening Variables." *The American Sociologist*, 1969, *4*, 29–34.

Einstein, A., and Freud, S. *Why War?* Paris: International Institute of Intellectual Cooperation, 1932.

Eisen, G. "Physical Activity, Physical Education, and Sport in the Old Testament." *Canadian Journal of History of Sport and Physical Education*, 1975, *6*, 44–65.

Eisenstadt, S. N. *From Generation to Generation: Age Groups and Social Structure.* New York: Free Press, 1956.

Eisenstadt, S. N. *Modernization: Protest and Change.* Englewood Cliffs, N.J.: Prentice-Hall, 1966.

Eisenstadt, S. N., and Curelaru, M. *The Form of Sociology: Paradigms and Crises.* New York: Wiley, 1976.

Eister, A. W. "An Outline of a Structural Theory of Cults." *Journal for the Scientific Study of Religion*, 1972, *11*, 319–333.

Eitzen, D. S. "Sport and Status in American Public Secondary Education." *Review of Sport and Leisure*, 1976, *1*, 139–155.

Ekehammar, B. "Interactionism in Personality From a Historical Perspective." *Psychological Bulletin,* 1974, *81,* 1026–1048.

Elder, G. H., Jr. *Adolescent Socialization and Personality Development.* Chicago: Rand McNally, 1968.

Elder, G. H., Jr. "Age Differentiation and the Life Course." In A. Inkeles, J. Coleman, and N. Smelser (Eds.), *Annual Review of Sociology.* Vol. 1. Palo Alto, Calif.: Annual Reviews, 1975.

Eldersveld, S. J., Jagannadham, V., and Barnabas, A. P. *The Citizen and the Administrator in a Developing Democracy.* Glenview, Ill.: Scott, Foresman, 1968.

Eldersveld, S. J., and Kubota, A. "Party Identification in India and Japan—In the Context of Western Theory and Research." Paper delivered at the Canadian Political Science Association Meeting, Montreal, 1973.

Elifson, K. W. "Religious Behavior Among Urban Southern Baptists: A Causal Inquiry." *Sociological Analysis,* 1976, *37,* 32–44.

Elkin, F. *The Child and Society.* New York: Random House, 1960.

Ellenwood, R. S., Jr. *Religions and Spiritual Groups in Modern America.* Englewood Cliffs, N.J.: Prentice-Hall, 1973.

Ellul, J. "The Psychology of a Rebellion: May–June 1968." In G. A. Kelly and C. W. Brown, Jr. (Eds.), *Struggles in the State: Sources and Patterns of World Revolution.* New York: Wiley, 1970.

Elms, A. C. "The Crisis of Confidence in Social Psychology." *American Psychologist,* 1975, *30,* 967–976.

Enck, H. *The Burden Borne: Northern White Philanthropy and Southern Black Industrial Education, 1900–1915.* Unpublished doctoral dissertation, Department of History, University of Cincinnati, 1970.

Endler, N. S., and Magnusson, D. *Interactional Psychology and Personality.* Washington, D.C.: Hemisphere, 1975.

Engel, J. F., Kollat, D. T., and Blackwell, R. D. *Consumer Behavior.* (2nd ed.) New York: Holt, Rinehart and Winston, 1973.

Engström, L. "Physical Activities During Leisure Time." *International Review of Sport Sociology,* 1974, *9,* 83–102.

Enloe, C. *Ethnic Conflict and Political Development.* Boston: Little, Brown, 1973.

Enroth, R. M., Breckenridge, P. C., and Ericson, E. E., Jr. *The Jesus People.* Grand Rapids, Mich.: Eerdmans, 1972.

Enroth, R. M., Breckenridge, P. C., and Ericson, E. E., Jr. "Christian Communes." In E. Heenan (Ed.), *Mystery, Magic and Miracle.* Englewood Cliffs, N.J.: Prentice-Hall, 1973.

Erbe, W. "Social Involvement and Political Activity." *American Sociological Review,* 1964, *29,* 198–215.

Erickson, P., and others. "Families in Disasters: Patterns of Recovery." *Mass Emergencies,* 1976, *1,* 203–216.

Eriksen, C. W., and Pierce, J. "Defense Mechanisms." In E. F. Borgatta and W. W. Lambert (Eds.), *Handbook of Personality Theory and Research*. Chicago: Rand McNally, 1968.

Erikson, E. H. "Identity and the Life Cycle." Monograph 1. *Psychological Issues*, 1959, *1*.

Erikson, E. H. *Childhood and Society*. (2nd ed.) New York: Norton, 1963.

Eron, L., Walder, L., and Lefkowitz, M. *Learning of Aggression in Children*. Boston: Little, Brown, 1971.

Etzioni, A. *The Active Society*. New York: Free Press, 1968.

Etzkorn, P. K. "Leisure and Camping: The Social Meaning of a Form of Public Recreation." *Sociology and Social Research*, 1964, *49*, 76–89.

Eulau, H. *Class and Party in the Eisenhower Years*. New York: Free Press, 1962.

Fagence, M. T. "Citizen Participation in the Planning Process." *Journal of the Royal Town Planning Institute*, 1973, *59*, 188–191.

Fairchilds, C. "Changing Patterns of Charity: Aix-en-Provence in the Seventeenth and Eighteenth Centuries." Unpublished paper presented at annual meeting of the American Historical Association, San Francisco, 1973.

Fallding, H. "A Proposal for the Empirical Study of Values." *American Sociological Review*, 1965, *30*, 223–233.

Faris, R.E.L. (Ed.). *Handbook of Modern Sociology*. Chicago: Rand McNally, 1964.

Farner, R. F., Jr., and others. *National Assessment of Educational Progress, 1970–1975*. Washington, D.C.: U.S. Office of Education, 1977.

Feierabend, I. K., and Feierabend, R. L. "Systemic Conditions of Political Aggression: An Application of Frustration-Aggression Theory." In I. K. Feierabend and others (Eds.), *Anger, Violence and Politics: Theories and Research*. Englewood Cliffs, N.J.: Prentice-Hall, 1972.

Feierabend, I. K., Feierabend, R. L., and Nesvold, B. A. "Social Change and Political Violence: Cross-National Patterns." In I. K. Feierabend and others (Eds.), *Anger, Violence and Politics: Theories and Research*. Englewood Cliffs, N.J.: Prentice-Hall, 1972.

Feinberg, H. and Staub, E. "Learning to be Prosocial: The Effects of Reasoning and Participation in Prosocial Action on Children's Prosocial Behavior." Paper presented at annual meeting of the Eastern Psychological Association, New York, 1975.

Feldman, K. A., and Newcomb, T. M. *The Impact of College on Students*. Vols. 1 and 2. San Francisco: Jossey-Bass, 1969.

Feldstein, M. "Report to the Commission on Private Philanthropy and Public Needs." Cited in P. Kihss, "Tax Deductions and Gifts Studied." *New York Times*, May 11, 1975.

Fenn, R. K. "A New Sociology of Religion." *Journal for the Scientific Study of Religion*, 1972, *11*, 11–32.

Ferge, S. "Social Differentiation in Leisure Activity Choices." In A. Szalai and others (Eds.), *The Use of Time*. The Hague, Netherlands: Mouton, 1972.

Ferge, S., and others. "Statistical Appendix." In A. Szalai and others (Eds.), *The Use of Time*. The Hague, Netherlands: Mouton, 1972.

Ferris, A. L. "The Social and Personality Correlates of Outdoor Recreation." *Annals of the American Academy of Political and Social Science*, 1970, *389*, 46–55.

Feshback, S. "The Drive-Reducing Function of Fantasy Behavior." *Journal of Abnormal and Social Psychology*, 1955, *50*, 3–11.

Feshback, S., and Singer, R. D. *Television and Aggression: An Experimental Field Study*. San Francisco: Jossey-Bass, 1971.

Festinger, L., Schachter, S., and Back, K. *Social Pressures in Informal Groups*. New York: Harper & Row, 1950.

Feuer, L. S. *The Conflict of Generations*. New York: Basic Books, 1969.

Fichter, J. H. "Profile of Catholic Religious Life." *American Journal of Sociology*, 1952, *58*, 45–149.

Fichter, J. H. *The Catholic Cult of the Paraclete*. Mission, Kans.: Sheed Andrews & McMeel, 1975.

Field, D. R. "Interchangeability of Parks with Other Leisure Settings." Paper presented at annual meeting of the American Association for the Advancement of Science, Philadelphia, 1971.

Field, D. R. "The Telephone Interview in Leisure Research." *Journal of Leisure Research*, 1973, *5*, 51–59.

Field, D. R., and O'Leary, J. T. "Social Groups as a Basis for Assessing Participation in Selected Water Activities." *Journal of Leisure Research*, 1973, *5*, 16–25.

Finifter, A. W. "Dimensions of Political Alienation." *American Political Science Review*, 1970, *64*, 389–410.

Finifter, A. W., and Miller, A. H. "Alienation: So What?" Paper presented at the Conference on Political Alienation and Support, San Francisco, 1975.

Fishbein, M. "The Relationship Between Beliefs, Attitudes, and Behavior." In S. Feldman (Ed.), *Cognitive Consistency*. New York: Academic Press, 1966.

Fishbein, M. "Attitude and the Prediction of Behavior." In M. Fishbein, (Ed.), *Readings in Attitude Theory and Measurement*. New York: Wiley, 1967.

Fishbein, M., and Ajzen, I. "Attitudes and Opinions." In P. H. Mussen and M. R. Rosenzweig (Eds.), *Annual Review of Psychology*. Vol. 23. Palo Alto, Calif.: Annual Reviews, 1972.

Fishbein, M., and Ajzen, I. *Belief, Attitude, Intention and Behavior.* Reading, Mass.: Addison-Wesley, 1975.

Fisher, A.C., and Driscoll, R. G. "Attribution of Attitudes Toward Physical Activity as a Function of Success." *Movement,* 1975, *9,* 239–241.

Fisher, J. D., and Nadler, A. "The Effect of Similarity Between Donor and Recipient on Recipient's Reaction to Aid." *Journal of Applied Social Psychology,* 1974, *4,* 230–243.

Fisher, J. D., and Nadler, A. "Effect of Donor Resources on Recipient of Self-Esteem and Self-Help." *Journal of Experimental Social Psychology,* 1976, *12,* 139–150.

Fiske, D. W., and Maddi, S. R. *Functions of Varied Experience.* Homewood, Ill.: Dorsey Press, 1961.

Flacks, R. "Who Protests: A Study of Student Activists." In J. Foster and D. Long (Eds.), *Protest: Student Activism in America.* New York: Morrow, 1970.

Flavell, J. H. *The Developmental Psychology of Jean Piaget.* New York: D. Van Nostrand, 1963.

Fletcher, R. L. "Selected Personality Characteristics and Activity Participation of Male College Freshman." Unpublished doctoral dissertation, Department of Physical Education, Texas A&M University, 1970.

Fletcher, R., and Dowell, L. "Selected Personality Characteristics of High School Athletes and Non-Athletes." *Journal of Psychology,* 1971, *77,* 39–41.

Flynn, J. P., and Webb, G. E. "Women's Incentives for Involvement in Policy Issues." *Journal of Voluntary Action Research,* 1975, *4,* 137–147.

Foley, D. L. "The Use of Local Facilities in a Metropolis." *American Journal of Sociology,* 1950, *56,* 238–246.

Form, W. "Comparative Industrial Sociology and the Convergence Hypothesis." In A. Inkeles, J. Coleman, and R. H. Turner (Eds.), *Annual Review of Sociology.* Vol. 5. Palo Alto, Calif.: Annual Reviews, 1979.

Form, W., and Nosow, S. *Community in Disaster.* New York: Harper & Row, 1958.

Forrest, T. R. *Structural Differentiation in Emergent Groups.* Columbus, Ohio: Disaster Research Center, 1974.

Forsey, S. D. "The Influence of Family Structures Upon the Patterns and Effects of Family Viewing." In L. Aarons and M. A. May (Eds.), *Television and Human Behavior.* New York: Appleton-Century-Crofts, 1963.

Forward, J. R., and Williams, J. R. "Internal-External Control and Black Militancy." *Journal of Social Issues,* 1970, *26,* 75–92.

Foster, C. R. (Ed.) *Comparative Public Policy and Citizen Participation: Energy, Education, Health and Local Governance in the U.S. and Germany.* Elmsford, N.Y.: Pergamon, 1980.

Fowler, J. W. "Stages in Faith: The Structural-Developmental Approach." In T. Hennessy (Ed.), *Values and Moral Development.* New York: Paulist Press, 1976.

Frederickson, R. "Toward a Taxonomy of Situations." *American Psychologist,* 1972, *27,* 114–124.

Freedman, J. L. "Transgression, Compliance, and Guilt." In J. Macaulay and L. Berkowitz (Eds.), *Altruism and Helping Behavior.* New York: Academic Press, 1970.

Freedman, J. L., and Fraser, S. C. "Compliance Without Pressure: The Foot-in-the-Door Technique." *Journal of Personality and Social Psychology,* 1966, *4,* 195–202.

Freeman, J. "The Origins of the Women's Liberation Movement." *American Journal of Sociology,* 1973, *78,* 792–811.

Freese, L. "Cumulative Sociological Knowledge." *American Sociological Review,* 1972, *37,* 472–482.

Freidson, E. *The Profession of Medicine.* New York: Dodd, Mead, 1970.

Freud, A. *The Ego and the Mechanisms of Defense.* London: Hogarth Institute of Psychoanalysis, 1932.

Freud, S. *Beyond the Pleasure Principle.* London: International Psychoanalytic Press, 1922.

Freud, S. *Collected Papers of Sigmund Freud.* (E. Jones, Ed.) 5 Vols. New York: Basic Books, 1959.

Freund, R. J., and Wilson, R. R. "An Example of a Gravity Model to Estimate Recreation Travel." *Journal of Leisure Research,* 1974, *6,* 241–256.

Fried, M., Havens, J., and Thrall, M. *Travel Behavior: A Synthesized Theory.* Chestnut Hill, Mass.: Laboratory for Psychosocial Studies, Boston College, 1977.

Friedman, N. *The Social Nature of Psychological Research.* New York: Basic Books, 1967.

Friedmann, K. A. *Complaining: Comparative Aspects of Complaint Behavior and Attitudes Toward Complaining in Canada and Britain.* Sage Professional Papers in Administrative and Policy Studies. Vol. 2. Series No. 03-019. Beverly Hills, Calif.: Sage, 1974.

Frisch, E. *An Historical Survey of Jewish Philanthropy.* New York: Cooper Square Publishers, 1969. (Originally published 1924.)

Fritz, C., and Mathewson, J. H. *Convergence Behavior in Disasters: A Problem in Social Control.* Washington, D.C.: National Academy of Sciences, 1957.

Fritz, C. E., Rayner, J. F., and Guskin, S. L. *Behavior in an Emergency Shelter: A Field Study of 800 Persons Stranded in a Highway Restau-*

rant During a Heavy Snowstorm. Washington, D.C.: National Academy of Sciences, 1958.

Fromm, E. *Man for Himself.* New York: Rinehart, 1947.

Fromm, E. *The Sane Society.* New York: Rinehart, 1955.

Fukuyama, Y. "The Major Dimensions of Church Membership." *Review of Religious Research,* 1961, *2,* 154–161.

Gallimore, R., Weiss, L. B., and Finney, R. "Cultural Differences in Delay of Gratification: A Problem of Behavior Classification." *Journal of Personality and Social Psychology,* 1974, *30,* 72–80.

Gallup, G. *Religion in America—The Gallup Opinion Index.* Report No. 130. Princeton, N.J.: American Institute of Public Opinion, 1976.

Gallup, G. *The Gallup Opinion Index.* Report No. 140. Princeton, N.J.: American Institute of Public Opinion, 1977.

Gamble, C. W. *How to Raise Money: Fund Raising Programs for Social and Religious Organizations.* New York: Association Press, 1942.

Gamer, R. *The Developing Nations: A Comparative Perspective.* Boston: Allyn & Bacon, 1976.

Gamson, W. A. *Power and Discontent.* Homewood, Ill.: Dorsey Press, 1968.

Gamson, W. A. *The Strategy of Social Protest.* Homewood, Ill.: Dorsey Press, 1975.

Gannon, T. M. "The Role of the Non-Professional in the Harlem Domestic Peace Corps." *Sociology and Social Research,* 1967, *52,* 348–362.

Garcia, F. C. *Political Socialization of Chicano Children.* New York: Harper, & Row, 1973.

Garson, G. D., and Smith, M. P. (Eds.). *Organizational Democracy.* Sage Contemporary Social Science Issues 22. Beverly Hills, Calif.: Sage, 1976.

Gartner, A., and Riessman, F. *The Service Society and the Consumer Vanguard.* New York: Harper & Row, 1974.

Geertz, C. "The Integrative Revolution: Primordial Sentiments and Civil Politics in the New States." In C. Welch (Ed.), *Political Modernization.* Belmont, Calif.: Wadsworth, 1967.

Geismar, L. L. *555 Families: A Social-Psychological Study of Young Families in Transition.* New Brunswick, N.J.: Transaction Books, 1973.

George, A. L., and George, G. L. *Woodrow Wilson and Colonel House: A Personality Study.* New York: Dover, 1956.

Gerber, E., and others. *The American Woman in Sport.* Reading, Mass.: Addison-Wesley, 1974.

Gergen, K. J. *The Concept of Self.* New York: Holt, Rinehart and Winston, 1971.

Gergen, K. J. (Ed.). "Reactions to Receiving Aid." *Journal of Applied Social Psychology*, 1974, *4*, 187–294.

Gergen, K. J., Gergen, M. M., and Meter, K. "Individual Orientations to Prosocial Behavior." *Journal of Social Issues*, 1972, *28*, 105–130.

Gergen, K. J., and others. "Obligation, Donor Resources and Reactions to Aid in Three Cultures." *Journal of Personality and Social Psychology*, 1975, *3*, 390–400.

Gerlach, L. P., and Hine, V. H. *People, Power, Change: Movements of Social Transformation*. Indianapolis, Ind.: Bobbs-Merrill, 1970.

Gerth, H. H., and Mills, C. W. *Character and Social Structure*. New York: Harcourt Brace Jovanovich, 1953.

Gerth, H. H., and Mills, C. W. (Eds.). *From Max Weber: Essays in Sociology*. New York: Oxford University Press, 1958.

Gettleman, M. "Charity and Social Classes in the United States, 1874–1900." *American Journal of Economics and Sociology*, 1963, *22*, 313–329, 417–426.

Gibbs, J. P. "Issues in Defining Deviant Behavior." In R. A. Scott and J. D. Douglas (Eds.), *Theoretical Perspectives in Deviance*. New York: Basic Books, 1972.

Gibbs, J. P., and Erickson, M. L. "Major Developments in the Sociological Study of Deviance." In A. Inkeles, J. Coleman, and N. Smelser (Eds.), *Annual Review of Sociology*. Vol. 1. Palo Alto, Calif.: Annual Reviews, 1975.

Gilmour, S. C. "What Does Fowler Have to Say to Adult Educators?" *Living Light*, 1976, *13*, 524–536.

Ginsberg, H., and Opper, S. *Piaget's Theory of Intellectual Development*. (2nd ed.) Englewood Cliffs, N.J.: Prentice-Hall, 1979.

Glaser, B. G., and Strauss, A. L. *Theory of Status Passage*. Chicago: Aldine, 1971.

Glenn, N. D., and Grimes, M. "Aging, Voting and Political Interest." *American Sociological Review*, 1968, *33*, 563–575.

Glenn, N. J. *Cohort Analysis*. Beverly Hills, Calif.: Sage, 1977.

Glock, C. Y. "The Role of Deprivation in the Origin and Evolution of Religious Groups." In R. Lee and M. E. Marty (Eds.), *Religion and Social Conflict*. New York: Oxford University Press, 1964.

Glock, C. Y. "Consciousness Among Contemporary Youth: An Interpretation." In C. Y. Glock and R. N. Bellah (Eds.), *The New Religious Consciousness*. Berkeley: University of California Press, 1976.

Glock, C. Y., and Stark, R. *Religion and Society in Tension*. Chicago: Rand McNally, 1965.

Goble, F. G. *The Third Force: The Psychology of Abraham Maslow*. New York: Grossman, 1970.

Gockel, G. L., Bradburn, N. M., and Sudman, S. "Community Organizations in Integrated Neighborhoods." In I. A. Spergel (Ed.), *Community Organization*. Beverly Hills, Calif.: Sage, 1972.

Godbey, G., and Kraus, R. "Citizen Participation in Urban Recreation Decision-Making." *Community Development Journal*, 1973, *8*, 155–160.

Goel, M. L. "Distribution of Civic Competence Feelings in India." *Social Science Quarterly*, 1970, *51*, 755–768.

Goel, M. L. "Urban-Rural Correlates of Political Participation in India." *Political Science Review*, 1971, *10*, 51–64.

Goel, M. L. *Political Participation in a Developing Nation: India*. New York: Asia Publishing House, 1975.

Goffman, E. *Asylums*. Garden City, N.Y.: Anchor Books, 1961.

Goffman, E. *Frame Analysis*. Cambridge, Mass.: Harvard University Press, 1974.

Goldberger, A. S., and Duncan, D. D. (Eds.). *Structural Equation Models in the Social Sciences*. New York: Academic Press, 1973.

Goldin, G. J., and others. *Dependency and Its Implications for Rehabilitation*. (Rev. ed.) Lexington, Mass.: Heath, 1972.

Gonos, G. "Situation Versus Frame: The Interactionist and the Structuralist Analyses of Everyday Life." *American Sociological Review*, 1977, *42*, 854–867.

Goode, W. J. "Family Disorganization." In R. K. Merton and R. A. Nisbet (Eds.), *Contemporary Social Problems*. New York: Harcourt Brace Jovanovich, 1961.

Goodspeed, C. E. *Angling in America: Its Early History and Literature*. Boston: Houghton Mifflin, 1939.

Gordon, C. *Looking Ahead: Self-Conceptions, Race and Family as Determinants of Adolescent Orientation to Achievement*. Washington, D.C.: American Sociological Association, Rose Monograph Series, 1972.

Gordon, C. "Development of Evaluated Role Identities." In A. Inkeles, J. Coleman, and N. Smelser (Eds.), *Annual Review of Sociology*. Vol. 3. Palo Alto, Calif.: Annual Reviews, 1976.

Gordon, C., Gaitz, C. M., and Scott, J. "Leisure and Lives: Personal Expressivity Across the Life Span." In R. H. Binstock and E. Shanas (Eds.), *Handbook of Aging and the Social Sciences*. New York: D. Van Nostrand, 1976.

Gordon, C., and Gergen, K. J. (Eds.). *The Self in Social Interaction*. New York: Wiley, 1968.

Gore, P. M., and Rotter, J. B. "A Personality Correlate of Social Action." *Journal of Personality*, 1963, *31*, 59–69.

Gorer, G. *Death, Grief, and Mourning*. New York: Doubleday, 1967.

Goslin, D. *Handbook of Socialization Theory and Research*. Chicago: Rand McNally, 1969.

Gough, H. G. "Predicting Social Participation." *Journal of Social Psychology*, 1952, *35*, 227–235.

Gould, D. R., and Landers, D. M. "Dangerous Sport Participation: A Replication of Nisbett's Birth Order Findings." Paper presented at North American Society for Psychology in Sports and Physical Activity, Houston, Tex., 1972.

Gould, M., and Kern-Daniels, R. "Toward a Sociological Theory of Gender and Sex." *The American Sociologist*, 1977, *12*, 182–189.

Gould, R. L. "The Phases of Adult Life: A Study in Developmental Psychology." *American Journal of Psychiatry*, 1972, *129*, 521–531.

Gould, R. L. "Adult Life Stages: Growth Toward Self-Tolerance." *Psychology Today*, February 1975, pp. 74–78.

Goulden, J. C. *The Money Givers.* New York: Random House, 1971.

Gouldner, A. W. "The Norm of Reciprocity: A Preliminary Statement." *American Sociological Review*, 1960, *25*, 161–178.

Gouldner, A. W. *The Coming Crisis of Western Sociology.* London: Heinemann, 1970.

Goulet, L. R., and Baltes, P. B. *Life-Span Developmental Psychology: Research and Theory.* New York: Academic Press, 1970.

Graney, M. J., and Graney, E. E. "Communications Activity Substitutions in Aging." *Journal of Communication*, 1974, *24*, 88–96.

Greeley, A. "Superstition, Ecstasy, and Tribal Consciousness." *Social Research*, 1970, *37*, 203–210.

Greeley, A. M., and Gockel, G. L. "The Religious Effects of Parochial Education." In M. P. Strommen (Ed.), *Research on Religious Development: A Comprehensive Handbook.* New York: Hawthorn Books, 1971.

Greeley, A. M., and Rossi, P. H. *The Education of Catholic Americans.* Chicago: Aldine, 1966.

Greenberg, B. S. "Gratifications of Television Viewing and Their Correlates for British Children." In J. Blumler and E. Katz (Eds.), *The Uses of Mass Communications.* Beverly Hills, Calif.: Sage, 1974.

Greenberg, B. S., and Dominick, J. R. "Race and Social Class Differences in Teenagers' Use of Television." *Journal of Broadcasting*, 1969, *13*, 331–344.

Greenberg, B. S., and Kumata, H. "National Sample Predictors of Mass Media Use." *Journalism Quarterly*, 1968, *45*, 641–646, 705.

Greenberg, C. "Work and Leisure Under Industrialism." In E. Larrabee and R. Meyersohn (Eds.), *Mass Leisure.* New York: Free Press, 1958.

Greenberg, E. "Orientations of Black and White Children to Political Authority." *Social Science Quarterly*, 1970, *51*, 934–943.

Greenberg, M. S. "A Preliminary Statement on a Theory of Indebtedness." Paper presented at annual meeting of the Western Psychological Association, 1968.

Greenberg, M. S. "A Theory of Indebtedness." In K. Gergen, M. S. Greenberg, and R. Willis (Eds.), *Exchange Theory*. New York: Wiley, forthcoming.

Greenberg, M. S., and Saxe, L. "Importance of Locus of Help Initiation and Type of Outcome as Determinants of Reactions to Another's Help Attempt." *Social Behavior and Personality*, 1975, *3*, 101–110.

Greenberg, M. S., and Shapiro, S. P. "Indebtedness: An Adverse Aspect of Asking for and Receiving Help." *Sociometry*, 1971, *34*, 290–301.

Greene, T. H. *Comparative Revolutionary Movements*. Englewood Cliffs, N.J.: Prentice-Hall, 1974.

Greenley, J. R., and Mechanic, D. "Social Selection in Seeking Help for Psychological Problems." *Journal of Health and Social Behavior*, 1976, *17*, 249–262.

Greenstein, F. I. "The Benevolent Leader: Children's Image of Political Authority." *American Political Science Review*, 1960, *54*, 934–945.

Greenstein, F. I. *Children and Politics*. New Haven, Conn.: Yale University Press, 1965.

Greenstein, F. I. *Personality and Politics*. Chicago: Markham, 1969.

Greenstein, F. I. "The Benevolent Leader Revisited: Children's Images of Political Leaders in Three Democracies." *American Political Science Review*, 1975, *69*, 1390.

Greenwald, A. C. "On Defining Attitude and Attitude Theory." In A. C. Greenwald, T. C. Brock, and T. M. Ostrom (Eds.), *Psychological Foundations of Attitudes*. New York: Academic Press, 1968.

Greer, S., and Winch, R. F. *Kinship and Voluntary Organization in Post-Thermonuclear Attack Society, Some Exploratory Studies*. McLean, Va.: Human Sciences Research, 1965.

Gronseth, E. "The Political Role of Women in Norway." In M. Duverger, *The Political Role of Women*. Paris: UNESCO, 1955.

Gross, A. E., and Latané, J. "Receiving Help, Reciprocation, and Interpersonal Attraction." *Journal of Applied Social Psychology*, 1974, *4*, 210–223.

Gross, A. E., and Lubell, B. B. "Reciprocity and Liking for the Helper." Unpublished data, University of Wisconsin, 1970.

Gross, A. E., and Somersan, S. "Helper Effort as an Inhibitor of Help-Seeking." Paper presented at Psychonomic Society Annual Meeting, 1974.

Gross, A. E., and others. "The Effects of Imposed, Offered and Requested Help: Three Pilot Studies." Unpublished manuscript, University of Wisconsin, 1971.

Groves, D. L., and Kahalas, H. "The Behavioral Dimensions of Free Time." *Society and Leisure*, 1975, *7*, 135–153.

Grundy, J. "Non-Voting in an Urban District." *Journal of the Manchester School of Economic and Social Studies*, 1950, *18*, 83–99.

Gruneau, R. S. "Class or Mass: Notes on the Democratization of Canadian Amateur Sport." In R. S. Gruneau and J. G. Albinson (Eds.), *Canadian Sport: Sociological Perspectives.* Don Mills, Ontario: Addison-Wesley, 1976.

Grupp, F. W., and Newman, W. M. "Political Ideology and Religious Preference: The John Birch Society and the Americans for Democratic Action." *Journal of the Scientific Study of Religion*, 1973, *12*, 1–13.

Grusec, J. E. "Demand Characteristics of the Modeling Experiment: Altruism as a Function of Age and Aggression." *Journal of Personality and Social Psychology*, 1972, *22*, 139–149.

Guilford, J. P. *The Nature of Human Intelligence.* New York: McGraw-Hill, 1967.

Guilford, J. P., and Hoepfner, R. *The Analysis of Intelligence.* New York: McGraw-Hill, 1971.

Gurr, T. R. *Why Men Rebel.* Princeton, N.J.: Princeton University Press, 1970.

Gurr, T. R. "A Causal Model of Civil Strife: A Comparative Analysis Using New Indices." In I. K. Feierabend and others (Eds.), *Anger, Violence and Politics: Theories and Research.* Englewood Cliffs, N.J.: Prentice-Hall, 1972a.

Gurr, T. R. "Psychological Factors in Civil Violence." In I. K. Feierabend and others (Eds.), *Anger, Violence and Politics: Theories and Research.* Englewood Cliffs, N.J.: Prentice-Hall, 1972b.

Gutenschwager, G. "The Time-Budget-Activity Systems Perspective in Urban Planning and Research." *Journal of the American Institute of Planners*, 1973, *39*, 378–387.

Gyman, H. "Altruism and Power in Interpersonal Exchanges." Paper presented at annual meeting of American Sociological Association, Denver, 1971.

Haan, N., Smith, M. B., and Block, J. "The Moral Reasoning of Young Adults: Political-Social Behavior, Family Background and Personality Correlates." *Journal of Personality and Social Psychology*, 1968, *10*, 183–201.

Hadden, J. K. *The Gathering Storm in the Churches.* New York: Doubleday, 1969.

Hage, J. *Techniques and Problems of Theory Construction.* New York: Wiley-Interscience, 1972.

Haggstrom, W. C. "The Power of the Poor." In F. Reissman, J. Cohen, and A. Pearl (Eds.) *Mental Health of the Poor.* New York: Free Press, 1964.

Hagopian, M. N. *The Phenomenon of Revolution.* New York: Dodd, Mead, 1974.

Hahn, C. L. "Review of Research on Sex Roles: Implications for Social

Studies." Paper presented at annual meeting of the National Council for the Social Studies, Washington, D.C., 1976.

Hahn, H. "Black Separatists: Attitudes and Objectives in a Riot-Torn Ghetto." *Journal of Black Studies*, 1970, *1*, 35–53.

Hall, C. S., and Lindzey, G. *Theories of Personality*. New York: Wiley, 1957, 1970 (2nd ed.), 1978 (3rd ed.).

Hall, E. T. *The Silent Language*. New York: Doubleday, 1959.

Hall, E. T. *The Hidden Dimension*. New York: Doubleday, 1966.

Hall, M. A. "Women and Physical Recreation: A Causal Analysis." Paper presented at the Women and Sport Symposium, University of Birmingham, Birmingham, England, 1973.

Hamblin, R. *The Humanization Process*. New York: Wiley, 1971.

Hamby, W. C. "The Allelulia Community." Paper presented at annual meeting of the Society for the Scientific Study of Religion, Milwaukee, 1975.

Hamilton, H. D. "The Municipal Voter: Voting and Non-Voting in City Elections." *American Political Science Review*, 1971, *65*, 1135–1140.

Hampden-Turner, C. *Radical Man*. Garden City, N.Y.: Anchor Books, 1971.

Hampden-Turner, C. *From Poverty to Dignity: A Strategy for Poor Americans*. New York: Doubleday, 1974.

Hands, A. R. *Charities and Social Aid in Greece and Rome*. Ithaca, N.Y.: Cornell University Press, 1968.

Hannan, M. T. *Aggregation and Disaggregation in Sociology*. Lexington, Mass.: Heath, 1971.

Hannan, M. T., and Tuma, N. B. "Methods for Temporal Analysis," In A. Inkeles, J. Coleman, and R. H. Turner (Eds.), *Annual Review of Sociology*. Vol. 5. Palo Alto, Calif.: Annual Reviews, 1979.

Hapgood, D., and Hall, R. *The Average Man Fights Back*. New York: Doubleday, 1977.

Harder, M., Richardson, J. T., and Simmonds, R. "The Jesus People." *Psychology Today*, 1972, *6*, 45–50, 110–113.

Hardt, H. "The Plight of the Daily Press in Western Europe." In H. D. Fischer and J. G. Merrill (Eds.), *International Communication*. New York: Hastings House, 1970.

Hardy, R. E., and Cull, J. C. *Applied Voluntarism in Community Development*. Springfield, Ill.: Thomas, 1973.

Hargrove, B. W. "The New Religious and Structural Change." Paper presented at annual meeting of the Society for the Scientific Study of Religion and Religious Research Association, Washington, D.C., 1974.

Harned, L. "Authoritarian Attitudes and Party Activity." *Public Opinion Quarterly*, 1961, *25*, 393-399.

Harris, D. V. "Physical Activity Attitudes of Middle-Aged Males." In G. S. Kenyon and T. M. Grogg (Eds.), *International Society of Sports Psychology Congress* (Second), *Contemporary Psychology of Sport Proceedings*. Chicago: Athletic Institute, 1970.

Harris, D. V. *Involvement in Sport: A Somatopsychic Rationale for Physical Activity*. Philadelphia: Lea and Febiger, 1973.

Harris, L. *The Harris Survey Yearbook of Public Opinion 1972*. Louis Harris & Associates, 1976a.

Harris, L. *The Harris Survey Yearbook of Public Opinion 1973*. Louis Harris & Associates, 1976b.

Harris, M. B. "Reciprocity and Generosity: Some Determinants of Sharing Behavior." *Child Development*, 1971, *41*, 313-328.

Harrison, G. S. "The Mass Media in Native Villages of Alaska." *Journalism Quarterly*, 1972, *49*, 373-376.

Harrison, M. I. "Preparation for Life in the Spirit: The Process of Initial Commitment to a Religious Movement." *Urban Life and Culture*, 1974a, *2*, 387-414.

Harrison, M. I. "Sources of Recruitment to Catholic Pentecostalism." *Journal for the Scientific Study of Religion*, 1974b, *13*, 49-64.

Harriss, C. "Philanthropy and Federal Tax Exemption." *Journal of Political Economy*, 1939, *47*, 526-541.

Harry, J. "Socio-Economic Patterns of Outdoor Recreation Use Near Urban Areas—A Comment." *Journal of Leisure Research*, 1972, *4*, 218-219.

Hartshorne, H., and May, M. A. *Studies in the Nature of Character*. New York: Macmillan, 1929.

Hartup, W. "Peer Interaction and Social Organization." In P. H. Mussen (Ed.), *Carmichael's Manual of Child Psychology*. New York: Wiley, 1970.

Hathaway, S. R. "Where Have We Gone Wrong? The Mystery of the Missing Progress." In J. Butcher (Ed.), *Objective Personality Assessment*. New York: Academic Press, 1972.

Hauser, P. M. "Demographic and Ecological Changes as Factors in Outdoor Recreation." In Outdoor Recreation Resources Review Commission, *ORRRC Study Report 22: Trends in American Living and Outdoor Recreation*. Washington, D.C.: U.S. Government Printing Office, 1962.

Hauser, R. M. "On 'Social Participation and Social Status.'" *American Sociological Review*, 1969, *34*, 549-553.

Hausknecht, M. *The Joiners*. New York: Bedminster Press, 1962.

Havighurst, R. J. "The Leisure Activities of the Middle Aged." *American Journal of Sociology,* 1957, *62,* 152–162.

Havighurst, R. J. "The Nature and Value of Meaningful Free-Time Activity." In R. W. Kleemeier, (Ed.), *Aging and Leisure.* New York: Oxford University Press, 1961.

Havighurst, R. J., and Feigenbaum, K. "Leisure and Life-Style." *American Journal of Sociology,* 1959, *64,* 396–404.

Havighurst, R. J., and Keating, B. "The Religion of Youth." In M. P. Strommen (Ed.), *Research on Religious Development: A Comprehensive Handbook.* New York: Hawthorn Books, 1971.

Havighurst, R. J., and others (Eds.). *Adjustment to Retirement.* Assen, Netherlands: Van Gorcum, 1969.

Hawes, G. "Academic Philanthropy—The Art of Getting." *Saturday Review,* December 16, 1967, pp. 65–67, 77–78.

Hecock, R. "Public Beach Recreation Opportunities and Patterns of Consumption on Cape Cod." Unpublished doctoral dissertation, Department of Geography, Clark University, 1966.

Heeman, E. F. "Which Witch? Some Personal and Sociological Impressions." In E. F. Heeman (Ed.), *Mystery, Magic, and Miracles.* Englewood Cliffs, N.J.: Prentice-Hall, 1973.

Heider, F. *The Psychology of Interpersonal Relations.* New York: Wiley, 1958.

Heinilä, K. *Leisure and Sports: A Sociological Study of Men's Use of Leisure and Sports Activities.* Helsinki, Finland: Porvoo, 1959.

Heinilä, K. "The Preferences of Physical Activities in Finnish High Schools." In E. Joki and E. Simon (Eds.), *International Research in Sport and Physical Education.* Springfield, Ill.: Thomas, 1964.

Heirich, M. *The Spiral of Conflict: Berkeley, 1964.* New York: Columbia University Press, 1973.

Hempel, C. G. *Fundamentals of Concept Formation in Empirical Science.* Chicago: University of Chicago Press, 1952.

Hendee, J. C. "Rural-Urban Differences Reflected in Outdoor Recreation Participation." *Journal of Leisure Research,* 1969, *1,* 333–341.

Hendee, J. C., and Burdge, R. J. "The Substitutability Concept: Implications for Recreation Research and Management." *Journal of Leisure Research,* 1974, *6,* 157–162.

Henderson, R. *Early American Sport.* New York: Barnes & Noble, 1953.

Hendricks, J. "Leisure Participation as Influenced by Urban Residence Patterns." *Sociology and Social Research,* 1971, *55,* 414–428.

Hendry, L. B. "Some Notions on Personality and Sporting Ability: Certain Comparisons with Scholastic Achievement." *Quest,* 1970, *13,* 63–73.

Hendry, L. B., and Douglass, L. "University Students: Attainment and Sport." *British Journal of Educational Psychology,* 1975, *45,* 299–306.

Hennessy, B. "Politicals and Apoliticals: Some Measurements of Personality Traits." *Midwest Journal of Political Science,* 1959, *3,* 336–355.

Hershey, M. R., and Hill, D. B. "Watergate and Pre-Adults' Attitudes Toward the President." *American Journal of Political Science,* 1975, *19,* 703–726.

Hervey, J. *Racing in America, 1665–1865.* 2 Vols. New York: Jockey Club, 1944.

Hess, B. B. "Stereotypes of the Aged." *Journal of Communication,* 1974, *24,* 76–85.

Hess, R. D., and Easton, D. "The Child's Changing Image of the President." *Public Opinion Quarterly,* 1960, *34,* 632–644.

Hess, R. D., and Torney, J. V. *The Development of Political Attitudes in Children.* Chicago: Aldine, 1967.

Hewitt, C. "Brazil: The Peasant Movement of Pernambuch, 1961–1964." In H. A. Landsberger (Ed.), *Latin American Peasant Movements.* Ithaca, N.Y.: Cornell University Press, 1969.

Hill, C. E. "Restructuring Through Religion: The Children of God." Unpublished manuscript, Georgia State University, 1975.

Himmelweit, H. T., Oppenheim, A. N., and Vince, P. *Television and the Child.* New York: Oxford University Press, 1958.

Hine, V. H. "Pentecostal Glossolalia: Toward a Functional Analysis." *Journal for the Scientific Study of Religion,* 1969, *8,* 211–226.

Hine, V. H., and Gerlach, L. "Five Factors Crucial to the Growth and Spread of a Modern Religious Movement." *Journal for the Scientific Study of Religion,* 1968, *7,* 23–40.

Hobart, C. W. "Active Sports Participation Among the Young, the Middle-Aged and the Elderly." *International Review of Sport Sociology,* 1975, *10,* 27–44.

Hoch, P. *Rip Off the Big Game.* New York: Doubleday, 1972.

Hodge, R. W. "Social Integration, Psychological Well-Being, and Their Socioeconomic Correlates." *Sociological Inquiry,* 1970, *40,* 182–206.

Hodge, R. W., and Trieman, D. J. "Social Participation and Social Status." *American Sociological Review,* 1968, *33,* 722–740.

Hodges, H. M. *Social Stratification: Class in America.* Cambridge, Mass.: Schenkman, 1964.

Hoffman, M. L. "Moral Development." In P. M. Mussen (Ed.), *Carmichael's Manual of Child Development.* New York: Wiley, 1970.

Hoffman, M. L. "Development of Internal Moral Standards in Children." In M. P. Strommen (Ed.), *Research on Religious Development: A Comprehensive Handbook.* New York: Hawthorn Books, 1971.

Hoffman, M. L. "Altruistic Behavior and the Parent-Child Relationship." *Journal of Personality and Social Psychology,* 1975a, *31,* 937–944.

Hoffman, M. L. "Altruistic Motivation and the Developmental Synthesis of Affect and Cognition." In D. DePalma and J. Folley (Eds.), *Moral Development.* New York: Halstead Press, 1975b.

Hoffman, M. L., and Saltzstein, H. "Parent Discipline and the Child's Moral Development." *Journal of Personality and Social Psychology,* 1967, *5,* 45–47.

Hogan, D. P. "Order of Events in the Life Course." *American Sociological Review,* 1978, *43,* 573–588.

Hoge, D. R., and Keeter, L. G. "Determinants of College Teachers' Religious Beliefs and Participation." *Journal for the Scientific Study of Religion,* 1976, *15,* 221–235.

Hollender, J. W. "Motivational Dimensions of the Camping Experience." *Journal of Leisure Research,* 1977, *9,* 133–141.

Hollingshead, A. *Elmtown's Youth.* New York: Wiley, 1949.

Hollstein, M. "Burma." In J. A. Lent (Ed.), *The Asia Newspapers' Reluctant Revolution.* Ames, Iowa: Iowa State University Press, 1971.

Homans, G. C. *The Human Group.* New York: Harcourt Brace Jovanovich, 1950.

Homans, G. C. *Social Behavior: Its Elementary Forms.* New York: Harcourt Brace Jovanovich, 1961. (Rev. ed. 1974.)

Homans, G. C. *The Nature of Social Science.* New York: Harcourt Brace Jovanovich, 1967.

Hood, R. W., Jr. "Differential Triggering of Mystical Experience as a Function of Self-Actualization." *Review of Religious Research,* 1977, *18,* 264–270.

Horn, J. L. "Human Abilities: A Review of Research and Theory in the Early 1970's." In M. R. Rosenzweig and L. W. Porter (Eds.), *Annual Review of Psychology.* Vol. 27. Palo Alto, Calif.: Annual Reviews, 1976.

Hornstein, H. A. "The Influence of Social Models on Helping." In J. R. Macaulay and L. Berkowitz (Eds.), *Altruism and Helping Behavior.* New York: Academic Press, 1970.

Hornstein, H. A. "The Basis of Prosocial Behavior from a Lewinian Perspective." *Journal of Social Issues,* 1972, *28,* 191–218.

Hosay, P. *The Challenge of Urban Poverty: Charity Reformers in New York City, 1835–1890.* Unpublished doctoral dissertation, Department of History, University of Michigan, 1969.

Hovland, C. L., and Janis, I. L. *Personality and Persuasibility.* New Haven, Conn: Yale University Press, 1959.

Howard, J. A., and Sheth, J. N. *The Theory of Buyer Behavior.* New York: Wiley, 1969.

Huggins, N. *Protestants Against Poverty: Boston's Charities, 1870–1900.* Westport, Conn.: Greenwood Press, 1971.

Hunt, J. M. "Traditional Personality Theory in the Light of Recent Evidence." *American Scientist,* 1965, *53,* 80–96.

Hunter, T. W. *The Tax Climate for Philanthropy.* Washington, D.C.: American College Public Relations Association, 1968.

Huntington, E. *Mainsprings of Civilization.* New York: Wiley, 1945.

Huntington, S. P. *Political Order in Changing Societies.* New Haven, Conn: Yale University Press, 1968.

Husman, B. F. "Sport and Personality Dynamics." In *Proceedings,* 72nd annual meeting of the National College Physical Education Association for Men. Durham, N.C., 1969.

Hyman, H. H. *Political Socialization.* New York: Free Press, 1959.

Hyman, H. H., and Singer, E. (Eds.). *Readings in Reference Group Theory and Research.* New York: Free Press, 1968.

Iglitzen, L. B. "The Making of the Apolitical Woman: Femininity and Sex Stereotyping." In J. S. Jaquette (Ed.), *Women in Politics.* New York: Wiley, 1974.

Inglehart, R. *The Silent Revolution.* Princeton, N.J.: Princeton University Press, 1977.

Inkeles, A. "Personality and Social Structure." In R. K. Merton, L. Broom, and L. S. Cottrell (Eds.), *Sociology Today.* New York: Basic Books, 1959.

Inkeles, A. "Participant Citizenship in Six Developing Countries." *American Political Science Review,* 1969, *63,* 1120–1141.

Inkeles, A. Coleman, J., and Smelser, N. (Eds.). *Annual Review of Sociology.* Vol. 1. Palo Alto, Calif.: Annual Reviews, 1975.

Inkeles, A., Coleman, J., and Smelser, N. (Eds.). *Annual Review of Sociology.* Vol. 2. Palo Alto, Calif.: Annual Reviews, 1976.

Inkeles, A., Coleman, J., and Smelser, N. (Eds.). *Annual Review of Sociology.* Vol. 3. Palo Alto, Calif.: Annual Reviews, 1977.

Inkeles, A., and Levinson, D. J. "National Character: The Study of Model Personality and Sociocultural Systems." In G. Lindzey and E. Aronson (Eds.), *The Handbook of Social Psychology.* (2nd ed.) Reading, Mass.: Addison-Wesley, 1969.

Inkeles, A., and Smith, D. H. *Becoming Modern: Individual Change in Six Developing Countries.* Cambridge, Mass.: Harvard University Press, 1974.

International Bureau of Fiscal Documentation. "The Tax Treatment of Charitable Institutions and Charitable Donations in Europe." *European Taxation,* 1965, *5,* 178–181.

Isen, A. M. "Success, Failure, Attention, and Reaction to Others: The

Warm Glow of Success." *Journal of Personality and Social Psychology*, 1970, *15*, 294–301.

Isen, A., Horn, N., and Rosenhan, D. "Effects of Success and Failure on Children's Generosity." *Journal of Personality and Social Psychology*, 1973, *27*, 239–248.

Isen, A., and Levin, P. "Effect of Feeling Good on Helping: Cookies and Kindness." *Journal of Personality and Social Psychology*, 1972, *21*, 384–388.

Iskrant, A. P., and Joliet, P. V. *Accidents and Homicide.* Cambridge, Mass.: Harvard University Press, 1968.

Iso-Ahola, S. "Leisure Patterns of American and Finnish Youth." *International Review of Sport Sociology*, 1975, *10*, 63–81.

Jaccard, J., and Davidson, A. R. "A Comparison of Two Models of Social Behavior: Results of a Survey Sample." *Sociometry*, 1975, *38*, 497–517.

Jackson, J. S., III. "Alienation and Black Political Participation." *Journal of Politics*, 1973, *35*, 849–885.

Jackson, L. R., and Johnson, W. A. *Protest by the Poor: The Welfare Rights Movement in New York City.* Lexington, Mass.: Heath, 1974.

Jacobson, H. H. "Mass Media Believability: A Study of Receiver Judgments." *Journalism Quarterly*, 1969, *46*, 10–28.

Jacoby, J. "Consumer Psychology: An Octennium." In M. R. Rosenzweig and L. W. Porter (Eds.), *Annual Review of Psychology.* Vol. 27. Palo Alto, Calif.: Annual Reviews, 1976.

James, W. *Varieties of Religious Experience.* New York: Modern Library, 1950. (Originally published 1936.)

Janowitz, M., and Marvick, D. "Authoritarianism and Political Behavior." *Public Opinion Quarterly*, 1953, *17*, 185–201.

Jaros, D., Hirsch, H., and Fleron, F. J., Jr. "The Malevolent Leader: Political Socialization in an American Sub-Culture." *American Political Science Review*, 1968, *62*, 572–575.

Jeffres, L. W. "A Study of Similarities in the Use of Print Media by Fathers and Sons." Unpublished master's thesis, Department of Communication, University of Washington, 1968.

Jeffres, L. W. "The Print Tradition in a Rural Philippine Province." *Gazette*, 1973, *19*, 248–257.

Jeffres, L. W. "Factors Affecting the Print Media: Media as Dependent Variables." Paper presented to Intercultural Communication Division, International Communication Association, Chicago, Ill., 1975a.

Jeffres, L. W. "Functions of Media Behaviors." *Communication Research*, 1975b, *2*, 137–161.

Jeffres, L. W., and Hur, K. K. "Ethnic Communication in Cleveland."

Communication Research Center in conjunction with the Ethnic Heritage Study Center, Cleveland State University, August, 1978.

Jenkins, E. *Philanthropy in America.* New York: Association Press, 1950.

Jennings, M. K. *The Student-Parent Socialization Study: Codebook* (Variable 119). Ann Arbor: Inter-University Consortium for Political Research, University of Michigan, 1971.

Jennings, M. K., and Niemi, R. G. *The Political Character of Adolescence.* Princeton, N.J.: Princeton University Press, 1974.

Jennings, M. K., and Niemi, R. G. "Continuity and Change in Political Orientations: A Longitudinal Study of Two Generations." *American Political Science Review,* 1975, *69,* 1316-1335.

Jensen, J. "Political Participation: A Survey in Evanston, Illinois." Unpublished master's thesis, Department of Political Science, Northwestern University, 1960.

Jessor, R., and Jessor, S. L. *Problem Behavior and Psychosocial Development: A Longitudinal Study of Youth.* New York: Academic Press, 1977.

Joffe, J. M. *Prenatal Determinants of Behavior.* Oxford, England: Pergamon Press, 1969.

Johnson, B. "Church and Sect Revisited." *Journal for the Scientific Study of Religion,* 1971, *10,* 124-137.

Johnson, D. B. *The Fundamental Economics of the Charity Market.* Unpublished doctoral dissertation, Department of Economics, University of Virginia, 1968.

Johnson, D. W. *Reaching Out: Interpersonal Effectiveness and Self-Actualization.* Englewood Cliffs, N.J.: Prentice-Hall, 1972.

Johnson, G. "The Hare Krishna in San Francisco." In C. Y. Glock and R. N. Bellah (Eds.), *The New Religious Consciousness.* Berkeley: University of California Press, 1976.

Johnson, G. W., "Research Note on Political Correlates of Voter Participation: A Deviant Case Analysis." *American Political Science Review,* 1971, *65,* 768-776.

Johnson, M. A. "Family Life and Religious Commitment." *Review of Religious Research,* 1973, *14,* 144-150.

Johnson, W. A. *The Search for Transcendence: A Theological Analysis of Nontheological Attempts to Define Transcendence.* New York: Harper & Row, 1974.

Johnston, W. E., and Elsner, G. H. "Variability in Use Among Ski Areas: A Statistical Study of the California Market Region." *Journal of Leisure Research,* 1972, *4,* 43-49.

Johnstone, J.W.C. "Social Integration and Mass Media Use Among

Adolescents: A Case Study." In J. G. Blumler and E. Katz (Eds.), *The Uses of Mass Communications*. Beverly Hills: Calif.: Sage, 1974.

Johnstone, J.W.C., and Rivera, R. J. *Volunteers for Learning: A Study of the Educational Pursuits of American Adults*. Chicago: Aldine, 1965.

Johnstone, R. L. *Religion and Society in Interaction: The Sociology of Religion*. Englewood Cliffs, N.J.: Prentice-Hall, 1975.

Jones, E. E., and Davis, K. E. "From Acts to Dispositions." In L. Berkowitz (Ed.), *Advances in Experimental Social Psychology*. New York: Academic Press, 1965.

Jones, E. E., and Nisbett, R. C. *The Actor and the Observer: Divergent Perceptions and the Causes of Behavior*. New York: General Learning Press, 1971.

Jones, J. P. *The American Giver*. New York: Inter-River Press, 1954.

Jordan, W. K. *Philanthropy in England, 1480–1660: A Study of the Changing Patterns of English Social Aspirations*. London: Allen & Unwin, 1959.

Jordan, W. K. *The Charities of London, 1480–1660*. London: Allen & Unwin, 1960.

Jordan, W. K. *The Charities of Rural England, 1480–1660*. London: Allen & Unwin, 1961a.

Jordan, W. K. "The Development of Philanthropy in England in the Early Modern Era." *Proceedings of the American Philosophical Society*, 1961b, *105*, 145.

Jourard, S. M. *The Healthy Personality*. New York: Macmillan, 1974.

Judah, S. S. *Hare Krishna and the Counter Culture*. New York: Wiley, 1974.

Judge, A.J.N. (Ed.). *Yearbook of World Problems and Human Potential*. Brussels, Belgium: Union of International Associations, 1976.

Juster, F. T. (Ed.). *Studies in the Measurement of Time Allocation*. Ann Arbor: Institute for Social Research, University of Michigan, forthcoming.

Kadushin, C., Hover, J., and Tichy, M. "How and Where to Find Intellectual Elite in the United States." *Public Opinion Quarterly*, 1971, *35*, 1–18.

Kagan, J., and Moss, H. A. *Birth to Maturity: A Study in Psychological Development*. New York: Wiley, 1962.

Kahan, I. M. *Abavath Chesed*. (L. Oschrz, trans.). New York: Feldheim, 1967.

Kahn, C. H. "Personal Deductions in the Individual Income Tax." In *Tax Revision Compendium*. Vol. 1. Washington, D.C.: U.S. Government Printing Office, 1959.

Kahn, C. H. *Personal Deductions in the Federal Income Tax*. New York: National Bureau of Economic Research, 1960.

Kalish, R. A. "Of Children and Grandfathers: A Speculative Essay on Dependency." *The Gerontologist,* 1967, *7,* 185–196.

Kando, T., and Summers, W. C. "The Impact of Work on Leisure: Toward a Paradigm and Research Strategy." *Pacific Sociological Review,* 1971, *41,* 310–327. (Also in T. B. Johannis, Jr., and C. N. Bull [Eds.], *Sociology of Leisure.* Beverly Hills, Calif.: Sage, 1971.)

Kane, J. E. "Report: Personality and Physical Abilities." In G. S. Kenyon (Ed.), *Contemporary Psychology of Sport.* Chicago: Athletic Institute, 1970.

Kaplan, H. B. *Self-Attitudes and Deviant Behavior.* Pacific Palisades, Calif.: Goodyear, 1974.

Kaplan, H. B. "Increase in Self-Rejection as an Antecedent of Deviant Responses." *Journal of Youth and Adolescence,* 1975a, *4,* 281–292.

Kaplan, H. B. "Sequlae of Self-Derogation: Predicting from a General Theory of Deviant Behavior." *Youth and Society,* 1975b, *7,* 171–197.

Kaplan, M. *Leisure in America: A Social Inquiry.* New York: Wiley, 1960.

Kaplan, M. "Jewish Philanthropy: Traditional and Modern." In E. Faris and others (Eds.), *Intelligent Philanthropy.* Chicago: University of Chicago Press, 1930.

Kaplan, S. *The Dream Deferred: People, Politics, and Planning In Suburbia.* New York: Seabury, 1976.

Kardiner, A. *The Individual and His Society.* New York: Columbia University Press, 1939.

Kardiner, A. *Psychological Frontiers of Society.* New York: Columbia University Press, 1945.

Kassarjian, H. H., and Robertson, T. S. (Eds.). *Perspectives in Consumer Behavior.* Glenview, Ill.: Scott, Foresman, 1968.

Katz, E., Blumler, J. G., and Gurevitch, M. "Utilization of Mass Communication by the Individual." In J. G. Blumler and E. Katz (Eds.), *The Uses of Mass Communications.* Beverley Hills, Calif.: Sage, 1974.

Katz, E., and Foulkes, D. "On the Use of the Mass Media for 'Escape': Clarification of a Concept." *Public Opinion Quarterly,* 1962, *26,* 377–388.

Katz, E., and Gurevitch, M. *The Secularization of Leisure: Culture and Communication in Israel.* Cambridge, Mass.: Harvard University Press, 1976.

Katz, E., Gurevitch, M., and Haas, H. "On the Use of Mass Media for Important Things." *American Sociological Review,* 1973, *38,* 164–181.

Katz, E., and Lazarsfeld, P. F. *Personal Influence.* New York: Free Press, 1955.

Katz, J. "Four Years of Growth, Conflict and Compliance." In J. Katz and associates (Eds.), *No Time for Youth: Growth and Constraint in College Students.* San Francisco: Jossey-Bass, 1968.

Kay, H. "Toward an Understanding of News-Reading Behavior." *Journalism Quarterly*, 1954, *31*, 15–32.

Keeley, B. J. "Generations in Tension: Intergenerational Differences and Continuities in Religion and Religion-Related Behavior." *Review of Religious Research*, 1976, *17*, 221–231.

Keith, J. E., and Workman, J. P. "Opportunity Cost of Time in Demand Estimates for Nonmarket Resources." *Journal of Leisure Research*, 1975, *7*, 121–127.

Keith-Lucas, A. *Giving and Taking Help.* Chapel Hill: University of North Carolina Press, 1972.

Kelley, H. H. "Attribution Theory in Social Psychology." In D. Levine (Ed.), *Nebraska Symposium on Motivation.* Lincoln: University of Nebraska Press, 1967.

Kelley, H. H., and others. "An Experimental Comparative Study of Negotiation Behavior." Unpublished manuscript, Department of Psychology, University of California, Los Angeles, 1969.

Kelley, H. H., and Stahelski, A. J. "Errors of Perception of Intentions in a Mixed Motive Game." *Journal of Experimental Social Psychology*, 1970a, *6*, 379–400.

Kelley, H. H., and Stahelski, A. J. "Social Interaction Basis of Cooperators' and Competitors' Beliefs About Others." *Journal of Personality and Social Psychology*, 1970b, *16*, 66–91.

Kelley, S., Jr., Ayers, R. E., and Bowen, W. G. "Registration and Voting: Putting First Things First." *American Political Science Review*, 1967, *61*, 359–377.

Kelly, J. "Socialization Toward Leisure: A Developmental Approach." *Journal of Leisure Research*, 1974, *6*, 181–193.

Kelly, J. "Leisure Socialization: A Replication." *Journal of Leisure Research*, 1977, *9*, 121–132.

Kelly, S. L. "Personality Characteristics of Female Highschool Athletes and Non-Participants in Athletics." Unpublished master's thesis, Department of Physical Education, University of Iowa, 1969.

Kelly, T., and Schieber, G. *Factors Affecting Medical Service Utilization: A Behavioral Approach.* Washington, D.C.: Urban Institute, 1972.

Kelman, H. C. "Processes of Opinion Change." *Public Opinion Quarterly*, 1961, *25*, 57–78.

Kemper, T. D. "Power, Status and Love." In D. Heise (Ed.), *Personality and Socialization.* Chicago: Rand McNally, 1972.

Kemper, T. D. "The Fundamental Dimensions of Social Relationship: A Theoretical Statement." *Acta Sociologica*, 1973, *16*, 41–58.

Keniston, K. *The Uncommitted: Alienated Youth in American Society.* New York: Harcourt Brace Jovanovich, 1965.

Keniston, K. *Young Radicals: Notes on Committed Youth.* New York: Harcourt, Brace Jovanovich, 1968.

Keniston, K. "Notes on Young Radicals." *Change,* 1969, *1,* 25–33.

Keniston, K. *Youth and Dissent.* New York: Harcourt Brace Jovanovich, 1971.

Kennedy, D. B., and Kerber, A. *Resocialization: An American Experiment.* New York: Behavioral Publications, 1973.

Kennedy, J. *Philanthropy and Science in New York City: The American Museum of National History, 1868–1968.* Unpublished doctoral dissertation, Department of History, Yale University, 1968.

Kennedy, W. C. "Police Departments: Organization and Tasks in Disaster." *American Behavioral Scientist,* 1970, *13,* 354–361.

Kenyon, G. "The Use of Path Analysis in Sport Sociology with Special Reference to Involvement Socialization." *International Review of Sport Sociology,* 1970, *5,* 191–203.

Kenyon, G. S. *Manual for the Attitudes to Physical Activity Inventory.* Ontario: University of Waterloo Press, 1972.

Kenyon, G. S., and McPherson, B. D. "An Approach to the Study of Sport Socialization." *International Review of Sport Sociology,* 1974a, *9,* 127–138.

Kenyon, G. S., and McPherson, B. D. "Becoming Involved in Physical Activity and Sport: A Process of Socialization." In G. L. Rarick (Ed.), *Physical Activity, Human Growth and Development.* New York: Academic Press, 1974b.

Kerpelman, L. *Activists and Non-Activists: A Psychological Study of American College Students.* New York: Behavioral Publications, 1972.

Key, V. O., Jr. *Public Opinion and American Democracy.* New York: Knopf, 1961.

Kie-chang Oh, J. "The Nichiren Shoshu of America." *Review of Religious Research,* 1973, *14,* 169–177.

Kiesler, S. "The Effect of Perceived Role Requirements on Reactions to Favor Doing." *Journal of Experimental Social Psychology,* 1966, *2,* 198–210.

Kildahl, J. *The Psychology of Speaking in Tongues.* New York: Harper & Row, 1973.

Kim, C. L. "Socio-Economic Development and Political Democracy in Japanese Prefectures." *American Political Science Review,* 1971, *65,* 184–186.

Kim. J., Nie, N., and Verba, S. "The Amount and Concentration of Political Participation." *Political Methodology,* 1974, *1,* 105–132.

594					References

King, J. P., and Chi, P.S.K. "Personality and the Athletic Social Structure: A Case Study." *Human Relations,* 1974, *27,* 179–193.

King, M., and Hunt, R. *Measuring Religious Dimensions.* Dallas: Southern Methodist University, 1972.

Kirstein, G. "Philanthropy: The Golden Crowbar." *The Nation,* 1968, *16,* 235–240.

Klapper, J. T. *The Effects of Mass Communication.* New York: Free Press, 1960.

Kleemeier, R. W. (Ed.). *Aging and Leisure: A Research Perspective into the Meaningful Use of Time.* New York: Oxford University Press, 1961.

Kline, F. G. "Media Time Budgeting as a Function of Demographics and Life Style." *Journalism Quarterly,* 1971, *48,* 211–221.

Knapp, R. J. "Authoritarianism, Alienation, and Related Variables: A Correlational and Factor-Analytic Study." *Psychological Bulletin,* 1976, *83,* 194–212.

Knoke, D. "A Causal Synthesis of Sociological and Psychological Models of American Voting Behavior." *Social Forces,* 1974, *53,* 92–101.

Knoke, D., and Thomson, R. "Voluntary Association Membership Trends and the Family Life Cycle." *Social Forces,* 1977, *56,* 48–65.

Knopp, T. B., and Tyger, J. D. "A Study of Conflict in Recreational Land Use: Snowmobiling vs. Ski-Touring." *Journal of Leisure Research,* 1973, *5,* 6–17.

Knutson, J. N. *The Human Basis of the Polity.* Chicago: Aldine-Atherton, 1972.

Knutson, J. N. (Ed.). *Handbook of Political Psychology.* San Francisco: Jossey-Bass, 1973.

Knutson, J. N. "The Political Relevance of Self Actualization." In A. R. Wilcox (Ed.), *Public Opinion and Political Attitudes.* New York: Wiley, 1974.

Kobayashi, B. Y. "Political Alienation and Political Participation: A Problem of Conceptualization and Theory as Applied to College Students." Paper presented at annual meeting of the American Political Science Association, Chicago, 1974.

Kohlberg, L. "Development of Moral Character and Ideology." In M. L. Hoffman and L. W. Hoffman (Eds.), *Review of Child Development Research.* Vol. 1. New York: Russell Sage Foundation, 1964.

Kohlberg, L. "Stage and Sequence: The Cognitive-Developmental Approach to Socialization." In D. A. Goslin (Ed.), *Handbook of Socialization Theory and Research.* Chicago: Rand McNally, 1969.

Kohlberg, L. "Indoctrination Versus Relativity in Value Education." *Zygon,* 1971, *6,* 368–383.

Kohlberg, L. "Education, Moral Development and Faith." *Journal of Moral Education,* 1974, *4,* 5–16.

Kohn, M. "Social Class and Parent-Child Relationships: An Interpretation." *American Journal of Sociology,* 1968, *74,* 471–480.

Koltai, I. "Development and Long-Term Forecast of Leisure Time Expenditure in Hungary." *Society and Leisure,* 1972, *4,* 91–109.

Korchin, S. J. "Psychological Variables in the Behavior of Voters." Unpublished doctoral dissertation, Department of Psychology, Harvard University, 1946.

Kornhauser, A., Mayer, A. J., and Sheppard, H. *When Labor Votes.* New York: University Books, 1956.

Kornhauser, W. *The Politics of Mass Society.* New York: Free Press, 1959.

Kothari, R. *Politics in India.* Boston: Little, Brown, 1970.

Kramer, R. M. *Participation of the Poor.* Englewood Cliffs, N.J.: Prentice-Hall, 1969.

Krantz, D. L. (Ed.). *Schools of Psychology.* New York: Appleton-Century-Crofts, 1969.

Kraus, S., and Davis, D. K. *The Effects of Mass Communication on Political Behavior.* University Park: Pennsylvania State University Press, 1976.

Krebs, D. L. "Altruism—An Examination of the Concept and a Review of the Literature." *Psychological Bulletin,* 1970, *73,* 258–302.

Kreimer, A. "Environmental Preferences: A Critical Analysis of Some Research Methodologies." *Journal of Leisure Research,* 1977, *9,* 88–97.

Kruglanski, A. W. "The Human Subject in the Psychological Experiment, Fact, and Artifact." In L. Berkowitz (Ed.), *Advances in Experimental Social Psychology.* Vol. 8. New York: Academic Press, 1975.

Kueneman, R. M., and Wright, J. E. "News Policies of Broadcast Stations for Civil Disturbances and Disasters." *Journalism Quarterly,* 1976, *53,* 670–677.

Kühl, P. H., Koch-Nielsen, I., and Westergaard, K. *Fritidsvaner I Danmark. [Leisure Time Activities in Denmark].* Copenhagen, Denmark: Teknisk Forlag, 1966.

Kuhn, A. *The Study of Society: A Unified Approach.* Homewood, Ill.: Dorsey Press, 1963.

Kuhn, T. S. "The Function of Dogma in Scientific Research." In A. C. Crombie (Ed.), *Scientific Change.* London: Heinemann, 1963.

Kuhn. T. S. *The Structure of Scientific Revolutions.* Chicago: University of Chicago Press, 1964.

Kuroda, Y. "Sociability and Political Involvement." *Midwest Journal of Political Science,* 1965, *9,* 133–147.

Kuroda, Y. "Measurement, Correlates, and Significance of Political Participation in a Japanese Community." *Western Political Quarterly*, 1967, *22*, 660–668.

Kutner, L. *Legal Aspects of Charitable Trusts and Foundations: A Guide for Philanthropoids.* New York: Commerce Clearing House, 1970.

Kyogoku, J., and Ike, N. *Urban-Rural Differences in Voting Behavior in Postwar Japan.* No. 66, *Proceedings*, Department of Social Sciences, University of Tokyo. Stanford, Calif.: Stanford University Press, 1959.

Ladieu, G., and others. "Studies in Adjustment to Visible Injuries: Evaluation of Help by the Injured." *Journal of Abnormal and Social Psychology*, 1947, *47*, 169–192.

Lallemand, L. *Histoire de la Charité [History of Charity].* 3 Vols. Paris: 1902–1906.

Lamale, H., and Clorety, J. "City Families as Givers." *Monthly Labor Review*, 1959, *82*, 1303–1311.

Lamb, C. *Political Power in Poor Neighborhoods.* Cambridge, Mass.: Schenkman, 1975.

Lamb, M. E. (Ed.). *The Role of the Father in Child Development.* New York: Academic Press, 1976.

Landers, D. M. "Sibling-Sex-Status and Ordinal Position Effects on Females' Sport Participation and Interests." *Journal of Social Psychology*, 1970, *80*, 247–248.

Landers, D. M. "Sibling-Sex and Ordinal Position as Factors in Sport Participation." Paper presented at 3rd International Symposium on the Sociology of Sport. University of Waterloo, Waterloo, Ontario, Canada, 1971.

Landers, D. M. "The Effect of Ordinal Position and Sibling's Sex on Males' Sport Participation." Paper presented at 4th annual meeting of the Canadian Association of Sport Sciences, 1972.

Landsberger, H. *Latin American Peasant Movements.* Ithaca, N.Y.: Cornell University Press, 1969.

Lane, C. L., Byrd, W. P., and Brantley, H. "Evaluation of Recreational Sites." *Journal of Leisure Research*, 1975, *7*, 296–300.

Lane, R. E. "Political Personality and Electoral Choice." *American Political Science Review*, 1955, *49*, 173–190.

Lane, R. E. *Political Life: Why People Get Involved in Politics.* New York: Free Press, 1959.

Langner, T. S., and Michael, S. T. *Life Stress and Mental Health.* New York: Free Press, 1963.

Lansbury, R. "Careers, Work and Leisure Among the New Professionals." *The Sociological Review*, 1974, *22*, 385–400.

Lapsley, J. N., and Simpson, J. A. "Speaking in Tongues from Infantile Babble or Song of the Self." *Pastoral Psychology*, 1964, *15* (Pt. I and II), 16–24; 48–55.

Larrabee, E., and Meyersohn, R. *Mass Leisure*. New York: Free Press, 1958.

Laski, M. *Ecstasy: A Study of Some Secular and Religious Experiences.* London: Cresset Press, 1961.

Lasser, J. K. *How Tax Laws Make Giving to Charity Easy.* New York: Funk & Wagnalls, 1948.

Lasser, J. K., and Casey, W. "The Family Foundation: Bulwark Against High Taxes." *Dun's Review*, August 1951, pp. 22–23.

Lasswell, H. D. *Psychopathology and Politics.* Chicago: University of Chicago Press, 1930. (Reprinted in *The Political Writings of Harold Lasswell.* New York: Free Press, 1951.)

Lasswell, H. D. "The Structure and Function of Communication in Society." In W. Schramm and D. Roberts (Eds.), *The Process and Effects of Mass Communication.* (rev. ed.) Urbana: University of Illinois Press, 1971.

Laszlo, E. *The Systems View of the World.* New York: Braziller, 1972.

Latané, B., and Darley, J. M. *The Unresponsive Bystander: Why Doesn't He Help?* New York: Appleton-Century-Crofts, 1970.

Latané, B., and Rodin, J. "A Lady in Distress: Inhibiting Effects of Friends and Strangers on Bystander Intervention." *Journal of Experimental Social Psychology*, 1969, *5*, 189–202.

Latané, B., and Wheeler, L. "Emotionality and Reactions to Disaster." *Journal of Experimental Social Psychology*, 1966, *1*, 95–102.

Laurence, J. E. "White Socialization: Black Reality." *Psychiatry*, 1970, *30*, 179.

LaVey, A. S. *The Santanic Bible.* New York: Avon Books, 1969.

LaVey, A. S. *The Satanic Rituals.* New York: Avon Books, 1972.

Lazarsfeld, P. F., Berelson, B., and Gaudet, H. *The Peoples' Choice.* New York: Duell, Sloan and Pearce, 1944.

Lazarus, R. S. *Psychological Stress and the Coping Process.* New York: McGraw-Hill, 1966.

Lazarus, R. S. "Emotions and Adaptation: Conceptual and Empirical Relations." In M. Arnold (Ed.), *Nebraska Symposium on Motivation.* Vol. 16. Lincoln: University of Nebraska Press, 1968.

Lazarus, R. S., and others. "A Laboratory Study of Psychosocial Stress Produced by a Motion Picture Film." *Psychological Monographs*, 1962, *76* (whole no. 553).

Lecky, P. *Self Consistency.* New York: Island Press, 1945.

Lee, J. "English-Language Press of Asia." In J. A. Lent (Ed.), *The Asian*

Newspapers' Reluctant Revolution. Ames: Iowa State University Press, 1971.

Lee, P. R., and others. *Symposium on Consciousness.* New York: Penguin Books, 1977.

Lefcourt, H. M., and Lading, G. W. "The American Negro: A Problem in Expectancies." *Journal of Personality and Social Psychology,* 1965, *1,* 377–380.

Lefkowitz, M. M., and others. *Growing Up to be Violent.* Elmsford, N.Y.: Pergamon Press, 1977.

Lehman, E. C., Jr. "Academic Discipline and Faculty Religiosity in Secular and Church-Related Colleges." *Journal for the Scientific Study of Religion,* 1974, *13,* 205–220.

Lehman, E. C., Jr., and Shriver, D. W., Jr. "Academic Discipline as Predictive of Faculty Religiosity." *Social Forces,* 1968, *47,* 171–182.

Leiden, C., and Schmitt, K. M. *The Politics of Violence: Revolution in the Modern World.* Englewood Cliffs, N.J.: Prentice-Hall, 1968.

Leigh, J. *Young People and Leisure.* London: Routledge & Kegan Paul, 1971.

Lemert, C. C. "Defining Non-Church Religion." *Review of Religious Research,* 1975, *16,* 186–197.

Lemert, E. M. *Human Deviance, Social Problems and Social Control.* (2nd ed.) Englewood Cliffs, N.J.: Prentice-Hall, 1972.

Leming, M. R., and Smith, T. C. "The Children of God as a Social Movement." *Journal of Voluntary Action Research,* 1975, *3,* 77–83.

Lemon, M., Palisi, B. J., and Jacobson, P. E. "Dominant Statuses and Involvement in Formal Voluntary Association." *Journal of Voluntary Action Research,* 1972, *1,* 30–42.

Lenski, G. E. "Status Crystallization: A Non-Vertical Dimension of Social Status." *American Sociological Review,* 1954, *19,* 405–413.

Lentnek, B., VanDoren, C. S., and Trail, J. R. "Spatial Behavior in Recreational Boating." *Journal of Leisure Research,* 1969, *1,* 103–124.

Leonard, E. M. *The Early History of English Poor Relief.* New York: Barnes & Noble, 1965.

LePage, W. F., and Ragain, D. P. "Family Camping Trends—An Eight-Year Panel Study." *Journal of Leisure Research,* 1974, *6,* 101–112.

Lerner, D. *The Passing of Traditional Society.* New York: Free Press, 1958.

Lester, D. *Why People Kill Themselves: A Summary of Research Findings on Suicidal Behavior.* Springfield, Ill.: Thomas, 1972.

Leuschen, G. (Ed.). *The Cross-Cultural Analysis of Sport and Games.* Champaign, Ill.: Stipes, 1970.

LeVine, R. A. "The Role of the Family in Authority System: A Cross-

Cultural Application of Stimulus-Generalization Theory." *Behavioral Science*, 1960, *5*, 291–296.

Levine, S., and Kozloff, M. A. "The Sick Role: Assessment and Overview." In R. H. Turner, J. Coleman, and R. C. Fox (Eds.), *Annual Review of Sociology*. Vol. 4. Palo Alto, Calif.: Annual Reviews, 1978.

Levinson, D. J. *The Seasons of a Man's Life*. New York: Knopf, 1978.

Lewin, K. *Field Theory in Social Sciences*. New York: Harper & Row, 1951.

Lewis, P. "The Female Vote in Argentina, 1958–1965." *Comparative Political Studies*, 1971, *3*, 425–442.

Lidz, T. *The Parson: His Development Through the Life Cycle*. New York: Basic Books, 1968.

Liebert, R. *Radical and Militant Youth*. New York: Praeger, 1971.

Liebert, R. M., Neale, J. M., and Davidson, E. S. *The Early Window: Effects of Television on Children and Youth*. Elmsford, N.Y.: Pergamon Press, 1973.

Liebert, R. M., Sobol, M. P., and Davidson, E. S. "Catharsis of Aggression Among Institutionalized Boys: Fact or Anti-Fact?" In G. A. Comstock, E. A. Rubenstein, and J. P. Murray (Eds.), *Television and Social Behavior*. Vol. 5. *Television's Effects: Further Explorations*. Washington, D.C.: U.S. Government Printing Office, 1972.

Lifton, R. *The Life of the Self*. New York: Simon & Schuster, 1976.

Lilienfeld, R. *The Rise of Systems Theory: An Ideological Analysis*. New York: Wiley, 1978.

Lime, D. "A Spatial Analysis of Auto-Camping in the Superior National Forest of Minnesota: Models of Campground Selection Behavior." Unpublished doctoral dissertation, Department of Geography, University of Pittsburgh, 1969.

Lind, A. "The Future of Citizen Involvement." *The Futurist*, 1975, *9*, 316–328.

Lindsay, J. J., and Ogle, R. A. "Socioeconomic Patterns of Outdoor Recreation Use Near Urban Areas." *Journal of Leisure Research*, 1972, *4*, 19–24.

Lindzey, G., and Aronson, E. (Eds.). *The Handbook of Social Psychology*. (2nd ed.) 5 vols. Reading Mass.: Addison-Wesley, 1968–1969.

Linton, R. *The Cultural Background of Personality*. New York: Appleton-Century-Crofts, 1945.

Lipman, A., and Sterne, R. "Aging in the United States: Ascription of a Terminal Sick Role." *Sociology and Social Research*, 1962, *53*, 194–203.

Lipman, E. J., and Varspan, A. *A Tale of Ten Cities*. New York: Union American Hebrew Congregation, 1962.

Lippitt, R. "Improving the Socialization Process." In J. A. Clausen (Ed.), *Socialization and Society*. Boston: Little, Brown, 1968.

Lipset, S. M. *Political Man*. New York: Doubleday, 1960.

Lipset, S. M. *The First New Nation*. New York: Basic Books, 1963.

Lipset, S. M., and Raab, E. *The Politics of Unreason: Right-Wing Extremism in America, 1790–1970*. New York: Harper & Row, 1970.

Lipset, S. M., Trow, M. A., and Coleman, J. S. *Union Democracy*. New York: Free Press, 1956.

Liska, A. E. "Emergent Issues in the Attitude-Behavior Consistency Controversy." *American Sociological Review*, 1974, *39*, 61–72.

Lodahl, J. B., and Gordon, G. "The Structure of Scientific Fields and the Functions of University Graduate Departments." *American Sociological Review*, 1972, *37*, 57–72.

Loeser, H. *Women, Work, and Volunteering*. Boston: Beacon Press, 1974.

Loevinger, J., Wessler, R., and Redmore, C. *Measuring Ego Development*. 2 vols. San Francisco: Jossey-Bass, 1970.

Lofland, J., and Stark, R. "Becoming a World-Saver: A Theory of Conversion to a Deviant Perspective." *American Sociological Review*, 1965, *30*, 862–875.

London, P. "The Rescuers: Motivational Hypotheses About Christians Who Saved Jews from the Nazis." In J. R. Macaulay and L. Berkowitz (Eds.), *Altruism and Helping Behavior*. New York: Academic Press, 1970.

Long, S. H. *Essays on the Voluntary Finance of Collective Consumption Goods*. Unpublished doctoral dissertation, Department of Economics, University of Wisconsin, 1975.

Lorenz, K. *On Aggression*. New York: Bantam, 1967.

Lowenthal, M. F., and others. *Four Stages of Life: A Comparative Study of Women and Men Facing Transitions*. San Francisco: Jossey-Bass, 1975.

Lowrey, G. A. "A Multivariate Analysis of the Relationship Between Selected Leisure Behavior Variables and Personal Values." Unpublished doctoral dissertation, Department of Physical Education, University of Illinois, 1969.

Loy, J. W. "A Paradigm of Technological Change in the Sports Situation." *International Review of Sport Sociology*, 1966, *1*, 175–193.

Loy, J. W. "The Nature of Sport: A Definitional Effort." *Quest*, 1968, Monograph 10, 1–15.

Loy, J. W., and Donnelly, P. "Need for Stimulation as a Factor in Sport Involvement." Paper presented at 1st national conference on the Mental Health Aspects of Sports, Exercise, and Recreation of the American Medical Association, Atlantic City, N.J., 1975.

Lubell, S. *The Hidden Crisis in American Politics.* New York: Norton, 1972.

Lubove, R. *The Professional Altruist: The Emergence of Social Work as a Career, 1880–1930.* Cambridge, Mass.: Harvard University Press, 1965.

Luckmann, T. *The Invisible Religion.* New York: Macmillan, 1967.

Lueptow, L. B., and Kayser, B. D. "Athletic Involvement, Academic Achievement, and Aspirations." *Sociological Focus,* 1973, *7,* 24–36.

Lundberg, G. A., Komarovsky, M., and McInerny, M. A. *Leisure: A Suburban Study.* New York: Columbia University Press, 1934.

Lüschen, G. "Prolegomena zu einer Sociologie des Sports" ["Preliminaries to a Sociology of Sport"]. *Kolner Zeitschrift fur Soziologie und Sozial-psychologie,* 1960, *12,* 505–515.

Lüschen, G. "Soziologische Aspekte de Leistung" ["Sociological Aspects of Achievement"]. *Allgemeine deutsche Lehrerzeitung,* 1964. *14,* 5–7.

Lüschen, G. "The Sociology of Sport." *Current Sociology,* 1967, *15,* 1–140.

Lüschen, G. "Social Stratification and Social Mobility Among Young Sportsmen." In J. S. Loy, Jr., and G. S. Kenyon (Eds.), *Sport, Culture and Society.* London: Macmillan, 1969.

Lutterman, K. *Giving to Churches: A Sociological Study of the Contributions to Eight Catholic and Lutheran Churches.* Unpublished doctoral dissertation, Department of Sociology, University of Wisconsin, 1962.

Lyle, J., and Hoffman, H. R. "Children's Use of Television and Other Media." In E. A. Rubinstein, G. A. Comstock, and J. P. Murray (Eds.), *Television and Social Behavior.* Vol. 4. *Television in Day-to-Day Life: Patterns of Use.* Washington, D.C.: National Institute of Mental Health, 1971.

Lynn, D. B. *The Father: His Role in Child Development.* Monterey, Calif.: Brooks/Cole, 1974.

Lynn, R. *Personality and National Character.* Oxford, England: Pergamon Press, 1971.

Lynn, R., Phelan, J., and Kiker, V. "Beliefs in Internal-External Control of Reinforcement and Participation in Groups and Individual Sports." *Perceptual and Motor Skills,* 1969, *29,* 551–553.

Lyons, S. R. "The Political Socialization of Ghetto Children: Efficacy and Cynicism." *Journal of Politics,* 1970, *32,* 294–295.

Maas, H. S., and Kuypers. J. A. *From Thirty to Seventy: A Forty-Year Longitudinal Study of Adult Life Styles and Personality.* San Francisco: Jossey-Bass, 1974.

McAlister, J. T., Jr., and Mus, P. *The Vietnamese and Their Revolution.* New York: Harper & Row, 1970.

Macaulay, J. R., and Berkowitz, L. (Eds.). *Altruism and Helping Behavior.* New York: Academic Press, 1970.

McCarthy, J. D., and Zald, M. N. *The Trends of Social Movements in America: Professionalization and Resource Mobilization.* Morristown, N.J.: General Learning Press, 1973.

Maccoby, E. E. "Why Do Children Watch Television?" *Public Opinion Quarterly,* 1954, *18,* 239–244.

Maccoby, E. E. "The Development of Moral Values and Behavior in Childhood." In J. Clausen (Ed.), *Socialization and Society.* Boston: Little, Brown, 1968.

McCombs, M. E. "Mass Communication in Political Campaigns: Information, Gratification, and Persuasion." In F. G. Kline and P. J. Tichenor (Eds.), *Current Perspectives in Mass Communication Research, Sage Annual Reviews of Communication Research.* Vol. 1. Beverly Hills, Calif.: Sage, 1972.

McConaughy, J. "Certain Personality Factors of State Legislators in South Carolina." *American Political Science Review,* 1950, *44,* 897–903.

McCready, W. C. "Faith of Our Fathers: A Study of the Process of Religious Socialization." Unpublished doctoral dissertation, Department of Sociology, University of Illinois at Chicago Circle, 1972.

McCrone, D. J., and Cnudde, C. F. "Toward a Communications Theory of Democratic Political Development." *American Political Science Review,* 1967, *61,* 72–79.

McEvoy, J. "Hours of Work and the Demand for Outdoor Recreation." *Journal of Leisure Research,* 1974, *6,* 125–139.

McGrath, J. E., and Altman, I. *Small Group Research.* New York: Holt, Rinehart and Winston, 1966.

McGuire, M. B. "Toward a Sociological Interpretation of the Catholic Pentecostal Movement." *Review of Religious Research,* 1975, *16,* 94–104.

McGuire, W. J. "Psychological Motives and Communication Gratification." In J. G. Blumler and E. Katz (Eds.), *The Uses of Mass Communications.* Beverly Hills, Calif.: Sage, 1974.

Machalek, R., and Martin, M. "Invisible Religions." *Journal for the Scientific Study of Religion,* 1976, *15,* 311–321.

McHugh, P. *Defining the Situation: The Organization of Meaning in Social Interaction.* Indianapolis, Ind.: Bobbs-Merrill, 1968.

McIntosh, P. C., and others. *Landmarks in the History of Physical Education.* London: Routledge & Kegan Paul, 1957.

McKechnie, G. E. "The Psychological Structure of Leisure: Past Behavior." *Journal of Leisure Research,* 1974, *6,* 27–45.

McKillop, W. "Wilderness Use in California: A Quantitative Analysis." *Journal of Leisure Research*, 1975, *7*, 165–178.

McKinney, J. P. "The Development of Values—Prescriptive or Proscriptive?" *Human Development*, 1971, *14*, 71–80.

McKnelly, P. K. "Leisure Behavior Patterns: A Study of Residents in the Lower Brazos Valley of Texas." Unpublished doctoral dissertation, Department of Sociology, Texas A & M University, 1973.

McLeod, J. M., Atkin, C. K., and Chaffee, S. "Adolescents, Parents, and Television Use: Adolescent Self-Report Measures from Maryland and Wisconsin Samples." In G. A. Comstock and E. A. Rubinstein (Eds.), *Television and Social Behavior, Reports and Papers.* Vol. 3: *Television and Adolescent Aggressiveness.* Washington, D.C.: National Institute of Mental Health, 1971a.

McLeod, J. M., Atkin, C. K., and Chaffee, S. "Adolescents, Parents, and Television Use: Self-Report and Other-Report Measures from Wisconsin Sample." In G. A. Comstock and E. A. Rubinstein (Eds.), *Television and Social Behavior, Reports and Papers.* Vol. 3: *Television and Adolescent Aggressiveness.* Washington, D.C.: National Institute of Mental Health, 1971b.

McLeod, J. M., and Becker, L. B. "Testing the Validity of Gratification Measures Through Political Effects Analysis." In J. G. Blumler and E. Katz (Eds.), *The Uses of Mass Communications.* Beverly Hills, Calif.: Sage, 1974.

McLeod, J. M., Becker, L. B., and Byrnes, J. E. "Another Look at the Agenda Setting Function of the Press." *Communication Research*, 1974, *1*, 131–166.

McLeod, J. M., Becker, L. B., and Elliott, W. R. "Communication and Political Change During the College Years." Madison Mass Communications Research Center, University of Wisconsin, 1972.

McLeod, J. M., and Byrnes, J. E. "Another Look at the Agenda-Setting Function of the Press." *Communication Research*, 1974, *1*, 131–166.

McLeod, J. M., and Elliott, W. R. "Communication and Political Change During the College Years." Madison: Mass Communication Research Center, University of Wisconsin, 1972.

McLeod, J. M., and O'Keefe, G. J., Jr. "The Socialization Perspective and Communication Behavior." In F. G. Kline and P. J. Tichenor (Eds.), *Current Perspectives in Mass Communication Research, Sage Annual Reviews of Communication Research.* Vol. 1. Beverly Hills, Calif.: Sage, 1972.

McLeod, J. M., Ward, L. S., and Tancill, K. "Alienation and Uses of the Mass Media." *Public Opinion Quarterly*, 1965–66, *29*, 583–594.

McMartin, P. A. "A Cross-Lag Test of Lerner's Model of Modernization." *Journalism Quarterly*, 1974, *51*, 120–122.

McNees, S. "Deductibility of Charitable Bequests." *National Tax Journal*, 1973, *26*, 79–98.

McPhee, W. N., and Glaser, W. A. (Eds.). *Public Opinion and Congressional Elections.* New York: Free Press, 1962.

McPherson, B. D. "The Black Athlete: An Overview and Analysis." In D. M. Landers (Ed.), *Social Problems in Athletics: Essays in the Sociology of Sport.* Urbana: University of Illinois Press, 1976.

McPherson, B. D., and Kozlik, C. A. "Canadian Leisure Patterns by Age: Disengagement, Continuity or Ageism." In V. W. Marshall (Ed.), *Aging in Canada: Social Perspectives.* Pickering, Ontario: Fitzhenry and Whiteside, 1979.

MacPherson, J. M. "The Dynamics of Voluntary Affiliation: A Multivariate Reanalysis." *Journal of Voluntary Action Research*, forthcoming.

McQuail, D., Blumler, J. G., and Brown, J. R. "The Television Audience: A Revised Perspective." In D. McQuail (Ed.), *Sociology of Mass Communications.* Harmondsworth, England: Penguin, 1972.

Macy, B. A. "The Bolivar Quality of Working Life Experiment: 1972–1977." Paper prepared for the Quality of Working Life Workshop on Collaborative Labor-Management Problem Solving, 37th annual meeting of the Academy of Management, Kissimmee, Fla., 1977.

Macy, B. A., and Nurick, A. J. "The Tennessee Valley Authority Quality of Working Life Experiment." Paper prepared for the Quality of Working Life Workshop on Collaborative Labor-Management Problem Solving, 37th annual meeting of the Academy of Management, Kissimmee, Fla., 1977.

Maddi, S. R. *Personality Theories: A Comparative Analysis.* Homewood, Ill.: Dorsey Press, 1968.

Magill, R. S. "Joining Formal Voluntary Associations and Social Action Among the Poor." *Journal of Voluntary Action Research*, 1973, *2*, 224–229.

Magnitz, R. "Leisure, Social Participation and Political Activity." *International Social Science Journal*, 1960, *12*, 561–574.

Malikin, D. *Social Disability: Alcoholism, Drug Addiction, Crime and Social Disadvantage.* New York: New York University Press, 1973.

Maloney, T. L., and Petrie, B. M. "Professionalization of Attitude Toward Play Among Canadian Schools Pupils as a Function of Sex, Grade, and Athletic Participation." *Journal of Leisure Research*, 1972, *4*, 184–195.

Manchester, H. *Four Centuries of Sport in America, 1490–1890.* New York: Blom, 1968. (Originally published in 1931.)

Mann, M. *Workers on the Move: The Sociology of Relocation.* Cambridge, England: Cambridge University Press, 1973.

March, J. G. "Making Artists Out of Pedants." In R. Stogdill (Ed.),

The Process of Model-Building in the Behavioral Sciences. Columbus: Ohio State University Press, 1970.

Marcus, P., "Survey of Lansing Employee Perceptions of Capital Area United Way: Report #1: Givers and Non-Givers." Unpublished paper, Department of Sociology, Michigan State University, 1973.

Marks, E., and others. *Human Reactions in Disaster Situations.* Chicago: National Opinion Research Center, 1954.

Marks, S. R. "Multiple Roles and Role Strain: Some Notes on Human Energy, Time and Commitment." *American Sociological Review,* 1977, *42,* 921–936.

Marquette, J. F. "Social Mobilization and the Philippine Political System." *Comparative Political Studies,* 1971, *4,* 339–348.

Marsland, D., and Perry, M. "Variations in 'Adolescent Societies'— Exploratory Analysis of the Orientations of Young People." *Youth and Society,* 1973, *5,* 61–83.

Martin, H. T., and Siegel, L. "Background Factors Related to Effective Group Participation." *Journal of Abnormal and Social Psychology,* 1953, *48,* 599–600.

Martindale, C. A. *Sport Involvement as a Function of Social Class and Ethnic Group Background.* Unpublished master's thesis, Department of Sociology, University of Wisconsin, 1971.

Marts, A. C. *Philanthropy's Role in Civilization: Its Contributions to Human Freedom.* New York: Harper & Row, 1953.

Marts, A. C. *The Generosity of Americans: Its Source—Its Achievements.* Englewood Cliffs, N.J.: Prentice-Hall, 1966.

Marty, M. E. "Religious Development in Historical, Social, and Cultural Context." In M. P. Strommen (Ed.), *Research on Religious Development: A Comprehensive Handbook.* New York: Hawthorn Books, 1971.

Marvick, D., and Nixon, C. "Recruitment Contrasts in Rival Campaign Groups." In D. Marvick (Ed.), *Political Decision-Makers.* New York: Free Press, 1961.

Marx, G. *Protest and Prejudice.* New York: Harper & Row, 1967a.

Marx, G. "Religion: Opiate or Inspiration of Civil Rights Militancy Among Negroes?" *American Sociological Review,* 1967b, *32,* 64–77.

Marx, G. "Thoughts on a Neglected Category of Social Movement Participant." *American Journal of Sociology,* 1974, *80,* 402–442.

Marx, G., and Wood, J. L. "Strands of Theory and Research in Collective Behavior." In A. Inkeles, J. Coleman, and N. Smelser (Eds.), *Annual Review of Sociology.* Vol. 1. Palo Alto, Calif.: Annual Reviews, 1975.

Maslog, C. "Images and the Mass Media." *Journalism Quarterly,* 1971, *48,* 519–525.

Maslow, A. H. *Motivation and Personality*. New York: Harper & Row, 1954.

Maslow, A *Toward a Psychology of Being*. New York: D. Van Nostrand, 1962.

Maslow, A. "The Need to Know and the Fear of Knowing." *Journal of General Psychology*, 1963, *68*, 111–125.

Masterman, M. "The Nature of a Paradigm." In I. Lakatos and A. Musgrave (Eds.), *Criticism and the Growth of Knowledge*. Cambridge, England: Cambridge University Press, 1970.

Mathiasen, J. R., and Powell, J. D. "Participation and Efficacy." *Comparative Politics*, 1972, *4*, 303–329.

Matthews, D. R., and Prothro, J. W. *Negroes and the New Southern Politics*. New York: Harcourt Brace Jovanovich, 1966.

Matza, D. *Becoming Deviant*. Englewood Cliffs, N.J.: Prentice-Hall, 1969.

Mauss, A. L. "Dimensions of Religious Defection." *Review of Religious Research*, 1969, *10*, 128–135.

Mauss, M. *The Gift: Forms and Functions of Exchange in Archaic Societies*. London: Cohen and West, 1966. (Originally published in French 1925.)

May, J. V. *Citizen Participation: A Review of the Literature*. Monticello, Ill.: Council of Planning Librarians, No. 210-211, 1971.

Mayer, H. *Charity in the Western Roman Empire*. Unpublished doctoral dissertation, Department of History, Washington University, 1973.

Mayntz, R. "Leisure, Social Participation and Political Activity." *International Socal Science Journal*, 1960, *12*, 561–574.

Mayntz, R. "Citizen Participation in Germany: Nature and Extent." Paper presented at 5th World Congress on the International Political Science Association, Paris, 1961.

Mazziotti, D. F. *Neighborhoods and Neighborhood Planning*. Monticello, Ill.: Council of Planning Librarians, No. 596, 1974.

Mead, G. *Mind, Self, and Society*. Chicago: University of Chicago Press, 1934.

Mead, M. "The Cross-Cultural Approach to the Study of Personality." In J. L. McCary (Ed.), *Psychology of Personality: Six Modern Approaches*. New York: Logos, 1956.

Mead, M. "Christian Faith and Technical Assistance." In W. Cowan (Ed.), *What the Christian Hopes for in Society*. New York: Association Press, 1957.

Mehrabian, A., and Russell, J. A. *An Approach to Environmental Psychology*. Cambridge, Mass.: M.I.T. Press, 1974.

Meier, D. L., and Bell, W. "Anomie and Differential Access to the

Achievement of Life Goals." *American Sociological Review*, 1959, *24*, 189–202.

Melbin, M. "Night as Frontier." *American Sociological Review*, 1978, *43*, 3–22.

Meldrum, K. I. "Participation in Outdoor Activities in Selected Countries in Western Europe." *Comparative Education*, 1971, 7, 137–142.

Menanteau-Horta, D., and Carter, R. E. "La Communicacion Colectiva en Chile: Algunas Caracteristicas del Campo y de la Ciudad" ["Collective Communication in Chile: Rural and Urban Characteristics"]. *Revista Espanola de la Opinion Publica*, 1972, *28*, 107–120.

Mendelsohn, H. "Radio in Contemporary American Life." Unpublished paper, Communication Arts Center, University of Denver, 1968.

Menke, F. *The Encyclopedia of Sports*. South Brunswick, N.J.: A.S. Barnes, 1969.

Mercer, D.C."Discretionary Travel Behavior and the Urban Mental Map." *Australian Geographical Studies*, 1971a, *9*, 37–43.

Mercer, D. C. "The Role of Perception in the Recreation Experience: A Review and Discussion." *Journal of Leisure Research*, 1971b, *3*, 261–276.

Merritt, R. "The Tax Incentives for Lifetime Gifts to Charity." *Taxes—The Tax Magazine*, 1961, *39*, 104–130.

Merton, R. K. *Social Theory and Social Structure*. New York: Free Press, 1949.

Merton, R. K. *Social Theory and Social Structure*. (rev. ed.) New York: Free Press, 1957.

Merton, R. K., Broom, L., and Cottrell, L. S. (Eds.) *Sociology Today*. New York: Basic Books, 1959.

Metcalfe, A. "Working Class Physical Recreation in Montreal, 1860-1895." Kingston, Ontario: *Working Papers in the Sociological Study of Sports and Leisure*. 1978, *1* (2).

Meux, E. P. "Concern of the Common Good in an N-person Game." *Journal of Personality and Social Psychology*, 1973, *28*, 414–418.

Meyer, J. W., Boli-Bennett, J., and Chase-Dunn, C. "Convergence and Divergence in Development." In A. Inkeles, J. Coleman, and N. Smelser (Eds.), *Annual Review of Sociology*. Vol. 1. Palo Alto, Calif.: Annual Reviews, 1975.

Meyer, M. W. "Size and the Structure of Organizations: A Causal Analysis." *American Sociological Review*, 1972, *37*, 434–440.

Meyers, W. R., and Sorwart, R. A. *Citizen Participation in Mental Health*. Monticello, Ill.: Council of Planning Librarians, No. 559, 1974.

Meyersohn, R. "Television and the Rest of Leisure." *Public Opinion Quarterly*, 1968, *32*, 102–112.

Michelson, W. "Some Like It Hot: Social Participation and Environmental Use as Functions of the Season." *American Journal of Sociology*, 1971, *76*, 1072–1083.

Midlarsky, E. "Aiding Responses: An Analysis and a Review." *Merrill Palmer Quarterly*, 1968, *14*, 229–260.

Midlarsky, E., Bryan, J., and Brickman, L. "Aversive Approval: Interactive Effects of Modeling and Reinforcement of Altruistic Behavior." *Child Development*, 1973, *44*, 315–321.

Miermans, C.G.M. *Voetbal in Nederland* [*Soccer in Netherlands*]. Assen, Netherlands: Van Gorcum, 1955.

Mihovilovic, M. "An Analysis of Some Factors Influencing the Time-Budget of Employed and Unemployed Women in Yugoslavia." *International Journal of Sociology of the Family*, 1973, *3*, 70–85.

Milbank, D. "Intervention and Transnational Terrorism: Diagnosis and Prognosis." Paper presented at the State Department Conference on International Terrorism, Washington, D.C., 1976.

Milbrath, L. W. "Measuring the Personalities of Lobbyists." Unpublished paper, Department of Political Science, State University of New York, Buffalo, 1960.

Milbrath, L. W. *Political Participation*. Chicago: Rand McNally, 1965.

Milbrath, L. W. "The Nature of Political Beliefs and the Relationship of the Individual to the Government." *American Behavioral Scientist*, 1968, *12*, 28–36.

Milbrath, L. W. "Political Participation in the States." In H. Jacob and K. Vines (Eds.), *Politics in the American States*. (2nd ed.) Boston: Little, Brown, 1971.

Milbrath, L. W. "Individuals and the Polity." Unpublished paper, State University of New York, Buffalo, 1972.

Milbrath, L. W., and Goel, M. L. *Political Participation*. (2nd ed.) Chicago: Rand McNally, 1977.

Milbrath, L. W., and Klein, W. "Personality Correlates of Political Participation." *Acta Sociologica*, 1962, *6*, 53–66.

Milgram, S. "Some Conditions of Obedience and Disobedience to Authority." *Human Relations*, 1965, *18*, 57–76.

Milgram, S., and Toch, H. "Collective Behavior: Crowds and Social Movements." In G. Lindzey and E. Aronson (Eds.), *The Handbook of Social Psychology*. (2nd ed.) Vol. 4. Reading, Mass.: Addison-Wesley, 1969.

Miller, A. H. "Political Issues and Trust in Government: 1964–1970." *American Political Science Review*, 1974, *68*, 951–972, 989–1001.

Miller, D. C. *Handbook of Research Design and Social Measurement*. (3rd ed.) New York: McKay, 1977.

Miller, G. A., Galanter, E., and Pribram, K. H. *Plans and the Structure of Behavior.* New York: Henry Holt, 1960.

Miller, H. *The Legal Foundation of American Philanthropy: 1776–1844.* Madison: State Historical Society of Wisconsin, 1961.

Miller, J. G. *Living Systems.* New York: McGraw-Hill, 1978.

Miller, M. "The Waukegan Study of Voter Turnout Prediction." *Public Opinion Quarterly,* 1952, *15,* 381–398.

Miller, N. E., and Dollard, J. *Social Learning and Imitation.* New Haven, Conn.: Yale University Press, 1941.

Miller, S. M., and Rein, M. "Participation, Poverty, and Administration." *Public Administration Review,* 1969, *29,* 15–24.

Mirande, A. M. "Social Mobility and Participation: The Dissociative and Socialization Hypotheses." *Sociological Quarterly,* 1973, *14,* 19–31.

Mischel, W. *Personality and Assessment.* New York: Wiley, 1968.

Mischel, W. "Continuity and Change in Personality." *American Psychologist,* 1969, *24,* 1012–1018.

Mischel, W. *Introduction to Personality.* New York: Holt, Rinehart and Winston, 1971.

Mischel, W. "Toward a Cognitive Social Learning Reconceptualization of Personality." *Psychological Review,* 1973, *80,* 252–283.

Mishlove, J. *The Roots of Consciousness.* New York: Random House, 1975.

Mitchell, B. *Fluoridation Bibliography.* Monticello, Ill.: Council of Planning Librarians, No. 268, 1972.

Moberg, D. O. *The Church as a Social Institution.* Englewood Cliffs, N.J.: Prentice-Hall, 1962.

Moberg, D. O. "Religious Practices." In M. P. Strommen (Ed.), *Research On Religious Development: A Comprehensive Handbook.* New York: Hawthorn Books, 1971.

Mogulof, M. B. *Citizen Participation: A Review and Commentary on Federal Policies and Practices.* Washington, D.C.: Urban Institute, 1970.

Moody, E. J. "Magical Therapy: An Anthropological Investigation of Contemporary Satanism." In I. I. Zaretsky and M. P. Leone (Eds.), *Religious Movements in Contemporary America.* Princeton, N.J.: Princeton University Press, 1974.

Moore, B., Jr. *Social Origins of Dictatorship and Democracy.* Boston: Beacon Press, 1966.

Moore, B., Jr., Underwood, B., and Rosenhan, D. "Affect and Altruism." *Developmental Psychology,* 1972, *8,* 99–104.

Moore, S. M. "Personality Traits of Physically Active, Moderately Active, and Inactive College Women." Unpublished master's thesis, University of Kansas, 1969.

Moos, R. H. "Conceptualization of Human Environments." *American Psychologist,* 1973, *28,* 652–665.

Moos, R. H. "Systems for the Assessment and Classification of Human Environments: An Overview." In R. H. Moos and P.N. Insel (Eds.), *Issues in Social Economy: Human Milieus.* Palo Alto, Calif.: National Press, 1974.

Morgan, J., and others. *Income and Welfare in the United States.* New York: McGraw-Hill, 1962.

Morgan, J. N., Dye, R. F., and Hybels, J. "Some Results from Two National Surveys of Philanthropic Activity." Paper commissioned by the (Filer) 1975 Commission of Private Philanthropy and Public Needs, Denver, Colo., 1975.

Morris, C. *Varieties of Human Values.* Chicago: University of Chicago Press, 1956.

Morris, S. C., and Rosen, S. "Effects of Felt Adequacy and Opportunity to Reciprocate on Help Seeking." *Journal of Experimental Social Psychology,* 1973, *9,* 265–276.

Morrison, D., and Centers, L. "Investigation of the Convergent Validity of Different Measures of Cognitive Style." *Journal of Projective Techniques and Personality Assessment,* 1969, *33,* 168–172.

Morse, S. J., and Gergen, K. J. "Material Aid and Social Attraction." *Journal of Applied Social Psychology,* 1971, *1,* 150–162.

Morse, S. J., and others. "Reactions to Receiving Expected and Unexpected Help from a Person Who Violates or Does Not Violate a Norm." *Journal of Experimental Social Psychology,* 1977, *13,* 397–402.

Mortimer, J. J., and Simmons, R. G. "Adult Socialization." In R. H. Turner, J. Coleman, and R. Fox (Eds.), *Annual Review of Sociology.* Vol. 4. Palo Alto, Calif.: Annual Reviews, 1978.

Mousseau-Glaser, M. "Consommation des Mass Media: Biculturalisme des Mass Media ou Bilinguisme des Consommateurs?" ["Mass Media Consumption: Biculturalism of the Mass Media or Bilingualism of Consumers?"] *Canadian Review of Sociology and Anthropology,* 1972, *9,* 325–346.

Moynihan, D. P. *Maximum Feasible Misunderstanding.* New York: Free Press, 1969.

Mulford, C. L., and Klonglan, G. E. "Attitude Determinants of Individual Participation in Organized Voluntary Action." In D. H. Smith, R. D. Reddy, and B. R. Baldwin (Eds.), *Voluntary Action Research: 1972.* Lexington, Mass.: Heath, 1972.

Muller, E. N. "Cross National Dimensions of Political Competence." *American Political Science Review,* 1970, *64,* 792–809.

Muller, E. N. "A Test of a Partial Theory of Potential for Political Violence." *American Political Science Review*, 1972, *66*, 928–959.

Muller, E. N. "Relative Deprivation and Aggressive Political Behavior." Paper presented at annual meeting of the American Political Science Association, San Francisco, Calif, 1975.

Mullins, N. C. "Theory Construction from Available Materials: A System For Organizing and Presenting Propositions. *American Journal of Sociology*, 1974, *80*, 1–15.

Mullins, N. C., and Mullins, C. *Theories and Theory Groups in Contemporary American Sociology*. New York: Harper & Row, 1973.

Muramatsu, Y. "Views of the Japanese Youths Toward Television." In H. Eguchi and K. Sata (Eds.), *Studies of Broadcasting*. Tokyo: Radio and T.V. Culture Research Center, 1975.

Murdock, G. P. "The Common Denominators of Cultures." In R. Linton (Ed.), *The Science of Man in World Crisis*. New York: Columbia University Press, 1949.

Murphy, L. B. *Social Behavior and Child Personality*. New York: Columbia University Press, 1937.

Murphy, P. E. "The Role of Attitude in the Choice Decision of Recreational Boaters." *Journal of Leisure Research*, 1975, *7*, 216–224.

Murray, H. A., and others. *Explorations in Personality*. New York: Oxford University Press, 1938.

Mussari, A. J. *Appointment With Disaster*. Wilkes-Barre, Pa.: Northeast Publications, 1974.

Nadel, M. V. "Consumerism: A Coalition in Flux." *Policy Studies Journal*, 1975, *4*, 31–35.

Nadel, S. F. *The Theory of Social Structure*. London: Cohen and West, 1957.

Nadler, A., Fisher, J. D., and Streufert, S. "The Donor's Dilemma: Recipient's Reactions to Aid from Friend or Foe." *Journal of Applied Social Psychology*, 1974, *4*, 275–285.

Nagel, E. *The Structure of Science*. New York: Harcourt Brace Jovanovich, 1961.

Nandy, A. "Engagement and Alienation in Indian Politics." *Comparative Political Studies*, 1974, *7*, 334–356.

Naroll, R., and Cohen, S. *A Handbook of Method in Cultural Anthropology*. New York: Columbia University Press, 1973.

Nash, D., and Berger, P. L. "The Child, the Family, and the Religious Revival in Suburbia." *Journal for the Scientific Study of Religion*, 1962, *2*, 85–93.

Nash, J. B. "The Enlarging Role of Voluntary Leisure-Time Associations in Outdoor Recreation and Education." In Outdoor Recreation Resources Review Commission, *Trends in American Living and*

Outdoor Recreation, Study Report No. 22. Washington, D.C.: U.S. Government Printing Office, 1962.

Nathanson, J. "Sixty-Four Million Americans Do Not Go To Church: What Do They Believe?" In L. Roslar (Ed.), *A Guide to Religion in America.* New York: Simon & Schuster, 1955.

Naylor, H. H. "Citizen Participation by Volunteers." Unpublished paper, Office of Volunteer Development. Washington, D.C.: Department of Health, Education, and Welfare, 1976.

Nayman, O. B., Atkin,C. K., and Gillette, B. "The Four-Day Workweek and Media Use: A Glimpse of the Future. *Journal of Broadcasting,* 1973, *17,* 301–308.

Neal, A., and Rettig, S. "On the Multi-Dimensionality of Alienation." *American Sociological Review,* 1967, *32,* 54–61.

Neal, M. A., *Values and Interest in Social Change.* Englewood Cliffs, N.J.: Prentice-Hall, 1965.

Nebolsine, G. *Fiscal Aspects of Foundations and Charitable Donations in European Countries.* Amsterdam, Netherlands: European Cultural Foundation, 1963.

Needleman, J. *The New Religions.* New York: Doubleday, 1970.

Needler, M. C. "Political Development and Socioeconomic Development: The Case of Latin America." *American Political Science Review,* 1968, *62,* 889–897.

Neel, A. *Theories of Psychology, A Handbook.* (rev. ed.) Cambridge, Mass.: Schenkman, 1977.

Nelson, J. "The Urban Poor. Disruption or Political Integration in Third World Cities." *World Politics,* 1970, *22,* 393–414.

Nelson, L. D. "The Orientational Function of Religion: An Empirical Investigation of Religion and Helping Action." Unpublished doctoral dissertation, Department of Sociology, Ohio State University, 1971.

Nelson, L. D. "Proximity to Emergency and Helping Behavior: Data from the Lubbock Tornado Disaster." *Journal of Voluntary Action Research,* 1973, *2,* 194–199.

Nettler, G. "Cruelty, Dignity and Determinism." *American Sociological Review,* 1959, *24,* 375–384.

Neugarten, B. L. "Personality Change in Late Life: A Developmental Perspective." In C. Eisdorfer and M. P. Lawton (Eds.), *The Psychology of Adult Development and Aging.* Washington, D.C.: American Psychological Association, 1973.

Neugarten, B., and Havighurst, R. J. "Disengagement Reconsidered in a Crossnational Context." In R. J. Havighurst and others (Eds.), *Adjustment to Retirement.* Assen, Netherlands: Van Gorcum, 1961.

Neulinger, J. *The Psychology of Leisure.* Springfield, Ill.: Thomas, 1974.

Neulinger, J., Light, S., and Mobley, T. "Attitude Dimensions of Leisure in a Student Population." *Journal of Leisure Research*, 1976, *8*, 175–176.

Newcomb, T. M. *Personality and Social Change: Attitude Formation in a Student Community*. New York: Dryden Press, 1943.

Newcomb, T. M., and others. *Persistence and Change: Bennington College and Its Students After 25 Years*. New York: Wiley, 1967.

Newman, E. *Law of Philanthropy*. New York: Ocean Publications, 1955.

New York City Office for the Aging. "The Elderly in the Inner City." Unpublished report, New York City, 1970.

New York Times. "Polls: Not Yet the Last Word." Review of the Week, September 24, 1972.

New York Times. "A Test Finds Public Less Honest Than Police." September 6, 1974, p. 48.

Niblock, N. W. "Personality Traits and Intelligence Level of Female Athletes and Non-Participants from McNally High School." Unpublished master's thesis, Department of Physical Education, University of Washington, 1967.

Nicosia, F. M. *Consumer Decision Processes*. Englewood Cliffs, N.J.: Prentice-Hall, 1966.

Nie, N. H., Powell, G. B., Jr., and Prewitt, K. "Social Structure and Political Participation: Development Relationships." *American Political Science Review*, 1969, *63*, 361–378, 808–832.

Nie, N. H., and Verba, S. "Political Participation." In F. Greenstein and N. Polsby (Eds.), *Handbook of Political Science*. Reading, Mass.: Addison-Wesley, 1975.

Nie, N. H., Verba, S., and Kim, J. "Political Participation and the Life Cycle." *Comparative Politics*, 1974, *6*, 319–340.

Nieburg, H. L. *Political Violence*. New York: St Martin's, 1969.

Nielsen, A. C. *The Television Audience/1969*. New York: Media Research Division, A. C. Nielsen, 1969.

Nielsen, A. C. *Nielsen Television, 1973*. Chicago: A. C. Nielsen, 1973.

Nimmo, D. "Political Image Makers and the Mass Media." *Annals*, 1976, *427*, 33–52.

Nisbett, R. E. "Birth Order and Participation in Dangerous Sports." *Journal of Personality and Social Psychology*, 1968, *8*, 351–353.

Nix, J. B. "Motivational Reasons for Participation and Nonparticipation in Interscholastic Athletics." Unpublished master's thesis, Department of Physical Education, Sacramento State College, 1969.

Nixon, R. "Factors Related to Freedom in National Press Systems." In H. D. Fischer and J. C. Merrill (Eds.), *International & Inter-Cultural Communication*. New York: Hastings House, 1976.

Nordlinger, E. A. "Political Development: Time Sequences and Rates of Change." *World Politics*, 1968, *20*, 494–520.

Oberschall, A. *Social Conflict and Social Movements*. Englewood Cliffs, N.J.: Prentice-Hall, 1973.

O'Connor, C. A. "A Study of Personality Needs Involved in the Selection of Specific Leisure Interest Groups." Unpublished doctoral dissertation, Department of Physical Education, University of Southern California, 1970.

Ogilvie, B. C. "The Sweet Psychic Jolt of Danger." *Psychology Today*, 1974, *8*, 88–94.

O'Keefe, G. J. "Political Campaigns and Mass Communication Research." In S. H. Chaffee (Ed.), *Political Communication: Issues and Strategies for Research*. Beverly Hills, Calif.: Sage, 1975.

O'Keefe, J., and Spetnagel, H. T. "Patterns of College Undergraduates' Use of Selected News Media." *Journalism Quarterly*, 1973, *50*, 543–548.

Olejnik, A. B., and McKinney, J. P. "Parental Value Orientation and Generosity in Children." *Developmental Psychology*, 1973, *8*, 311–318.

Olsen, M. E. "Two Categories of Political Alienation." *Social Forces*, 1969, *47*, 288–299.

Olsen, M. E. "Social and Political Participation of Blacks." *American Sociological Review*, 1970, *35*, 682–697.

Olsen, M. E. "Social Participation and Voting Turnout: A Multivariate Analysis." *American Sociological Review*, 1972, *37*, 317–333.

Olsen, M. E. "A Model of Political Participation Stratification." *Journal of Political and Military Sociology*, 1973, *1*, 183–200.

Olsen, M. E. "Interest Association Participation and Political Activity in the U.S. and Sweden." *Journal of Voluntary Action Research*, 1974, *3*, 17–32.

Olson, M., Jr. "Rapid Growth As a Destabilizing Force." *Journal of Economic History*, 1963, *23*, 529–552.

Onibokun, A. G., and Curry, M. "An Ideology of Citizen Participation: The Metropolitan Seattle Transit Case Study." *Public Administration Review*, 1976, *36*, 269–277.

Oppenheimer, J. R. "The Tree of Knowledge." *Harper's*, 1958, *217*, 55–57.

Orbell, J. M., and Uno, T. "A Theory of Neighborhood Problem Solving: Political Action vs. Residential Mobility." *American Political Science Review*, 1972, *66*, 471–490.

Organski, A.F.K. "Fascism and Modernization." In S. J. Woolf (Ed.), *The Nature of Fascism*. New York: Vintage Books, 1969.

Orlick, T. D. "An Analysis of Expectancy as a Motivational Factor Influencing Sports Participation." In *Proceedings*, Third World Congress of the International Society of Sports Participation. Vol. 2. Madrid: Instituto Nacional de Educacion Fisica y Deportes, 1973.

Orlick, T. D., "Sport Participation—A Process of Shaping Behavior." *Human Factors*, 1974, *16*, 558–561.

Ornstein, R. E. (Ed.). *The Nature of Human Consciousness*. San Francisco: W.H. Freeman, 1973.

Ornstein, R. E. *The Psychology of Consciousness*. (2nd ed.) New York: Harcourt Brace Jovanovich, 1977.

O'Rourke, B. "Travel in the Recreational Experience—A Literature Review." *Journal of Leisure Research*, 1974, *6*, 140–156.

Otto, L. B., and Alwin, D. F. "Athletics, Aspirations and Attainments." *Sociology of Education*, 1977, *50*, 102–113.

Outdoor Recreation Resource Review Commission (ORRRC). *National Recreation Survey*, Study Report 19. Washington, D.C.: U.S. Government Printing Office, 1962a.

Outdoor Recreation Resource Review Commission (ORRRC). *Participation in Outdoor Recreation: Factors Affecting Demand Among American Adults*, Study Report No. 20. Washington, D.C.: U.S. Government Printing Office, 1962b.

Outdoor Recreation Resource Review Commission (ORRRC). *Trends in American Living and Outdoor Recreation*, Study Report 22. Washington, D.C.: U.S. Government Printing Office, 1962c.

Owen, J. D. "The Demand for Leisure." *Journal of Political Economy*, 1971, *79*, 56–76.

Page, C. "The World of Sport and Its Study." In J. Talamini and C. Page (Eds.), *Sport and Society*. Boston: Little, Brown, 1973.

Palmore, E. (Ed.). *Normal Aging: Reports from the Duke Longitudinal Study, 1955–1969*. Durham, N.C.: Duke University Press, 1970.

Parker, S. *The Future of Work and Leisure*. London: MacGibbon and Kee, 1971.

Parkum, K. H., and Parkum, V. C. *Voluntary Participation in Health Planning*. Unpublished doctoral dissertation, Department of Sociology, University of Wisconsin, 1973.

Parkim, K. H., and Parkum, V. C. *Voluntary Participation in Health Planning*. Harrisburg: Pennsylvania Department of Health, 1973.

Parkum, V. C. *Citizen Participation: A Bibliography of Theory and Practice, with Special Emphasis on Comprehensive Health Planning*. Harrisburg: Pennsylvania Department of Health, 1974.

Parkum, V. C. *Efficacy and Action: An Extension of the Efficacy Concept in Relation to Selected Aspects of Citizen Participation*. Unpublished doctoral dissertation, Department of Political Science, University of Mannheim, West Germany, 1976.

Parkum, V. C. *Social Planning and Citizen Participation.* New Haven, Conn.: Yale School of Organization and Management, Working Paper, A-10, Condensation of *Efficacy and Action.* 1978.

Parsons, T. *The Structure of Social Action.* New York: Free Press, 1949.

Parsons, T. *The Social System.* New York: Free Press, 1964.

Parsons, T. *Societies: Evolutionary and Comparative Perspectives.* Englewood Cliffs, N.J.: Prentice-Hall, 1966.

Parsons, T. "Durkheim's Contribution to the Theory of Integration of Social Systems." In T. Parsons, *Sociological Theory and Modern Society.* New York: Free Press, 1967.

Parsons, T. "The Sick Role and the Role of the Physician Reconsidered." *Milbank Memorial Fund Quarterly: Health and Society,* 1975, *53,* 257–278.

Parsons, T., Bales, R. F., and Shils, E. *Working Papers in the Theory of Action.* New York: Free Press, 1953.

Parsons, T., and Shils, E. *Toward a General Theory of Action.* Cambridge, Mass.: Harvard University Press, 1951.

Pateman, C. *Participation and Democratic Theory.* Oxford, England: Clarendon Press, 1970.

Payne, B. P. "Age Differences in the Meaning of Leisure Time." Unpublished paper presented to the Gerontological Society, Miami, Fla., 1973a.

Payne, B. P. "Voluntary Association of the Elderly." Unpublished paper presented to the Society for the Scientific Study of Religion, New York, 1973b.

Payne, B. P., and Whittington, F. J. "Aged Women: Variables Unique to Women and Common to the Sexes." Paper presented at annual meeting of the Southern Sociological Society, Atlanta, Ga., 1974.

Payne, R., Payne, B. P., and Reddy, R. D. "Social Background and Role Determinants of Individual Participation in Organized Voluntary Action." In D. H. Smith, R. D. Reddy, and B. R. Baldwin (Eds.), *Voluntary Action Research: 1972.* Lexington, Mass.: Heath, 1972.

Pearson, J. W. *The Eight Day Week.* New York: Harper & Row, 1973.

Peled, T., and Katz, E. "Media Functions in Wartime: The Israel Home Front in October, 1973." In J. G. Blumler and E. Katz (Eds.), *The Uses of Mass Communications.* Beverly Hills, Calif.: Sage, 1974.

Penrose, J., and others. "The Newspaper Nonreader 10 Years Later: A Partial Replication of Westley-Severin." *Journalism Quarterly,* 1974, *51,* 631–638.

Perlman, J. C. "Rio's Favelas and the Myth of Marginality." *Politics and Society,* 1975, *5,* 131–160.

Pesonen, P. "The Voting Behavior of Finnish Students." In Finnish Political Science Association, *Democracy in Finland.* Helsinki, Finland: Finnish Political Science Association, 1960.

Pesonen, P. "Citizen Participation in Finnish Politics." Paper presented at 5th World Congress of the International Political Science Association, Paris, 1961.

Pesonen, P. *An Election in Finland.* New Haven, Conn.: Yale University Press, 1968.

Peterson, D. W., and Mauss, A. L. "The Cross and the Commune: An Interpretation of the Jesus People." In C. Y. Glock (Ed.), *Religion in Sociological Perspective.* Belmont, Calif.: Wadsworth, 1973.

Peterson, P. E. "Forms of Representation: Participation of the Poor in the Community Action Program." *American Political Science Review,* 1970, *64,* 491–507.

Peterson, V. "Trends in U.S. Collegiate Voluntary Associations in the Twentieth Century." In D. H. Smith (Ed.), *Voluntary Action Research, 1973.* Lexington, Mass.: Heath, 1973.

Petrinovich, L. "Probabilistic Functionalism." *American Psychologist,* 1979, *34,* 373–390.

Pettigrew, T. F. *Racially Separate or Together?* New York: McGraw-Hill, 1971.

Pfeiffer, D. G. "Volunteers within the Formal Public Policy Making Process." Paper presented at annual meeting of the Association of Voluntary Action Scholars, Boston, 1976.

Phares, E. J., and Lamiell, J. T. "Personality." In M. R. Rosenzweig and L. Porter (Eds.), *Annual Review of Psychology.* Vol. 28. Palo Alto, Calif.: Annual Reviews, 1977.

Phillips, D. "Mental Health Status, Social Participation and Happiness." *Journal of Health and Social Behavior,* 1967a, *8,* 285–291.

Phillips, D. "Social Participation and Happiness." *American Journal of Sociology,* 1976b, *72,* 479–488.

Phillips, D. *Knowledge from What?* Chicago: Rand McNally, 1971.

Phillips, J. L. *The Origins of Intellect: Piaget's Theory.* San Francisco: W. H. Freeman, 1969.

Phillips, J., and Schafer, W. "The Athletic Sub-Culture: A Preliminary Study." Paper presented at annual meeting of the American Sociological Association, 1970.

Phillips, L. *Human Adaptation and Its Failures.* New York: Academic Press, 1968.

Piaget, J. *The Moral Judgment of the Child* (M. Gabain, Trans.). New York: Free Press, 1965.

Piazza, J. "Jewish Identity and the Counter Culture." In C. Y. Glock and R. N. Bellah (Eds.), *The New Religious Consciousness.* Berkeley: University of California Press, 1976.

Pierce, M. C. *Participation in Decision-Making.* Monticello, Ill.: Council of Planning Librarians, No. 558, 1972.

Pierson, G. W. *The Moving American.* New York: Knopf, 1973.

Piliavin, I., and Gross, A. E. "The Effects of Separation of Services and Income Maintenance on AFDC Recipients." *Social Service Review,* 1977, *51,* 389–406.

Piliavin, I. M., Rodin, J., and Piliavin, J. A. "Good Samaritanism: An Underground Phenomenon." *Journal of Personality and Social Psychology,* 1969, *13,* 289–299.

Pilskaln, R., and Hirsch, P. "Protest Rock and Drugs." *Journal of Communication,* 1976, *26,* 125–136.

Pittard-Payne, B. *The Meaning and Measurement of Commitment to the Church.* Unpublished doctoral dissertation, Department of Religion and Society, Emory University, 1963.

Pittard-Payne, B. "The Meaning and Measurement of Commitment to the Church." Atlanta: Research Paper No. 13, Georgia State University, 1966.

Pittard-Payne, B., and others. *Protestant Parish.* Atlanta: Communication Arts Press, 1963.

Plowman, E. F. *The Jesus Movement in America.* Elgin, Ill.: D. C. Cook, 1971.

Plutchik, R. *Emotion: A Psychoevolutionary Synthesis.* New York: Harper & Row, 1980a.

Plutchik, R. " A Language for the Emotions." *Psychology Today,* 1980b, *13,* 68–78.

Poor, R. *4 Days, 40 Hours.* Cambridge, Mass.: Bursk and Poor, 1970.

Powell, J. "Venezuela: The Peasant Union Movement." In H. A. Landsberger (Ed.), *Latin American Peasant Movements.* Ithaca, N.Y.: Cornell University Press, 1969.

Pred, A. *Behavior and Location: Foundations for a Geographic and Dynamic Location Theory.* Lund, Sweden: Department of Geography, Royal University of Lund, 1967.

Prince, S. H. *Catastrophe and Social Change.* New York: Columbia University Press, 1920.

Prizzia, R., and Sinsawasdi, N. "Evolution of the Thai Student Movement." *Asia Quarterly,* 1975, *1,* 3–54.

Proctor, C. "Dependence of Recreation Participation on Background Characteristics of Sample Persons in the September 1960 National Recreation Survey." In Outdoor Recreation Resource Review Commission, *National Recreation Survey,* Study Report No. 19. Washington, D.C.: U.S. Government Printing Office, 1962.

Proshansky, H., Ittelson, W., and Rivlin, L. (Eds.). *Environmental Psychology.* New York: Holt, Rinehart and Winston, 1970.

Przeworski, A., and Teune, H. *The Logic of Comparative Social Inquiry.* New York: Wiley-Interscience, 1970.

Pudenz, H. "Vom Zeitvertreib der Overschicht zum Sport für Alle. Zur Geschicte des Sports in England von 1850–1950" ["A History of Sport in England 1850–1950"]. Unpublished doctoral dissertation, Department of History, University of Kiel, West Germany, 1960.

Pye, L. W. *Politics, Personality, and Nation Building.* New Haven, Conn.: Yale University Press, 1962.

Pye, L. W. *Aspects of Political Development.* Boston: Little, Brown, 1966.

Quarantelli, E. L. "Emergent Accommodation Groups: Beyond Current Collective Behavior Typologies." In T. Shibutani (Ed.), *Human Nature and Collective Behavior: Papers in Honor of Herbert Blumer.* Englewood Cliffs, N.J.: Prentice-Hall, 1970.

Quarantelli, E. L. (Ed.). *Disasters: Theory and Research.* Beverly Hills, Calif.: Sage, 1977.

Quarantelli, E. L., and Dynes, R. R. "Response to Social Crisis and Disaster." In A. Inkeles, J. Coleman, and N. Smelser (Eds.), *Annual Review of Sociology.* Vol. 3. Palo Alto, Calif.: Annual Reviews, 1977.

Quinley, H. E. "The Dilemma of an Activist Church: Protest Religion in the Sixties and Seventies." *Journal for the Scientific Study of Religion,* 1974, *13*, 1–21.

Quinney, R. *The Social Reality of Crime.* Boston: Little, Brown, 1970.

Rabushka, A. "A Note on Overseas Chinese Political Participation in Urban Malaya." *American Political Science Review,* 1970, *64*, 177–178.

Ranney, A., and Epstein, L. D. "The Two Electorates: Voters and Non-Voters in a Wisconsin Primary." *Journal of Politics,* 1966, *28*, 598–616.

Ransford, H. E. "Isolation, Powerlessness, and Violence: A Study of Attitudes and Participation in the Watts Riots." *American Journal of Sociology,* 1968, *73*, 581–591.

Rao, Y.V.L. *Communication and Development: A Study of Two Indian Villages.* Minneapolis: University of Minnesota Press, 1966.

Rapoport, R., and Rapoport, R. N. *Leisure and the Family Life Cycle.* London: Routledge & Kegan Paul, 1975.

Ready, W. E. "The Consumer's Role in the Politics of Health Planning." *Health Education Monographs,* 1972, *32*, 51–58.

Reddy, R. D. *Personal Factors and Individual Participation in Formal Volunteer Groups.* Unpublished doctoral dissertation, Department of Sociology, Boston College. 1974.

Reddy, R. D., and Smith, D. H. "Personality and Capacity Determinants of Individual Participation in Organized Voluntary Action." In D. H.

Smith, R. D. Reddy, and B. R. Baldwin (Eds.), *Voluntary Action Research: 1972*. Lexington, Mass.: Heath, 1972.

Reed, G. *The Psychology of Anomolous Experience*. Boston: Houghton Mifflin, 1974.

Rees, M. B. "Achievement Motivation and Contest Preferences." *Journalism Quarterly*, 1967, *44*, 688–692.

Rehberg, R. A., and Cohen, M. "Political Attitudes and Participation in Extracurricular Activities." In D. M. Landers (Ed.), *Social Problems in Athletics*. Urbana: University of Illinois Press, 1976.

Reich, C. M. "Socioeconomic Factors Related to Household Participation in Community Recreation." Unpublished doctoral dissertation, Department of Physical Education, Pennsylvania State University, 1965.

Reich, C. M. *The Greening of America*. New York: Random House, 1970.

Resnick, H.L.P. (Ed.). *Suicidal Behavior, Diagnosis and Management*. Boston: Little, Brown, 1968.

Rhys-Williams, J. *Taxation and Incentive*. New York: Oxford University Press, 1953.

Rice, L. N., and Gaylin, N. L. "Personality Processes Reflected in Client Vocal Style and Rorschach Performance." *Journal of Consulting and Clinical Psychology*, 1973, *40*, 133–138.

Rich, R. C. "Leadership in Neighborhood Organizations." Paper presented at annual meeting of the Association of Voluntary Action Scholars, Boston, 1976.

Richardson, B. M. "Political Attitudes and Voting Behavior in Contemporary Japan: Rural and Urban Differences." Unpublished doctoral dissertation, Department of Political Science, University of California, 1966.

Richardson, B. M. "Urbanization and Political Participation: The Case of Japan." *American Political Science Review*, 1973, *67*, 433–452.

Richardson, B. M. *The Political Culture of Japan*. Berkeley: University of California Press, 1974.

Riesman, D. "Leisure and Work in Post-Industrial Society." In E. Larrabee and R. Meyersohn (Eds.), *Mass Leisure*. New York: Free Press, 1958.

Riesman, D., and Denny, R. "Football in America." In D. Riesman, *Individualism Reconsidered*. New York: Free Press, 1954.

Riesman, D., Denney, R., and Glazer, N. *The Lonely Crowd*. New Haven, Conn.: Yale University Press, 1950.

Riesman, D., and Glazer, N. "Criteria for Political Apathy." In A. Gouldner (Ed.), *Studies in Leadership*. New York: Harper & Row, 1950.

Riley, M. W., and Foner, A. *Aging and Society*. Vol. 1: *An Inventory of Research Findings*. New York: Russell Sage Foundation, 1968.

Riley, M. W., and others (Eds.). *Aging and Society*. Vol. 2.: *Aging and the Professions*. New York: Russell Sage Foundation, 1969a.

Riley, M. W., and others. "Socialization for the Middle and Late Years." In D. A. Goslin (Ed.), *Handbook of Socialization Theory and Research*. Chicago: Rand McNally, 1969b.

Riley, M. W., and others (Eds). *Aging and Society*. Vol. 3: *A Society of Age Stratification*. New York: Russell Sage Foundation, 1972.

Ritchey, P. N. "Explanations of Migration." In A. Inkeles, J. Coleman, and N. Smelser (Eds.), *Annual Review of Sociology*. Vol. 2. Palo Alto, Calif.: Annual Reviews, 1976.

Ritchie, J.R.B. "On the Derivation of Leisure Activity Types—A Perceptual Mapping Approach." *Journal of Leisure Research*, 1975, 7, 128–140.

Ritzer, G. *Sociology: A Multiple Paradigm Science*. Boston: Allyn & Bacon, 1975.

Robbins, J. *Citizen Participation and Public Library Policy*. Metuchen, N.J.: Scarecrow Press, 1975.

Robbins, T. and Anthony, D. "Getting Straight with Meher Baba." *Journal for the Scientific Study of Religion*, 1972, 11, 122–140.

Roberts, D. F. "Communication and Children: A Developmental Approach." In I. de S. Poole and W. Schramm (Eds.), *Handbook of Communication*. Chicago: Rand McNally, 1973.

Roberts, J. M., Arth, M. J., and Bus, R. R. "Games in Culture." *American Anthropologist*, 1959, 61, 597–605.

Robertson, R. *The Sociological Interpretation of Religion*. New York: Schocken Books, 1970.

Robertson, T. S., and Rossiter, J. R. "Children and Commercial Persuasion: An Attribution Theory Analysis." Paper presented at annual meeting of the Association of Consumer Researchers Convention, Boston, 1973.

Robinson, J. A., and Standing, W. H. "Some Correlates of Voter Participation: The Case of Indiana." *The Journal of Politics*, 1960, 22, 96–111.

Robinson, J. P. "Public Information About World Affairs." Ann Arbor: Institute for Social Research, University of Michigan, 1967a.

Robinson, J. P. "Time Expenditures on Sports Across Ten Countries." *International Review of Sport Sociology*, 1967b, 2, 67–84.

Robinson, J. P. "Social Change as Measured by Time Budgets." *Journal of Leisure Research*, 1969, 1, 75–77.

Robinson, J. P. "The Audience for National TV News Programs." *Public Opinion Quarterly*, 1971a, 35, 403–405.

Robinson, J. P. "Mass Media Usage by the College Graduate." In S. Withey (Ed.), *A Degree and What Else?* New York: McGraw-Hill, 1971b.

Robinson, J. P. "Mass Communication and Information Diffusion." In F. G. Kline and P. J. Tichenor (Eds.), *Current Perspectives in Mass Communication Research.* Beverly Hills, Calif.: Sage, 1972.

Robinson, J. P. "Interpersonal Influence in Election Campaigns: Two Step-Flow Hypotheses." *Public Opinion Quarterly,* 1976a, *40,* 304–319.

Robinson, J. P. "The Press and the Voter." *Annals,* 1976b, *427,* 95–103.

Robinson, J. P. *How Americans Use Time: A Social-Psychological Analysis of Everyday Behavior.* New York: Praeger, 1977.

Robinson, J. P., Athanasiou, R., and Head, K. B. *Measures of Occupational Attitudes and Occupational Characteristics.* Ann Arbor: Institute for Social Research, University of Michigan, 1969.

Robinson, J. P., and Converse, P. E. "The Impact of Television on Mass Media Usage." In A. Szalai and others (Eds.), *The Use of Time: Daily Activities of Urban and Suburban Populations in Twelve Countries.* The Hague, Netherlands: Mouton, 1972.

Robinson, J. P., Converse, P. E., and Szalai, A. "Everyday Life in Twelve Countries." In A. Szalai and others (Eds.), *The Use of Time: Daily Activities of Urban and Suburban Populations in Twelve Countries.* The Hague, Netherlands: Mouton, 1972.

Robinson, J. P., and Jeffres, L. W. "The Changing Role of Newspapers in the Age of Television." *Journalism Monographs,* September 1979, No. 63.

Robinson, J. P., Pilskaln, R., and Hirsch, P. "Protest Rock and Drugs." *Journal of Communication,* 1976, *26,* 125–136.

Robinson, J. P., Rusk, J. G., and Head, K. B. *Measures of Political Attitudes.* Ann Arbor: Institute of Social Research, University of Michigan, 1969.

Robinson, J. P., and Shaver, P. R. *Measures of Social Psychological Attitudes.* (rev. ed.) Ann Arbor: Institute of Social Research, University of Michigan, 1973.

Robinson, W. S. "Ecological Correlations and the Behavior of Individuals." *American Sociological Review,* 1950, *15,* 351–357.

Roff, M., and Ricks, D. F. (Eds.). *Life History Research in Psychopathology.* Minneapolis: University of Minnesota Press, 1970.

Roff, M., Robins, L. N., and Pollack, M. (Eds.). *Life History Research in Psychopathology.* Vol. 2. Minneapolis: University of Minnesota Press, 1972.

Rogers, D. L. "Contrasts Between Behavioral and Affective Involvement in Voluntary Associations: An Exploratory Analysis." *Rural Sociology,* 1971, *36,* 340–358.

Rogers, D., and Bultena, G. L. "Voluntary Associations and Political Equality: An Extension of Mobilization Theory." *Journal of Voluntary Action Research*, 1975, *4*, 172–183.

Rogers, E. M., and Shoemaker, F. F. *Communication of Innovations*. New York: Free Press, 1971.

Rogers, R. "Normative Aspects of Leisure Time Behavior in the Soviet Union." *Sociology and Social Research*, 1974, *58*, 369–379.

Rohter, I. S. "The Genesis of Political Radicalism: The Case of the Radical Right." In R. S. Siegel (Ed.), *Learning About Politics: A Reader in Political Socialization*. New York: Random House, 1970.

Roistacher, E., and Morgan, J. N. "Charitable Giving, Property Taxes and Itemization on Federal Tax Returns: A Final Report from a National Survey." Ann Arbor: Institute for Social Research, University of Michigan, 1974.

Roistacher, E. A., Morgan, J. N., and Juster, F. T. "Preliminary Report to the Commission on Private Philanthropy and Public Needs." Ann Arbor: Institute for Social Research, University of Michigan, 1974.

Rokeach, M. *The Open and Closed Mind*. New York: Basic Books, 1960.

Rokeach, M. *Beliefs, Attitudes, and Values: A Theory of Organization and Change*. San Francisco: Jossey-Bass, 1968.

Rokeach, M. "Paradoxes of Religious Belief." In W. A. Sadler, Jr. (Ed.), *Personality and Religion*. New York: Harper & Row, 1970.

Rokeach, M. *The Nature of Human Values*. New York: Free Press, 1973.

Rokkan, S. "The Comparative Study of Political Participation: Notes Toward a Perspective on Current Research." In A. Ranney (Ed.), *Essays on the Behavioral Study of Politics*. Urbana: University of Illinois Press, 1962.

Rokkan, S., and Campbell, A. "Norway and the United States of America." *International Social Science Journal*, 1960, *12*, 69–99.

Romsa, G. H. "A Method of Deriving Outdoor Recreational Activity Packages." *Journal of Leisure Research*, 1973, *5*, 34–46.

Romsa, G. H., and Girling, S. "The Identification of Outdoor Recreation Market Segments on the Basis of Frequency of Participation." *Journal of Leisure Research*, 1976, *8*, 247–255.

Roof, W. C. "Traditional Religion in Contemporary Society: A Theory of Local-Cosmopolitan Plausibility." *American Sociological Review*, 1976, *41*, 195–208.

Rooney, J. F. *A Geography of American Sport*. Reading, Mass.: Addison-Wesley, 1974.

Roper, B. W. *A Ten-Year View of Public Attitudes Toward Television and Other Mass Media, 1959–1968*. New York: Television Information Office, 1969.

Rose, A. M. "Incomplete Socialization." *Sociology and Social Research*, 1960, *44*, 244–250.

Rose, R., and Mossawir, H. "Voting and Elections: A Functional Analysis." *Political Studies*, 1967, *15*, 173–201.

Rosegrant, J. "Impact of Set and Setting on Religious Experience." *Journal for the Scientific Study of Religion*, 1976, *15*, 301–310.

Rosen, B. C. *Adolescence and Religion: The Jewish Teenager in American Society*. Cambridge, Mass.: Schenkman, 1965.

Rosen, B., and Salling, R. "Political Participation as a Function of Internal-External Locus of Control." *Psychological Reports*, 1971, *29*, 880–882.

Rosenau, J. N. *Citizenship Between Elections: An Inquiry into the Mobilizable American*. New York: Free Press, 1974.

Rosengren, K. E. "Uses and Gratifications: A Paradigm Outlined." In J. G. Blumler and E. Katz (Eds.), *The Uses of Mass Communications*. Beverly Hills, Calif.: Sage, 1974.

Rosengren, K. E., and Windahl, S. "Mass Media Consumption as a Functional Alternative." In D. McQuail (Ed.), *Sociology of Mass Communications*. Middlesex, England: Penguin Books, 1972.

Rosenhan, D. "The Natural Socialization of Altruistic Autonomy." In J. R. Macaulay and L. Berkowitz (Eds.), *Altruism and Helping Behavior*. New York: Academic Press, 1970.

Rosenhan, D., and White, G. "Observation and Rehearsal as Determinants of Prosocial Behavior." *Journal of Personality and Social Psychology*, 1967, *5*, 424–431.

Rosenthal, J. *The Purchase of Paradise: Gift-Giving and the Aristocracy, 1307–1485*. London: Routledge & Kegan Paul, 1972.

Rosenthal, R., and Rosnow, R. L. (Eds.). *Artifact in Behavioral Research*. New York: Academic Press, 1969.

Ross, A. "Philanthropic Activity and the Business Career." *Social Forces*, 1954, *32*, 274–280.

Ross, A. *Modes of Guilt Reduction*. Unpublished doctoral dissertation, Department of Psychology, University of Minnesota, 1965.

Ross, A. "Philanthropy." In D. Sills (Ed.), *International Encyclopedia of the Social Sciences*. New York: Macmillan, 1968.

Ross, A. "Effect of Increased Responsibility on Bystander Intervention: The Presence of Children." *Journal of Personality and Social Psychology*, 1971, *19*, 306–310.

Rossi, P. H. *Why Families Move*. New York: Free Press, 1955.

Roszak, T. *The Making of a Counter Culture: Reflections of the Technocratic Society and Its Youthful Opposition*. New York: Doubleday, 1969.

Rude, G. *The Crowd in History*. New York: Wiley, 1964.

Rummelhart, D. E. *Introduction to Human Information Processing.* New York: Wiley, 1977.

Rushton, J. P. "Generosity in Children: Immediate and Long Term Effects of Modeling, Preaching, and Moral Judgment." *Journal of Personality and Social Psychology,* 1975, *31,* 459–466.

Russett, B. M. "Inequality and Instability: The Relation of Land Tenure to Politics." In I. K. Feierabend and others (Eds.), *Anger, Violence and Politics: Theories and Research.* Englewood Cliffs, N.J.: Prentice-Hall, 1972.

Russett, B. M., and others. *World Handbook of Political and Social Indicators.* New Haven, Conn.: Yale University Press, 1964.

Rutherford, E., and Mussen, A. P. "Generosity in Nursery School Boys." *Child Development,* 1968, *39,* 755–765.

Ruzek, S. B. *The Women's Health Movement.* New York: Praeger, 1978.

Ryan, M. "News Content, Geographical Origin and Perceived Media Credibility." *Journalism Quarterly,* 1973, *50,* 312–318.

Salisbury, R. H. "Research on Political Participation." *American Journal of Political Science,* 1975, *19,* 323–341.

Salisbury, W. S. "Religious Identity and Religious Behavior of the Sons and Daughters of Religious Intermarriage." *Review of Religious Research,* 1970, *11,* 128–135.

Sallach, D. L., Babchuk, N., and Booth, A. "Social Involvement and Political Activity: Another View." *Social Science Quarterly,* 1972, *52,* 874–892.

Samuelson, M., Carter, R. F., and Ruggles, W. L. "Education, Available Time and Use of the Mass Media." *Journalism Quarterly,* 1963, *40,* 491–496.

Sanford, N. *Issues in Personality Theory.* San Francisco: Jossey-Bass, 1970.

Sanford, N. "Authoritarian Personality in Contemporary Perspective." In J. N. Knutsen (Ed.), *Handbook of Political Psychology.* San Francisco: Jossey-Bass, 1973.

Sarason, I. G., Smith, R. E., and Diener, E. "Personality Research: Components of Variance Attributable to the Person and Situation." *Journal of Personality and Social Psychology,* 1975, *32,* 199–204.

Sarbin, T. R., and Allen, V. L. "Role Theory." In G. Lindzey and E. Aronson (Eds.), *The Handbook of Social Psychology.* (2nd ed.) Vol. 1. Reading, Mass.: Addison-Wesley, 1968.

Schafer, W., and Rehberg, R. "Athletic Participation, College Aspirations, and College Encouragement." *Pacific Sociological Review,* 1970, *13,* 182–186.

Schendel, J. "Psychological Differences Between Athletes and Non-

Participants at Three Educational Levels." *Research Quarterly*, 1965, *36*, 52–67.

Scherer, R. P. "The Church as a Formal Organization." In D. H. Smith, R. D. Reddy, and B. R. Baldwin (Eds.), *Voluntary Action Research, 1972*. Lexington, Mass.: Heath, 1972.

Schevitz, J. M. "The Militarized Society and the Weapons-Makers." *Sociological Inquiry*, 1970, *40*, 49–60.

Schiffman, L. G., and Kanuk, L. I. *Consumer Behavior*. Englewood Cliffs, N.J.: Prentice-Hall, 1978.

Schilt, T. "Muziekkorps en Band, Twe Vormen van Sociale Participatie" ("Marching Band and Rock Group: Two Forms of Social Participation"). *Sociologische Gids*, 1969, *16*, 228–237.

Schmitt, D. E. (Ed.). *Dynamics of the Third World: Political and Social Change*. Cambridge, Mass.: Winthrop, 1974.

Schmitt, R. L. *The Reference Other Orientation: An Extension of the Reference Group Concept*. Carbondale, Ill.: Southern Illinois University Press, 1972.

Schopler, J. "An Attribution Analysis of Some Determinants of Reciprocating a Benefit." In J. R. Macaulay and L. Berkowitz (Eds.), *Altruism and Helping Behavior*. New York: Academic Press, 1970.

Schopler, J., and Thompson, V. D. "Role Attribution Processes in Mediating Amount of Reciprocity for a Favor." *Journal of Personality and Social Psychology*, 1968, *10*, 243–250.

Schramm, W. *Mass Media and National Development*. Stanford, Calif.: Stanford University Press, 1964.

Schramm, W. *Men, Messages, and Media*. New York: Harper & Row, 1973.

Schramm, W., and Carter, R. "Effectiveness of a Political Telethon." *Public Opinion Quarterly*, 1959, *23*, 121–126.

Schramm, W., Lyle, J., and Parker, E. *Television in the Lives of Our Children*. Stanford, Calif.: Stanford University Press, 1961.

Schramm, W., Lyle, J., and Pool, I. de S. *The People Look at Educational Television*. Stanford, Calif.: Stanford University Press, 1963.

Schuman, H., and Johnson, M. P. "Attitudes and Behavior." In A. Inkeles, J. Coleman, and N. Smelser (Eds.), *Annual Review of Sociology*. Vol. 2. Palo Alto, Calif.: Annual Reviews, 1976.

Schwartz, D. *Political Alienation and Political Behavior*. Chicago: Aldine, 1973.

Schwartz, M., and Stryker, S. *Deviance, Selves and Others*. Washington, D.C.: American Sociological Association, 1971.

Schwartz, R. *Private Philanthropic Contributions: An Economic Analysis*. Unpublished doctoral dissertation, Department of Economics, Columbia University, 1966.

Schwartz, R. "Personal Philanthropic Contributions." *Journal of Political Economy*, 1970, *78*, 1264–1291.

Schwartz, S. H. "Elicitation of Moral Obligation and Self-Sacrificing Behavior." *Journal of Personality and Social Psychology*, 1970a, *15*, 283–293.

Schwartz, S. H. "Moral Decision Making and Behavior." In J. R. Macaulay and L. Berkowitz (Eds.), *Altruism and Helping Behavior*. New York: Academic Press, 1970b.

Schwartz, S. H. "Normative Explanations of Helping Behavior: A Critique, A Proposal and Empirical Test." *Journal of Experimental Social Psychology*, 1973, *9*, 349–364.

Schwartz, S. H. "Awareness of Interpersonal Consequences, Responsibility Denial and Volunteering." *Journal of Personality and Social Psychology*, 1974, *30*, 57–63.

Schwartz, S. H., and Clausen, C. "Responsibility, Norms and Helping in an Emergency." *Journal of Personality and Social Psychology*, 1970, *11*, 299–310.

Scott, E. M. "Personality and Movie Preference." *Psychological Reports*, 1957, *3*, 17–19.

Scott, E. M. *An Arena for Happiness*. Springfield, Ill.: Thomas, 1971.

Scott, J. *The Athletic Revolution*. New York: Free Press, 1971.

Scott, R. A., and Douglas, J. D. *Theoretical Perspectives on Deviance*. New York: Basic Books, 1972.

Searing, D. D., Schwartz, J. J., and Lind, A. E. "The Structuring Principle: Political Socialization and Belief Systems." *American Political Science Review*, 1973, *67*, 415–432.

Searing, D. D., Wright, G., and Rabinowitz, G. "The Primacy Principle: Attitude Change and Political Socialization." *British Journal of Political Science*, 1976, *6*, 83–113.

Sears, D., "The Paradox of De Facto Selective Exposure Without Preferences for Supportive Information." In R. Abelson and others (Eds.), *Theories of Cognitive Consistency*. Chicago: Rand McNally, 1968.

Sears, D. "Political Socialization." In F. I. Greenstein and N. Polsby (Eds.), *Handbook of Political Science*. Vol. 2. Reading, Mass.: Addison-Wesley, 1975.

Sears, D., and Freedman, J. "Selective Exposure to Information: A Critical Review." *Public Opinion Quarterly*, 1967, *31*, 194–213.

Sears, D., and McConahay, J. B. *The Politics of Violence*. Boston: Houghton Mifflin, 1973.

Sechrest, L., "Personality." In M. R. Rosenzweig and L. W. Porter (Eds.), *Annual Review of Psychology*. Vol. 27. Palo Alto, Calif.: Annual Reviews, 1976.

Seeley, J., Sim, R., and Loosley, E. *Crestwood Heights*. New York: Wiley, 1963.

Seeley, J., and others. *Community Chest*. Toronto, Canada: University of Toronto Press, 1957.

Seeman, M. "On the Meaning of Alienation." *American Sociological Review*, 1959, *24*, 783–791.

Seeman, M. "Alienation and Engagement." In A. Campbell and P. Converse (Eds.), *The Human Meaning of Social Change*. New York: Russell Sage Foundation, 1972.

Sennott, R. *Egoism and Philanthropy*. Unpublished doctoral dissertation, Department of Sociology, University of Pennsylvania, 1971.

Senters, J. M. "A Function of Uncertainty and Stakes in Recreation." *Pacific Sociological Review*, 1971, *14*, 259–269.

Sermat, V., and Gregorovich, R. P. "The Effect of Experimental Manipulation on Cooperative Behavior in a Chicken Game." *Psychonomic Science*, 1966, *4*, 435–436.

Sessoms, H. D. "An Analysis of the Selected Variables Affecting Outdoor Recreational Patterns." *Social Forces*, 1963, *42*, 112–115.

Sessoms, H. D., and Oakley, S. R. "Recreation, Leisure and the Alcoholic." *Journal of Leisure Research*, 1969, *1*, 21–32.

Seward, G. H., and Williamson, R. C. (Eds.). *Sex Roles in Changing Society*. New York: Random House, 1970.

Shafer, E. L., Hamilton, J. F., and Schmidt, E. A. "Natural Landscape Preferences: A Predictive Model." *Journal of Leisure Research*, 1969, *1*, 1–19.

Shafer, E. L., and Tooby, M. "Landscape Preferences: An International Replication." *Journal of Leisure Research*, 1972, *4*, 60–65.

Shapiro, D., and Crider, A. "Psychophysiological Approaches in Social Psychology." In G. Lindzey and E. Aronson (Eds.), *The Handbook of Social Psychology*. (2nd ed.) Reading, Mass.: Addison-Wesley, 1969.

Shapiro, M. S. *Tzedaka—An Aspect of Jewish Uniqueness*. New York: Council of Jewish Federations and Welfare Funds, 1966.

Sharon, A. T. "Racial Differences in Newspaper Readership." *Public Opinion Quarterly*, 1973–74a, *37*, 611–617.

Sharon, A. T. "What Do Adults Read?" *Reading Research Quarterly*, 1973–74b, *9*, 148–169.

Shaskolsky, L. "Volunteerism in Disaster Situations." Preliminary Paper No. 1. Columbus, Ohio: Disaster Research Center, 1967.

Shaw, E. F. "Media Credibility: Taking the Measure of a Measure." *Journalism Quarterly*, 1973, *50*, 306–311.

Shaw, M. E., and Wright, J. W. *Scales for the Measurement of Attitudes*. New York: McGraw-Hill, 1967.

Sheehy, G. *Passages: Predictable Crises of Adult Life*. New York: Dutton, 1974.

Sheinkopf, K. G., Atkin, C. K., and Bowen, L. "How Political Party Workers Respond to Political Advertising." *Journalism Quarterly*, 1973, *50*, 334-339.

Sherif, M., and Sherif, C. A. (Eds.), *Interdisciplinary Relationship in the Social Sciences*. Chicago: Aldine, 1969.

Sherman, J. A. *On the Psychology of Women: A Survey of Empirical Studies*. Springfield, Ill.: Thomas, 1971.

Sheth, J. N. (Ed.). *Models of Buyer Behavior*. New York: Harper & Row, 1974.

Shively, W. P. "Voting Stability and the Nature of Party Attachments in the Weimar Republic." *American Political Science Review*, 1972, *66*, 1203-1225.

Shuttleworth, F. K., and May, M. A. *The Social Conduct and Attitudes of Movie Fans*. New York: Macmillan, 1933.

Sieber, S. D. "Toward a Theory of Role Accumulation." *American Sociological Review*. 1974, *39*, 567-578.

Sillitoe, K. K. *The Pilot National Recreation Study. Report No. 1*. Keele, England: University Press and the British Travel Association, 1967.

Sillitoe, K. K. *Planning for Leisure*. London: Governmental Social Survey, Her Majesty's Stationery Office, 1969.

Sills, D. *The Volunteers*. New York: Free Press, 1957.

Silverman, I. *The Human Subject in the Psychological Laboratory*. New York: Pergamon, 1976.

Simmonds, R. B., Richardson, J. T., and Harder, M. W. "Jesus Movement: Adjective Check List Assessment." *Journal for the Scientific Study of Religion*, 1976, *15*, 323-337.

Simon, H. A. "Motivational and Emotional Controls of Cognition." *Psychological Review*, 1967, *74*, 28-39.

Skilling, C. "Charitable Contributions." *Tax Lawyer*, 1970, *23*, 35-39.

Skinner, B. F. *Science and Human Behavior*. New York: Free Press, 1965.

Skinner, B. F. *Contingencies of Reinforcement*. Englewood Cliffs, N.J.: Prentice-Hall, 1969.

Skjelsbeck, K. "The Growth of International Non-Governmental Organizations in the Twentieth Century." In D. H. Smith (Ed.), *Voluntary Action Research, 1973*. Lexington, Mass.: Heath, 1973.

Sloan, A. K., *Citizen Participation in Transportation Planning: The Boston Experience*. Cambridge, Mass.: Ballinger, 1974.

Slovic, P., Fischhoff, B., and Lichtenstein, S. "Behavioral Decision Theory." In M. R. Rosenzweig and L. W. Porter (Eds.), *Annual Review of Psychology*. Vol. 28. Palo Alto, Calif.: Anuual Reviews, 1977.

Slusher, H. S. "Personality and Intelligence Characteristics of Selected High School Athletes and Nonathletes." *Research Quarterly* (AAHPER), 1964, *35*, 539-545.

Smith, A. *Powers of the Mind.* New York: Ballantine Books, 1976.

Smith, D. H. "The Religious Behavior of Latin American University Students: An Explanatory Survey." Unpublished manuscript, Boston College, no date.

Smith, D. H. "A Psychological Model of Individual Participation in Formal Voluntary Organizations; Application to Some Chilean Data." *American Journal of Sociology,* 1966, 72, 249–266.

Smith, D. H. "Evidence for a General Activity Syndrome." *Proceedings,* 77th Annual Convention of the American Psychological Association, Washington, D.C., 1969.

Smith, D. H. *Voluntary Activity in Eight Massachusetts Towns.* Draft of unpublished manuscript, Boston College, 1972.

Smith, D. H. "The Impact of the Voluntary Sector on Society." In D. H. Smith (Ed.), *Voluntary Action Research: 1973.* Lexington, Mass.: Heath, 1973a.

Smith, D. H. *Latin American Student Activism.* Lexington, Mass.: Heath, 1973b.

Smith, D. H. "Modernization and the Emergence of Volunteer Organizations." In D. H. Smith (Ed.), *Voluntary Action Research: 1973.* Lexington, Mass.: Heath, 1973c.

Smith, D. H. "Preface." In D. H. Smith (Ed.), *Voluntary Action Research: 1973.* Lexington, Mass.: Heath, 1973d.

Smith, D. H. "Voluntary Action and Voluntary Groups." In A. Inkeles, J. Coleman, and N. Smelser (Eds.), *Annual Review of Sociology.* Vol. 1. Palo Alto, Calif.: Annual Reviews, 1975.

Smith, D. H. "Determinants of Church Attendance: A Review and a Model." Unpublished paper, Department of Sociology, Boston College, 1979a.

Smith, D. H. "Explaining the Apparent Direct Effects of Sociodemographic Variables by Intervening Social Psychological Variables: An Example from the Study of Voluntary Action." Unpublished paper, 1979b.

Smith, D. H. "Political Psychology and the Proliferation of Interdisciplinary Fields in the Social-Behavioral Sciences." Unpublished paper, Department of Sociology, Boston College, 1979c.

Smith, D. H. "The Psychopathology of Human Decisions: In by Image, Out by Reality." Unpublished paper, Department of Sociology, Boston College, 1979d.

Smith, D. H. "Wave-Particle Duality and the Inability of Social-Behavioral Scientists to Accept Duality in Theory and Research." Unpublished paper, Department of Sociology, Boston College, 1979e.

Smith, D. H. "Why Have the Human Sciences Lagged the Physical and

Biological Sciences in Their Intellectual Advancement?" Unpublished paper, Department of Sociology, Boston College, 1980.

Smith, D. H., and Fisher, A. "Toward a Comparative Theory of the Incidence and Prevalence of Voluntary Associations in Territorial Social Systems." Paper presented at annual meeting of the Association for Asian Studies, Washington, D.C., 1971.

Smith, D. H., and Fried, M. "The General Activity Syndrome. I: Evidence of Positive Covariation Among Valued Discretionary Activities." Unpublished paper, Boston College, 1979a.

Smith, D. H., and Fried, M. "The General Activity Syndrome. II: Correlates of the Primary Pattern and Its Variations." Unpublished paper, Boston College, 1979b.

Smith, D. H., and Inkeles, A. "The OM Scale: A Comparative Socio-Psychological Measure of Individual Modernity." *Sociometry*, 1966, *29*, 353–377.

Smith, D. H., and Inkeles, A. "Individual Modernizing Experiences and Psycho-Social Modernity Scores: Validation of the OM Scales in Six Developing Countries." *International Journal of Comparative Sociology*, 1975, *16*, 155–173.

Smith, D. H., and Reddy, R. D. "An Overview of the Determinants of Individual Participation in Organized Voluntary Action." In D. H. Smith, R. D. Reddy, and B. R. Baldwin, (Eds.), *Voluntary Action Research: 1972*. Lexington, Mass.: Heath, 1972a.

Smith, D. H., and Reddy, R. D. "Contextual and Organizational Determinants of Individual Participation in Organized Voluntary Action." In D. H. Smith, R. D. Reddy, and B. R. Baldwin (Eds.), *Voluntary Action Research: 1972*. Lexington, Mass.: Heath, 1972b.

Smith, D. H., Reddy, R. D., and Baldwin, B. R. "Types of Voluntary Action: A Definitional Essay." In D. H. Smith, R. D. Reddy, and B. R. Baldwin (Eds.), *Voluntary Action Research: 1972*. Lexington, Mass.: Heath, 1972a.

Smith, D. H., Reddy, R. D., and Baldwin, B. R. (Eds.). *Voluntary Action Research: 1972*. Lexington, Mass.: Heath, 1972b.

Smith, K. U. *Work Theory and Economic Behavior*. Bloomington: Foundation for Economic and Business Studies, Indiana University, 1962.

Smith, M., and Nustrom, W. C. "A Study of Social Participation and of Leisure Time Leaders and Nonleaders." *Journal of Applied Psychology*, 1937, *21*, 251–259.

Smith, M. B. "A Map for the Analysis of Personality and Politics." *Journal of Social Issues*, 1968, *24*, 15–28.

Snook, J. "Social Indicators and Religious Indicators." *Review of Religious Research*, 1973, *14*, 77–90.

Snook, J. "An Alternative to Church Sect." *Journal for the Scientific Study of Religion*, 1974, *13*, 191–204.

Snyder, E. E., "A Longitudinal Analysis of the Relationship Between High School Student Values, Social Participation, and Educational-Occupational Achievement." *Sociology of Education*, 1967, *42*, 261–270.

Snyder, E. E., and Kivlin, J. E. "Women Athletes and Aspects of Psychological Well-Being and Body Image." *Research Quarterly*, 1975, *46*, 191–199.

Snyder, E. E., and Spreitzer, E. "Orientations Toward Work and Leisure as Predictors of Sports Involvement." *Research Quarterly*, 1974a, *45*, 398–406.

Snyder, E. E., and Spreitzer, E. "Sociology of Sport: An Overview." *The Sociological Quarterly*, 1974b, *15*, 467–487.

Snyder, E. E., and Spreitzer, E. "Correlates of Sport Participation among Adolescent Girls." *Research Quarterly*, 1976, *47*, 804–809.

Sommer, R. *Personal Space*. Englewood Cliffs, N.J.: Prentice-Hall, 1969.

Sorokin, P. A. "Affiliative and Hostile Tendencies in College Students." In P. A. Sorokin (Ed.), *Explorations in Altruistic Love and Behavior: A Symposium*. Boston: Beacon Press, 1950.

Sorokin, P. A. *Social and Cultural Dynamics*. Boston: Horizon Books, 1957.

Sorokin, P. A., and Berger, C. Q. *Time Budgets of Human Behavior*. Cambridge, Mass.: Harvard University Press, 1939.

Soule, G. "The Economics of Leisure." In P. F. Douglass (Ed.), *Recreation in the Age of Automation. Annals of the American Academy of Political and Social Sciences*, 1957, *313*, 16–24.

Soyka, F., and Edmunds, A. *The Ion Effect*. New York: Dutton, 1977.

Sparer, G., Dines, G. B., and Smith, D. "Consumer Participation in OEO-Assisted Neighborhood Health Centers." *American Journal of Public Health*, 1970, *60*, 1091–1102.

Spenner, K. I., and Featherman, D. L. "Achievement Ambitions." In R. H. Turner, J. Coleman, and R. C. Fox (Eds.), *Annual Review of Sociology*. Vol. 4. Palo Alto, Calif.: Annual Reviews, 1978.

Spiegel, H.B.C. *Citizen Participation in Urban Development*. Vol. 1: *Concepts and Issues*. Washington, D.C.: NTL Institute for Applied Behavioral Science, 1968.

Spiegel, H.B.C. *Citizen Participation in Urban Development*. Vol. 2: *Cases and Programs*. Washington, D.C.: NTL Institute for Applied Behavioral Science, 1969.

Spiegel, H.B.C. "Citizen Participation in Federal Programs: A Review." In D. H. Smith (Ed.), *Voluntary Action Research: 1973*. Lexington, Mass.: Heath, 1973.

Spiegel, H.B.C. (Ed.). *Citizen Participation in Urban Development.* Vol. 3: *Decentralization.* Fairfax, Va.: Learning Resources Corporation/NTL, 1974a.

Spiegel, H.B.C. *Not for Work Alone: Services at the Workplace.* New York: Urban Research Center, Hunter College of the City University of New York, 1974b.

Spierer, H. *Major Transitions in the Human Life Cycle.* New York: Academy for Educational Development, 1977.

Spitzer, S., Couch, C., and Stratton, J. *The Assessment of Self.* Iowa City, Iowa: Escort Sernoll, 1971.

Spreitzer, E., and Snyder, E. "Socialization into Sport: An Exploratory Path Analysis." *Research Quarterly,* 1976, *47,* 238-245.

Srole, L. "Social Dysfunction, Personality, and Social Distance Attitudes." Paper presented at annual meeting of the American Sociological Society, Chicago, 1951.

Srole, L. "Social Integration and Certain Corollaries: An Exploratory Study." *American Sociological Review.* 1956, *21,* 709-716.

Staats, A. W. "Social Behavioralism and Human Motivation: Principles of the Attitude-Reinforcer-Discriminative System." In A. C. Greenwald, T. C. Brock, and T. M. Ostrom (Eds.), *Psychological Foundations of Attitudes.* New York: Academic Press, 1968.

Stallings, R. "Hospital Adaptations to Disaster: Flow Models of Intensive Technologies." *Human Organization,* 1970, *29,* 294-302.

Stallings, R. "Differential Response of Hospital Personnel to a Disaster." *Mass Emergencies,* 1975, *1,* 44-54.

Stallings, R. "The Structural Patterns of Four Types of Organizations in Disaster." In E. L. Quarantelli (Ed.), *Disasters: Theory and Research.* Beverly Hills, Calif.: Sage, 1977.

Stanford, N., and Comstock, C. *Sanctions for Evil.* Boston: Beacon Press, 1971.

Stanwick, M. E. *Patterns of Participation.* Boston: Institute for Responsive Education, 1975.

Starck, K. "Media Credibility in Finland: A Cross-National Study." *Journalism Quarterly,* 1969, *46,* 790-795.

Stark, R. "Psychopathology and Religious Commitment." *Review of Religious Research,* 1971, *12,* 165-176.

Staub, E. "A Child in Distress: The Effects of Focusing Responsibility of Children on their Attempts to Help." *Developmental Psychology,* 1970a, *2,* 152-154.

Staub, E. "A Child in Distress: The Influence of Age and Number of Witnesses on Children's Attempts to Help." *Journal of Personality and Social Psychology,* 1970b, *14,* 130-140.

Staub, E. "A Child in Distress: The Influence of Modeling and Nurturance on Children's Attempts to Help." *Developmental Psychology*, 1971a, *5*, 124–133.

Staub, E. "The Use of Role Playing and Induction in Children's Learning of Helping and Sharing Behavior." *Child Development*, 1971b, *42*, 805–817.

Staub, E. "The Effects of Persuasion and Modeling on Delay of Gratification." *Developmental Psychology*, 1972a, *6*, 168–177.

Staub, E. "Instigation to Goodness: The Role of Social Norms and Interpersonal Influence." *Journal of Social Issues*, 1972b, *28*, 131–151.

Staub, E. "Helping a Distressed Person: Social, Personality, and Stimulus Determinants." In L. Berkowitz (Ed.), *Advances in Experimental Social Psychology*. Vol. 7. New York: Academic Press, 1974.

Staub, E. *The Development of Prosocial Behavior in Children*. Morristown, N.J.: General Learning Press, 1975a.

Staub, E. "Personality, the Situation, and the Determinants of Social Behavior." Unpublished manuscript, University of Massachusetts, 1975b.

Staub, E. "To Rear a Prosocial Child: Reasoning, Learning by Doing, and Learning by Teaching Others." In D. DePalma and J. Folley (Eds.), *Moral Development*. New York: Halstead Press, 1975c.

Staub, E. *Positive Social Behavior and Morality*. Vol. 1: *Social and Personal Influences*. New York: Academic Press, 1978.

Staub, E. *Positive Social Behavior and Morality*. Vol. 2: *Socialization and Development*. New York: Academic Press, 1979.

Staub, E., and Baer, R. S., Jr. "Stimulus Characteristics of a Sufferer and Difficulty of Escape as Determinants of Helping." *Journal of Personality and Social Psychology*, 1974, *30*, 279–285.

Stebbins, C. *Achievement in Sport as a Function of Personality and Social Situation*. Unpublished master's thesis, Department of Physical Education, University of Wisconsin, 1969.

Steele, P. D., and Zurcher, L. A., Jr. "Leisure Sports as 'Ephemeral Roles': An Exploratory Study." *Pacific Sociological Review*, 1973, *16*, 345–356.

Steggert, F. X. *Community Action Groups and City Governments*. Cambridge, Mass.: Ballinger, 1975.

Stein, A. H., and Freidrich, L. K., with Vondracek, F. "Television Content and Young Children's Behavior." In J. P. Murray, E. A. Rubenstein, and G. A. Comstock, *Television and Social Behavior*. Vol. 2: *Television and Social Learning*. Washington, D.C.: National Institute of Mental Health, 1972.

Stein, M. R. *The Eclipse of Community*. New York: Harper & Row, 1960.

Steiner, J. F. *Americans at Play*. New York: Arno Press, 1970. (Originally published 1933).

Stensaasen, S. "School Sport on a Voluntary Basis." *International Review of Sports Sociology*, 1974, *9*, 33–44.

Stockfelt, T. "Psychological Analyses of Swedish Elite Athletes." In G. Kenyon (Ed.), *Contemporary Psychology of Sport*. Chicago: Athletic Institue, 1970.

Stöckman, P. "More Leisure for Employed Mothers." *Society and Leisure*, 1974, *6*, 141–153.

Stokols, D. "Origins and Directions of Environment-Behavior Research." In D. Stokols (Ed.), *Psychological Perspectives on Environment and Behavior*. New York: Plenum, 1977.

Stone, A. A., and Onqué, G. C. *Longitudinal Studies of Child Personality*. Cambridge, Mass.: Harvard University Press, 1959.

Stone, G. P. "Some Meanings of American Sport." *60th Proceedings* of the annual meeting of the College Physical Education Association, Columbus, Ohio, 1957.

Stone, G. P. "Some Meanings of American Sport: An Extended View." In G. S. Kenyon (Ed.), *Aspects of Contemporary Sport Sociology*. Chicago, Ill.: Athletic Institute, 1968.

Stotland, E. "Exploratory Investigations of Empathy." In L. Berkowitz (Ed.), *Advances in Experimental Social Psychology*. Vol. 4. New York: Academic Press, 1969.

Straus, M. A. *Family Measurement Techniques*. Minneapolis: University of Minnesota Press, 1969.

Strauss, A. *Mirrors and Masks: The Search for Identity*. New York: Free Press, 1959.

Streicher, L. H., and Bonney, N. L. "Children Talk About Television." *Journal of Communication*, 1974, *23*, 54–61.

Strommen, M. P. (Ed.). *Research on Religious Development: A Comprehensive Handbook*. New York: Hawthorn Books, 1971.

Struening, E. L., and Richardson, A. H. "A Factor Analytic Exploration of the Alienation, Anomie and Authoritarianism Domain." *American Sociological Review*, 1965, *30*, 768–776.

Suchman, E. A. "Accidents and Social Deviance." *Journal of Health and Social Behavior*, 1970, *11*, 4–15.

Super, D. E., and others. *Career Development: Self-Concept Theory*. New York: College Entrance Examination Board, 1963.

Survey Research Center. *1960 Election Study*. Ann Arbor: Interuniversity Consortium for Political Research, University of Michigan, 1960.

Survey Research Center. *1964 Election Study*. Ann Arbor: Interuniversity Consortium for Political Research, University of Michigan, 1964.

Survey Research Center. *1968 Election Study*. Ann Arbor: Interuniversity Consortium for Political Research, University of Michigan, 1968.

Sussman, L. "Mass Political Letter Writing in America: The Growth of an Institution." *Public Opinion Quarterly,* 1959, *13,* 203–212.

Sutherland, E. H. *Principles of Criminology.* (3rd ed.) New York: Lippincott, 1939.

Sutherland, E. H., and Cressey, D. R. *Criminology.* (8th ed.) Philadelphia: Lippincott, 1970.

Sutherland, J. W. *A General Systems Philosophy for the Social and Behavioral Sciences.* New York: George Braziller, 1973.

Sutton-Smith, B. "Game Involvement in Adults." *Journal of Social Psychology,* 1963, *60,* 15–30.

Sutton-Smith, B., and Rosenberg, B. G. "Sixty Years of Historical Change in the Game Preferences of American Children." *Journal of American Folklore,* 1961, *74,* 17–46.

Symonds, P. M. *The Ego and the Self.* New York: Appleton-Century-Crofts, 1951.

Szalai, A. "Appendix to Multinational Comparative Social Research." *American Behavioral Scientist,* 1966, *10,* 3–8.

Szalai, A., and others. *The Use of Time.* The Hague, Netherlands: Mouton, 1972.

Taft, P., and Ross, P. "American Labor Violence: Its Causes, Character and Outcome." In H. D. Graham and T. R. Gurr (Eds.), *The History of Violence in America.* New York: Bantam, 1969.

Tan, A., and Vaughn, P. "Mass Media Exposure, Public Affairs Knowledge, and Black Militancy." *Journalism Quarterly,* 1976, *53,* 271–279.

Tannenbaum, A. S., and Bachman, J. G. "Structural versus Individual Effects." *The American Journal of Sociology,* 1964, *44,* 585–595.

Tanter, R., and Midlarsky, M. "A Theory of Revolution." *Journal of Conflict Resolution,* 1967, *11,* 264–280.

Tarrow, S. "The Urban-Rural Change in Involvement: The Case of France." *American Political Science Review,* 1971, *65,* 341–359.

Tart, C. (Ed.). *Altered States of Consciousness: A Book of Readings.* (2nd ed.) New York: Doubleday, 1972.

Tart, C. *States of Consciousness.* New York: Dutton, 1975.

Tatham, R. L., and Dornoff, R. J. "Market Segmentation for Outdoor Recreation Research." *Journal of Leisure Research,* 1971, *3,* 5–16.

Taussig, M. K. *The Charitable Contributions Deduction in the Federal Personal Income Tax.* Unpublished doctoral dissertation, Department of Economics, Massachusetts Institute of Technology, 1965.

Taussig, M. K. "Economic Aspects of the Personal Income Tax Treatment of Charitable Contributions." *National Tax Journal,* 1967, *20,* 1–19.

Taylor, C. E., and Knudson, D. M. "Area Preferences of Midwestern Campers." *Journal of Leisure Research,* 1973, *5,* 39–48.

Taylor, J. B., Zurcher, L. A., and Key, W. H. *Tornado: A Community Responds to Disaster.* Seattle: University of Washington Press, 1970.

Taylor, V. "The Delivery of Mental Health Services in the Xenia Tornado: A Collective Behavior Analysis of an Emergency System Response." Unpublished doctoral dissertation, Department of Sociology, Ohio State University, 1967.

Taylor, V., Ross, A., and Quarantelli, E. L. *Delivery of Mental Health Services in Disasters: The Xenia Tornado.* Columbus, Ohio: Disaster Research Center, 1976.

Tedin, K. L. "The Influence of Parents on the Political Attitudes of Adolescents." *American Political Science Review,* 1974, *67,* 1579–1592.

Tedin, K. L., Brady, D. W., and Vedlitz, A. "Sex Differences in Political Attitudes and Behavior: The Case for Situational Factors." *Journal of Politics,* 1977, *39,* 448–456.

Templeton, F. "Alienation and Political Participation." *Public Opinion Quarterly,* 1966, *30,* 249–261.

Terman, L. M., Burks, B. S., and Jensen, D. W. *Genetic Studies of Genius: III. The Promise of Youth: Follow-Up Studies of a Thousand Gifted Children.* Stanford, Calif.: Stanford University Press, 1930.

Terman, L. M., and Oden, M. H. *Genetic Studies of Genius: IV. The Gifted Child Grows Up: Twenty-Five Years Follow-Up on the Superior Group.* Stanford, Calif.: Stanford University Press, 1947.

Terman, L. M., and Oden, M. H. *Genetic Studies of Genius: V. The Gifted Group at Mid-Life.* Stanford, Calif.: Stanford University Press, 1959.

Terman, L. M., and others. *Genetic Studies of Genius: I. Mental and Physical Traits of a Thousand Gifted Children.* Stanford, Calif.: Stanford University Press, 1925.

Tessler, M. A. "The Application of Western Theories and Measure of Political Participation to a Single-Party North African State." *Comparative Political Studies,* 1972, *5,* 175–192.

Tessler, R. C., and Schwartz, S. H. "Help Seeking, Self-Esteem, and Achievement Motivation: An Attributional Analysis." *Journal of Personality and Social Psychology,* 1972, *21,* 318–326.

Thayer, R. L., and others. "Validation of a Natural Landscape Preference Model as a Predictor of Perceived Landscape Beauty in Photographs." *Journal of Leisure Research,* 1976, *8,* 292–299.

Thelen, H. A. "Tutoring by Students." *School Review,* 1969, *77,* 229–244.

Theodore, A. "The Voluntary Participation of College Students as a Catalyst for Social Change." In D. H. Smith (Ed.), *Voluntary Action Research, 1973.* Lexington, Mass: Heath, 1973.

Thibaut, J. J., and Kelley, H. H. *The Social Psychology of Groups.* New York: Wiley, 1959.

Thiessen, V. *Who Gives a Damn? A Study of Charitable Contributions.* Unpublished doctoral dissertation, Department of Economics, University of Wisconsin, 1968.

Thomas, D., and others. *Family Socialization and the Adolescent.* Lexington, Mass.: Heath, 1974.

Thompson, D. F. *The Democratic Citizen: Social Science and Democratic Theory in the Twentieth Century.* Cambridge, England: Cambridge University Press, 1970.

Thompson, J.A.F., "Piety and Charity in Late Medieval London." *Journal of Ecclesiastical History,* 1965, *16,* 178–195.

Thompson, W. E., and Horton, J. E. "Political Alienation as a Force in Political Action." *Social Forces,* 1960, *38,* 190–195.

Thornton, R., and Nardi, P. M. "The Dynamics of Role Acquisition." *American Journal of Sociology,* 1975, *80,* 870–885.

Tichenor, P. J., Donohue, G. A., and Olien, C. N. "Mass Media and Differential Growth in Knowledge." *Public Opinion Quarterly,* 1970, *34,* 158–170.

Tichenor, P. J., and others. "Community Issues, Confict, and Public Affairs Knowledge." In P. Clarke (Ed.), *New Models for Mass Communication Research.* Beverly Hills, Calif.: Sage, 1973.

Tierney, K., and Taylor, V. "EMS Delivery in Mass Emergencies: Preliminary Research Findings." *Mass Emergencies,* 1977, *2,* 151–157.

Tilly, C. "Collective Violence in European Perspective." In H.G. Davis and T. R. Gurr (Eds.), *The History of Violence in America.* New York: Praeger, 1969.

Tingsten, H. *Political Behavior Studies in Election Statistics.* London: King, 1937.

Tinsley, H.E.A., Barrett, J. C., and Kass, R. A. "Leisure Activities and Need Satisfaction." *Journal of Leisure Research,* 1977, *2,* 110–120.

Titmuss, R. *The Gift Relationship: From Human Blood to Social Policy.* New York: Random House, 1972.

Tomeh, A. K. "Formal Voluntary Organizations: Participation, Correlates, and Interrelationships." *Sociological Inquiry,* 1973, *43,* 89–122.

Tomeh, A. K. "Birth Order, Club Membership and Mass Media Exposure." *Journal of Marriage and the Family,* 1976, *38,* 151–164.

Tompkins, S. "The Psychology of Commitment. Part 1. The Constructive Role of Violence and Suffering for the Individual and for His Society." In S. Tompkins and C. E. Izard (Eds.), *Affect, Cognition, and Personality.* New York: Springer-Verlag, 1965.

Torbert, W. R. *Being for the Most Part Puppets: Interactions Among Men's Labor, Leisure, and Politics.* Cambridge, Mass.: Schenkman, 1973.

Torney, J. M., and Buergenthal, T. "Alternative Conceptions of Politically Relevant Socialization." Paper delivered at the International Conference of Political Socialization and Political Education, Tutzing, F.R.G., 1977.

Torney, J. V., Oppenheim, A. N., and Farnen, F. R. *Civic Education in Ten Countries.* New York: Halsted Press, 1975.

Townsend, E. J. "An Examination of Participants in Organizational, Political, Informational, and Interpersonal Activities." *Journal of Voluntary Action Research,* 1973, *2,* 200–211.

Treble, G., and Neil, J. "Folklore and Women's Participation in Sports." *Australia Journal of Physical Education,* 1972, *55,* 38–41.

Tresemer, D. "Assumptions Made about Gender Roles." In M. Millman and R. M. Kanter (Eds.), *Another Voice.* New York: Anchor Press/Doubleday, 1975.

Triandis, H. C., Malpass, R. S., and Davidson, A. R. "Psychology and Culture." In M. R. Rosenzweig and L. W. Porter (Eds.), *Annual Review of Psychology.* Vol. 24. Palo Alto, Calif.: Annual Reviews, 1973.

Triandis, H., and others (Eds.). *The Analysis of Subjective Culture.* New York: Wiley-Interscience, 1972.

Troeltsch, E. *The Social Teachings of the Christian Churches.* New York: Macmillan, 1950. (Originally published 1931.)

Troeltsch, E. *Social Teachings of the Church.* (O. Wyon, Trans.). New York: Harper & Row, 1960.

Truzzi, M. "The Occult Revival or Popular Culture: Some Random Observations on the Deviant Nouveau Witch." *Sociological Quarterly,* 1972, *13,* 16–36.

Tschudnowski, P. Paper presented at Conference on Mechanisms of Pro-Social Behavior, sponsored by the Committee of Psychological Sciences of the Polish Academy of Science, Warsaw, Poland, 1974.

Tuan, Y. *Topophilia: A Study of Environmental Perception, Attitudes and Values.* Englewood Cliffs, N.J.: Prentice-Hall, 1974.

Tuma, E., and Livson, N. "Family Socio-Economic Status and Adolescent Attitudes Toward Authority." *Child Development,* 1960, *31,* 387–399.

Tuma, N. B., and Hannan, M. T. "Approaches to the Censoring Problem in Analysis of Event Histories." In K. F. Schuessler (Ed.), *Sociological Methodology 1979.* San Francisco: Jossey-Bass, 1979.

Tuma, N. B., Hannan, M. T., and Groeneveld, L. P. "Dynamic Analysis of Event Histories." *American Journal of Sociology,* 1979, *84,* 820–854.

Turk, A. T. *Criminality and Legal Order.* Chicago: Rand McNally, 1969.

Turner, R. "The Real Self: From Institution to Impulse." *American Journal of Sociology*, 1975, *81*, 989–1016.

Turner, R., Coleman, J., and Fox, R. (Eds.). *Annual Review of Sociology*. Vol. 4. Palo Alto, Calif.: Annual Reviews, 1978.

Ulhorn, G. *Christian Charity in the Ancient Church*. New York Scribner's, 1883.

Unger, R. K. "Status, Power and Gender: An Examination of Parallelisms." In J. A. Sherman and F. Denmark (Eds.), *New Directions for Research on Women*. New York: Psychological Dimensions, 1978.

U.S. Department of Health, Education, and Welfare. *Television and Growing Up: The Impact of Televised Violence*. G. A. Comstock, and E. A. Rubenstein (Eds.), Vol. 1: *Media Content and Control;* J. P. Murray, E. A. Rubinstein, and G. A. Comstock (Eds.), Vol. 2: *Television and Social Learning;* G. A. Comstock and E. A. Rubinstein (Eds.), Vol. 3: *Television and Adolescent Aggressiveness;* E. A. Rubinstein, G. A. Comstock, and J. P. Murray (Eds.), Vol. 4: *Television in Day-to-Day Life: Patterns of Use;* G. A. Comstock, E. A. Rubinstein, and J. P. Murray (Eds.), Vol. 5: *Television's Effects: Further Explorations*. Washington, D.C.: U.S. Government Printing Office, 1972.

U.S. Department of Health, Education, and Welfare. "Summary Report: New Jersey Graduated Work Incentive Experiment." Washington, D.C.: U.S. Government Printing Office, 1973.

U.S. Department of Labor. *Americans Volunteer*. Manpower Administration, Research Monograph No. 10. Washington, D.C.: U.S. Government Printing Office. 1969.

Vaillant, G. *Adaptation to Life*. Boston: Little, Brown, 1977.

Valen, H. "The Motivation and Recruitment of Political Personnel." Paper presented at UNESCO Seminar, Bergen, Norway, 1961.

Valen, H., and Katz, D. *Political Parties in Norway*. Oslo, Norway: University of Oslo Press, 1964.

Valkonen, T. "Individual and Structural Effects in Ecological Research." In M. Dogan and S. Rokkan (Eds.), *Quantitative Ecological Analysis in the Social Sciences*. Cambridge, Mass.: M.I.T. Press, 1969.

van Meter, E. C. "Citizen Participation in the Policy Management Process." *Public Administration Review*, 1975, *35*, 804–812.

Verba, S. *Small Groups and Political Behavior*. Princeton, N.J.: Princeton University Press, 1961.

Verba, S., Ahmed, B., and Bhatt, A. *Caste, Race and Politics: A Comparative Study of India and the United States*. Beverly Hills, Calif.: Sage, 1971.

Verba, S., and Brody, R. "Participation, Policy Preference and the War in Vietnam." *Public Opinion Quarterly*, 1970, *34*, 330.

Verba, S. and Nie, N. *Participation in America: Political Democracy and Social Equality*. New York: Harper & Row, 1972.

Verba, S., Nie, N., and Kim, J. *Modes of Political Participation*. Beverly Hills, Calif.: Sage, 1971.

Verba, S., and others. "The Modes of Participation: Continuities in Research." *Comparative Political Studies*, 1973, *6*, 235–250.

Vernon, G. "The Religious 'Nones': A Neglected Category." *Journal for the Scientific Study of Religion*, 1968, *7*, 219–229.

Videbeck, R., and Knox, A. "Alternative Participatory Responses to Aging." In A. M. Rose and W. A. Peterson (Eds.), *Older People and Their Social World*. Philadelphia: Dane, 1965.

Villani, K. B. "Personality, Life Style, and Television Viewing Behavior." *Journal of Marketing Research*, 1975, *12*, 432–439.

Vinyard, D., and Sigel, R. "Newspapers and Urban Voters." *Journalism Quarterly*, 1971, *48*, 486–493.

Viver, L. "Glossolalia." Unpublished doctoral dissertation, Department of Psychiatry, University of Chicago and Union Theological Seminary, 1960.

von der Mehden, F. R. *Comparative Political Violence*. Englewood Cliffs, N.J.: Prentice-Hall, 1973.

von Feilitzen, C. "The Function Served by the Media." In R. Brown (Ed.), *Children and Television*. Beverly Hills, Calif: Sage, 1976.

Wackman, D. B., and Wartella, E. "A Review of Cognitive Development Theory and Research and the Implication for Research on Children's Responses to Television." *Communication Research*, 1977, *4*, 203–223.

Wackman, D. B., Wartella, E., and Ward, S. "Learning to Be Consumers: The Role of the Family." *Journal of Communication*, 1977, *27*, 138–151.

Wade, S. E., and Schramm, W. "The Mass Media as Sources of Public Affairs, Science and Health Knowledge." *Public Opinion Quarterly*, 1969, *33*, 197–209.

Wagner, F. W., and Donohue, T. R. "The Impact of Inflation and Recession on Urban Leisure in New Orleans." *Journal of Leisure Research*, 1976, *8*, 300–306.

Wakeman, E., Jr. "Rebellion and Revolution: The Study of Popular Movements in Chinese History." *Journal of Asian Studies*, 1977, *36*, 201–237.

Wallace, A. *Tornado in Worcester: An Explanatory Study of Individual and Community Behavior in an Extreme Situation*. Washington, D.C.: National Academy of Sciences, 1956.

Wallston, B. S. "The Effects of Sex-Role Ideology, Self-esteem, and Expected Future Interactions with an Audience on Male Help Seeking." *Sex Roles*, 1976, *2*, 353–356.

Walster, E., Walster, G. W., and Berscheid, E. *Equity: Theory and Research*. Boston: Allyn & Bacon, 1978.

Warburton, F. W., and Kane, J. E. "Personality Correlates of Sport and Physical Abilities." In J. E. Kane (Ed.), *Readings in Physical Education*. London: Physical Education Association, 1966.

Ward, S., and Wackman, D. B. "Children's Information Processing of Television Advertising." In P. Clarke (Ed.), *New Models for Mass Communication Research*. Beverly Hills, Calif.: Sage, 1973.

Ward, S., Wackman, D. B., and Wartella, E. *How Children Learn to Buy: The Development of Consumer Information Processing Skills*. Beverly Hills, Calif.: Sage, 1977.

Warner, W. K., and Rogers, D. L. "Some Correlates of Control in Voluntary Farm Organizations." *Rural Sociology*, 1971, *36*, 326–329.

Warwick, P., and Bishop, D. "A Bibliography of Literature Dealing with the General Concept of Time, Time-Related Data Analysis and Time-Budget Studies—With an Emphasis on Leisure." *Journal of Leisure Research*, 1972, *4*, 232–244.

Washnis, G. J. *Citizen Involvement in Crime Prevention*. Lexington, Mass.: Heath, 1975.

Watanuki, J. "Social Structure and Political Participation in Japan." Tokyo: Sophia University Institute of International Relations, 1972.

Watts, D. P. "Changing Conception of Competitive Sports for Girls and Women in the United States from 1880–1960." Unpublished doctoral dissertation, Department of History, University of California, Los Angeles, 1960.

Watts, W., and Free, L. A. *State of the Nation, 1974*. Washington, D.C.: Potomac Associates, 1974.

Waxman, J. "Local Broadcast Gatekeeping During Natural Disasters." *Journalism Quarterly*, 1973, *50*, 751–758.

Weaver, R. B. *Amusements and Sports in American Life*. Westport, Conn.: Greenwood Press, 1968. (Originally published 1939.)

Weaver, W. *U.S. Philanthropic Foundations*. New York: Harper & Row, 1967.

Webb, E. J., and others. *Unobtrusive Measures*. Chicago: Rand McNally, 1966.

Webb, H. "Professionalization of Attitudes Toward Play Among Adolescents." In G. S. Kenyon (Ed.), *Sociology of Sport*. Chicago: Athletic Institute, 1969.

Weber, M. *From Max Weber: Essays in Sociology*. (H. H. Gerth and C. W. Mills, Trans. and Eds.) New York: Oxford University Press, 1946.

Weber, M. *The Protestant Ethic and the Spirit of Capitalism*. (T. Parsons, Trans.) New York: Scribner's, 1958.

Weber, M. *Economy and Society*. Vol. 3. (G. Roth and C. Wittich, Eds.) New York: Bedminster Press, 1968.

Webster, M., Jr., and Sobieszek, B. *Sources of Self Evaluation: A Formal Theory of Significant Others and Social Influence*. New York: Wiley-Interscience, 1974.

Wedge, B. "Students and Political Violence: Brazil, 1964, and the Dominican Republic, 1965." In I. K. Feierabend and others (Eds.), *Anger, Violence and Politics: Theories and Research*. Englewood Cliffs, N.J.: Prentice-Hall, 1972.

Weigert, A. J., and Thomas, D. L. "Parental Support, Control and Adolescent Religiosity: An Extension of Previous Research." *Journal for the Scientific Study of Religion*, 1972, *11*, 389–393.

Weiss, C. H. "What America's Leaders Read." *Public Opinion Quarterly*, 1974, *38*, 1–22.

Weiss, R. S. *Marital Separation*. New York: Basic Books, 1975.

Weiss, W. "Effects of the Mass Media of Communication." In G. Lindzey and E. Aronson (Eds.), *The Handbook of Social Psychology*. Reading, Mass.: Addison-Wesley, 1969.

Weissberg, R. *Political Learning, Political Choice, and Democratic Leadership*. Englewood Cliffs, N.J.: Prentice-Hall, 1974.

Weissman, H. H. *Community Councils and Community Control: The Workings of Democratic Mythology*. Pittsburgh: University of Pittsburgh Press, 1970.

Welch, S. "Dimensions of Political Participation in a Canadian Sample." *Canadian Journal of Political Science*, 1975, *8*, 553–559.

Welch, S., Comer, J., and Steinman, M. "Political Participation Among Mexican Americans: An Exploratory Examination." *Social Science Quarterly*, 1973, *53*, 799–813.

Weller, J. and Quarantelli, E. L. "Neglected Characteristics of Collective Behavior." *American Journal of Sociology*, 1973, *19*, 665–686.

Wells, L., and Marwell, G. *Self-Esteem: Its Conceptualization and Its Measurement*. Beverly Hills, Calif.: Sage, 1976.

Wenner, L. "Functional Analysis of TV Viewing for Older Adults." *Journal of Broadcasting*, 1976, *20*, 77–88.

Westerhoff, J. H., III. "A Changing Focus: Toward an Understanding of Religious Socialization." *Andover Newton Quarterly*, 1973, *14*, 18–29.

Westerhoff, J. H., III, and Neville, G. K. *Generation to Generation: Conversations on Religious Education and Culture*. Philadelphia: United Church Press, 1974.

Westley, B. H., and Severin, W. J. "A Profile of the Daily Newspaper Nonreader." *Journalism Quarterly*, 1964, *41*, 45–51.

Wexler, P. "Children of the Immigrants: A Study of Education, Ethnicity, and Change in Israel." Unpublished doctoral dissertation, Department of Sociology, Princeton University, 1972.

White, G. M. "Immediate and Deferred Effects of Model Observation and Guided Rehearsal on Donating and Stealing." *Journal of Personality and Social Psychology*, 1972, *21*, 139–148.

White, R. C. "Social Class Differences in the Use of Leisure." *American Journal of Sociology*, 1955, *61*, 145–150.

White, T. H. "The Relative Importance of Education and Income as Predictors in Outdoor Recreation Participation." *Journal of Leisure Research*, 1975, 7, 191–199.

Whiting, J.W.M., and Child, I. L. *Child Training and Personality: A Cross-Cultural Study*. New Haven, Conn.: Yale University Press, 1953.

Whiting, J.M.W., and Whiting, B. "The Behavior of Children in Six Cultures." Unpublished manuscript, Department of Anthropology, Harvard University, 1969.

Wicker, A. W. "Attitudes Versus Actions: The Relationship of Verbal and Overt and Behavioral Responses to Attitudinal Objects." *Journal of Social Issues*, 1969, *25*, 41–78.

Wilensky, H. L. "The Uneven Distribution of Leisure: The Impact of Economic Growth on 'Free Time.'" *Social Problems*, 1961, *9*, 32–56.

Wilensky, H. L. "Mass Society and Mass Culture: Interdependence or Independence." *American Sociological Review*, 1964, *29*, 173–197.

Wilensky, H. L. *The Welfare State and Equality*. Berkeley: University of California Press, 1975.

Wilkinson, P. F. "The Use of Models in Predicting the Consumption of Outdoor Recreation." *Journal of Leisure Research*, 1973, 5, 34–48.

Williams, F., Dordick, H. S., and Horstmann, F. "Where Citizens Go for Information." *Journal of Communication*, 1977, *27*, 95–106.

Williams, R. M. *American Society*. New York: Knopf, 1970.

Willner, A. R. *Charismatic Political Leadership: A Theory*. Monograph 32. Princeton, N.J.: Center of International Studies, 1968.

Wilson, B. *Religious Sects*. New York: McGraw-Hill, 1970.

Wilson, E. O. *Sociobiology: The New Synthesis*. Cambridge, Mass.: Harvard University Press, 1975.

Wilson, E. O. *On Human Nature*. Cambridge, Mass.: Harvard University Press, 1978.

Wilson, W. "Correlates of Avowed Happiness." *Psychological Bulletin*, 1967, *67*, 294–306.

Winch, R. G. *Mate-Selection: A Study of Complementary Needs*. New York: Harper & Row, 1958.

Winham, G. R. "Political Development and Lerner's Theory: Further Tests of a Causal Model." *American Political Science Review*, 1970, *64*, 810–818.

Winter, D. G. *The Power Motive*. New York: Free Press, 1973.

Wippler, R. *Social Determinants of Leisure Behavior*. Groningen, Netherlands: Van Gorcum, 1968.

Wispé, L. G. "Positive Forms of Social Behavior: An Overview." *Journal of Social Issues*, 1972, *28*, 1–19.

Witt, P. A. "Factor Structure of Leisure Behavior for High School Age Youth in Three Communities." *Journal of Leisure Research*, 1971, *3*, 213–219.

Witt, P. A., and Bishop, D. W. "Situational Antecedents to Leisure Behavior." *Journal of Leisure Research*, 1970, *2*, 64–77.

Wolf, E. R. *Peasant Wars of the Twentieth Century*. New York: Harper & Row, 1969.

Wolf, E. R. "Peasant Rebellion and Revolution." In N. Miller and R. Aya (Eds.), *National Liberation: Revolution in the Third World*. New York: Free Press, 1971.

Wolf, E. R., and Hansen, E. *The Human Condition in Latin America*. New York: Oxford University Press, 1972.

Wolfe, R. I. "The Inertia Model." *Journal of Leisure Research*, 1972, *4*, 73–76.

Wolfenstein, E. V. *The Revolutionary Personality*. Princeton, N.J.: Princeton University Press, 1967.

Wolfenstein, M. "The Emergence of Fun Morality." In E. Larrabee and R. Meyersohn (Eds.), *Mass Leisure*. New York: Free Press, 1958.

Wolfgang, M. W., Figlio, R. M., and Sellin, T. *Delinquency in a Birth Cohort*. Chicago: University of Chicago Press, 1972.

Wonneberger, I. "The Role of Physical Culture and Sport in Leisure Pursuits of Women as Compared with that of Men." *International Review of Sport Sociology*. 1968, *3*, 116–124.

Wood, J. L. *The Sources of American Student Activism*. Lexington, Mass.: Heath, 1974.

Wood, W. W. *Culture and Personality Aspects of the Pentecostal Holiness Religion*. The Hague, Netherlands: Mouton, 1965.

Woodward, J. L., and Roper, E. "Political Activity of American Citizens." *American Political Science Review*, 1950, *44*, 872–885.

Woodworth, R. S. *Contemporary Schools of Psychology*. New York: Ronald Press, 1948.

Wrong, D. "The Oversocialized Conception of Man in Modern Sociology." *American Sociological Review*, 1961, *26*, 189–193.

Wuthnow, R. "The New Religion in Social Context." In C. Y. Glock and R. N. Bellah (Eds.), *The New Religious Consciousness*. Berkeley: University of California Press, 1976.

Wylie, R. C. "The Present Status of Self Theory." In E. F. Borgatta and W. W. Lambert (Eds.), *Handbook of Personality Theory and Research.* Chicago: Rand McNally, 1968.

Wylie, R. C. *The Self-Concept.* (Rev. ed.) Lincoln: University of Nebraska Press, 1974.

Yakimovich, D., and Saltz, E. "Helping Behavior: The Cry For Help." *Psychonomic Science,* 1971, *23,* 427–428.

Yalman, A. E. "Notes on the Development of the Turkish Press." *Gazette,* 1964, *10,* 3–9.

Yancy, W. L., and Snell, J. "Parks as Aspects of Leisure in the Intercity: An Exploratoy Investigation." Paper presented at annual meeting of the American Association for the Advancement of Science, Philadelphia, 1971.

Yarrow, M. R., and Scott, P. M. "Imitation of Nurturant and Nonnurturant Models." *Journal of Personality and Social Psychology,* 1972, *23,* 259–270.

Yarrow, M. R., Scott, P. M., and Waxler, C. Z. "Learning Concern for Others." *Developmental Psychology,* 1973, *8,* 240–261.

Yates, D. *Neighborhood Democracy.* Lexington, Mass.: Heath, 1973.

Yiannakis, A. "Birth Order and Preference for Dangerous Sports Among Males." *Research Quarterly,* 1976, *47,* 62–67.

Yin, R. K., and Yates, D. *Street-Level Governments: Assessing Decentralization and Urban Services.* Lexington, Mass.: Heath, 1975.

Yin, R. K., and others. *Citizen Organizations: Increasing Client Control over Services.* Rand publication No. R 1196-HEW. Santa Monica, Calif.: Rand, 1973.

Yinger, J. M. *Sociology Looks at Religion.* New York: Macmillan, 1963.

Yinger, J. M. *The Scientific Study of Religion.* New York: Macmillan, 1970.

Yinger, J. M. "Anomie, Alienation and Political Behavior." In J. N. Knutson (Ed.), *Handbook of Political Psychology.* San Francisco: Jossey-Bass, 1973.

Yoesting, D. R., and Burkhead, D. L. "Significance of Childhood Recreation Experience on Adult Leisure Behavior: An Exploratory Analysis." *Journal of Leisure Research,* 1973, *5,* 25–36.

Zaltman, G., Pinson, C.R.A., and Angelman, R. *Metatheory and Consumer Behavior.* New York: Holt, Rinehart and Winston, 1973.

Zaretsky, I. I., and Leone, M. P. (Eds.). *Religious Movements in Contemporary America.* Princeton, N.J.: Princeton University Press, 1974.

Zeisel, J. "The Workweek in American Industry, 1850–1956." In E. Larrabee and R. Meyersohn (Eds.), *Mass Leisure.* New York: Free Press, 1958.

Zeitlin, M. *Revolutionary Politics and the Cuban Working Class.* Princeton, N.J.: Princeton University Press, 1967.

Zeitlin, M. *Rethinking Sociology: A Critique of Contemporary Theory.* New York: Appleton-Century-Crofts, 1973.

Ziblatt, D. "High School Extracurricular Activities and Political Socialization." *Annals of the American Academy of Political and Social Science*, 1965, *361*, 20-31.

Zigler, E., and Child, I. "Socialization." In G. Lindzey and E. Aronson (Eds.), *Handbook of Social Psychology.* Vol. 3. Reading, Mass.: Addison-Wesley, 1969.

Ziller, R. C. *The Social Self.* Elmsford, N.Y.: Pergamon Press, 1972.

Zimbardo, P. G., Ebbesen, E. B., and Maslach, C. *Influencing Attitudes and Changing Behavior.* Reading, Mass.: Addison-Wesley, 1977.

Zinger, C. L., Dalsemer, R., and Magargle, H. *Environmental Volunteers in America.* Washington, D.C.: National Center for Voluntary Action, 1973.

Zipf, G. K. *Human Behavior and the Principle of Least Effort.* Reading, Mass.: Addison-Wesley, 1949.

Zurcher, L. "Socialpsychological Functions of Ephemeral Roles: A Disaster Work Crew." *Human Organization*, 1968, *27*, 281-297.

Zurcher, L. A. *The Mutable Self.* Beverly Hills, Calif.: Sage, 1977.

Zweers, W. "Research on Dutch Theatre Audiences." *Sociologia Neerlandica*, 1971, *7*, 42-49.

Name Index

118, 120, 122–123, 125, 126, 127, 129, 130, 131, 132, 138, 149, 520
Vernon, G., 222
Vernon, P. E., 55
Villani, K. B., 269
Vince, P., 270
Vinyard, D., 271
Viver, L., 238–239
von der Mehden, F. R., 136, 137
von Feilitzen, C., 247

Wackman, D. B., 246, 255–256
Wade, S. E., 270
Wagner, F. W., 182
Wakeman, E., Jr., 136
Walbek, N. H., 293
Walder, L., 298
Walker, J. L., 138, 148
Wallace, A., 326, 340
Wallston, B., 355–369
Walster, E., 358, 361
Walster, G. W., 358, 361
Walters, J., 198
Walters, R. H., 50, 88, 144, 322
Warburton, F. W., 192
Ward, L. S., 247, 253, 266, 271, 273
Ward, S., 246, 255–256
Warner, W. K., 449
Wartella, E., 246, 255–256
Warwick, P., 15
Washnis, G. J., 157, 159
Watanuki, J., 110, 116, 117, 167
Watts, D. P., 181
Watts, W., 270
Waxler, C. Z., 291, 293, 294
Waxman, J., 339
Weatherford, W. C., 222
Weaver, R. B., 180
Weaver, W., 373, 374, 375, 376
Webb, E. J., 403
Webb, G. E., 162
Webb, H., 175
Weber, M., 128, 155, 329, 331, 332
Webster, M., Jr., 432
Wedge, B., 146
Weigert, A. J., 207
Weinstein, M. S., 286
Weiss, C. H., 263
Weiss, L. B., 315, 336
Weiss, R. S., 417, 450
Weiss, W., 270

Weissberg, R., 88, 89, 90n, 91, 96, 99, 100, 101, 105
Weissman, H. H., 156, 157, 162, 165
Welch, S., 114, 127
Weller, J., 340
Wells, L., 432
Wenger, W. D., Jr., 197
Wenner, L., 262
Wessler, R., 432
Westergaard, K., 184, 187, 190
Westerhoff, J. H., III, 203, 208
Westley, B. H., 265, 266, 270
Wexler, P., 316–317, 336
Whaley, R. S., 199, 403
Wheeler, L., 347
Wheeler, S., 202
White, G. M., 293, 295
White, T. H., 184, 187, 188, 190
Whiting, B., 295
Whiting, J.W.M., 87, 93, 295
Whittington, F. J., 208
Wicker, A. W., 57
Wilde, R. J., 272
Wilensky, H. L., 156, 182, 262–263
Wilkinson, P. F., 197
Willets, F. K., 206
Williams, F., 268
Williams, J. R., 149
Williams, R. M., 181
Williamson, R. C., 42
Willner, A. R., 140
Wilson, B., 216, 218
Wilson, D., 249, 250, 255, 256
Wilson, E. O., 425, 442
Wilson, M., 233
Wilson, R. R., 191, 197
Wilson, W., 6
Winch, R. G., 417, 449
Windahl, S., 271
Wingrove, C. R., 237
Winham, G. R., 259
Winter, D. G., 192
Wippler, R., 185, 186, 188, 190, 191, 194, 199
Wispé, L. G., 317, 330–331
Withey, S. B., 6
Witt, P. A., 191, 198
Wolf, E. R., 136, 139, 140, 141, 142
Wolfe, R. I., 178, 197
Wolfenstein, E. V., 144
Wolfenstein, M., 181

Subject Index

Access. *See* Resources, access to

Accommodation: and humanization, 462; importance of, 462; of individual with culture, 22, 457, 462; and nonassociational religious participation, 240; reasons for, 462; research on, 486; secondary, 477–485

ACTION, 428

Action tendency, 282–283

Active-effective character: analysis of, 466–472; and levels of activity, 473–474; research on, 495–501

Activity: and access, 465, 486–487, 513–514, 522; categories of, 9–13, 16–17; correlates of, 485–520; cumulative pattern of, 462; diachronic covariation of, 528–529; individual character, body, and context in, 463–466; levels of, 462–463; nonlinear covariation

of, 463; nonrandom patterns in, 461; situation/role and, 463; social-structural conditions for, 489–495; synchronic covariation of, 520–528. *See also* Behavior; Discretionary time use

Adolescence, 247

Adult education participation, correlates of, 486, 505, 506, 511, 513, 514, 516, 518, 525

Adulthood, 247–251

Africa: media consumption in, 260; race in, 518; unconventional political activity in, 133

Age: and community activity, 158–159; and conventional political activity, 118–120; correlates of, 516–517; and leisure and sport socialization, 173; and media consumption, 261–262; and nonassociational religious participa-

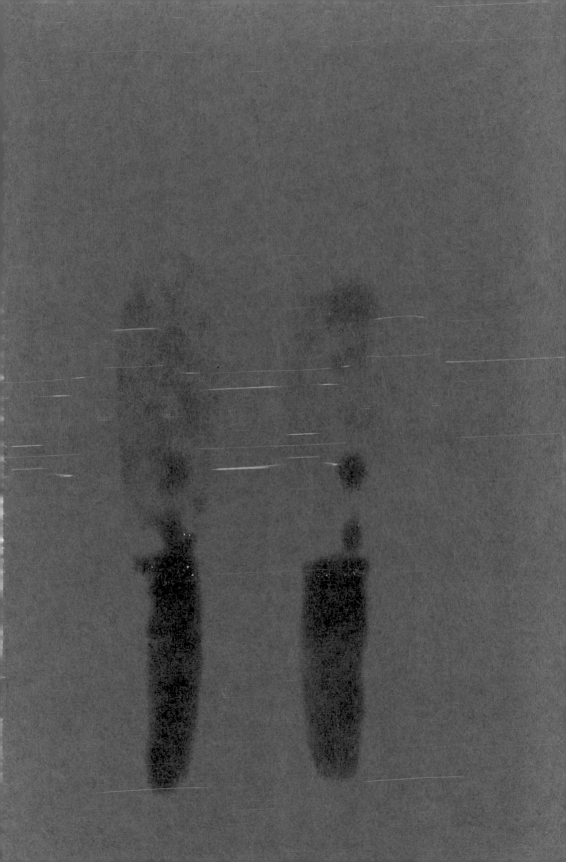

MAR 3 1982
JUL 0 6 1983   OCT 4 1987

  AUG 1 3 1984
JUN 5   1986   OCT 2 7 1987
  MAY   4 1986
    NOV 1 9 1986
    NOV 1 8
APR   1 1987

              4 1992

MAY 0 1 1988

JAN   3 1990
  APR 2 7 1992